T0355317

Age of Wolf and Wind

Age of Wolf and Wind

Voyages through the Viking World

DAVIDE ZORI

OXFORD
UNIVERSITY PRESS

OXFORD
UNIVERSITY PRESS

Oxford University Press is a department of the University of Oxford. It furthers
the University's objective of excellence in research, scholarship, and education
by publishing worldwide. Oxford is a registered trade mark of Oxford University
Press in the UK and certain other countries.

Published in the United States of America by Oxford University Press
198 Madison Avenue, New York, NY 10016, United States of America.

© Oxford University Press 2024

Library of Congress Cataloging-in-Publication Data
Names: Zori, Davide, author.
Title: Age of wolf and wind : voyages through the Viking world / Davide Zori.
Description: New York, NY : Oxford University Press, 2024. |
Includes bibliographical references and index.
Identifiers: LCCN 2023022734 (print) | LCCN 2023022735 (ebook) |
ISBN 9780190916060 (hardback) | ISBN 9780190916084 (epub)
Subjects: LCSH: Vikings. | Scandinavia—Antiquities. | Vikings—North
Atlantic Region. | Old Norse literature—History and criticism. |
Scandinavia—History—To 1397.
Classification: LCC DL31 .Z675 2024 (print) | LCC DL31 (ebook) |
DDC 948/.022—dc23/eng/20230520
LC record available at https://lccn.loc.gov/2023022734
LC ebook record available at https://lccn.loc.gov/2023022735

DOI: 10.1093/oso/9780190916060.001.0001

Printed by Sheridan Books, Inc., United States of America

To all the voyagers in my family

skeggǫld, skalmǫld, skildir ro klonir, | axe age, sword age, shields are shattered,
vindǫld, vargǫld, áðr verǫld steypisk, | wind age, wolf age, before the world sinks,
mun engi maðr ǫðrum þyrma. | men will not spare each other.

Vǫluspá, stanza 45, a seeress foretells the end of the old world to Odin

Contents

Figures

Acknowledgments

I am grateful to many people and institutions for support and encouragement while I wrote this book. My views on the Viking Age have been formed in great part through collaborations and discussions with friends and colleagues, including Fedir Androshchuk, Terri Barnes, Rhonda Bathurst, Egil Bauer, Marianna Betti, Bjarki Bjarnason, Doug Bolender, Stefan Brink, Jesse Byock, Tara Carter, Colin Connors, Florin Curta, Matthew Delvaux, Jørgen Dencker, Ásdís Egilsdóttir, Bjarni Einarsson, Jackie Eng, Jon Erlandson, Egill Erlendsson, Véronique Forbes, Vaughan Grimes, Magnús Guðmundsson, Greg Mumford, Per Holck, Margrét Hallmundsdóttir, Sice Hansen, Volker Hilberg, Elín Ósk Hreiðarsdóttir, Sven Kalmring, Gunnar Karlsson, Steinar Kristensen, Rúnar Leifsson, Gavin Lucas, Kevin Martin, Steve Martin, Karen Milek, Sarah Morris, Guðmundur Ólafsson, Sarah Parcak, Ben Raffield, Klavs Randsborg, Scott Ridell, Angelos Parigoris, Neil Price, Flemming Rieck, Howell Roberts, David Scott, Dagfinn Skre, Poul Skaaning, Magnús Sigurgeirsson, John Steinberg, Jennica Einebrant Svensson, Óskar Gísli Sveinbjarnarson, Björn Þráinn Þórðarson, Helgi Þorláksson, Guðrún Þráinsdóttir, Ragnheiður Traustadóttir, Nikola Trbojevic, Torfi Tulinius, Mark Tveskov, Claus von Carnap-Bornheim, Tom Wake, Phillip Walker, Bryndís Zöega, and Guðný Zoëga. This book has benefited in tangible ways from my discussions with each of these colleagues.

I want to especially thank my friend and colleague Terri Barnes, who read the entire book manuscript and provided astute suggestions that have notably improved the text. Our discussions of each chapter have been a true pleasure and always filled with good laughs. Also, Jesse Byock, my PhD mentor and my research collaborator for over two decades, has had a profound influence on my thinking about the sagas and interdisciplinarity. For his support and friendship, I am immensely grateful. From my time at UCLA, John Papadopoulos, Patrick Geary, and Chip Stanish have been lasting intellectual inspirations. My perspective on the Vikings has been formed through spending most of my life living in, visiting, and conducting research in the Scandinavian lands. Denmark and Iceland are second homes for me, and I want to express my gratitude to friends and family, especially Karen and Aksel Hansen, Hans and Birgit Bødker, Claus Jensen and Maria Falden, Lenni Mose, the Pedersen clan, Ólafur Júlíusson, Brooks Walker, Herdís Ólafsdóttir, Pilar Coello, Nicolas Barreiro, Valur Þorvaldsson and Guðrún Sigurðardóttir. At key moments for me, each of you warmed the long Scandinavian winter nights or joyfully extended the summer evenings.

The images and illustrations in this book are many and so are the people and institutions that have granted permission for their use. Roberto Fortuna, photographer at the National Museum of Denmark, took the beautiful photo used for the cover. For institutional permissions to reproduce photographs, I thank the National Museum of Denmark, the Royal Danish Library, the British Museum, the British Library, Museum of London, the National Museum of Iceland, the Swedish National Heritage Board, the National Historical Museums (Sweden), the City of Bayeux, the Corpus of Anglo-Saxon Sculpture, Canadian Museum of History, the Maine State Museum, Compost Creative, Headland Archaeology Ltd., the Minnesota Historical Society, the Viking Ship Museum (Denmark), and the American Numismatic Society. For personal permissions, I am grateful to Gavin Lucas (Hofstaðir map), Pétur Reynisson (Thingvellir photo), Ragnar Børsheim (Tissø digital reconstruction), Neil Price (Birka Grave Bj 581), and Thomas Guntzelnick Poulsen (St. Knut coin).

Publishing with Oxford University Press has been a pleasure. I thank the myriad people at OUP who made this book possible, including the many project managers and copy and image editors. I want to extend my thanks to the anonymous reviewers of the proposal and the finished book draft. Particularly, I thank my editor at OUP, Stefan Vranka, who believed in this project from the beginning and has guided it to the finish line. Even if we disagree on the ideal caption lengths, we agree about nearly everything else, including the qualities of Italian wines.

This book has been written mostly in central Texas, far away from the Viking world and Italian wines. Here Baylor University has generously supported my work, and I particularly thank my former and current program directors Anne-Marie Schulz, Chuck McDaniel, and Darren Middleton, and the former and current Honors College deans Thomas Hibbs and Douglas Henry for steadfast encouragement and support. My intellectual community here is a source of great happiness, and I particularly thank Jeff Hamilton, Alden Smith, and Jason Whitlark for early and wise council. Always ready for commiserating and sound advice over a beer, my dear friends, Sam Perry and Paul Carron, have many times helped me laugh when I instead wanted to throw up my hands. The Baylor students in my Vikings courses have been tremendous sounding boards. They have repeatedly reconfirmed for me the critical role that teaching plays in the formulation of good questions and lucid explanation of data.

My family has been an unwavering source of strength and encouragement through the writing process. My parents, Åse and Roberto, could not be more supportive, and although they were endlessly incredulous at how long it could take me to finish this book, I hope they will be pleased with the result. For the most profound patience, I thank my wife, Colleen, who keenly read and incisively edited several chapters. After listening to countless hours of musings about the Viking Age and rants at various levels of panic, this book should feel nearly as much yours as mine. To our kids, Lucas and Irene, who sort-of enjoy hearing stories about Vikings and have been forced to voyage across the Atlantic more times than they would care to count in pursuit of archaeology, thank you for not protesting too much; at least we didn't have to do it in open wooden ships.

A Note on Spelling and Pronunciation

Many people and places from across the Viking world are discussed in this book, including especially names of archaeological sites and personal names from various cultures in Europe, Asia, the North Atlantic, and the Mediterranean region. Standardization in spelling of Old Norse—the language of the Vikings—is challenging, and consistency is nearly impossible. There was no uniformity for spelling in the Viking Age, nor in the letters in the Scandinavian runic alphabet, which varied regionally and changed over time. The various languages used in the texts, both ancient and modern, also pose significant challenges. To take just one example: one of the most famous Viking Age kings is Knut the Great. His name is written in many different forms in modern scholarship ranging from Old Norse versions with or without nominative endings to those that are anglicized or use modern Scandinavian spelling, resulting in many variations: Knútr, Knút, Canute, Cnut, Knut, Knud, and Knútur. For simplicity, this book uses the anglicized Old Norse version Knut without accents. As a rule, I aim for readability and consistency in English. Therefore, names and places are often anglicized in the main text, especially names that are familiar to the reader. For instance, I write Odin and not Óðinn, and Thor rather than Þórr. The original language of direct quotes in Old Norse, Latin, Anglo-Saxon (Old English), and all the modern Scandinavian languages is provided in the endnotes.

A word about pronunciation is useful as some readers will be unfamiliar with the letters used to write Old Norse and the modern Scandinavian languages. Most scholars prefer to follow modern Icelandic pronunciation for Old Norse even though differences existed in space and time. For instance, the sounds of the letters ǫ and ø letters were distinguished from each other in Old Norse in the Middle Ages before converging into the single ö letter, which has since been used in Icelandic and Swedish, but not in Danish and Norwegian, where the single ø is retained. The ä/aa/å vowel, which emerged from the Old Norse long a (á), varies a bit more in pronunciation in the modern Scandinavian languages but the Icelandic pronunciation is close to the *ou* in house. The chart below offers the English sound equivalents for the modern Icelandic pronunciations commonly used for Old Norse.

Á á	*ou* in house
É é	*ye* in yellow
Í í	*ea* in ear
Ó ó	*ow* in *slow*
Ú ú	*oo* in *cool*
Ý ý	*ee* in beet
Þ þ ("thorn")	soft *th* as in thin
Ð ð ("eth")	hard *th* as in father
Æ æ, Œ œ	*i* as in Nile
Ø ø, Ö ö, Ǫ ǫ	*oo* in book

For personal names from the ancient sources, I anglicize unfamiliar letters and drop accents for ease of reading, while often giving the original in parenthesis at the first mention of a name. Þ/þ is replaced with th, while Ð/ð is anglicized as d, such that the female names Þorgerður and Þórdís are written as Thorgerdur and Thordis. I also drop the final consonants of many male names, which are actually only the nominative case ending, as in for example the double *n* in Óðinn, and more commonly the final -*r*, as in Knútr. Names of modern scholars are retained in their native Scandinavian forms for bibliographical accuracy. Viking Age people were often given nicknames based on appearances, characteristics, and accomplishments. I retain these nicknames, such as Harald Bluetooth and Eirik Bloodaxe, to help distinguish the many Haralds and Eiriks of the period.

Finally, for place names, which the reader often still needs to find on modern maps, I retain the spellings used in their respective modern countries. So, in Iceland for instance, I will refer to Hrísbrú and Borgarfjörður, while in Denmark we will encounter Tissø and Toftegård. At times, the acute accents can crucially change the meaning of a word, such as for example in Vínland (Wine-land) versus Vinland (Pasture-land). In these cases, the accents are preserved. A few larger geographical areas, besides modern countries, are given in their well-known anglicized form, such as Jutland rather than Jylland.

1

Introduction

Viking Voyages through History and Archaeology

Viking Voyages

The story of the Vikings is one of voyages. In the Viking Age, Scandinavian voyagers from today's Denmark, Norway, and Sweden encountered new people and novel landscapes with an unprecedented intensity. The movement of people brought transfers of ideas, sharing of technologies, trade in material goods, inter-marriage, and warfare. The Viking Age (c. 790–1100) is primarily represented in popular culture as a violent age, and it was. It was also much more. Vikings were farmers, raiders, traders, and settlers. Most Viking Age Scandinavians probably would not have thought of themselves as "Vikings." The word *víking* did exist at the time, but it referred strictly a to sea-borne raider, essentially a pirate. It was an occupation, and it could be seasonal work, a multi-year engagement, and at times a lifetime commitment. In fact, Scandinavian víking raiding parties could and did incorporate peoples from other linguistic, ethnic, and cultural groups. Nonetheless, for convenience and because of broadly understood conventions, scholars often use the term Vikings to refer broadly to Viking Age Scandinavians.

Like most people in most ages, Viking Age Scandinavians were opportunists looking for ways to better their own situation in life, and that of their family and offspring. The overwhelming majority of people were farmers, but at an unprec-edented scale, leaving the farm for other economic activities became possible and lucrative. People could pursue craft production or trading in the growing urban centers or get aboard the increasing numbers of ships leaving the na-tive shores to trade at foreign ports, or if the centers of wealth concentration—monasteries and trading sites—seemed vulnerable, then they could raid. As the Viking Age progressed, permanent migration to unpopulated or newly conquered lands opened new venues for Scandinavians seeking to better their fortunes. Scandinavians struck out far beyond the western extent of any European travelers, settling the North Atlantic islands of Iceland and Greenland and reaching the eastern shores of North America. To the modern reader, these voyagers seem perhaps overly intrepid, boarding open wooden boats to cross the North Atlantic and travel into the unknown. This is also why the Vikings

Age of Wolf and Wind. Davide Zori, Oxford University Press. © Oxford University Press 2024.
DOI: 10.1093/oso/9780190916060.003.0001

continue to fascinate us, because their compelling stories connect with the universal human desire for exploration and adventure.

The Viking Age was the most dynamic period in the pre-modern history of Scandinavia. Scandinavians have long considered it a Golden Age in which their ancestors' impact on the world extended far beyond the region's borders. Inter-regional connections stimulated trade as Scandinavians traveled farther from their homelands. At the start of the Viking Age, Scandinavia had no urban centers. When the age ended, cities had emerged as the centers of trade and government administration. Economic exchange at the start of the Viking Age took the form of barter, while the end of the Viking Age had seen the emergence of state-controlled currencies on the model of coins used in Western Europe. Christianity arrived as ideas were exchanged in the nascent urban centers. At the start of the Viking Age, Scandinavia was divided into chiefdoms and petty kingdoms. At its close, the states of Denmark, Norway, and Sweden emerged united under single monarchies. As we shall see in the chapters ahead, the turn of the millennium around 1000 was a time of transition that saw tremendous changes in Scandinavia in urbanization, monetization of the economy, Christianization, formation of powerful unified states, and comprehensive Europeanization. When these factors took hold thoroughly by the end of the eleventh century, Scandinavia became fully incorporated into *Christianitas*, as Christian Europe was known, and the Viking Age came to a close.

The Vikings had a tremendous impact on the peoples and lands they encountered in their maritime movements along coastlines and along the rivers of Eurasia. The Viking ship, which was the culmination of centuries of native Scandinavian innovations, gave them privileged access to these maritime and riverine superhighways. These fast, shallow-drafted, and sturdy ships gave them advantages everywhere they traveled. Scandinavians played key roles in connecting far-flung regions into a Viking-dominated trade system, sometimes called the Northern Arc, which connected Western Europe to the Middle East and the western ends of the Silk Roads leading east to China. This trade system was even more important because the trade across the Mediterranean Sea, once overseen by the Roman Empire, had largely collapsed after the fall of the Western Roman Empire and the rapid Arab conquests of the Middle East and North Africa. The Mediterranean was split between polities with diverse cultures, languages, and religions. Trade across the Mediterranean certainly did not disappear, but it was much decreased. The Vikings filled the void by redirecting trade through the river superhighways of Russia and Ukraine—especially the Dnieper and the Volga Rivers—and across the Baltic Sea to the emergent Scandinavian trading centers, and on to Britain, Ireland, and Francia (Figure 1.1). The vast numbers of coins from the Islamic Caliphates that have been found in Scandinavia attest to the strength of this trade. This trade had its dark side

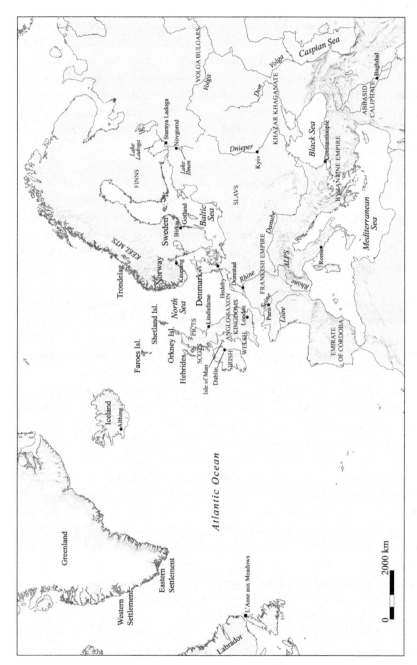

Figure 1.1 The Viking World *Source: map by author*

too: one of the most important commodities that Scandinavians brought south to the large urban centers of Constantinople and Baghdad were slaves.

The traditional historical date for the beginning of the Viking Age is taken from the raid on the English monastery of Lindisfarne in 793, which sent shock waves across Western Europe. Although this does not appear to have been the first Scandinavian raid in Britain, letters exchanged between appalled clerics in Britain and Francia show that this raid had a reverberating impact. In one of the most famous of these letters, written by the Anglo-Saxon scholar Alcuin from the court of Charlemagne to King Æthelred of Northumbria, we find evidence of the shock that most contemporaries felt.

> Behold, we and our forefathers have inhabited this most beautiful land for almost three hundred and fifty years and never before has such terror appeared in Britain as we have now suffered from a pagan people; nor was it thought that such an incursion across the sea was possible. Behold St. Cuthbert's church spattered with the blood of God's priests and deprived of its holy ornaments. Britain's most venerable site has been left as prey to the pagans.[1]

With the help of their ships, recently equipped with a sail, Scandinavians could now surprise any community in Britain by crossing the North Sea directly instead of hugging the European continental coast to cross at the English Channel. The late fifth- to sixth-century Anglo-Saxon invasions of England had been accomplished in row boats without sails. The threat from the pagan lands was transformed.

When Vikings emerged from the sea to sack Lindisfarne, what is today England was divided into separate and often warring kingdoms. In the late eighth century, there were seven kingdoms, known as the heptarchy: Wessex, Essex, Sussex, Kent, East Anglia, Mercia, and Northumbria. By the early ninth century, however, Wessex had absorbed Essex, Sussex, and Kent. Viking attacks and conquests over the next half century would eliminate East Anglia, Mercia, and Northumbria, leaving only Wessex. Forced by Vikings to rearm, refortify, and reform, the kingdom of Wessex would eventually reconquer these lands and create a unified kingdom of England. In this way, the Viking Age was the crucible in which the English state was formed. In the areas of Scotland's northern and western islands—the Hebrides, Orkneys, and Shetlands—the Vikings dominated local populations, and the Norse culture and language took over. In Orkney, Shetland, and some areas of mainland Scotland, people spoke a Scandinavian language called Norn until the nineteenth century.

Vikings raided in Ireland by 795 and began to settle there permanently in the early 800s. The Viking story in Ireland was different from the rest of the British Isles. Here, among decentralized Celtic chiefdoms, and in the absence of any urban centers, Vikings became intimately involved in the process of urbanization and the fostering of inter-regional trade. A nationalistically charged debate still simmers about whether the Vikings started the first towns in Ireland. What can certainly be said is that there is a direct correlation between the arrival of the Vikings and the appearance of the first Irish towns, which were all coastal and located on rivers. Many of these towns have Norse names: Waterford (Veðrarfjörðr), Wexford (Viegsfjörðr), and Limerick (Hlymrekr). These early Irish towns, especially Dublin, have yielded Scandinavian burials of both males and females, reminding us that Viking migrants were not just men. The Scandinavian influx was coastal, and little archaeological evidence of Scandinavian settlement exists internally in Ireland. Nonetheless, DNA studies show that up to 20 percent of the modern Irish population has Norwegian ancestry, deriving presumably from a sizable influx of Scandinavians in the Viking Age.[2] The intermixing of populations in Ireland resulted in a rich hybridized culture, referred to as Hiberno-Norse.

In contrast to most other Viking ventures, the settlement of the large North Atlantic islands was a peaceful process, as there was no one there to raid, fight, or conquer. Instead, Viking Age Scandinavians brought their traditional ways of subsistence and political organization to these remote islands. The Scandinavian seafarers' encounter with these islands at the far margins of the known world are just as central to the story of the Vikings as are their violent encounters with Northumbrian monks. Vikings probably discovered the Faroe Islands on their voyages from Norway to Britain, setting in motion the island-hopping Scandinavian settlement of the North Atlantic that followed a pattern of accidental discovery, purposeful exploration, and planned settlement. The Faroes were quickly settled in the mid-ninth century. Iceland was discovered soon after, and permanent settlers began arriving around 870. By 930, the extensive lands of Iceland had all been claimed by Scandinavians from the homelands and Vikings retiring from their more violent activities in the British Isles. Island-hopping farther across the North Atlantic Ocean, Vikings, who are usually called Norse in this region, settled within the sheltered fjords on the southwestern coast of Greenland in the 980s. Less than twenty years later, the Norse sagas tell us that mariners blown off course on their way to Greenland discovered the eastern shores of the Americas. Irrefutable archaeological evidence of at least one Viking Age Scandinavian settlement on Newfoundland, Canada, now validates these old stories. Through the Viking Age, these islands of the North Atlantic remained in direct contact with the Scandinavian homelands. But as the large-scale people movements of the Viking Age came to an end, the contact with these distant colonies dwindled. Icelandic culture continued to thrive, preserving for us some of the most significant literature of the Middle Ages in the Icelandic Sagas, but the more remote outposts in Greenland declined in increasing isolation and disappeared sometime before 1500.

On the European continent, Vikings had dramatic impacts on coastal regions of what is today Germany, France, Netherlands, and Belgium. The Carolingian dynasty of the Franks, who ruled these lands, had built Western Europe's most powerful medieval state. After striking a mutually beneficial alliance with the pope, the most famous Carolingian king, Charlemagne, had been crowned Roman emperor and king of the Lombards in 800. Especially after the end of Charlemagne's strong reign, no places on the coast, or along the European river systems of the Rhine, Seine, Loire, and Garonne, were safe from Viking incursions. The numbers of communities, towns, and cities that endured Viking attacks is staggering. It puts the period into perspective to remember that each of the brief historical mentions of raids represents great suffering as people were violently dragged from their homes, killed, raped, or enslaved, while their wealth was stolen, and their lands and houses burned. It is sometimes said that the Vikings were no more violent than other peoples of the Middle Ages, and there is some truth to that. But they were certainly not less violent. The non-Christian Vikings, who depended on raiding and slaving for wealth accumulation, did not have any of the ideological taboos in dealing out this type of violence on peaceful Christian sites. Some scholars have gone as far as to suggest that Viking raids represented a religiously motivated vengeful assault on Christian sites. But their frequent attacks on monasteries is more likely to have been an opportunistic strategy targeting places of great wealth inhabited by folks that were relatively less capable of self-defense.

In the ninth-century heyday of Viking activity on the European Continent, Viking fleets that had established permanent bases at the mouths of the great French rivers would have heard stories of even greater wealth farther south. From these bases, Vikings entered the Mediterranean Sea through the Straits of Gibraltar. Scandinavian sagas of mythic proportions about men like Bjorn Ironside (Bjǫrn Járnsíða) include much fantasy, but their grounding in a historic voyage from 859 to 862 is substantiated by Frankish annals and accounts in Arab sources from North Africa and the powerful Muslim Caliphate of Córdoba that controlled the Iberian peninsula. The Viking fleet, said to number sixty-two ships, raided Spain and North Africa, capturing the Moroccan town of Mazimma, where wealthy citizens were ransomed. The fleet continued to southern France and sacked Pisa in central Italy, but as they continued east, the corroborating Frankish and saga sources become less reliable. We are left with a particularly colorful account of a siege of a town in Italy that Bjorn Ironside and his partner Hastein believed to be Rome. The late tenth-century Norman historian Dudo of St. Quentin resorts to a storytelling cliché when he recounts how Hastein faked his death, complete with a pre-death conversion to Christianity, in order that he might be allowed into the city for Christian burial. Once his coffin had been carried through the city gates and Mass had been said over his body, Hastein jumped out fully armed and led the Vikings in a surprise attack. The ruse worked and the town was sacked, but only thereafter did the Vikings realize that the town they had sacked was the provincial city of Luni.[3] Later Norman historians, like William of Jumièges (mid-eleventh century), retold this story and applied Hastein's trick to stories of other daring siege breakers. Several sagas, including *The Saga of Ragnar Lodbrok and His Sons* and *The Tale of Ragnar's Sons*, also recount the story of the capture of Luni, albeit without Hastein's elaborate ruse and without the Vikings' implausible misidentification of Luni as Rome. Stories such as these, even if based on memories of real journeys, cannot of course be trusted in their details, and no archaeological evidence has been recovered that can be tied directly to the voyage and Mediterranean raids of Bjorn and Hastein.

By the tenth century, the French and German inheritors of the Frankish Empire were mounting increasingly effective resistance against the Vikings. As fortification of towns and bridges, as well as reorganization of local defenses and navies, made traditional Viking activities more difficult, some Scandinavians looked for other opportunities elsewhere while others tried to make deals with local rulers to settle. The West Frankish king, Charles the Simple, pursuing a policy of appeasement, granted land to a Viking leader by the name of Hrolf (Rollo in Latin sources) around the mouth of the Seine River in 911. In return for this grant of land, Hrolf swore fealty to the French king and promised to defend the mouth of the Seine from incursions by other Vikings. Hrolf's descendants would forge a powerful state here that became known as the Duchy of Normandy, or Duchy of the Northmen. The impact of this geographically small polity was extraordinary. Hrolf's descendent William the Bastard became William the Conqueror after his Norman Conquest of England in 1066. Other Norman knights, operating as mercenaries in the central Mediterranean in the decades after the Norman Conquest, would forge for themselves a kingdom on the island of Sicily. The Normans who conquered England and formed the kingdom of Sicily were French speakers but retained cultural aspects of their Scandinavian background, including a rich tradition of saga-like storytelling and, as we see on the Bayeux Tapestry, which depicts William's victory at the Battle of Hastings, ships of the Viking tradition (Figure 1.2).

The Vikings' effect on the Carolingian Empire was disruptive and destructive of imperial control, contributing in the longer term to the splintering of the regional political order into feudal lordships. During Charlemagne's reign (768–814), Carolingian military strength held Viking attacks mostly in check, but the situation began to deteriorate already in the reign of his son, Louis the Pious (814–840), and especially after Charlemagne's grandsons—Lothar, Charles the Bald, and Louis the German—divided the Frankish Empire into three kingdoms at the Treaty of Verdun in 843. These internal troubles, exacerbated by the Viking assaults, eroded centralized power and revealed the inability of the Frankish

Figure 1.2 William the Conqueror's fleet sailing across the English Channel during the Norman Invasion of 1066 as depicted on the Bayeux Tapestry (c. 1075). The Normans, or "North Men," spoke French but had Scandinavian ancestry and sailed across the channel in ships built in the Scandinavian tradition.
Source: detail of the Bayeux Tapestry courtesy of the City of Bayeux

kings to protect local populations. Local lords increasingly assumed this role as provincial protectors, building castles and forming their own private armies to defend against external threats, such as the Vikings. The Vikings were not the only force assaulting the empire, but they did play a role in the flowering of feudalism, especially in what is today France. This type of lord- and castle-based feudalism spread from its Frankish center to other places in Europe, like northern Italy, where Carolingian power was waning, and was subsequently transplanted to England and Southern Italy with the Norman conquests of both those regions.[4]

Viking voyages to the east of their homelands often sound incredible as they are recounted in sagas, commemorated on runestones, and remembered in post–Viking Age East Slavic texts. Nevertheless, these Scandinavian exploits are also recounted in Byzantine and Arabic sources, and documented through ever-mounting archaeological evidence. The journeys to the east appear in fact to predate the raids of Lindisfarne in 793. The earliest evidence for Scandinavian activity in the east comes from archaeology rather than historical sources. Archaeological remains bear witness to settlements with significant Scandinavian presence along the southern shore of the Baltic Sea already in the eighth century. A spectacular discovery at Salme in Estonia of two crews of Vikings buried in their ships bears witness to a failed raid around 750. Buried far from home by friends who survived the battle, the dead were accompanied by animals, food, gaming pieces, and an array of weapons comparable to examples from central Sweden. Predating the Lindisfarne raid by over forty years, the largest of the two ships had a substantial keel and was covered by an immense textile, providing possibly the earliest evidence of a Viking ship with a sail. Perhaps the Viking Age as we know it began in the Baltic.[5]

The Viking story farther east began with trading ventures in search of movable wealth. The major expansion occurred as Scandinavian traders passed east beyond the Baltic Sea and into the Russian/Ukrainian river systems that led south to Byzantium, the Silk Roads, and the Abbasid Caliphate of Baghdad. Offering furs, amber, and slaves to lands in the south, Vikings returned to Scandinavia with prestige goods such as beads, silk, and especially silver. From the Baltic Sea, Vikings entered the Gulf of Finland and navigated up the Nema River to Europe's largest lake, Lake Ladoga. By the mid-eighth century, they had established a trading center at Staraya Ladoga, which was strategically positioned at the mouth of the Volkhov River, where it flows into Lake Ladoga from the south. The Scandinavian settlement at Staraya Ladoga became the key gateway in the Northern Arc trade route. The presence of Scandinavians at Staraya Ladoga (Aldeigjuborg in Old Norse) is evidenced by excavated ruins of longhouses and large burial mounds that are still visually imposing, along the shores of the Volkhov River. Sailing south along the Volkhov River, the Vikings reached Lake Ilmen, and here they established a second base overlooked by a hillfort at Novgorod (Holmgarðr, or "Island-town or fort" in Old Norse). From Lake Ilmen the routes split, with the Dnieper River system leading south to the Black Sea and Constantinople, while the Volga River system leads east and south to the Caspian Sea and the Abbasid Caliphate.

The Scandinavians came to function as a minority merchant elite within the trading sites and forts linked together by the Viking Age long-distance riverine trade system. These connected sites, politically dominated by Scandinavians for a time, formed a cultural area that the sagas refer to as Garðaríki ("Realm of towns/ forts"). These emergent towns were melting pots of Scandinavians and Slavs, and they drew in influences from neighboring peoples, such as the Finno-Ugric speaking peoples, Balts of the northern forests, Volga Bulgars, and semi-nomadic Turkic-speaking Khazars and Pechenegs. Greek, Arabic, and Latin sources agree that the Scandinavians in this region were called Rus, an ethnic designation that is the root of the name Russia. The original meaning of Rus is probably related to "rowers" of boats (Old Norse róðr = rowing), presumably referring to the crews of Viking ships plying the rivers.[6] By the late ninth century, Scandinavians had established a southern fortified base at Kyiv on the Dnieper, closer to the wealth of the Byzantine Empire. In the tenth century, Kyiv became the capital of the nascent Rus or Russian state. As the elite, the Scandinavians played a vital role in the formation of Russia, although the extent of this influence has been a matter of significant debate. In early tenth-century treaties between the Rus from Kyiv and the Byzantine Greeks, the names of the Rus leaders are Scandinavian names such as Karl, Farulf, Vermund, Gunnar, Hroar, and Angantyr. The Scandinavian elite origins were also remembered in the earliest Russian written sources. A hybrid identity developed, but by the eleventh century, a separate Rus identity emerged that was governed by leaders who spoke Old East Slavic, bore Slavic names, and followed Byzantine modes of Christianity. The longstanding cultural and economic connections between Scandinavians and the Rus state were not forgotten, however, and continued well beyond the Viking Age.

Viking groups attempted raids on Byzantium in the mid-ninth and early tenth centuries, but were mostly repelled by the strength of the Byzantine army, which possessed such novel weapons as Greek Fire, a napalm-like substance propelled from a tube. Instead, Vikings from Kyiv negotiated treaties and established trade relationships with Byzantium. Scandinavian warriors subsequently became mercenaries in the Byzantine military forces as the emperor's personal bodyguard, known as the Varangian Guard. The name Varangian derives from another self-ascribed designation based on the Old Norse word *vár*, meaning pledge or oath. Varangians probably meant "men of the pledge," as in the pledge a crew would make to one another before setting out on a sea-borne business venture.[7] Varangians left some archaeological traces, including their names—such as Halfdan and Ari—carved in runes as graffiti into the balustrade on the second floor of the Hagia Sophia Church in Constantinople and a long rune-scroll chiseled into a larger-than-life marble lion that used to sit overlooking the harbor of Athens at Piraeus (Figure 1.3).[8] The most famous Scandinavian warrior in the Byzantine army was Harald Sigurdsson, also known as Harald the Ruthless (Harðráði). Icelandic sagas recount Harald's lucrative adventures as a leader in the Byzantine emperor's army, which included daring sieges in Africa, Sicily, and Palestine. As fantastic as these ventures sound, Greek chronicles confirm that Harald (called Araltes) and his five hundred warriors were integrated into the Byzantine wars in Sicily and Bulgaria around 1040 and that Harald was named leader of the emperor's bodyguard as a reward for his services.[9] The sagas talk of his romantic involvement with the empress and subsequent imprisonment. By contrast, the Greek sources say only that Harald was detained in Byzantium against his will before he made an escape back to his homeland. The sagas tell of his travels back to Norway, where he used his great wealth to become king of Norway before launching an invasion of England, just weeks before William the Conqueror and his Normans reached the southern shores of Britain. The sagas and English sources concur that Harald's story ended with his death on the

Figure 1.3 The Piraeus Lion, which once stood guard over the port of Athens, now stands outside the military ship construction facilities in Venice. The runic inscriptions carved into its flanks and shoulders bear witness to the Scandinavian mercenaries among the Byzantine military. The text is difficult but might read: "They cut [the runes], the men of the host. . . but in this harbor those men cut runes after Haursi, the free farmer. . . Svear (Swedish) men applied this on the lion. He fell before he could receive payment. Young warriors cut the runes. Asmund carved these runes, they, Eskil, Thorlev, and. . . ." (Adapted from Snædal 2016: 187–214.)
Source: photo by author

battlefield of Stamford Bridge in 1066, a date that has traditionally been used as the historical end of the Viking Age.

Methodological Voyages

This book too is about voyages, not just those of the Vikings, but voyages through historical sources, archaeological evidence, and new scientific approaches to the Vikings. The book offers an optimistic yet critical methodology that explores the complexities of weaving together narratives of text and material culture. Recent advances in excavation methods and archaeological science, coupled with a re-evaluation of oral traditions and written sources, inspire the telling of new stories that further our understanding of the Viking Age. This book draws equally on archaeology and historical sources, and capitalizes on the increasingly impactful results of scientific analyses of people, things, and landscapes. This is certainly not the first book that draws on interdisciplinary lines of evidence to understand the Viking Age—many do so—but the novelty of this book is that it explicitly seeks balance among the sources, treating each source type separately before drawing them together for conclusions.

This book proposes that we directly address "the three Cs"—confirmation, contradiction, and complementarity—that emerge when we juxtapose the independent data sets of archaeology, written sources, and scientific analysis. The dialogues created among history, archaeology, and hard scientific analyses result in an entanglement of **confirmation** (texts, archaeology, and science confirming the same story), **contradiction** (texts, archaeology, and science telling incompatible stories), and **complementarity** (texts, archaeology, and science telling supporting stories). By exploring these three arenas and checking the sources against one another, we can arrive at new synthetic understandings of the Vikings and resolve some of the key controversies of the Viking Age.

Although the sources of evidence can be broadly divided into written texts, archaeology, and scientific analyses, the reality is that within each of these broad groups there are different and diverse types of data sets that require specific disciplinary approaches and interpretation. Written sources, for instance, include those sources that traditional historians are more confident about, namely contemporary documents—such as chronicles, annals, church inventories, letters, and travelers accounts—written at or around the time of the events that they describe. For the vast majority of the Viking Age, these were all written by non-Scandinavians living outside of Scandinavia, who had their own preconceptions of the Vikings. These views are mostly colored by hostility and fear, and they sometimes show awe and curiosity and, less frequently, genuine understanding. The external nature of these sources means that the Viking Age in Scandinavia can be viewed as a proto-historical period in which there are almost no contemporary written sources composed by Scandinavians themselves. Instead, we must rely on foreign accounts, oral traditions written down several generations after the Viking Age, and snippets of text written in the runic alphabet on objects and stones (Figure 1.4). Strictly speaking, the short runic inscriptions in Old Norse—the language of the Vikings—are the only primary sources from Scandinavia in this period. This has led some scholars to want to write the history of the Vikings based almost exclusively on runic inscriptions.[10] This is rather limiting, when so many other sources of information exist. For example, orally transmitted poetry from the Viking Age was passed down through several generations before being committed to writing, embedded within prose sagas and as poetic compendia. Among these poems, the so-called Eddic poetry provides a wealth of information about Viking legends and mythology, while skaldic poetry composed in the courts of Viking Age leaders preserves deeds and ideals of the elite and their supporters. In addition, some post-Viking Age law code compilations, such as the Icelandic *Grágás* and the Norwegian *Gulathing's Law*, contain elements of Viking Age law. The largest corpus of written sources preserving Viking Age oral tradition are the Icelandic prose sagas. The Icelanders had a reputation—even in the Viking Age—for their excellence in skaldic poetry that preserved old stories and immortalized contemporary achievements. These stories were written down in Iceland in a time of great literary fluorescence beginning in the twelfth

Figure 1.4 The runic alphabet, called Futhark after the first six letters, was used in the Viking Age to carve short inscriptions into wood, bone, and stone. None of the runes employ horizontal lines, suggesting that the alphabet was designed to avoid obscuring lines in horizontal wood grains. The older runic alphabet (Elder Futhark), which appeared by the second century AD, had twenty-four letters. In the century leading up to the Viking Age the alphabet was reduced to the sixteen runes that make up the Younger Futhark. The runic alphabet was originally an elite technology primarily used for magical and curative purposes. The state of literacy in the Viking Age is debated, but at least by the tenth century, the messages and placements of runestones indicate a desire for their inscriptions to be read.
Source: graphic by author

century. Today, the sagas make up the largest corpus of medieval vernacular texts in all of Europe.

Since the sagas are the most controversial of the historical sources used in this book, it is worth exploring the methodological challenges that they present in greater detail. After the waning of Romantic notions that the sagas could be taken at their word as true historical accounts, modern saga scholarship split between adherents of Bookprose Theory, who believed that the sagas were fictional literary creations, and adherents of Freeprose Theory, who held that the sagas were orally composed works that were transferred intact into the their current written form.[11] The study of the sagas as a source of history has subsequently revolved around the interlinked issues of orality and historicity. The first question is whether the sagas derive from a stable oral tradition that stretches back into the Viking Age. The second question is whether they retain historically accurate information. If the sagas were not orally transmitted, then they cannot retain material from the Viking Age. On the other hand, if they contain historically accurate information, then this historical material must derive from transmission through oral tradition.

Recent breakthroughs in the understanding of the potential stability of oral tradition derived from ethnographic field work,[12] laboratory work of cognitive psychologists,[13] and the study of preserved oral traditions in Icelandic Sagas,[14] as well as independent verification of saga stories by archaeological research,[15] have led to a more nuanced understanding of the relationship between orality and historicity. Most modern scholars now agree that the sagas do retain information from oral tradition and that they have been shown to portray sociological and historical realities from the Viking Age. The sagas are now regularly employed as historical texts that provide sociological and anthropological insights into the medieval Icelandic society in which the sagas were written, as well as—although with more caution—insights into the earlier Viking Age society that they describe.[16] Scholars agree that the most important element of saga historicity lies not in their retention of specific historical events or characters, but rather in their preservation of information regarding societal patterns and social memory of general historical conditions.

The oral background of the prose sagas that were written down mostly in the thirteenth century can be illustrated by the correspondence of saga stories with mythological scenes from much earlier picture stones and rune stones across the Viking world. For example, multiple monuments depict scenes described in the Icelandic saga legend of Sigurd the Dragon Slayer, including such distinct scenes as the roasting of the dragon Fafnir's heart and Sigurd's horse Grani loaded with Fafnir's treasure (Figure 1.5).[17] The Sigurd legend of the prose sagas is supported by poetic stanzas that helped to retain the story in oral tradition from at least the ninth century until the thirteenth century. The historicity of sagas, in the general

Figure 1.5 The Ramsund Stone carving (Mora, Sweden, c. 1030) depicts episodes from the story of Sigurd the Dragon Slayer that are also recorded in poetry and prose written down in Iceland after the end of the Viking Age. The correspondence of the stories on stone and in text exemplifies the common stories circulating in the Viking Age. The numbered story elements include Sigurd killing the dragon Fafnir (5), Sigurd's horse loaded with the dragon's treasure (4), Sigurd roasting Fafnir's heart (1) and learning the speech of birds (2) after he ingests Fafnir's blood by sucking his burned thumb.

Source: photo from Swedish National Heritage Board, public domain; drawing from Nordisk Familjebok *1876–1899, public domain.*

sense that they depict societal realities of the Viking Age, is supported by both textual and archaeological correspondence. Even some very fantastic accounts in the sagas have been shown to hold historical truth. The case of Harald the Ruthless' travels to Russia and his service in the Byzantine army has already been discussed. Here we can be sure that the Icelandic and Greek traditions are completely separate and preserved distinct recollections of the same historical reality. Probably the most dramatic support for the historical tradition maintained in the sagas, however, came from the archaeological discovery of the Scandinavian Viking Age site at L'Anse aux Meadows on Newfoundland. This discovery confirmed the seemingly fantastic voyages to North America recorded in the Icelandic *Greenlanders' Saga* and *Eirik the Red's Saga*.

Precisely because the Viking Age is a proto-historic period, the importance of archaeological evidence cannot be overstated. The material culture used by the Vikings shows us their world in a different light, simultaneously more mundane and more intimate. At the same time, grand new discoveries of massive monuments that had been forgotten—or purposefully ignored—by the textual record have also reshaped our understanding of the organizational capabilities of Viking Age chieftains and kings. For example, the extraordinary system of centrally planned ring forts in Denmark (addressed in Chapter 5), which changed our view of royal power at the end of the tenth century, have gone completely unmentioned in any historical source. The archaeology of the Vikings is a flourishing field and with every field season, our understanding of the Vikings continues to evolve. Archaeological evidence also comes in many forms, ranging from surveys of habitation sites, roads, and barriers in landscapes, to classic excavations and careful analyses of individual objects.

Straddling the divide between archaeology and texts are the magnificent Viking Age runestones, which carry short written statements and are meaningfully situated in the landscape. They preserve the language of the period, chiseled into stone and embedded in beautiful and intricate artwork. The limitation of runestone texts is that they are mostly very short and contain restricted types of information: most, in fact, are formulaic memorials of inheritance. But even these short messages still provide key insights into inheritance patterns, family structure, and the rights of Viking women.[18] Other ways to look at these monuments provide additional insights into the Viking Age. For instance, their position in the landscape points to important travel routes, meeting sites, and settlements. Their relative frequency through time and space also reveals distinct patterns that help us understand periods of social instability that require more overt statements of inheritance by the elite. Proliferation of runestones with Christian symbols and statements about God and the human soul tells us about the timing of Christianization in local communities, as well as conceptions of the new religion in the early years after conversion. Although not strictly called runestones, as they are typically devoid of text, the Gotlandic picture stones make up another class of decorated commemorative monuments. The artwork on these stones is extraordinary in the preservation of images of ships and scenes related to myth and ritual practices, many of which remain open to interpretation (Figure 1.6).

Also embedded in the landscape as snippets of text are the names that Viking Age people gave to places. Analysis of place names can reveal aspects of local economics, social structure, patterns of religious worship, and even interactions between ethnic and linguistic population groups. Some settlement names indicate local economic resources, like forests or iron-bearing streams. Names containing prefixes or suffixes referring to a large manor or a large house may point to centers of political power. For instance, Uppsalir, meaning "The High Halls," is a famous Swedish royal site, while a series of sites called Husby or Huseby, meaning simply "House-settlement," appear to be linked to royal resource control. Other names point to the use of sites in pre-Christian worship, such as those containing the element -vé (shrine or sacrificial grove). One example of this is the Danish city of Odense, originally Odins-vé. Viking conquests can sometimes be charted in place names. In eastern England, for instance, the proliferation of names bearing the suffixes -by and -thorpe mirror Scandinavian settlement in the region known as the Danelaw (the region of England that followed the law of the Danes). When the Vikings settled the uninhabited islands of the North Atlantic, they had an

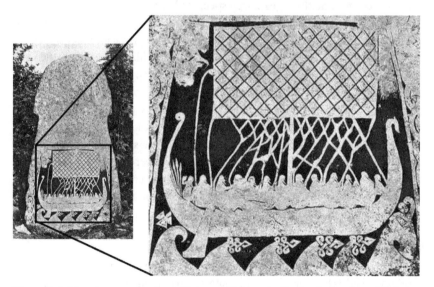

Figure 1.6 The picture stone from Hejnum-Riddare in Gotland, showing a Viking ship in full sail.

Source: Lindqvist 1941: fig. 79.

empty landscape to name. They gave names based on natural features, such as hot springs (Reykjavík or Steam-bay), and important resources such as walrus (Rosmhvalanes or Walrus-peninsula). They also named their farms in systematic ways that hint at settlement order and political hierarchy. The first settlers, for instance, who usually claimed the best lands in a given area, typically named his or her farm after a large landscape feature, such as a prominent or even suggestively shaped mountain. Settlers who arrived later usually employed smaller landscape features or specific suffixes, such as -staðir, in the naming of their farms.

Finally, scientific analyses of things, landscapes, and people are now revolutionizing our understanding of the Vikings. Lab sciences have a long history of use within archaeology, particularly dating techniques such as radiocarbon dating and dendrochronology (tree-ring dating). More recent breakthroughs in tephrochronology (dating by use of volcanic ejecta layers), aided by ice cores extracted from glaciers, are now able to produce dating precision of stratigraphical breaks to within a few years. Analysis of objects recovered from excavations is the oldest of the scientific approaches. Older technologies such as x-rays can for instance reveal the true form of iron objects obscured within a mass of corrosion. But new techniques now abound that reveal an artifact's sub-structural composition, including elemental composition (x-ray fluorescence) and crystalline structure (x-ray diffraction). The vast increase in collecting and sampling in archaeology has contributed assemblages of human and animal bones, plant remains, insect remains, and soils now available for testing using laboratory sciences. Great breakthroughs have especially been made by study of ancient DNA from human remains, which has helped to illustrate differing degrees of replacement and admixture of populations in areas where Scandinavians settled occupied lands, as well as the mixture of genetic populations in the settlement of previously uninhabited landscapes. Further insight into an individual's place of origin can be obtained by studying the signatures of stable and radiogenic isotopes in archaeologically recovered teeth and bones. Since people's skeletons and teeth incorporate isotopic signatures specific to the local geology where their food was produced, isotopic analysis of elements such as strontium, nitrogen, and oxygen can indicate where people were raised and thereby also reveal patterns of migration. The interdisciplinary study of anthropogenic landscapes now routinely includes geologists, geomorphologists, oceanographers, palynologists, and more. From palynologists' study of pollen, for instance, we learn what grains were cultivated, where animals were grazed, and how and when people made changes in their agricultural use of the landscape.

The methodological challenge of studying the Viking Age is determining how (and not whether) to use all of these datasets in combination with one another. Text, archaeology, and scientific techniques provide independent data sets, which is precisely why they constitute such a powerful combination for understanding the past. My approach grew out of my own field research, focusing on integrating archaeological evidence with the Icelandic sagas. In this work, I have come to favor an optimistic view that attempts to directly seek and maximize this integration, allowing an exploration of the interplay among the various data sources. Closing our eyes to archaeological evidence when writing history—or conversely, neglecting textual sources when drawing conclusions from archaeology—results in an incomplete understanding of the past. The challenges are substantial in making sense of vastly different data sets. The pitfalls in interpretation, such as the historically problematic and ever-threatening "tyranny of the text"—that the written record will determine the directions of archaeological research and subsequently dictate the interpretation of the archaeological record—are sizable.[19]

As I hope to show with this book, however, capitalizing on inter-dependencies of archaeology and written sources yields more complete, nuanced, and interesting conclusions.[20] Each chapter presents a case study illustrating how the productive combination of data sets has resulted in breakthroughs in our understanding of the Vikings. I have selected case studies that reveal important insights and that make rich stories, from both a narrative and an analytical perspective. Together, the chapters provide a holistic picture of the Viking Age. I have developed topics that I know well through my own archaeological fieldwork. For example, I have led excavations for many years on early settlers in Iceland (Chapter 6), sought evidence of Viking feasting in the archaeological record (Chapter 3), and excavated in Newfoundland, seeking evidence of Scandinavian colonization in the Americas (Chapter 7). A case-study approach allows an in-depth focus on the selected cases and a close engagement with the myriad interdisciplinary lines of evidence that enrich these stories. The case studies show a focus on the North Atlantic expansion to Iceland and the Americas, drawing on my own fieldwork in Iceland and Newfoundland, and my work on the Icelandic saga material. The North Atlantic region and evidence of Vikings in North America, nearly always treated peripherally in introductory books on the Vikings, are given special attention here.

This book is intended to be useful as an introduction to those wishing to dive directly into the datasets that underlie our knowledge about the Vikings. Additionally, because of its thematic approach, offering interpretation of new and original data on key issues, the book provides more in-depth information for readers already familiar with the Viking Age. As a result, this book does not attempt to cover all aspects or areas of the Viking world equally. For instance, instead of charting Viking raids in France, Germany, Spain, England, Ireland, Scotland, the Baltic lands, and Russia, we will zero in on the case of Britain. In addition to a rich tradition of Viking scholarship there, the Viking experience in Britain has also seen a great deal of new archaeological discoveries and the applications of novel scientific studies that have advanced our understanding of

Scandinavian interactions with Anglo-Saxons, as well as the Celtic and Pictish people who inhabited northern Britain and the islands of the Orkneys, Hebrides, and Shetlands. By contrast, the eastern Viking expansion does not have a chapter of its own in this book, although several chapters do incorporate part of the Viking experience in Eastern Europe and western Asia. Focusing on strategically selected case studies allows for a more thorough treatment of each. Readers are encouraged to seek out other books that provide overview treatments of regions minimally covered in this book.[21]

The case studies that make up the chapters of this book are organized thematically and regionally, and each follows the chronology of the Viking Age. Each chapter offers new conclusions about the Vikings—their views on death, their raiding tactics, their forging of powerful medieval states—by juxtaposing evidence from written sources, archaeology, and new scientific analyses. Each chapter treats evidence from texts and from archaeology before offering examples of rich integrated stories and conclusions. This introductory chapter provides an overview of the Viking expansion and the characteristics of Viking society, aiming to give readers unfamiliar with the Vikings a foundation that will enrich their reading of the case studies in the remainder of the book. With this background, Chapter 2 explores the onset and evolution of Viking raids, with a focus on the Viking experience in Britain. Chapter 3 returns to Scandinavia to understand the traditional political economics that structured Viking society. Chapter 4 continues the explanation of traditional Viking society with an exploration of pre-Christian belief systems, before unpacking the complex and dramatic changes to belief, politics, and economics brought about by Christianization. Chapter 5 focuses on Denmark, analyzing the economic and political development through the Viking Age that culminated in the emergence of a centralized Danish state. Chapter 6 turns to the North Atlantic to understand the forces behind peaceful Viking Age expansion into unoccupied territories and their efforts at colonization. Here, the successful peopling of Iceland, which has such a wonderfully rich textual and archaeological record, is the focus of the story. Chapter 7 interweaves the limited, fascinating, and—at times—controversial data that we have on the farthest Viking expansion into North America. The remainder of this introduction provides an overview of key aspects of Viking economics, politics, and ideology that will help to frame the rest of the book.

Scandinavia at the Dawn of the Viking Age

The Scandinavian homelands of the Vikings are geographically vast and geologically varied. The northernmost tip of arctic Norway lies 2,000 km from the Danevirke ramparts that demarcate the southern border of Viking Age

Denmark. This is farther than the distance from Danevirke to the southernmost tip of the toe of the Italian peninsula. The three modern nations of Denmark, Norway, and Sweden cover an area of nearly 900,000 km², and together they have a coastline of over 110,000 km. In general, the extensive coastline of Scandinavia is characterized by fjords, inlets, and archipelagos of island clusters and island strings. The sea has been a dominant force for Scandinavians, shaping population movements and economic adaptations, and ameliorating the climate. No place in Denmark is farther than 55 km from an arm of the sea, and Norway— the North Way—takes its name from the maritime navigational route leading north into the arctic.

Scandinavia lies between 54°30′ and 71°15′ north, roughly the same north-south extent as Alaska. Scandinavia is cold, but not *that* cold. This northerly region is saved, climatically speaking, by the Gulf Stream, which brings warmer weather and a great deal of rain to Northwestern Europe from the South Atlantic. The Gulf Stream blesses Denmark, western Norway, and southern Sweden with a temperate marine climate that includes cool summers and mild winters. Even far north toward the Arctic Circle, the coastal region of western Norway has a relatively mild climate. The Keel Mountain Range that separates Norway from Sweden blocks some of the effects of the Gulf Stream from moving farther east, leaving eastern Norway and central Sweden with a more continental climate, comprising humid summers and colder winters. Progressing north in the inland regions of Norway and Sweden sub-arctic and then arctic conditions prevail.

A glance at an aerial photograph of Scandinavia from mid-March 2002 shows the large portions of the region that are covered with snow for much of the year, while also offering some keys to understanding the settlement pattern of the pre-modern periods (Figure 1.7). The northern part of the Scandinavian peninsula, protruding from today's Finland and Russia, was and still is sparsely populated. Northerly inland and highland areas were inhabited by the nomadic Sámi who spoke a Finno-Ugric language. Interactions between Scandinavians and Sámi were constant and varied throughout the Viking Age, involving peaceful trade, tribute extraction, and intermarriage. Scandinavian people speaking various dialects of the mutually intelligible Old Norse language lived in the southern and coastal regions of Scandinavia and in low-lying riverine valleys stretching farther inland. Settlements were often situated along rivers and beside lakes with access to the sea. The densest settlements stretched across the fertile lowlands of Denmark and southern Sweden. Other population centers were concentrated around the fjords and lakes of eastern central Sweden and in the plains of the Oslo and Trondheim fjords in Norway, with sparser settlements clustered in the narrow strips of inhabitable lands along the coast and glacial fjords of Norway.

Figure 1.7 Scandinavia and the Baltic Sea region in mid-March of 2002.
Source: image by Jacques Descloitres, MODIS Land Rapid Response Team at NASA GSFC, public domain,

Economics: Settlement and Exchange

Viking Age Scandinavians were primarily a rural, agricultural, and agro-pastoral people. Most people were farmers who lived in villages and farms. They culti-vated grains in fields and vegetables in gardens, while rearing domesticated ani-mals. Cultivated crops included mainly barley and rye, but also oats and wheat. In small gardens, they grew cabbage, beans, and peas. Cereals were eaten in por-ridge, as bread, and consumed as beer. Wild plants and berries were used for flavoring. Hay fields were also of crucial importance as they provided fodder for animals, especially through the winter. In southern Scandinavia, this was easier as animals could be left outdoors for longer portions of the winter to fend for themselves. In places like northern Norway and the North Atlantic islands, however, hay production was the key to survival for a predominantly sedentary pastoral economy.

Viking households kept a variety of domesticated animals, including cattle, horses, pigs, sheep, goats, and chickens, as well as geese and ducks. As might be expected, Viking Age livestock ratios utilized in Scandinavia varied by region. Cattle rearing for meat and milk was popular everywhere, but the southern regions of Denmark and southern and central Sweden were more suitable to this practice. Sheep were kept universally and had the advantage of being better adapted to environmental conditions in northern Scandinavia, the western coast of Norway, and in the North Atlantic islands settled during the Viking Age. Pigs were prized for meat and could be kept in forested regions, while goats were kept especially in highland areas where they could forage on steeper hillsides and mountains. Chickens, geese, and ducks were less common. Animals were typically slaughtered in the autumn, before winter set in. Thereafter meat was preserved by drying, salting, and smoking, and in the North Atlantic, especially by pickling in the sour whey left over from cheese production. Most animals, except for pigs, had other uses besides meat, as transportation, traction, and for secondary products used to make clothes, tools, and decorative items. Sheep were particularly important for their wool, necessary in large quantities not only for clothes but also for the sails on ships.

Farms supplemented agricultural production with hunting and gathering strategies appropriate to the varied regions. Fishing in the sea, as well as in rivers and lakes, was important nearly everywhere; this is demonstrated by the nearly ubiquitous presence of fishing equipment like net sinkers, fishhooks, and eel spears in archaeological excavations, as well as the fish bones found in houses and middens. Along the northern coast of Norway and in the North Atlantic, they hunted seal and walrus and utilized whales that drifted ashore for meat and blubber. They hunted birds in wetlands and highlands, and gathered eggs from lowlands and cliff-sides alike.

Settlement was primarily rural, with people living mostly in villages and dispersed farmsteads. Villages were the norm in the low-lying lands of Denmark and southern Sweden, where the climate and topography allowed extensive agriculture combining cereal cultivation with stock-rearing. A dispersed settlement pattern of individual farmsteads predominated in more northerly areas and the North Atlantic islands, where cereal cultivation was more difficult and economies centered on stock-rearing, especially of sheep. Villages consisted of a cluster of farms that retained economic self-sufficiency. Individual farm units

were often demarcated by a fence surrounding a central house, a series of ancillary buildings, and a garden. The lack of central administrative buildings and
the absence of communal storage facilities in villages reinforce that individual
farming households retained these functions. Each farm in the village replicated
many of the same buildings and features that would have allowed the units to
retain independent agricultural function. For instance, in the Danish village of
Vorbasse, individual farms had their own well, hay-storage facility, and smithy.

Whether in villages or as separate farms, the main houses were three-aisled
longhouses, following a long Scandinavian house-building tradition. In most
places in Scandinavia, the internal layout of these houses was similar, consisting
of a wide central aisle and two flanking side aisles. In a central room, the middle
aisle often had an open fireplace, while the side aisles consisted of raised living
platforms or benches upon which people worked and slept. In the early Viking
Age, livestock was often kept in rooms flanking the central room. Later in the
Viking Age, animals were moved out into separate stall buildings. Although the
internal framing and superstructural support system of the longhouses were
consistently made of wood across the Viking world, the external walls varied
greatly in construction material depending on the natural materials available
in the environment. In tree-rich areas of central Scandinavia, wooden planks
were employed, while wattle-and-daub construction was used in many areas of
Denmark, and stone and turf walls were the norm in the North Atlantic. Smaller
ancillary buildings for additional living quarters, workshops, and storage were
clustered around the central longhouses. Sometimes these buildings were dug
down as semi-subterranean structures known as pit houses, which may have had
humid conditions particularly suited to the work of weaving.[22]

The Viking Age saw the exponential expansion of trade, the emergence of
urbanism, and a significant movement of people from rural farms and villages
into towns. This process was associated with a rise in centralized royal power,
and the nascent towns of the Viking Age were sponsored by ambitious kings
seeking to control and benefit from the growing trade. Of course, the urban dynamism of the age also grew out of pre-existing conditions. In fact, the onset of
the Viking Age—which saw the large-scale movements of Scandinavians beyond
their homelands—was predicated on the pre-existence of a flourishing system
of inter-regional exchange. Scandinavians participating in this trade brought
back stories of wealth and opportunity abroad. Already before the onset of the
Viking Age, urban characteristics had started to appear at Ribe in southwestern
Denmark, where trade flourished with neighbors to the south and across the
English Channel.

The first urban centers in Scandinavia were seasonal marketplaces. Even from
the early period, these sites show signs of centralized planning, with formal
boundaries and consistent plot sizes for craftsmen and merchants. The largest

trading centers, known as emporia, served primarily as nexuses of interregional trade, linking the Viking homelands with the outside world. The four major emporia of Ribe, Hedeby, Kaupang, and Birka each served as hubs oriented toward different directions in the interregional exchange beyond Scandinavia. Ribe, located close to the southwestern border of Denmark, was directed toward the trade of the Carolingian Empire and Anglo-Saxon Britain. Hedeby on the eastern coast of southern Jutland faced east toward the Baltic Sea trade and south toward the Saxon lands in Germany. Kaupang, located in the Oslo Fjord, linked trade networks especially to northern Norway, while Birka looked farthest east toward the goods and markets of the eastern Baltic and the Russian/Ukrainian river systems. The emporia were linked both to smaller regional marketplaces and to the local agricultural hinterlands, which provided food in exchange for the imports that are often found in nearby villages. Smaller marketplaces that continued to be seasonally occupied longer into the Viking Age served to link local areas to the larger network.

Lively trade took place between these emporia, such that goods from everywhere in the Viking world are found at each emporium. The archaeological remains from the emporia reveal sites with an international and multi-ethnic composition. While archaeology indicates the presence of foreign merchants and craft specialists, written sources from beyond Scandinavia attest to visits by missionaries, merchants, and probably even spies from as far afield as the Umayyad Caliphate of Córdoba.[23] A diverse range of products made their way into the system from the contacts beyond the homelands. Silver, silk, and gems flowed in from the east; intricate Anglo-Saxon metalwork arrived from across the North Sea; and Frankish swords, worked glass, high-quality quern stones, wine, and Rhenish pottery entered the Scandinavian ports from the Carolingian lands to the south. Many of these imports were directed toward elite households, but the presence of imports in villages and on farms across Scandinavia testifies to the penetration of this trade into rural communities.

Long-distance trade also flourished within Scandinavia. Right at the start of the Viking Age and perhaps earlier, important trade networks had developed that connected the emporia with the far reaches of northern Norway. A series of offshore islands protected ships plying the long distances between northern Norway and the rest of Scandinavia. The motivation for these journeys was in large part marine and terrestrial animal products of the Arctic. Walrus tusks fetched high prices in Europe, while walrus and seal hide made the best ship ropes and cables and blubber was useful in oil lamps. Western Norway was also a source of stone products deriving from the Keel Mountains. Soapstone, which is easily workable, was used to make bowls, spindle whorls, and other objects. Significant quantities of whetstones used to sharpen iron edges, which were quarried in the Trondelag region, have been found in the emporium of Ribe. The name Norway—the North Way—was already used in the Viking Age and likely refers to this trade route.

The Viking Ship: Catalyst of the Viking Age

Advances in ship technology transformed the economics and politics of Scandinavia during the Viking Age. Long before the Viking Age, the maritime focus of Scandinavian society meant that boats held vital importance to economics, politics, and ideological belief systems. The boat technology that was revolutionized in the Viking Age relied on an indigenous Scandinavian technological trajectory stretching deep into the prehistory of Scandinavia. Evidence of dug-out canoes used for fishing and hunting in lakes and wetlands dates back to the Mesolithic period (7000–5000 BC). By the Scandinavian Bronze Age (2000–500 BC), rock carvings depict double-prowed boats being employed for ritual displays, as well as economic activity. The art reveals a cosmological system in which a boat transports the sun on its nightly journey, as well as the souls of the dead to the next world. This period also saw the first appearance of the so-called ship-settings—stones erected linearly in the shape of a ship—that often contain graves or mark special locations in the landscape. This tradition would continue in Scandinavia into the Viking Age and up until the conversion to Christianity. In the Pre-Roman Iron Age (500–1 BC), boats of similar appearance have been recovered from bogs, where they were sacrificed along with the equipment of defeated raiding parties. Boats and weapon assemblages from places like Hjortspring, where four or five boats were found accompanied by the equipment of 80–130 warriors, show that complex maritime raiding parties were already roaming Scandinavia by the fourth century BC. The Hjortspring boat, which measured about 2 x 20 m, was propelled by paddling, as is done in a canoe. The boats were, in fact, essentially enhanced and upgraded canoes: the bottoms consisted of hollowed-out tree trunks, with overlapping planks added on either side and lashed together with rawhide cords.

Boat sizes increased in the Roman Iron Age (AD 1–500), as exemplified by the fourth-century boat from the Nydam bog, measuring 4 x 23 m. These boats were built in what is called clinker-style construction, in which increasing numbers of overlapping planks were fastened to one another with iron rivets. The Nydam boat also shows a major advance in boat propulsion, as it was rowed rather than paddled, allowing for a significant increase in speed. Like the later Viking ships, the prow and stern were interchangeable so that the boat could be rowed in to shore in one direction and rowed back in the opposite direction. Evidence of the further evolution of the indigenous Scandinavian boat-building tradition was found in Kvalsund Norway, where a boat built right at the dawn of the Viking Age (AD 780–800) came to light in the straits off the island of Nerlandsøy.[24] The Kvalsund boat was rowed, like the Nydam boat, but its keel was much more solidly built, and it possessed the detachable rudder on the right or starboard—from Old Norse *stýriborð*. Both these were characteristics of later Viking ships.

Nonetheless, the Kvalsund ship still lacked the key innovation that transformed Iron Age boats into Viking ships. This innovation was the sail, and it would usher in the Viking Age. This essential improvement in ship technology required the addition of structural wooden elements above the keel to support the force acting upon a mast with raised sail. The Salme ship from circa 750 may have had a mast and sail, but incontrovertible evidence of these innovations is clearly visible for the first time in the Oseberg ship, built around 800 and interred in a burial mound in 834. The key innovation was the addition of two large wooden supports for the mast: (1) a keelson placed on top of the keel to serve as a mast slot, and (2) a deck-level mast fastener, which is known as a "mast fish" because of its suggestive shape. A removable wedge in the massive mast fish allowed the mast to be lowered. Finally, the production of the massive sails is too often overlooked in the story of the development of Scandinavian ship technology. Sail making demanded a comparable labor investment as the construction of the wooden ship itself. At the start of the Viking Age, the increased need for sheep's wool required an expansion of grazing lands and an economic reorganization of farms and villages, where women spun and wove the cloth for sails on traditional vertical standing looms.[25] The ramifications of the invention of the sail-bearing ship, which added wind power to the methods of aquatic propulsion, transformed the economics of raiding and trading and revolutionized the ability of the Scandinavians to interact with people far beyond their regional borders.

In contrast to the ships of the Mediterranean tradition, which were built from the inside-out, Viking ships were built from the outside-in. The shell of the ship was built first, with overlapping planks made from logs split radially with an axe so that each timber retained the natural strength of the tree. The planks were fastened together by the clinker method, using a type of iron rivet known as a clench bolt, and then caulked with animal hair and tree sap. Once the shell was complete, an internal wooden frame of larger timbers was lashed and pegged into place to brace the external shell. The Viking shipwrights' final product was light-weight, yet flexible and strong. In the waves of the open sea, the natural strength of the planks allowed the outer shell to flex and bend without breaking, while the internal frame fastened to the shell with wooden pegs and cords allowed the ships' composite parts to shift and adjust to water pressure. Simultaneously, this construction method permitted the keel of the ships to sit high in the water, so that the ships could be navigated in shallow waters and pulled ashore easily.

Scandinavian boat builders made increasingly specialized ships as the Viking Age progressed, beginning with all-purpose ships and over time creating ships designed specifically for war and for trade. The Oseberg ship exemplifies the early type of all-purpose ship. By 830, this type of ship—known in the later literature as a karv—was perfected in the Gokstad ship. Like the Oseberg ship, the Gokstad ship was equipped with a single sail, a steering oar on the right side, and sealable oar-holes, which would have served to keep out the higher waters of the open sea. As the ships became increasingly specialized, a clear distinction developed between warships built for speed, and trading vessels built to maximize cargo space. Called longships, warships were relatively narrow, with high length-to-width ratios. Longships were designed to carry large numbers of rowers who could propel the ships quickly up and down rivers once the sails were taken down. These warships, as illustrated by ships found in Roskilde Fjord in Denmark, could be well over 30 m long and accommodate a crew of over a hundred. Specialized trading vessels, known as knerrir (sing. knǫrr), were much wider in relation to the length to accommodate a large trading cargo. The carrying capacity of a knǫrr recovered from the Hedeby harbor was between 13 and 38 tons. The high sides of the knǫrr also made them exceptionally sea-worthy and safe for voyaging on the open seas. Smaller vessels called byrdings, with a crew of perhaps half a dozen, were used as coastal and riverine transport and trading vessels.[26] The various Viking ship types provided the means of connectivity that tied together the communities of Scandinavia and linked them to the economic potentials of far-flung foreign lands.

Social Structure and Politics

Scandinavia was a class-based society from the start of the Viking Age. The social organization of Viking Age Scandinavia comprised slaves, attached workers, free farmers, chieftains, and kings. Social class difference can be seen in farmsteads and grave sites. Farm sizes varied both within villages and in dispersed farms, indicating a significant level of hierarchical differentiation. Large manors occupied by chieftains enclosed more extensive farm areas, had bigger central longhouses, and had more numerous and varied ancillary structures. Modest farms may have housed extended families and a few attached workers, while larger farms accommodated larger numbers of workers and political supporters, as well as slaves. Wealthier farms can also often be recognized by larger stall areas, wherein were housed a greater number of livestock. Viking Age burials also show wide variety in the amount of wealth invested. A great many graves are rather simple, with few grave goods accompanying the dead. Others, such as the famous mound burials containing enormous amounts of wealth, include ships and carts, weapons, animal sacrifices, and other grave goods. Even human sacrifices have been recognized in a few high-status burials. These sacrifices are assumed to have been slaves accompanying their masters in death.[27]

A useful—although perhaps oversimplified—view of Viking society is provided in the Old Norse poem *Rígsþula* (*The Poem of Ríg*). Composed in the Viking Age and preserved in an early fourteenth-century Icelandic vellum codex, *Rígsþula* describes how the god Heimdall visited three successive earthly households and, by sleeping with the wife of each household, became the progenitor of the three human social classes: slaves, free farmers, and the elite.[28] Heimdall, traveling disguised as a visitor named *Ríg*, first accepts hospitality at a poor household. He is given a lumpy loaf of bread and a bowl of broth to eat before settling in for three successive nights, during which he lies in bed between the couple of the house. Nine months after his visit, a son, named Thrall (Slave), is born. Thrall, described as physically unattractive with wrinkled skin and a stooped back, grows up to marry a woman named Thir (Slave Woman). Their union is described as happy, but the work of their children is that expected of slaves: building fences, spreading manure on fields, herding goats, and cutting peat. The account of this visit ends with a list of the pejorative names of Thrall and Thir's children—like Stinky, Crooked-back, Skinny-hips, and Stumpy—followed by the explicit statement that all the slave families are descended from them.

Heimdall spends his next three nights with a well-dressed couple living in a longhouse with expensive wooden flooring, where he is fed "boiled veal and fine delicacies."[29] Here, too, he lies between the couple for three nights, and nine months later, a son named Karl (Free Farmer) is born. Karl marries Snor (Daughter-in-Law) and performs work that is fitting for his station: breaking oxen, plowing fields, building houses, and erecting barns. The work described for a woman in the free-farmer household is spinning yarn and weaving cloth. Again, the poem gives a list of their children's names—like Manly, Landowner, and Sparkling—before stating that all the free-farmer families are descended from this union.

At the third household, Heimdall finds a wealthy man making a bow and arrows, sitting beside his wife, who is dressed in fine colored linen. They offer an extravagant meal served on silver dishes and heaped with a variety of meats, including fish, bacon, and roasted fowl. For the first time, he is offered alcohol: fine wine poured from a jug into decorated cups. Nine months later, the wife gives birth to a boy named Jarl (Earl), who grows up learning the arts of war. While learning to fight with sword, shield, bow, and spear, he also practices horseback riding, hunting with dogs, and competitive swimming. This is the only child that Ríg revisits and recognizes as his own child by giving him his name, teaching him runes, and encouraging him to conquer other lands. The boy takes his task to heart, conquering eighteen estates before engaging in the classic chieftain behaviors to reward followers and generate loyalty: he "shared out wealth, gave to all gifts and treasures, and slender horses. He distributed finger rings, cut up arm rings."[30]

The *Rígsþula* poem reveals an explicitly class-conscious society that associates the three classes of unfree, free, and elite with distinct clothing, work, food, and even skin color—Thrall is dark-skinned, while Karl is red and ruddy, and Jarl is blond with bright cheeks. Although the description would certainly have been seen as oversimplified, even in the Viking Age, it gives a clear impression of the conceptual models of each class. The signaling of status through house size, clothing, serving dishes, food, and drink is consistent with archaeological evidence from excavated Viking Age households and cemeteries. The focus on the elite household and the role of the elite in battle, conquest, and redistribution of wealth to generate loyalty is also completely consistent with other historical sources, our anthropological understating of Germanic chiefdoms, and the archaeological record. Interestingly, the end of the poem turns ominous with the story of Jarl's youngest son, Kin, whose name might well be an allusion to a King.[31] Kin learns magic runes and the speech of birds before outwitting Ríg with trickery and thereby taking forcefully his inherited name. Kin spends his time killing birds before a lone crow advises him to turn his attention back to the killing of men. The crow's enticing words also contain a warning that rich, nearby chieftains know well how to "command ships, sharpen sword blades, and rip open wounds."[32] The ambiguous and even anxious feelings toward kings betrayed by the poem reveal real Viking Age societal tensions generated as kings forcefully centralized power through warfare and conquest. In Iceland, for instance, where the *Rígsþula* poem was preserved, the immigration narrative contained recollections of fleeing the growing power of the Norwegian king and establishing a polity that was purposefully designed to be free of kings.

The sources of power available to early Viking Age Scandinavians—whether farmers, chieftains, or kings—were derived from kinship relationships, economic wealth, military strength, political functions, and ideological conceptions. The kings, at least at the start of the Viking Age, were not so different from the chieftains who had to use constellations of these sources to grow and retain their power.[33] The basic support network of any Viking Age Scandinavian began with their kin group, both real and fictive, through marriage. Inherited family land was part of inalienable allodial (i.e., freely held without obligation) property known as oðal.[34] The land was important as the basis of a family's economic output, but also for political standing, as land ownership was the basis of political rights. Through the Viking Age, kings attempted to wrest allodial property from farmers and local leaders.

Economic power was primarily derived from landed estates. Kings and chieftains had larger estates than most farmers and thereby more power. Kings, who had been instrumental in establishing the early trading emporia, might have charged rent for the well-organized plots and surely charged some form of toll on merchant passage in emporia and along the travel routes that they controlled. The positioning of elite manors overlooking the emporia in places like Birka, Kaupang, and Hedeby indicate a level of royal oversight and control. Excavations at Füsing, overlooking Hedeby and Huseby above Kaupang, revealed large houses and settlement complexes rich in high-status prestige goods.[35] The hall at Huseby, for instance, measured 40 m in length and included elite objects such as imported glass drinking vessels, precious metal jewelry, and glass beads, as well as weapons typically associated with high-status sites.[36] The inclusion of the name prefix Hus- ("house") followed by the settlement suffix -bú ("farm") in the site overlooking Kaupang and at other sites across Scandinavia often indicates the presence of a royal estate where the king centralized and redistributed goods.[37] The written sources mention kings residing in the trading sites, but no elite residences within the early towns have been discovered to date. It is likely that when the sources talk of kings residing in towns, they are in fact referring to these rich manors positioned strategically just outside and overlooking the towns. Toward the end of the Viking Age, the royal residences—along with other key functions of governance, like coin minting and religious worship—moved into towns (see Chapter 5).

Military prowess, achieved through the ability to recruit warriors for local conflicts and overseas ventures, was arguably the most important source of power for Viking leaders. Yet, military power was limited by the absence of any real standing armies. Powerful leaders, whether kings or chieftains, sought in-stead to surround themselves with bands of skilled warriors. This warrior band, known as a hirð, followed a long Germanic tradition of warriors personally loyal to war leaders described already by the Roman historian Tacitus in the first century AD. These warriors formed the core and elite members of a leader's war party. Leaders formed bonds of personal loyalty by rewarding warriors with valuable gifts, food, and shelter, and through lavish feasts that simultaneously in-debted supporters and accentuated the special status of the host (see Chapter 3). A key challenge for Viking leaders was to convince people beyond their core group of followers to board ships and set out on raiding and trading expeditions far from home. The limited scope of the power of early Viking leaders meant that this is unlikely to have been accomplished by coercion alone. Rather, leaders offered shares in the spoils of war achieved through plunder, tribute, and ransom or through profitable trading, in many cases exchanging for profit products, like slaves, which were violently taken during raiding expeditions. In addition, leaders might be able to summon a levy of warriors from villages and farms over which they exerted a measure of control, although the extent that this was achievable in practice during the early Viking Age is unclear. By the late Viking Age, the increasingly powerful kings do appear to have been able to summon a levy from wide geographical areas, but even then, the levy could be unreliable and even dangerous. For one king, the Danish Saint Knut, violence inflicted by a mob disgruntled by a levy led to his martyrdom.[38]

Popular assemblies—called þings—were the major arenas for public political action outside of the households of individual leaders. These assemblies, held at regular times and places during the year, served legislative and judicial purposes. The formal purpose of these assemblies was to make and recite laws, and to resolve disputes. Each assembly had a law speaker, who was responsible for reciting a certain portion of the law and for leading proceedings. Landowning males and especially chieftains were the main participants at assemblies, but landowning women could actively participate in some legal matters, especially if widowed or unmarried. Based on percentages of runestones sponsored by women who presumably owned land, it has been suggested that women may have comprised up to 10 percent of legal participants in assemblies.[39] Beyond the direct participants in legal proceedings, a large number of non-participants attended the assemblies because assemblies also served many other social functions. These sorts of popular assemblies, like the warrior bands, had been a feature of Germanic society for centuries and are described by Tacitus and even depicted on the column of Marcus Aurelius in Rome from 193.

Assemblies can be divided broadly into local þings representing smaller geographical areas, and macro-regional þings serving larger geographical zones encompassing the jurisdiction of more than one local assembly. Each macro-regional or top-level assembly appears to have made and upheld independent laws, as evidenced by the preservation of law books from several different districts of Norway and Sweden.[40] The geographic extent of the regional þings varied significantly, but none of the traditional assemblies had powers that extended across the geographical areas of the Scandinavian kingdoms of the late Viking Age. Instead, later medieval documents suggest that Norway had six law provinces, while Sweden had a dozen. Denmark may have had the fewest, as documents suggest that there may have been only three macro-regional assemblies at Viborg, Ringsted, and Lund. This may have been a result of the smaller geographical size of Denmark, but also perhaps testifies to a greater political centralization. Interestingly, and by contrast, Iceland, where native kings never developed, had a single macro-regional assembly, known as the Alþingi (anglicized as Althing), where the Icelanders made laws and resolved disputes for the whole island.

The assemblies were led by chieftains, called goðar (singular, goði), who were duty- bound to attend local and regional assemblies together with their supporters or thingmen (þingmen). The name goði is cognate with the word "god," indicating that these chieftain-priests possessed leadership roles in both politics and in the pre-Christian cult worship that was practiced in elite halls, in temples, in sacred groves, and at assemblies. The lawspeaker for each assembly was typically drawn from the goði-chieftain class. The role of kings at assemblies is not so clearly defined. The top-level assemblies needed to accept kings publicly when they inherited or violently took power. The need for public acceptance of kings is probably linked to a sacral role that kings had in maintaining the fertility of their lands. Some legendary narratives about early kings suggest that the sacral role could be enacted at the assemblies, although this did not always work out to their benefit.[41] For instance, the legendary King Domaldi was sacrificed by the congregation of assembly-goers at Uppsala in Sweden in a plea to the gods to return fertility to their lands.[42] In general, as royal power grew in Scandinavia, the power of the popular assemblies to make laws, resolve conflicts, and organize political society declined.[43]

The macro-regional assemblies, typically lasting up to a week in the middle of the summer, allowed for ancillary social functions that may well have been just as important as law- making and conflict resolution. These events involved substantial portions of society beyond the participants in the official proceedings of the courts. The saga literature from Iceland is particularly rich in describing the events that surrounded assemblies (see Chapter 6). The sagas describe how people in attendance exchanged valuable information, formed friendships and political alliances, exchanged goods, fell in love, and arranged marriages. Tensions could run high in such public arenas, and interactions could turn hostile as insults flew, swords were drawn, and fights erupted. The risk of vio-lence in these settings was mitigated by strict legal provisions that sanctified the ground of the assembly. Spilling of blood was punished severely, and at least one runestone indicates that asylum could be sought within the bounded area of the assembly.[44]

Assembly sites were commonly located in prominent places along travel routes, beside bodies of freshwater, and along traditional district borders. Human-made features often demarcated assembly boundaries and lent promi-nence to the proceedings. Old burial mounds from centuries before the Viking Age are common at such sites. Sometimes the old mounds were built up further during the Viking Age, to add prominence to the location and elevate the posi-tion of a speaker addressing the assembled group. Recent archaeological work has shown that these sites were more carefully planned than previously thought, with complex arrays of burial mounds, runestones, ship settings, standing stones, temporary houses or booths, and wooden posts arranged in carefully chosen locations that appear physically and symbolically distinct from the sur-rounding landscape. Entry into these sites was given special attention, as indi-cated by lines of wooden posts as high as 6–8 m that form processional routes for entering and leaving sites such as Anundshög and Gamla Uppsala (Figure 1.8). Cooking and brewing pits excavated at Anundshög indicate that communal feasting took place.[45] Substantial work was invested in the creation of these

Figure 1.8 The Anundshög assembly site in central Sweden encompasses burial mounds and ship settings. Recent excavations have revealed rows of wooden posts and standing stones that form a processional road to the left of the two large, paired ship settings.
Source: aerial photo 1935, AB Flygtrafik / Västmanlands läns museum, public domain

sites, and it is likely that local chieftains built these sites as part of their claims to local power. Perhaps they asserted ancestral ties to leadership by the proximity of the burial mounds of the ancestors. Runestones still standing at some assemblies certainly read like advertising of ancestry and perhaps even reveal dueling interests of chieftains competing with one another for local power. In eleventh-century eastern Sweden, for instance, a newly established Christian elite appears to lay down claims to local power through the raising of runestones and construction of assemblies. One of these new leaders, a chieftain named Jarlabanke, constructed a þing site sometime between 1020 and 1075 in order to rival an older pre-Christian þing site that lay just 2 km away.[46] He also erected a series of runestones in the wider area, at least one of which, now found at a nearby church, is connected to the þing site. It reads: "Jarlabanke had this stone raised in memory of himself, and he made this assembly site, and owned the entirety of this hundred."[47] Jarlabanke suggests that his efforts in organizing the labor to construct a þing site should translate into a leadership role for himself at the assembly proceedings. He also overtly connects the assembly site to the ownership of an area known as a hundred, which probably encompassed an area from which one hundred warriors could be recruited. In this short inscription, then, Jarlabanke explicitly links economic, military, and political power, and immortalizes it in stone for all to read.

Mythology and Worldview

The Viking Age Scandinavians believed their world was inhabited by a wide range of supernatural beings, including land spirits, elves, giants, and gods. There was no religious text that produced uniformity of faith or practice. Peoples across Scandinavia had diverse approaches to divine beings and their veneration. At the same time, these beliefs fell under a common umbrella of beliefs that would have been recognizable across the Scandinavian cultural area.

The most well known of the supernatural beings—both to modern readers and to the Viking Age Scandinavians themselves—were the Asgardian gods, who are comparable in many respects to the pantheon of Greco-Roman gods. Mythological stories about these gods were likely known in some form by nearly all Old Norse speakers of the Viking world. Written sources, archaeology, and place names suggest shared beliefs in the primary gods, although veneration of particular gods seems to have varied from region to region. What we know about these gods comes mostly from written sources drawn together in Iceland from oral traditions over a hundred years after the end of the Viking Age. The most important of these written sources are the anonymous compilation of poems known as the *Poetic Edda* and the guide for aspiring poets known as the *Prose Edda*, which was written by the Icelandic chieftain Snorri Sturluson in the early thirteenth century.

Intimately known for Viking Age Scandinavians were the beings and spirits that inhabited the world of humans. Some elves, or *álfar*, were thought to live in a heavenly realm called Álfheimar, while others appear to have been tied to the earth and had to be placated with sacrifices. Dwarves too were mythological beings, dwelling in seemingly otherworldly mountains where they fashioned great metalworking treasures, but they also might be expected in earthly mountains. Trolls might also be found in such places, far removed from human society. The hidden people or *huldufólk* were a class of being that were related to elves, living next to humans on borders of fertile lands in adjacent hills and forests. Huldufólk could be threatening if transgressed. Land spirits in one's homeland could typically be trusted, but other spirits guarding newly discovered lands were unknown quantities that had to be engaged carefully to see if they welcomed new arrivals. Ancestors were venerated and sometimes thought to continue to live within their places of burial on earth. Ancestors could be visited at their grave mounds, and contemplation there could provide more direct access to otherworldly knowledge. Whether an ancestor or not, the dead could rise from their graves and walk again as corporal zombie-like revenants, paying friendly visits to relatives or haunting and violent visits to enemies. Individual living people also had personal spirits called *fylgjur* (sg. fylgja). People with heightened connections to the spirit world might sense these fylgjur before the arrival of a friend or enemy. At times of death, a person's fylgja might become especially visible and might even at that time transfer to another family member. Encounters with all of these supernatural beings might come at unanticipated times or could be sought through ritual specialists by sacrifice, prophecy, or shamanistic practices. Such contact could be a source of danger but also of great power.

The non-Christian belief system of early Viking Age Scandinavians was one of the primary features that distinguished them from other people of Western Europe. The writings of the people that the Vikings encountered placed great importance on their belief system and how it made them more vicious, frightening, and dangerous. Descriptions of Viking raids, such as the letter by Alcuin quoted above, stress the pagan beliefs of the Vikings as the key differentiating characteristics of the godless and merciless raiders. Foreign descriptions of their practices in the Scandinavian homelands also focus on the strangeness of their rituals. Adam of Bremen, a German bishop and chronicler, describes with horror a religion with ritual performances at a temple in Uppsala. Worship of the gods here required the sacrifice of nine of every type of animal, including humans, every nine years. Muslims too found their belief systems of particular interest. The Arab diplomat Ibn Fadlan, who encountered Vikings in a peaceful setting, describes at length their raucous rituals of burial that involved destruction of great wealth and both animal and human sacrifice in a gruesome multi-day feast.

Narrative sources, including the Icelandic sagas, provide parallel views of the types of pagan ritual practices described by foreign observants. Pagan ritual practice, generally called *blót* (blood), included sacrifices of animals (and occasionally of humans), feasting, and veneration of idols made in images of gods such as Thor, Odin, and Frey.[48] Sacrifices occurred in specialized temple buildings, in chieftains' houses, at public assemblies, and outdoors in groves, and sometimes involved "reddening" a *hörgr* or altar of stone with sacrificial blood.[49] Sacrifices were also made to other spirits at certain times of the year.

Archaeology provides another window into pre-Christian Scandinavian cult, with a particular strength in yielding views of actual ritual practices that can be compared with the general mythological conceptions, foreign observances, and saga descriptions. The evidence recovered from chieftains' longhouses, temples, sacrificial sites, and graves complement the views of the rituals described in the written sources by revealing the diversity of ritual activities that still fit within a shared general framework. General confirmation of the belief system described in the mythological poems and the *Prose Edda* is found in the widespread distribution of iconographical representations of gods, heroes, and myths chiseled into stone, woven into textiles, and carved into wood. Recovery of Thor's hammer pendants from many archaeological sites shows devotion to Thor, while figurines that presumably depict Thor, Odin, and Frey indicate their local veneration (Figure 1.9). Invocations of individual gods are also sometimes found in runic messages and protective charms (Figure 1.10).

The remainder of this section deals with Norse mythology and cosmology, providing a background for future chapters in which the myths and gods appear frequently. Pre-Christian ritual practices in temples and open-air sites will be covered further in Chapter 3 on ritual feasts and Chapter 4 on conceptions of death, burial, and the afterlife. The coming of Christianity and the impacts of Christianization on Scandinavian society are treated in several chapters. Chapter 3 discusses the impact of Christianity on politics, while Chapter 4 treats

Figure 1.9 Figurine found at the Eyrarland farm in northern Iceland, showing a seated figure that is usually interpreted as the god Thor gripping a stylized, inverted hammer.

Source: courtesy of the National Museum of Iceland

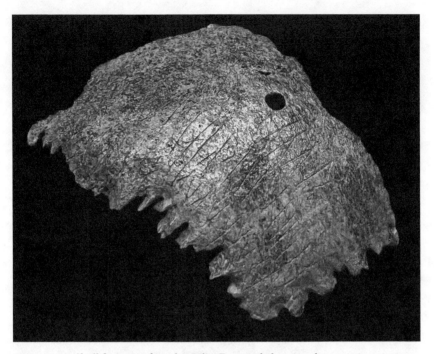

Figure 1.10 Skull fragment found at Ribe, Denmark, bearing the runic inscription "Ulf and Odin, and High Tyr, is help for Bur, against pain and dwarf stroke, [signed] Bur." (Modified by author from MacLeod and Mees 2006: 24.) The drilled hole at the top might indicate that it was suspended on a necklace and worn as a protective talisman or possibly hung in a doorway. Although Odin is seen generally as a fickle god, at least one Viking Age person felt that Odin could be trusted as a protector against sickness and supernatural assaults.
Source: photo by author, Museet Ribes Vikinger

the impacts on conceptions of death and burial, and Chapter 6 details the interesting case of the peaceful Christianization of Iceland.

The Viking mythological world had temporal depth, with events split among those occurring in the mythic past, the mythic present, and the mythic future.[50] In the deep mythic past, before the creation of the cosmos, there existed only a primeval void known as Ginnungagap. This proto-space was suffused with magic powers that were activated when frost from a northerly realm called Niflheim collided with heat from the southerly realm of Muspelheim. Drops of water from the northerly ice condensed to form a primordial frost giant named Ymir. Ymir fed on milk from a primordial cow that also appeared from the thawing frost. The sweat from Ymir's underarms created more giants, as did a strange sexual pairing of his right leg with his left. When the primordial cow began to lick the salty frost blocks, another male being named Buri emerged. He became the forefather of the gods. A series of procreation events ensued. First, Buri begot Bor. Bor then partnered with a giantess named Bestla, who subsequently gave birth to the three gods Odin, Vili, and Vé. The three brothers killed the primordial giant Ymir and formed the world with his body, making the soil with his flesh, the rocks with his bones and teeth, the waters with his blood, and using his skull to form the firmament and his brains to make clouds. Importantly, they shaped his eyebrows to separate the land of men, called Midgard (Middle Enclosure or Middle Earth), from the various lands of the giants, called Jotunheimar (Jǫtunheimar, Homes of the Giants). Only subsequently did the three creator gods fashion the first man, Ask (Ash-tree), and the first woman, Embla (possibly Elm-tree), from driftwood they found on the beach. The sources, which disagree on other details, do agree that Odin was one of the three creators of men and that the three gods vivified the humans with the breath of life, mental faculties, speech, and lifeblood. Uniting the whole completed cosmos was the world tree, Yggdrasil, which extended its limbs over the world. The trunk of Yggdrasil makes the vertical axis of the cosmos, with an underworld below, the world of men in the middle, and the world of the gods above. The roots of Yggdrasil make a horizontal axis, extending down and out beyond the lands of men and gods, and toward the marginal lands of the giants.

In the more recent mythic past, the gods multiplied and crystalized into a stable pantheon. In the mythic present, the gods live in the divine realm of Asgard (Ásgarðr, Enclosure of the Gods), where they each inhabit separate halls and interact with one another in many ways, much like humans on the earth albeit on a grander scale. From Asgard the gods, especially the powerful male gods, could visit the humans of Midgard or venture out to contest with the giants in Jotunheimar. Odin (Óðinn), referred to as the All-father, fostered many of the main family of gods called Æsir (sg. Ás) that inhabit Asgard. Odin is the head of the pantheon, as well as the god of wisdom, war, and magic. The poetry informs that Odin acquired his wisdom by sacrificing himself to himself on the World Tree:

> I know that I hung
> On the windswept tree [Yggdrasil]
> Nine whole nights,
> Spear wounded,
> And given to Odin,
> Myself to myself . . .[51]

Odin's self-sacrifice is usually interpreted as a shamanistic act that allowed a trance-like communion with otherworldly forces. Odin, like many of the gods, also possesses animals and special objects. He rides the eight-legged horse, Sleipnir, bears the magic spear Gungnir, and when sitting in the high-seat, Hliðskjálf, he can see across the entire world. He possesses two ravens, Huginn (Thought) and Muninn (Mind), to whom he taught speech. He sends out his ravens daily to gather information about occurrences in the world of men. He has two wolves, Geri (Hungry) and Freki (Ravenous), whom he feeds from his table. It is no accident that ravens and wolves are animals that could be expected to feast on dead bodies. Humans who died on the battlefield were chosen by Odin's Valkyries (Choosers of the Slain), who brought the dead into Odin's hall, Valhalla (Hall of the Slain). In Valhalla, they fought one another on the battle-field during the day and feasted in the evening, only to get up and do it again the next day. These Odinic warriors trained and waited for the final battle, when they would fight the forces of chaos.

Thor (Þórr), Odin's son from a union with the personified earth (Jǫrð), is Asgard's main defender against external aggression from giants. Thor, riding his goat-drawn chariot across the sky, is also a thunder god who brings rain. The wheels of his goat-drawn chariot made thunder, while his short-handled hammer (Mjǫllnir) generates lighting when thrown. Thor is the god of farmers and more trustworthy than his father, Odin. Perhaps this is why his cult is represented by so many place names across the Scandinavian landscape. It is probably also the reason that so many of the Scandinavian names we know from the period have Thor as a prefix, such as the male names Thorgrim (Þórgrímr), Thorstein (Þórsteinn), and Thorhall (Þórhallr), but also women's names, such as Thorgunna (Þórgunna), Thordis (Þórdís), and Thora (Þóra).

Other important sons of Odin include Heimdall, the guardian of the gods. Standing guard at the rainbow bridge Bifrost (Bifrǫst) that gives access to Asgard from Midgard, Heimdall needs almost no sleep, has keen eyesight, and can hear even the growing of grass. He possesses the trumpet-like horn, Gjallarhorn, which he will sound to awaken the gods when the forces of chaos approach at the end of the world. Another of Odin's sons, Balder (Baldr), is described as the best and the most beautiful, but his main role in the mythology is to be the first god to die in the recent mythic past, mistakenly killed with an arrow shot by his blind half-brother, Hod (Hǫðr). This killing among Odin's sons, which precipitates the end of the world, was masterminded by the enigmatic but important trickster god, Loki. Loki was born a giant but lived with the gods in Asgard into the re-cent mythic past. During this time, he accompanied Odin and Thor on multiple journeys and often helped save the gods, such as when he makes the threatening giantess Skadi laugh by tying his testicles to the chin hair of a goat and engaging in a game of tug-of-war. But Loki is by nature hateful and causes trouble for the gods as often as he saves them, even before the final betrayal that leads to Balder's death. In the end, in the mythic future, he will side with the forces of chaos.

The Æsir goddesses are powerful but given less attention than the gods in our preserved stories. Significantly, they reside in their own halls, separate apparently from their god husbands. Most goddesses are associated with fertility, rejuvenation, and motherhood. Frigg—Odin's wife, Balder's mother, and the foremost of the Æsir goddesses—is the goddess of motherhood and family. Sif, Thor's wife, is a goddess of the earth, whose golden hair should likely be seen as a reflection of the golden color of ripe grain. Idunn, a goddess of eternal youth, is the keeper of the apples of immortality that the gods eat whenever they start to feel old.

In the mythic past, the Æsir were joined in Asgard by members of another family of gods called the Vanir. The Vanir are usually interpreted as old Germanic fertility gods. They were seen—even in the Viking Age—as distinct from the warlike Æsir and therefore in need of a mythological backstory, envisioned as a great mythical war between the two families of gods. As part of the peace negotiations, the two groups of gods exchanged hostages so that three of the Vanir—Njord, Frey, and Freyja—came to live with the Æsir in Asgard. Njord (Njǫrðr) is a sea god, associated with the wealth of the sea and venerated for success in seafaring and fishing. Njord's children, Frey and Freyja, are fertility gods associated with the earth and reproduction. Frey was said to rule over rain, sunshine, and the productivity of the earth and the wealth of men. Freyja is the goddess of lust and love, but interestingly, she also has aspects of a warrior goddess, as she brings half of the dead with her when she rides into battle in a cart pulled by cats. Freyja was also, like Odin, a master of a type of sorcery called *seiðr* and at least one poem suggests that she is no less sexually promiscuous than Odin.

Representing the struggle between the forces of order and chaos, the gods and the giants continually compete and raid each other's lands, primarily for women and objects of magical power. Although the gods are not always victorious, the flow of wealth and women is always from the giants to the gods. The male Æsir gods seem all to take concubines from among the giants, while the Vanir males take their actual wives from among the giants, possibly indicating a hierarchical relationship between the Æsir and Vanir. The gods also steal valuable items from the giants, such as a beer-making cauldron that Thor took by force from the giant Hymir after smashing Hymir's drinking cup on his rock-hard forehead. In another example, Odin stole the mead of poetic inspiration from the giant Suttung by using deceit and a shape-changing disguise. The nature of the two gods—Thor's brute strength and Odin's trickery—is on display in these stories. Attempts by the giants to raid the gods, to extract for instance Idunn's apples of immortality or to steal away the goddess Freyja, are repelled by Odin or Loki's scheming, or more commonly, beaten back by Thor and his hammer.

Key occurrences in the recent mythic past and into the mythic present involve binding and containing the forces of chaos that threaten to overturn the order of the cosmos. The greatest threats are the monstrous children that Loki fathered with the giantess Angrboda, namely Hel, the Midgard Serpent, and the Fenris Wolf. When Odin foresees the dangers of these children, he banishes Hel to rule over the underworld, called Niflheim (Fog-world), and casts the Midgard Serpent into the sea that surrounds the earth.[52] The Fenris Wolf, also called just Fenrir, is harder to deal with, and the gods have to resort to trickery to bind him with a magic chain crafted by the dwarves. Loki is himself bound underground after he plans and executes the death of Balder. Loki, his children, and all the forces of chaos lie in wait in the mythic present until the waning power of the gods will allow them to break free from their confinement and launch their final assault on Asgard.

Ragnarok (Ragnarǫk "The Twilight of the Gods") is a multi-part series of events in the mythic future that will lead to the destruction of the world. The main event is the battle between the gods and the forces of chaos. Other events precede the battle. First, several successive extreme winters will descend on the world, with no summer between them. The sun will be of no use, and hardships will take a toll on humanity as kinship ties shatter, justice is no longer upheld, and relatives kill one another. Next, the wolves that have been chasing the sun and moon across the sky since the beginning of the world will finally catch and swallow them. Then mountains will shake and fall, bringing down the trees. Even the great tree Yggdrasil will shudder. Then the supernatural bonds holding back the forces of chaos will break. The sea will flood Midgard and the Midgard Serpent will writhe ashore. The Fenris Wolf will break his bonds, as will his father Loki, who will arrive with the Frost Giants from Jotunheimar. As the forces of chaos cross the Bifrost bridge from Midgard to Asgard, the bridge will break and Heimdall will blow his horn and awaken the gods to action. Humans will have a role to play at the end of the world, as well. All those who died in battle and spent their time as part of Odin's retinue in Valhalla will pour forth from its many doors to fight on the side of the Æsir. The dead who inhabit the underworld with Hel will board a ship made from the fingernail clippings of the dead and sail to fight on the side of the forces of chaos. In this last battle, all of the main gods will die. Odin will be swallowed by Fenrir but be avenged by his son Vidar. Thor will manage to kill the Midgard Serpent but then succumb to its poison. Heimdall and Loki also battle to their mutual destruction. The fire giant Surt, bearing a flaming sword, will kill Frey and then use it to burn the earth before it sinks beneath the sea. The end is grimly reported in the poem *Vǫluspá* ("Prophecy of the Seeress"):

> The sun grows black,
> The earth sinks into the sea.
> The bright stars
> Vanish from the heavens.

Steam surges up
And the fire rages.
Heat reaches high
Against heaven itself.[53]

The fatalistic worldview of the Vikings, in which they knew—and their gods knew—that what ultimately awaited them was a losing battle and a grim Armageddon, must have impacted the way they lived their lives. Perhaps it emboldened them to make daring journeys and to throw themselves into earthly battles with the hope of joining Odin's warriors in a last, albeit futile, attempt to defend the world order. But the mythic future will not end with the demise of this world. After an unspecified amount of time, a new world will rise out of the sea and a new sun emerge. We learn that two sons of Thor and two sons of Odin will somehow survive Ragnarok, and the god of light, Balder, will return from the underworld. Together they will find the relics of the past world in the grass, including Thor's mighty hammer, and then remember and tell stories about the past world. Maybe the promise of these stories further drove Viking Age Scandinavians to desire great deeds in this world and on the final mythological battlefield.

The worldly deeds of the Vikings as they crossed the North Sea to plunder, dominate, and settle the British Isles are the focus of the next chapter. It is appropriate that we begin here since the movement of peoples out of Scandinavia is the central characteristic of the Viking Age. The focus on Britain will allow us deep exploration of the sources—the written texts, the archaeology, and the new sciences—as we seek to understand the motivations of Viking Age Scandinavians and the impact that their diasporas had on local populations.

2

Raiding, Conquering, and Settling Down in Britain

Viking Ways

The raid on the Lindisfarne monastery in 793 marks the traditional start of the Viking Age in Britain. Even if this was not the first contact Vikings had with the Anglo-Saxons, Alcuin's letter to King Æthelred, quoted in the introduction, shows the impact this raid had on contemporary perceptions of the new Viking threat. Although founded in the Celtic tradition of isolation from worldly distractions, Britain's island monasteries had become rich by the mid-eighth century. On their island retreats, the monks were safe from threats of violence from the Anglo-Saxon mainland. However, this same island isolation, combined with their growing wealth, made them prime targets for early sea-based Viking raids. The monastery of St. Cuthbert, located on an island off the coast of northeast England near the modern border with Scotland, exhibits all these characteristics of great wealth, isolation, and vulnerability to sea-borne raids (Figure 2.1). Founded in the seventh century by a mission from the venerable monastery of Iona on the western coast of Scotland, Lindisfarne became both the seat of a bishop and an outpost of Celtic Christianity's influence on the Anglo-Saxons. The monastery took its name from St. Cuthbert, a seventh-century monk and bishop at Lindisfarne who became the patron saint of Northumbria. The *Life of St. Cuthbert*, particularly the stories of the posthumous travels of his relics, is a valuable source on the interactions between Vikings and Anglo-Saxons in this region of England.

The *Life of St Cuthbert* tells of the monks who fled Viking raids, bringing St. Cuthbert's coffin with them on their travels around northern England seeking refuge. The saint was eventually reinterred in Durham, where his grave became a pilgrimage site. When his tomb was reopened in 1827, the eighth-century objects placed beside the saint as part of his original burial and subsequently as gifts to the dead saint revealed the wealth of the Lindisfarne monastery. The grave goods included a garnet-embellished golden cross, a comb of elephant ivory, a silver-covered portable altar, and an eighth-century pocket gospel with a binding covered in jewels and metals.[1] These items are precisely the type of valuables that the Vikings plundered from monastic cells, church altars, and graves. The metal

Age of Wolf and Wind. Davide Zori, Oxford University Press. © Oxford University Press 2024.
DOI: 10.1093/oso/9780190916060.003.0002

Figure 2.1 The British Isles in the Viking Age

Source: map by author

objects in particular were inherently valuable as means of exchange. Such raided items were also imbued with social value because they carried with them the stories of Viking raids across the sea. The objects acquired during raids were integrally linked with—and indeed became material manifestations of—the stories of the raids. Beginning from this premise, the present chapter weaves together insights about objects, raids, and new information from the biological sciences into a textured tapestry depicting the interactions between the Vikings and the Anglo-Saxons.

This chapter begins with an examination of the evidence of Viking raiding by interlacing written texts from clerical communities together with archaeological evidence of destroyed settlements and raided objects brought back to Scandinavia or deposited in hoards in Britain. These more traditional lines of evidence can be augmented with new scientific data, including an isotopic analysis of the teeth of a massacred Viking raiding party. The strontium and oxygen isotopes in their dental enamel reveal that the Viking raiders originated from a variety of geographic regions and that the party comprised men of a range of ethnic origins. To shed light on how these multi-regional raiding parties came into existence, we then turn to a consideration of anthropological models of group formation. The act of going on a raid, combined with textually and archaeologically attested acts of reciprocity and feasting, provided the crucible in which the raiding party became a unified group. In this reconsideration of the Viking raid, we see groups that bear closer resemblance to our image of eighteenth-century pirates than our classic views of the uniform Viking throngs from the north. Viking aggressive activities abroad were not at all stagnant or uniform. Even in general terms these activities evolved over time from seasonal raids to multi-seasonal expeditions with wintering camps, and then to campaigns and state-sponsored invasions with the goal of permanent settlement. Viking raiding strategies and goals shifted over time with fluctuations in the underlying push-and-pull factors that drove these peregrinations. As the influences of these forces altered, Scandinavian involvement in Britain became more peaceful and shifted to processes of acculturation and identity re-formation, which we can now be seen more clearly than previously through the combined study of place names, hybridized Anglo-Norse material culture, and genetic research.

Raids in Britain—The Written Sources

Anglo-Saxon texts and Old Norse sagas are complementary sources, and in fact each can be used to compensate for weaknesses inherent in the other. The Anglo-Saxon sources like the *Anglo-Saxon Chronicle* organize events by year, thereby providing a relatively trustworthy chronological framework for events. The sagas, on the other hand, cannot be relied upon for dating, but provide insight into the mentality and objective of the raiders.

The *Anglo-Saxon Chronicle*, a collection of annals written in Old English, survives in nine manuscripts dating from between the end of the ninth to the early twelfth century. These manuscripts are the main source of events, including Viking raids, that took place in England from the eighth to the end of the eleventh century. The earliest manuscripts date to the reign of King Alfred (871–899), the king who first drew various earlier regional annals into a unified form. Although the earliest entry dates to 60 BC, the reliability and length of the entries increases the closer the years draw to the reign of Alfred. Scribes in various parts of Britain continue the *Chronicle* after the reign of Alfred and occasionally include other source material, such as poems about tenth-century battles involving Scandinavian warriors. Although the *Chronicle* has clear biases, these various versions of the text provide the basis of the chronological framework for Viking activity in England.

Native Scandinavian texts about raids in Britain consist of short runic inscriptions on runestones and stories about Scandinavians in Britain contained in the Icelandic saga literature. The runestone texts concerning raids in Britain date to the late tenth to early eleventh century but are devoid of references to the first raids in the last years of the eighth century and the heyday of raiding in the ninth century. The runic sources are, however, immensely useful for understanding the mentality, motivations, and goals of Viking overseas aggression. The motivations for Viking voyages were similar in many respects for the smaller raids of the late eighth and ninth centuries and the large-scale Viking enterprises of the late tenth and eleventh centuries. Key differences also exist, meaning that we need to proceed with care in using even the runic material as sources for the mentality of early Viking activities. The sagas, by contrast, provide longer accounts and colorful details of Scandinavian heroic ventures. But the stories in the sagas are removed by several generations from the events they describe. Furthermore, with a few exceptions and similar to the runestones, the sagas are mostly about late tenth- and eleventh-century Viking expeditions, rather than the first raiders. When used together, however, the runic inscriptions and saga texts provide a clearer window into the latter half of the Viking Age and the processes attendant upon permanent Scandinavian settlement in England and the large eleventh-century invasions led by kings of the increasingly consolidated Scandinavian kingdoms.

Voices of the Raided—Anglo-Saxon texts

The *Anglo-Saxon Chronicle* shows the progression of Viking activities in Britain through the four phases—seasonal raids, multi-year expeditions, permanent settlement, and state-sponsored invasion—while also revealing specific periods of intensity and hiatus in raiding. The first phase—seasonal raids—is anticipated in the *Chronicle* even three years before the raid on Lindisfarne. The *Chronicle* records that in 789 "three ships of Northmen from Horðaland" came to Portland in southern England. The description of the subsequent encounter is rife with tensions and uncertainty of what is expected from both sides. "Then the reeve rode there and wanted to compel them to go to the king's town because he did not know what they were; and then they killed him. These were the first ships of the Danish men which sought out the land of the English race."[2] The encounter, which was initiated by the Anglo-Saxon reeve (a local royal official, like the later sheriffs), leads to killing, but this is perhaps based on a misunderstanding rather than any premeditation to do violence. Neither side seems to know what to expect from the other. Interestingly, although the reeve does not know who he is dealing with, the text identifies the Northmen (called Danes interchangeably) as coming from Horðaland in western Norway, showing significant familiarity with Scandinavia. On the part of the Northmen, their killing of the reeve may be partially explained by their reticence to follow him to the king's hall. No raid or other motive is documented for these Northmen. Perhaps the ships were on a fact-finding mission, looking for easy and lucrative targets. Such targets were found farther north in places such as Lindisfarne, where the Scandinavians initiated sudden violent encounters with the explicit goal of looting valuables.

The first phase of Viking activity in Britain focused on monasteries. The British monasteries were relatively easy targets, being nearly undefended and inhabited by monks who were not trained in warfare. As noted above, the monasteries were built on islands, following Celtic models of monastic isolation, making them easily accessible by ship but impossible to get to on foot for possible Anglo-Saxon reinforcements from the mainland. Although many of these monasteries were physically remote from the secular power centers on the mainland, they were not socially or even economically isolated. They were thoroughly integrated into the gift economies of the time, and donations to monasteries from the rich elites had made these monasteries repositories of wealth. Viking raids targeted monasteries precisely because of this combination of wealth, isolation, and martial weakness.

The *Chronicle* records ongoing raiding in the 790s, such as a raid on the Jarrow monastery in 796: "the heathen raided in Northumbria and looted Ecgfrith's minster at the Don mouth; and there one of their commanders was killed, and also some of their ships were broken up by bad weather, and many of them drowned there; and some came to shore alive, and then were immediately killed at the river mouth."[3] The recorded death of a Viking leader and the execution of shipwrecked raiders underscores the risks of undertaking raiding expeditions, even when they targeted monasteries. It is noteworthy, however, that the raid itself was a Viking victory. After the raids in the late 790s, there was a hiatus of raids on Britain, probably related to the shift in the focus of Viking activity to Ireland and Francia (the lands of the Franks) during the early years of the 800s.[4] In the 830s, the Vikings returned again to England in increased numbers, and virtually every year thereafter in the chronicle is dominated by conflicts in Kent, Sussex, Wessex, Mercia, and Northumbria between the Anglo-Saxons and the Vikings, who are described frequently as a Danish raiding-army. The geographical reach of this wave of attacks was much more extensive than the previous raids in the 790s. The Viking raiders targeted a variety of sites and were willing to fight pitched battles with local lords and kings.[5] The Viking tactics included making alliances locally, and in 838, the Danes arrived in Cornwall and allied with the local Cornish Britons and as the *Chronicle* says "turned into one" army to fight against King Egbert of Wessex.[6] The phrase "turned into one" significantly indicates that these Viking raiding parties were ethnically inclusive and flexible in their constituency. As we will see, the archaeological and biological evidence also bears out this multi-ethnic aspect of Viking raiding parties.

The *Anglo-Saxon Chronicle* announces the onset of the second phase of Viking activity in Britain—multi-season expeditions—with descriptions of raiding parties establishing coastal wintering bases. The *Chronicle* recognizes the significance of this shift in 851: "and for the first time the heathen men stayed over the winter."[7] Some versions of the *Chronicle* say they wintered on the island of Thanet, while Alfred's biographer Asser claims the wintering was on the island of Sheppey (literally "Sheep-island" in Old Norse; see Figure 2.1). Islands in estuaries, which were often repositories for local sheep that could feed Viking raiders during their stay, made ideal wintering camps for the sea-based raiders. From these islands, the Vikings could escape quickly and monitor ships moving along the coast and into/out of major rivers. Establishing bases on islands was a strategy used across Britain and also on the continent on islands such as Walcheren (842) in the Scheldt estuary and Noirmoutier (843) in the Loire estuary.

The scale and character of Viking activities intensified in 865 with the arrival of the Great Heathen Army (*micel hæþen here*). The actions of the Great Army in England over the next fifteen years led to the destruction of three of the four Anglo-Saxon kingdoms (East Anglia, Northumbria, and Mercia) and ushered in the third phase of the Viking Age in Britain: permanent settlement. From the start, the Great Army's goals exceeded those of the earlier raids. The aims went beyond looting and ransom to include systematic tribute extraction, territorial conquest, and political control. The historical sources indicate that the Great Army was larger than previous Viking forces—thousands rather than hundreds—and consisted of a loose confederation of chieftains (called "kings" and "jarls" in the sources) and their supporters. The Great Army splintered, reformed, and aggregated fluidly as chieftains and their retinues pursued their separate interests and strategies of wealth accumulation. At several points, new arrivals from Scandinavia and from raiding parties operating in Francia supplemented the Great Army. For example, in 871 a group described as the Great Summer Army arrived from Scandinavia, while the early 880s saw Viking groups shifting back and forth across the English Channel, joining into larger armies when it was advantageous and profitable.[8]

Arriving first in 865 and wintering in safety on the island of Thanet, the Great Heathen Army extracted tribute from the people of Kent in return for peace. The next winter, the Great Army wintered in East Anglia, where the local population gave them horses in exchange for peace. In 866, the Army proceeded overland to occupy York, where they routed a combined Northumbrian army and killed two rival kings (Osberht and Ælla) who had set aside their differences to fight the Vikings. The Vikings installed a puppet king in York and invaded Mercia in 867. In the following years, the army shifted between kingdoms, taking advantage of local weaknesses, and wintering in defensible locations. In 870 the army returned to East Anglia, defeating, and killing King Edmund. The *Anglo-Saxon Chronicle* recalls that the Vikings "conquered all that land," while the Peterborough Manuscript version adds that "they came to Peterborough [monastery]: burned and demolished, killed the abbot and monks and all that they found there, brought it about so that what was earlier very rich was as it were nothing."[9] The *Chronicle* in the following years is solely concerned with the Viking incursions. In 871 alone the *Chronicle* records nine large-scale battles fought within the kingdom of Wessex alone.[10] In these battles, nine jarls and one Scandinavian king were killed, reminding us of the confederative nature of the army consisting of allied Viking bands. In 874 the Great Army wintered at the Mercian royal site of Repton and expelled Burgred, king of Mercia. In his place they installed a king named Ceolwulf II, who swore oaths and granted hostages to the invaders, promising the Vikings that the kingdom of Mercia "should be ready for them whichever day they might want it, and he himself should be ready with all who would follow him, at the service of the raiding-army."[11]

After wintering in Repton in 873–874, the Great Army split in two. One army, led by Halfdan, returned to Northumbria, raiding widely into Scotland, before settling the army permanently in 876: "Halfdan divided up the land of Northumbria; and they were ploughing and were providing for themselves."[12] The other half of the Great Army, led by Guthrum, Oscytel, and Anund, continued the attacks on Wessex, the single remaining Anglo-Saxon kingdom. Wessex, led by the young King Alfred, had been successful in resisting the Viking incursions by a combination of forceful resistance and periodic payment of tribute for peace. The tides turned in 878 when Alfred defeated "the whole raiding-army" at the Battle of Edington.[13] After the battle, Guthrum gave hostages, swore to leave Wessex, and in a show of subservience received baptism with King Alfred as his godfather.[14] Guthrum withdrew to East Anglia, where in 879 he "settled that land, and divided it up," adding another permanent Scandinavian-ruled kingdom to the British political landscape.[15] Alfred's new strength is indicated also in the same year by another Viking group's departure to the lands of the Franks, where the recent death of Emperor Charles the Bald left West Francia weak and ripe for Viking exploitation. During the 880s and into the 890s the *Anglo-Saxon Chronicle* records a sort of stalemate between Alfred and the Vikings with victories on both sides. The chronicle records as many attacks abroad in Francia as it does in England. A preserved treaty from this period between Alfred and Guthrum embodies this stalemate.[16] The treaty, which implies equality by calling both men kings, defined the boundary between Alfred's English kingdom and Guthrum's kingdom of East Anglia (Figure 2.1). The document also defines the legal relationship between Danes living in Britain and the native English, thereby suggesting a permanence to the Scandinavian settlers' presence. The stalemate reached between Alfred the Great and the Vikings resulted in permanent Scandinavian settlement in eastern England. This area, which subsequently followed Scandinavian laws, became known as the Danelaw.

During the 880s and 890s, the kingdom of Wessex gradually gained the upper hand, often going on the offensive against the Scandinavian areas of control, for instance capturing London in 886. The Viking raiders did reappear to raid Wessex, and the *Chronicle* makes clear that when they returned, they received assistance and raised recruits among the Scandinavian settlers in Northumbria and East Anglia. But entries in the *Chronicle* show that various groups of Viking raiders increasingly pursued opportunities in Francia. The kingdom of Wessex withstood the renewed raids, and in 897 the last major Viking raiding party disbanded. The *Chronicle* states, "the army left, some to East Anglia, some to Northumbria, and those who were without property got themselves ships there, and went south over the sea to the river Seine."[17] King Alfred was successful against the Vikings where other kings were not because he organized defenses and responsive military units in Wessex that made it more profitable for the Scandinavian raiders to settle down in Danelaw or pursue raiding elsewhere. The *Chronicle* records Alfred's early use of ships to counter Viking raiders in the 870s, while he began to actively construct an updated navy in the 890s to face the Vikings at sea.[18] He also adopted successful tactics of building fortified bridges that blocked Vikings from freely navigating rivers, thereby neutralizing the main military advantage of their shallow-drafted ships. A remarkable document from the 880s, *The Burghal Hidage*, shows how Alfred reorganized the tax base to construct fortified sites or burhs for the defense of Wessex.[19] The burhs, which were built anew or refashioned from Roman fortifications or Iron Age forts, were positioned strategically across Wessex so that nearly all rural settlements in Alfred's kingdom were no more than 25 km from a burh (see Figure 2.1).

The *Burghal Hidage* also lists the tax levied on local communities for the construction and maintenance of the burhs. At the time of his death in 901, Alfred had created a well-organized and militarily powerful kingdom of Wessex from which his descendants would subsequently launch conquests of the Danelaw. As such, the creation of a single English kingdom was a legacy of local Anglo-Saxon responses to the Viking incursions.

In the early tenth century, the Wessex Dynasty, especially Alfred's son Edward and grandsons Æthelstan and Edmund, gradually established control over the Danelaw. This was not a reconquest, but rather an expansion of the kingdom of Wessex—by conquest, purchases, and political pressure—to form, for the first time, a kingdom that encompassed most of what is today England. The success of the Wessex kings in establishing control over northeastern England generated resistance in neighboring populations, epitomized by the alliance of forces that opposed Æthelstan at the Battle of Brunanburh in 937.[20] Æthelstan met a combined invading force of Scots, Picts, Strathclyde Britons, and Vikings from Dublin, who had allied to counter the growing power of Wessex. Æthelstan's victory at Brunanburh was commemorated in an Anglo-Saxon battle poem, which opens with "Æthelstan the King, captain of men, ring giver of warriors—and with him his brother Edmund the Atheling—unending glory won in that strife by their sword's edges that there was about Brunanburh." The poem identifies the main opponents as Scots led by King Constantine and Dublin-based Northerners, "who with Anlaf [Olaf] over the ocean's courses in the bosom of a ship had sought our land and their doom in that fight."[21] The complex alliances in which the Vikings were embroiled in the Battle of Brunanburh show the Scandinavian settlers as a firmly established population in Britain.[22] Subsequent Viking invaders for the remainder of the Viking Age would find ready allies among this group of Anglo-Scandinavians in Danelaw.

In the last decade of the tenth century, Viking expeditions returned to England with a renewed force that opened the fourth phase of the Viking Age: royal invasions. This phase was heralded by the arrival of aspiring kings with large armies. In 991, the *Anglo-Saxon Chronicle* records the arrival of a large Viking armada led by Olaf Tryggvason, the future king of Norway. The *Anglo-Saxon Chronicle* notes, "In this year Anlaf came with ninety-three ships to Folkestone and ravaged the neighborhood, went on to Sandwich, and then to Ipswich, and overran the whole area, and so to Maldon."[23] The Battle of Maldon, like Brunanburh, is a battle commemorated in near-contemporary Anglo-Saxon poetry. This battle, however, was a Viking victory that resulted in the death of an Anglo-Saxon Ealdorman (i.e., a local magistrate over a shire or group of shires) named Byrhtnoth and the defeat of his bodyguard and the local levy (fyrd). The negotiations as recalled in the poem *The Battle of Maldon* show continued Viking strategies of ransoming captives and tribute extraction. A Viking spokesman presents the following typical terms to the English:

> ". . . if you take this course of action,
> are willing to pay your people's ransom,
> will give to Vikings what we think right,
> buying our peace at our price,
> we shall with that tribute turn back to our ship,
> sail out on the sea, and hold you as friends."[24]

Also apparent is the Anglo-Saxon desire to resist by force, possibly driven by renewed confidence in the Wessex dynasty. The Ealdorman Byrhtnoth answers angrily and ends his speech with a promise of resistance: "English silver is not so softly won: first iron and edge shall make arbitrement, harsh war-trial, before we yield tribute."[25] His confidence in this case and in the following decades was misplaced. The Scandinavian armies had grown in numbers, and their organizational strength drew from new state-level institutions in Denmark and Norway. The successes of the initial royal invasions encouraged ever-larger Viking fleets with heighted ambitions that ultimately aimed for territorial conquest. After crushing the Anglo-Saxons at the Battle of Maldon, Olaf's army of ninety-three ships was given 10,000 pounds of silver to cease their attack. This payment notwithstanding, in 994 Olaf Tryggvason returned with the Danish king, Svein Forkbeard, and a fleet of ninety-four ships. Despite an unsuccessful attempt to take London, Olaf and King Svein were nonetheless given tribute payment of 16,000 pounds of silver. Olaf received baptism and promised never to return to England. He kept his promise, although his reasons were at least partially based on the advantages he gained through his newly acquired English treasure, which he used to make himself king of Norway upon his return to his homeland. The Danish King Svein had no such reservations, and in 1002, Svein's army returned to English shores with renewed force and motivated by the desire to avenge Danes massacred by Æthelred on St. Brice's Day. Svein's army was paid a massive tribute of 24,000 pounds of silver. As a result of Svein's continued military pressure, the tribute quantities continued to increase, and in 1006, the Danish army was paid 36,000 pounds. In 1011, Svein's army took Canterbury and captured its archbishop, Ælfheah. The archbishop refused to be ransomed. Consequently, Svein's men pelted him with bones and cattle skulls from their feast before one Viking martyred the archbishop by striking him with the back of an axe. King Æthelred paid Svein's army 48,000 pounds of silver in 1012 to leave his country.

These early eleventh-century Viking attacks on England were different from the earlier ninth- and early tenth-century armies—even the Great Heathen Army—because they possessed a unity based on the power of increasingly powerful kings in Scandinavia. These kings had established means of control in their homelands that allowed both increased royal revenue extraction (from various forms of taxation and dues) and a more comprehensive mandatory military service in the form of a wide-cast net of the naval levy. King Svein was invading England with the full strength of the Danish nascent state's military resources.[26]

State power could still fray as powerful chieftains exercised their independence. Thorkel the Tall, a Danish chieftain supporter of King Svein, entered Æthelred's service after 1012 and pledged to defend his kingdom. A different form of tribute called *heregeld* (army tribute) financed mercenaries like Thorkel. When King Svein arrived in 1013 with an army intent on the conquest of all of England, Thorkel stayed loyal to Æthelred. Svein began his conquest in sympathetic Danelaw and from there quickly received the submission of all of England. When Svein died in early 1014, his son Knut was elected king by the Danish army but could not hold on to the English crown. Upon his return to the throne, Æthelred gave Thorkel's army 21,000 pounds of silver for his loyalty. It took King Knut only one year to regroup. He returned to England with a Danish fleet supported by his brother Harald, the new king of Denmark. It was then that the erstwhile supporter of Æthelred, Thorkel the Tall, switched his allegiance back to Knut. Knut's victory over Æthelred's son, Edmund, at the Battle of Ashingdon resulted in a division of the English kingdom between Knut and Edmund. Edmund died later that year, however, leaving Knut as the sole king of England. In the reorganization of his realm into four earldoms (Wessex, East Anglia, Mercia, and Northumbria), Knut rewarded Thorkel the Tall with the Earldom of East Anglia. Knut's power continued to grow. In 1018, Knut's brother Harald died, making Knut king of Denmark as well. Knut's kingdom had become an empire straddling the North Sea. Knut ruled like a Christian king on par with other kings in Western Europe. He attended the coronation of the Holy Roman Emperor Conrad in Rome. While in Rome, he sent a letter to the English people calling himself "King of all England, and of Denmark, of the Norwegians, and part of the Swedes."[27]

The heregeld-type payment that Æthelred paid Thorkel to stay and fight for the English kingdom replaced the earlier Danegeld tribute that had simply paid Vikings to leave. The Vikings who accepted this payment became mercenaries paid to defend England. The replacement in tribute type especially took hold after the complete conquest of England by Svein in 1014 and by Knut in 1016. These conquests resulted in Scandinavian armies remaining in England to defend the new Scandinavian kings. Knut's royal rule and peace in England, lasting from his victory at the Battle of Ashingdon to his death in 1035, was enforced by his personal army (his lið). This portion of his army, consisting of forty shiploads of professional Viking warriors, remained with the king even after the rest of his army dispersed in 1018 upon receiving 82,500 pounds of silver in tribute from

England. Knut's kingship in England, as many generations of Anglo-Saxon kings before him, was in large part legitimized by the protection that he could provide against Viking raids. In a letter sent from Denmark while he was consolidating his power there in the winter of 1019–1020, Knut legitimized his rule by employing Christian kingship language and stressing his role in preventing further attacks from Denmark: "Then I was informed that greater danger was approaching us than we liked at all; and then I went myself with the men who accompanied me to Denmark, from where the greatest injury had come to you, and with God's help I have taken measures so that never henceforth shall hostility reach you from there as long as you support me rightly and my life lasts."[28] Knut underscored his role as a Christian king by sponsoring the English Church and formally seeking public penance for his and his Danish people's violent Viking relations with the English. In a show of his repentance as well as the shift away from previous Viking motivations, he atoned for his father's army's murder of Archbishop Ælfheah by exhuming and transporting Ælfheah's body to Canterbury for reburial.

Voices of the Raiders—Runestones and Sagas

The Anglo-Saxon written accounts of Viking raids in Britain are largely responsible for the quintessential image of the Vikings as a marauding horde. In contrast, the Scandinavian accounts of Viking activities have had less influence on the popular view of Vikings. In traditional scholarship, native Scandinavian sources have been overshadowed by sources like the *Anglo-Saxon Chronicle*, conventionally considered more trustworthy than sagas written in Iceland several hundred years after the onset of the Viking raids in Britain. To balance the etic (external observer) viewpoint of foreign sources with an emic (internal subject) perspective, it is necessary to turn to runestones and sagas to hear the voices of Scandinavians.

Runestones

Nearly thirty Scandinavian runestones, mostly from Sweden, refer to voyages to Britain. Although the runestones date from the tenth–eleventh centuries, the texts are our closest native Scandinavian articulation of the motivations and perceptions of Viking raids. There is a distinct focus on wealth, glory, and memorializing the relationship between raiders and expedition leaders. Consistency in what the Vikings considered honorable and worthy of remembrance suggests that the ethos was likely the same for Vikings of the last years of the eighth and the ninth centuries.

Acquisition of wealth is the primary motivation discernable from the runestones. The runestone evidence dates mostly to the tenth and eleventh centuries, when the initial raids had transformed into expeditions aimed at tribute extraction and permanent settlement. The stones, therefore, unsurprisingly, show the economics of tribute extraction rather than direct plunder. The Danegeld tribute seen in the Anglo-Saxon texts is explicitly mentioned in the runestone texts.[29] One of two Lingberg Runestones, found in Uppland province in Sweden and dating to the early eleventh century, reads: "And Dan and Huskarl and Svein had the stone erected in memory of Ulfrik, their father's father. He had taken two payments in England. May God and God's mother help the souls of the father and son."[30] The cross prominently positioned at the top of the runestone shows that the erectors of the monument were Christians (Figure 2.2). The sole Norwegian runestone concerning Viking activity in Britain (N184) also bears a Christian message, as well as a reminder of the risks of Viking raids: "Arnstein raised this stone in memory of Bjor his son who died in the retinue when Knut attacked England. God is one."[31]

The runestones show chieftains redistributing wealth to followers. This is exemplified by an early eleventh- century runestone (U344) from Uppland commemorating multiple Viking ventures from the late tenth to the early eleventh century. The text reads, "And Ulf has taken three payments in England. That was the first that Tosti paid. Then Thorkel paid. Then Knut paid."[32] Ulf, who must have been from the area of eastern Sweden where his runestone was found, joined his first Viking voyage in 991 as a follower of the legendary Swedish Viking Skoglar Tosti, who was from western Sweden, around modern-day Göteborg. Ulf's second voyage was with Thorkel the Tall, the chieftain from Scania, whom we met earlier. Ulf probably joined Thorkel in the invasion of 1012, when Thorkel was a chieftain in King Svein's invasion of England. In his third voyage (c. 1018), Ulf joined the new Danish King, Knut the Great, in his conquest of England. Ulf's Viking career spanned almost twenty years, and we may safely assume that the three adventures commemorated on his runestone were only the most prominent and successful of his Viking enterprises. The runestone texts show more clearly than the etic Anglo-Saxon documents how Viking leaders brought together fluid and interregional groups of warriors in their attacks on Britain.

A second key motivating factor for Viking activity is also revealed by the runestones that commonly highlight the glory and honor conferred in Viking raiding ventures. For Ulf, in the example above, his Viking voyages comprised his life's most memorable and praiseworthy moments. In another example, a Danish runestone from Tirsted in Lolland (DR 216) remembers the glory gained by Fradi from being the fiercest in a chieftain's raiding party: "Astrad and Hildulf raised this stone in memory of Fradi, their kinsman. And he was then the terror of men. He died in Sweden and was . . . the first in Friggir's retinue of all Vikings."[33] Friggir's retinue's raid from Lolland in Denmark into what is today eastern Sweden provides a rare record of what must have been the most common

Figure 2.2 The Lingberg 2 runestone, positioned beside a causeway in Sweden, memorializes Ulrik, who journeyed twice to England to extract tribute (Danegeld) in the late tenth or early eleventh century. The runic text, written within the body of a serpent, is crowned by a Christian cross, a reminder that Viking activity and Christianity were not mutually exclusive.
Source: photo by Pål-Nils Nilsson, Swedish National Heritage Board (CC BY 4.0)

Viking raids, namely those directed toward other Scandinavian lands. Voyages to more distant lands brought even greater renown. That Vikings considered runestones a way to immortalize connections to particular Viking voyages and their famous leaders is borne out in a group of twenty-six runestones from Sweden known as the Ingvar stones. These stones memorialize Vikings who joined Ingvar in a legendary voyage east to Serkland, the Muslim lands centered on the Caliphate of Baghdad. One of these Ingvar stones (the Gripsholm

Runestone) underscores the goal of wealth acquisition and the honor attainable through battle: "Tola had this stone raised in memory of her son Harald, Ingvar's brother. They traveled valiantly far for gold, and in the east gave [food] to the eagle. [They] died in the south in Serkland."[34] Even if they resulted in failure and death, Viking voyages such as this were commemorated and viewed as conferring honor to participants. The Ingvar runestones also corroborate *Ingvar the Far-traveler's Saga*, an Icelandic saga written in the twelfth century that had long been considered a purely legendary account of Ingvar's voyages to the Caspian Sea. The parallels between the runestones and the saga account suggest that the saga account has at least a kernel of historical truth.[35]

Sagas

The Icelandic saga literature forms the other major native Scandinavian textual corpus providing insight into the motivations of Viking expeditions. These texts—better than any others—provide a sense of the Viking raider experience. The Icelandic sagas contain vivid narratives of Viking activities in England, especially from the late ninth century and until the end of the Viking Age. The sources are rich for the last decades of the ninth century, as the Viking expeditions were part of the historic-legendary material that comprised the founding stories of the Icelanders. In the subsequent tenth and eleventh centuries, young Icelanders seeking to acquire wealth and fame regularly returned to Scandinavia and the British Isles to participate in Viking ventures. During this period, the relationships among Anglo-Saxons, Celtic Britons, and Scandinavians were dynamic and alliances and ethnic identities quite fluid. The saga literature is vast. This section draws out examples focused on motivations for raiding as well as peaceful Viking voyages to England, while pointing out the difficulty of using saga texts as historical sources in combination with the non-Scandinavian texts.

By the mid- to late ninth century, Scandinavian permanent settlement had begun in Danelaw, and Norse earldoms had emerged in island clusters of the Orkneys, Shetlands, and Hebrides (Figure 2.1). The Anglo-Scandinavian power center in York waxed and waned, while overlordship over the town shifted between English and Scandinavian kings. At the margins of these polities and within the often-antagonistic relationship between them, there was still ample room for Viking-style raiding. Young would-be Vikings could band together or go it alone; alternatively, and more commonly, they could seek out patronage and sponsorship from local chieftains, earls, or kings, and join their raiding parties. One such young Icelandic Viking was Gunnlaug Worm-tongue, an unruly warrior poet from western Iceland, who joined the supporters of Earl Sigurd of Orkney. After staying with the earl through the winter, enjoying his hospitality, Gunnlaug joined the Earl's raiding party: "in the summer they raided widely in the Hebrides and the fjords of Scotland, and they fought many battles. Wherever they went Gunnlaug was reckoned the bravest and manliest of men and the hardest fighter."[36]

Simultaneously, the space for peaceful interaction had grown, and we see Scandinavians arriving to join English kings or docking peacefully at English markets for trading. Although the saga sources paint the most vivid pictures of these interactions, we must remember that they were written in Iceland a century after the end of the Viking Age. Moreover, nearly absent from these sagas are the stories of the first encounters or even the first phases of the Viking Age in Britain. As with the runestones evidence, the sagas do not contain records of the first raids. Memories of these early raids are simply absent from the native Scandinavian textual tradition.

The saga accounts of mid-ninth-century raiding, however, do provide very believable accounts of preparations, organization, and motivations for the types of seasonal raids that characterized the first phase of Viking activity in Western Europe. For instance, in the opening of *Egil's Saga*, Egil's uncle Thorolf, who is the eldest son of Kveld-Ulf ("Night-Wolf") Bjalfason, prepares for a Viking expedition:

> When Thorolf was about twenty years old he decided to go raiding and Kveld-Ulf gave him a longship. Kari's sons, Eyvind and Olvir, joined him. They had a large following and another longship. They went on a Viking expedition that summer and they gained so much loot that each of them got a large share. For some years they spent their summers on Viking raids and spent their winters at home with their fathers. Thorolf brought home many expensive items to him father and mother. There was plenty of opportunity to get rich and famous.[37]

This passage describes the situation for a son of a chieftain living in the western Norwegian province of Fjordane in the 870s before Harald Fairhair's victory at Hafrsfjord in circa 880.[38] Thorolf's motivations are wealth and fame. His father Kveld-Ulf provides the means for the raid, including the longship. After successful raids, Thorolf pays part of his debt back to his father in the form of movable wealth. The family's friendship network provides parts of the crew, including the sons of Kari, who in the earlier generation had raided as Kveld-Ulf's partner. Such kinship and friendship networks provided the social glue that bound together raiding parties. The loot from raiding is shared among the young men, but significant wealth also flows back to the older generation that had provided the means for the raid.

This general sociological view of the raids and the raiders' mentality is credible, but we are on much less firm ground when seeking historical facts about the early ninth-century raids. The sagas about Ragnar Lodbrok and his sons are of particular interest because they describe two generations of raiding practices in the early and mid-ninth century that directly parallel the events surrounding the invasion of the Great Army recorded in the *Anglo-Saxon Chronicle*. These sagas (*The Saga of Ragnar Lodbrok* and *The Tale of Ragnar's Sons*) have been grouped together with the Mythic-Legendary Sagas, such as *Saga of the Volsungs*, dealing with events in the Migration Period. The sagas about Ragnar and his sons, how-ever, mix legend and history, thereby bearing a closer resemblance to the more historically reliable King's Sagas than to the Mythic-Legendary Sagas.[39] The Ragnar sagas provide a Scandinavian backstory to the Great Army's invasion of England. Ragnar Lodbrok, having reached old age after a lifetime of raiding, decides on a foolhardy attack on England with only two merchant-style knǫrr ships. He is defeated by King Ælla, described as the king of all of England, who devises a gruesome death for Ragnar in a pit of snakes. Before he dies Ragnar utters the memorable line, "The piglets would grunt now if they only knew the suffering of the old boar."[40] In the saga tradition, avenging Ragnar's gruesome death provides the key motive for the sons of Ragnar to launch their invasion of England remembered in the Anglo-Saxon sources as the invasion of the Great Army. The sagas stay focused on the elite motivations, and the subsequent events revolve around the interactions between Ragnar's sons as they achieve their revenge on King Ælla. Although many of the apparently historical people are largely the same in the Scandinavian and the Anglo-Saxon sources, it is diffi-cult to draw historical facts from the sagas beyond what can be confirmed by the *Chronicle*. Significant contradictions are also found between the sources. For ex-ample, Ragnar's supposed raid on England could not have taken place while Ælla was king because he had only just become king the year that the sons of Ragnar invaded. The saga also makes Ælla out to be king of all of England, whereas we know him from the *Chronicle* to be king only of Northumbria. Also, the saga has Ragnar's sons attack Ælla first to exact their vengeance, whereas the *Chronicle* indicates that the Great Army's first target was East Anglia. Perhaps we might say that these are details, but the contradictions are too great to look for much more historically believable information in the sagas about Ragnar and his sons.

In the broader sociological perspective, however, these sagas do offer views on the motives of Viking expeditions that are consistent with the runestone evidence and the Anglo-Saxon sources. The motivation for raids in the sagas is wealth, but the wealth acquisition is tied integrally to the resulting renown and honor achieved through successful raiding. For instance, when the sons of Ragnar de-cide to begin raiding, it is for "riches and fame."[41] The acquisition of wealth in itself was most significant in its use for increasing their raiding force: "wherever they fought, they plundered more loot, and won for themselves both a large con-tingent of followers and great wealth."[42]

Before his final raid on England, Ragnar composes a poem that voices similar sentiments:

> Let no man spare the Rhine's amber [treasure]
> if he wants seasoned warriors;
> it's harmful for the helm-wise [leaders]
> to hoard rings, rather than troops.[43]

Wealth is for using, and primarily for using to reward loyal supporters. The motive for Ragnar's sons to attack Ælla is vengeance, which they are honor-bound to seek. This could and has often been attributed to saga literary fancy. But considering the nature of Viking society, where feuding in the form of reciprocal violent offenses was closely tied to honor, perhaps vengeance in addition to promises of personal gain for leaders as well as followers, might have been powerful motivators. The sagas speak of this, but the runestones and Anglo-Saxon sources are silent on this possibility.

The voyages to England were not always violent affairs. The sagas also hold stories of peaceful trading trips. *Egil's Saga* details the economic life of Egil's uncle Thorolf Kveldulfsson, after he has become one of Harald Fairhair's chieftains in the northern Norwegian province of Halogaland. Thorolf administers a successful farming estate, extracts tribute from the semi-nomadic Sámi reindeer herders, mounts raiding expeditions to the east in Karelia and into the Baltic Sea, and stations men on the Vago Islands to fish for cod and herring. Thorolf also sends one of his men, Thorgils Gjallandi ("the Bellower"), on a trading expedition to England on a large ocean-going ship:

> Then Thorolf had his ship loaded with dried fish, hides and sheep wool, as well as a large amount of white animal furs and other pelts that he had obtained from the mountains [of northern Norway]. The load was extremely valuable. He had Thorgils sail the ship west to England to buy cloth and other goods that he needed. They sailed south along the land, then out into the sea. They landed in England, where they did lucrative trading. They loaded the ship with wheat and honey, wine, and cloth, and sailed back home in the fall.[44]

The opportunism is apparent. It is also noteworthy that Thorolf himself carries out the most heroic occupations, such as raiding and tribute extraction, while the more mundane fishing and trading expeditions are left to his followers.

The next generation in *Egil's Saga*, including Egil and his older brother Thorolf, named after his paternal uncle, continue to engage in raiding in the Baltic and the British Isles. Their engagements last multiple seasons and correspond to the second phase of the Viking Age, in which winters were spent abroad. They also serve Viking rulers who have settled down in the foreign lands as rulers, corresponding to the third phase of the Viking Age. But opportunity lay also with foreign non-Scandinavian kings. For instance, Egil and Thorolf joined the retinue of King Æthelstan of England after hearing that the king was willing to handsomely reward warriors. Egil composed a skaldic poem while serving Æthelred against an invading force led by King Olaf the Red of Scotland, who was of mixed Scandinavian and Scottish descent as well as a descendent of Ragnar Lodbrok. The poem connects the glory of violence and the spilt blood with the generosity of chieftains.

> One earl fled from Olaf,
> Life ended for the other
> The lusty war-leader
> Was lavish in blood-gifts.
> England's enemy conquered
> Half of Alfgeir's earldom,
> While the great Godrek
> Rambled on the gore-plain.[45]

To join Æthelstan, the saga informs that Egil and Thorolf had accepted preliminary baptism (*prima signatio*), "as that was customary both for merchants and mercenaries serving Christian rulers."[46] The events described in *Egil's Saga*, which take place in the tenth century and are supported by skaldic poetry likely composed by Egil himself, contain more historical information than the sagas about Ragnar and his sons. The broad-brush events recorded in *Egil's saga*, such as the battle at Brunanburh between Olaf and Æthelstan, are consistent with the Anglo-Saxon sources. However, the sagas provide a different, more personal view of the Viking raiders, the details of which cannot be confirmed in the Anglo-Saxon sources. In this manner, the sources offer complementary views. For instance, *Egil's Saga* with its focus on the lives of somewhat average Viking raiders such as Egil provides a counterbalance to the elite-centered *Anglo-Saxon Chronicle* and a useful reminder that Scandinavians fought on both sides of many of the battles that are described in Anglo-Saxon, Irish, and Frankish chronicles as pitting Anglo-Saxons or Irishmen or Franks against Scandinavians. In this manner, *Egil's Saga* depicts war bands of the Viking Age as opportunistic groupings of international and heterogenous warriors of fortune. This saga view is certainly consistent with the runestones evidence and, as we shall see, also with the mounting archaeological and biological evidence.

The Archaeology of Raiding in Britain: Hoards, Vanished Settlements, Viking Camps, and Mass Burials

The archaeology of the early phases of Viking activities in Britain is ephemeral. In his survey of Viking Age England, Julian D. Richards begins his chapter on raids with the observation that "any account of Viking raids has to be derived from historical sources, which for England means the *Anglo-Saxon Chronicle*. Archaeological evidence is a poor witness to particular events."[47] Significant progress has been made since Richards wrote in 2004, especially in the scientific investigations—such as genetics and isotopic analysis—of archaeological materials. This section addresses phases one (seasonal raids) and two (multi-year raids). The archaeology of phases three (permanent settlements) and four (eleventh-century conquest) is addressed below in the last section, "The Raiders Settle Down." As observed above, phase one and most of phase two lack native Scandinavian textual sources, while even the Anglo-Saxon texts are limited and problematic until the reign of Alfred the Great (871–899), at which time they may be more accurate in their basic information, but still retain an intense bias against Scandinavian activities in England. Archaeological data is therefore critical to our understanding of this dynamic period.

Archaeological evidence for successful Viking raids can be gleaned from looted objects and raid-associated destruction inflicted on settlement sites. Unsuccessful Viking expeditions have only recently been identified, in the material remains of defeated Viking raiding parties. Viking bases and forts constructed in England are mentioned in texts and implied by place names, but archaeological evidence for these bases is now being discovered through excavations at sites such as Repton and Torksey. This evidence goes far beyond confirming the existence of fortified bases recorded in the texts and are instead shedding new light on the economics, make-up, and social interactions of the Viking war bands.

Viking Loot and Hoards

Vikings deposited high-value objects in hoards, graves, and settlements in Britain and in the Scandinavian homelands. But how can we distinguish objects acquired by peaceful means—such as trade or gift-exchange—from objects acquired by plunder? In fact, it is probably impossible to be completely sure. Certain artifacts, however, are unlikely to have been traded or gifted to Vikings, including objects related to the practice of the Christian faith (Figure 2.3). Other items that appear to have been (forcibly) removed from the context in which they had more intrinsic value, such as metal book bindings, are equally unlikely to have been considered suitable for exchange between Anglo-Saxons and Scandinavians.

Viking treasure stolen from Britain appears not infrequently as grave goods deposited in Scandinavian graves. Reliquaries stolen from churches are recalled in historical sources and several have been found redeposited in pre-Christian

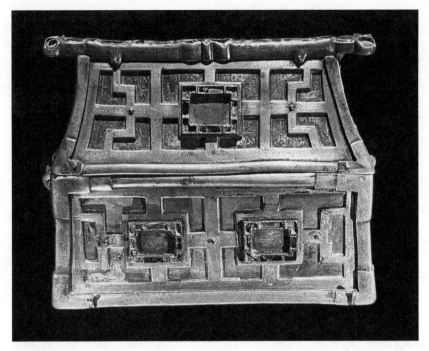

Figure 2.3 A portable reliquary shrine originally crafted and used in a monastic setting in the Gaelic Irish Sea area. The shrine was found deposited in a pagan grave in Norway, dating to the late-eighth to early ninth century. It is known as "Ranveig's Casket" because of the female name inscribed in runes on the bottom: RANVEIK. Ecclesiastically holy and expensive items such as this shrine would almost certainly have been acquired through raids. Back in Scandinavia such items were often retained intact and must have provided mementos of raiding success and served as valued objects that could be invested in the gift-giving economy.
Source: photo by author, National Museum of Denmark

pagan graves.[48] A number of late eighth- to early ninth-century Viking Age graves, at sites such as Melhus and Setnes in Norway, have produced complete Celtic-style house-shaped reliquaries.[49] An object that appears to be such a house-shaped reliquary is depicted on the remarkable Hostage Stone found in the eighth- to ninth-century scriptorium in the Inchmarnock monastery in the Hebrides (Figure 2.4).[50] The stone shows a bound hostage being led to a ship by a wild-haired warrior. The hostage—presumably a monk—appears to have a reliquary hanging around his neck. Other ecclesiastical objects that originated in the British Isles but ended up as grave goods in Scandinavia include at least five bishops' croziers.[51] In fact, the Setnes grave with a house-shaped reliquary also contained a crozier fragment. Neither the reliquary boxes nor the bishops'

Figure 2.4 An inscribed slate tablet found at the monastery of Inchmarnock dating to the late-eighth or early-ninth century. Monks used such slates to practice in the scriptorium school. The monk who worked on this stone appears to have etched an image of his fear of Viking raiders. An armored and long-haired warrior leads a smaller figure towards a ship by a rope or chain. The smaller and somewhat cowering figure, whose hands appear to be bound, holds an object that bears resemblance to the portable reliquary shrines that have been found in Viking Age graves (see Figure 2.3).
Source: image used with permission from Headland Archaeology (UK) Ltd.

croziers were likely to have been given up willingly by their original owners, and it seems unlikely that they belonged to early missionaries to Scandinavia, particularly as so many ended up as grave goods in pre-Christian burials.[52] For instance, the Melhus reliquary was found in a boat burial that held a man and a woman, each accompanied by a range of objects.[53] The same Melhus woman wore a dress-pin refashioned in Scandinavia from a bronze mount of British or Irish origin. Melhus reliquary and other intact looted objects deposited in graves indicate that these items had high social value in their intact form. These imported objects became prestige goods, valued for their exotic origins and for the stories that could be told about their daring acquisition. The social "lives" of the objects provided value and continued to be inalienable from the objects as long as they were retained intact.

Beyond graves, Viking treasure hoards collate a large sample of precious objects, providing our most archaeologically visible evidence of the products that motivated Viking activities. Hoards, as collections of treasure accumulated over time and purposefully deposited together, tell us about where the Vikings went, what they valued, how their economy functioned, and how their political order was maintained. Silver is by far the most common material in Viking hoards, suggesting that it was a primary target for raiding. Silver had value by weight as a means of exchange and as display items indicating status. Vikings often melted and cast silver into easily transportable objects of uniform weight such as ingots or arm rings. Although consistent locally, the weight of such objects often varied regionally. Weights of silver were checked with folding scales and lead weights, which are found in graves and settlements across the Viking world. Since the silver was valued as bullion (i.e., by weight), silver ingots or other objects were commonly cut into smaller weights for use in exchange. Called hacksilver, these distinctly cut fragments of larger standardized silver objects are a distinguishing characteristic of Viking hoards. For instance, ingots often show evidence of having been cut at either end to remove specific measures of silver, possibly to pay for supplies or reward followers. The Silverdale hoard—discovered in 2011 in northwest England and dated to circa 900—contained 129 ingots, of which all but thirteen had been cut on one or both ends.[54] Also distinctive of Viking hoards is evidence of nicking and pecking of silver objects with a knife to verify the quality of the silver: silver that was too soft had been mixed with lead, while silver that was too hard had copper added.[55] In the beginning of the Viking Age, in particular, the value lay in the weight and purity of the silver, and the quest for silver to a large extent fueled Viking economics as well as the social relations that united raiding parties.

Much silver acquired abroad was melted down and refashioned into ingots or decorative objects in Scandinavia. The origins of looted objects can be investigated through style if the object is retained in this original form. Even if the object is refashioned, geochemical methods can seek the origins in the make-up of the silver. The geochemical signature of silver objects can point to the location where the silver was mined, but unless impurities were added in the production process, this method will not be able to pinpoint the location of production and certainly not the place from which Vikings acquired the object. Comparing the silver composition of coinage from different parts of Europe and Eurasia (e.g., Carolingian Empire, Anglo-Saxon kingdoms, Abbasid Caliphate) with objects refashioned into Scandinavian-style jewelry, ingots, and ring money could estab-lish connections. One current research project seeks to use isotopes to examine how silver moved around the Viking world. Preliminary research has for instance indicated that the silver in two Hiberno-Scandinavian style arm rings from the Bedale Hoard (deposited c. 900) has a lead isotope signature that matches the

Carolingian coins minted in Messel, western France, in the ninth century.[56] This suggests that the Vikings who buried their treasure in Bedale in northern England had employed silver acquired in Francia to produce standardized silver arm rings commonly used as a means of exchange in the Irish Sea zone.

Other objects, including silver that was not re-melted and cast into ingots or rings, tell clearer stories about where the Vikings went and provide more definitive evidence that this wealth was not acquired peacefully. Foreign coins, especially Anglo-Saxon coins, found in the Scandinavian homelands have often been interpreted as deriving from raids or Danegeld tribute extraction. Calculations indicate that of the roughly 70,000 silver coins found in Denmark and southwest Sweden, over 15,000 are Anglo-Saxon Viking Age coins.[57] The coin hoards provide temporal resolution for the Viking activity, showing that the majority of the English coins come from the late tenth and early eleventh centuries, centered in the phase of Viking activities led by Svein Forkbeard and Knut the Great. Farther afield and indicating the involvement of peoples from wide geographical reaches of the Viking world, even the Gullberjar hoard found in Iceland (c. 1015) included 180 Anglo-Saxon coins that have been interpreted as deriving from Danegeld extracted in the late tenth or early eleventh century.[58]

Variations in coin percentages suggest where particular Vikings focused their activities. An incredible density of hoards, nearly 400, have been found on the Swedish island of Gotland. Although the coin evidence shows that the economy of Gotland was clearly directed toward the eastern Baltic, Russia, Ukraine, Byzantium, and Baghdad, the hoards evidence the international character of Viking activities across Scandinavia. For instance, the Gotlandic Ocksarve Hoard deposited shortly after 999 and found in 1997 included 370 silver coins that showed a focus on the East Frankish lands (340 German coins, eight Bohemian, six English, six ancient Roman, three Italian, three Arabic, two Scandinavian, and one Byzantine).[59] Yet, another hoard found at the same site of Ocksarve in 1912 had an eastern and specifically Byzantine focus including 123 millerisia (silver Byzantine coins dating from the eighth to the eleventh century) minted in the reign of Constantine IX Monomachos (1042–1055).[60] The eastern focus is also abundantly clear in Gotland's Spillings Hoard—the largest Viking hoard yet recovered—weighing 67 kg and consisting of 486 silver arm rings and just over 14,300 coins, the latest coin dating to 870/871. The hoard contained coins from across Europe, including England, as well as imitations of Islamic coins minted in the Khazar and Bulgar kingdoms in the zone between the Dnieper and Volga Rivers, but over 99 percent of these coins are from the Muslim world.[61] Excavations of the hoard find spot revealed building foundations and floor deposits, indicating that the hoard had been buried beneath a house floor. From these three hoards, three regional foci of the Viking voyagers are discernable: Francia for Ocksarve 1997, Byzantium for Ocksarve

1912, and the Muslim lands for Spillings. Importantly, based mostly on textual analogy, common assumptions about the activities that generated this wealth vary: the Frankish wealth is assumed to be generated by raiding, the Byzantine riches by service to the Byzantine emperor in his personal bodyguard, while the Islamic silver is believed to have derived primarily through trade. In reality, we do not know for certain which of these or which combination of these Viking activities led to the accumulation of this great wealth buried in Gotland.

Beyond the Scandinavian homelands, several hoards found in Britain are identified as Viking hoards based on their date, context, and most importantly, their contents. The Cuerdale Hoard, excavated in 1840, is the largest Viking hoard discovered in Britain. It comprises over 8,600 pieces buried in a lead box in the early tenth century (c. 905–910).[62] The Cuerdale Hoard's international character includes coins minted in England, Scandinavia, Italy, the Carolingian Empire, and Central Asia. The hoard includes around 1,000 Carolingian coins. These Carolingian coins may have been acquired through raiding or as payoff in Francia. The movement of raiding parties back and forth across the English Channel suggested by the texts is here consistent with hoard evidence. The accumulation of wealth from multiple regions deposited in areas far-removed from the Viking homelands also suggests extended stays abroad, consistent with wintering bases and the onset of permanent settlement mentioned in the texts.

The Vale of York Hoard found in 2007 was likely buried in a lead or lead-lined container by a Viking elite, who may have been fleeing the advancing English armies during the conquest of Scandinavian-dominated northeast England by Edward the Elder of Wessex. The most recent coin that entered the hoard is an Æthelstan coin from 928.[63] The hoard held a spectacular silver cup with gilding inside and outside and animal and floral motif decorations. The cup's internal gilding and the likelihood that it originally had a lid indicates that it was originally used as a ciborium (a cup used for holding consecrated bread during Mass).[64] The cup was looted from northern Francia. Such an ecclesiastical object is unlikely to have been given as a gift or as tribute, which was typically paid in coin.[65]

The Galloway Hoard, discovered in 2014 in southwest Scotland and dating to around 900, is particularly instructive because professional archaeologists excavated a large area around the find spot initially identified by a metal-detectorist. At the top, the hoard consisted of a dozen flattened silver arm rings, which would have served as means of exchange in the bullion economy. Just below, but still in the upper layer of the hoard, was an Anglo-Saxon silver cross on a chain. Immediately below was a layer of gravel, followed by a second layer of the hoarded wealth that contained increasingly valuable objects in three separately deposited parcels. One parcel contained an even greater number of silver ingots and arm rings, four of which had runic inscriptions that corresponded to four groupings of rings with ends folded in four distinct ways. If the short runic inscriptions are names, then perhaps this is a rare opportunity to see the jointly hoarded wealth of four Vikings. A second parcel contained larger and unfolded arm rings still meant for wearing with a wooden box in the middle that itself contained three gold objects, including a bird-shaped pin. The third parcel contained a silver-gilt lidded Carolingian vessel wrapped in textile and filled with a carefully wrapped collection of objects not meant for use in the bullion economy: silver Anglo-Saxon disc and quatrefoil brooches, an Irish silver brooch, two Anglo-Saxon hinged mounts, silk, and gold objects including a gold pendant that probably held saintly relics.[66] At the bottom of the vessel was a pouch containing three layers of textile (leather, linen, and silk) wrapping a rock crystal jar from the Islamic world. The Carolingian vessel itself had probably been used originally in Christian worship, possibly as ciborium, like the one found in the Vale of York Hoard. Subsequent open-area excavations (30 x 30 m) and geophysical survey at the find spot—not typically conducted at hoard find sites—uncovered further evidence of Viking Age remains, including evidence of a timber building under which the hoard was deposited.[67]

Why Viking Age people chose to bury their treasures in hoards is a question that has long been asked. Most hoards were probably buried for safekeeping and then never recovered, although the theory that some Vikings permanently buried their hoarded wealth so that they could use it in the afterlife remains a possibility supported by Old Norse literature.[68] The hoards found under house floors, such the Galloway Hoard and the Spillings Hoard found in Gotland, were probably stores of wealth meant to be used later. The untimely death of the hoards' owners provides the most likely explanation for the fact that the hoards were not recovered and used by their owners. Wealth may have been buried in times of conflict. For instance, twenty-six hoards have been recovered in England that date to the 870s, when the Viking Great Army was devastating the Anglo-Saxon kingdoms, while only an average of three hoards per decade have been recovered from the other four decades from 850 to 900.[69] The clustering of tenth-century hoards along the likely very dangerous road from Dublin to York provides some support for this interpretation. The massive hoards of Cuerdale and Vale of York, for instance, have both been interpreted as the wealth of Viking chieftains fleeing advancing Anglo-Saxon forces. These defeats, recorded in the historical sources, are typically given as reasons for the hoard depositions. However, the find spot of the Galloway Hoard in the corner of a house beneath the floor importantly hints that perhaps the hoards clustered along the old Roman roads and river crossings between the Irish Sea (leading to Dublin) and York are buried under settlements along the roads established by the first wave of permanent settlers in this area rather than by fleeing nobles connected to specific events of Viking defeats in the centers of Dublin and York. In either case, the clustering of hoards in northwest

England on the travel axis between the Hiberno-Scandinavian center of Dublin and the Anglo-Scandinavian center of York underscores the importance of these two Viking urban centers that became key nodes in the international exchange system in the late ninth and early tenth centuries. The hoards, in fact, cluster chronologically in the early tenth century, when the Scandinavian influence on these centers was at its height.

The contents of hoards bear witness to Viking activities, while the geographical distribution of hoards in Britain provides evidence of both transient and permanent Scandinavian presence. The hoards are evidence of the raids and tribute extraction, which are activities that characterize Phase 1, but which took place throughout the Viking Age. In fact, most hoards date to the tenth century, at which time permanent settlement was well established. Further evidence of Phase 1- and Phase 2-type activities can be sought in settlements subjected to raids, which is the topic of the following section. Archaeological evidence of Phase 2 wintering forts will be sought in a subsequent section on Viking forts and encampments.

Raided Settlements

The Scandinavian raids on Britain destructively impacted monasteries, settlements, and trading sites. Nevertheless, identifying archaeological evidence of Viking attacks is difficult. The earliest hit-and-run raids have been especially hard to identify. The evidence of a devastating Viking raid on the Scottish monastery of Portmahomack is therefore even more remarkable. Portmahomack was a Pictish coastal monastery on the Tarbat Peninsula located between the Firths of Dornoch and Moray in northeastern Scotland. The flourishing eighth-century monastery that produced vellum for manuscripts, liturgical metalwork, and beautiful Pictish Christian stone sculpture met an abrupt end when its buildings were burned and the monumental stone crosses that marked the edge of its sacred grounds were toppled and deliberately smashed sometime between 780 and 810.[70] In the eighth-century cemetery, two of the circa fifty male skeletons showed evidence of bladed weapon wounds. One of these two individuals, who were presumably monks, suffered two cranial fractures from behind with a bladed weapon that instantly killed him.[71] The violence done to the four monumental stone crosses in particular suggests a Viking incursion, one that targeted these crosses not just as symbols of Christianity, but also as political symbols of Pictish overlordship.[72]

After the raid, Portmahomack was restructured as a secular metal-production and trading site, producing among other objects cast acorn-shaped weights used for bullion-economy transactions.[73] The site continued to be occupied by

Picts, but interactions—possibly subservient ones—were now common with Scandinavians, as evidenced by the presence of Scandinavian material culture, including Viking style combs, a ring, and a gaming board. Isotopic analysis of the eighth-century burials in the Portmahomack monastery cemetery indicated that two of the individuals were from Scandinavia. Multiple interpretations are possible, and most involve a level of non-violent interaction either before or soon after the violent Viking raid of circa 800.[74] As the Vikings settled and gained control of northern Scotland and the islands north of the mainland, Portmahomack occupied a position on the border between the Scandinavian-controlled northern part of Scotland and the Celtic- and Pictish-controlled south. Around 1000 a silver hoard was deposited at Portmahomack that contained English and Frankish coins as well as four silver arm rings. Martin Carver raises the possibility that this was a metalworkers' hoard awaiting refashioning into objects intended for either Vikings or Scots.[75] Whatever the silver was to be used for, its accumulation most likely derived from piratical activities, while its owner may well have buried it in the wake of one of the battles involved in the power struggle for this area. *Orkneyinga Saga*, for instance, records a sea battle between Thorfinn the Mighty (Earl of Orkney) and Karl Hundison that took place in 1035 just a few kilometers from Portmahomack.[76] Repton, another religious center, deeply reshaped by Viking incursion, is addressed below—although in Repton the footprint of the Vikings is clearer as they remained for a time and from there began their settlement of England.

Winter Camps of the Great Army

Archaeological correlates of the second-phase Viking activities involving multi-seasonal campaigns are evident in fortified camps where Vikings stayed more permanently. The first Viking bases, situated along the coasts and in estuaries, have been identified archaeologically in places such as the small, defended site of Cronk ny Merriu on the Isle of Man and the larger fort of Camp de Péran in Brittany, which lies 10 km from the sea along the Urne River.[77] The largest and most illuminating Viking bases in Britain are associated with the Viking Great Army that caused the downfall of three of the four Anglo-Saxon kingdoms in the late 860s and into the early 870s. These camps moved farther inland, still strategically situated along rivers. The discovery of three Viking winter camps in England provide evidence for the second phase of Viking activity: wintering. The archaeological remains of these camps correlate in location, character, and date with Viking encampments mentioned in the *Anglo-Saxon Chronicle*, while expanding exponentially our understanding of Viking armies.

The *Anglo Saxon Chronicle* entry from 873 states, "here the raiding army went from Lindsey to Repton and took winter-quarters there, and drove King Burgred [of Mercia] across the sea 22 years after he had the kingdom; and conquered all the land."[78] From Repton, the Viking leaders dismantled Mercia and set up a puppet king who swore to "be ready with all who would follow him, at the service of the raiding-army."[79] Archaeological excavations at Repton that began in the 1970s have unearthed the remains of a fortified camp and Scandinavian-style burials. The defensive center of the camp was a D-shaped rampart and ditch (1.2 m deep and 2.7 m wide) built along the east bank of the river Trent. The Vikings reused the Mercian royal church of St. Wystan as a gatehouse, employing the south doorway of the church as a gated entry into the fortification. The north side of the enclosure culminated in a cliff-side facing the river, which was unwalled and open for docking ships. The investment in the fortification was a defensive measure, but even more so, this winter base was a conspicuous show of power by the Great Army employed at a crucial time as they took power in Mercia. Repton was a royal center for the Mercian kings that held a monastic community and a mausoleum used as a place of burial for multiple eighth- and ninth-century Mercian kings.[80] Among the Mercian kings buried in the church's eighth-century crypt was King Wystan. After Wystan was made a saint, the Repton church became a pilgrimage site.[81]

The Vikings manifested their victory in the Mercian landscape by choosing to set their camp within this major royal center and transforming the monuments of the Anglo-Saxon Church and State. They desecrated and retooled the church to make their gatehouse, causing such damage in the process that "the upper half of its walls had to be completely rebuilt, including the windows and roof."[82] The ditch and rampart disturbed and covered the earlier Christian burials within the churchyard. The church was damaged, with debris appearing in subsequently inhumed Scandinavian style graves.[83] Grave 529, dating to the early 870s, contained a man buried with five silver pennies. He was interred up against the church chancel's north wall and his grave dug into large deposits of charcoal, burnt sandstone from the church, and other debris.[84] By burying several of their dead with overt pagan symbols, the Vikings were appropriating the old Christian graveyard. Close to Grave 529 and also north of the chancel, Grave 511 held the remains of a thirty-five to forty-five-year-old man who died in battle from multiple weapon wounds, including a blow to his skull and a piercing sword thrust to his eye socket, suggesting that he might have been wearing a helmet. After he had fallen, he suffered a cut to his groin that cut deep into his right femoral head and may have severed his genitals. He was interred with a Viking-style sword, a silver Thor's hammer pendant, a crow bone, and boar's tusk placed between his legs. The crow bone may be a reference to Odin's ravens, while some have suggested that the boar's tusk—a symbol of the fertility god Frey—might have been a symbolic replacement of his possible emasculation. A younger male (aged seventeen to twenty), who also died in battle, was buried in Grave 295 shortly after and just to the north of Grave 511. The tombs of both men were marked by a single large post by their feet and then covered by a stone cairn that incorporated five pieces of a purposefully destroyed Anglo-Saxon cross from the Christian graveyard. Radiocarbon dating pinpointed their deaths to the years between 873 and 886, while strontium isotope analysis of teeth from both men indicates that they grew up in the same part of southern Scandinavia, probably in Denmark.[85] The connection between the two apparent Viking warriors grew closer after analysis of their DNA showed a first-degree link on the paternal line, meaning that they could very well have been father and son.

The excavators of Repton in the 1970s and 1980s, Martin Biddle and Birthe Kjølbye-Biddle, thought that additional deceased Vikings from the Great Army were represented in a remarkable collection of neatly arranged bones placed within a reutilized seventh- to eighth-century Anglo-Saxon subterranean mausoleum (Figure 2.5). This mass burial was first recorded in the seventeenth century, when a local man dug into a mound located west of the church. Within the mound, he found a two-roomed structure. In the eastern room, beneath a collapsed roof formerly held up by wooden beams, he uncovered a large skeleton within a stone box surrounded by "one hundred humane skeletons, with their feet pointing to the stone coffin."[86] Excavations in the 1980s largely confirmed this story. The mausoleum contained the bones of at least 264 individuals, and over 80 percent of them were robust males. The sex ratio, the large stature of the males, as well as an age profile favoring people in their physical prime (93% aged between seventeen and forty-five), suggested to the excavators that these were dead warriors. The recovery of Viking weapons and five silver coins dated to the early 870s connected the warriors to the Great Army. This attribution was subsequently challenged on the basis of radiocarbon dates that placed a number of the graves in the seventh and eighth centuries. However, recent re-dating of the skeletal material that adjusted for the high marine diets of these individuals has shown that all dated burials within the mass grave are consistent with an internment around the year 873–874. Moreover, strontium and oxygen isotope analysis showed that the vast majority of the sixty-one individuals sampled could not have grown up in the Repton area, while most showed isotopic signatures consistent with having spent their childhoods in Scandinavia.[87]

The burial monument constructed from the old Anglo-Saxon mausoleum showed an extravagant investment of time and energy that indicated the high status of the centrally buried individual. The ritual complexity of the mass burial included leveling the earlier Anglo-Saxon semi-subterranean structure to the height of the surrounding ground. After a phase of destruction evidenced by broken glass and fragments of plaster scattered in the entrance room, the inner

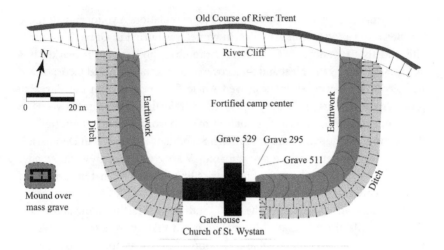

Figure 2.5 The fortified Viking camp at the Anglo-Saxon royal monastic site of Repton, where the Great Army wintered in 873/874. Vikings converted the church to a gatehouse leading into a fortification constructed to abut the river. Archaeological investigations have revealed a more substantial camp that extends beyond the fort, as shown in the digital reconstruction.

Source: map by author after Jarman et al. 2017; image created by Compost Creative

room of the subterranean space was prepared for use as a mass burial chamber. The floor onto which the dead were placed was first cleaned and then covered with red a layer of marl stone sand imported from several kilometers away. After the interment of the dead, timber planks were laid over the chamber and a mound of stone and earth was heaped over the old building. The closing of the mound was marked by four pits dug into the side of the mound. One of these pits contained the carefully arranged bodies of four children buried together and interpreted by the excavators as a sacrificial deposit marking the burial event of the Great Army's leader who would have occupied the central burial within the newly constructed mound. Two of the children's remains showed evidence of violent death. Their strontium and oxygen isotope levels varied substantially from one another, meaning that they had grown up in different places and were probably taken to Repton as slaves by the Vikings.[88] Viking Age Scandinavians did practice human sacrifice, but it was reserved for very solemn occasions, such as the death of important leaders. The central burial must clearly have held a person of great social importance.

The excavators have argued based on the evidence from historical sources—including Irish Annals, English historical traditions, and the sagas—that the central grave within the mound might have contained Ivar the Boneless. Ivar is the only historically known leader of the Great Army who is not mentioned after the Vikings left Repton. The Irish *Annals of Ulster* inform that Ivar (Imar) died in 873, while the *Saga of Ragnar Lodbrok* explains that Ivar was buried in England under a barrow at a place that was a frontier exposed to attack from his enemies.[89] Perhaps the death of the "king of the Norsemen of all Ireland and Britain," as the *Annals of Ulster* calls Ivar, was a partial cause for the splintering of the Great Army. After wintering at Repton, the Great Army never again fought together as a whole.[90] The *Anglo-Saxon Chronicle* tells that Halfdan took half of the army north to Northumbria, while Guthrum went south with his followers. Whoever the leader buried at Repton was, the Great Army had made a clear claim to be the new masters of the land by reshaping the Mercian royal site and making an old Christian mausoleum into a pagan Scandinavian burial mound on par with the ritual complexity and economic investment required for any royal burial in the Viking homelands.

A second Viking cemetery that appears also to be associated with the Viking Great Army's overwintering at Repton has been partially excavated at Heath Wood, 4 km from Repton.[91] In contrast to the inhumation graves at Repton, the Heath Wood cemetery consists of fifty-nine mounds covering cremation graves. Some of the mounds show evidence of cremation on the spot, whereas other mounds include remains cremated elsewhere and then transported to Heath Wood for interment. Swords, spears, shields, dogs, and horses were placed on the pyres, while cuts of beef, pork, and mutton thrown into the pyre indicate that feasting took place at the graveside. The graves are distinctly and conservatively Scandinavian, making intentional statements of difference from the local population and group unity among the individuals interred there. In fact, the difference in burial rites—inhumation at Repton and cremation at Heath Wood—might signal two ideological constituencies within the Great Army, which in turn might correlate with separate war bands. Newly reported metal-detecting work within eyesight of Heath Wood at a place called Foremark (Old Norse, Forn-verk, meaning Old Fortification) has yielded preliminary evidence of Viking Age Scandinavian objects such as dirhams (Islamic silver coins) and a Thor's hammer that further connect this cremation cemetery with the Great Army's fortification at Repton. The Repton fortification is too small (c. 0.46 hectares) to have encompassed the whole army for the winter of 873–874, even though archaeologists have begun to find remains of a larger camp extending beyond the D-shaped ramparts.[92] Foremark, on the other hand, is strategically placed on a broad bluff overlooking the river Trent between Repton and Heath Wood at a place ideal for anchoring ships. Foremark then might have served as the location of the larger camp with a small lookout force positioned on still higher ground at Repton.[93]

Repton's relatively small D-shaped fortification was until very recently used as *the* type site for Vikings forts.[94] But recent discoveries of the site of Foremark and two additional Viking bases of the Great Army showed that the Viking camps varied according to local conditions and political circumstances. The year before the Great Army stayed at Repton, the *Anglo-Saxon Chronicle* pinpoints another Viking wintering base (872–873): "Here the raiding-army went into Northumbria, and it took winter-quarters at Torksey in Lindsey."[95] The modern village of Torksey, which has origins dating back to the period immediately after the Viking Age, showed no evidence of a D-shaped fortification or any other fortification thought to resemble a Viking base. With the recent advent of productive relationships between metal detectorists and professional archaeologists, loose finds have increasingly been documented with GPS and entered into the Portable Antiquities Scheme (PAS) database.[96] This collaboration resulted in mounting evidence for a clustering of Viking metalwork in multiple fields lying to the north of Torksey village.[97] The concentration of Scandinavian-style metalwork, which stretches across a site of 55 hectares, includes four Thor's hammers and production debris from bronze casting and lead strips with die impressions suggesting minting of coins imitating Louis the Pious' solidus (a gold coin of high value based on Byzantine standards) as well as silver stycas (small pennies from Northumbria).[98] The metalwork includes remnants of the thriving Viking-style dual-economy (also evidenced in hoards) in which transactions could be made with standard weights of silver or with coinage. Ingots, hacksilver, fragments of silver arm rings, and cut dirhams indicate bullion-economy transactions, while a large number of intact English pennies, especially the Northumbrian stycas, show the presence of coinage transactions. Characteristic of Viking economics are over 350 weights, including 99 cubo-octahedral and 6 truncated spheroid weights that were both adopted by Scandinavian merchants from the Arab world.[99] More than 400 coins recovered at Torksey show a short occupation following the issue of the latest coins in the early 870s. The site yielded 144 Islamic dirham coins cut into fragments, more than any other site in the British Isles.[100] Importantly, the latest of these dirhams, minted in the late 860s, arrived in England after the beginning of the campaigns of the Great Army, showing the army's continued contacts stretching through Scandinavia and to the Caliphate of Baghdad.[101] Also characteristic of Scandinavian culture were the more than 300 conical pieces of lead measuring 2–3 cm in height used to play the chess-like game of hnefatafl (meaning "fist-table," or perhaps "game of the fist").[102] The rules of the game are unknown, but the gaming pieces have been found throughout the Viking world and especially in elite graves. Distinctive oval brooches worn by Scandinavian women have also been recovered, suggesting the presence of women in the Viking camps.[103] Geophysical survey, fieldwalking, and excavation yielded no evidence of Viking Age ditches, ramparts, or permanent structures at Torksey. This work, however, did yield seventy human skeletal fragments distributed in two discrete burial zones. Radiocarbon dating of two bones gave mid-ninth-century dates, consistent with the Great Army's occupation of the site. The bones from both zones are from unburned inhumations, but the separation of the bone fragments into two burial zones could speak of separate groups within the camp.[104]

Recent archaeological excavations following the discovery of extensive clandestine metal detectorist findings have revealed a third Viking base located about 20 km northwest of York at a place called Aldwark (Old English, meaning "Old Fortification").[105] Accessible directly from York along the navigable Ouse River, Aldwark is situated where there is both a natural crossing point and a suitable place for pulling ships up onto the riverbank. The large assemblage of finds is similar in character to those from Torksey with weapons, looted objects, and a great deal of items related to trade and exchange. Hack-silver, cut Islamic dirhams, ingots, scales, and weights (of the Arab-influenced cubo-octahedral types found at Torksey) co-occur with Northumbrian styca coins. Tied explicitly to Norse beliefs are a Thor's hammer, a lead fragment showing the Fenris wolf, and a lead amulet in the form of a shield-bearing female or Valkyrie. The distinctive objects and a hoard of coins that date the site to the mid-to-late 870s suggest an intensive temporary occupation shortly after the occupations of Torksey and Repton. The site is not mentioned in the *Anglo-Saxon Chronicle*, but such a date for Aldwark corresponds with the return of Halfdan and half of the Great Army to Northumbria in 874 after the winter in Repton.[106] In contrast to

Torksey, a possible fortification at Aldwark has been identified in the shape of a "large sub-rectangular enclosure."[107] The enclosure encompasses an area of 31 hectares, which more comparable to the size of the Torksey camp (55 hectares) than to Repton's D-shaped rampart and ditch (0.46 hectares). In light of the size of the Torksey and Aldwark sites, the expected footprint of the Viking camps has grown exponentially as has their expected impact on the local populations.

Controlling the navigable rivers that allowed reinforcement, provisioning, and tactical advantages was paramount in choosing winter camps for the Viking Great Army. All three archaeologically verified bases are situated on rivers, and Repton and Torksey are both located on high bluffs overlooking the landscape at the junction of riverine and land-based travel routes. Fortification of some sort existed at both Repton and Aldwark. The naturally defensible site of Torksey may not have necessitated a fortification. Landscape reconstruction and survey showed that Torksey would have been a virtual island, occupying a bluff bounded on the west by the River Trent and on the east by a marshland. Marshes form barriers to the north and south of the Torksey base, while silt deposits on both these sides show the presence of ancient tidal pools with sandy slopes that would have been ideal for beaching ships.[108] The Torksey bluff served as a strategic vantage point elevated 10 m above the surrounding lowland that extended in all directions. The Torksey camp also occupied a nodal point in the early medieval landscape, a place where the land-based Roman road crossed the riverine travel route. Ships could follow the River Trent to the Humber and through the Humber enter the North Sea or by way of the River Ouse arrive in York.[109] The strategically located positions of the Viking encampments on rivers and at river crossings would have been ideal for smaller parties to strike out to raid, trade, and gather supplies in the surrounding countryside, even when the larger army was not on the move. It is precisely such smaller Scandinavian raiding parties that have now been evidenced at about thirty sites in northeastern England on the basis of a "Great Army signature" that includes (1) objects used in the Viking bullion economy (hacksilver, lead and copper weights, and deliberately cut and potentially looted dress accessories), (2) Anglo-Saxon coins found outside their normal circulation area (Northumbrian stycas and other Anglo-Saxon silver pennies), and (3) lead gaming pieces for playing hnefatafl.[110]

The date and locations of the three archaeologically documented Viking camps are consistent with the written sources. Yet, the archaeological evidence has expanded our knowledge immeasurably. The Viking army's strategic adaptability can be appreciated in both the tactical location chosen for each camp site and the decisions made about the kinds of fortification that each site needed. The graves at Repton and at Heath Wood reveal the remains of a conquering army that distinguished itself by adherence to the Scandinavian belief system while conspicuously burying its dead in places of traditional sacral importance.

The enormous size of the bases and the diverse finds assemblages are the most stunning aspects of the Viking winter camps. They bear witness to massive and mobile proto-urban camps that possessed a previously unappreciated economic integration with the Anglo-Saxon hinterland.

A Mass Burial of Interregional Vikings

The search for the physical remains of Vikings in Britain is complex, and chemical analyses of skeletal material often yield unclear results.[111] But results can also be spectacularly successful, as was the case with the fifty individuals uncovered by a road-construction project on Ridgeway Hill in Dorset, southern England.[112] The individuals, mostly young men, had been decapitated with a sword.[113] Their heads were severed brutally with each victim suffering an average of four blows somewhere between the shoulder blades and the bottom of their skulls. Their executioners had collated the severed heads in a pile at the southern edge of their mass grave. Their bodies had been carelessly thrown down within an old, reused quarry pit. The excavation yielded more bodies than skulls, suggesting that some heads were kept as trophies and possibly put on stakes besides the mass grave or elsewhere. The mass grave's location—on the top of Ridgeway Hill, along an old Roman road, on a parish boundary, and beside a prehistoric barrow used in the tenth century as an assembly site—had been specifically selected for visibility and to make an example of the executed individuals.[114] Radiocarbon dating of bone samples from the top, middle, and bottom of the mass grave all showed dates around 1000 with a combined calibrated date range of 970–1025.

The dead were buried without any objects, meaning that cultural affinity could not be determined through grave goods as has often been the practice, for example with the Scandinavian graves at Repton. However, six individuals among the dead had dental modification including polished and filed horizontal grooves in their front incisors. Similar dental modification has been identified in over ninety individuals from Viking Age graves in Scandinavia, whereas no such examples have been found in England.[115] One man, aged twenty-six to thirty-five, had two parallel horizontal lines filed into both upper front teeth.[116] The lines, probably filled with dye, would be visible when the man smiled broadly and may be indicative of status or occupational display. At first, the executed individuals were thought to have been victims of a Viking raid, but the dental modification suggested otherwise. Subsequent isotopic analysis of the skeletons turned the interpretation on its head by showing that the individuals assessed for isotopic signatures of strontium and oxygen had grown up and lived the years prior to their death outside of Britain in diverse geographical localities ranging from northern Iceland and Arctic Norway to the southern Baltic region.

Surprisingly, a core group of twenty out of thirty-one sampled individuals showed shared oxygen, strontium, and lead isotopic signatures. Members of this core group appear to have grown up on the southern coast of Baltic, probably in modern-day Poland. The remainder of the sample group appeared to be from diverse regions of northern Scandinavia and possibly Iceland, but not Denmark or southern or southwestern Norway.[117] This contrasts with written sources and archaeological assumptions of the Danish and Norwegian origins of the Vikings who attacked Britain. The men with dental modifications, who were excluded from this testing to preserve their teeth for future study, remain mysterious but considering their affinity with cultural practices overwhelmingly concentrated in Scandinavia, this origin seems the most likely. In any case, the group's diverse origins and numbers are consistent with one shipload of young males recruited from across the Viking world to carry out an ultimately unsuccessful Viking raid on southern England during the reign of Æthelred the Unready (978–1016).

Models for Understanding Raids and Raiding

The imminent historian Peter Sawyer saw the Viking incursions as "an extension of normal Dark Age activity, made possible by special circumstances."[118] This may be broadly true. Viking leaders were status-seeking chieftains pursuing personal gain by mobilizing bands of followers with social mechanisms of gift giving, feasting, and loot redistribution. But the Viking raids were an "extension" to the point that they became, as Patrick Wormald says, "abnormal." Wormald explained this abnormality of the Viking expansion as rooted in an "abnormal crisis" of internal political upheaval rooted in the shift from sacral to military kingship in Scandinavia.[119] But if we consider the Viking Age in global perspective, then we see also particular historical circumstances that offered a set of opportunities for Scandinavians to serve their individual personal interests by striking out beyond their homelands at an unprecedented scale. These population movements, whether engaged in raids, trade, exploration, or migration, needed broad-based support at home, extending beyond the not-yet-very-powerful elite. In other words, leaders still had to convince fellow raiders and their wider community that the voyages were worth undertaking.

Viking expeditions were a risky business for those people who participated. Launching such expeditions was also an expensive endeavor for the Scandinavian communities from which the voyages were launched. One way to approach a phenomenon such as the Viking expansion is to try to understand the motivations of the individual actors involved.[120] Following an economic anthropological approach, the participants in Viking voyages were individuals making rational decisions in their own best interests. Such a model recognizes individual agency and the cumulative outcomes of many individuals' decisions as drivers of historical phenomena. The individual decisions are based on constellations of biological, environmental, political, and ideological factors. Once the underlying conditions favor decisions that draw in large portions of the population into new networks of cooperation, these networks can and often do intertwine larger portions of the population. Scandinavian people's actions in response to specific combinations of motivations—the pushes and pulls—and the specific opportunities of the period led to the Viking Age. When the set of conditions—demographic, economic, political, and ideological—no longer favored raiding or conquest for enough leaders and enough followers to put together Viking groups that could challenge societies overseas, the Viking Age came to a close.

Biologically Driven Push Factors: Population Pressure and Bride Prices

Population pressure, one of the most widely cited motivations for migrations in the past, has also been proposed for the Viking expansion. This explanation was offered already during the Viking Age by Dudo of St. Quentin around the turn of the millennium (996–1015) in his account of the Norman dynasty and its Viking roots:

> Now these people burn with too much wanton lasciviousness, and with singular depravity debauch and mate with as many women as they please; and so, by mingling together in illicit coupling, they generate innumerable children. When these have grown up, they clamor fiercely against their fathers and their grandfathers, or more frequently against each other, for shares of property; and, as they are over-many, and the land they inhabit is not large enough for them to live in, there is a very old custom by which a multitude of youths is selected by lot and expelled into the realms of other nations, to win kingdoms for themselves by fighting, where they can live in uninterrupted peace.[121]

But there is no documentable evidence for dramatic spikes in populations in Scandinavia in the mid- to late eighth century.[122] Furthermore, the first Vikings to descend on Europe were raiders that had the intention of returning home, not seeking land to settle.[123]

A recently rejuvenated idea sees unequal access to mates as a primary driving force behind Viking raids. Scandinavian social practices, including female infanticide, and more probably polygamy and concubinage, may have resulted in high-status males having multiple mates, while low-status males were left without mates.[124] While the evidence for female infanticide is slight, historical sources such as Ibn Fadlan's account of his encounter with Scandinavians on the Volga do record chieftains having multiple and even many wives. Anthropological examinations of societies with high male-biased operational sex ratios (the ratio of males to females who are ready to mate) show increased aggressive behavior by low- as well as by high-status males.[125] In this model, the timing of the advent of raiding in the late eighth century is dependent on the increases in centralization in the early Viking Age that triggered ever-richer chieftains to acquire ever-growing numbers of wives and concubines. Under these conditions, low-status males might have accepted the dangers of a Viking voyage with the hope of acquiring portable wealth with which to return home and pay the bride price for a wife. High-status males' interests in increasing their own political power would coincide with the lower-status males' interests in raiding, making it easier for chieftains to re-cruit and gently coerce marriage-age men to join Viking expeditions. Upon their return from raiding, chieftains could use newly acquired movable wealth to invest in political bouts of feasting and reciprocal gift giving, while attracting followers with stories of their past successes and debt-inducing wealth redis-tribution. The advantage of this model, which draws heavily on evolutionary anthropology, is that it considers the individual motivations of both high- and low-status people. The proponents of this model suggest that an influx of silver into Scandinavia in the mid-eighth century was the likely trigger that set this economy of raiding in motion.[126] This evolutionary model uses the biological drive for reproduction as the main underlying motivational pressure while proposing specific historical triggers, such as growing social complexity and an influx of silver. The weakness of this otherwise attractive interdisciplinary model is the tenuous link between the underlying biological drive and the his-torical triggers that are rooted in the political economy.

Socially Driven Push Factors: Politics and Ideology

The most satisfying explanations for the push toward raiding consider the role of eighth-century Scandinavian political economics. From the perspective of the historical sources, political centralization was itself a particularly forceful push factor that appeared sporadically in the Viking Age. According to these texts, the conquests of aspiring kings and chieftains resulted in the banishment or forced migration of the members of the losing parties. One example is Harald Fairhair's Norwegian territorial conquests in the mid- to late 800s that have been blamed for migrations to uninhabited parts of Scandinavia, the unsettled islands in the North Atlantic, and the new Norse colonies in Ireland, Britain, and Francia.[127] Egil's Saga recounts these wide-ranging effects.

In every district, King Harald took possession of all the inherited estates and all the land, inhabited and uninhabited. He took over the sea and the lakes as well. All farmers had to become his tenants. All foresters, salt-workers, and hunters both on sea and land had to pay him tribute. Because of this oppression, many fled the country and settled in uninhabited places both to the east in Jämtland and Hälsingland, and in west in the British Isles, the Hebrides, Dublin shire, Ireland, Normandy in France, Caithness in Scotland, the Orkneys, Shetlands, and Faroes. And at that time, Iceland was discovered.[128]

But *Egil's Saga* is describing ninth-century events, and archaeological evidence for state formation is most obvious for the tenth century rather than the mid- to late eighth century.[129] Nevertheless, scholars have held up increasing political centralization in the late eighth century—seen not in texts but interpreted from the archaeological record of growing urban centers—as a trigger to explain the timing of the beginning of Viking raiding.[130] In this model, political centralization made it harder to acquire wealth within Scandinavia at the same time that a flourishing silver economy made acquisition of storable wealth through raiding more attainable. The formation of state-level apparatuses was a start-and-stop process in the Viking Age (see Chapter 5). Each step in the direction of tighter state-level control resulted in disenfranchisement of chieftains and free farmers. No overwhelming lurch in the direction of state formation can be documented at the opening of the Viking Age. But as the Viking Age progressed and increasing amounts of wealth from abroad arrived back home in Scandinavia, centralization quickened.

Economic and Political Pull Factors: Wealth and Opportunistic Exploitation of Weakness

Seeing the Vikings as opportunists seeking to maximize biological, social, and economic benefits while limiting personal danger helps underscore that a major pull factor for raiding was not just wealth, but more specifically movable wealth stored in places that were militarily weak. The runestones and sagas suggest that the strongest motivation for going abroad on Viking expeditions was acquisition of personal wealth and prestige, whether for private use or for investment into the political economics of chiefly power negotiations. The most valuable economic entities in Viking Age Scandinavia were land and cattle. This raises the question of why groups of Scandinavians made the massive expenditures and took the huge risks of boarding ships, crossing the seas, and going on raids to acquire precious metals.

To explain the motivations of Viking raiders, most recent scholarship has focused on portable material wealth in the form of silver and prestige goods used for social interactions, such as paying bride prices, establishing alliances, increasing status, or collecting followers for further raiding.[131] Consistent with the biological/evolutionary model presented above, Sindbæk suggests that silver was the main target especially because it was very movable, storable, and easy to invest in social and political relationships at home.[132] But the value of the raided objects lay not just in the precious metal. The social value of raided objects more generally is stressed by Ashby, who suggests that the stories created by the raid and retold in conjunction with the display of looted treasure was invaluable in the martially charged pre-Christian Scandinavian society.[133] Objects that were retained intact, such as the reliquary box found in the late seventh- to early eighth-century boat burial at Melhus, were material repositories of the memories of military prowess. Plundered objects were prestige goods, obviously rare, foreign, and beautiful, but they also embodied the success of a tale-worthy voyage. The Melhus reliquary box found in a double male-female grave was placed beside the female. In general, in fact, the raided objects found in late eighth- to ninth-century Norwegian graves appear to be associated more with females than males. Reworked pieces of British metalwork from these graves appear to have been worn and prominently displayed as part of the female dress. For example, the Melhus woman was buried with an imported bronze mount from the British Isles refashioned with a pin to function as a brooch to fasten her fur cloak around her shoulders.[134] This association between females and raided objects offers evidence that appears to corroborate the bride-wealth theory presented above.

The Hostage Stone discussed above provides a rare view of the other main valuable commodity—besides silver—that was essential in motivating Viking raids and driving the trade network: slaves. Slaves are less visible in the archaeological record than silver and other material loot. Nevertheless, we know slaves were crucially important in Viking Age trade, especially with large state-level polities such as the Byzantine Empire, the Caliphate in Baghdad, and the Islamic Emirate of Córdoba in Spain. Scholars have suggested that up to 25 percent of the Scandinavian Viking Age population was unfree, although this seems too high according to recent reassessments.[135] Scandinavian mythological texts, narrative sources, and later medieval laws deal extensively with slaves as significant components of Scandinavian society. The taking of slaves is also mentioned with horror in British and Irish texts.[136] The challenges of seeing this nearly invisible (archaeologically speaking) trade within the maritime raiding economy has meant that slaving and the commodification of human beings as slaves has received too little attention.[137] Slaves were—like silver—movable wealth. Both were valued widely as trade commodities in Scandinavian and foreign markets. Young males who could not find mates at home might find their sexual partners in slaves as was clearly the case for the Vikings encountered by Ibn Fadlan on the Volga River (see Chapter 4).

A significant challenge is how to determine forced versus voluntary mobility. Furthermore, personal ethnicity and geographical origins are typically impossible to determine with skeletal material itself. But support for the sexual enslavement of females from the British Isles can be found in the disproportionate contribution of female Celtic mitochondrial DNA to the settler population of Iceland (see Chapter 6). This discrepancy is unlikely to be explainable as Celtic women willingly accompanying male Scandinavians to Iceland.

The pull of the Viking expansion depended on knowledge or belief that wealth and opportunity existed beyond Scandinavia. The growth in trade during the eighth century, before the Viking Age, especially centered in trading emporia on either side of the English Channel and around the rim of the Baltic Sea, would have caught the eye of Scandinavians. Scandinavian participation in this trade, especially from Ribe on the west coast of Jutland, provided further knowledge of the wealth and potential weaknesses of the rich trading centers in Britain and Francia. The movable wealth in these urban centers of production and exchange made kings and merchants wealthy. The exchange network with wealth flowing between major urban trade centers interlinked the North Sea and the Baltic Sea, drew in the village hinterlands that lay behind the trading centers, and made the Viking Age an international phenomenon.[138] The ready availability of wealth moving along the coastlines and between the many islands of Scandinavia likely enticed those who were not directly benefiting from this trade to turn to pirating. The Viking Age probably began with local pirating in Scandinavia. But once pirating was shown to be a productive and status-garnering activity, the impetus that gathered increasing participants was redirected toward centers beyond Scandinavia, where sea-based merchants knew of great stores of wealth in places like Dorestad and Quentovic in Francia and London and Southampton in England. Dorestad was an early and frequent target of raids in Francia. In Britain, however, early Viking energy shifted to target wealthy monasteries more so than trading sites. This was likely just a utilitarian decision in which raiders chose opportunistically to target monasteries because they were isolated repositories of wealth with weak defenses. However, it has also been suggested that the targeting of Christian religious sites was purposeful as a response to eighth-century Frankish Christian militaristic expansionism.[139]

The Ideological Pull Factors

The Viking Age Scandinavians were not the only politically centralizing chieftain-level society in Northern Europe that had knowledge of the wealth accumulating in emporia and monasteries in northwest Europe. So why did the Scandinavians cause such havoc, rather than for instance the Picts of Scotland, the Celts of Ireland, or for that matter the Anglo-Saxons of England? Scandinavian ship technology had taken a dramatic leap in the eighth century with the addition of the sail to the old native clinker-type boat (see Chapter 1). This allowed crossings of open seas and the launching of surprise attacks of the type that so shocked Alcuin, but other peoples in Northern Europe also had sail-powered ships. So, although the Viking ship may have been an important technological catalyst for the Viking Age, the ships themselves did not provide motivation or justification.

Justification for the violence of raiding and conquest can be sought in the Viking worldview, which amounted to a disorganized but potent ideology that urged the acquisition of fame and wealth in a manner that was both fatalistic and enterprising. This ideology was the most important distinction between the Vikings and their victims, particularly those in Western European Christianity. In an interesting but extreme view, Patrick Wormald sees the Viking raids as a response to external pressures favoring Christianity and a decoupling of Scandinavian kingship from the pagan gods. In Wormald's model, these pressures for internal religious change generated a leadership crisis in Scandinavia and thereafter ideologically motivated defensive actions against threatening Christian neighbors.[140] Although ideology and religious differences have clearly driven large-scale aggressive movements of people in the past, this is usually the preserve of centralized state-level polities, rather than the regional chiefdoms of the early Viking Age. Vikings were perfectly content raiding non-Christians or partnering with Christians in wealth- and honor-seeking exploits. The Viking belief system held violence as an arena for gaining honor and wealth. Valiant death was praised and was the clearest path to an afterlife among Odin's chosen warriors in Valhalla.

The worldview of Viking Age Scandinavians probably did not drive them abroad on raids, but it did help to legitimize voyages for the sake of fame and violent raids for the sake of wealth accumulation. Violence in itself was neither positive nor negative. This meant, on the one hand, that dishonor did not arise inherently from killing or even from killing without cause. But on the other hand, directing violence in an honorable way toward self-improvement was positive. Death in battle was honorable, even if that death came in an unprovoked raid on an island monastery. *Hávamál* (*Sayings of the High One*), a collection of poems attributed to Odin, sums up the importance of honor:

> Cattle die,
> kinsmen die,
> You yourself will die too,
> but one thing will never die,
> the fame of one who earns it.[141]

The Viking worldview was fatalistic and one's time for death was thought of as being preordained. Until then, each person controlled his or her actions that would resound in this life and carry them into the next life. Beyond worldly fame of the type commemorated on runestones, an afterlife of the Viking good life awaited one who went into battle without fear. The Eddic poem *Krákumál* commemorates the ideal warrior's emotions and the joy such a warrior feels in anticipation of joining Odin's chosen warrior in Valhalla.

> We struck with our swords!
> My soul is glad, for I know
> That Balder's father's benches
> For a banquet are made ready
> We'll toss back toasts of ale
> From bent trees of the skulls,
> No warrior bewails his death
> In the wonderous house of Fjolnir.
> Not one word of weakness will I speak in Vidrir's hall.[142]

Great critique has been leveled on Adam of Bremen's *Gesta Hammaburgensis Ecclesiae Pontificum* (1073–1076) as a source because of its Christian ecclesiastical bias and Adam's own secondhand knowledge of Scandinavia obtained from the Danish King Svein Estridsen. However, in Adam's work we find a clear medieval explanation for both the cause and the cessation of raiding. Concerning Norway, Adam states, "on account of the roughness of its mountains and the immoderate cold, Norway is the most unproductive of all countries, suited only for herds . . . Poverty has forced them thus to go all over the world and from piratical raids they bring home in great abundance the riches of the lands." However, after the arrival of Christianity, Norwegians "learned to love the truth and peace and be content with their poverty."[143] It is not surprising that Adam, who aims to show the success of the archbishops of Hamburg-Bremen in bringing Christianity to the heathens of the north, would attribute the pacification of Vikings to the expansion of Christianity. In fact, for Adam, the cessation of raiding not only of the Norwegians but also of the Danes and Swedes was due to the pacifying effects of Christianity: "behold that piratical people, by which, we read, whole provinces of the Gauls and of Germany were once devastated and which is now content with its bounds and can say with the Apostle, 'For we have not here a lasting city, but we seek one that is to come.'"[144] By circa 1075, then, Adam feels that the Viking Age is in the past. Adam is of course biased, and other factors were at play simultaneously with Christianization—most importantly the formation of states that built their financial structure on internal taxation rather than external raiding— but in general the correspondence between Christianization and decreasing external raids holds up to scrutiny. Once the Scandinavian Christian kingdoms emerge, raiding ceases. Although invasions are still carried out by kings like King

Knut the Great and the barely Christian Harald Hardrada, the Viking Age drew to an end and subsequent wars and invasions had very different justifications, exemplified by the Scandinavian Baltic Crusade, which also usefully reminds us that the Christian medieval kingdoms were far from peaceful.[145]

The Raiders Settle Down: A Multi-Disciplinary View of the Vikings Who Stayed in Britain

The Viking Age Scandinavians who boarded ships to go to Britain had a series of goals—to raid, to trade, and to settle—that varied broadly across time and geography. The process and the scale of the impact of the Vikings remains much debated, particularly for the area of Danelaw and northwestern England, where the sources indicate that Danish and Norwegian Vikings settled, respectively. With the backdrop of the textual and archaeological evidence provided above, this section focuses on the interdisciplinary investigation of these areas. For the northern Scottish Isles—Shetland and Orkney—the replacement of local populations or at least the replacement of local culture and language is clearly indicated by the shift to Viking-style domestic structures and artifacts, and the takeover by the Old Norse language as represented by the ubiquitous Norse place names for islands and local topographical features as well as the survival of the Scandinavian language in Orkney, Shetland, and Caithness until the 1800s.[146]

The new settlers in Britain, whether in Danelaw or the Isle of Man, or the Hebrides, had choices to make in representing their new identity. The archaeological remains and linguistic relics in the landscape and in the English language speak of the different choices made by these settlers: some conservative, stressing Scandinavian identity, others more progressive, displaying diplomatic hybridity between Scandinavians and local practices, and still others, favoring assimilation with a quick adoption of the ways and styles of the new lands. The conservative assertions of Scandinavian identity are the most visibly distinct in the archaeological record. Examples of this doubling-down on Scandinavian identity can be seen at sites such as the cremation cemetery at Heath Wood, the refashioning of the royal establishment at Repton, and boat burials on the Isle of Man (Balladoole) and Orkney (Scar).[147] The middle path of hybridity can be seen in naming practices, the range of syncretic stone monuments found in churchyards in Britain, and in the culture of Anglo-Scandinavian towns, particularly evident in the coinage of York. Fuller assimilation is more difficult to identify archaeologically or through place names precisely because these social choices are meant to adopt local styles that blend in with the local populations. We can, however, see efforts at this assimilation, which often has a strong political dimension, in the historical sources.

Acculturation, Syncretism, and the Creation of New Identities in the Danelaw

Scandinavian permanent settlement in Britain varied dramatically in the different regions of Britain. In the Northern Isles—Shetland and Orkney—and the Hebrides, the evidence suggests a thorough Scandinavianization occurring through a combination of extermination and acculturation of the local communities of Britons, Picts, and Celts. The Danelaw represents a particularly complex area of Viking settlement and integration with locals that resulted in a flowering of hybrid culture and bilingualism perhaps unmatched elsewhere in the Viking world. Perhaps not the beginnings of Scandinavian settlement in England, but the largest infusion of settlers came as a direct result of the territorial conquests of the Great Army. The makeup of the Great Army—as well as its regional successes and failures—therefore became reflected in the Scandinavian settlement of England.[148] The areas in which the leaders of the Great Army shared out land in 876, 877, and 880, according to the written sources, correspond to regional concentrations of Scandinavian place names and loose finds of Scandinavian metalwork.

In examining material culture, language, and naming practices of ninth- to eleventh-century Danelaw, we see less the biological ethnicity than the identity that Viking Age people living in Britain chose to represent. Viking Age people's statements about identity drew from their background and exposure to variability within linguistic and material expression of culture. Individual choice of personal names and dress styles varied but was more limited and conservative than for modern people in the Western World. Styles changed to mimic neighboring styles through exposure that involved movement of people, direct contact, and the examples set by elites. Certainly, the many Scandinavian names that continued up through the twelfth century as well as the stylistically Viking objects found in Danelaw could be borne by Anglo-Saxons. But more than likely, they were worn by individuals who felt they had a kinship and/or cultural affinity with Scandinavia. The importance of lineage and kinship were still paramount. The broad patterns visible in our textual, archaeological, and linguistic datasets show realities of these affinities even if an individual place name using a Scandinavian name might not always indicate a Scandinavian settlement. Going further, the overwhelmingly convincing evidence of these patterns of Scandinavian impacts on Britain come from correspondences between the patterns from independent datasets. The correspondence between the clustering of Scandinavian place names, naming practices, objects, and textual references indicates that the northern and eastern portion of England saw extensive immigration of Scandinavians from the ninth to the early eleventh century.

Scandinavian Influence on English Language, Names and Place Names

Linguists and place name scholars generally argue that the Viking settlement of Danelaw must have been substantial, including numbers large enough to impact the English language and names of minor topographical features, such as fields cultivated and presumably named by people who farmed the land.[149] Old Norse influenced the English language quite dramatically—a fact most easily seen in the wide range of loan words. Possibly most fundamentally, English adopted the Old Norse third-person plural pronouns: they (þeir), them (þeim), their (þeirra). Words of seafaring, such as keel (kiolr) and bait (bæit), and words of exchange such as sale (sala) and thrift (þrift) also perhaps unsurprisingly come from Scandinavian. But so do common words, such as knife (knifur) and husband (hús-bóndi), as well as the legal terms of law (lag) and bylaw (bylög, meaning village law).

Scandinavian personal names used in England appear in historical texts and are engraved on monuments. For instance in the William the Conqueror's *Domesday Book*, which made a comprehensive record of English landholdings in 1086, Scandinavian names are very common in place names of the Danelaw area, such that Scandinavian names make up 40 percent of names employed in place names in Derbyshire and 50 percent in Nottinghamshire and Cheshire.[150] Scandinavian names might have become fashionable in periods of Viking domination, especially among the elite, and it is therefore possible that the use of Scandinavian names in place names reveals as much about people's politics as about their place of origin.[151] Although some of the proliferation of Scandinavian names can be explained by elite landholding and naming practices, Townend has argued convincingly that the diversity of these names—the range of different names in addition to the numbers of place names—recorded in the *Domesday Book* shows a widespread settlement by simple farmers as well as elite leaders.[152]

The study of place names in Britain has a vast literature, and opinions therein vary about how many Scandinavian settlers might be needed for the massive place-name change in Danelaw. The debate pivots around whether the settlements with Scandinavian names were actually inhabited by Scandinavians. At least some of the settlements might have been given names by Scandinavian elites—and by locals emulating elite Scandinavian naming preferences—but have been inhabited by the native populations. Some support is provided to this interpretation by the existence of place names such as Ingleby ("Settlement of the Angles").[153] Another complicating factor is that the majority of the Scandinavian place names date to the tenth century rather than the ninth century when the leaders of the Great Army redistributed land to their followers.[154] The proliferation of tenth-century Scandinavian place names in the Danelaw corresponds instead with a trend toward fragmentation of large landholdings into smaller privately owned farms. It is possible, therefore, that the tenth-century process of landholding fragmentation augmented the proportion of Scandinavian place names as the landscape happened to be dominated by Scandinavian elites precisely when new smaller farms were being given new names.[155] Both of these caveats—elite naming and land reforms—do not explain, however, the vast diversity of names given not only to farms but also to small topographical features named by people working the land.

The general patterns in the *Domesday Book* (1086) names and particularly the clustering of place names in areas that are known from the historical sources to fall within the Danelaw indicate that the Scandinavian settlement was substantial.[156] Very few place names of Scandinavian origin appear south of Danelaw (Figure 2.6).[157] In general, place names that end in a Scandinavian suffix, such as -by (farmstead or village) or -thorp (secondary settlement), or -thwaite (forest clearing), indicate influence of Norse speakers on the naming of settlements. To take just the -by names, there are 850 -by place names in the *Domesday Book*, making up compounds such as Kirby, Dalby, and Balby. Many of these suffixes are preceded by Scandinavian personal names (e.g., Thirkleby [Þorketill] and Ormesby [Ormr]). Still other names take their prefix from a landscape feature (e.g., Dalby = Valley or Dale Settlement) or from a cultural feature (e.g., Kirkby = Church Settlement). A second class of Scandinavian-influenced place names involves a hybrid construction combining Scandinavian and English elements—for instance, the common English village suffix of -ton combined with a Scandinavian personal name (e.g., Grimston = Grim's Village). A third class consists of place names whose pronunciation have been Scandinavianized for easier pronunciation by Norse speakers (e.g., Shipton to Skipton). These names suggest substantial mutual intelligibility between the two languages. A fourth class, consisting of translated names, also indicates communication between Old English and Norse speakers, but embeds a Scandinavian show of new dominance over the landscape. By this translation process, for instance, a settlement previously known from documents to have been named Church-ton became Kirk-by through the influence of Norse speakers.

Most convincing of all is the correspondence of evidence for extensive Scandinavian settlement in the Danelaw that comes from names, place names, loose finds, and genetics. The increasing numbers of loose finds of Scandinavian-style artifacts that are turning up, even in rural areas, as part of metal-detectorist work further supports the clustering of Scandinavian settlements in the Danelaw, with a few noteworthy differences.[158] The precise numbers of Viking Age Scandinavians who immigrated to Danelaw is elusive, although recently numbers between 25,000 and 35,000 for all England have been suggested based on modeling of loose metal finds and a very rough estimate of south Scandinavian genetic input into the modern English population.[159] Although this is probably in the higher range of estimates, it has the advantage of drawing on quantifiable

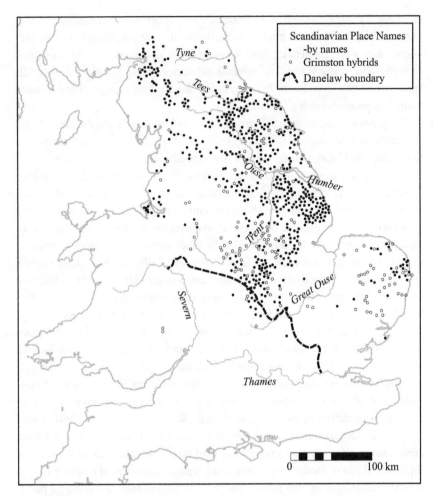

Figure 2.6 Distribution of two Scandinavian place name types in England. The place names are dense throughout Danelaw, particularly in what had been the southern portion of the Kingdom of Northumbria and northeastern Mercia (compare with Figure 2.1). East of the Great Ouse River a cluster characterized by high incidence of the Grimston hybrid names is typically attributed to Scandinavians who settled in East Anglia after 880 when Guthrum made peace with Alfred and shared out land to his followers.

Source: map by author; place name locations follows Richards 2004

data. The issue of numbers of settlers will be taken up below in a discussion of the results of recent projects on the genetics of Britain. First, however, we turn to deeper consideration of the syncretic culture that emerged in the Danelaw as Scandinavian farmers and elites were integrated into and transformed the countryside and the urban fabric of Anglo-Saxon England.

Hybrid Symbols in Anglo-Scandinavian Elite Culture

Especially in the islands to the north and the west of Britain monuments and linguistic changes show Scandinavians—and certainly Scandinavian identity—as dominant. The complete change in place name and language use in the Shetland and Orkney Islands for instance shows cultural if not biological population replacement. Dramatic shifts in the archaeology of daily life in the form of houses, tools, and economic adaptations show a Scandinavianization of the islands of Shetland, Orkney, and the Hebrides, as well as the Isle of Man. Particularly changes in burial rituals with the introduction of cremation graves and boat burials emphasized a distinctive Scandinavian mortuary ritual and ideology. The rituals performed at the Ingleby cremation cemetery of the Great Army that was addressed above emphasized the army's pagan Scandinavian identity. Boat burials, further discussed in Chapter 4, provide a conspicuous ritual and representational link back to Scandinavia. Within the burials at Pierowall beach market in Orkney, for instance, the local population chose to bury their dead with horses in the Scandinavian fashion to signal their participation in the Viking world system that controlled trade from the Irish Sea and around northern Britain and the North Sea to Scandinavia.[160] These graves showed that a new elite was in charge. The boat burial from Balladoole on the Isle of Man perhaps illustrates this most clearly.[161] The boat was dug into the top of an old burial ground, scattering the early graves and skeletal remains to the sides. In the new lands, boat burials and cremation graves were the conservative, obstinately Scandinavian monuments of a conquering population.

In the Danelaw, however, the Scandinavian influences were typically more assimilative. Scandinavians adopted local practices and by the tenth century new syncretic identities were emerging. For instance, the Scandinavian settlement of northern and eastern England resulted in the flowering of secularized stone sculpture in the tenth and eleventh centuries. The sculptures—all Christian monuments—were placed in churches and churchyards, but the art styles were Scandinavian, and the themes and impetus for creation were more secular than the ecclesiastical focus of earlier Anglo-Saxon sculpture.[162] The sculptural monuments offer combinations of "material and verbal culture" placed in prominent positions designed to be seen by people visiting the churches and churchyards.[163] The monuments are syncretic in their blending of Anglo-Saxon Christianity and the Old English language with Scandinavian styles, names, and linguistic influences. These were a new form of monument, representing the creation of new identities within the Anglo-Scandinavian milieu. These new material expressions extend beyond syncretic statements in their use by the local elite as manifestations of novel Anglo-Scandinavian identity.

The most well known of these Scandinavianized monuments is the hogback, a type of grave marker that takes its name from a characteristic arched and downward-curving top.[164] About 120 hogbacks are found clustering in northern England and southern Scotland (Figure 2.7). None are exactly alike, but in general they are about 1.5 m in length and their form mimics Scandinavian-type longhouses, with many having characteristic bowed side walls. The roofs are curved, and some are decorated with shingles, while the decorated sides often include iconography drawn from Scandinavian, Anglo-Saxon, and Celtic traditions. Although clearly Christian monuments associated with cemeteries, many hogbacks exhibit secular art themes, and some depict scenes from Norse mythology. Different beasts—mostly bears—which may represent spirits of the home, grasp and bite the gable ends of the houses (Figure 2.8).[165] Although few—or possibly none—have been found in situ, these large carved stones were not moved far from their original context of use.[166] Many for instance were incorporated into church walls during phases of structural alteration. Originally, they probably functioned as individual grave covers, although it is possible that at least some marked family grave sites. Regionally, the hogbacks cluster in areas with matching concentrations of Scandinavian place names, and they further appear to cluster around riverine and maritime sites. Traditionally seen as colonial monuments tied closely to the Scandinavian diaspora, recent work on hogbacks links them specifically to local elite identity formation. Part of the formation of this new identity draws on an array of material citations to a range of other structures and objects that are "bow-backed and beast-guarded," such as Scandinavian runestones and Christian house shrines.[167] Most interesting is the idea that they represent houses for the dead and that each individual hogback might conjure images of ancestral family homes and symbolize mythological halls, such as Odin's Valhalla. For a Scandinavian and Anglo-Scandinavian elite that still looked to the traditions of the afterlife influenced by pre-Christian conceptions, the house-like hogbacks, which mimicked the appearance of ideal elite halls, were both a suitable earthly resting place in this world and a fitting material metaphor for the anticipated post-life existence in a heavenly hall.

Prominent—and expensive—grave markers and monumental stone crosses showing Scandinavian influence suggest that an elite class in northern and eastern England were assimilating Scandinavian elite ideologies into the sacred context of burial. These Scandinavianized monuments, although seeming to contrast with traditional Anglo-Saxon Christian art styles, may well have been meant to make similar statements as earlier pagan burial but in a more palatable medium. The monuments are self-conscious and confident in their material conspicuousness, and the newness of these sculptural types means that they must have made a significant visual impact on the society. They signaled that there had been a change within the socio-political elite and that this elite was referencing its Scandinavianess within the fabric of the local Christianity. The Middleton Cross, for instance, is covered in Scandinavian-style decoration on the cross shaft's two

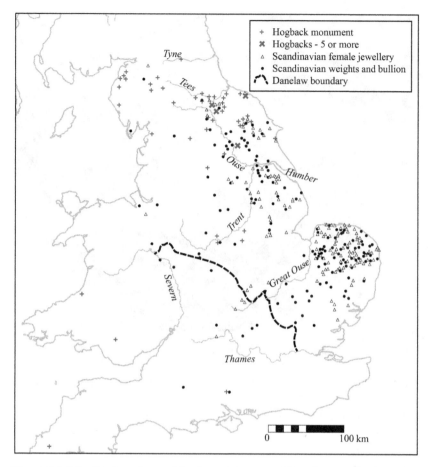

Figure 2.7 Distribution of material culture signatures of Scandinavian settlement. As with the place name evidence (Figure 2.6), the finds are concentrated in Danelaw with a distinct cluster centered in the Kingdom of York (southern Northumbria and Danish Mercia) and East Anglia. The distribution of the hogback monuments are manifestations of the Scandinavianized tenth- to early eleventh-century elite in the Kingdom of York and are absent from the East Anglian Scandinavian zone.

Source: map by author; artifact locations according to Kershaw 2008, hogback locations follow Richards 2004.

pictorial panels, including a serpent-like beast that envelops the lower panel on the reverse side (Figure 2.9).[168] The front panel of the cross depicts a warrior surrounded by his weapons, including a distinctively Scandinavian axe. One interpretation sees this as a depiction of a warrior in his grave. Instead of burying the warrior with his weapons in the old Scandinavian style, the monument

Figure 2.8 The Brompton Hogbacks. Beasts that appear to be muzzled bears clutch and crawl on the gable ends of these grave markers shaped like Viking Age longhouses. The shingles on the roofs are particularly visible on the stones in the foreground and the middle.

Source: photo by T. Middlemass, © Corpus of Anglo-Saxon Stone Sculpture

depicts this same warrior identity carved into the stone cross. Christian practice did not typically allow warriors to be buried with their possessions, but carving the weapons in stone served a similar purpose. A second interpretation, which views the balls visible on either side of the warrior's head as the tops of a chair, sees the warrior as seated in his chair or throne surrounded by his weapons.[169] In fact, there may not be a significant difference between these two explanations. As we will see in Chapter 4, both written sources and archaeological evidence suggest that Viking elites were often positioned in chairs within their grave so that they appeared still seated in an authority-giving chair.[170] In either case, the pre-Christian warrior ideal previously represented at the graveside by inclusion of weapons within elite graves was here represented carved in a stone monumental cross positioned in a Christian graveyard beside a church that the dead man is likely to have patronized in life.

In a final example, five small carved stone sundials, originally situated beside the main southern entrance into churches clustered in Yorkshire, provide

Figure 2.9 Middleton Cross, with the front panel (left) showing a warrior either seated in his throne or inhumed in his grave. The main panel on the back (right) of the cross features a Scandinavian-style serpent or monster in primitive Jelling style. Adorning the top, a cross signals the Christian context of this grave marker.

Source: photos by T. Middlemass, © Corpus of Anglo-Saxon Stone Sculpture

another material marker of the new Anglo-Scandinavian identity. This class of sculpture dating to the eleventh century is very Christian and Anglo-Saxon in appearance, with the sundial itself being a nod to the Christian ordering of time and the position of the dial beside the door referencing entrance into holiness. The language too is Old English, and the alphabet is the Latin one. But the Old English shows influence of Old Norse, including the use of loanwords "solmerca" (sun-mark) and "huscarl" (house-man or warrior).[171] Furthermore, and significantly, the names of the producers and patrons on the sundials are all Scandinavian.[172] One of the sundials, a fragmentary one found at Skeleton-in-Cleveland, shows use of Scandinavian runes alongside Latin letters. The runes are difficult to read but are used to spell the Old Norse word "ok" (and). The rest of the inscription is unreadable and may represent a hybridized language, possibly in use in Yorkshire at the time when King Knut invaded England, 150 years after the Great Army's invasion.

Despite Knut's conquest of all of England, less evidence of lasting Scandinavian impacts appears in England outside of the Danelaw. Knut's conquest and rule over all of England appear to have affected the country more at the elite culture level than on the level of settlement. Returning to the literary record of the eleventh century, the Anglo-Saxon sources show little pride in the Scandinavian conquering cultural assertion. But if we shift our view to the Old Norse skaldic praise poems that were recited at the English court of King Knut, the confident assertion of Viking identity within the English court is evident. Knut's court poet Ottar the Black composed the following lines: "Strong Skjǫldungr, you performed a feat of battle under your shield; the blood-crane [raven] received dark morsels at Ashingdon. Prince, you won by fighting a great enough name with a mighty sword near to the north of the Forest of the Danes [or of Dean], and it seemed a slaughter to your retinue."[173] The vocative use of Skjǫldungr to address Knut directly pins his identity to the Danish Skjǫldungr dynasty of kings and sets his identity in opposition to the English whom he slaughters at Ashingdon to the delight of the raven.[174] Simultaneously, the court poetry stresses the Christian kingship of Knut within the old pagan skaldic style. The poet Sighvat Thordarson offered this stanza about pilgrimage after several stanzas about classic warrior journeys of the Viking type: "Desire for a journey came upon the ruler bearing a staff, who bore warfare in his heart. The leader, dear to the emperor, close to Peter, enjoyed some of the glory of Rome."[175] Although Knut's virtuous warrior heart is praised, the pull of Christian pilgrimage makes him a king on par with the emperor and makes him a friend of St. Peter.

One member of Knut's court, who would have heard recitations of poems such as those by Ottar the Black and Sighvat Thordarson, had his (or her) grave at St. Paul's Church in London marked with a grave slab that prominently displays a self-conscious Scandinavian identity. The grave slab, carved from local

English stone, has a protrusion from the bottom meant to be inserted into the ground, presumably over the head or the foot of a grave placed in the church-yard of London's main church (Figure 2.10). But the monument is completely Scandinavian in style, language, and letters.[176] The iconography on the grave-marker is in the Scandinavian early eleventh-century Ringerike style, with the central image depicting a stag-like beast with elongated curled horns (or ears), bared canine teeth, and a protruding curled tongue. The animal's shoulder joints are indicated by spirals, whereas the visible legs terminate in two-toed claws. Remnant paint indicates that the stone was painted blue, red, and white. Along one thin side the rune carver employed Scandinavian runes to spell a commemo-rative sentence in Old Norse: "Ginna and Toki had this stone laid."[177] The person buried below this stone is unknown. But the find context within the Old St. Paul's churchyard indicates that the person was Christian, while the artwork shows a focus on Scandinavian heritage and a display of apparent cultural paganism, al-beit not necessarily syncretic beliefs. Found well beyond the Danelaw, this grave marker indicates Scandinavian tastes and identity brought to England in the eleventh century with Knut's conquest and reflects a Scandinavian consciousness at the heart of the king's court.

Figure 2.10 Grave marker with runic inscription from St. Paul's Cathedral in London, originally used to mark the grave of one of the elite Scandinavians who served Knut the Great in the early eleventh century. The drawing on the left shows the undecorated lower portion of the stone, which was likely inserted into the ground above the grave.
Source: Left: Beckett 1924: 30, fig. 36; Right: © Museum of London

The Politics of Land, Contrasting Exchange Systems, and Coinage in the Danelaw

The Viking settlement of Danelaw began with the "sharing-out" of land by the leaders of the Great Army. As we have already seen, however, the complex process involved not just transfer of land to Scandinavians, but also the adaptation of Scandinavians to the realities of local land ownership and political economics. The assimilative aspect of Scandinavian settlement in Danelaw can be sought in the Anglo-Saxon texts, and especially the *Life of St. Cuthbert*, one of the very few preserved texts actually written in northern England during the Viking Age.[178] Of interest in this section particularly is the text's perspective on the lands of the monastic guardians of the saint's relics as well as the monastic community's apparent collaboration with the new Scandinavian rulers. Appearing in a vision to Abbot Eadred, the saint explains that the next king of Northumbria is to be a Scandinavian slave named Guthred who was traveling with the Viking Great Army. The saint instructs the abbot to propose to the invaders that if the Vikings accept the saint's choice from among them, then the saint will support his reign. The saint adds the following conditions, "Tell him also, after he has been made king, to give me all the land between the Tyne and the Wear and [to grant to me] whoever shall flee to me, whether for homicide or for any other necessity, may have peace for thirty-seven days and nights."[179]

The events described took place soon after the death of the Viking leader Halfdan, who had shared out land in Northumbria. This would have been a crucial period for the Scandinavian settlers, involving negotiation of local power in the absence of a leader. The blessing and support of the influential monks of St. Cuthbert validated their rule. The ceremony of kingship is also described in *The Life of St. Cuthbert* as dictated by Saint Cuthbert himself: "lead him before the whole multitude so that they may elect him king . . . lead him with the whole army upon the hill which is called Oswigesdune and there place on his right arm a golden armlet, and thus they shall all constitute him king."[180] All this was done and included direct involvement of the saint: "Then bishop Eardulf brought to that host and to that hill the body of St. Cuthbert, over which the king himself and the whole host swore peace and fidelity."[181] The ceremony combined pagan rites using a sacred arm band with Christian rites of saintly legitimization through the presence of the saint's relics. Furthermore, they enacted the syncretic ceremony on a hill named after the seventh-century Northumbrian King Oswiu, thereby linking the new Viking-monastic alliance to the landscape, and bestowing the authority of past royal traditions on the new king. In return, the monastic community received new lands and an alliance with the new rulers. The strategy appears to have worked for the monastic community, as they not only maintained their previous lands but also acquired additional lands during the later ninth and tenth centuries.[182] This example, showing the agency of both the invaders and the monastic elite in forming the new politico-economic order, provides an instructive backdrop from which to examine the archaeological evidence for the hybrid economy and innovative coinage of Viking Danelaw.

The economics of Danelaw provides a case for a cultural encounter between the Scandinavian international bullion (weight-based) silver economy and the coin-based Anglo-Saxon economy. The encounter resulted in a dual-currency economy in which both systems of exchange operated concurrently from at least 865 until 940.[183] Scandinavian rulers of York and East Anglia both minted their own coins imitating earlier Anglo-Saxon coinage, including symbols of the Christian faith.[184] The payoff in terms of leadership propaganda would have been limited as long as the coins emulated coins from Wessex and even included the picture and names of kings like Alfred. But there was an economic payoff: silver coins were worth more than the raw silver that went into the coins. Furthermore, private moneyers sanctioned by the king had to pay the king a portion of the profits from the sale of his minted coins.[185] If rulers could convince populations to switch to a coinage economy, then they stood to benefit, especially during periods of coin debasement. The initial Viking conquest of York saw the complete disruption of the production of Northumbrian coinage.[186] After thirty years, the Scandinavian kings of York began to mint their own silver coinage that lasted from 895 until 954, when the last Viking king of York was expelled. These coins, inscribed with the kings' names, were produced prolifically and widely accepted. The kings of York seem to have convinced the populace within their capital city to use this coinage ubiquitously as the extensive excavations there have shown very few examples of the typical products used in the bullion economy, that is, ingots and hacksilver.[187] This situation contrasts markedly with excavations of early towns in Scandinavia, such as Kaupang and Hedeby, where ninth-century exchange was based primarily on bullion.[188]

The bullion economy continued in most of rural Danelaw, however, where single finds document widespread use of distinctive Scandinavian-style ingots, hacksilver, weights used to measure bullion, and Arabic dirhams employed for their weight rather than any intrinsic value of the coin. The date ranges of the known dirhams show import at least until 940. The reasons for the continued use of bullion in most of Danelaw, especially in rural areas, should be sought in the intersection of economics, power-politics, and cultural identity. The area of Scandinavian Mercia known as the Five Boroughs (Leicester, Lincoln, Stamford, Derby, and Nottingham) also does not show evidence of pervasive bullion exchange even though historical documents and place-name research show that Scandinavians densely settled these areas (see Figures 2.1 and 2.6). So why did Scandinavians in York and the Five Boroughs shift more quickly to coinage while rural populations retained the bullion economy? Although the explanation could be as prosaic as coinage being less available in the rural areas of Danelaw, this seems unlikely, especially because of the dearth of bullion found in the rural areas of the Five Boroughs. The choice made by northern and eastern Danelaw communities to use bullion in part must reflect a purposeful decision to main-tain a Scandinavian identity through their means of exchange. Use of bullion also linked these communities to an international medium of exchange that could be used beyond the political borders of Danelaw in other parts of the Viking world.

The coins of York provide one of our clearest insights into the new Scandinavian leadership's shrewd and varied use of hybridized material culture to entrench their rule.[189] Early coins from York mimic Anglo-Saxon exemplars, as do many of the earlier Viking coins, such as those minted in the 870s in East Anglia by the Viking ruler Guthrum in imitation of King Alfred's coins.[190] Although the new Viking coinage emulated aspects of the Wessex currency, the kings employed the old weight standard set by the Northumbrian stycas, often employed Carolingian moneyers (indicated in inscriptions), and declared their independence with their own names inscribed on the coins. After an initial phase of substantial imitation, the Kings of York used their coinage to visually stress their independence from the Wessex dynasty. At times they confidently underscored their Scandinavian identity in a self-conscious manner reminiscent of the placement of a ship burial atop an earlier burial ground. The message is clear: new rulers had arrived. The most dramatic of these statements is made by the ruler Olaf (Anlaf) Guthfrithsson. We have met Olaf in the discussion above concerning the Battle of Brunanburh during which he was on the losing side of a Scandinavian-Scottish alliance against King Æthelstan of Wessex. After Ælthelstan's death in 939, Olaf returned, captured York, reconquered Danelaw, and re-established the old boundary of Watling Street agreed to in the treaty between Alfred and Guthrum. The triumphant Olaf minted a large number of "intensely Scandinavian" coins that have been described as "victory coinage."[191] Olaf's coinage minted from 939 to 941 shows an Odinic raven on the obverse surrounded by a Norse inscription using Latin letters that reads Anlaf Konungr (King Olaf; Figure 2.11). Other coins are more diplomatic and make visual ap-peals to both Scandinavian and Anglo-Saxon audiences. The St. Peter coinage from the early tenth century, which takes its name from the saint whose name is imprinted on the reverse of the coin, is adorned with crosses on both the ob-verse and reverse. However, between the saint's name is an unmistakable Viking sword, and most creatively, at the bottom, an upside-down Thor's hammer is inserted between the R and I of St. Peter's name (SCI PETRII; Figure 2.12). The coins of the violent Eirik Bloodaxe from 952 to 954 also include a Viking style sword in the center of the obverse, but his title is written in the traditional Latin (ERIC REX), and a central cross adorns the reverse (Figure 2.13). The juxtapo-sition on these coins of seemingly contrasting Viking militarism with Christian piety was likely an attempt to appeal to both the identities of Scandinavian and

Figure 2.11 Silver penny minted for Olaf Guthfrithsson, the Norse King of York, between 939 and 941. The iconography is syncretic, mixing Scandinavian and Anglo-Saxon elements. The obverse shows a self-consciously Scandinavian and even pagan Odinic raven, while the reverse features a cross. The use of the Old Norse language with the Latin alphabet—the earliest known example of this practice—is remarkable. Instead of the common Latin term rex (king), Olaf (spelled ANLAF) chose to use konungr (here spelled CUNUNC), the Scandinavian word for king.
Source: © The Trustees of the British Museum

Figure 2.12 Silver penny minted in York around 915. The reverse includes a central cross, while the obverse also appeals to Christianity with a small cross at the top and a two-line inscription with the name Saint Peter: SCIPE (first line), TRIIO (second line). In the center, however, a Viking style sword points to the right, while an upside-down Thor's hammer separates the R and the first I of the lower line of text. The pairing of pagan Scandinavian iconography with Christian text and traditional Anglo-Saxon iconography probably served the purpose of appealing to the dual audiences of Anglo-Saxons and Scandinavians living in Viking Age York.
Source: © The Trustees of the British Museum.

Figure 2.13   Eirik Bloodaxe's silver penny, minted in York from 952 to 954. The reverse with the name of moneyer Ingelgar (ING Æ LGAR) and a central cross bears resemblance to contemporary Anglo-Saxon coins. The inscription on the obverse is in Latin, reading Eric Rex (King Eirik), but the iconography is distinct from Anglo-Saxon coinage in its confident martial and Scandinavian message included in the use of a distinctive Viking-style sword.

Source: © The Trustees of the British Museum

Anglo-Saxon audiences. The tensions in the appeals to both identities, which are apparent in all the York coinage, created the hybrid art styles that the Anglo-Scandinavian elite employed to communicate a great deal of their political messages to each other and the people they wished to rule.

The Genetic Legacy of the Vikings

The shift toward questions of identity—whether ethnic or class-based—and away from the older dilemmas of invasion size and settlement numbers has greatly nuanced the discussion of the Viking impact on Britain. Nevertheless, the debate about the scale of the migrations remains a lingering question for understanding Viking Age Britain. The range of estimates for Scandinavian immigrants ranges wildly with some (although no longer most) holding that immigrants were an elite conquering group numbering in the hundreds,[192] while other recent estimates have suggested "perhaps a few thousand,"[193] and still others arrive at numbers around 30,000.[194] Dawn Hadley, who was among the pioneers of new synthetic approaches centered on identity, expressed the feelings of the field in 2006: "Certainly, the scale of the settlement has been the focus of often quite ferocious debate, although in recent studies by historians there has been a tendency to avoid the issue of scale entirely, given the dearth of evidence that would allow the matter to be settled conclusively."[195] However, the scale of migrations is a key to understanding how local people's lives changed and how the cultural transformations were enacted. For instance, it matters immensely for our understanding of life in this period whether the persons buried under the hogbacks and living in Kirkby were descended from a local population who had been living in Britain for hundreds if not thousands of years, or whether those individuals had just recently killed or violently displaced the multi-generational residents. What were the relationships of intermarriage, mate-stealing, apartheid, and/or ethnic cleansing that underlay the apparent mixed marriages and name adoption that are visible on stone sculpture? To a significant extent our modern view of this period relies on the answers to these questions that had at least partially been abandoned by the shift of focus to representations of identity. The fast-moving science of genetics seems ideal to finally answer these questions.

For Iceland, the genetic research has revolutionized our understanding of the make-up of the settler population. The surprise there was that although 80 percent of the male population of Iceland shows closest biological relationships to Scandinavians, less than 50 percent of the females do so. The majority of females show closer genetic affinity with the Celtic peoples of the British Isles. These percentages are perhaps the clearest indication that Scandinavian men took—sometimes probably forcibly—women from the British Isles. Although some of these women may have gone willingly, it is difficult to imagine a scenario where all of them did so.

But the genetics of Britain holds more difficulties than that of Iceland. Iceland had only one substantial migration stream, dated to the late ninth to early tenth century. This migration settled a previously unoccupied land. Britain on the other hand has been continuously occupied by humans, in parts at least, for 17,000 years and has seen multiple large-scale migrations. Besides the Viking diaspora, the Middle Ages saw substantial migrations of Anglo, Saxons, and Jutes in the fifth and sixth centuries and Normans in the late eleventh century. At least a portion of the Anglo-Saxon migrations derived from southern Jutland and portions of northern Germany that fall within the later Viking homelands, meaning that the population genetics of the Anglo-Saxons and Viking Age Danes partially overlap. This is further complicated by the relatively—genetically speaking—narrow time range between Anglo-Saxon (mostly sixth cent.) and Viking (mostly ninth cent.) migrations. These factors complicate the search for the genetic legacy of Viking Age Scandinavian migrations to Britain. This section will explore the promise and the difficulty of interpreting the genetics research by looking at three recent projects: (1) comparative genetics of the islands to the north and west of Scotland, (2) the Vikings in the Wirral and West Lancashire Project, and (3) People of the British Isles Project.[196]

Genetics research on the populations of the islands to the north and north-west of Britain—the Hebrides, Orkney, and Shetland—has potential to illuminate the population dynamics underlying the Viking Age dominance of Scandinavians that is apparent from the linguistic, place-name, and archaeological evidence.[197] A genetic study by Sara Goodacre and her colleagues of people on these island groups revealed significant differences in the percentage contribution of Scandinavian and native British/Celtic groups to the current population. The researchers examined both the Y-chromosome and mitochondrial DNA (mtDNA) of a large sample of the modern populations on the islands. The Y-chromosome, possessed only by males, is transferred with very little change from father to son in a direct line, meaning that it can be used to chart male ancestry. Mitochondrial DNA is passed almost exclusively from mothers to their children, meaning that it can be used to study female ancestry.[198] The study showed differences in percentages of Scandinavian male and female genetic contributions to the various island groups. Perhaps unsurprisingly, Scandinavian contributions to the gene pool—both male and female—were greatest in the islands closest to Scandinavia. Scandinavian patrilineal ancestry (Y-chromosome) was highest in Shetland (c. 44%), followed by Orkney (c. 31%), the Hebrides and Skye (c. 22%), and the Scottish northwest coast (c. 15%). Scandinavian matrilineal ancestry (mitochondrial DNA) showed the same patterning of decreasing Scandinavian genetic contributions with distance from the homelands: Shetland (c. 43%), Orkney (c. 30.5%), Scottish northwest coast (c. 14.5%), and Hebrides and Skye (c. 11%). The nearly identical contribution of Y-chromosomes and mtDNA to the islands of Shetland and Orkney, as well as the Scottish northwest coast, suggest that a similar number of Scandinavian males and females immigrated to these islands. The authors interpret this to mean that families settled these islands. The notable percentage difference in the Hebrides between male Scandinavian ancestry (22%) and female ancestry (11%), in contrast, suggests that these islands were settled by more Scandinavian males than females. Interestingly, Iceland shows a similar dichotomy between Scandinavian male (80%) and female (37%) ancestry with British/Irish genetic contributions accounting for 25 percent of male ancestry and 66 percent of female ancestry. Both the Hebrides and Iceland therefore appear to show a situation whereby Scandinavian males took reproductive partners from the British/Celtic populations. Whether these women were wives, willing concubines, or slaves taken forcefully is impossible to determine genetically. The archaeological and place-name evidence shows cultural domination of the Scandinavians in these islands, but the genetic evidence indicates a population with a more substantial local contribution, suggesting acculturation of the local population to Scandinavian culture.

The Viking impact in Wirral and West Lancashire on the Irish Sea coast of northwest England—sandwiched between northeast Wales and the western extent of the Danelaw—has long been recognized through a dense distribution of Norse place names, dialect words of Norse origin, and clusters of Scandinavian style loose finds and hoards (Figure 2.1).[199] Importantly, two sites named Thingvollr (Thing-plain) indicate that a substantial Scandinavian settlement resulted in the establishment of Scandinavian-style political organization administered from these local parliament sites.[200] The Scandinavian settlement is thought to be from Norwegian Vikings who were active in the Irish Sea. The specific circumstances of their engagement in this area are typically associated with the historically attested expulsion of the Viking elite from Dublin in 902. The Vikings in the Wirral and West Lancashire Project targeted modern DNA from males living in this part of England to investigate the Y-chromosome. The study used two effective strategies to limit the amount of influence recent migrations might have had on the samples. First, as is standard practice, only males whose paternal grandfather lived in the area were sampled. The more novel approach was the targeted sampling of individuals with surnames that could be documented in historical texts predating 1572, thereby helping to exclude more recent post-medieval male immigrants.[201] The admixture analysis of the general population showed a 38 percent Scandinavian contribution in both West Lancashire and Wirral. When considered by itself, however, the "medieval" group of males with old local surnames showed an even higher proportion of Scandinavian admixture: circa 51 percent in West Lancashire and circa 47 percent in Wirral. Further removal of samples from people with very common surnames to focus on characteristic surnames from the area resulted in an even higher proportion of Scandinavian ancestry: circa 53 percent for West Lancashire and circa 51 percent for Wirral. These percentages are higher even than those estimated for Scandinavian male ancestry documented in Shetland.[202]

The estimated percentages discussed so far are calculated by admixture analysis that relies on a series of assumptions. To avoid some of these assumptions, which are discussed further below, the research group also examined frequencies of Y-chromosome haplogroups. Haplogroups are genetic changes throughout the genome that are associated with a common ancestor. The Wirral/West Lancashire Project documented significantly higher proportions of a haplogroup named R1a1 in Wirral (14%) and West Lancashire (17%), which is rare in Britain (1%) but common in Norway (35%). The results of both the admixture analysis and haplogroup frequency analysis show a local area of concentrated Scandinavian settlement on the British Irish Sea coast. The correspondence with archaeological data and place names is convincing. The potential correspondence with historical accounts of exiled Norwegian/Irish Vikings is not more than suggestive. But this potential correspondence has also led the genetic community to build historical assumptions into their genetic models.

For the admixture analysis, the Wirral/West Lancashire project used Norwegian males as the representative comparison group for Scandinavian Vikings, while using samples from central Ireland and Scotland to represent the local population. The creation of comparison groups that represent "native British" and "non-native Scandinavian" is of essential importance for admixture analysis of modern populations. This is especially the case because the percentages generated for this project—and in fact for many DNA projects—assumes a binary contribution to the modern populations from British/Celtic and Scandinavian sources. For example, the model used in this project assumed that 100 percent of the ancestry must come from a combination of Norwegian and Celtic British/Irish sources. Not modeled therefore are Danish, Swedish, and Anglo-Saxon genetic contributions. The importance of such assumptions in admixture modeling can be illustrated by comparing the results from the Goodacre group's results with those of an earlier study by Capelli and colleagues. Both groups found substantial Scandinavian male ancestry contributions in the islands north and west of Britain, but the percentages varied quite dramatically. The Capelli group's study showed Scandinavian ancestry consistently higher than the Goodacre group: Shetland (68.3% vs. 44.5%), Orkney (55.3% vs. 31%), Hebrides (61.6% vs. 22.5). The Goodacre group explained these variances as potentially resulting from differences in modeling and the fact that the Goodacre group created the "Celtic parental population" from samples from central Ireland and Scotland, while the Cappelli group defined their Celtic parental population by using samples from central Ireland and the Basque region of Spain.[203] Admixture percentages estimated through genetic modeling are a powerful tool for approaching the scale and impact of the Scandinavian population incursions. But the discrepancies show that the percentages provided by these studies should be used cautiously with the recognition that different methods will yield different, and even substantially different, results. The underlying assumptions of the make-up of Viking settlers as being Danish (for Danelaw) or Norwegian (for the Northern Isles, Ireland, and Wirral/West Lancashire), or even consisting uniformly of people from Scandinavia is called into question by the isotopic studies of raiding parties such as the one uncovered at Ridgeway Hill, where most of the apparent Vikings grew up in Eastern Europe around Poland. The genetics focused on modern populations, and the isotopic examination of Viking Age remains do not contradict each other, but there is a gulf to be bridged. Study of ancient DNA from skeletons from sites such as the mass graves at Ridgeway Hill and Repton might help. Beyond these exceptional cases, studies will hopefully also turn to less characteristically Scandinavian graves to examine genetic diversity of Viking Age Britain as compared with the areas of the Scandinavian homelands and the other areas of the diaspora, whether in Iceland or in Eastern Europe.

Our final example shows the complexities of interpreting modern DNA data by looking at the debate about the results of the People of the British Isles project (PoBI). The project sought to create a fine-scale population genetics map of the United Kingdom by sampling large numbers of individuals from diverse rural areas across Britain. The results that concern the Viking Age sparked debate because of the project's conclusions about the genetic contributions of Scandinavians to the Danelaw region of England. The complexities of the analysis are amplified here in comparison with the northern British Isles and even with the Wirral/Lancashire region for several reasons. Genetic population differences are more marked between the mostly Celtic populations of northern Britain and Scandinavia than are the mixed Celtic and Anglo-Saxon populations of southern Britain. The Anglo-Saxons came from areas that overlap partially with the Danes of the Viking Age (e.g., southern Jutland in Denmark and Schleswig in modern Germany), meaning that the creation of separate comparison groups that represent "Anglo-Saxons" versus "Danes" has proven methodologically problematic.[204]

The PoBI project used genetic material from the whole genome rather than just Y-chromosome and/or mitochondrial DNA and sampled only individuals who had four grandparents who were born within 80 km of each other. The results from analysis of a subset of 2,039 individuals showed clustering of genetic haplotypes (groups of genes inherited from a single parent) in seventeen discrete geographical areas. The genetic hierarchical relationships among these seventeen groups showed four coarser population clusters that also organized according to geography: (1) Orkney, (2) Scotland/north England, (3) central and south England, and (4) Wales. Among these four groups, Orkney was the most distinctive followed by Wales, while northern Scotland and all of England showed closer relatedness. Significantly, the geographical clusters showed great genetic differences between the traditional "Celtic" areas of Britain. For instance, central Scotland, which has been used to create a surrogate old Celtic signature for admixture analysis, showed closer genetic affinity with central England than with other supposedly Celtic areas such as Wales and Cornwall. Future projects will need to take this into consideration as they form their baseline "Celtic" comparison group for admixture analysis.

The project then compared the genetic clusters with clusters of genetic samples from mainland Europe. The aim was to map regionally variable genetic input from mainland Europe and estimate the timing of the admixture(s). The results were impressive. The project explained the uniqueness of the Orkney cluster by an overall 25 percent contribution of DNA from Norway in an admixture event taking place around 1100 (between 830 and 1418 with 95% confidence).[205] These conclusions are consistent with the previous studies although it estimates a much smaller contribution from Scandinavians (compare with 31% by Goodacre's group and 55% by Capelli's group based on Y-chromosome modeling). It also places the date of admixture rather later than expected as will be discussed further below.

The most controversial findings, however, related to the largest genetic cluster dominating lowland eastern and southern Britain. Unsurprisingly, the lowland British cluster showed substantial affinity with genetic groups from northern France, Belgium, northern Germany, and Denmark.[206] The controversy concerned the project's conclusions about the relative contributions of the medieval-period migrations to the lowland British gene pool. The project estimated that a migration from northwestern Germany dated to circa 858 (802–914 with 95% certainty) led to a circa 35 percent genetic contribution to the population of Britain. Based on these numbers, the study's authors concluded that that Anglo-Saxons had contributed under half of the genetic material in lowland Britain, whereas they found "no clear genetic evidence of the Danish Viking occupation and control of a large part of England, either in separate UK clusters in that region, or in estimated ancestry profiles."[207] This conclusion appears to contradict results from the projects discussed above.

Soon after the publication of the People of the British Isles project, a reinterpretation of the data was offered that demonstrates the importance and difficulties in establishing useful genetic comparison groups from modern populations. Just as with the analysis of the Orkney samples, the authors of the original study used genetic changes that happen generationally as material is passed from parent to child to provide a date estimate for an influx of genetic material into the southeastern British population from the northwestern German genetic group. As noted above, the authors identified a migration event that contributed circa 35 percent of genetic material from northern Germany to lowland Britain around 858.[208] The original project authors believe that the population admixture of Anglo-Saxon and Britons happened about 150–200 after the Anglo-Saxon invasions. Kershaw and Royrik's subsequent reinterpretation of the data argues that the original study erred in two assumptions: (1) that northern German and Danish DNA are distinguishable enough from each other to serve as two separate comparison groups, (2) that the admixture event dated to 858 excluded Danish Viking Age contributions to the gene pool. The Danish DNA used as a comparison group was drawn from around Copenhagen without any control for recent immigration, meaning that this population probably does not represent the Viking Age population from the whole area of Denmark. In fact, Denmark of the Viking Age would have included portions of the locations sampled for the northern German comparison group (i.e., those from Schleswig-Holstein). Kershaw and Royrik's reinterpretation also held that the date of the admixture event better represented an average of two admixtures deriving from the fifth- to sixth-century Anglo-Saxon migration and the ninth- to tenth-century Viking migration. They pointed to the mounting evidence from archaeology, place-name studies, and the reanalysis of the written sources to argue that Danes must have had a genetic impact on England. The discrepancy of the interpretations of the data for Britain is a bit unsettling and certainly shows the limitations of the current state of genetics research. DNA research in Iceland had more success because of the relative simplicity of a Viking Age migration event in which people moved into an unoccupied landscape.[209] Britain is a very different case. So, although DNA research is immensely valuable for our understanding of the Viking Age migrations to Britain, the analyses have not yet provided the final answers to the questions of scale and impact of the Scandinavian migrations.

What can we take from the DNA analysis done up to this point? Some general conclusions such as the substantial input of Scandinavian DNA into the population Shetland and Orkney are upheld by all published projects, even if the precise percentage estimates vary. But how are we to reconcile the estimates of over 50 percent Norwegian Viking contribution to the medieval male populations of Wirral and West Lancashire with the estimates of an undetectable contribution of Viking Age Scandinavian DNA to the Danelaw area? Part of the answer lies in the comparison groups. The different scale of the sampling also plays a role. The Wirral/West Lancashire project focused intentionally on a geographically confined locality believed to be an epicenter of Scandinavian immigration. Here we see evidence of the intense local variation in the Scandinavian migration process. The PoBI project used broad-based sampling and illuminated wider general genetic distribution patterns that showed complex layers of genetic influence beyond the Celtic versus Viking dichotomy. This project showed that when extending analysis beyond this binary approach to other genetic groups across Europe, the particular migrations become less clear. Date estimates are helpful here, but the estimates themselves date admixture rather than immigration (addressed further below). The reality is that as long as we are using modern DNA for ancient migrations, we ignore so much of the movement of people that happened between the Viking Age and the modern period, even with the ingenious application of sampling according to specific surnames. Ongoing analyses of large samples of ancient DNA from populations across Europe promises to help, but even then, we will need to build models on assumptions and evidence from texts, archaeology, and place-name studies.

Conclusions

In this chapter, the tensions among scientific, archaeological, and textual datasets were seen clearly in the interpretation of the genetics results. Reflecting back on Orkney from a native British perspective, 75 percent of the DNA appears to derive from older, pre-Viking migrations. The ways in which this part of the population integrated with the dominant elite Viking Age Scandinavians who renamed their landscape and completely altered their material and cultural landscape remain even more invisible than the Vikings themselves. An aspect worth revisiting at the close of the chapter is the expected delay in interbreeding that the People of the British Isles project documented in the analysis of the Orkney population. The estimate of an admixture date of circa 1100 postdates Viking domination of the islands by 250–300 years. The Orkney estimates do not have the same issues of interpretation as the data from lowland Britain. The PoBI project assumes at least eight to ten generations passed between settlement and genetic admixture between the populations. This assumption would require an apartheid period in which the populations remained separate biologically if not culturally. However, gradual interbreeding and intermarriage is indicated by historical sources at least at the highest level of society. Interbreeding and intermarriage are also strongly suggested by hybridized material culture and language in the Danelaw. The PoBI project's conclusions in one way had lessened the grizzly possibilities of ethnic cleansing by Vikings in the northern British Isles by documenting such a low contribution of Scandinavian DNA to current populations. But lasting apartheid conjures other unpleasant and, in many ways, surprising images.

In Viking studies in Britain, a revitalized interdisciplinarity drawing on modern sciences has made Scandinavian impacts more visible. Overall, the discipline of Viking studies has documented quick assimilation of Scandinavians into Christian English culture after periods of creative syncretization in most of the British Isles, while a near ubiquitous cultural assimilation to Scandinavian culture in the northern Scottish Isles was seen in archaeological remains, place names, and language change. The disciplinary shift to focus on identities formed in the interrelationships between Scandinavians and locals has shown that the new communities dominated by Scandinavians were creative in forming not just hybrid identities but new identities that were expressed in novel ways and forms such as the hogback monuments and the coinage from York. Some traditional narratives are supported by correspondence between traditional datasets and the new sciences. For instance, conclusions based on historical sources and place-name influences concerning the Norwegian Viking domination of the Irish Sea have been supported if not confirmed by the DNA project in Wirral/West Lancashire, which has collected robust data on the high incidence of a haplogroup common in Norway, but less so in Denmark or Sweden. Simultaneously, the mounting archaeological evidence is giving scholars renewed confidence that Scandinavians are visible—for instance in the Viking winter camps of Repton and Torksey as well as widespread loose finds of Scandinavian-influenced metalwork. The archaeological and genetic visibility of Scandinavians makes it possible to revisit questions of scale and impact. Yet, the narrative is complicated by the realization that Viking groups were multi-ethnic, as shown clearly by the diverse childhood homes of the executed raiders at Ridgeway Hill. Had a diverse group of Vikings such as this settled in Britain, they would have had a complex and distinctively un-Scandinavian impact on the gene pool. Historical accounts of Vikings in Britain and traditional assumptions of the Scandinavianess of these Viking bands underlie modern genetic models that seek to measure Viking impacts by comparison with modern Scandinavian genetics. The isotopic analysis of skeletons can be a corrective as can further comparative study of ancient DNA samples from Britain and Scandinavia. With further micro- and macro-regional studies of genetics and isotopes from ancient samples, Viking studies in Britain is likely at the beginning of a massive data revolution. The coming flood of hard data can now be approached through the lens of mutable identities and the flexibility of Viking group formation. The bands of warriors that showed up on the shores of Britain were made into Vikings in the crucible of battle and in the shared pursuit of simple common goals: to increase social and biological success.

3

From Subsistence Economy
to Political Order

Viking Feasts

The image of the hard-drinking convivial Viking raising his horn at a raucous feast has become a cliché in popular culture and to an extent also within academic literature. However, this is at least in part because there is substantial historical truth to the image. Throughout history feasting practices have had immense importance for human societies and social change.[1] Many scholars now believe that efforts to produce food and drink for feasts played key roles in the advent of inequality, the food-production revolution, and the emergence of the state. Chiefdom-level societies, such as those that existed in Scandinavia in the Viking Age, appear to have been particularly structured by feasting. Many scholars of the Viking Age have recognized the importance of feasting, even if the space given to these practices is underrepresented when compared to discussion of raiding or trading. For instance, Aaron Gurevich called feasting "the most important social institution" in pre-Christian Scandinavia while Else Roesdahl describes feasting as "the key stone of the Scandinavian political system."[2]

The reality of the importance of feasting is borne out in the texts and in the archaeological record examined in this chapter. It is also true that anthological study of pre-industrialized societies has shown that feasting is one of the key venues for alliance building and status negotiation in pre-modern societies. This chapter argues that it was the main way that surplus food production could be used to make statements of political power. So why should it be different for the Vikings, especially as we have such plentiful texts describing feasts? In fact, the sagas provide some of the best ethnohistorical accounts of feasting available from any pre-modern European society. Some scholars have lamented the simplified cliché of the feast and downplayed the role that feasting played as "social glue" in the Viking Age.[3] In reality, Viking Age feasts were not at all simple. The hosts and guests who attended had complex motivations that extended well beyond the joy of communal drunken revelry. Feasts are complex events that are rife with opportunities for social statements of solidarity, exclusion, and competition. Feasts can unite friends, divide social classes, and form arenas for status jockeying. Feasts were very public and emotionally charged arenas that amplified

Age of Wolf and Wind. Davide Zori, Oxford University Press. © Oxford University Press 2024.
DOI: 10.1093/oso/9780190916060.003.0003

the gravitas of verbal and material statements. This chapter will unravel these motivations and show how feasts served as arenas for negotiating a wide range of social relationships and power plays.

As agriculturalists, Viking Age Scandinavians produced their food primarily from domesticated plants and animals. The products of agriculture fed the population, while surplus foods could be accumulated for use in social interactions that structured the political hierarchy. Marcel Mauss sums up his view on the reasons for surplus accumulation in archaic economies: "They hoard, but in order to spend, to place under obligation, to have their own 'liege men.' On the other hand, they carry on exchange, but it is above all in luxury articles, ornaments or clothes, or things that are consumed immediately, as at feasts."[4] Scandinavian leaders praised for generosity are referred to with epitaphs such as "ring-giver," or "ring-poor" (because they have given their wealth to others), precisely because they have bestowed luxury goods, such as rings and weapons, on potential followers. Feasts often provide the public arenas for such gift-giving, while as Mauss points out, the feasts themselves also provide the venues for bestowing sumptuous foods and drink on guests. The seemingly inexplicable excess of the Viking feasts is not so strange when seen in comparison with other anthropologically documented feasts in which the host explicitly seeks to destroy wealth. Over-eating and over-drinking are the corollary of this wealth destruction as enacted by the guests who have accepted the excessive show of wealth in surplus resources. In essence, this mandatory overindulgence in food and drink provides the appropriate honor to the host.[5] The honor raises the host's rank, showing him or her to be superior to guests, at least until the commensal gifts of the feast are returned on another occasion.

At its simplest, a feast is an unusual meal shared on an unusual occasion, like a special dinner cooked for friends who have returned from a long trip.[6] The Viking feasts described in sagas and poetry are generally on a larger scale and more akin to what Michael Dietler has described as "a form of public ritual activity centered around the communal consumption of food and drink."[7] As seen in the sagas and cross-culturally, the combined ritual and public aspects make feasts ideal stages for other social transactions, such as reciprocal gift giving, that establish and reproduce social relations.[8] The term most often used for feasting in the Old Norse sources is *veizla* (noun sg. *veizlur*) meaning to feast or even to support or help. Veizla derives from *veita* "to grant/confer," underscoring the role of providing goods and hospitality that is central to the feast.[9]

Sponsorship of feasts is undertaken to conspicuously display wealth, make alliances, and impress both rivals and potential followers. Feasts create relationships of reciprocal obligation between hosts and guests by the same social principle of reciprocity that governs the flow of material gifts from donors to receivers.[10] No gift or feast is free. The host or host group will expect something in return. This could be another feast, or might also be labor, or loyalty or political support. Feasts are laden with manifestations of hierarchy—who provides and who consumes, where people are seated, who is served first, who can procure the most extravagant food and drink. They are therefore ideal arenas to establish and reproduce social relations. Since "feasts are inherently political" and "constitute a fundamental instrument and theater of political relations," the Viking feast offers an analytical venue for understanding how political action operated in the Viking Age.[11]

Many efforts have been made to articulate feast types. On the one hand, the simplest way to divide feasts is by the overt occasions of the feast: such as wedding feast, funeral feast, and seasonal transitional feasts, such as the feasting around Yule (*jól* in Old Norse, a pre-Christian winter feast that becomes integrated into Christian Christmas). All these can be found in the texts concerning the Vikings. Anthropologists on the other hand often categorize feasts by their apparent functional goals. An overarching category for feasts that operate in the realm of uninstitutionalized power has been called the *empowering feast*.[12] In general, the host of an empowering feast aims to acquire social power, prestige, and alliances through a generous display of commensal hospitality that serves to indebt guests. Successful hosts are accorded respect and deference, which translate into uninstitutionalized forms of political power and influence.[13] This prestige attracts admirers, allies, potential spouses, and trading partners. Although the feasts of the lower classes are less frequently visible in our saga texts, every Viking Age household with sufficient resources would have hosted this type of promotional feast. These feasts, which were often reciprocal, served as a foundation for friendship and cooperation. Subcategories of empowering feasts are also readily identifiable. For instance, some feasts are meant to create stronger social bonds of cooperation. Feasts that solidify an in-group are often called *group-solidarity feasts*, while feasts that create bonds between two or more social groups are called *alliance feasts*. Other feasts are competitive and pit rivals against each other in displays of their wealth.

More one-sided affairs, the *Patron-role feasts* affirm unequal social power between elites and followers because the person of higher status perpetually holds the role of host. Like all feasts, the patron-role feasts function on a logic of reciprocity, meaning that the guest who never returns the favor instead owes allegiance. Therefore, patron-role feasts generate inequalities, legitimize asymmetrical social relationships, and institutionalize obligations of political support. These feasts might simultaneously promote feelings of solidarity among social groups and ease the friction between leaders and supporters.[14] Nevertheless, the social relations remain continually inequitable because in-kind reciprocation from subordinate supporters is neither expected nor possible.[15]

Unequal power relations are also visible in the type of feasts, often called *diacritic feasts*, that function primarily to show and uphold class/status differences between those who can afford expensive feasting products and those who cannot. Hosting lavish feasts is often an obligation of leaders, but moreover it is also often the monopolized preserve of institutionalized power.[16] In a sense, then, these diacritic elitist feasts function by a logic of social exclusion and are meant to reaffirm and exhibit elite class alliances.

We can also think about feasts as targeting social relationships that are either *horizontal* (between equals) or *vertical* (between people of unequal status). Horizontal feasting between equals or near equals can be friendly and work to create solidarity and alliances. Vertical feasting between people of unequal status can still facilitate creation of social groups, such as the chieftain support groups that were often created by patron-client feasts. Conversely, vertical feasts can also be antagonistic, as exemplified by taxation feasts during which the person of lower status is compelled to provide food and drink for a political superior as a primitive form of taxation. This last feast type, the taxation feast, is important for understanding the emergence of nascent states in Scandinavia.

As they play out over days with many different actors, feasts often have several distinct functions, blending together the types of feasts articulated above. For instance, a lavish funeral feast might unite a kin group, while simultaneously aweing a neighboring chieftain and showing off the chieftain's wealth to potential followers. Perhaps if the funeral feast's guest list is limited to the upper echelons of society, it may also function diacritically to demarcate social class.

This chapter will first seek the ideal feast in the poems and myths of the Viking Age. A close examination of these texts will show a preoccupation with the essential products of the feast—alcohol and meat—and stress the importance of the socially constructed arena of feasting within the feasting hall. Looking closely at the sagas, we will then be able to unravel the dynamics of feasting first among kings in Scandinavia—Norway specifically—and then among chieftains and farmers in Iceland. We will then interrogate these conclusions with the help of the archaeological evidence by specifically focusing on traces of feasting found inscribed on stones, left in graves, and preserved in feasting halls. Finally, by combining our datasets, we will examine the interesting challenges and potentials of maintaining Scandinavian feasting customs on the margins of the Viking world, in Iceland, and take up a case study that shows the importance of an elite family's feasting potential for their changing political fortunes.

A Politics of Commensal Hospitality in the Written Sources

The written sources—from contemporary foreign texts to thirteenth-century sagas—show that feasting was an important strategy for social integration and power plays among the Viking Age Scandinavians. The texts written by non-Scandinavians about Viking feasts show them as important political and religious events. They describe feasts at funerals, at religious events, and at the courts of kings. The feasting at the graveside of a Viking chieftain on the Volga River as observed by an Arab traveler is one of the most enlightening (and in fact terrifying) of any description of feasting among the Vikings. These views, however, are snapshots from the outside that do not show the broader picture of how feasts were embedded in intricate power plays and hierarchical relations.

For an inside view that reveals individual agency on a wide canvas of political power brokerage, we need to turn to the Norse poetry and sagas. The chapter gives priority to the poetry, as much of it derives from that Viking Age. The sagas, largely from the thirteenth century, provide a much larger corpus with feasts embedded in narratives of kings in the *Kings Sagas* and wealthy farmers in the *Family Sagas*. The sagas show a view of feasting that is consistent both with the poetry and with the foreign texts written in the Viking Age. With only a few exceptions, I employ the sagas for a generalized view of the social realities of feasts in the Viking Age. It probably stretches the saga evidence to attempt to use them to chart temporal changes in feasting practices. The exceptions I make show my inclination to view the chronologically earliest feasts as involving a stronger focus on royal sacrifice and my opinion that the sagas retain reliable memories of a late eleventh-century shift in feasting practices that brought Scandinavian customs more into line with the rest of Christian Europe.

The Strange Feast: Outsiders Observing Viking Feasts

Foreign sources, like Adam of Bremen's eleventh-century chronicle *Gesta Hammaburgensis Ecclesiae Pontificum*, are invaluable as they provide the only contemporary accounts of Viking feasts. These sources show that feasts were essential political and religious events. But since these sources provide biased views colored by exaggeration and Christian moralizing, we should hold them up against the later native sagas and archaeological evidence. For example, Adam of Bremen fancifully describes feasting and sacrifice at the pagan temple in Uppsala in Sweden. At least as valuable—and certainly more trustworthy—is Adam's matter-of-fact description of occurrences during the archbishop Adalbert's mission to the Danish king Svein Estridsen's court: "as is the custom among the barbarians, they feasted each other sumptuously on eight successive days to confirm the treaty of alliance."[17] Adam indicates that the feast that occurred over the course of multiple days in Svein's court—presumably within his hall—was reciprocal insomuch as "they feasted each other" and that the overarching aim was to cement a political alliance. Many of the key elements of the political feast described by anthropologists are glaringly present in Adam's brief sentence.

On the eastern reaches of the Viking world, the Arab traveler Ibn Fadlan observed a funeral feast in which a group of Scandinavians on the Volga River bury their dead chieftain with an extravagant feasting display of food and alcohol.[18] Animals, including a dog, a rooster, and a horse, were sacrificed and placed in the Viking chief's burial ship along with other foods, alcohol, and selected personal possessions. The feast involves immense destruction of wealth in the burning of a ship, but also in the conspicuous consumption of copious amounts of alcohol (a strong drink referred to as *Nabīdh*) and real and symbolic meat consumption (many types of meat are mentioned, including notably cattle). Animals not normally eaten, like dogs and a rooster, are also sacrificed. The role of meat and sacrificed animals is striking in Ibn Fadlan's description. Cross-culturally, the ultimate culinary wealth display during feasting is often the slaughter of the largest domesticated animals. These animals were both sources and symbols of wealth for agricultural societies, particularly societies in Scandinavia where livestock, rather than plant domesticates, were the main form of stored wealth. These animals became symbols of strength, vitality, reproduction, and group leadership. Sacrificed animals are consumed by feasting participants while the dead chieftain joins in the feast through meat deposited in his boat. The gruesome rape and sacrifice of a slave girl during the culmination of the funeral feasts and her eerie transcendence to the next world through a symbolic doorway will be considered in detail in Chapter 4. For the purposes of this chapter, we are seeking primarily the setting and the products of the feast. We can conclude that the feast on the Volga was conducted in the open air and in a temporary structure while the main products of the feast were various types of meat and copious amounts of alcohol.

The Mythological Feast: Banqueting among the Gods and Ancient Heroes

The role of the feast among Viking Age Scandinavians can be approached through examining the realm of the gods and mythology. Old Norse literature allows us to peer into this realm mainly through Snorri Sturluson's thirteenth-century *Prose Edda* and compilations of mythological and legendary poetry (Eddic poetry), some of which was composed in the Viking Age.[19] In mythic poetry and prose, the Norse gods are humanized, but are also idealized. The gods are like humans but also superhuman. Their power is greater than any human king could possess, their knowledge is greater than any human mind's capacity, and their resources extend beyond earthly potential. In turn, the feasts of the gods are depicted as the ideal—but unachievable—feasts. Odin—the ruler of the gods, the god of chieftains and war-leaders, and the afterlife lord of the fiercest fallen warriors—was the most powerful of the gods. Odin's hall and the activities undertaken therein therefore offer a picture of the ideals of perfection for Viking political ideology.

Most people know the image from Norse mythology of the Viking honorable dead feasting on an inexhaustible supply of meat and alcohol in Odin's hall, Valhalla. This ideal feast image is a good starting point as it emphasizes three main aspects of feasting discussed in this chapter: the ritualized meal in a hall setting, the extravagant consumption of meat, and the drinking of large quantities of alcohol. As well as being an arena for sumptuous displays of hospitality, Valhalla is a place of ideal masculine values. *Grímnismál*, an Eddic poem composed around 1000, describes Odin's hall:

> Valhalla
> is easily recognized
> if one comes to see it.
> The hall is held up by spear shafts,
> it is roofed by shields,
> chainmail is on the benches.[20]

The martial ethos of the hall underscores the violent potential of Odin and his followers, known as the Einherjar ("the army of one").[21] Odin's hall signals his capacity to host and sustain warriors by its pure size:

> I think Valhalla
> has six-hundred and forty doors,
> if all are counted.
> Eight hundred Einherjar
> Will walk through each
> when the day comes to fight Fenrir.[22]

Described in this way, the hall is the pinnacle of chiefly grandiosity. The size of the hall is matched by the extravagant and unending feasting products that show Odin's access to unlimited food and drink. *Grímnismál* describes the quality of the meat at Odin's nightly feasts, which derives from an unidentified animal named Sæhrimnir (Sæhrímnir): "the best meat."[23] Although unclear in the poetry, Snorri's *Prose Edda* identifies Sæhrimnir as a boar: "Never are there so many in Valhalla that they run out of meat from the boar called Sæhrimnir."[24] Sæhrimnir is cooked every evening and regenerates the next day to serve as feasting meat the following evening. The meat from Sæhrimnir is paired with mead that flows from the udders of a goat named Heidrun (Heiðrún) that perpetually stands atop Valhalla's roof:

> That goat fills Valhalla's cups
> with bright mead from her udders,
> and that drink will never diminish.[25]

The *Prose Edda* expands on the poetic imagery by articulating expectations that a high-status host such as Odin provide high-quality alcohol to guests. The wanderer Gangleri asks Odin whether water is served in Valhalla. Odin responds, "That is a strange question. Would All-father invite kings, jarls, and other men of rank to his hall and give them water to drink?"[26] Those who sacrificed on the battlefield "would think a drink of water dearly bought if no better greeting were available."[27] Reciprocity is implied between the warriors who offer battle to their chieftain in exchange for costly provisions provided in the hall. Besides mead, Odin's Valkyries ("choosers of the slain") bring beer in cups and drinking horns to the dead men of Valhalla.[28] Beer/ale, wine, and mead often appear to be interchangeably used in the poetry.[29] Although the flavor may vary, the poetry makes clear that alcoholic beverages are necessary for Odin's hospitality.

The female Valkyries who serve Odin and the slain warriors in Valhalla do reify the male-centric martial ethos of the Viking Age, but these women are also formidable warriors and powerful entities in their own right. The act of serving at a high-status feast would not be seen as a low-status or servile activity. In fact, the best of the goddesses serve at the feasts of the gods, such as for instance when Freyja, the prominent goddess of love, serves ale at the competitive drinking feast between the gods and the boastful visiting giant Hrungnir, who aggressively vows that he will drink all the ale of the gods.[30] High-status women were also respectfully referred to in poetry with reference to the alcoholic drink or the drinking vessels used at feasts: "ale-giver," "wine-bestower," "cup-bearer."[31] Generously bestowing drink and food to guests was a sign of status for women of the Viking Age. Simultaneously, the status of the feast itself and the respect offered to a guest were highlighted by the status of the female serving the drink. That is why Thor's second question, when he returns to Asgard to find Hrungnir drinking with the gods in Valhalla, is ". . . why should Freyja be serving him as though he were feasting among the Æsir?"[32] Thor clearly feels that Hrungnir's presence at the feast and especially his service from Freyja overvalues the giant's status. Hrungnir, the strongest of the giants, is assaulting the mythical hierarchy through aggressive feasting. The feast provides a context for challenging the mythological social order. That arena—like other arenas of status competition such as duels and open battles—had rules. Because Hrungnir is an invited guest, it would be dishonorable to assault him in the hall. Thor and Hrungnir therefore arrange a duel in a neutral location where Thor defeats Hrungnir and returns the mythological hierarchy to its appropriate order.

Eddic and Skaldic poetry further reveals the symbolic importance of the feast through playful poetic constructions for the halls of legendary kings, such as "mead-house," "beer-hall," and "beer-happy hall."[33] The most valued feasting product as well as the most important political activity undertaken within these halls are clear from the name. Moreover, the typical poetic description of heroes approaching kings' halls invariably finds warriors feasting within. For instance, the poems about legendary kings from the Migration Period (c. 375–700), including the story of Sigurd the Dragon Slayer, have frequent messengers sent among the Goths, Burgundians, and Huns. One poem, *Atlakviða* (*The Song of Attila*), describes the scene when the Burgundian warriors Gunnar and Hogni approach the legendary hall of Attila the Hun, whom the poem treats as the most powerful of kings:

> They saw the hall of Attila
> where Huns stood guard;
> men patrolled
> outside that high hall.
> That Hunnish hall
> was full of seats for drinking,
> of iron-bound shields
> and yellow shields,
> of spearpoints and javelins,
> and there sat Atilla
> drinking wine.[34]

Atilla's hall is the center of his power, and within the hall martial ethos and feasting prowess are combined in vivid poetic style.

The myths articulate the material objects used in the feast. Inside halls, the gods and heroes encounter warm fires, laden tables, drinking horns, and glass cups. The gods' original acquisition of feasting equipment in the mythic past is even the focus of the poem *Hymiskviða* (Hymir's Song). Thor orders the giant Ægir to provide a feast for the gods, to which Ægir responds that he would if he only had a cauldron of sufficient size to brew enough beer to satisfy the gods. The god Tyr suggests that solve their problem by stealing an appropriately sized brewing cauldron from the giant Hymir, who possess one that is said to be "a mile deep."[35] This proposal is quickly accepted, and Thor and Tyr set out to visit Hymir. Hymir reluctantly welcomes them with a feast that includes three sacrificed bulls:

They beheaded
the bulls,
and brought them
to the cook-pot;
and before he went to bed,
Thor, son of Odin,
ate two whole bulls
of Hymir's.[36]

Hymir—a giant and an adversary of the gods—is reluctant to provide beer and beef for the feast.[37] The ritual killing of a large bull is an extreme expenditure of wealth, and Thor's appetite is equally extreme as is expected from a divine feaster. At the end of the feast, Thor breaks Hymir's wine glass on Hymir's forehead. Thor has thereby assaulted Hymir's store of feasting products and broken Hymir's most prized consumption vessel. Finally, Thor takes away Hymir's brewing cauldron and with it his means to produce alcohol. At the end of the poem Thor has destroyed Hymir's ability to host feasts and taken away his political potential. A defeated Hymir responds to his new reality:

I know my loss is great
when I see my cup
fall broken at my knees;
I know that I will
never again say,
"The drinks are ready!"[38]

The gods are not "good guests" in this story, but the social relationship between gods and giants is based on negative rather than positive reciprocity, and the poetry always praises aggressive actions from the gods—especially Thor. At the poem's end, Thor returns to Asgard with the cauldron:

And now the gods
drink good beer
every winter's day
in Ægir's hall.[39]

As seen in *Hymiskviða*, feasts are loaded with social potential, both positive and negative. Navigating a feast is often risky. Marcel Maus refers to this tension as the "unstable state between festival and war" that can turn a rather friendly commensal rivalry into violent combat.[40] Honorable consumption and acceptance of a host's largesse would ideally be balanced with a moderation that allowed quick thinking in the face of aggressive political or violent challenges. In the Norse wisdom poetry contained in *Hávamál* (Sayings of the High One), Odin himself warns of the risks of overindulgence at feasts:

> There is not as much good
> As men claim there is
> In alcohol for one's well-being.
> A man knows less
> As he drinks more, and loses more and more of his wisdom.[41]

> The best kind of feast
> Is one you go home from
> With all your wits about you.[42]

> Don't hold on to the mead-horn
> But drink your fair share.
> Say something useful or stay quiet.
> And no one else
> Will judge you poorly
> If you go to sleep early.[43]

By no means is Odin advising abstinence and he is certainly encouraging active participation in feasting and drinking. Moderation though is offered up as an ideal. The results of overindulgence are highlighted in another Eddic poem, *Sigdrífumál*, in which the Valkyrie Sigrdrifa (Victory-driver) gives this warning to the famous warrior, Sigurd the Dragon Slayer:

> Often a night
> of song and beer
> has caused men unhappiness;
> it's sometimes caused their death,
> it's sometimes gotten them cursed.
> Drunkenness has caused untold sorrows.[44]

Even the gods do not always fare well in the contests of the feast. During one of his most memorable trips to the land of the giants, Thor, his companion Loki, and his servant Tjalfi are feasted in the hall of Utgard-Loki (Útgarða-Loki, or "Loki of the Outer Enclosures").[45] Just as the feast in Hymir's hall, this feast is not a feast between friends. Rather, this aggressive feast is aimed at destroying the honor and political power—if not the life—of an adversary. In a series of feasting contests, the giants emerge on top through trickery and magic. The contests are telling in character and involve the competitive consumption of the essential products of the feast. Thor is challenged to a drinking competition in which he must empty Utgard-Loki's drinking horn. The significance of a leader's own drinking vessel—Hymir's glass cup and Utgard-Loki's horn—underscores the role of these items in political action. In the mythic narratives, these drinking vessels must be mastered before the chieftain can be vanquished. If Thor cannot empty Utgard-Loki's horn, then the implication is that he is a lesser leader than his adversary. Thor's demoralizing failure is achieved by trickery as the end of the horn had been attached to the ocean. The audience learns only later that Thor was in fact such a powerful drinker that his drinking caused the sea to recede and engendered the tides of the ocean. Loki's challenge is to compete in the eating of meat, the other key product of the feast. Loki too fails by trickery alone as his competitor, Logi, is the personification of fire, who consumes meat and even the wooden feasting platters at incomparable speed. Having been routed at the games of feasting as well as in equally deceptive feats of strength (against the personification of death and the Midgard Serpent) and speed (against the personification of thought), Thor and his companions leave Utgard-Loki's hall in defeat. We are reminded in the end of Odin's warning to keep your wits about you at feasts.

The Eddic poems and prose stories of Viking mythology show a world in which the main political action, besides that which takes place on the battlefield, occurs at elite feasting events hosted by political leaders in their sumptuous halls. The ideals of providing food and drink in excess for the host are tempered, however, with voices urging guests to be cautious of overindulgence as the risk of lost honor and violence are amplified in the public setting of the feast.

Feasting among Kings: The Sagas of Kings

The Scandinavian kings of the sagas aspired to join Odin's retinue in Valhalla, while wanting to emulate Asgardian scenes of plentiful feasting in their own halls. The kings' aspirations are beautifully remembered in one of the oldest references to Valhalla preserved in a skaldic praise poem for the Norwegian King Eirik Bloodaxe that was composed shortly after his death on the battlefield in England in 954.[46] The poem, known as *Eiríksmál*, opens with Odin recounting his dream about Eirik's arrival to Valhalla:

> What kind of dream is this, that I thought that a little
> before daybreak I was preparing Valhalla for a slain army?
> I awakened the einherjar, I asked them to get up
> to strew the benches, to rinse the drinking cups,
> [I asked] Valkyries to bring wine, as if a leader should come.[47]

Since the Icelanders had closer contact with Norway than the other mainland Scandinavian lands, the sagas about the Norwegian kings are by far the most plentiful and reliable of the kings' sagas (see Table 3.1 for Viking Age Norwegian kings). These sagas offer legends and memories about the importance of feasts stretching from legendary ancestral kings to the post-Viking Age medieval kings.[48] The kingdom ruled by the saga kings, which has been described as a "constellation of political bonds," fluctuated in size and degree of political centralization.[49] In the maneuverings of expanding and fracturing polities, feasting remained a primary—if not the primary—way these political bonds were formed and negotiated. Feasting also retains primacy as a political, economic, and ideological strategy through the Christianization process. The saga about the earliest legendary kings, *Ynglinga Saga*, tells short and often fantastic stories about pagan feasts and royal sacrifice. The sagas of the kings around the time of the Christian conversion (early eleventh century) also offer detailed descriptions of pagan feasts as the Christian kings try to quash pagan ritual practice in favor of the new religion. Finally, the kings at the very end of the Viking Age host feasts that are transformed and come more thoroughly to emulate the High Medieval feasts of the continental Christian kings. Throughout the processes of nascent state formation and Christianization, the feast remained a key arena for the articulation and construction of royal power.

Ideal kingship in the *Kings' Sagas* includes providing generous feasts and gifts to supporters as well as competitive feasting with rivals. The *Kings' Sagas* also bring to the forefront feasts as events of compulsory hospitality for the purposes of taxation. The Norwegian kings of the Viking Age were not yet rulers of a unified state and were therefore constantly struggling against local rulers and rivals to the throne. Feasting played a key role in this struggle as an arena for expressions of power and alliances, and for the extraction of surpluses in a society where official taxation was not yet organized. The kings always needed to be formally recognized by the regional political assemblies and often had to forcibly make local magnates submit to their authority. After submission to the king, local leaders were typically made to swear allegiance through oaths and then make a public display of hosting the king at feasts. This type of feast was not friendly and provided the social glue for society only in the sense that it structured the hierarchy of rulership.

An Opening Anecdote about Kings

One of the best anecdotes on the sources of royal power comes from a story recounting King Olaf the Saint's analysis of his own half-brothers' potential for kingship. St. Olaf is the paragon of kingship in Snorri's *Heimskringla*, wherein his saga takes up the central third of the whole work. St. Olaf's views and opinions therefore hold significant weight. Toward the end of his saga, Olaf attends a feast

Table 3.1 The Viking Age kings of Norway with the dates of their reigns and the portion of Snorri Sturluson's *Heimskringla* that covers their reigns.

Viking Age Kings of Norway		
King	Dates	Saga within *Heimskringla*
Mythic/legendary Yngling Dynasty kings of Sweden	?	*Ynglinga Saga*
Halfdan "White-legs" Olafsson	?	
Eystein Halfdansson	?	
Halfdan "the Mild and Stingy with Food" Halfdansson	810s?	
Gudrod "the Hunter" Halfdansson	d. 820?	
Halfdan "the Black" Gudrodsson	840s–860s?	*Saga of Halfdan the Black*
Harald "Fairhair" Halfdansson	c. 872–932	*Saga of Harald Fairhair*
Eirik "Bloodaxe" Haraldsson	c. 932–934	
Hakon "the Good" Haraldsson	934–961	*Saga of Hakon the Good*
Harald "Greycloak" Eiriksson	c. 961–970	*Saga of Harald Greycloak*
Earl Hakon Sigurdsson (de facto) under the rule of Harald "Bluetooth" Gormsson of Denmark	970–995	*Saga of Harald Greycloak and Saga of Olaf Tryggvason*
Olaf Tryggvason	995–1000	*Saga of Olaf Tryggvason*
Earl Eirik Hakonarson and Earl Svein Hakonarson (de facto) under the rule of Svein "Forkbeard" Haraldsson of Denmark	1000–1015	*Saga of St. Olaf*
Saint Olaf Haraldsson	1015–1028	
Earl Hakon Eiriksson (de facto) under the rule of Knut "the Great" Sveinsson of Denmark	1028–1029	
Svein Knutsson and his mother Ælfgifu under Knut of Denmark	1030–1035	
Magnus "the Good" Olafsson	1035–1047	*Saga of Magnus the Good*
Harald "the Hardruler" Sigurdsson	1046–1066	*Saga of Harald Hardrada*
Magnus Haraldsson	1066–1069	
Olaf "the Peaceful" Haraldsson	1067–1093	*Saga of Olaf the Peaceful*
Magnus "Barefoot" Olafsson	1093–1103	*Saga of Magnus Barefoot*

Note: The legendary kings in *Ynglinga Saga*, whose history is doubtful, are said to be descended from Odin. Their ancestors lived in Sweden before moving to Norway where they became petty kings of various regions of southern Norway. Harald Fairhair is said to have been the first king of all of Norway, although this is debated, and after his reign the kingdom did not always remain united. Periodically, the Earls of Lade functioned as de facto rulers, while acknowledging the overlordship of Danish kings, especially over the southern region of Norway around Oslo Fjord.

offered by his mother, Queen Asta. As part of the events, Olaf meets his half-brothers, Guthorm, Halfdan, and Harald (the future King Harald Hardrada or Harðráði, the "Hard Ruler"). Olaf's evaluation of his half-brothers' meddle as potential kings perfectly articulates the Viking ideals of kingship. Olaf observes the three boys playing. Guthorm and Halfdan were playing by a lakeside with "big farms, large grain storage barns, and many cattle and sheep," while their brother Harald was playing with wood chips that he explains are warships.[50] Olaf asks each boy in turn what they would most like to possess in this world. Guthorm chooses grain fields: "I want so much grain sown each summer that it covers the whole headland sticking out into the lake." Olaf acknowledges the wisdom in this and responds, "a great deal of grain could be grown there."[51] When it is Halfdan's turn, he selects cattle: "so many [cattle] that when they went to drink water, they would stand side by side around the whole lake."[52] Olaf also approves of Halfdan's answer. Finally, Olaf comes to Harald, who answers, "warriors . . . so many that they would eat all my brother Halfdan's cattle in one meal." At this, Olaf laughs (a very Viking sign of approval) and says to his mother, "here you are raising a king, mother."[53]

The story is meant to show that Harald Hardrada will be an aggressive and powerful warrior king, but moreover, it demonstrates the key resources necessary to be a successful king: grain, cattle, and warriors on warships. The warriors that Harald imagines he will gather around him will be made loyal to him in part by feeding them beef. Grain is food as well, for cattle and for men, and also necessary to make beer. The mode in which these products are acquired matters less than the ultimate leadership goal of indebting and maintaining warriors through provisioning them with food and drink. The ultimate symbolic representation of that provisioning is a lavish feast.

The Generous King's Feasting Prowess

In the last section of the Prose Edda called *Háttatal* (Catalog of Meters), Snorri provides an explanation of poetic verse forms exemplified with wide-ranging poems. Several of them composed by Snorri himself for his Norwegian patrons—King Hakon and Earl Skuli—pertain to the general expectations of leaders to generously provide feasts and gifts for their followers in exchange for their support of the king in battle.

> The happy band of men is able to receive mead together with gold from the ruler. He lets the troop drink at his hall the fair wine served in silver.[54]

In his praise poems, Snorri refers often to royal generosity shown in halls crowded with warriors. The hall itself is referred to with poetic circumlocutions, such as "there where the lord drinks," that reference the symbolic activities carried out in the king's hall.[55] Poetic references to kings underscore their generosity by calling them names such as "wealth-thrower," "ring-flinger," "ring-damager," "ring-spoiler," "gold-breaker," "gold-cutter," and "bracelet-hating bracelet flinger." The gifts given by kings often took the form of rings worn around their arms. Sometimes kings cut rings to give weights of gold or silver as gifts to followers. The following skaldic verse demonstrates the intensity of the hyperbolic praise for generous kings, who are so generous that they seem to destroy their own wealth:

> The gold-generous gold-diminisher gives the troop of men gold. I hear the ring liberal ring-spoiler throws away rings. The bracelet-hating bracelet-flinger honors men with bracelets. The gold-breaker, dangerous to gold, causes complete destruction to gold.[56]

The most frequent site of royal feasts in the *Kings' Sagas* is within the king's hall. *St. Olaf's Saga* describes the royal residence that the Christian King Olaf built for himself in the recently founded town of Nidaros. The seating within Olaf's reception hall is carefully arranged with the king's high-seat in the center flanked by the bishop and priests on one side and his secular councilors on the other side. Opposite the king sat his military commander in another high-seat surrounded by the king's *hirð* (warrior retinue), consisting of a bodyguard of thirty men. The saga informs that when important visitors arrived, the fires were lit on the floor of the hall, and ale was served.[57]

The martial ethos of the hall seen in Odin's hall of Valhalla is also praised in the poetry about kings. As the poet Sigvat enters St. Olaf's hall, he utters this verse:

> Our king's hall is hung with
> helmets and eke with mailcoats
> of hirð-men back from harrying—
> hall and eke the wall-posts.
> No better found, nor fitter
> furnishings than those byrnies,
> a king nor comelier hangings
> could find: thy hall is goodly![58]

The decorations of the hall are themselves arms and armor and the hall itself is idealized as "goodly."

The sagas of the earliest Norwegian kings are rife with feasts in which the kings have a ritual role as leaders of the communal sacrifices to the gods. Sacrificial feasts for prosperity and agricultural fertility required the participation of kings in the consumption of ritual food and drink. The king at times ritually appears to wed a goddess of fertility. Particularly dire situations require that the king be killed alongside the animals of the feast. When the legendary Swedish King Domaldi is sacrificed on an altar, his blood is described as a gift to the gods offered in hope of ending a severe famine.[59] In other stories, when matters are especially dire, the king seems literally to be subsumed into the feast. The legendary Swedish King Fjolnir, for instance, who is engaged in reciprocal feasting with the Danish King Frodi at Lejre (Hleiðrar), gets so drunk that he falls into Frodi's massive mead cauldron and drowns. The story is told in prose in *Ynglinga Saga* and preserved in the *Ynglingatal* poem, wherein his drowning in a mead vat is recalled, but the manner in which he entered the mead is left unspecified.[60] The inclusion of the king's body into the sacrificial feast would be the highest sacrifice.

The link between the pre-Christian gods and the feasting meat is also illustrated by a story of Odin's visitation of the Christianizing Norwegian King Olaf Tryggvason during a feast. The disguised Odin deems the meat of the feast unworthy of serving to the king and gives the cook "two sides of beef, thick and fat."[61] The cook boils the meat, but when the Christian king suspects that the meat was provided by Odin, he orders it destroyed. The story underscores the sacral nature of the feasting meat, while also showing the Christian attempt to sever the link of the feast with pagan worship.

Reciprocal Feasts of "Friendship"
Feasting between equal allies (or near-equals) involved alternating and reciprocal hosting arrangements. One such arrangement was forced upon two rivals in the Orkney Islands—Earl Einar and the powerful Thorkel from Sandvík—as part of a peace deal. The arrangement held that they should be bound in "friendship" by trading feasts although they intensely hated each other. The arrangement ends badly, especially for Einar, who is hewn down in his own hall at one of these peace-making feasts. Einar's fate confuses all present "because they all thought that it had been agreed that there should be friendship between the earl and Thorkel."[62] The use of the feast as a method of alliance was ingrained in the political action repertoire, but the highly charged events were risky with high chances of deadly violence. This story also underscores just how unfriendly these types of public political "friendships" could be.

St. Olaf's Saga remembers a genuinely friendly reciprocal Yule feasting arrangement between two rich kinsmen in the Swedish province of Jämtland. In this case, the local lawspeaker and his "powerful and wealthy" relative celebrated the long yuletide by alternating celebrations at each other's farmsteads. These feasts do not feature any explicit pagan elements, although the Swedes had considered using St. Olaf's visiting tax-collectors as unspecified sacrifices. The alternating hosts get on fine, but the visiting Norwegians are drawn into a drinking competition that devolves into comparisons of the stature of their respective kings, the outcomes of past battles, and finally insults and threats of violence, which are subsequently carried out. Again, we see that feasts are contests and often not about peacemaking.[63]

Inheritance/Funeral Feasts

Funeral feasts were celebrated to send the dead king to the next world as well as to elevate the heir ritually and publicly to kingship. The hosts of funeral feasts were typically those who stood to inherit the power of the deceased. The verb *erfa*, in fact, means both to honor someone with a funerary feast, and to inherit. The role of the feast in the rituals of transition from this world to the next is addressed in greater detail in Chapter 4, while the focus here is on the role of the feast in politics. Upon his father's death, the legendary King Ingjald of Uppsala in Sweden invites all neighboring kings to a funeral feast for which he had constructed a special hall, which he called the Hall of Seven Kings. At the feast inside this new funerary feasting hall a ritual of transition is described in *Ynglinga Saga*:

> It was the custom at that time, when a funeral feast (*erfi*) was prepared to honor a [departed] king or earl, that the one who prepared the feast and was to be inducted into the inheritance, was to sit on the step before the high-seat until the beaker called the *bragafull* [the foremost cup] was brought in; and then he was to stand up to receive it and make a vow, then drink deeply from the beaker, whereupon he was to be inducted in the high-seat which his father had occupied. Then he had come into the [rightful] inheritance to succeed him.[64]

Once the new King Ingjald had undertaken the ritual and all his guests were drunk, he exited the hall and set it on fire with his six rival kings and their men still inside. This last part of the story is another reminder of the dangers embedded in political rivalry feasts, but might also hold a memory of funerary feasts involving human sacrifice, possibly even of high-ranking men.

The practice of the funeral feast carried over relatively seamlessly into the Christian period with toasts to the memory of the deceased that had been previously paired with toasts to pagan gods simply being replaced by toasts to the dead paired with toasts to Christ and the saints. *The Saga of Olaf Tryggvason* recounts such a funerary feast hosted by Danish King Svein Forkbeard after the death of his father, Harald Bluetooth. To publicly enter into his inheritance and to reinforce the loyalty of the Danish elite, Svein invites all the chieftains in his kingdom, including the legendary Jomsvikings, who made up a formidable warrior band with a fortified base at Jomsborg in present-day Poland.[65] As Svein takes his place in his father's high-seat, he offers a series of toasts to the memory of his father, Christ, and the Archangel Michael. At each toast, the memorial drinking horns were drunk completely. In each toast, the status of the

Jomsvikings is underscored as they were each time served "the largest horns with the strongest drink."[66] After Svein's toast to his father, he makes a public hallowed vow, promising to invade England. After Svein's three toasts, a series of paired toasts and vows are made by the Jomsviking leaders, starting with Earl Sigvaldi, who toasts his own dead father and vows to invade Norway. Subsequent toasts promise to aid Sigvaldi. The saga concludes the episode by suggesting that the Jomsvikings regretted their vows the next day, but that they were now honor-bound to carry out the ill-fated invasion because of the hallowed and public nature of their vows. As the saga says, "this all became widely known throughout the surrounding lands."[67]

The scene highlights the fundamental themes of feasting, including the expectation of overindulgence and the obligation to consume food and drink when it is offered in a feast setting. The multi-dimensional aspect of feasting in structuring politics and in motivating future action is clear from the special treatment of the Jomsviking and the public vows that cannot be broken. Odin's advice to keep your wits about you and be careful what you say while drinking become abundantly clear to the Jomsviking the morning after their drinking bout.

Seasonal Transition Feasts during the Pagan Period

Many feasts were held at key transitional moments in the calendar and included sacrifices to the gods for prosperity. The traditional Norse calendar included two seasons: summer and winter. The transition from each more or less fell on the equinoxes. In addition, feasts were held at mid-winter and mid-summer. These four expected seasonal feasts were sometimes reduced to three by omitting the mid-summer feast. These three major sacrificial feasts—transition to winter, mid-winter, and transition to summer—are also dictated by Odin in *Ynglinga Saga*: "People should sacrifice at the beginning of the winter for a good year, and in the middle of the winter for fertility of the soil, and at the beginning of summer for victory in battle."[68]

The most frequently described feasts were those occurring during the mid-winter or Yuletide period. In the Christian period, this mid-winter feast retained its pagan name, *jól* (Yule), and Christmas time continues to this day to involve brewing of special beer in Scandinavia.[69] Yuletide—a period of darkness and transition—could be dangerous and the sagas describe many supernatural occurrences during these times. Even the Yule feasts could be supernaturally assaulted. In *The Saga of Halfdan the Black*, for instance, a Finnish stranger makes all the food and ale of King Halfdan's Yule feast disappear in front of his guests. The stranger's assault on the products of the king's feast is equivalent to an assault on the king's power. Halfdan's promising but underappreciated son, Harald Fairhair, helps the Finn to escape and accompanies him to a chieftain's home where he is feasted generously. That this was a supernatural theft of the king's feast is subsequently revealed by the magic chieftain: "Your father thought it was a mighty great injury when I took some of his food this winter, but I will reward you with good news. Your father is dead now, and . . . you will inherit his entire realm and with that you shall possess all of Norway."[70] The demise of the king immediately follows the decimation of his feasting potential.

The sagas describe Yule feasts in lavish detail as they are repressed and extinguished by the early Christian Norwegian kings starting with Hakon the Good in the late tenth century and up through St. Olaf in the 1020s. The main pagan stronghold was the Trondelag region, where earls and farmers persisted in their great sacrifices at Lade (Hlaðir) and at Mærin. *The Saga of Hakon the Good* records a Yule sacrificial feast at the Norwegian Earl Sigurd's temple in Lade, which the earls oversaw on the king's behalf. All farmers in the region were to be in attendance and partake in the communal drinking. Moreover, each person was responsible for bringing their own food for the feast:

> All kinds of livestock were killed in connection with it, horses, also; and the blood from them was called *hlaut* (sacrificial blood), and *hlautbolli*, the vessels holding that blood; and *hlautteinar*, the sacrificial twigs (aspergills). These were fashioned like sprinklers, and with them were to be smeared all over the blood the pedestals of the idols and also the walls of the temple within and without; and likewise the men present were to be sprinkled with blood. But the meat of the animals was to be boiled and to be served as food at the banquet.[71]

The chieftain who hosted the feast blessed the meat as well as a large sacrificial cup, which he used in a series of toasts: the first to Odin for victory and power to the king, the second for prosperity from the Vanir gods Njord and Frey, the third for the king, and a fourth in memory of departed kinsmen. Communal alcohol consumption during these feasts allowed access to divine favor, particularly for the host and the king, who were not necessarily the same person.

The saga also describes how Earl Sigurd of Lade earned fame and distinguished himself by provisioning the Yule feast and defraying costs for the farmers. A skaldic poem that describes Sigurd as "the fender of the temple" praises his openhandedness:

> Bring not there your beer, vat-
> brewed, to lord free handed,
> nor fare with baskets filled with food.[72]

At a similar feast, the newly Christianized King Hakon the Good (reign c. 934–961), who attends as a guest, is compelled to participate in sacrificial rituals that include communal consumption of horse meat. His reluctant participation goes noticed as he is absent from the high-seat position at the feast and refuses to dedicate his beaker to Thor or to eat horse meat that is forbidden by Christian laws. A negotiation begins as the pagan chieftains and farmers are insistent that the king must consume some horse meat, even if in broth form, before the sacrifice can be effective. This harkens back to the king's participation in sacrifices being requisite for the community's prosperity. Eventually they reach an elaborate compromise in which the king gapes his mouth over a cloth that lies on the ladle's handle upon which steam from the kettle with horse meat had settled.[73]

Over fifty years after Hakon was forced to inhale horse-meat steam, King Olaf the Saint (reign c. 1015–028) was still faced with pagan sacrifice and feasting in the Trondelag district. Word reaches him that these great winter feasts still followed heathen custom in toasting the old Æsir gods and sacrificing horses and cattle, whose blood was smeared on pagan idols for good harvests. Olvir, a visiting Trondelager at the king's court, objects, claiming that these get-togethers at the onset of winter were merely "communal drinking bouts" among friends.[74] Olvir's description is clearly meant to mislead the king concerning the religious nature of the feasts, but it does provide us with a good idea of what these events were like. When additional pagan feasts were again rumored at mid-winter, the king summons Olvir to his estate at Nidaros (Niðarós, the old name for the site that would later become the town of Trondheim). Olvir again insists that this Yuletide social drinking had merely lasted a little longer than expected because the farmers had provided for ample food and drink to avoid running out. He also explained that the monumental feasting halls at the large estate of Mærin were just meant to serve the local people who consider it "good fun to drink many in a large company."[75] Olaf does not believe Olvir and soon learns that the people in the interior of Trondheim fjord remain committed pagans who still uphold the custom of sacrifices at the three traditional times each year: in the late fall to welcome winter, at midwinter, and at the start of the summer. His informant further explains that twelve leading men take it upon themselves to arrange the feasts and the substantial efforts of gathering provisions at the large halls in the central settlement of Mærin. When the king attacks Mærin, his men sack the halls, and the saga describes them hauling away not only provisions but also furniture, valuables, and clothing that had been brought there for use in the festivities. These additional objects of the feast are unfortunately not further described, and the saga moves on to the execution, mutilation, enslavement, and banishment of the heathen revelers.[76] The communal nature of the feasting, as well as the role of the elite in providing for these communal events, is clear, as is the king's need to destroy this politico-religious feasting network in order that his own political power could effactually extend over the northern Norwegian power-wielders who lived in the inner fjords of Trondelag.

Royal Feasting after Christianization

Feasting was not of course the preserve of pagans alone, and feasting as a political strategy continued after Christianization. In fact, the earliest Norse account of the Norwegian Kings, *Ágrip af Nóregskonungasögum* (*Summary of the Norwegian Kings' Saga*), which was written around 1190 in western Norway and preserved in an Icelandic manuscript, tersely recounts how King Olaf Tryggvason (reign 995–1000) purposefully Christianized pagan feasting practices: ". . . he first built churches on his own large farmsteads and then eliminated pagan sacrifice rituals (*blót*) and ritual drinking (*blótdrykkjur*), and instead established, on account of the people, feast-drinking at Christmas and Easter, and St. John's mass ale (*mungát*) and harvest-beer (*haustǫl*) at the Feast of St. Michael."[77] Olaf thereby co-opted the four seasonal transition feasts: winter solstice with Christmas, spring equinox with Easter, mid-summer with St. John's day (June 24), and autumn equinox (harvest) with Michaelmas (September 29). Each seasonal transition continued to be marked by feasting and drinking. The account specifies that Olaf does this in consideration of the people's traditional practices. We can be fairly sure that his own interests and those of the elite are also at stake here as these feasting events publicly reified the social structure through communal commensal ritual.

In general, the kings of the late Viking Age—after around 1000—were increasingly spending time and therefore also feasting in the towns that were solidifying across Scandinavia. The royal halls—and the royal feasts—moved from farmsteads into the heart of the towns to be paired with Christian churches and royal burial within these churches. St. Olaf, for example, arranges great Easter feasts at the town of Nidaros to which he invites townspeople as well as farmers from the surrounding districts.[78] But it is the saga accounts of King Olaf the Peaceful (reign 1067–1093), who is described as "cheerful at beer-drinking and a great drinker," that best show the growing importance of towns as well as the continued role of royal feasting.[79] The young king offers his main advisor, Skuli, the governance of an entire Norwegian county with its attendant revenues. To this Skuli responds that he would rather be granted "some properties close to the market towns where you, lord, are accustomed to living and having your Yule feasts."[80] In response, the king grants Skuli estates adjacent to five early Norwegian towns: Konungahella, Oslo, Tunsberg, Borg, and Bergen.[81] These estates put Skuli in prominent places in the growing interregional economy and in a strategic position to host and be hosted by the king in the emergent power centers.

During Olaf the Peaceful's reign—right at the very end of the Viking Age—*Heimskringla* directly addresses a significant shift in feasting practices. This description indicates a knowledge of past social practices that will comfort anyone who seeks historical information concerning the Viking Age in the sagas.

Since it is very clear from this description that the sagas are not just discussing thirteenth-century social practices, it is worth an extended quotation:

> It was old custom in Norway that the high-seat of the king was in the middle of the long bench in the hall. And the ale was carried around the fire. King Olaf [the Peaceful] was the first to have his high-seat placed on the elevated dais which ran across the hall [on the short side] . . . In the days of King Olaf the market towns grew fast, and some new ones were established . . . King Olaf established the Great Guild in Nidaros, and many others in the market towns. Before there had been only banquets at various places . . . there arose clubs and drinking bouts in the market towns. At the time new fashions in dress made their appearance. Men wore court-breeches laced tight around the legs . . . They wore trailing gowns . . . There were many other striking new fashions at the time. King Olaf introduced these customs in his court that he had cup-bearers stand by his table to pour out the drink from pitchers, both for himself and for all men of high rank who sat at his table. He had also candle-bearers who held candles for him at the table, as many as there were men of high rank sitting there. There was also the seat for the king's marshal, farther out from the side-board, and there sat the marshals and other persons of rank; and they sat facing inward toward the high-seat. King Harald [the Hard Ruler] and other kings before his time used to drink out of horns and to have the ale borne from the high-seat around the fireplace, and to toast those whom they wished.[82]

Guild feasts, trailing capes, the disappearance of drinking horns, and the replacement of Valkyrie-like high-status women serving ale with professional male waiters standing beside each guest; the fashions indicate an integration of feasting practices into the medieval Christian European world. The classic image of the Viking Age hall was transformed, and quite possibly this is as good a point as any to declare the end of the Viking Age.

Feasting Itinerant Kings

Kings of the Viking Age, especially the early Viking Age, had private manors, but they lacked permanent residences in capitals. Instead, they often moved across the landscape with the expectation that their subjects would house, feed, and entertain them and their retinues. This obligatory hospitality functioned as a form of taxation, meaning that the king was not honor-bound to return the feast reciprocally. These types of feasts are often called "touring feasts" and have been recognized as ruling strategies in chiefdoms and early states cross-culturally from Polynesia to Europe.[83] Without a functional bureaucracy to systematically extract wealth, these kings extracted wealth by forced feasting. They ruled their kingdom through their physical presence in the most important regions of their realm. Simultaneously the public events of the feasts themselves re-enforced the kings' rule and reified the personal relationships between kings and their most prominent chieftains and farmers in their realms. These kings who ruled through their physical presence and extracted a form of taxation during visits to their subordinates are called itinerant kings because of the *iter*—or journey—that they repeatedly made across their kingdoms.[84] Nearly every meal with an itinerant king on tour appears to be a feast. These delicate moments of wealth extraction through feasts had to be carefully navigated. The risk for both parties was greater in this type of commensal taxation since both the host and king risked being exposed to violence.

At first glance, these enforced feasts might appear to run counter to the ideals of royal generosity: here the politically inferior person hosts the king, while the king is not seen to reciprocate. The cost of maintaining kings and their retinues that accompanied them could exhaust the means of local leaders, especially later in the Viking Age as the kings' retinues grew in size. But the laws of reciprocity are still at work. The fundamental principle is that the king is owed something inherently because of his position as king; the subservient landowners owe their position to the king and therefore must give of the produce of their farms. The intrinsic debt owed to the king is reinforced in the sagas that occasionally use the term *veizlugjöld* "feasting debt" to describe payments made to the king in lieu of the feast itself.[85] A challenge for the king was instating this royal principle of commensal taxation over regional chieftains who had previously ruled independently without subservience to a paramount ruler. As a part of the state-formation process in Norway, the kings therefore confiscated and redistributed newly acquired lands to loyal servants. These newly appointed elites—often called landed men (*lendir menn*)—owed the king hospitality because they ruled at the king's behest.

When the king arrived at a farm to be feasted, he brought with him a large number of retainers that also had to be fed and housed. The sagas do not typically provide the exact numbers of retainers, but in a few places customary law appears to prescribe 60 retainers (*hirðmen*). *Fagrskinna* tells that "Harald Fairhair had 60 hirðmen with him when he attended feasts in peacetime."[86] Harald also brought servants with him in his retinue and there is no indication of how many hirðmen he might bring in wartime. The saga notes additional attached servants as well. At the end of the Viking Age this number is reiterated for Olaf the Peaceful when the farmers complain that he has doubled his retinue from the customary 60 to 120, while also adding 60 servants and 60 "guests" to his court.[87] The size of the retinue matters of course in order to understand the financial burden on the local leading farmers subjected to forced hospitality. What is clear based on these numbers is that feasting a king's court was something that only the wealthiest farmers or leaders could have done. In all likelihood, the responsibility was often shared among the well-off farmers of a region visited by the king. *St. Olaf's Saga* reports this type of arrangement for King Olaf the Saint's progression through Raumaríki, where he ordered local farmers to contribute to the households that were offering hospitality.[88]

Although feasting the king was an economic burden and could be risky if violence erupted, elites had great possibilities for honor and alliance building while hosting the king. The itinerant feasts of the sagas are aristocratic events that reinforce class difference, and as such they also fit the mold of the diacritic feast type identified by anthropologists. Symbolically, the hosts of the itinerant royal feast were not the kings' equals, but it was as close as one could come. The host would also benefit from the reaffirmation of his power by the presence of the king. In visiting a particular local leader, the king was also affirming the political interdependence (albeit a hierarchical one) between himself and the host.

Prominent chieftains living in areas claimed by multiple kings had increased risk, but also increased potential for their own claims and building fruitful alliances. The *Saga of Harald Fairhair* records the story of a rich ninth-century farmer named Aki who lived in Vermaland and was caught in a feasting dilemma between the power of the ascendant Norwegian King Harald Fairhair and the Swedish King Eirik. Both kings were making their rounds in this disputed territory, such that Aki felt obligated to feast both kings at his estate. Aki, who had an old feasting hall, built an equally grand second hall especially for this purpose, so that each king could have an equal-sized hall. Aki assigned the new hall to the younger Harald and the old hall to the older King Eirik. New tapestries were used to decorate the new hall so as to equal the old tapestries in the old hall. The saga explains Aki's thoughtful preparations for the table service:

> King Eirik and his company all had old drinking vessels and horns, gilt and beautifully ornamented; and King Harald and his men had all new drinking vessels and horns, all adorned with gold. They were polished and smooth as glass. The drink was equally excellent in both parties.[89]

King Harald was well pleased and promised to "repay" Aki by taking in his son as his personal attendant. But despite Aki's efforts, King Eirik sees an affront to his honor and questions Aki: "Why did you differentiate in the hospitality you offered to me and King Harald, such that he received the best of everything? You know well that you are my man [owe your allegiance to me]."[90] Aki replies that the feasts were equivalent, but then adds the fateful words: "But when you remind me that I am your man, then I consider it no less true that you are my man."[91] At this, King Eirik drew his sword and killed Aki on the spot. Eirik feels insulted by having been given the old feasting vessels, but he cannot abide Aki's suggestion that there might be equality between himself and the farmer. Aki is suggesting here too that the feast—which Eirik believes inferior—has indebted Eirik to Aki, in effect reversing the hierarchical relationship. In the end, although Aki successfully uses his feast to create a family alliance with the young King Harald—who is well pleased to be given the same honor as King Eirik—he fails to delicately maneuver his relationship with Eirik and therefore pays the ultimate price.

Feasting as taxation is also substantially riskier for the king than taxation through tax collectors because the king has to be physically present at the feasts. Two generations after Harald Fairhair, his grandsons vie for power in Norway. When his grandson Gudrod (Guðröð) arrives from England and begins subjugating the Viken region, the people offer to summon an assembly to name him king. As he awaits the gathering of the assembly, Gudrod demands maintenance tribute (*vistagjald*) to feed his men. The saga continues, "but the farmers chose rather the cost of preparing feasts for as long as the king needed. The king accepted this offer and traveled through the country feasting with some of his supporters (his *lið*), while others guarded the ships."[92] His rivals, knowing of Gudrod's presence, ambush him one night while he is feasting and kill him and most of his men. This case underscores both the tributary aspect of forced hospitality imposed by kings as well as the violence—both economic and physical—that often underpinned feasting.

The aristocracy understood Gudrod's vulnerability, and perhaps this is why they chose feasting instead of direct food tribute. Kings had to be careful. A similar case occurs in *St. Olaf's Saga* when Olaf seeks affirmation of his kingship in northern Norway. The local earl, Svein, plans to ambush and kill Olaf while he feasts at a local farm. Olaf sniffs out the ambush, and the saga describes how he literally takes the feast from the farm and loads it onto his ship. In this case, the movable feast is simply the products of the feast, which the saga describes as "both food and drink."[93]

Both King Olaf and his aggressive half-brother, Harald Hardrada, violently subjugated parts of Norway and subsequently enforced itinerant feasts on the local leaders. The violence of these enforced feasts and the displeasure with which they are offered are particularly clear in their dealings with the people of the landlocked region of Uppland, where resistance to royal authority was strong. *Heimskringla* recounts Harald on a feasting tour of the Upplands early in his reign, but then his strategy shifts as he tries sending emissaries to collect "dues and taxes."[94] When the Upplanders refuse to pay these unprecedented dues, Harald lives up to his nickname ("Hard Ruler") with his response, which is recorded in poetry:

> No poet can with justice
> Describe the royal vengeance

That left the Uppland's farmsteads
Derelict and empty.[95]

Harald Hardrada incorporated the marginal inland areas of Norway into the nascent Norwegian state through the royal feasting regime and eventually through violence. After his reign, the feasting reforms of Olaf the Peaceful described above indicate a shift to urban feasting in capital towns and a decline in royal itinerancy paired with the growth of formalized bureaucratic modes of taxation.[96] Feasting remained an important arena for public enactments of royal power, but the heyday of the itinerant king and aggressive forced hospitality was over.

Feasting among Farmers: The Sagas of Icelanders

The *Sagas of the Icelanders*, also called the *Family Sagas*, offer a view of feasting at a smaller scale than the *Kings' Sagas*. The petty chieftains, free farmers, attached workers, and slaves who settled Iceland in the ninth century created a society without kings.[97] The chieftain and farmer leaders of Iceland did not have the coercive power or the resources of the Scandinavian kings. Scarcer natural resources and the challenges of transplanting and sustaining cattle rearing and grain cultivation made lavish feasts more difficult on this North Atlantic island. As a result, the feasts of the *Family Sagas* tend to be more modest, with a few anomalous and therefore noteworthy cases of extreme expenditures. Feasts were surely held at all levels of society, but it is important to note that nearly all of the feasts that appear in the *Family Sagas* are still those held by the wealthy population: chieftains and affluent farmers. This is not surprising since the sagas are interested in the power brokers of society. Absent therefore are the feasts of the poorer farmers, who would still surely have hosted their friends and kin in less lavish feasts of great importance to their own social lives.

The realities of Iceland affected the types of feasts held there. Alliance feasts were very common, such as those around weddings and funerals that target kinship groups, as well as current and potential allies. The importance of friendship alliances mean that reciprocal feasts appear frequently in the sources. Political feasts of the *diacritic feast* type (see above), signaling membership in the elite group, often take a reciprocal form too. Simultaneously, political feasts of the patron-client type were hosted by chieftains and rich farmers for their supporters. Less common are the aggressive competitive feasts meant to show overlordship. Importantly, also, the absence of royal coercive force and territorial overlordship meant that the forced hospitality feasts of the itinerant kings were not employed in Iceland, except in extremely rare cases. Instead, feasts are more commonly used as a ritualized public arena to establish peace and maintain social order.

Following patterns in Scandinavia, Icelanders held feasts at individual farmsteads on a number of occasions during the year, such as the autumn slaughter-time, around Yule, and in association with pre-Christian rituals and Christian worship. The most common large feasts in the sagas mark weddings and funerals. These events were also the times when the largest amount of property and wealth exchanged hands; feasts facilitated and made public this wealth transfer. Smaller more ad hoc feasts occurred at times when hospitality might be expected, such as the arrival from a long journey of an esteemed friend or a potential ally.

Empowering Feasts: Settlement Structuring, Weddings, Funerals, and Inheritance

Chieftains and farmers hosted *empowering feasts* to reify claims to wealth and status, to build alliances, and to compete in displays of prestige that could attract potential supporters. The sagas suggest that feasts helped to structure even the emigration from Norway and the process of the settlement of Iceland. *Vatnsdæla Saga* (*The Saga of the People of Vatnsdal*) begins as many sagas do in Norway before the emigration to Iceland. The founding father of the Vatnsdal (Lake Valley) region, Ingimund, was a successful Viking in Norway, who in contrast to many of the immigrants to Iceland fought on the side of King Harald Fairhair in his efforts to unite Norway. After their victory, Harald wants to reward him, particularly because Ingimund was not obligated to fight for Harald: "I will reward your support with a feast and friendship gifts."[98] The feast, in this case, is offered after the support is provided, but the exchange is the same as in other patron-role feats: feasting in exchange for military and political support. After the feast, Ingimund becomes tied to Harald to the point that he feels he must ask Harald's permission to leave Norway for Iceland. After that permission is granted, Ingimund holds a feast to attract supporters who will follow him to Iceland and, once there, support his claim to authority as a chieftain (goði) in the newly claimed region of Vatnsdal. In his speech during the feast, Ingimund makes his point: "Those who want to come with me are welcome; those who want to remain behind may do so freely."[99] The saga continues, "Many people prepared to go with Ingimund: people of great worth, both free farmers and landless men."[100] Ingimund's feast is a recruitment feast for a communal undertaking of which Ingimund is the leader. In Iceland, Ingimund continues his generosity and hospitality to the people of his region. Ingimund's son, Thorstein, also hosts a yearly autumn feast as part of his maintenance of his father's chieftaincy.[101]

The role of feasts in structuring the settlement of Iceland is also illustrated in
Laxdæla Saga (*The Saga of the People of Laxardal*), which begins with the story of
one of the most fascinating settlers, the female chieftain Unn the Deep-Minded.
After the death of her husband and son in Scotland, Unn leads a group of settlers
to Iceland. Upon arrival she seeks out her two brothers who had arrived before
her. Unn is insulted when her brother Helgi extends hospitality only to her and
nine companions. Unn refuses and seeks out her other brother Bjorn, who honors
her by hospitably entertaining her entire company over the winter: "provisions
were plentiful and wealth was not spared."[102] Unn settled close to her brother
Bjorn, claiming a whole region around Hvammsfjord in western Iceland. The
clarity and richness of *Laxdæla saga*'s feasting events make it ideal to follow this
saga through several generations.

Feasts are essential in Unn's strategy of land distribution and in passing
power to her grandchildren. She marries her granddaughter, Thorgerd, to
one of her followers, Koll, who is of chieftain rank. Unn shows her position
of authority by bearing the entire cost of the wedding feast and giving the
whole of Laxardal (Salmon River Valley) to the newlyweds as a dowry. As her
death approaches, Unn prepares a grand wedding feast for her grandson Olaf
Feilan, who she intends to take over her farm of Hvamm and her position of
authority. She plans the feast for the end of the summer because, as she says,
"that is the best time for getting all the necessary provisions."[103] When the
large numbers of relatives and "important people" were seated in her hall,
she gives a speech making clear that this wedding feast is an inheritance feast
as well: "My brothers, Bjorn and Helgi, and my other kinsmen and friends,
I call upon you to witness that I place my farmstead and everything in sight
that belongs to this household in the hands of Olaf, my kinsman to own and
administer."[104]

She then orders ale served to the entire company before retiring to die. The
inheritance feast now incorporates a funerary feast that lasts for several days.
On the last day of the celebrations, the feasters lay Unn in a treasure-laden ship
and inter her within a burial mound. The saga then reiterates the kinsmen's acceptance of Olaf's new status: "Olaf Feilan then took over the farm and household management at Hvamm with the assent of his relatives who had been at the
feast."[105] The scene ends as Olaf bestows magnificent parting gifts on the distinguished guests to reinforce their kinships and friendship alliances.

The moments of family inheritance, especially at the deaths of chieftains,
were delicate as *Laxdæla Saga* illustrates when Unn's great-grandson, Hoskuld
Kollsson, passes away. His sons by two different women bury their father and
then discuss a great memorial feast. Olaf Hoskuldsson is the most prominent
among them, but also the one with the most to prove because he is the son of
Hoskuld's concubine rather than his wife. Olaf suggests that they delay the feast

for one year so that they can gather provisions and ensure maximum attendance. Olaf's feasting ambitions are great, and he plans to assert his status as equal to his brothers: "I suggest that this summer at the Althing I should undertake to invite the guests to this feast; and, I will put forth one third of the feast's costs."[106] Splitting the cost evenly with his brothers places Olaf on equal footing with them concerning their father's legacy and inheritance. He gives himself added honor by being responsible for the public invitation. Olaf uses the annual Althing meeting attended by all the chieftains and farmers in Iceland as an ideal public arena for his feast announcement:

> Now many men are present who were his [Hoskuld's] kinsmen and relatives. Now it is the will of my brothers that I invite all you chieftains to a funeral feast for Hoskuld, our father, because most of the noteworthy men here had kinship ties to him. I also declare that none of the more worthy people shall leave the feast without gifts. In addition, we want to invite all the free farmers and anyone else who will accept this invitation, whether rich or poor, to attend a half-month-long feast at Hoskuldstaðir ten weeks before winter.[107]

The saga states that 1,080 guests attended the feast and that it was the second largest feast ever held in Iceland. Even if the attendance numbers are likely exaggerated, this observation shows that early Icelanders were carefully attentive to the size of feasts. The feast was a success, and as a result "the brothers greatly enhanced their prestige"; yet the saga adds, "but Olaf was the foremost leader among them."[108] The feast and the extensive guest list can also be read as a competitive feast pitting brother against brother. Olaf's half-brothers are not happy about the feast's costs but feel obligated to join him as co-hosts. After Olaf's invitation at the Althing, the saga laconically remarks, "they [his brothers] were not pleased and thought he had overdone it."[109] Olaf, who is wealthier than his brothers, challenges them, especially his oldest brother Thorleik, who thinks himself the true inheritor of their father's wealth and power. After the ostentatious display at their father's memorial feast, however, Olaf emerges as the leading brother and the inheritor of the family chieftaincy. To patch matters up with his brother Thorleik, Olaf offers to foster his son in a show of respect. Although Olaf conciliatorily adds, "for he is called the lesser man, who fosters another's child," the power has already passed to Olaf.[110]

Reciprocal Alliance Feasting in Iceland

Feasts held reciprocally to build alliances and friendships are a particularly common type of *empowering feast* visible in the sagas. The friendship engendered in the sagas is not really about feelings of mutual love, but rather about conduct and action. That is not to say that the actions do not show love or animosity.

They certainly do that too, but it is action that obligates and engenders power, friendship, and violence. The eponymous character in *Njal's Saga* (*Brennu-Njáls saga*), one of the wisest characters in all of the *Family Sagas*, employs feasting strategies extensively to form friendship alliances with powerful men in his region of southern Iceland. The most heralded friendship in this saga—the friendship between Njal and the heroic warrior Gunnar Hallmundarson—is also held together by reciprocal feasting. A short mention such as the following from *Njal's Saga* is a common way for the sagas to indicate alliances: "It was Gunnar and Njal's custom, on account of their friendship, to take turns inviting each other to a winter feast."[111] Such statements carry deep implications of mutual support. The following passage concerning the friendship between Njal's family and a soon-to-be chieftain, Hoskuld of Hvítanes, explains some of these implications and perfectly demonstrates the function of reciprocal feasting in alliance building:

> The affection was so great between them all that none made any decision without consulting the others. Hoskuld lived for a long time at Ossabær while they supported each other's honor, and Njal's sons were in his company whenever he traveled. Their friendship was so strong that they exchanged autumn [harvest] feasts every year and each gave the other generous gifts.[112]

The alliance feasts commonly lasted for days or even weeks, leaving ample time for planning mutual action, but also for mutual animosity to grow. The sagas excel at describing such tensions. Returning to *Laxdæla Saga*, Olaf the Peacock and his friend Osvif are allies: "The friendship was great between Olaf and Osvif and they took turns attending each other's feasts."[113] However, despite the depth of their friendship, intrigues that develop over love and honor among their children cause the friendship to fray. Olaf the Peacock and Osvif try to sustain this friendship with reciprocal autumn feasts as the young love between their children, Kjartan Olafsson and Gudrun Osvifsdottir, goes awry when Kjartan's extended absence abroad provides space for Gudrun's father to pressure her into marrying Kjartan's friend Bolli. The reciprocal feasts, so rife with signals of prestige, now become arenas for jealousy, insults, and offended honor. Upon his return to Iceland, Kjartan first refuses to attend Osvif's feast at Laugur, but is convinced by his father to come along. At the feast, Bolli offers Kjartan a beautiful white fighting stallion and three white mares as gifts, seeking to reestablish their friendship alliance. In the first overt sign of severe enmity, Kjartan refuses the gifts. The public refusal of a friendship gift within a feasting arena is a serious matter, and the saga ominously notes, "they parted thereafter with little warmth."[114] In the next round of reciprocal feasts, the animosity increases when Kjartan insists that his new wife Hrefna be given the honor of sitting in the high-seat rather than Gudrun, who because of her high status had always been given pride of place at previous feasts.[115] An insult is then dealt back to Kjartan when his sword, given to him by the Norwegian King Olaf, is not-so-mysteriously stolen at the end of the feast. Kjartan seeks redress, but his father cautions him not to disrupt the friendship alliance. At the next feast, hosted by Osvif, a final insult is dealt when Kjartan's wedding gift to his wife, a headdress of unparalleled beauty, goes missing. Kjartan publicly accuses Osvif's household of theft. The saga notes that, "The invitations to feasts now ceased."[116] The friendship alliances between the households are finished, and the animosity soon devolves into open violent feuding that culminates in the deaths of the young leaders of both social groups, Kjartan and Bolli. In this case, the reciprocal feasts provided the social glue of friendship to the old generation, but in the next generation the feasts become a public arena for reciprocal actions of animosity driven by envy and betrayed love. In the end, though, once the feasts end, so does the peace.

Feasts of Inequality: Patron Client Feasts in Iceland

A different class of feasts visible in the *Family Sagas* are not reciprocal, but instead generate long-term asymmetrical social relationships. Oriented toward vertical social relations, these feasts are one-sided and repeatedly hosted by the person of higher status. In these *patron-role feasts*, the host aims to maintain inequalities in social power by the same operative principle of reciprocal obligation created through feasts. In this type of feasting, however, reciprocation between the chieftain and the subordinate supporter is neither expected nor possible, and therefore, the social relations remain continually inequitable.[117] This type of feast has the potential to institutionalize inequality and obligations of support for chieftains in violent and political altercations. In Iceland, chieftains held this type of feast for supporters or thingmen who were obligated to support their chieftains at political assemblies (things, or þingjar in Old Norse). In patron-role feasts, the feasting group is therefore often equivalent to the chieftain's support group. The attention paid by the Icelandic sagas to the identities of attendees of feasts and the seating arrangement of guests in relation to the chieftain bears witness to the social and political weight of attending such events.

Attendance by a farmer at a chieftain's feast, particularly at formalized ceremonial feasts, was understood as a public declaration of a chieftain-supporter relationship between the host and the attendee. *Hrafnkel's Saga* tells of a conflict between rivals Hrafnkel and Sam. Sam is a rich farmer who challenges Hrafnkel's status as chieftain. To do so he needs the backing of Hrafnkel's thingmen followers. In a moment in which Sam has the upper hand, he invites Hrafnkel's thingmen to a feast at the farm that he has recently confiscated from Hrafnkel:

Sam established his household at Aðalból after Hrafnkel's departure. Thereafter
he hosted an honorable feast and invited all those who had previously been his
[Hrafnkel's] thingmen. Sam proposed that he should be their chieftain instead
of Hrafnkel. They accepted this proposal, but feelings were mixed.[118]

Sam uses a feast to publicly signal his forceful takeover of Hrafnkel's chieftaincy.
Not all of Hrafnkel's political supporters are pleased, but they do not feel like they
have a choice. This is one of the most overt examples of formal political support
being dictated through a feast, and it indicates the occurrence of many similar
events.[119]

Patron client feasts were recurring. For example, *Valla-Ljot's Saga* presents
a recurring patron-role feast hosted by one of the most powerful chieftains
in the saga corpus, the aptly named Gudmund the Powerful (Guðmundr
dýri): "Gudmund held a well-attended feast at Möðruvellir, and Halli was there,
as he was at all the feasts that Gudmund hosted."[120] Halli and his brothers are
Gudmund's thingmen. Halli and his brothers do not reciprocate by hosting a
feast of their own. Instead, the violent and troublesome brothers form part of
Gudmund's political and military support unit. Their hierarchical relationship is
signaled and reaffirmed at each of Gudmund's unilateral feasts.

Gudmund the Powerful is a rather àtypical and immoderate chieftain who
pushes the boundaries of the power potential of leaders in Viking Age Iceland.
He is the only chieftain of the Viking Age in Iceland who, according to the sagas,
presses some of his followers into forced hospitality in a way similar to the kings
of Norway depicted in *Heimskringla*. Gudmund's practices are the subject of an
entire separate þáttr (tale), *Ofeig's Tale*, which opens with the problems that enforced feasting causes for Icelandic farmers:

> He [Gudmund] had the habit of traveling north around the district during
> the spring to meet his thingmen and discuss the management of the district
> and people's individual legal cases. Those who had not sufficiently prepared
> provisions at their farms found themselves short of supplies. He typically rode
> with thirty men and just as many horses, and stayed for seven nights.[121]

Gudmund's nickname indicates the atypical nature of his power, and significantly, the local farmers resist Gudmund's practices, albeit peacefully. In fact,
Ofeig's Tale is entirely the story of how local farmers come together to ask a local
power broker, Ofeig, to intervene on their behalf to lighten the burden imposed
by Gudmund. Ofeig gently makes the case to Gudmund, who somewhat reluctantly follows Ofeig's advice to decrease his traveling companions to ten. The
interaction causes tension as Gudmund suspects that Ofeig will challenge his
power in the region. The tale ends as the two men make an uneasy peace through

the exchange of gifts in the form of two pairs of oxen. This tale appears to be a very unusual situation of tax-like obligatory hospitality, which does not appear anywhere else in the saga corpus about Viking Age Iceland.

Materialized Hospitality: Another Politics of Food and Drink

The prominence of the politics of feasting in the diverse range of written sources is striking. The myths and sagas show the efforts taken especially by the elite—gods, kings, chieftains, prominent farmers—to signal their commensal prowess to rivals, enemies, allies, and supporters. Archaeological evidence from picture stones, runestones, graves, and settlements tells equally evocative stories of the importance of the feasting for Viking Age politics. The images from picture stones from the island of Gotland show prominent scenes of welcoming to large halls and depict ritual communal drinking. Runestones—so terse in most of their written expressions—explicitly praise leaders for generosity in provisioning their guests and followers, while also underscoring the importance of feasting during important moments such as funerals, when power transfers from one generation to the next. Elite Viking Age graves are direct materialized expressions of funerary rituals that are infinitely more complex and diverse than those described in written sources. The events visible in the graves reveal a complexity of the visceral pre-Christian expressions of resource destruction that is perhaps only approximated by Ibn Fadlan's description of the chieftain's funeral on the Volga River. Meanwhile, Scandinavian settlement sites, and particularly sites with large halls and pagan temples, offer archaeological remains accumulated over a long period that show recurring feasts in spaces designed for hosting large groups of people. In the settlement evidence, we see most clearly the evidence that lower classes would also have aspired to express their ability to be convivial hosts able to provide a setting, the food, and the drink for a memorable social event.

Feasting on Picture Stones and Runestones

Like feasts, picture stones and runestones erected in prominent locations by the elite and landowning classes signal status, commemorate the deceased, and reinforce inheritance rights. These monuments function as Viking Age billboards on which iconography and short texts offer unique windows into the cultural values of social power. The beautiful Viking Age picture stones from Gotland show cultural values in images.[122] The lower parts of the stones frequently depict exquisite ships in full sail, underscoring the economic wealth, political power, and ideological importance of seaborne voyages of raiding, trading, and migration. The images on these monuments—most of which are probably burial markers—also include depictions of hospitality and feasting. The Lärbro Tängelgårda IV picture stone shows a group of bearded feasters lifting drinking horns, probably preparing to drink in honor of the deceased at a funeral feast (Figure 4.5). In the bottom left, two men inside a structure—possibly a temporary structure erected for the funeral feast—invert their horns as if ready to dip and refill them in a large vat. If this stone shows the event that sends the dead to the next world, then the Alskog Tjängvide I stone shows the welcome a hero can expect in the next world (Figure 3.1). Here a woman, perhaps a Valkyrie, holds up a drinking horn to a warrior arriving at a hall on Odin's eight-legged horse, Sleipnir. The warrior appears already to be holding a drinking cup in his left hand, and behind the woman is a large hall—probably Valhalla—which is surely the warrior's destination. Inside a great feast awaits. At least fourteen Gotlandic picture stones show this welcome scene, sometimes with a walking rather than a mounted warrior. The recurring image might sometimes refer to hospitality in this world and other times to the welcome into the afterlife.[123] A different but related scene appears on the Levide Kyrka stone, which depicts a female figure holding a drinking horn while traveling on a horse-drawn wagon (Figure 3.2).[124] The welcoming figure can typically be identified as female based on the long dress and hair tied in a bun, but in a few examples the gender is ambiguous. This stock scene then reiterates the role of the high-status woman—whether the wife of a chieftain or one of Odin's Valkyries—as the direct dispenser of the honorary welcoming drink of a feast.[125]

Another reference to feasting in the form of a triskelion of three interlocking drinking horns appears above the mounted warrior on the Lillbjärs III stone (Figure 3.3). The same triskelion appears on a number of other picture stones, such as the pre-Viking Age Sandagårda II stone, where two figures jointly lift a cup toward the symbol (Figure 3.4).[126] Below them three figures also raise their hands and at least one drinking horn. The age of this stone indicates the depth of the Viking Age symbols of the drinking horn and the triskelion. The triskelion could reference the mead of wisdom and poetic inspiration (skáldskaparmjöðr) that Odin stole from the giant Suttung by taking three massive drinks from three enigmatically named mead horns (Óðrœrir, Boðn, and Són). The possible Odinic association of the triskelion symbol as well as the funerary association of the Gotlandic stones in general makes it likely that the welcoming scene should be interpreted in most cases as a welcome into Odin's feasting unit in Valhalla.

Runestones from the rest of Scandinavia cannot match the striking imagery preserved on the Gotlandic stones, but instead provide short texts that reinforce the importance of feasting prowess for the status of leaders. In general, only the upper and upper middle classes were commemorated on these stones.

Figure 3.1 The Gotlandic Alskog Tjängvide I picture stone showing a fully equipped ship in the bottom register and a welcoming scene at the top in which a woman offers a drinking horn to a warrior mounted on Odin's horse, Sleipnir. Behind the woman stands the hall of Valhalla where eternal feasting awaits the warrior.

Source: photo by Ola Myrin, Historiska museet/National Historical Museums, Sweden (CC BY 4.0)

Runestones were erected to signal local power, especially during times of transition, such as moments of familial inheritance or transfer of power to a new elite.[127] One of the rare ornamental depictions on Danish runestones is a triskelion of drinking horns on the Snoldelev runestone. The correlation of this symbol with wisdom and performative poetics is made more likely because

Figure 3.2 The picture stone from Levide Kyrka shows a female figure on a cart with a drinking horn, probably on the way to the afterlife.
Source: photo by Alfred Edle, Riksantikvarieämbetet, Sweden (public domain)

the commemorated individual on this stone, Gunnvald, is called a thul (*þulr*), meaning speaker, or skjald from Salhaugar.[128] Salhaugar means "Hall-mounds," which connects the formal position of skjald/or speaker and the mythical mead horns to a place of elite residence.

Contrary to the Gotlandic picture stones, which show generosity through depicting ale horns, direct references to provisioning of alcohol in runic texts on runestones are rarer. Nevertheless, the link of alcohol consumption with funerals is probably retained in the enigmatic poetic riddles on the Malt Stone in Denmark. The text has been translated in various ways, but one translation includes the following reference to funerary beer: "[he] made strong spiced beer for his beloved father. Kolfinn placed therein [in the funerary beer] happiness runes and eternal runes."[129] The Skadeberg stone from western Norway (c. 1100) is more direct in connecting funerary feasting to bands of supporters or comrades in arms: "The drinking-companions raised this stone in memory of Skardi when they drank his funeral-feast."[130]

The runestones reveal attention to feasting prowess in the epithets used for high-status individuals commemorated on the stones. Rather than references to

Figure 3.3 The Lillbjärs III stone shows a warrior being welcomed with a mead horn. Visible above the horse's head is a symbol known as the triskelion, which consists of three interlocking drinking horns.

Source: photo by Gabriel Hildebrand, Historiska museet/National Historical Museums, Sweden (CC BY 4.0)

alcohol provisioning, the runic inscriptions stress generalized generous food distribution. The convention was to highlight a person's generosity through an expression of liberality with food such as *góðr matar* (good with food), *mildr matar* (generous with food), or *maðr matar* (man of food), which bear the meaning of generous with food. In her survey of 2,307 runic inscriptions, Birgit Sawyer found that 330 of these contained epithets and that 15 of those were references to such generosity with food.[131] This considerable number is second only to

Figure 3.4 Feasters raising a cup to the triskelion symbol on the Sandagårda II picture stone.

Source: photo by employee of Historiska museet/National Historical Museums, Sweden (CC BY 4.0)

epithets that refer to social status with some elaboration of the term *góðr* (good), which appears in 263 of the 330 epithets. The Sövestad 2 stone in Scania includes the following inscription, "Tonna placed this stone in memory of Bram, her husband, and (so did) Asgaut, his son. He was the best of estate-holders and the most generous with food."[132] The claim to generosity read from bottom to top is placed prominently and centrally on the stone, showing the importance of this feasting potential to elite morality and social power.[133] Another stone from Småland in Sweden links the commensal generosity to personal followers: "Vemund placed this stone . . . his brother Svein, gentle with his followers and free with food, greatly praised."[134] Neatly then, while the Gotlandic picture stones refer to the feast in the afterlife primarily through depictions of the drinking horns and cups, the runes carved on stones on the mainland praise the feast of this world by reference to elite generosity with food.

Feasting in Graves

The written sources as well as the picture stones and runestones indicate that Viking Age Scandinavians held feasts at funeral sites, at cultic sites, and in domestic (mostly elite) halls. Viking graves—treated in more detail in Chapter 4—include both evidence of actual feasts as well as symbolic feasts in which the deceased will participate for eternity in the afterlife. Graves provide critical information on the symbolic importance of feasting, as well as practical insights into the types of foods and beverages served. Excavation of pre-Christian graves has yielded impressive objects used for conspicuous consumption during the feast. The most diagnostic of such artifacts consist of drinking equipment found in pre-Christian graves. These include objects used to drink alcohol, like drinking horns, glass beakers, cups, and mixing bowls. Other objects found in graves were used for showing and consuming food, like elite ceramic tableware, roasting spits, metal plates, and silverware.

Elite ship burials are some of the most iconic of all archaeological discoveries of the Viking Age. Evidence of the symbolic feast as well as funerary feasting abounds within and besides these magnificent burials. Ship graves—like those found at Ladby in Denmark and Oseberg in Norway—contain particularly striking evidence of the symbolic feast, animal sacrifice, and the consumption of alcohol and meat.

Sometime in the early to mid-tenth century, a group of mourners dragged a 21.5 m longship up the hill at Ladby from the banks of Kerteminde Fjord on the Danish island of Fyn.[135] After interring the ship in a prepared pit so the gunwales lay below the ground level, the mourners carried out extensive funerary rituals before enclosing the dead person and a rich grave assemblage within a chamber created by laying a wooden covering across the entire ship. Over the ship they constructed a mound with strips of turf and encircled the mound with large wooden posts positioned 15 m from the center of the ship. The funeral took time—days or weeks. Burnt bone, charcoal, and fragments of broken pottery found in the bottom of the grave chamber and within the mound itself are most likely the remnants of a funerary feast purposefully incorporated into the grave mound.[136] Cereal grains, including oats and other grains, were also spread within the chamber. Whether these grains were symbolic, or part of funerary feasting, or intended as animal fodder is unclear. The funeral also involved the sacrifice of eleven horses and four or five dogs, all interred at the front of the ship. These animals may have been killed with an axe that lay beside the horse skeletons, but the animals do not show any sign of butchering for meals. Instead, the sacrificed animals signaled very high status of a martial nature. The horses were of various ages and both sexes, and the horse closest to the center of the ship was interred wearing one of four sets of riding gear, suggesting that this was the chieftain's own riding horse. Three of the dog skeletons were of a robust type similar to Greenlandic sled dogs, while a fourth was a smaller terrier-like dog. An elaborate dog harness found in the grave suggests that four of the larger dog types made up the chieftain's hunting dogs. The human body and the greatest portion of the grave assemblage were placed toward the ship's stern, behind the mast.[137]

Among the grave goods were a number of martial items—a shield, a sword hilt, a bundle of forty-five arrows—that have been used to suggest that the buried individual was male. Also among these goods are several examples of tableware employed in serving and presenting feasting food and drink, including two iron-plated buckets, a silver plate, a bronze dish, and a pair of fine knives. One of the large buckets—40 cm tall and circa 50 cm in diameter—was made of oak wood covered in panels of decorated iron with mountings for iron handle rings. The second bucket of yew wood is of a very rare type that was probably imported. The shallow silver plate, measuring 15 cm diameter with gilding and interlacing decorations on the collar, was also imported, probably from the Anglo-Irish area of the British Isles. Perhaps used to hold the host in Christian liturgical services, the plate was repurposed for aristocratic dining in Scandinavia, where it would recall international connections and probably success in raiding, since silver plates from churches were rarely given away voluntarily. The scattered remains of two larger bronze dishes had also been placed beside the deceased. Analytical techniques—X-ray fluorescence, instrumental neutron activation analysis, and atomic absorption spectrometry—revealed nearly identical elemental compositions with high levels of tin in fragments that clearly derived from two different vessels as shown by decorative differences on the rims and variable rim diameters 15 and 25 cm. The levels of tin indicate an origin from Anglo-Saxon England, while the similarity in elemental composition suggest that these bronze vessels used for food and/or drink were crafted in the same workshop. Finally, two distinctively slender iron knives with silver inlay and handle decoration had been placed together with a silver spoon in a wooden box, also possibly decorated with silver. These knives, which are nearly unique in Scandinavia, were part of the chieftain's formal feasting utensils. All these objects of the feast were fragmented and difficult to piece together because they had been purposefully dismantled already in the Viking Age.

Not many years after the deposition of the Ladby ship, people broke into the grave in an effort that would have taken days and been publicly visible. They dug from the side of the mound approaching the ship's port side. Appearing to understand the layout of the burial, they targeted the back area that contained the chieftain and his most personal items. Once they broke through the wooden covering that was still intact, they may have looted a few weapons that are expected in male ship graves, such as a sword and a battle axe. The body itself appears to have been dismantled and strewn across the open chamber where scattered pieces of human bone were recovered during excavation. The digging disturbed and redistributed the burnt animal bone and ceramic cooking pots within the chamber and earth of the mound. Significantly, the feasting equipment appears to have been especially targeted for violence and destruction since the silver plate, the bronze dish, and the two imported buckets were found in small pieces strewn widely across the back and middle of the ship. Whoever broke into this grave did so to do violence to the key aspects of social power represented in the burial. The looters attacked the grave mound itself as a visible reminder of the chieftain's power. They attacked the ship, a symbol of the chieftain's earthly power and probably his vehicle to the next world. Symbols of his martial status on which much of his earthly power rested, including his sword, axe, and stirrups, were either taken or in the case of the sword and one of the stirrups thrown about the ship's deck. The symbols of his feasting prowess suffered most in the attack as these items were mostly intently dismantled and most widely strewn across the ship.

The ship grave at Oseberg in Norway provides even clearer material reference to feasting prowess, especially since wooden objects were spectacularly preserved in the underlying clay and turf of the burial mound.[138] In the summer of 834, about a century before the Ladby funeral, mourners dragged a beautifully decorated 21-meter-long ship up from a navigable stream 4 km from the western side of the Oslo Fjord in Norway. They rolled the ship into a dug hollow in the clay before beginning an elaborate season of performative ritual that lasted several months, eventually resulting in an elaborate archaeological assemblage of humans, animals, and rich grave goods. The funeral created three distinct areas aboard the ship. A tent-shaped wooden chamber constructed in the center of the ship held the bodies of two women and items of an elite bedroom, including two beds with down- and feather-filled bedding, two standing looms, decorated tapestries, and wooden bowls and ladles for drinking. Here, too, other personal possessions were kept in up to eight wooden chests and buckets containing food items such as grain, blueberries, and wild apples. Four posts with evocative animal heads attached to iron ringed rattles were attached to the chamber, perhaps in reference to the specialist ritual power of one or both women buried within the chamber. Behind the chamber, a full kitchen was outfitted, and a cow was sacrificed in reference to the ideal feasting food. The items in the Oseberg kitchen, which compare favorably to later medieval upper-class Norwegian castle kitchen inventories, included three large iron cauldrons, an iron cauldron tripod with a suspension chain, an iron frying pan, two axes, three knives, a millstone for grain, four wooden troughs, wooden ladles, dishes, drinking bowls, at least five buckets, a barrel, a cheese strainer, and a kitchen bench. These utilitarian kitchen items mostly stress food production rather than food consumption. The barrels represent stored food, while the troughs represent food production—as exemplified by a baker's trough containing rye flour. Yet, some of the finely decorated bowls, ladles, and dishes were intended for public drinking and are similar in form to later Norwegian examples known to be used as beer bowls.[139] The front third of the ship between the prow and the burial chamber contained the largest quantity of grave goods in several complex layers representing multiple phases of funerary ritual. This front portion contained several beautiful vehicles for travel including an exquisitely ornate wagon, four sleighs, as well as three travel tents. The sense of a long voyage was completed by heaping these objects on the ship that was prepared for departure with all the rigging ready to set sail, a raised mast, and multiple oars positioned in their oar holes. Here, too, ten decapitated horses, three dogs, and the severed head of a large ox were carefully placed on a bed designed for travel. Right outside of the front third of the ship lay three additional decapitated horses and a beheaded cow.

The assemblage within the Oseberg ship was carefully structured in a way that mimics the rooms of a traditional elite longhouse.[140] Food storage and production were located out of sight in the back of the house behind the private chambers, while the front of the house was often the large public feasting hall. The foredeck of the ship may therefore logically have been the site of communal feasting displays during the long funeral. Such an interpretation finds support in the phases of the mound's construction. The back of the mound—constructed of a dark turf—was built first to cover the stern of the ship, including the kitchen area and right up to the front gable of the tent-like wooden chamber. Spring flowers found underneath these turf layers show the season of construction. It was not until several months later that the front part of the ship was covered in a lighter turf, probably in late September as indicated by autumn flowers found beneath this construction phase. This means that at least four months passed during which the foredeck of the ship was exposed and entry into the private burial chamber was possible. In the chamber, items of the feast have also been found, including wooden drinking vessels, fragments of a ceramic bowl, and a barrel containing a decorated drinking bowl that surely would have originally held the funeral ale.[141] The grave goods and sacrificed animals on the foredeck bear witness to the protracted and repeated ritual performances. At the funerary feasting, the two deceased women lay as symbolic hosts within the burial chamber that remained open but also covered in earth, placing the women in the liminal space between life and death. When the last ritual was over, the chamber was closed and the rest of the mound constructed over the prow of the ship.

Like the Ladby grave, the Oseberg grave was also violently and publicly opened during the Viking Age in order to assault the symbols of power within. The symbols of power were similar in many ways in both mounds, although we can see that the Ladby burial highlights warrior ethos and items of food consumption, while the Oseberg grave lays more weight on food production. In their assault on the Oseberg mound, the grave robbers dug a 2–3-meter-wide and 10-meter-long trench from the south side of the mound toward the middle. They cut down the ship prow's serpentine ornamentation before entering the foredeck and smashing a hole in the intact grave chamber. Here they broke apart most of the chests and removed costly items, including any potential vessels of feasting display. The typical personal adornments of the high-status females—jewelry and other items of public display—are also absent. The bodies of the females were themselves desecrated, torn apart, and thrown into the looters' trench in front of the chamber. The remaining skeletal elements have been examined multiple times, with the most recent analysis estimating that the older woman was at least eighty years old and suffered from gigantism, which would have made her look and sound more masculine. She appears to have died of cancer, probably ruling out an old theory that she could have been sacrificed to accompany the younger woman. The younger woman, who may have been around fifty at death, may have been a servant to the high-status older woman, but this is uncertain, especially as cause of death could not be determined from the meager skeletal elements that remain from the younger woman. Isotopic analysis of the bones of both women yielded similarly low ratios of carbon-13 (^{13}C) to carbon-12 (^{12}C) that result from having eaten primarily terrestrial plants and animals rather than marine foods.[142] Such diets, including relatively large quantities of terrestrial meat and grain as opposed to fish, are consistent with the high-status diets described in the written sources. Dental wear on the teeth of the younger woman also indicates the probable use of iron toothpicks, a feature often associated with high-status dining practices. The political context of the looting has been wonderfully illuminated by recent dendrochronological work on digging tools left by the looters in their open trench.[143] The assault on the grave took place between 953 and 975, during a time when historical sources indicate that the Danish King Harald Bluetooth was extending his power over this region of Norway (see Chapter 5). Harald may then have orchestrated a public performance of destroying the monument of the old entrenched Norwegian elites, as well as the symbols of power held therein.

A final example from Swordle Bay in northwestern Scotland illustrates display of feasting prowess at one rung lower on the social ladder.[144] Although the objects in this tenth-century grave are fewer and of lesser value, they still echo the same key representations of Viking Age prowess in nautical travel, warfare, production of food and drink, and feasting. The burial took place in a small rowboat (5.1 m long) rather than a large ship. The mound was low, and the funeral—although surely dramatic—included a fraction of the wealth investment of the graves at Ladby and Oseberg. But this burial was intact, meaning that the personal items stolen from the larger Scandinavian burial mounds were found in situ at Swordle Bay. A sword and an axe on the left side of the body reduplicate the ideal warrior ethos. A hammer, tongs, and a large iron ladle (27 cm diameter) for serving drink were positioned above the head of the deceased. Within the ladle were found organic remnants of food. Placed on the deceased's right side, a sickle represented fertility in the harvest, while a drinking horn symbolized the consumption of alcohol at feasts. Finally, a shield and a purposefully broken spear were thrown into the top of the partially closed grave in an act of ritual closing.

The prominence of archaeological remains of feasting in elite graves correlates well with the written sources, which show the importance of feasting for the gods and legendary heroes in the myths and for the chieftains and kings in the sagas. The discussion of the material evidence of feasting in graves in this section has focused on the richest class of burials in the Viking world. Certainly, the feast as a political tool was particularly vital for the ruling classes. But the nature of our sources—both textual and archaeological—makes the elite more visible than the lower classes. For instance, the graves of the average villagers and inhabitants of the nascent Viking Age towns contain few grave goods that might be used to interpret the importance of feasting.[145] This is not to say that the middle classes, or even lower middle classes, did not engage in the social strategies of commensal politics and reciprocal provisioning of food and drink. Rather, it means that the symbolic value of the feast—seen both in the written sources and represented in the carefully orchestrated burial events—was especially fundamental for the elite in structuring power in the Viking world.

Feasting in Settlements: Halls and Cult Sites

Studies of domestic settlements provide a balance to the idealized pictures presented in graves. Graves are carefully constructed theatrical and symbolic statements of power that provide compelling evidence of feasting in the form of sacrificed animals and museum-worthy artifacts. Archaeology of settlement sites, in contrast to burial archaeology, deals with spaces that people occupied continually and used daily. Fewer deposits are symbolically constructed.

Instead, the finds are largely discarded as trash or accidentally lost. This often makes the archaeological correlates of feasting more difficult to identify as they are subsumed within the long-term accumulation of daily life. One approach to detecting feasting in settlement sites relies on identifying special deposits where objects for feasts or animal bones are treated in an unusual manner or found in a special location. Found individually concentrated in certain houses, elite table-ware and drinking vessels, like horns with intricate mounts or delicate imported glass cups can help pinpoint specific households that engaged in public display during meals. Arenas for feasts can also be located based on concentrations of feasting waste from beer brewing or large concentrations of animal bone. At times we also get lucky, as did excavators of eleventh-century Sigtuna when they found a pig bone that bears a satisfied runic statement: "good beer."[146] Here was a happy feaster.

Out of political necessity, Viking Age elites engaged in feasting on a larger scale than did the rest of the population. Feasting is therefore mostly archae-ologically identifiable at elite settlements. The power of the elite in the Viking Age encompassed control over land, labor, craft production, exchange, and monumental display. This control conferred increased feasting potential that is visible archaeologically in special types or quantities of food and drink, expen-sive items for consumption of food and drink, and magnificent buildings for hosting banquets. For instance, as has been suggested throughout this chapter, the Viking Age elite shared a dietary profile that focused on the consumption of meat.[147] The focus on meat as a food especially suited for special socially charged occasions is detectable by scientific analyses. A comparative study that extracted lipids from pottery from Swedish graves and settlements revealed that meat was nearly ubiquitous on ceramics from funerary contexts (91%), but not from ceramics used in daily food preparation where vegetables were dominant and meat appeared in combination with vegetables as would be ex-pected in stews. In other words, meat was associated with special occasions, such as feasts and funerals.[148] The elite meat consumption sometimes included special rare animals, but mostly centered on large, domesticated animals, like cattle and pigs. Consumption of large domesticates is difficult at the scale of a single domestic household. Cattle, for example, yield up to 200 kg of meat.[149] Communal feasting facilitated the consumption of this meat, storing the wealth as social obligations.

At times, however, archaeologists have located evidence of nearly ubiquitous feasting across society. One potential archaeological signal of beer-brewing for feasts is the presence of large deposits of fire-cracked rocks in mounds or pits. According to long-lasting practices still recalled in mid-nineteenth-century Norway, these stones—often called "beer stones"—were heated before being deposited in large wooden barrels to boil water for beer brewing.[150] After use

in brewing they were discarded in midden layers and probably sometimes conspicuously piled up over time to display feasting prowess. A careful strategy of
survey and test excavation in the Trondelag region of Norway showed that nearly
all (over 90%) of the known farms in selected coastal and inland areas showed
evidence of beer-brewing on a significant scale in the form of dense layers of
brewing stones.[151] Radiocarbon dating of the midden layers containing these
stones yielded dates from 600 to 1600, showing that the practice began around
600 and disappeared when metal vats for boiling water became widely available
after the end of the Middle Ages. Fire-cracked rock could also be used for baking
meat in pits dug in the ground, but the author of this study argues that the larger
and more thoroughly cracked stones, such as those encountered in Trondelag,
are more likely to derive from beer brewing than food preparation. Both these
strategies utilizing hot rocks would have been meant for preparation of large
quantities of beer and/or meat. The survey results from the Trondelag farms are
significant because it suggests that a broad spectrum of society engaged in commensal hospitality. These feasts are likely to have been rare and special occasions,
like weddings and funerals, and may have been politically very modest in scope.
Although these are noteworthy results, we cannot say how common these feasts
were, and we certainly cannot say that this type of ubiquity is present in other
parts of the Viking world.

The pre-Viking date of circa 600 appears to mark a shift in cooking and eating
conventions. This shift brought new aspects of elite feasting practices that continued into the Viking Age. At this time, cooking in open-air pit sites decreased
and shifted into settlements where the elite could extend control. Evidence of a
shift in food preparation and feast setting is evident from the traces of cooking
pits at the Norwegian site of Guåker in Hedmark, where sporadic feasts are apparent from proliferation of cooking pits dating to the period before 700. The
author suggests that the feasts held at this open-air site far from any farmstead
functioned to enhance community solidarity.[152] After 700, the cooking evidence
is more sporadic as the events probably shifted into settlements under the more
direct auspices of leaders.

New kitchen utensils also appeared in the century before the Viking Age as the
communal feast shifted increasingly into the elite leader's personal hall. Food-
preparation utensils that highlighted the visual and auditory aspects of food
preparation—such as iron roasting spits and frying pans—proliferated, while
baking in inconspicuous subterranean pits decreased.[153] Within the confines of
the hall, the point was to see and hear the meat sizzling over the fire. Roasting
meat, a preparation strategy that requires fresh meat, is wasteful in terms of
both the caloric value and fuel usage when compared to baking or boiling. The
implements used for roasting and frying were designed to display status, and,
just as they began to be used within the hall, they proliferate in elite graves. These

costly food-preparation items and strategies functioned as diacritical devices that separated the elite from the non-elite.

Elite settlements exhibit evidence for feasting that is tied both to political power and to pre-Christian cultic activity, as suggested by the written sources. A basic organizational pattern at elite sites includes a fence or palisade enclosing a large domestic house and a cult building. The century leading up to the Viking Age witnessed an increased privatization of the feast inside elite farmsteads, and specifically within elite-controlled halls and associated special buildings that appear to have had pre-Christian cult associations. The hall—a large, ostentatious house with a room for hosting visitors and supporters—is in fact the clearest indicator of elite presence within a settlement.[154] The halls were commonly the centerpiece of elite settlements where the occupant of the hall sponsored feasts, controlled craft production and trade, and housed attached retinue. In marginal places, like Iceland, as will be seen below, the scale of society meant that some of these functions were minimized. Most often, ancillary structures for storage, craft production, and habitation are also located within the elite site enclosures. Most of these elite sites have a trajectory that stretches back into the pre-Viking period, showing a significant continuity of places of power, both political and ideological. The sites, which often include pre-Christian elements in their place name, are frequently abandoned around or right after the conversion to Christianity, showing both the importance of the link between pre-Christian religion and political power, as well as the tendency for a shift in the location of political power during the co-evolving processes of state formation and Christianization around the turn of the millennium.

The Swedish island of Helgö (Holy Island), which lies to the west of modern Stockholm in Lake Mälaren, was an elite habitation site with evidence of feasting, cult practice, and craft production stretching from the fifth to the tenth century.[155] Lake Mälaren was open to the Baltic Sea in the Viking Age, giving Helgö direct access to the sea-routes of the wider Viking world. The site's zenith came in the centuries immediately prior to the Viking Age, but cult practices including feasting continued into the Viking Age. Excavations over twenty-five seasons unearthed eight occupation areas (or Building Groups) and six cemeteries, but one specific area, Building Group 2, was clearly the dominant location of the elite. Here excavations revealed multiple phases of large dwelling halls measuring up to 35 m in length (Building Group 2: Terrace III) located beside a series of smaller (c. 20 m long) and sturdily constructed buildings (Building Group 2: Terrace I). The impressive buildings on Terrace III could accommodate large gatherings. Particularly noteworthy are the arrangements of internal posts in the houses that immediately predate the Viking Age, which were designed to create a large open room in the east end of the house. The smaller structures on Terrace I have been interpreted as multiple phases of a long-lasting pre-Christian cult building or temple. From the beginning, the distinct phases of the temple, which contained a spectacular array of finds that indicate religious cult purposes, was constructed with widely spaced posts on the western end to create a large meeting room. Recovery of over two dozen guldgubber (i.e., gold foils with figurines linked to fertility worship across Scandinavia) shows cult practice in the period immediately before the Viking Age, while Thor's hammer amulets, amulet rings, and miniature sickles (fertility symbols) support that the temple was used into the Viking Age. Also, from within the temple were objects for feasting, including elite drinking wares in the form of imported eighth-century reticella glass cups, ninth-century glass funnel beakers, and bronze cups and ladles. Together, over 1,500 glass shards from drinking vessels were recovered from the general temple area in Building Group 2.[156]

The finds from Helgö also include objects obtained by raiding or trading from three continents: a sixth-century Buddha figurine from what is today Pakistan, an Irish bishop's crozier from the early ninth century, and a Coptic bronze ladle (Figure 3.5). The Buddha figurine was already an antique when, as suggested by its find associations, it was hung by a strap from the external gable end of the temple structure. The objects found in association with the temple not only point toward elite status and use in feasting, but hint also at a gift-giving economy in which visiting elites might present the local leader with prestige items acquired through trade (e.g., the Buddha figurine) or through raiding (e.g., the Irish bishop's crozier). They highlight the prowess of leaders engaging in ideal Viking activities abroad. The gifts bestowed were key tokens of friendship and memorials of the feast during which they were given. This explains why the gifts given at feasts in the written sources are not only expensive but typically have a character that allows them to be prominently displayed in public, such as for example weapons, items of dress, or the exceptionally rare objects found at Helgö, rather than items that are tucked away out of site or passed on or consumed quickly (e.g., coins and inconspicuous foods). The objects become inalienable symbols of a personal relationship, worn to signal and recall the alliance. The items such as the decorated gold foil guldgubber found in both the domestic dwellings and the temple building might visually represent specific lineages or regional chieftaincies that could be commemorated at future feasts if hung on the wall or on centrally located posts. The latter case is supported by excavations where the guldgubber are found beside or within post holes, perhaps having originally been displayed prominently on posts or walls to signal alliances while also linking different social groups to the fertility rituals enacted as part of the feasts.

Atop a man-made platform (Terrace 4) around a distinctive stone ledge 20 m to the east of the temple at Helgö, thick cultural layers dating from the third to the ninth century cover a vast area that is topped by a triangular stone setting.[157] This was the location of open-air feasting, as indicated by in-situ fireplaces and large

Figure 3.5 These two objects, a figurine of Buddha from sixth-century Pakistan and an Irish crozier head from c. 800, were both found in association with a pre-Christian cult building at the Swedish site of Helgö. This building was the structural culmination of a long sequence of cult-related feasting halls located on the same terrace and stretching back into the 400s. Black scale boxes are 1 cm long.
Source: photos by Ola Myrin, Historiska museet/National Historical Museums, Sweden (CC BY 4.0)

quantities of fire-cracked rock. A nearby enclosure with no buildings but very elevated phosphate levels measured in the soil may have been the site of ritual animal sacrifice. Feasting on animals at this open-air site is further witnessed by the recovery of 120 kg of cremated and uncremated animal bone; this amounts to over half of the animal bone excavated at the entire Helgö site.[158] Carbonized bread also found here in greater quantities than elsewhere on the site provides further support of commensal gatherings. Links to a bread-fertility cult is additionally suggested by the purposeful placement of carbonized bread in pits and graves, as well as deposits of fragments of clay ovens and quern stones at the open-air site.

The ritual continuity at Helgö is striking, but certain key changes also point toward shifts in the locations and the character of feasting and ritual from the pre-Viking to the Viking periods. Over time, the center of the cult activity—including feasting—shifted away from the domestic dwelling site on Terrace 3 and the open-air site on Terrace 4 and into the cult building on Terrace 1. The buildings on Terrace 3 up until 600 were extravagantly large and contained objects of ritual significance such as gold foil guldgubber. Thereafter the size of the buildings and finds became more mundane just as the temple on Terrace 1 was being elaborated and the ritual objects therein were exploding in number and quality. Rituals at the open-air site continued into the Viking Age but decreased in importance and were discontinued in the ninth century, some time before the end of cult activity at the temple. This might be just a locational shift, or it might be related to a Viking Age trend toward locating cult inside social spaces that were more controllable by elites. This trend reached an apex in the hierarchical Christian church buildings. But Helgö and its prominence was a pagan phenomenon, and its importance did not extend into the time of the arrival of Christianity.

Another elite site linking prominent pagan cult practice and feasting was discovered beside the appropriately pagan-sounding lake of Tissø (Tyr's Lake) in Denmark. This site belongs to a class of elite residences characterized by large halls paired with probable temples and enclosed by fences or palisades. This type of elite residence has been found at several places in Scandinavia, including the Danish sites of Lisbjerg and Erritså in Jutland and Toftegård and Tissø on Sjælland, as well as at Järrestad in Scania, Sweden.[159] Of these, Tissø provides probably the clearest example and will be used here to exemplify the pattern of sites that were founded in the sixth to seventh century and lasted until around 1000 with the advent of Christianity.[160] The first manifestation of the elite residence that included a large hall (43 m long) and a smaller structure with its own enclosure grew in the sixth century to be three times larger than the normal contemporary Danish farm. After the farm burned around 700, a new farmstead with similar layout developed to the south. This later farm had two main phases, the first dating to the eighth to ninth century, and the second to the tenth century.

The eighth- to ningh-century settlement at Tissø consisted of a large hall (c. 35 m long) and a separately enclosed cult building or temple. The hall appears to have been divided into a public feasting/assembly area in the eastern half and private quarters in the western end. Artifacts related to feasting found in the eastern part of the hall include elite drinking vessels and a tuning-peg from a lyre, which was no doubt used to entertain revelers with poetic songs such as those recalled in the literature. A large quantity of animal bones, including special elite food animals like osprey and spoonbill birds, was also recovered in the eastern half of the hall and interpreted as evidence of communal feasting. The sheer volume of animal bones recovered—over 200 kg—was interpreted by the excavators as evidence of feasting. In noteworthy contrast, the western part of the hall where the chieftain had his private quarters was nearly devoid of animal bones and elite drinking vessels. Just to the northwest of the hall, excavators found a pile of several cubic meters of fire-cracked stone with no charcoal or charring. As was the case with the fire-cracked rocks from the Norwegian study in Trondelag, such stones, especially when they are not associated with charcoal, suggest use in brewing beer. The probable temple building, which was accessible only through the hall building, was devoid of animal bones, a hearth, and drinking vessels, indicating that the feasts at Tissø were centered in the hall rather than the temple. But inside the enclosure around the temple, elevated phosphate levels may indicate animal sacrifices with large quantities of spilled blood. Evidence of ritualized feasting comes from a long row of thirty-four cooking pits that extend south in a straight line for 80 m from the southeast corner of the temple enclosure. Finally, in the northwest corner of the larger farm enclosure, a small pit house was positioned next to a thick layer of charcoal and bone that contained atypically pristine objects such as strike-a-lights and sickles, which the excavator felt were sacrificially deposited. In fact, the site in general appears to be sacrificial in nature with large quantities of weapons being destroyed and purposefully deposited in the lake, which is of course connected by its name to the god Tyr.

In the tenth century, the Tissø elite-ritual complex retained the same basic layout within the fenced farmstead, while both the hall and the temple were transformed in ways that impacted the visibility of communal rituals at the site (Figure 3.6). The hall was refashioned to a larger scale measuring circa 40 m in length. The new hall was given a larger, unobstructed space in the interior by replacing the two rows of internal roof-supporting posts of the three-aisled building with external diagonal support posts. This shift followed a general shift in the tenth century at elite sites, especially those connected with the formation of the Danish state (see Chapter 5). The cult space was reshaped as well to make the temple more impressive and to transform the interrelationship between the hall and the temple. First, the temple was rebuilt as a square building with large corner posts, probably supporting a higher roof. Second, the fence or palisade surrounding the temple was altered so that it did not directly abut the large dwelling hall. Perhaps this slight decoupling of the hall from the specialized ritual structure reflects a change in ritual practice. By the end of the tenth century, the enclosure disappeared altogether, opening religious performance to a larger audience.

Excavations at a growing number of elite settlements across Scandinavia are revealing a similar settlement organization as the Tissø complex. A few particularly interesting aspects are worth drawing out to show some of the variations at such sites and the individual signals of feasting that are identifiable. For instance, the sequence of main halls (37–40 m in length) from Toftegård stretching from the seventh to the tenth century revealed the characteristic elite items of gold foil figurines (guldgubber), weapons, as well as Anglo-Saxon and Carolingian imported glass drinking ware. Three phases of smaller enclosed probable cult

Figure 3.6 The elite settlement at Lake Tissø in Denmark in the tenth century with a large elite hall and a separately enclosed square temple building.
Source: courtesy of Ragnar L. Børsheim, Arkikon AS

buildings at Toftegård are paired with these halls as are three distinct clusters of a considerable number of pits filled with fire-cracked stones. At Järrestad in Sweden, one of the Viking Age phases showed a main hall connected to a probable temple by an enclosure. Inside the enclosure higher phosphate levels may relate to animal sacrifice. In a nearby hollow, 60 m³ of fire-cracked rock was found, again probably relating to beer production and/or large-scale meat preparation. A special aspect at Järrestad includes presence of sacrificial wells into which significant but less meat-rich portions of sacrificed animals were deposited, such as heads and limbs of horses, cattle, sheep, and pigs. The torsos were no doubt saved for consumption by the feasters.

The elite sites addressed in this section show evidence of the convergence of chiefly power and pre-Christian religion. None of the sites in this section are mentioned in medieval texts, yet they are nexuses of political and ideological power. They all exhibit a deep continuity of place and a continuity of the main buildings: halls and temples. The shapes of buildings may change slightly, and new innovations may arrive, such as the external lean-to posts at Tissø, but their placement remains the same. Despite the centuries of continuity, stretching back to the Roman Iron Age (AD 1–500) in the case of Helgö, these types of sites mostly disappear with the arrival of Christianity when the landscape of power was transformed. A few sites, such as the royal site of Jelling that we will encounter in later chapters, were Christianized and played pivotal roles in the formation of the nascent Scandinavian states. But the sites that did not become incorporated into the new Christian system were forgotten and leave only their archaeological traces and echoes in place names. These traces show the deep-rooted pre-Christian elements of chiefly power. Their disappearance coincides with the dramatic changes indicated by the medieval texts that willfully forget the earlier power centers. Here then is a prime example of the complementary nature of written sources and archaeology.

Maintaining the Ideal Feasts at the Diasporic Margins: An Interdisciplinary Story from Iceland

The written sources and the archaeological evidence show that Viking ideals of social interchange and especially the expression of power involve food, drink, and an appropriate setting for feasting. In this chapter's final section, we turn to an example from Iceland that demonstrates both the complementarity of archaeology and texts as well as the extraordinary efforts made by Viking Age leaders to sustain the tradition-mandated feasts. Viking seafarers arrived in Iceland in the late ninth century and encountered an unoccupied landscape (Chapter 6 focuses on the Viking experience in Iceland and the North Atlantic). They found a variety of ecosystems, including sheltered fjords and ample pasturage. At the same time, this sub-arctic island exposed the settlers to new environmental constraints that meant that some subsistence adaptations from Scandinavia were harder to maintain. Among these were the larger meat-producing animals—pigs and cattle—that in Iceland were far beyond their original homelands in the Near East. Cultivating any sort of grain became much more difficult. The birch forests there were extensive, but the utility of the timber in constructing large buildings and ships was very limited. The distances to mainland Europe also meant that the trade became more costly. These new limitations on products utilized by Viking Age Scandinavians had implications not only for their subsistence economics, but also for their political economics that included a decreased availability of the goods used to sustain feasting. The Viking settlers of Iceland brought with them their ideals concerning the essential role of feasting. With this came the need to obtain the products consumed during feasts, despite the limitations imposed by the harsh environment and a relative isolation from mainland Europe. In this environment, chieftains found it increasingly difficult to acquire the resources to construct large houses and the basic feasting food and drink necessary for political action.

Icelandic feasts described in the sagas served to create alliances, build chiefly coalitions, and provide an arena for competitive displays of generosity and conspicuous consumption. The sagas also describe the feast settings and sometimes even the efforts undertaken by hosts to acquire food and drink. These descriptions can be supplemented by traditional information from archaeo-logical excavations of households. Moreover, advances in the archaeological sciences and in sampling strategies mean that we know much more about the consumption patterns of the Viking Age Icelanders. This final section examines three aspects of feasting in early Iceland that can be analyzed both through the written sources and the archaeological evidence. First, the house as the lo-cation of the feast. Second, the meat eaten during the feast. Third, the alcohol consumed. Comparing the variability of these aspects of feasting at the house-hold level shows how individuals created and maintained a stratified society in Iceland and thereby further illuminates how feasting functioned as a key founda-tional pillar of Viking Age social structure.

The Family Sagas reveal the importance and the challenges for chieftains in Iceland who sought to retain the feasting prowess of their forebears in Scandinavia. The heavy costs of a feast are evident in many of the examples provided above in the section on the feasts in the sagas. For instance, Unn the Deep Minded carefully plans the season of Olaf Feilan's wedding feast to coincide with the time of plenty around the slaughter season. Olaf the Peacock and his half-brothers let nearly a year go by to hold their father's me-morial feast so that they will have time to gather supplies. And Gudmund's thingmen cannot sustain the economic production necessary for his chiefly aspirations.

The saga feasts that include copious drinking suggest that grain was a major limiting resource, while the coincidence of feasts with slaughtering season indicates that meat from domesticated animals was a preferred feast dish. These are of course also the resources described in the mythological sources—both po-etry and prose—as the ideal feasting products. The North Atlantic environment presented new difficulties for the acquisition of the ideal feasting products, espe-cially grain for alcohol and cattle and pork for meat. The sagas show this strain as well as the careful calculus necessary for the transformation of economic goods into social power.

Characteristically, *Laxdæla Saga* is perfectly overt on the role of feasting and refreshingly clear on the powerful role of women. Toward the end of the saga, the wise and dangerous Gudrun Osvifsdottir advises Thorkel, her chieftain husband, to save no expense in hosting a winter feast:

> He [Thorkel] hosted a Yule-drinking feast at Helgafell, and a large number of people attended. He showed great magnificence with everyone that winter. Gudrun did not resist and said that this was what wealth was for—to increase prestige; and that the resources should be made available that Gudrun needed to make an extravagant display.[161]

The point of wealth for a chieftain was to generate prestige. The problem for chieftains in the North Atlantic was that wealth was not always easily sustained, a fact that will be made dramatically obvious from the saga examples and archaeological evidence.

Halls as Feast Settings in Iceland and the Example of the Excavated House at Hrísbrú

Iceland offers a unique potential to investigate feasting on the level of the individual households because of the rich saga descriptions of rural life combined with particular archaeological conditions that have led to intact Viking Age floor layers lying preserved beneath collapsed turf roofs in a still mostly rural landscape. This section draws on the results of my own fieldwork in Iceland to provide an example of how feasting functioned as a prime motivator of economic and political decision-making for the Viking Age elite. As the field director of the Mosfell Archaeological Project (MAP) I worked for over a decade together with a team directed by Jesse Byock to investigate a chieftain's farmstead at Hrísbrú in the Mosfell Valley, located just northeast of Reykjavík (Figures 3.7 and 3.8). Over the years we uncovered the remains of a tenth- to eleventh-century manor that encompasses a conversion-period church, a graveyard with mixed pagan and Christian burial traditions, and one of the largest Viking Age longhouses recorded in Iceland. The Icelandic sagas retain stories of this farmstead as the seat of local chieftains, one of whom, Grim Svertingsson, was the Lawspeaker of the Icelandic national assembly (Althing) around 1000. The Hrísbrú longhouse was the private home of people like Grim, and the archaeological evidence indicates that it served as a feasting hall.[162]

The chieftains who inhabited the monumental hall at Hrísbrú loomed large in the experience of people living in or traveling through the Mosfell Valley. Their farmstead was prominently located at the southern foot of Mosfell Mountain at the seaward entrance of the valley. The farm was in position to monitor a seasonal harbor site that was remembered in the sagas as controlled by the chieftains. The description in the sagas is rich and our team pinpointed the location of this harbor in the inner reaches of the Leiruvogur lagoon.[163] Travelers approaching from the west by land or by sea would see the Hrísbrú farmhouse long before entering the valley. After the construction of the Christian church at Hrísbrú around 1000, the timber structure would have stood out on the high knoll immediately in front of the longhouse. The church and the size of the house signaled status, while the location of the farm overlooking the entrance to the valley demonstrated the household's dominance over the region.

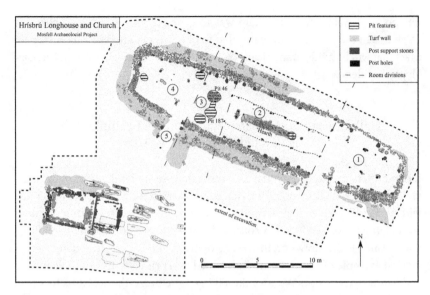

Figure 3.7 The tenth- to eleventh-century chieftain's farmstead at Hrísbrú in southern Iceland, showing the longhouse and the contemporary church built around 1000. The hall was divided into four rooms and an entryway. The central room (2) was the location of feasts and cooking over the central fireplace, while rooms 3 and 4 to the west were for food storage and preparation—including perhaps brewing in pits 46 and 187.
Source: map by author, Mosfell Archaeological Project

The longhouse at Hrísbrú was a domestic space designed for a large household that would likely consist of an extended family, attached laborers, and slaves. At least this is what the saga descriptions of the household tells us. For instance, *Egil's Saga* tells us that besides his own nuclear family, the chieftain Grim also housed his wife's aging uncle and several non-kin servants and slaves. Subsequently in the first decade of the eleventh century, *The Saga Gunnlaug Worm-Tongue* describes the household as including the chieftain Onund, his adult son, and several workers, including a servant whose job it was to monitor the harbor traffic at Leiruvogur. The longhouse excavated at Hrísbrú was occupied during this period, and the size of the house is appropriate for a household such as that described in the sagas. In fact, it was the description in *Egil's Saga* of the burial of the saga hero, Egil Skallagrimsson, in the church at Hrísbrú that led to the genesis of the Mosfell Archaeological Project. The site had not been found in previous archaeological surveys. But we located it with reference to the saga and in consultation with the current farmer of Hrísbrú, who pointed to a small hillock in his hay field, which was called Kirkjuhóll (Church Knoll). Under the grass of

Figure 3.8 Excavation of the longhouse at Hrísbrú, Iceland. Visible in the picture are the large central fireplace and the post holes along the raised side aisles where people worked, slept, and periodically feasted. The bay of Leiruvogur, where a seasonal harbor lay, can be seen in the background, and beyond that are the spires and high rises of modern Reykjavík.

Source: photo by author, Mosfell Archaeological Project

this hill, we uncovered a church from around 1000 (Chapter 4 explores this case more fully). The saga had preserved the story, oral tradition of the place name had retained the memory of the church's location, and finally, excavation discovered the farmstead. Without the combination of the three sources of information the reality of the Viking Age farm would have been lost. In the example of the Hrísbrú house, we have general confirmation between archaeology and written sources. But as will be further argued in this section, only the complementarity of the sources allows us insight into the full political agency of the chieftains who occupied this house. The limited narrative scenes from the sagas that take place at this farmstead do not describe feasts. The feasts have to be interpreted from the archaeological and paleoenvironmental evidence.

Chieftains, such as those who lived at Hrísbrú, needed large expensive halls to accommodate their guests and to serve as the arena for power plays. In the earliest sources, like runestones and skaldic poetry, the largest Viking Age houses were called salr (salir, pl.), and later the word höll (pl. höll) was introduced and used interchangeably with salr. In the sagas, a large hall in Iceland is called a skáli (skálar, pl.) or eldskáli (fire-hall), and it has been suggested that skálar were seen as categorically different, lesser, non-royal buildings.[164] For archaeologists, the character of a "hall" is not universally agreed upon, and there is somewhat of a split between those who see the hall as a large house with special public and political functions and others who have a narrower definition that defines the hall as being a single room or building that is completely separate from domestic occupation and therefore not used as a dwelling.[165] I favor the former definition because the evidence suggests that the private and public spheres of the Viking Age elite are often intermingled within the longhouse.[166]

Whatever we call these houses, their size provides a potential correlate for the types of feasts that might be hosted therein. Smaller feasts could be hosted in any house, but larger feasts, such as the chiefly patron-role type described above, necessitated a more spacious hall. Most excavated Viking Age longhouses in Iceland are 12–16 m long.[167] By contrast, several longhouses are significantly larger. The patterned variation in the sizes of excavated houses, capped by a limited number of larger houses suggests that the larger houses, including Hrísbrú, Hofstaðir in Mývatnssveit, and Skallakot in Þjórsárdalur, correlate with spaces suited for large chiefly feasts. The hall at Hrísbrú is among the largest Viking Age houses excavated in Iceland, measuring 28 m from end to end (25.2 m internally).[168] The form of the Hrísbrú longhouse is typical of Icelandic Viking Age houses, with bow-sided turf and stone walls, two rows of internal posts along the long axis, and doors at opposite ends of the long sides. The house had four separate rooms including a central room, two gable rooms, an anteroom, as well as a covered entryway outside of the western doorway (Figures 3.7 and 3.8). The western gable room and the anteroom next to the central room were used for food and drink storage. The feasts themselves would have taken place in the central room, measuring 9.5 m long and 5 m wide.

The Hrísbrú house would surely have been impressive, but of all the Icelandic longhouses, Hofstaðir at 35.9 m long is the most impressive.[169] Hofstaðir, occupied from around 940 until 1070, might also present the only possible exception to the rule that Icelandic chiefly houses were built primarily as private homes. The name Hofstaðir (Temple-farm) has always evoked special interest and may also explain the extraordinary size. The excavators believe that the very small fireplace, which measures 1.2 x 0.7 m (as compared for example with the hearth at Hrísbrú, measuring 4.3 x 0.75 m) would have been too small to heat the large house through the cold winters.[170] They suggest instead that the size of the Hofstaðir house was designed to accommodate large numbers of guests at seasonal feasts. Possible partitions observed as beam slots in the raised side aisles might have divided the hall into fourteen cubicles designated for specific visiting social groups.[171]

None of the halls excavated in Iceland, not even Hofstaðir, would have been able to accommodate the number of people articulated for the largest feasts in the sagas. Hoskuld's memorial feasts with over 1,000 guests is an outlier, but even the large wedding feasts where numbers of guests are articulated often include between 100 and 200 people.[172] This does not necessarily mean that the numbers are exaggerated, and we should probably imagine a scenario in which the highest-status individuals feasted in the main hall, while other guests congregated outside and in ancillary or temporary structures.

Nevertheless, saga chieftains who were expected to host large numbers of high-status guests simultaneously desired large and impressive halls. The raw material itself was expensive in the North Atlantic, where wood was scarce. *Njal's Saga* lingers on the fact that Gunnar Hammundarson's hall was entirely made of overlapping timbers, rather than the usual North Atlantic turf construction.[173] Gunnar's house is clearly special, but good building wood was a rare commodity in Iceland. Here too *Laxdæla Saga* offers one of the most famous feast settings in Olaf the Peacock's showy hall at Hjardarholt. Olaf first builds his hall from the local forest and driftwood collected from the beaches. The saga calls this hall "magnificent."[174] Not satisfied, the ambitious Olaf sails to Norway specifically to obtain and import wood to construct a new hall. The Norwegian timber allowed a much larger hall than the small native birch wood and salvaged driftwood. The saga describes Olaf's new hall at length:

> That summer Olaf had a hall built at Hjardarholt, larger and better than anyone had ever seen before. Old legends were carved on the internal wooden paneling and ceiling. They were so well carved that the hall was considered more impressive when the wall-hangings were not up.[175]

Olaf soon put his new hall to use for a wedding feast. In one of the great moments connecting feasting, poetry, and power, the poet Ulf Uggason, who is a guest at the feast, spontaneously composes a poem called *House Lay* (*Húsdrápa*) in honor of Olaf and his splendid hall. The poem, which is named but not recorded in *Laxdæla Saga*, is fortunately partially preserved in Snorri's *Prose Edda*. Ulf's poem lingers on the mythological scenes carved in the hall's wall panels and appropriately reveals one of these scenes to be the great funeral feast of Balder, the son of Odin: "There I perceive Valkyries and ravens accompanying the wise victory tree [Odin] to the drink of the holy offering [of Balder's funeral feast]."[176] Olaf the Peacock rewards the poet generously, gives gifts to all his guests, and although it goes without saying, the saga culminates the scene by stating, "Olaf's prestige grew from this feast."[177] The *Húsdrápa* poem composed in a hall during a feast, and recited by a guest to a host in praise of carved mythological scenes of feasting, is a vivid reminder of the dramatic events of a feast played out in a material setting.

The archaeological remains found within the Icelandic longhouses lack the poetics of *Laxdæla Saga*, and no timbers have been preserved that might have provided carved wooden panels such as those described in Ulf's poem. But other more durable artifacts from within the Viking Age Icelandic houses speak to the relative wealth of chiefly houses, albeit a lesser wealth than that possessed by mainland Scandinavian kings and chieftains. A comparison of beads and other status-related finds from excavated Viking Age Icelandic houses shows clear distinctions in the material wealth of the households. The largest houses at Hrísbrú, Hofstaðir, and Skallakot also contain the greatest number and diversity of prestige goods. Non-ferrous metals and glass objects were imported from Europe. Imported glass beads are particularly well suited for inter-site comparisons because of their value, likelihood of preservation, and the recovery of a quantifiable number from sites across Iceland. The wealth of the Hrísbrú household as well as their capacity to reward supporters can be gleaned from a relative abundance of imported prestige goods, including more imported beads than any other excavated Icelandic longhouse. The artifacts from Hrísbrú, Hofstaðir, and Skallakot represent the upper level of material wealth attainable in resource-impoverished Viking Age Iceland.

Cattle for Feasts in Iceland

The ideal economic organization of elite farms in Iceland would be capable of sustaining daily needs as well as providing provisions for politically motivated feasts. As has been argued throughout this chapter, this necessitated meat from large domesticates: cattle and pigs. Because of the colder climate, maintaining pigs and cattle was more difficult in Iceland than most regions of mainland Scandinavia. Pigs declined quickly in Iceland, but the Viking Age settlers held on particularly to their cattle herds. Cattle had to be provisioned with fodder and stabled for the winter, while sheep could remain outside and fend for themselves with minimal assistance from humans. Households seeking to optimize their subsistence production would have preferred sheep herding. Since pure subsistence pressures favored sheep pastoralism, other cultural preferences and/or political needs for cattle must have outweighed subsistence considerations at high-status farms. I previously have suggested that the Viking settlers of Iceland preferred cattle over sheep, at least in part, for reasons related to feasting displays.[178] A politically driven feasting profile in the food products can be recognized in the animal bones excavated from Viking Age Icelandic longhouses, both in the special treatment of animal remains and in the ratios of species represented within the collections.

The choice of cattle for elaborate feasting displays is exemplified by the excavations of the Hofstaðir hall in northern Iceland, where evidence from the cattle bones shows special treatment in slaughter and post-mortem treatment of cattle skulls (Figure 3.9).[179] As noted above, the name element Hof- means temple, suggesting that this was associated with the pre-Christian cult. In general, the faunal remains recovered in the excavation show a normal range of animal foods and products of the Icelandic Viking Age subsistence package. A strikingly unique feature, however, was recognized in twenty-three large cattle skulls that were recovered in three separate caches just outside the central hall and immediately below the collapsed turf walls. The skulls of animals in their prime were apparently placed in these groups as the site was abandoned. The teeth showed that these cattle were in their prime, while measurements of the horn cores indicated that the majority were bulls. The skulls showed that the animals had been killed by a blow with a blunt object—possibly a large hammer—between the eyes. Cut marks on the upper vertebrae of the neck showed that simultaneously a vertical slash with a sword or axe decapitated the standing animals. The result of decapitating these adult cattle in standing position was that blood, driven by the animal's still pumping heart, would rhythmically spray forth until the animal collapsed. This slaughtering method wasted calorie-rich blood to create a gruesome display that must be a local manifestation of the Viking tradition of animal sacrifice associated with ritual feasts, appropriately called simply blót (blood). Weathering on the front of the cattle skulls showed that they were hung for display, probably on the outer walls of the hall. Amplifying the visual impact, the horns were left on the skulls instead of being removed for craft production as is the norm. The skulls had been exposed to different degrees of weathering, suggesting that they had hung on the walls for different amounts of time. The most likely scenario is that one of these cattle was sacrificed and consumed at each major feast, after which the skull was added to the growing collection of skulls on the outer walls as trophies to display the feasting prowess of the household. Radiocarbon dating indicates that the last bull was slaughtered at Hofstaðir around 1000, right at the time when Iceland converted to Christianity. Seventy years later, the hall at Hofstaðir was abandoned and the cattle skulls buried permanently as the ritual feasting with pagan overtones ended.

At the farmstead of Hrísbrú we could detect no special slaughter methods or post-mortem display of animals.[180] Instead, an elite profile suitable for providing meat for feasts was discernible in the high ratios of cattle bones relative to sheep bones. The zooarchaeological profile of Hrísbrú reveals a farmstead that depended primarily on domesticated animals, especially sheep and cattle, with smaller quantities of pigs kept for meat. The diet was supplemented by wild birds, fish, marine mammals, and possibly even shellfish. In many respects, then, the Hrísbrú faunal assemblage with a mixture of domesticated and wild animals is characteristic of the zooarchaeological remains from other Viking Age farms in Iceland. Some anomalous characteristics stand out, however, in the faunal assemblage from Hrísbrú. The relative abundance of fish bones at Hrísbrú suggests

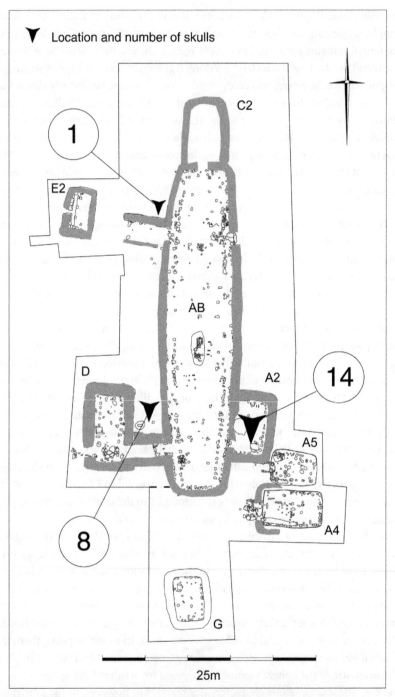

Figure 3.9 The tenth- to eleventh-century feasting hall at Hofstaðir in northern Iceland, showing the location of the caches of cattle skulls that were once mounted on the outside of the walls to signal the feasting prowess of the farm.

Source: courtesy of Gavin Lucas (Lucas and McGovern 2007)

that the farm had excellent access to the products of fishing that could also reflect trade or control over the coastal area to the west. The far reach of the farm's food catchment area extends to the east as well as indicated by the presence of highland birds. Most important for the feasting potential of the site is the high ratio of cattle to sheep bones, suggesting that the household of Hrísbrú consumed relatively large quantities of beef. Feasts featuring consumption of beef would create such a ratio.

The faunal assemblage from Hrísbrú has a ratio of cattle to sheep/goat bones that falls at the high end of the variation documented at other ninth- to eleventh-century Icelandic farms. The high-status eighth- to ninth-century farm at Aaker in southern Norway has been used as the model high-status Viking Age farm that aspiring chieftains in Iceland would have attempted to emulate. The faunal assemblage at Aaker shows an approximate ratio of two cattle bones for every one sheep/goat bone.[181] As stated above, the preference for cattle has been documented across the Viking North Atlantic, with high-status sites more able to sustain the efforts necessary for cattle rearing. The pattern is most clearly visible in the even more extreme environment of Greenland, where drastic inequalities in access to cattle are visible in comparisons of high- and low-status sites. These inequalities become more marked through time. For example, the high-status site called Sandnes W51 (Greenlandic sites are named using W or E for Western or Eastern Settlement followed by a number) showed a 1:1 ratio of cattle to sheep/goats in the eleventh to twelfth century and retained a 0.87 to 1 ratio into the fourteenth century. By contrast, the low-status W48 farm exhibited a relatively high 0.43 cattle to 1 caprine bone ratio in the Viking Age, but this ratio declined to 0.13 cattle to 1 caprine bone in the fourteenth century.[182] The Viking Age cultural and political preferences for cattle continued in Greenland until the demise of the Norse colonies in the fifteenth century.

Hrísbrú has a ratio of 1.92 cattle bones to 1 sheep bone, which is the highest ratio of any examined Viking Age faunal remains in Iceland. The Hrísbrú assemblage dates to the tenth to eleventh century, relatively soon after the initial settlement, when a high ratio of cattle to sheep was more easily retained. A favorable environment in southern Iceland and at the mouth of a valley that allowed extensive wetland meadow grazing might also have contributed to the Hrísbrú household's success at cattle rearing.[183] Nevertheless the cattle-to-caprine ratio from the Hrísbrú assemblage still stands out at the high end of the variation found in other contemporary assemblages from the ninth to eleventh century as well as among the assemblages from sites in southern Iceland (i.e., Aðalstræti, Herjólfsdalur, and Tjarnargata) (Figure 3.10). The high cattle ratio at Hrísbrú is therefore a clear reflection of conscious and costly choices made by the inhabitants to retain their social standing and feasting prowess.

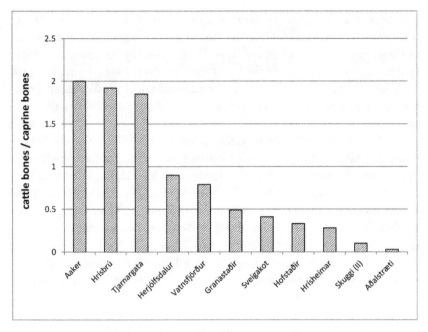

Figure 3.10 Status-conscious Vikings favored cattle over sheep and goats, even in North Atlantic environments that made cattle-rearing very costly. The graph compares the ratio of cattle to caprine (sheep/goat) in animal bone assemblages from Hrísbrú with the eighth- to ninth-century Norwegian chiefly farm of Aaker and Viking Age farms in Iceland. Aaker exemplifies the type of ideal elite farm that aspiring early Icelanders would have tried to replicate, at least in part to be able to provide meat for politically driven feasts.

Source: graph by author incorporating data from Mosfell Archaeological Project; Amorosi and McGovern 2000; McGovern 2003, 2005, and 2008; Palsdóttir et al. 2008; Tinsley and McGovern 2001; Vésteinsson et al. 2002.

Barley and Beer for Feasts in Iceland

The ideal Viking feast required the provisioning of alcohol by hosts for guests. Beer made from fermented barley was the only commonly available alcohol in Iceland. The acquisition of barley therefore became a priority for ambitious chieftains. But since the growing season is shorter and climate colder in Iceland than in the Scandinavian homelands, grain was never a dependable staple food.[184] Cultivation of barley in Iceland has always been suggested by place names such as that of the small offshore island of Akurey (Akur- means cultivated field, and -ey means island) and has been documented by pollen records and at least one instance of probable plowed furrows.[185] Barley consumption has additionally been documented in a number of primarily high-status farmsteads, especially in southern Iceland, but also in some instances in northern Iceland.[186] But since Iceland lies at the northern limits of grain cultivation, it required large labor inputs in soil improvement through manuring. Over time, and probably rather rapidly, barley cultivation likely became increasingly restricted to high-status households that could afford to invest labor and resources in the cultivation of a grain that did not make sense for subsistence alone.[187] Barley was surely used for porridge and bread as well, but the scarcity of barley in Iceland and the social value of beer make it highly likely that barley was reserved in large part for the production of alcohol.

Written sources indicate that grain import was necessary by the end of the Viking Age and that by the fifteenth century cultivation of grain was non-existent in Iceland.[188] The sagas include sparse mention of grain cultivation and very few mentions of people engaged in brewing.[189] The necessity of grain import already in the Viking Age is clear from the sources. *Eirik the Red's Saga* in particular makes clear the necessity of grain import for the purposes of upholding chiefly status in the North Atlantic already before 1000. Having just led a small fleet of Icelanders to Greenland in 985, Eirik the Red was the obvious leader of the newly settled landscape, and his farm therefore became the logical destination of traveling merchants from Scandinavia who needed to stay the winter in Greenland while awaiting the spring sailing season. When the Norwegian Thorfinn Karlsefni stays with Eirik after an unproductive summer, Eirik worries about his reputation:

> "I fear that when you visit other places it will be said that you have never had a worse Yule than this one when Eirik the Red feasted you all at Brattahlíð in Greenland." "That will not happen, farmer," said Karlsefni, "we have on our ship both malt and grain, and you should take from that as much as you want to make as magnificent a feast as you desire for yourself."[190]

Malt is grain that has been made to germinate by soaking in water before being made to redry for use in beer making. Malt is not necessary to make bread or porridge. According to the saga, then, the product that Eirik most desperately needs to support his power as the primary chieftain in Greenland is beer.

Returning to the specific archaeological evidence at the high-status farms of Hofstaðir and Hrísbrú, we find evidence of both grain production and consumption. Hofstaðir may have some features that recall the type of evidence that was used to suggest beer production in the archaeological examples from Norway discussed above. The large hall at Hofstaðir was divided into three spaces with food preparation likely taking place in both the central hall and the northern room. In the room to the north, several pits contained fire-exposed rocks that could have been used for boiling water for beer production. The highest concentration of barley seeds was also found in these pits.[191] The co-occurrence of grain and brewing-stones increases the likelihood the pits were used in beer production. The high elevation of the Hofstaðir site (270 m above sea level) makes it highly unlikely that barley was ever grown locally, and the paleobotanist examining the barley seeds concluded that the barley would have been imported from elsewhere in Iceland or from abroad.[192]

At Hrísbrú, there is evidence of both grain consumption as well as grain production locally, the latter of which was absent at Hofstaðir. Carbonized barley seeds found within the longhouse at Hrísbrú suggest that barley was consumed in the house. A total of 217 barley seeds were recovered from 196.2 liters of sampled soil that we sifted through a flotation machine. This density, 1.106 barley seeds/liter, is high in comparison to seed densities recovered from other domestic sites in Iceland. For Hofstaðir, the only other published longhouse excavation employing comparably detailed sampling methods, 1479.2 liters of soil samples yielded 23 barley seeds, a ratio of 0.016 seeds/liter. At Hrísbrú, a grindstone found on the northern bench probably bears witness to the processing of grain, but other local Icelandic wild seeds are also known to have been ground and included in porridge. At Hrísbrú, most of the barley seeds from inside the house were recovered in the two rooms west of the central hall room (see Figure 3.7). These two rooms were probably used for storage and some food/drink preparation, just as the northern room at Hofstaðir. One of the pits (pit 46) was also filled with fire-exposed rocks. As was suggested at Hofstaðir, it is possible that this pit was used for boiling water for beer brewing. Immediately adjacent and connected by a trail of charcoal and ash was a second pit (pit 187) in which high-temperature burning had created stratified layers of oxidized and black soil. This second pit may be connected to brewing as the place where the stones were heated before being repositioned into the adjoining pit.

Pollen research at the Hrísbrú farm aided by the chronological control offered by tephra layers with known ages shows that barley cultivation began at the time of the founding of the Hrísbrú farm around 870.[193] The presence of grazing-sensitive plants suggests that the grain fields were protected from grazing. Efforts at fertilization are reflected in the microscopic charcoal, bone, and coprophilous fungal spores identified in the pollen core. After the Viking Age, reduced counts of microscopic charcoal, barley pollen, and some cultivation-associated weeds in the pollen profile around 1200 provide evidence for declining agricultural activity. At the same time, plants sensitive to grazing disappear and pasture vegetation increases. The increase in pasture area suggests a change in subsistence strategy to focus on a less labor-intensive sheep-herding economy. Barley pollen disappears around or just before 1200, indicating the cessation of local cereal cultivation.

Cereal cultivation in Iceland was a marker of wealth and correlates with high-status farmsteads. The barley fields would be obvious to visitors, while barley-brewed beer and perhaps bread were used in feasting displays. The elite of Iceland had since the settlement of the island claimed the most fertile lands found at low altitudes with south-facing slopes that received more sunlight. We tested this idea in the Mosfell Valley with pollen cores taken close to the original archaeological remains of five medieval farms: Hrísbrú, Mosfell, Helgadalur, Leirvogstunga, and Skeggjastaðir. The neighboring farms of Hrísbrú and Mosfell were originally part of the same estate of the chieftains who lived in the longhouse at Hrísbrú (Chapter 6 further explores the settlement history of the valley). Our study showed that grain cultivation was limited only to the fields controlled by the chieftains at Hrísbrú/Mosfell with no evidence of grain cultivation at the other farms in the valley.[194] This does not mean that the farmers at the neighboring farms could not acquire grain through trade or purchase from places such as Hrísbrú, but it does mean that the Hrísbrú chieftains controlled local grain production and thereby also one of the key products for status-signaling and alliance-building feasts.

Returning to the written sources, the Mosfell Valley chieftains feature prominently in the saga literature in the late tenth and early eleventh centuries, and a powerful priest-chieftain is still resident there in the twelfth century. However, the chieftains are not mentioned in the sagas dealing with the late twelfth and thirteenth centuries.[195] Perhaps this absence indicates that the power of the Mosfell Valley chieftains declined toward the end of the twelfth century, when they cease to be mentioned in any sagas. The temporal correlation between this phenomenon and the cessation of grain production is probably not coincidental. Importantly, the cessation of barley cultivation precedes the cooling of the climate associated with the Little Ice Age, which began around 1250. The disappearance of barley from the pollen record therefore seems to be driven by social rather than environmental circumstances and may track the collapse of a chiefly economy.

The Hrísbrú example illustrates the potential of approaching the dynamic aspects of feasting through archaeological and environmental evidence. Even in a society such as Viking Age Iceland, for which we lack the shiny cups and drinking horns and for which the spatially separate arenas of ritual feasting have not been found, the residues or trash from feasting events present us with a window for exploration. The clues of feasting and social differentiation are embedded within the archaeological record of an apparently normal household.

Conclusions: Anthropological Models, Historical Generalities, and Archaeological Particulars

Anthropological study of chieftain and early state-level societies, such as those of the Viking Age, indicate that feasting was a pervasive social practice of immense

political significance for alliance building and status signaling. The myths preserved in the Prose and Poetic Eddas indicate that the social significance of
feasting was ingrained in the ideological system of Viking Age Scandinavians.
The sagas of the Norwegian kings and those of the Icelandic chieftains and
farmers show that feasts featured prominently in pre-Christian ritual practice,
among aggrandizing kings, and within the diasporic society of early Iceland.
These feasting generalities are aided by archaeology and the associated sciences
of paleoethnobotany (analysis of plant remains from excavations) and palynology (pollen research) that provide views into the economics of individual
households. Traditional objects of consumption—like drinking horns, cups,
cauldrons, and tripods—found in graves show the same ideals of rulership and
power as those treated in the texts. Excavated graves such as especially that of
the Oseberg ship show the theater of the feast at the grave site. The archaeology
of households such as Hrísbrú and Hofstaðir provide evidence of local production and consumption that goes beyond confirmation of the texts to offer a level
of detail that richly complements the written sources and the excavated graves.
Combined pollen and archaeological studies are particularly powerful because
they allow us to understand local differences in agricultural production in a social light. We see economic decision-making motivated by shifting subsistence
needs over time, but also politically driven efforts to create hierarchy with food
and drink. The story of the Mosfell Valley shows this potential. Yet, we come
to fully appreciate the social significance of the differences and changes in the
pollen profiles throughout the valley only when putting the pollen research into
the context of the feasting ideals engrained in Viking mentalities and the presence of a chieftain family at Hrísbrú as indicated by both sagas and archaeological excavation. The explosion of recent research in the archaeological sciences
and collaboration with the environmental sciences promises to teach us much
more about the politics of food and drink in the Viking Age, especially through
interdisciplinary collaborative approaches.

4

From Paganism to Christianization

Viking Death and Burial

How did the Vikings conceive of death, and what came after? This would have depended on where, and when, you were in the Viking Age. At the opening of the Viking Age in the late eighth century, the Scandinavian worldview coalesced around a deep mythological tradition and a broadly shared—yet diverse— set of pagan beliefs. In their travels, Viking Age Scandinavians encountered many other belief systems, most influentially the monotheistic faiths of Islam and Christianity. The Christian faith ultimately spread to the Scandinavian homelands through a variety of means, ranging from missionary priests to captured slaves to Scandinavian kings who were eager for the wealth and power associated with the new religious institution. The proximity of the Latin Christian lands meant that Western Christendom became dominant in Scandinavia, although the Scandinavians who settled along the Dnieper River in Russia and Ukraine would follow Eastern Orthodox Christianity. Islam remained an important although more remote influence, especially for Scandinavians who pursued expeditions down the Volga River and into the Caliphate of Baghdad.

The Viking Age was a dynamic period spanning pre-Christian paganism, the transition to Christianity, and the beginning of the institutionalization of the new faith in Scandinavia. The myriad ways in which Viking Age Scandinavians buried their dead offer unique insights into the pre-Christian religion and the shifting views of death that accompanied the transition from paganism to Christianity. Pre-Christian burial practices were heterogeneous and contingent on social status and wealth, ranging from simple interments with minimal accompaniments to elaborate burial rituals that left large monuments and richly appointed graves accompanied by prestigious artifacts and the sacrifice of various animal species and sometimes other human beings. Written sources and archaeological evidence reveal the cultural logic that structured the diversity of pagan mortuary practices. This cultural logic shifted during the process of Christianization. During the earliest period after the arrival of Christianity in the Viking world, the burials reflect a creative intermixing of the faiths. After this brief period of syncretism and before the twilight of the Viking Age, Christianity brought a simplification and increased standardization to the burial traditions as

Age of Wolf and Wind. Davide Zori, Oxford University Press. © Oxford University Press 2024.
DOI: 10.1093/oso/9780190916060.003.0004

the Scandinavians were increasingly tied into the cultural network of medieval Christian Europe.

Pre-Christian mortuary practices varied considerably across the extent of the Viking world. Pagan burial practices included both cremation and inhumation of the bodies. Some burials were grouped into cemeteries, and others were interred in isolation. Some burials were placed in house-like chambers under mounds, while others were deposited in carts, small boats, large ships, wooden coffins, or log coffins, over biers, within stone alignments, or without any receptacle at all. Nonetheless, a common ritual vocabulary provided the overarching cognitive framework for the mortuary practices of pagan Viking Age Scandinavians. This overarching vocabulary can be observed in pre-Christian Scandinavian burials. The burial rites performed at the graveside of a Viking merchant-raider on the river Volga certainly varied from those performed at the grave of a farmer-settler in North Iceland, or again from those seen in a proto-urban Danish town; however, the rites employed the same underlying ideology, and the rituals would have been mutually comprehensible.

Viking Age burials are a particularly fruitful arena to pursue the creation of the entangled dialogues of confirmation, contradiction, and complementarity. Multiple sources, including foreign texts, describe Viking Age burial rites. The chapter begins with a text written by an Arab Muslim who observed Scandinavian burial rites on the river Volga in Russia. As with other topics, no contemporary native Scandinavian texts describing burial practices exist. We therefore must turn to later Scandinavian records—including the *Eddas* and sagas written in Old Norse, but also Latin works such as Adam of Bremen's *Gesta Hammaburgensis Ecclesiae Pontificum* and Saxo Grammaticus' *Gesta Danorum*—for insights into earlier Viking mortuary practices. The archaeological data from pre-Christian graves are materially rich and therefore provide a complementary and vivid reflection of a community's purposeful statements about the dead. By looking carefully at these graves, we will see how the diverse Scandinavian mortuary rituals were structured by common ideals of hospitality, reciprocal exchange, feasting, and continued life after death.

A key to understanding Viking burial practice is the recognition that interactions between the dead and the living did not cease when the act of burial was complete. The dead were very present for the Viking Age Scandinavians. Roads passed within view of graves, through cemeteries, and below barrows. Graves provided antiquity and legitimacy to land claims, justification for inheritance, and connections to powerful ancestors and legendary heroes. Both written sources and archaeological records indicate that burials were entered, barrows were reshaped, human remains were moved, and objects were taken. The purposes of these mound breakings varied—re-establishing links to the ancestors, re-killing the un-dead, forming of new material memories, claiming political authority, retrieving objects, Christianizing the dead, and transferring bodies to new locations—but an underlying logic in the reopening of graves was grounded in the dead's continuing importance for the community of the living.

Pre-Christian Death Rites in the Written Sources

The often enigmatic written sources left to us regarding pre-Christian death and burial—ranging from Ibn Fadlan's outsider perspective to the echoes of the Viking Age found in the Icelandic sagas—represent people navigating the most significant life history crisis that humans face: death.[1] To help us approach the varied ways that Viking Age Scandinavians dealt with this crisis, this chapter considers Viking death beliefs and practices through the lens of anthropological work conducted on rites of passage.[2] Rites of passage accompany individuals as they pass from one stage of life to another, with death comprising the final transition. Arnold van Gennep, who coined the term, understood the rites of passage as being tripartite, involving distinct stages of initial separation, a liminal phase of transition, and a final phase of (re-)incorporation.[3] Funerals encompass all three stages. First, pre-liminal rites separate the individual from their previous social roles and connections. Second, liminal rituals ease the transition of the deceased from the world of the living to that of the dead, but they also constitute a dangerous period in which the dead occupies a place between this world and the next. Third, post-liminal rites incorporate the individual into their new social world.

A Viking Burial on the Volga River

In 921, an Arab ambassador from Baghdad named Ahmad ibn Fadlan encountered a group of Vikings on the river Volga as he was traveling north from the Caspian Sea. He calls them Russiyah, the Arab version of the word Rus, which refers to the ethnic Scandinavians who traveled the river systems of Eastern Europe and Western Asia. As discussed in the introductory chapter, the term Rus derives ultimately from the Old Norse word róðr, meaning "rowing." Appropriately for Scandinavians exploring the Eurasian river system in Viking ships, their ethnic name became essentially "the rowers."[4] In his encounter with these Rus, Ibn Fadlan witnessed a chieftain's funeral, and his careful description is an unparalleled source for understanding Scandinavian pre-Christian rituals of death and burial. The setting was an extended feast with excessive consumption, elaborate ritual, and unsettling violence. The whole community of Rus participated in the public ceremonies that culminated in the conflagration of the chieftain aboard his ship laden with grave goods and the body of a sacrificial victim. Ibn Fadlan's story of the chieftain's death feast and subsequent burial reveals that funerals were ritual theaters in which both the verbal and material statements were performed with particular intentions.

The Rus began the funerary ritual by interring the dead chieftain in a temporary grave, a subterranean chamber covered by a wooden roof and earth. The rites of separation occurred in this interim tomb, as the chieftain was physically separated from the living for ten days. During this time, his people prepared his funeral clothes, burial ship, and provisions for his final interment.

In death—as they had in life—Viking chieftains laid claim to personal loyalty through gift giving and feasting (see Chapter 3).[5] Ibn Fadlan records that feasting both materially and symbolically accompanied the burial of the dead. The mortuary feast is a separation rite that marks the beginning of the deceased's social transition between life and death. A third of the deceased chieftain's wealth was spent procuring alcoholic beverages consumed prior to and during his cremation. Ibn Fadlan elaborates: "they drink *nabīdh* unrestrainedly, night and day, so that sometimes one of them dies with a wine cup in his hand."[6] Nabīdh is a strong alcoholic beverage traditionally made with raisins or dates, but here the precise type of alcohol is less clear than its effect. In his temporary grave, the chieftain joins in the feast: "they had put nabīdh in the tomb with him, and fruit, and a drum."[7] His kin, successors, and supporters were responsible for organizing the death feast.[8] However, throughout the feast, the dead chieftain maintained the symbolic role of the feast-giver.

Ten days passed before the Rus transferred the chieftain to his second grave aboard his ship, which had been pulled up on the riverbank and secured in a wooden scaffolding. This second grave provides the setting for the rites of transition that conduct the dead chieftain to the next world. They placed the chieftain inside a tent aboard the ship, in a seated position supported by pillows and surrounded by food and alcohol. Here, the chieftain appeared as the host of the revelry, prominently engaging with his community in his final feast. Ibn Fadlan describes the food and animals deposited with the chieftain:

> Then they brought *nabīdh*, fruit and basil which they placed near him. Next they carried in bread, meat and onions which they laid before him. After that, they brought in a dog, which they cut in two and threw into the boat. Then they placed his weapons beside him. Next they took two horses and made them run until they were in lather, before hacking them to pieces with swords and throwing their flesh on to the boat. Then they brought two cows, which they also cut into pieces and threw them on to the boat. Finally, they brought a cock and a hen, killed them and threw them on to the boat as well.[9]

These sacrifices juxtapose potent symbols of life, death, and rebirth. The symbolic reference to life and death included shows of vitality, such as the running of the horses, immediately followed by their bloody sacrifice and dismemberment. The cock and hen were paired in reference to reproductive capacity, which is then extinguished when they are killed and tossed aboard the funeral ship. The Rus selected, sacrificed, and deposited specific animals on the chieftain's boat to channel their vitality toward the chieftain's rebirth into his next life. The sacrifices ease the transition.

A slave girl volunteered to accompany her master into the afterlife. She was attended by two female ritual specialists while singing and drinking alcohol liberally. Ibn Fadlan's account describes how she entered the tents of the chieftain's supporters, each of whom had intercourse with her and repeated the ritualized phrase: "Tell your master that I only did this for your love of him."[10] She bore the virility of these supporters to the chieftain's grave and into the next world.

Ibn Fadlan's account relates that "they led the slave girl towards something which they had constructed which looked like the frame of a door. She placed her feet on the palms of the hands of the men, until she could look over this frame."[11] Before entering the ship—the vehicle for transport to the next world—the girl must cross this symbolic threshold.[12] The male participants lift her three times so she can see over the frame into the other world. The first time she is lifted, she says, "There I see my father and my mother"; the second time she says, "There I see all my dead relatives sitting"; and on the third lift, "There I see my master sitting in Paradise and Paradise is green and beautiful. There are men with him and young people, and he is calling me. Take me to him."[13] The slave girl, already in a liminal state amplified by intoxication, relates the images of the chieftain in the afterlife that blend the ritual present (e.g., the chieftain calling her) with the ritual future (e.g., the chieftain's presence in Paradise). The images are positive and indicative of a successful transfer of the chieftain's spirit into the next world, presumably dependent on the imminent ritual union of the slave girl with the chieftain and the destruction of both of their physical bodies during the conflagration of the burial ship.[14]

Aboard the funeral ship, the progression of sacrifices culminates in the gruesome death of the slave girl. The female slave—sacrificed as the chieftain's ritual mate—is the ultimate fertility symbol and bearer of reproductive capacity conveyed into the next world. An old woman called the Angel of Death urges the slave girl to drink more alcohol, after which the girl grows very intoxicated and approaches the chieftain's burial tent aboard the ship. The Angel of Death drags the girl inside the tent, where six of the chieftain's supporters have intercourse with the slave girl while other men beat weapons on their shields, making a great noise—possibly to drown out her cries and/or to heighten the ritual tension.

Inside the tent, the men strangle the girl with rope while the Angel of Death stabs her repeatedly in the chest. The burial ship is then set ablaze.

The rites of transition culminate in cremation and the quick transfer of the chieftain through the liminal stage between this world and the next. As the chieftain's funeral ship blazes, a Rus participant explains, "we burn them [in the fire] in an instant, so that at once without delay they enter Paradise."[15] Through the ongoing funerary feast at the graveside, the chieftain and his material goods are destroyed: the feasters consume the chieftain's worldly resources while the chieftain's body is consumed on the pyre. The Rus complete the ritual by constructing an earthen mound over the cremation assemblage and raising a large wooden post bearing the name of the deceased chieftain.

The Rus man's statement on the efficacy of cremation echoes cross-cultural concerns about the dangers of the liminal state between death and the afterlife. The spirit is gone, but the body remains behind to decay slowly. In many cultures, the transfer of a dead person's soul to the afterlife cannot take place until the body has reached a point of stasis, where it is no longer undergoing the physical changes that accompany death and decomposition.[16] During the transition, dangers can arise both for the dead and for the living. Ibn Fadlan's Rus informant knows the danger of prolonged liminality both for the chieftain's successful transition and for his society in general. He mocks Ibn Fadlan: "You Arabs are fools! . . . you put the men you love most, [and the most noble among you] into the earth, and the earth and worms and insects eat them."[17] The Rus Vikings choose cremation to quickly render their chieftain's corpse into the stable form of ash and dry bone fragments, thereby freeing his soul to enter the afterlife.

The Rus in Ibn Fadlan's story anticipate that the chieftain's transition is complete when they build a commemorative mound over the cremation site. Although Ibn Fadlan's account terminates with the mound construction, we can turn to Old Norse literature and archaeology to examine the post-liminal stage of the Viking rites of passage. The saga accounts and the excavated pagan graves tell tales of the post-mortem existences of the dead.

Saga Accounts of Pre-Christian Burial

Viking Age Scandinavians' approaches to death and burial were dependent upon their view of the afterlife. This view appears varied, and there were many different afterlives within their cosmology. The most common modern conception of the Viking afterlife draws from the traditions of Odin's hall, Valhalla, found in sources like *The Prose Edda* and *The Poetic Edda*. As we saw in the previous chapter, these texts portray warrior males joining Odin's retinue in daytime battle and nightly feasting. In terms of the rites of passage, feasting in Valhalla is a rite of incorporation into the afterlife, one that is reiterated nightly. After the warriors hack each other to pieces on the battlefield, they are reincorporated into Odin's retinue by sharing in communal drink and food in his hall.

But Valhalla is just one of many halls in Asgard, the land of the gods. The sources speak of other possible destinations for the dead. For instance, the fertility goddess Freyja had a claim to half the warrior dead, although no source tells us what happens in Freyja's hall. The less fortunate dead—those who failed to perish on the battlefield—risked joining the ghastly Hel in the underworld, which takes her name. The view from the *Eddas* of two diametrically opposed afterlives in Asgard and Hel, in which the dead await a final confrontation at Ragnarok, can be seen as a part of a united belief system.[18] However, narrative sources that are not explicitly eschatological, as well as archaeological evidence, suggest additional and seemingly contradictory notions of the afterlife. In the sagas, the dead can continue to inhabit this earth in semi-permanent liminal states. These liminal dead, who have not fully crossed over into their next life, can be dangerous for the living. As we will see, however, not all of the dead who inhabit this earth are threatening.

A diversity of ritual options in burial were available to the Viking Age Scandinavians. These ritual solutions could be different pathways to the same afterlife, or they could give access to different afterlives. A major (possibly *the* major) ritual choice was between cremation and inhumation. Both were practiced across Scandinavia in various regional frequencies, as is clear from both texts and the archaeological record.

Snorri Sturluson's mythic-legendary *Ynglinga Saga* reflects back on the pagan period from thirteenth-century Christian Iceland and includes an attempt to understand the rite of cremation. In the deep past, Odin, who Snorri reimagined as an ancestral king, ordered "that all the dead should be burned on a pyre with their possessions. He said that thereby each person would arrive to Valhalla with the goods that they had with them on the pyre."[19] *Ynglinga Saga* recounts that Odin himself was burned with great expenditure of wealth after he died because "it was people's belief that the higher the smoke rose in the sky, the more elevated the cremated person would be in heaven; and so, the person was greater, the more wealth was burned with them."[20] Odin's mandate for cremation is consistent with the Rus man's argument that cremation transfers the dead quickly to Paradise. *Ynglinga Saga* provides the further indication that "riches"—surely including personal possessions, food, animals, and slaves—that were destroyed as part of death rituals (cremation or uncremated inhumation) would be useful for the chieftain in his next life.

Snorri Sturluson also explains the varied burial practices of the past according to both temporal shifts and regional differences. In his prologue to *Heimskringla*, placed just before the legendary material in *Ynglinga Saga*, Snorri divides the past into "ages" according to the most popular mortuary rituals and rationalizes that the some of the temporal and regional differences in burial style emerged following examples set by past kings:

> The first age is called the Age of Cremation. In that age it was the custom to burn all the dead and to raise memorial stones after them; but after Frey was put to rest in a burial mound at Uppsala, many chieftains used to erect burial mounds as often as memorial stones to commemorate departed relatives. However, after Dan the Proud, the Danish king, had a burial mound made for himself and decreed that he was to be carried into it when dead, in all his royal vestments and armor, together with his horse fully saddled, and much treasure besides, and when many of kinsmen did likewise, then began the Age of Sepulchral Mounds. However, the Age of Cremation persisted for a long time among the Swedes and Norwegians.[21]

The regional differences noted by Snorri are of special interest, as the preference for cremation in Sweden and Norway is consistent with the archaeological evidence. The memory of a pre–Viking Age king's burial at Uppsala also bears interesting parallels to the Migration Period burials excavated within the mounds at Uppsala in Sweden.

In general, our texts, and particularly the sagas, excel at providing individual stories of burial with particular detail afforded to wealthy burials. The portion of *Heimskringla* cited above is an example of the types of information offered concerning pagan graves in our sources. The objects indicated as grave goods in Dan the Proud's mound—clothes, armor, a horse, and generalized treasure—are items tied to the king's identity as a warrior ruler. Sagas about reopening old graves give yet another textual insight into the choices of grave goods. These goods come to light as heroes creep around the darkness searching for ancient treasure and legendary swords, typically finding first an animated corpse.

The Icelandic Family Sagas describe the deaths and burials of people in the pre-Christian period less regal than King Dan. These sagas typically recount burial in mounds and sometimes give the place name of the mound's location. The descriptions are so similar as to comprise what may be thought of as stock scenes. The burial of Thidrandi, a farmer's son, from *Thidrandi and Thorhall's Tale* (*Þiðranda þáttr ok Þórhalls*) provides an example: "He died that same morning at daybreak and was placed in a burial mound in accordance with heathen tradition."[22] When more detail is offered, place names and grave goods are mentioned, such as Skallagrim's funeral in *Egil's Saga*: "Skallagrim was put in a ship and rowed out to the Digranes. Egil [Skallagrim's son] had a burial mound built there at the tip of the promontory and Skallagrim was laid therein with his horse, weapons, and smith's tools; it is not told whether any money was placed in the mound with him."[23] Digranes is a narrow promontory that juts out prominently into the fjord of Borgarfjörður. A mound on the tip of this peninsula would be prominently visible for visitors arriving to the district from the sea. The grave goods in Skallagrim's mound echo a few of the items placed in King Dan's grave: weapons/armor and a horse. The expectation of treasure is there as well, although the saga author—possibly the same Snorri Sturluson—adds uncertainty to the grave wealth. Skallagrim, who was a skilled blacksmith, is also buried with his tools, as this trade was a significant part of his identity.

The sagas—perhaps because they were written in the Christian period or perhaps because it remained a mystery—do not speculate on the afterlife in Asgard or any other realm separate from the world of the living. The sagas do, however, provide rich details of afterlives in this world. *Ynglinga Saga* offers a mythic story of King Frey, who in life assured the fertility of his lands. After his death, his supporters hid his demise from the wider population by interring his body in a house-like chamber grave inside a burial mound, complete with a door and three windows. His supporters pour tribute of gold, silver, and copper in through the windows in order to assure peace and good harvests.[24] In his grave, King Frey remains very much alive—at least in a social sense—while his veneration continues. In cases where the soul continues to inhabit the grave, we can view the burial itself as the rite of incorporation: the dead have been re-incorporated into the social world of the living, albeit in a prolonged liminal state.

In the sagas, mound-dwellers often seem happy to proceed with their liminal existence within their grave. This existence can involve normal Viking joys, such as feasting, drinking, singing, and reciting poetry. One of the heroes in *Njal's Saga*, Gunnar of Hlidarendi, is overheard by passersby enjoying himself in his grave: "it happened one day at Hlidarendi that a shepherd and a servant woman were driving cattle past Gunnar's burial mound; Gunnar seemed to them to be in a good mood as he was singing poetic verses in his mound."[25] In this state, the dead could offer guidance to the living. In a second encounter with Gunnar, his son Hogni and his friend Skarphedin look toward the mound illuminated in the moonlight shining through the clouds: "It seemed to them that the burial mound was open, and that Gunnar had turned around to look at the moon . . . They saw that Gunnar was cheerful and looked happy."[26] Hogni and Skarphedin are undecided about how to respond in a blood feud, and Gunnar recites a poem in which he advises taking action against their opponents: "the shield-holding ghost [*vættidraugr*] would sooner wear his helmet high than falter in the fray, rather die for battle-Freyja."[27] Gunnar's existence in his mound thereby allows him to continue advice his relatives and friends, and thereby have a role in the conflicts among the living. Existence within a burial mound after death was not necessarily perceived as being a solitary experience. *Eyrbyggja Saga* tells of Thorstein Cod-biter who, after dying at sea, joins a feasting-group of the dead inside the distinctive natural hill called Helgafell (Holy Mountain). Thorstein takes his place in the high-seat as the leader of this company of undead revelers:

> One evening in the autumn Thorstein's shepherd was rounding up his sheep north of Helgafell when he saw the northern side of the mountain open up. He saw great fires burning inside and heard the sound of feasting and good cheer. When he listened closely, he heard that Thorstein Cod-biter and his men were being welcomed there and that Thorstein was being told to sit in the high-seat opposite his father.[28]

The death feast with the living, such as that observed by Ibn Fadlan, marks the Rus chieftain's departure from earthly existence. By contrast, feasting of the deceased with the community of the dead marks their incorporation into the next life. In Thorstein's case, this involves rejoining his dead kin inside Helgafell. Feasting marks both ends of the rite of passage: separation rites at the beginning and incorporation rites at the end.

Although the mound-dwellers like Gunnar and Thorstein remain in this world within their respective mound or mountain, they appear to have passed safely to their next existence and do not constitute threats to the living. Nonetheless, the sagas are rife with the dangerous un-dead. Bad people, bad deaths, or bad burial rites can lead to a failure to cross over to a peaceful post-life existence. Without having crossed over to the next world, these undead beings haunt the living. In the sagas, these wandering undead, called *draugr*, are not ethereal ghosts, but rather corporeal beings. The souls and the bodies of these revenants are still united such that the deceased can still act in the physical world. Such beings, characterized by Victor Turner as "threshold people," are dangerous because they are "neither here nor there" in the social categories typical of most cultures.[29] Those who have not had funeral rites performed are usually perceived as "the most dangerous dead."[30] They are hostile and aggressive because they cannot fully re-enter the world of the living, nor successfully join that of the dead. These homeless dead are wanderers, rising from their bodily resting places to roam the landscape and threaten the homes of the living.

Two Viking ghost stories from *Grettir's Saga* shed some light on the fears and potential results of an unsuccessful transition to the next world. The first story tells of the revenant Glam, who posthumously causes the desertion of an entire valley. After Glam's death, the local community fails to arrange proper interment of his corpse and does not perform the rites of passage necessary to allow Glam's spirit to pass beyond the state of liminality. Glam subsequently destroys both livestock and humans as part of his hauntings. The hauntings cease only after the monster-slaying Grettir the Strong decapitates Glam and follows a clearly insulting yet ritually important action to destroy the body: "He drew the sax and cut off Glam's head, placing it against his buttocks . . . They set to work and burned Glam, until only his cold ashes remained. Then they carried the ashes in a skin bag, burying them at a place farthest from where people would go or livestock might graze."[31] Ritually destroyed, Glam's ashes are still as a precaution set so far from human society that not even livestock would wander there.

In some cases, the dead continue living a corporeal existence inside their burial mounds, with the resting place of the soul being the grave itself. Such a *haugbúi* (mound-dweller) might meddle with the affairs of men, but not in a universally destructive manner. In the second Viking ghost story, the hero Grettir confronts a mound-dweller nicknamed Kar the Old, who is haunting a Norwegian district in an attempt to increase the power of his son. Grettir breaks into the house-like chamber grave within Kar's burial mound:

> It was dark inside, and not altogether sweet-smelling. He had to feel around to get an idea of what was inside. He found some horse bones, and next bumped into the back-posts of a seat. He realized that a man was sitting in the chair. There was a great pile of gold and silver all mixed together. There was also a chest full of silver under the man's feet.[32]

As Grettir pulls himself out of the mound with much treasure in tow, "something strong grabbed ahold of him."[33] The man in the grave has come alive to defend his possessions that he plainly still feels he needs in the afterlife. An epic fight ensues that breaks apart the chamber grave. The revenant Kar is, like Glam, only put to final rest after Grettir ritually decapitates him and places the severed head against the dead man's buttocks.

The dead clearly had interest in their material graves and in retaining control of the goods placed in their tombs. In *The Tale of the Cairn-Dweller* (*Kumlbúa þáttr*), a man named Thorstein gets lost and finds a burial cairn in a deserted valley. When he reaches into the grave, he gets ahold of a sword, pulls it out, and takes it home. That night in a dream, the dead man appears to Thorstein and tells him to return the sword to his mound. The dead man recites a poetic threat to Thorstein, to which Thorstein replies with an equally bombastic verse threat, finishing with "Raider, I'll repay you blow for blow in battle."[34] The cairn dweller quickly changes his tune telling Thorstein: "you have done just the right thing; nothing else would have been appropriate."[35] In the mound-dweller's poem, we learn that the dead man was also named Thorstein. The grave was unknown to Thorstein, but a kinship between him and the cairn-dweller is suggested by their shared name. When tested by the threats of the cairn-dwelling Thorstein, the living Thorstein is found to be worthy of inheriting the sword. Still later, Thorstein tries to return to the grave, but he fails to find it. The monument seems to have appeared from nowhere in order that the sword be imparted to the living

Thorstein. The final lesson from this ghost story seems to be that sometimes, when the living intruder is a worthy heir, the dead approve of the taking of their goods. As we shift our attention to the archaeology of graves, we should keep in mind that disturbing the graves of the dead might also have been perceived as desirable by those inhabiting the graves—not solely beneficial to the living in search of loot.

The Archaeology of Viking Pre-Christian Death

Graves and cemeteries dating to the pre-Christian period provide a complementary data source for understanding Viking Age perceptions of death. Such graves appear in Scandinavia and in the lands visited and settled by the Scandinavian diasporas. Typically, Scandinavian pagan graves have been identified by their position in the landscape, elaborate funerary ritual (e.g., cremation, mound burial, stone settings), and the presence of grave goods. The pagan burial rites are often set in contrast to the more standardized Christian burials that are oriented east-west, are positioned around or in churches, and lack grave goods. In areas with mixed pagan and Christian populations, identifying pagan graves can be problematic, and scholars have most frequently relied on the presence of grave goods within the burials as an indication of the religious orientation of the deceased. This is complicated by the fact that not all pagans—and specifically, those of the lower social classes—were buried with grave goods.

This section concerning the archaeological evidence begins by addressing the apparent variability in the pagan burial rituals. Within this variability, commonalities emerge, such as the attention that Viking Age Scandinavians paid to the mode of transport by which the deceased passed into the next world. In general, the items deposited in graves alongside the dead reveal the importance of war, trade, and generous hospitality in the Viking Age conceptions of people's identities. The sacrifice of animals—and sometimes of humans—provides another overarching commonality. Within this framework, we will look specifically at the mortuary ritual of co-burial with horses as an illustration of how within an overarching ritual vocabulary, specific uses of similar symbols can vary between cemeteries. Variability within cemeteries is also visible in the towns, as will be shown by looking at large grave fields connected to two early Scandinavian towns. The interrelationship between urban cemeteries and the inhabited towns demonstrates that the cemeteries occupied commandingly visible positions in the landscape and functioned to legitimize the residents' membership in diverse urban communities. Finally, we will look at recent scientific approaches applied to burial analysis that have challenged some previous assumptions and deepened our understanding of the Viking representation of identity in death.

Variability within the Archaeological Evidence

Pagan graves from the Viking period exhibit a great deal of heterogeneity, such that very few burial rites can be called the same.[36] Variability in graves can be expressed in many ways, with some of the key variables being treatment of the body (cremation/inhumation), the location of the burial (isolated burial/small cemetery/large cemetery), grave topography (mound/flat grave, stone settings, simple grave/chamber grave), grave receptacle (coffin/boat/cart), and grave offerings (objects, animals, simple/opulent). The archaeological remains derive from variability in mortuary practices that can be linked to many factors, such as settlement type, regional distinctiveness, social status, ethnicity, personal identity, and belief.

Probably the clearest basic variable is whether the body and burial assemblages were cremated or inhumed unburnt. Cremation was the most common mode of burial for pre-Christian Scandinavians of the Viking Age. Cremations were either placed in vessels like ceramic pots or more commonly spread as cremation layers that were then covered with mounds of various sizes and construction styles (Figure 4.1).[37] Cremation is preponderant in southern and eastern Norway, and in Sweden. In western Norway, cremations and inhumations appear in equal proportions, whereas in northern Norway, inhumation was the common mode of burial and cremations are almost non-existent.[38] In most of Denmark, except northern Jutland, inhumation was the norm.[39]

Across Scandinavia, pre-Christian Viking Age burials are situated near settlement sites. Burials can appear in isolation, in small groupings, or in larger cemeteries. Isolated burials are not as common as previously presumed. Recent excavation of larger areas around burials has revealed that many graves originally thought to be isolated graves are in fact parts of larger cemeteries. Broadly speaking, cemetery sizes correlate to at least three different settlement types: farms, villages, and urban trading centers. Anomalies exist, such as the mass burial of an apparent failed raiding party not associated with any settlement (Salme, Estonia), or the cemetery of Viking warriors from a military encampment in Britain (Ingleby, England), or even the short-lived cemeteries for the large state-controlled fortresses in Denmark (Trelleborg-type forts).[40]

In the marginal areas of the Viking world, such as the North Atlantic colonies, no towns or villages with concomitant large grave fields existed. In these colonies, the dead were buried in isolated graves or grave clusters with a small number of interments. In general, islands in the Viking world have distinct burial records.[41] For example, the Åland islanders living at the southern extent of the Gulf of Bothnia that separates modern Sweden and Finland placed the cremated remains of their dead in ceramic vessels. On top of these vessels, they placed unburned clay bear or beaver paws.[42] On the other side of the Viking world, Iceland

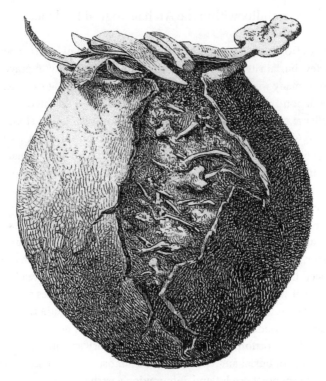

Figure 4.1 Cremation urn from the island of Föhr, located west of Jutland, Denmark. The ceramic urn was filled with burnt human remains and covered with a shield boss and a purposefully broken sword. Viking Age cremations were typically placed in urns or deposited in layers and covered by mounds of various sizes.
Source: Worsaae 1859: 120

has a burial record that fits well within the variability of pre-Christian graves, including burials in boats, in mounds, with weapons, and with animals, but only a single cremation grave has been identified among a large corpus of burials.[43] Other distinctive mortuary practices of island populations are discernible in the use of animals in burial rituals.

Variability in Co-burial with Animals: The Example of the Horse
Deposition of sacrificed animals in graves was common among pre-Christian Viking Age Scandinavians. Although some animal bones in graves are remains of funerary feasts, other bones clearly are not. Scholars have directed much attention toward graves with accompanying horses that were killed for the burial occasion. The prevalent and widespread practice of burying with horses shows that the animal was particularly suitable for inclusion in funerary contexts.[44]

Despite the typical variation between examples across the Viking world, the use of the horse in Scandinavian burials is a uniting ritual practice with a common ritual vocabulary.

A generally accepted assumption is that burials with horses indicate the status of the buried individual. In Danish Viking Age graves from the tenth century, the inclusion of horses, horse gear, and weapons has been associated with the rise of local elites during the formation of the Danish state.[45] In some wealthy inhuma-tion graves, the sheer quantity of sacrificed horses is arresting. The Oseberg ship burial contained fifteen decapitated horses, while the Ladby ship burial included eleven horses placed in the prow of the ship.[46] The significance of horse sacrifice was manifold. Horses interred in graves represent a means of transport to the next world, just as the ships, boats, and carts in which people were also interred. Scenes on Viking Age picture stones from Gotland in which mounted figures are welcomed into Valhalla support the notion that horses provided transport both to and within the afterlife (Figure 4.2). As prized possessions from the world of the living, horses might also have been considered a form of social capital for the deceased in the next life. The absence of evidence for butchery suggests that the sacrificed horses were not primarily meant as food for funerary feasting. This seems consistent with Ibn Fadlan's observations of the Rus funeral, during which two horses feature prominently, but were apparently not eaten. Rather, in these grand burials, the inclusion of horses intertwined symbolic statements of travel, sacrifice, and conspicuous destruction of resources for status display.

Some of the variety of customs subsumed within the rite of human co-burial with horses can be illustrated with two examples from the Viking diaspora into the North Atlantic: Iceland and the Orkney Islands. Viking Age Icelandic graves contained a low species diversity: specifically, Icelandic inhumation graves contain only dogs and horses.[47] But the ritual killing and deposition of horses in graves was more common in Iceland than elsewhere in the Viking world. Thirty-four percent of the excavated Icelandic pagan burials contain horse re-mains.[48] All horses that could be sexed and aged were males between five and fifteen years old. This age and gender profile indicate that full-grown male horses were considered most appropriate for use in funerary contexts. Kristján Eldjárn suggested that horses were chosen because they were more readily available in Iceland compared with other potential grave goods commonly seen in Viking graves elsewhere, such as weapons or brooches.[49] A more recent hypothesis, however, holds that horses were a more appropriate status symbol in the less militarized and more rural Icelandic society focused on familial rather than in-dividual status.[50]

In Scotland, horse remains have been found in 7 percent of the 130 Viking Age burials.[51] Most of these graves were associated with ninth-century beach markets. These beach markets competed for trading activity with other local

Figure 4.2 The Gotlandic picture stones, like Lärbro Tängelgårda I, often contain scenes of processions (probably funerary) and scenes of welcome (probably into the afterlife). On the panel above the ship, a rider is welcomed by a figure holding up a drinking horn.
Source: Lindqvist 1941: Fig. 86 [Taf. 31]

markets on the trade route from Ireland and northwest Britain to Scandinavia. Based on similarities between excavated graves from the Pierowall beach market in the Orkneys (dating to c. 850–950) and burials with horses in the towns of Birka and Kaupang, Siobhan Cooke argues that the inclusion of horses in Scottish graves is an emulation of a merchant burial type from these early Scandinavian towns.[52] A shared burial rite might establish trust through similarity of identity representation in death. The assumption is that traders moving between Scandinavia and the Irish Sea would have multiple options for beach markets and would choose the ones where social connections indicated a suitable trading environment eased by cultural similarity.[53] Scottish Vikings chose in death to underscore shared cultural identity with economic trading partners in the homeland.

The explanations offered above for the horse burials in Iceland and Scotland provide plausible stories, but they cannot be conclusively verified archaeologically. Other possible explanations exist. The symbolic meanings of horses deposited in graves are most likely variable, and the meanings may well incorporate multiple covalent explanations. For instance, in Iceland the economic availability of horses was probably coincidental with the social pressure to stress the value of the horse in early Icelandic settler graves. Such multivariate explanations have the advantage of recognizing that the killing of these large, strong, quick animals, with expressive eyes and manes of flowing hair, are particularly impactful props in the theater of death.

Cemetery Landscapes: Kaupang and Birka

The surface appearance of the Viking Age cemetery landscapes is often difficult to reconstruct. This makes even more valuable a cemetery at Lindholm Høje in Denmark that was preserved by shifting sand, providing a unique window into cemetery topography and the types of activities that the living carried out among the dead. Excavation of this cemetery showed graves marked with a variety of stone alignments or settings, including ovals, squares, and boat-shapes.[54] Besides graves, cemeteries also encompass other archaeological features that are now increasingly coming to light through excavation, features such as stone alignments, enigmatic walls, and post holes supporting grave superstructures.[55] These features reveal cemetery landscapes used during and after the deposition of the bodies, and they shed light on the stage employed for the enactment of funerary drama surrounding the burial act. This section discusses cemeteries as a whole by focusing on the large groupings of burials excavated at Kaupang and Birka. The more than 1,500 graves that have been documented at these two towns alone represent an unparalleled archaeological source of information about Viking Age funerary practice in Scandinavia.

Large cemeteries were a feature of the Viking Age settled landscape and were particularly associated with early towns or emporia (e.g., Birka, Hedeby, Kaupang). These trading and production centers attracted a diverse population of craftsmen and food producers from the surrounding hinterland, as well as traders and travelers from farther afield. Each of these sites had multiple burial grounds, situated beyond the edge of town. The grave types within these urban cemeteries are more variable than at smaller rural cemeteries, in part due to the sheer number of burials located in urban cemeteries. However, some of the variability reflects the diversity of the people who inhabited the towns, including people from other ethnic groups coming from beyond Scandinavia. Encompassing many messages, the interment of the dead in these established cemeteries probably provided townsfolk a sense of community, underscored kin group legitimacy, and served as an arena for status display. This section focuses on the cemeteries of Kaupang and Birka, which have both been well studied and seen multiple large excavations.[56] The explosion of recent scientific analysis of the Birka graves in particular will help to illustrate the new dialogues being opened up between text, archaeology, and the hard sciences.

Eight separate cemeteries dating from circa 800 to 950 are located around the trading center at Kaupang, once home to between 200 and 1,000 people (Figure 4.3).[57] Used over generations, the cemeteries encircle the site like villages of the dead that together contain about 700 graves, although the original number of graves is perhaps closer to 1,000. Grave forms vary between the town's cemeteries: Nordre Kaupang and Lamya are mound cemeteries, while Kikjholberget is a flat grave cemetery.[58] Inter-cemetery variation can also be seen in the distribution of cremation and inhumation graves. At Bikjholberget all graves are inhumations, while the burials at both Nordre and Sondre Kaupang are all cremations in mounds.[59] The inhumation graves often preserve the grave goods and structure of the burial chamber or receptacle, which also shows great variation. Particularly the inhumation burial ground at Bikjholberget includes a mixture of grave forms that includes boat graves, chamber graves, and coffin graves.

Cemeteries and even individual burials were meant to be seen. They were positioned adjacent to roads and close to habituation sites. Travelers to Kaupang, arriving by both land and sea, would pass the cemeteries before entering the town (Figure 4.3). The Nordre Kaupang cemetery, containing an estimated 263 mounds, was the largest and most visually impressive.[60] It was located on a subsidiary road leading to the major thoroughfare known as the Ridge Road, which served as the principal travel route along the western side of the Oslo Fjord. This connector road from the Ridge Road was the only land road into Kaupang. By sea, from the south, travelers passed by the island cemeteries of Vikingholmen and Lamøya with its estimated 200 mounds before coming to the settlement that was ringed closer by the three cemeteries of Bikjholberget, Hegejordet, and Søndre Kaupang.[61] Entering Kaupang demanded travel through and past the villages of the dead. Through any entryway into the town, the monuments of the dead would have welcomed relatives home and reminded visitors of the prominence, history, and wealth of the people of Kaupang.

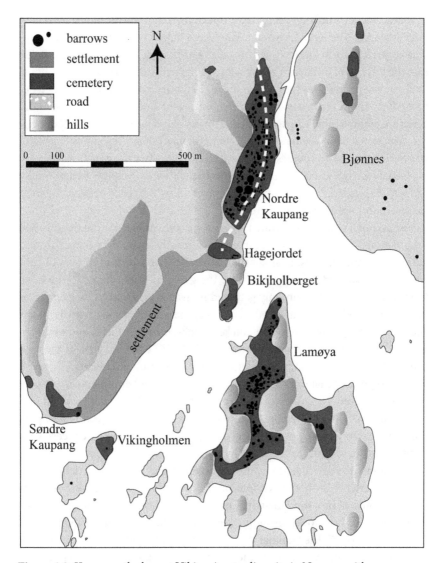

Figure 4.3 Kaupang, the largest Viking Age trading site in Norway, with surrounding burial grounds. The cemeteries associated with early towns comprise the largest corpus of graves from the period. The cemeteries feature prominently in the visual landscape of the town, particularly for anyone entering or leaving the town, whether by sea or by land.

Source: map by author redrawn and adapted from Stylegar 2007 [Fig 5.2] and Skre 2007 [Fig 1.3]. Original illustrations by Anne Engesveen

Birka, Sweden's major Viking Age emporium, lies on the island of Björkö, in Lake Mälaren. The large freshwater lake was a bay in the Viking Age. The waterway stretches 120 km from east to west and provides access from the Baltic into the interior of Sweden. The site, which at its tenth-century zenith was home to about 900 people, was founded in the mid-eighth century and abandoned before 980.[62] The seven cemeteries with an estimated 3,000 graves that surround Birka are highly visible and dominate the town's island location.[63] As at Kaupang, the cemeteries lie in clusters beyond the settlement. High-resolution dating of the burials at Birka provides insights into how the structure of the cemetery evolved over time: distinct and isolated burial clusters—possibly tied to family groups—expanded through time, with graves filling the space between them to make a more continuous burial ground.[64]

Just over half of Birka's excavated graves were cremations (566 cremations, 544 inhumations).[65] The cremation graves, which mostly lay on the original ground surface beneath mounds, bear substantial similarity to the local graves of central Sweden, suggesting that these were the graves of Birka locals.[66] The bone fragments were most commonly gathered in urns placed within the cremation layer. Some cremations included Thor's hammers and various food remains, such as bread, eggshells, unburnt chicken bones, hazelnut shells, and grains of wheat. A little over half the cremations (285 of 566) contain rivets of the type used in boat construction, possibly indicating cremation atop boats. Although analysis suggested that only 25 of these graves contained entire boats, it is very possible that even a few rivets are indicative of pieces of boats incorporated into the cremation.[67] In sum, symbols within Birka cremation graves echo the importance of the ship, a pre-Christian belief in Thor, and probably also a concern with fertility (and/or rebirth) as suggested by eggshells and chicken bones.

In contrast to the cremations, the inhumation graves—and particularly the rich chamber graves—have been interpreted as graves of non-native merchants or at least graves of a foreign style. The chamber graves cluster in prestigious locations around the town, including beside the hillfort guarding the town and the town rampart.[68] The fact that the chamber graves are also among the richest graves in the cemeteries has led to the idea that they belonged to an international merchant elite. Connections to Western European have been stressed especially for chamber-grave construction styles and the find material during Birka's early period in the ninth century. As the town grew in the late ninth century to early tenth century, imports found in both graves and the wider settlement indicate a shift in trade toward the East, whence flowed valuable and exotic trade goods such Byzantine silk and Arabic silver dirham coins.

The symbolic statements made in the Birka graves are dizzyingly manifold and often elusive. Clearly discernible meanings are, however, associated with grave goods connected to Norse gods, such as iron rings associated with Odin and hammer pendants associated with Thor. Symbols of more worldly status can also be discerned from grave goods such as miniature silver chairs found in both male and female graves that likely symbolize the seat of honor in a household. The large numbers of stone settings—found in four main types: circles, triangles, rectangles, and boat-shapes—contain both inhumations and cremations, but are also sometimes empty, representing cenotaph memorials.[69] Of the settings, the boat-shaped grave settings—one of which contained an actual boat—have the clearest meaning. All these boat settings point toward the beach market area, suggesting that the ships of the dead were poised to set sail from the harbor. These prominent graves—similar probably to the conception of many other conspicuous graves at early Viking Age towns—watched over the living conducting their business in the harbor, legitimizing their activities. Foreign travelers arriving in Birka or Kaupang likely looked at these monuments as an indication of the antiquity and importance of the sites. These cemeteries memorialized community members who had passed on to the afterlife and lent weight to claims of social belonging made by the living. Inhabitants whose relatives were interred in the town's cemeteries likely saw the graves as important links to their family's history, as the relatively novel processes of Scandinavian urbanization brought together many different kin groups in a single community.

New Scientific Analyses of Burials: Examples from Birka and Northern Norway

Recent work on the Birka graves illustrates the capacity of modern scientific methods to provide a dataset for cross-checking the encounter between text and archaeology. Scientific analyses of stable isotopes and human genetics of buried individuals have been particularly influential.

Grave goods have traditionally been used to determine the sex of buried individuals. In 1965, the eminent Danish archaeologist Johannes Brønsted wrote, "The race and sex of those who were buried in graves can be determined by the objects placed in these graves."[70] This method assumes that certain objects would only be placed with one or the other sex, for instance weapons with males and jewelry with females. This approach came into intense media focus in 2017 with the publication of a reanalysis of a grave from Birka buried with two swords, two horses, a spear, arrows, and a chess set. This "warrior grave" had become a prototypical Viking warrior man's grave in the scholarly literature.[71] Osteological analysis of the skeleton in the grave, however, indicated that the person was a biological female. The results presented at a conference were controversial and potential issues—such as the possibility of a

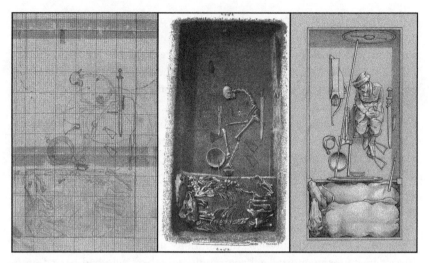

Figure 4.4 Three drawings of Birka Grave Bj 581 that held material culture indicative of a warrior identity—a sword, an axe, a spear, arrows, and two horses—and a skeleton that has been genetically identified as a biological female.

Source: Left: original field drawing by Hjalmar Stolpe; Center: illustration by Evald Hansen (after Stolpe 1889); Right: reconstruction by Þórhallur Þráinsson, courtesy of Neil Price

missing male skeleton or cataloging confusions—were brought forth. To address these issues, a femur and a tooth from the skeleton were subjected to genetic testing, which showed that the individual lacked a Y-chromosome and was therefore biologically female (Figure 4.4).[72]

A long-held and related assumption is that grave goods reflect occupation in life. Stable isotopes from human bones provide a well-established method for examining the diet and mobility of past individuals, potentially correlated with an individual's occupation. Such isotopic studies offer new potentials to confirm or undermine conclusions based upon grave goods. An exemplary study of the Birka graves analyzed the isotopic signatures from a sample of twenty-four individuals of both sexes and from chamber and simpler inhumation graves.[73] Carbon (^{13}C), nitrogen (^{15}N), and sulfur (^{34}S) isotopes were used to determine differences in protein consumption from marine and terrestrial sources. The results showed a correlation between grave goods and diet: people buried with weapons ate diets richer in marine-based protein than those buried without weapons, who had diets more reliant on local terrestrial and freshwater foods. The marine-based diets probably reflect mobility on the ocean, a type of travel that is consistent with an ocean-crossing Viking raiding and/or trading lifestyle. In this case, then, the weapons in their graves do appear to reflect the warrior activities in life.

It is typical in archaeology that the social status of buried individuals is measured by the comparative wealth of the accompanying grave goods. Although rife with methodological issues, this approach is made even more difficult when grave goods are lacking or contextual information from grave excavations is missing. Scientific methods provide new promise in resolving these issues. In one example, isotopic analysis of diet using ^{15}N and ^{13}C was applied to the ten Viking Age individuals buried in a small farm cemetery on the island of Flakstad in Northern Norway.[74] The ten dead were distributed in six graves: three single burials, two double burials, and one triple burial. In the double and triple burials, one person was buried as a complete skeleton while additional individuals were buried without their heads. Headless individuals are typically interpreted as slaves sacrificed to accompany elite burials. The Flakstad cemetery appears to show a three-tier social hierarchy: decapitated slaves, free commoners buried in single graves, and elites buried with sacrificed slaves. The results of the isotopic analysis identified a distinct terrestrial diet for the elite individuals. The surprise was that the diets of those presumed to be slaves and commoners were indistinguishable and equally heavily reliant on marine foods. The consumption of terrestrial protein—especially cattle and pig—was a status marker, and these animals probably comprised feasting foods in this high-latitude location.

Meaning of Burials in Text and Archaeology: The Theater and Drama of the Rites of Passage

There were many Viking conceptions of life after death and many corresponding ritual options to facilitate transitions into the afterlife. The appropriateness of these rituals depended upon the identity of the dead, the aspirations of the living, and the desired destination for the dead. We return now to the idea of funerary drama involving rites of passage: separation, transition, and incorporation. This tripartite ritual framework was used explicitly above to structure the discussion of the Ibn Fadlan and saga texts; this section now puts it into dialogue with the archaeological material.

Neil Price has suggested that the archaeologically excavated graves are "the 'stage set' at the close of a 'play.'"[75] The activity that goes before the actual burial is difficult to discern from the archaeological remains; texts are helpful here. Archaeology has the potential to provide important insights that were never contained in contemporaneous texts. These insights range from new information about specific individuals, such as biological sex, diet, and occupation, to activities in cemeteries that accompanied burials, as exemplified by recently discovered mortuary houses and other ephemeral structures near graves. This section draws attention to the ways in which texts, archaeology, and new methods of scientific analysis can be combined to provide insights that are richer and more nuanced than any one approach used in isolation. In particular, these insights shed light on how mortuary rituals were dramatic performances that used evocative imagery and ritual practices to consummate the separation, transition, and reincorporation of the deceased into the social world of the dead.

Interactions by the Grave: Feasting

Of the rites of passage addressed in texts such as Ibn Fadlan's account, funerary feasting is perhaps the most discernable in archaeological burial assemblages. Objects used for food and drink consumption, as well as actual food remains themselves, make up a significant percentage of the grave goods from burials of both males and females. As discussed in Chapter 3, The Scandinavian Viking Age elite ship burials like Ladby in Denmark and Oseberg in Norway contain references to feasting, with particularly striking evidence of animal sacrifice and meat consumption. In the rich Oseberg burial, for example, excavators found the bones of an ox in an area of the deck equipped for food preparation, including two large cauldrons and an iron tripod for boiling meat.[76] That portions of animal bones uncovered in burial assemblages represent food is apparent from the extensive evidence of dismemberment and butchery; in this way, they represent a significant departure from animals included in their entirety as sacrifices, such as horses. It is often unclear, however, whether funerary feasters consumed the meat before placing the bones into the grave or whether the animal remains were intended for consumption in the next life. A third possibility—one that draws from saga stories—is that the meat may have been meant for consumption in the limbo-like state of existence within the grave.

Participants in funeral feasts consumed ale and other types of alcoholic beverages such as wine, mead, or the Rus *nabīdh*. Drinking vessels ranged widely in form and material. The vessels described in texts, depicted in art, and found in graves are typically special drinking vessels meant to indicate high status, and include drinking horns, glass beakers, and silver cups. Drinking horns accompanied the dead in graves, including the Oseberg ship burial. Drinking horns are depicted on Gotlandic picture stones, such as Lärbro Tängelgårda IV (Figure 4.5). The Lärbro Tängelgårda IV stone depicts figures using drinking horns in a formalized ritual scene that likely represents a funerary drinking feast. Among the feasters are two bearded men standing inside what could be a temporary structure in a cemetery. These two men hold objects that look like upside-down drinking horns poised for plunging into a communal drink storage vessel. The vessels do not curve like typical drinking horns, so another interpretation is that the men hold presses or grinding objects for preparing the alcohol. Multiple

Figure 4.5 The Lärbro Tängelgårda IV picture stone showing a probable funerary feast. The men inside the possible funerary structure in the bottom left corner may either be holding items for processing alcohol or drinking horns that are tipped upside down. An almost identical scene appears in the top panel of the Lärbro Tängelgårda I stone in Figure 4.2.

Source: photo by Helena Bonnevier, Historiska museet/National Historical Museums, Sweden (CC BY 4.0)

excavated cemeteries have yielded remains of ephemeral buildings—funerary houses or canopies—that may be comparable to the structure depicted on Lärbro Tängelgårda IV.[77]

Picture stones, cemetery excavations, and textual sources agree that Viking rites of passage incorporated the metaphor and practice of feasting regularly and prominently. The graveside feast was an important arena for renegotiating the relationships between the living and the dead in the stages of separation and transition, as well as among the living as the deceased was incorporated into the social world of the afterlife and the lives of successors and kin resumed without the departed individual. The feast in the afterlife marks the deceased's entry into the next life, whether in a grave mound, a holy mountain, or Valhalla.

Interactions in Erecting the Grave: Making Mounds

The written sources about Viking Age Scandinavians indicate that some people experienced an extended liminal phase, such as King Frey's afterlife in his house tomb. Recall that King Frey's followers continued to make offerings of gold, silver, and copper after his death. Archaeological analysis of stratigraphic layers comprising grave mounds has shown that these mounds were constructed through a lengthy ritualized process, and that the living continued to interact with the dead even after the preliminary rites of interment were over.[78]

The ritual of mound construction was clear in 1946 to excavators of the Ballateare Viking grave mound on the Isle of Man.[79] At the bottom of the mound was a chamber containing a high-status male burial complete with weapons, whose interment had been followed by extended rituals of mound construction. A sword had been intentionally broken and the shield boss struck multiple times to ritually kill the objects, ending the life of the artifacts by purposefully damaging them. Two spears were positioned on top of the coffin before the grave was filled up with white sand. Over the sand, a mound was built using turfs stripped from an estimated 500 m² area. Toward the very top of the mound another series of features appeared, including the body of a female (aged twenty to thirty). The cause of her death appears to have been a blow to the back of the head with a bladed weapon, which cleaved the posterior portion of her skull. The arms of the skeleton were raised upward, suggesting rigor mortis had set in before the burial. The fact that rigor mortis had begun means that the woman was killed ten to seventy-two hours prior to her interment in the top of the mound. The absence of the skull fragment severed by the violent blow suggested that the woman died elsewhere. The burial shows some parallels with Ibn Fadlan's account of the slave girl's sacrifice. Above the woman's body a layer of burned animal bone was spread just below the mound's ancient surface. In the center of the old surface was a posthole, showing the location of a post or marker placed atop the mound, again with a parallel to the post erected with the chieftain's name in Ibn Fadlan's account.[80]

Other instances indicate that some tombs were left open to facilitate ongoing interaction with the dead, suggesting that the deceased was in an extended liminal phase comparable to King Frey's postmortem existence. One example is the Oseberg ship burial, where the mound was left half-open for a substantial period, probably to allow continued ritual action to be performed on the front of the ship deck.[81]

Interactions with the Grave: Burial Reopenings

The stage after the end of the funeral—after the successful (or failed) rite of incorporation—was explored with the saga texts above. Archaeological evidence of reopening of old graves provides another vantage point. These reopenings were structured as a drama that likely addressed a need to modify rites of incorporation. The goals may have included the transfer of the dead into the next world, recovery of an important object, or change of the location of the dead in the afterlife.

Reopenings of graves provide a particularly vivid enactment of the theater of death, with significance far beyond grave looting. Activities at the graveside well beyond the initial burial event continued to have great importance, not least because graves were loci of social memory about individuals, kinship bonds, and the wider social order. The elaborate and sometimes violent disturbance of graves shows that people often reopened graves publicly and not furtively in the night, as would be expected in instances of tomb robbery. For instance, as discussed in Chapter 3, the grave-openers of the Ladby ship burial in Denmark removed a circa 5-meter-long stretch of turf to facilitate access into the mound.[82] Archaeological evidence indicates that grave reopenings were very common, so common that most graves in Norway and Iceland were disturbed in antiquity. The sagas, as discussed above, are replete with instances of grave robbery and the recovery of important heirlooms and valuable weapons. The archaeological record also holds many examples of the opening of old monuments to eliminate the dangerous dead, erase or challenge past power structures, and reconnect with ancestors.[83]

The decapitations of Kar the Old and Glam in *Grettir's Saga* are prime examples of the destruction of the dead to control hauntings. Viking Age archaeological examples show parallel cases of ritualized solutions for controlling the dangerous dead. In their graves, potentially dangerous dead people are often physically held down or decapitated to ensure that their death is permanent. Grave T in the Bogøvej cemetery in Denmark consisted of a seemingly normal female burial placed in her grave with a knife and a few beads. Sometime after her initial burial, however, people broke into her grave, severed her head from her body, and placed the skull and her purposefully broken mandible on top of her left leg.[84]

Reopenings of elite burials may also have been politically motivated theater meant to destroy symbols of hereditary rule. The reopening of the Oseberg
mound, recently precisely dated to the third quarter of the tenth century (c.
120 years after its construction), provides such an example.[85] The skull of the
younger woman in the Oseberg burial appears to have been violently and forcefully crushed and then scattered inside the reopened grave. The Oseberg ship
itself was also treated violently, hacked with axes.[86] With reference to written
sources, the Oseberg reopening and the reopenings of other large mounds such
as Borre and Gokstad have been connected to the Danish King Harald Bluetooth's
takeover of the Oslo Fjord region of Norway.[87] Harald's public violence toward
the burial mounds reshaped their meaning to carry an explicit political message
that there had been a transfer of power. The modified mounds were left standing
but with new meaning.

Tomb reopenings often targeted specific items, while leaving others behind.
The items removed from male graves appear to be swords and shields, the carriers
of masculine warrior identity. Jewelry and dress ornaments, signals of female
wealth and status, were removed from female graves. Both males and females
also appear to have their objects of the feast targeted for theft and destruction.
Alison Klevnäs has argued that the grave openers aimed to take possession of
"inalienable" objects that were linked to the identity of the buried individuals.[88]
By recovering these objects, they could access part of the dead person's virtues,
such as strength, honor, or leadership. The warrior's sword—often named and
inherited through generations in the sagas—is a quintessential example. Some
special personal items were so intricately linked to particular individuals that the
separation of object and person was inconceivable even in death.

The combined evidence from the saga stories and the violently disturbed archaeological remains manifest this struggle over inheriting inalienable objects,
explicit symbols of power transfer. Sometimes the acquisition of such items required a forceful taking of the object and a re-killing of the dead, who invariably
struggle to retain their possessions. *Grettir's Saga* provides a compelling example.
After Grettir kills the revenant Kar and takes Kar's sword from his mound, he
returns the sword to Kar's living son, Thorfinn. Thorfinn's initial anger abates
when Grettir gives him the sword. Thorfinn explains: "I was never able to get it
from my father while he was alive."[89] He keeps the sword by his bedside. Later,
as a show of gratitude to Grettir for saving his family from twelve berserkers,
Thorfinn gives Kar's sword to Grettir. The gift carries significant importance and
social value, and Grettir carries it for the rest of his life.

This section has stressed violence to grave mounds and the dead. However,
reverent manipulation of the body of the dead was also practiced to reify inheritance claims and reinforce links to the past. One example addressed below
is the remolding and reopening of graves during the ideological transition to

Christianity. This specific type of grave reopening focused on moving the bodies of deceased to bring ancestors across the transition to the new religion.

Conclusions: Pre-Christian Death

Old Norse texts and archaeological remains support the idea of multiple Viking conceptions of the afterlife. Excavated graves from across the Viking world—especially those of the wealthy segment of society—are congruent with Ibn Fadlan's account of extravagant burial practices involving ships, feasting, sacrifices, and cremation. The narrative sources that are not explicitly eschatological, as well as the archaeological materials, suggest additional and seemingly contradictory notions of the afterlife. A clear contrast exists, for instance, between the quick transfer of the soul to the afterlife recommended in Ibn Fadlan's account and mirrored in archaeological cremation graves, and the mound-dwellers of the sagas, as manifested in some of the archaeological chamber graves and the extended periods of ceremonial mound construction.

Much of the ritual and display of Scandinavian pre-Christian death rites was directed toward statements about status, mourning, and inheritance for the living. For instance, the feast at the grave was likely a key rite reconstituting (re-incorporating) the community in the wake of a member's death. But in the pre-Christian conception, it is crucial to remember that the dead had needs too, regardless of whether they had traveled to the afterlife or lived on within the grave. These needs are represented in the archaeological record, for example, by food sacrifices.

Descriptions of burials in the texts demonstrate a cultural preoccupation with the successful navigation of the state of liminality, wherein the deceased person exists between this life and the next. This phase involved heightened contact with the world of the dead. This contact offered opportunities to harness otherworldly forces, but the connection to the other world was also dangerous, since the world of the dead can threaten the living. The post-mortem existence represented in saga accounts of mound-dwellers and revenants is complemented by the archaeological evidence of burials that were opened to manipulate the grave—and sometimes to re-kill the dead.

To conclude this section on pre-Christian death rites, let us return to Birka grave Bj 581 that generated so much media attention (Figure 4.4). The grave shows the versatility of the pre-Christian Scandinavian rites and is an illustration of the variability that leaves room for interpretation and reinterpretation. Since few graves are alike, the stories that can be told are many and often divergent. Bj 581 is an illustration of the potential of new sciences to aid in reinterpretation. Was this a female warrior, a shield-maiden straight from the Viking legendary texts? We cannot know for sure. The weapons may have been placed in the grave symbolically in order to reflect the female's status or her role in the community. The researchers who conducted the genetic research believed that gaming pieces from a strategic board game placed on the deceased's lap signify her role as a tactician in life, an example of symbolism supporting a lifetime occupation as a war leader. Others have countered that perhaps the weapons and chess pieces do not directly mirror her actual occupation in life, but instead that of her husband or male relatives. Broadly speaking, though, identities depicted in graves typically relate directly to people's occupations and identities in life. As such, they conform in realistic ways with the expectations that other community members would have had regarding the deceased individual. This basic idea is also supported by the isotopic analysis from Birka, suggesting that individuals buried with weapons also traveled on the oceans. Just as texts meant to be seen as "true" need to stay within the realm of plausibility for the intended audience, so also do public burial rituals need to be seen as consistent with reality. Skepticism is healthy, but a refusal to accept the most likely explanation—which in this case seems to be that the woman was a high-status warrior in life—is an exercise in academic over-skepticism for its own sake.

Conversion and the Process of Christianizing Viking Age Death

Across the Viking world, the change from paganism to Christianity was a gradual process. The moment of public conversion should be distinguished from the slower phenomenon of Christianization, emergent from widespread transformations in individual choices of worship. It is also clear that this complex process entailed a significant degree of syncretization of paganism and Christianity. Christian influences preceded the public moments of conversion, while after conversion, some pre-Christian beliefs and practices persisted.

During this Syncretization Period (c. 950–1100), Scandinavian ritual systems hybridized as ideology and practice shifted from pagan to Christian. The accommodation of old symbols and practices resulted in a period of intermixed ritual systems. This process is often flattened in the textual record: most of the texts about Viking Age Scandinavia were produced by backward-looking Christians who had particular agendas in the representation of their ancestor's ritual practices. Fortunately, however, archaeology is particularly well suited to explore the practices and material correlates of the Christianization process. Both textual and archaeological sources agree, however, that the pagan ritual landscape and mortuary ritual were completely transformed as a result of this Christianization.

In the texts, conversion moments are sudden and securely controlled by po-
litical leaders. This is exemplified in Denmark, where King Harald Bluetooth is
said to have converted to Christianity in 965 and with him followed the whole
Danish realm. Harald makes precisely this same claim on the larger of the two
Jelling runestones. The runic inscription reads: "King Harald commanded
these memorials made to Gorm, his father, and to Thyre, his mother. That
Harald who won for himself all of Denmark and Norway, and made the Danes
Christian."[90] A similar claim to conversion by the elite is made in texts about the
Christianization of Iceland; *Íslendingabók* (*The Book of Icelanders*, c. 1125) states
plainly that in 999/1000, the council of chieftains at the Althing decided that the
population of Iceland would be publicly Christian.[91]

The texts are best at capturing the moment of public conversion, but also provide glimpses at Christianization preceding the more propagandistic accounts of
public conversion. For Iceland, the sagas make mention of Christian settlers to
the island, although they suggest that Christian practice did not last past the first
generation or two.[92] For mainland Scandinavia, *Vita Anskarii* describes the wandering Bishop Anskar's missions to the Scandinavian towns of Hedeby, Ribe, and
Birka in the 820s and 830s. But *Vita Anskarii*, as well as Adam of Bremen's *Gesta
Hammaburgensis Ecclesiae Pontificum* (c. 1076) and Saxo Grammaticus' *Gesta
Danorum* (c. 1208), treat the successes of the Christian Church in centers such
as Hedeby as cyclically dependent upon the favor of local kings and heroic missionary journeys from the German-speaking Christian lands. These texts thus
present the Christianization process as one that is top-down and dependent on
the will of the king.

Archaeology, on the other hand, can provide further insight into the slower
process of Christianization from the bottom up. These can be seen most clearly
through the practices of individuals, as represented in graves and public
monuments. One example can be drawn from the burial practices at the early
town of Hedeby. Of all the urban centers in Scandinavia, Hedeby lay the farthest
south, closest to the Christian lands, and probably included the most international population. The cemetery at Hedeby shows evidence of Christian influence
pre-dating the conversion of Harald Bluetooth. The shift to inhumation burial—
a rite more compatible with Christian practice—from cremation happens in the
early ninth century at Hedeby, whereas in the rest of Denmark it occurs only in
the late ninth century. Other distinctly pagan burial practices such as mound
construction and inclusion of grave goods in burials cease early in the tenth century at Hedeby, well before Harald's conversion in 965.[93] Items with Christian
symbols, such as brooches with cross motifs, begin to appear in the Hedeby
graves at this same time. The organization of the cemeteries within the ramparts
shows three elements that bear similarities to Christian cemeteries: burials
oriented east-west, a row-like organization of graves, and only small distances

between graves. Since neither a church nor a boundary wall or fence has been found in conjunction with these burial clusters, it is unclear whether these are burials of Christians or simply graves exhibiting Christian influence.[94]

After the public moments of conversion, the pace of the Christianization process in the Viking world is gradual. The graveyard at Fyrkat, a fortress built by Harald Bluetooth circa 980, about fifteen years after his conversion, has yielded evidence of mixed pagan and Christian aspects.[95] Many of the graves include substantial grave goods, atypical of Christian burials. One female grave at Fyrkat was placed in a wagon, as per the pagan tradition, together with ritual items that included an iron staff connecting her to the pre-Christian sorcery called seiðr.[96] The graveyard does not have a central church, but rather, a central wood-paved road or raised platform. This structure has no parallels in Christian graveyards and may be a platform for conducting pagan rituals—or perhaps mixed pagan and Christian rituals (Figure 4.6). Other aspects of the graveyard, such as the

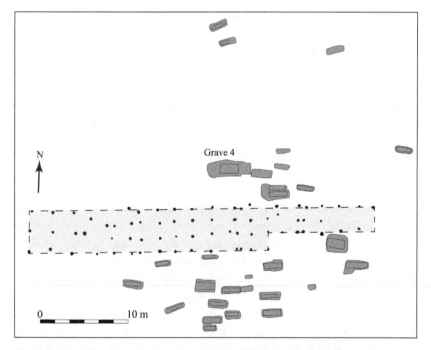

Figure 4.6 The graveyard associated with the Fyrkat circular fortress built by Harald Bluetooth c. 980, about fifteen years after his conversion to Christianity. The graveyard had a central wooden platform where burial rituals likely took place. The graves, located to the north and south of the central platform, include Grave 4, which contained the richly adorned remains of a sorceress buried in a wagon.
Source: map by author based on Roesdahl 1977: Figure 86

east-west orientation of most graves and the presence of many more child graves than is typical of pagan burial grounds, are suggestive of Christian influence.[97] The scarcity of archaeological examples of churches in Denmark—with the exception of those located in major centers, such as Jelling—before the mid-eleventh century (almost a hundred years after the conversion of Harald) also suggests a slower process of Danish Christianization.[98] By contrast, the relatively large number of archaeologically identified early Christian churches in Iceland dating to the early eleventh century may indicate, somewhat surprisingly, that Christianization proceeded at a faster pace in marginal Iceland. Perhaps the chieftains and prominent farmers in Iceland were quick to seize the initiative to wield control over the new faith. In the absence of a strong royal ruler, prominent individuals built their own churches on their own farms.

The character of ideological power changed radically as the ritual system shifted from the relatively diffuse power of pre-Christian paganism to the hierarchically organized and institutionalized Christian Church. In the pagan period, claims to status, group membership, and territory were expressed in mound burials that were strategically situated overlooking towns, along routes of travel and at the borders of old territorial divisions. After the conversion to Christianity, the locus for ritual practice became centralized at churches built and controlled by the elite. A handful of churches from the early period of Christianity have been excavated.[99] The earliest churches were built of wood in a simple rectangular or nave-and-chancel style. Burial became centralized around these churches.[100] The syncretization of pagan and Christian ritual systems, as well as the role of this process in the continuity of power, is visible in the archaeological record from early churchyards, such as the graveyard surrounding the conversion period church at Hrísbrú in southwest Iceland. Here two processes are evident: the continued use of the pre-Christian ship symbol in graves and retroactive Christianization of venerable ancestors.[101] Five burials from Hrísbrú contained clench bolts, suggesting that pieces of boats had been reused as covers for graves.[102] The reused boat fragments represent continuity of the ship symbol deeply rooted in the Norse ritual tradition. The second process of retroactive Christianization is the topic of the subsequent two sections.

Christianizing the Pagan Dead: King Gorm of Denmark and the Jelling Monuments

The role of the Jelling Dynasty in state formation, beginning with Gorm the Old and followed by Harald Bluetooth, is treated in Chapter 5. In this section, we turn to the monuments at Jelling to address Denmark's Christianization and how Christianity was materialized within a pagan ritual landscape. Jelling, located in south central Jutland, is a sleepy village today but was the political capital of tenth-century Denmark.

The large runestone erected by Harald Bluetooth between two massive mounds provides a contemporary textual starting point. In the text quoted above, King Harald claims to have built the surrounding monuments for his parents, Gorm and Thyre. Immediately next to Harald's runestone, however, sits a runestone attributed to Gorm with the following runic claim: "King Gorm made these monuments in memory of Thyre, his wife, Denmark's betterment."[103] But which monuments were Harald's and which were Gorm's? Did Svein, Harald's successor, build any of them? These questions have led to great scholarly debate that serves as an ideal illustration of the challenges and potential payouts of combining texts and archaeology. Chronology—particularly the intersection of textual and archaeological dating—is the key to answering the questions about the Jelling monuments and by extension, providing new insights into the process of Danish Christianization.

Multiple later texts recall the reigns of Gorm, Harald, and Svein, most importantly Saxo Grammaticus' *Gesta Danorum* (c. 1208), Sven Aggesen's *Brevis Historia Regum Dacie* (c. 1186), and Adam of Bremen's *Gesta Hammaburgensis Ecclesiae Pontificum* (c. 1076). According to chronologies established from these texts, Harald is said to have converted to Christianity c. 965 and died before 987 (probably in 986). After Harald, his son Svein ruled until his death in England in 1014.

Archaeological investigations of the monuments at Jelling have demonstrated that the visible features were part of a large palace-like royal complex that included an encircling palisade and several longhouses of the late tenth-century Trelleborg type (Figure 4.7). The palisade precisely encloses the massive ship setting (354 m long) that dominated the site in the earliest Viking Age phase. Diagonal lines from the corners of the palisade meet in the center of the North Mound, where nineteenth-century excavations found a chamber grave that had been re-opened in antiquity and from which grave goods and human bones were removed. The South Mound sits atop the southern end of the ship setting, such that its construction would have erased a portion of the setting's outline. Midway between the mounds stands Harald's runestone. Just north of the runestone and underneath the current Romanesque stone church lay a large wooden church with a burial chamber located beneath the floor, immediately west of the choir and adjacent to the location where the altar would have stood. Within this 2 × 3 m chamber lay seventy-three disarticulated bones of a male, circa 173 cm tall and between thirty-five and fifty years old. The nature of the disarticulation of the bones indicates that this man had been laid to rest somewhere else first and later moved to this position beside the altar. The grandeur of the monuments and the juxtaposition of pagan and Christian monuments show the importance of Jelling

Figure 4.7 **Above:** Reconstruction of the Jelling runestone raised by Harald Bluetooth around the time of his conversion to Christianity (see also Figure 5.4). As part of his Christian remodeling of the royal palace complex at Jelling, Harald placed this large runestone in the center of Scandinavia's largest ship setting and between two pagan-style mounds. **Below:** Aerial photograph of Jelling with white markers showing the extent of the palisade and the ship setting.

Source: Left: The National Museum of Denmark (CC BY-SA 2.0); Right: photo by Daniel Frank/ Colourbox.com

in materializing royal power and how the Danish ruler(s) navigated the process of Christianization. But understanding this historical process requires that the monuments be precisely dated, such that they can be matched to the chronology recreated from the texts discussed above and thereby tied to the efforts of particular Jelling kings (Gorm, Harald, or Svein).

The true breakthrough in the archaeological chronology of the building sequence came with the science of dendrochronology, which provided dates for the felled trees used in the construction of the North Mound's burial chamber (958/9), the palisade (968), the South Mound (970). Dendrochronology also provided a date of 964/5 for a tool used during the reopening of the North Mound's chamber that removed the human bone.[104] Although the chamber grave beneath the wooden church has only been dated via the included artifacts, these objects are from the late tenth century and closely match the so-called Jelling style of finds from within the North Mound. These dates fall within the reign of Harald Bluetooth. Perhaps most intriguingly, the date of the reopening of the North Mound aligns precisely with the likely 965 date of Harald's conversion to Christianity, and so is also the likely date for Harald's runestone with Denmark's first image of Christ (Figure 4.7).

The most widely accepted conclusion is that Harald retroactively Christianized his father Gorm by carefully removing him from his pagan mound—which he then faithfully reconstructed—and reinterred his father's bones beside the altar of Harald's new Christian church. Several finds showing Christian influence, such as a cross pendant and chalice, were found inside the chamber of the North Mound, and Knud Krogh has interpreted these as objects left inside the reopened grave during extended Christian rituals that surrounded the reclamation of Gorm's bones. The story is a good one and has widespread acceptance: even before the dendrochronological dating program had confirmed the chronology, the royalty and people of Denmark had accepted it to the degree that the seventy-three bones were reburied—again for political reasons—under the floor of the current church and covered by a slab with the inscription: "King Gorm buried in a mound 959 and later laid in a grave here."[105]

Not all, however, are fully ready to accept the story. For example, alternate interpretations of the textual chronology and the dating of the church suggest that the grave was Harald's and that Svein built the church.[106] Furthermore, recent excavations beneath the current Jelling church have revealed that the oldest building on this spot is not a church at all, but rather a large longhouse. If this was Gorm's royal hall then further archaeological work has promise to reveal an even more interesting story about the continuity of ritual space and the royal statements of conversion as inscribed on the landscape.

Christianizing the Pagan Dead: Archaeology and Egil Skallagrimsson's Grave

Returning now to the Hrísbrú graveyard in Iceland, the combined evidence of texts and archaeology reveals a parallel case of retroactive Christianization of an ancestor, albeit on a chiefly rather than royal scale. *Egil's Saga* tells of the burial and two subsequent reburials of the famous warrior poet Egil Skallagrimsson. At the end of his life Egil lived at the Mosfell farmstead with his stepdaughter Thordis and her chieftain husband, Grim Svertingsson. *Egil's Saga* recounts: "Egil became sick afterwards in the autumn, leading to his death. And when he died, Grim dressed Egil in fine clothes; then he let him be moved down to Tjaldanes and made a mound there and Egil was placed into the mound with his weapons and clothes."[107] According to the current place names in the valley, the procession carried Egil's finely dressed body 1.4 km down from the Mosfell farm (now called Hrísbrú) to Tjaldanes (Tenting-promontory). The mound was prominently visible at a place where travelers set up their tents during journeys along the main east-west route to the site of the Icelandic parliamentary meetings at Thingvellir. His burial mound would have been an enduring symbol of Mosfell's power and claim to the surrounding lands.

After the Icelandic chieftains agreed at the Althing to adopt Christianity in the year 1000, the people of Mosfell responded quickly by displaying prominently their own conversion to Christianity. They built a church at Mosfell (Hrísbrú), monumentally materializing the new ideology. They then disinterred and transferred the remains of their venerable ancestor to a prominent location within the new church:

> Grim of Mosfell was baptized when Christianity was adopted by law in Iceland; he had a church built there. And people say that Thordis had Egil moved to the church, and this is evidenced by the fact that afterwards when a church was built at Mosfell, and the church that Grim had had built at Hrísbrú was taken down, then the old churchyard was dug up. And under the location of the altar, human bones were found. Men thought that they knew from the stories told by old people that these must be Egil's bones. At that time Skapti the priest Thorarinsson, a wise man, lived there . . . The bones of Egil were reburied at the edge of the churchyard at Mosfell.[108]

The importance of Egil Skallagrimsson for the claims to status of the Mosfellingar—as the people of Mosfell were called—is evidenced by the fact that Egil's bones are moved not once but twice to follow the materialized focal point of their ideological power. In the pagan period, Egil's mound was a signal

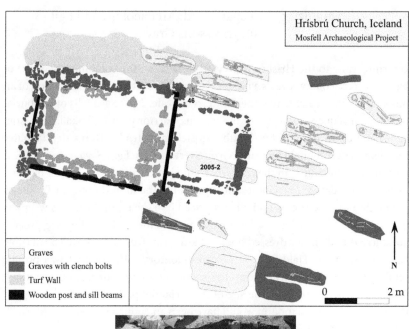

Hrísbrú Church, Iceland
Mosfell Archaeological Project

46

2005-2

4

Graves
Graves with clench bolts
Turf Wall
Wooden post and sill beams

N

0   2 m

Figure 4.8 The Hrísbrú church built around the year 1000. *Egil's Saga* tells of the reburial of the warrior poet Egil Skallagrimsson underneath the altar. Grave 2005-2,

of the Mosfellingar's power and land ownership, presented in the form of an ancestral burial. When Christianity arrived, the ritual focus and realm of the dead ancestors shifted closer to the domestic space of the living, and the people of Mosfell decided to give their most famous ancestor the most prominent place in the new church, under the holy altar at Hrísbrú. When the farmstead of Mosfell was moved to the location of the modern Mosfell farmstead in the time of Skapti Thorarinsson (middle of the twelfth century), the Mosfellingar again brought Egil's remains with them.[109] The incorporation of this presumed event into a saga written in the thirteenth century shows the tenacity and continued relevance of this social memory and the effectiveness of the efforts to incorporate an honored ancestor into the physical spaces of the new religious landscape.[110]

The Mosfell Archaeological Project (MAP) excavated a wooden church from circa 1000 at the farmstead of Hrísbrú, at the place where *Egil's Saga* says Grim Svertingsson built his church.[111] Enticingly, the archaeological excavations unearthed an empty grave beneath the altar area where Egil Skallagrimsson was supposedly reburied (Figure 4.8).[112] Excavations of the surrounding churchyard showed that bodies were moved both out of and into the cemetery. The transfer of bodies to the cemetery took place simultaneously with and shortly after the construction of the church. The removal of the bones appears to have taken place with the abandonment and relocation of the church to the nearby farm of Mosfell, where MAP identified a late-medieval church within the churchyard of the modern church.

Excavations at around the Hrísbrú church revealed two secondary burials placed along the exterior walls of the church chancel (Figure 4.9). The chancel contained the altar and was the holiest part of the church. The placement of these two reburials in symmetrical locations on either side of the chancel indicates the intentionality of their re-interments and the importance of the individuals. Both burials consisted of the disarticulated skeletons of tall adolescent males. The skeleton reburied beside the southern chancel wall has a calibrated ^{14}C date range of 780–980, indicating that the individual died well before the official conversion to

---

which appeared to match the saga description of an emptied tomb, generated significant excitement, and some locals asked to be photographed in "Egil's grave." This grave, as well as the reburials placed along the chancel (graves 4 and 46), are examples of early Christian Icelanders retroactively Christianizing pagan ancestors by bringing their remains into Christian graveyards. The five dark gray graves contained clench bolts, indicating that pieces of boats had been placed atop the graves. The presence of these boat fragments shows the enduring importance of the ship symbol, sustained across the transition to the new Christian religious system.

Source: map and photo by author, Mosfell Archaeological Project

Figure 4.9 The reburied remains of an adolescent male, most likely transferred from a pagan grave and then reinterred in a bundle beside the conversion-era Hrísbrú church in Iceland. A whalebone disc—interpreted as a curative amulet—was recovered with the bones of the young man, who suffered from a painful facial abscess that likely caused his death. The stones to the right are the foundation stones of the southern wall of the church chancel.
Source: Mosfell Archaeological Project

Christianity. These young men represent ancestors that warranted inclusion in the sacred burial space of the new religion.

Five of the graves in the Hrísbrú churchyard were empty, showing that the remains of some of the dead were moved elsewhere in antiquity. One of these empty graves extended underneath the eastern wall of the church chancel and is the only burial that predates the construction of the chancel. Since all other burials in the cemetery were placed around the church chancel, the burial under the chancel appears to be the first grave dug in the churchyard.

The excavation revealed that the grave underneath the chancel was emptied simultaneously with the church's abandonment. The exhumation event appeared as an archaeologically recognizable hole dug through the built-up gravel floor of the chancel and culminating in the grave. Those who dug this hole displaced gravel from the chancel floor and threw it over and beyond the chancel foundations, indicating that the wooden walls of the church were already removed when the grave digging took place. Since no bones were recovered in the grave under the altar at Hrísbrú, it is impossible to demonstrate conclusively whether the grave had contained a primary burial (a person buried here for the first time) or a secondary burial (a person reburied here from another original position). Nonetheless, it is probable that this grave contained a reburial interred immediately before the construction of the chancel as part of a foundation ritual that moved the remains of a recently deceased family member into the newly established Christian graveyard. Interment of a revered ancestor under the altar of Hrísbrú would have lent a sense of legitimacy and authority to the new religion and its church. Archaeology cannot tell us where the grave diggers subsequently moved the remains of the person buried beneath the altar when the church at Hrísbrú was taken down. The most logical location—as *Egil's Saga* also tells us—would be the medieval parish church at Mosfell, located 100 m to the east. Transfer of the remains of this important family member from the old church to the new church would have conferred the connection to a deep family history to the new medieval church.

Conclusions: Christianizing Death

Although the example from the Hrísbrú church is on a chiefly scale, while the Danish example is on a grander royal scale, the concept of retroactive Christianization is the same. During Christianization, powerful individuals who took a leading role in ideological change maintained their legitimacy by incorporating pagan bodies and pagan monuments into new Christian monumental landscapes. These acts were public events meant to demonstrate continuity with the past and the support of the ancestors for religious change.

Was the grave underneath the Hrísbrú chancel the second of three resting places of Egil Skallagrimsson? We cannot say. Whomever the historical person buried under the chancel was, the archaeological record and the textual sources agree that the earthly remains of certain special ancestors were important in retaining and reconstituting the ideological claims to status, power, and land. Broadly speaking, archaeological excavation confirmed the saga story of a church constructed at Hrísbrú around 1000 and the transfer of ancestral remains into the Christian graveyard. The story from *Egil's Saga* shows that retroactive Christianization was a concept that medieval Icelanders understood, while the archaeologically excavated reburials at Hrísbrú corroborate the text by strongly suggesting that this process was not just a perception, but a reality. The emptied grave underneath the altar of the Hrísbrú church generated intense public and media attention because it appeared to directly correspond with the account of

Egil's reburial from *Egil's Saga*. The wider message was that the sagas had been vindicated. The high degree of correspondence suggests to me that the saga retained a specific social memory, and that the most likely explanation is that this was Egil's grave. However, the nature of the archaeological evidence means that we will never know for certain whether the excavated tomb under the altar was indeed the grave of Egil Skallagrimsson.

The correspondence between the archaeology and the written sources at Hrísbrú is more specific than in the Jelling case. There are no textual references to the reburial of Gorm in the church at Jelling or, for that matter, to Harald having built a church at Jelling at all. The argument for the retroactive Christianization of Gorm is built on archaeological evidence. Instead of direct correspondence, the lines of evidence—textually derived dates of the reigns of the different kings, the inscriptions on runestones, archaeological excavations of the burial complex, and dendrochronological dating of the various features—complement one another in unusually detailed ways. Other text-aided arguments are also possible, but the story of Gorm's reburial by Harald remains the most widely accepted because it builds a compelling story that combines multiple independent lines of evidence.[113]

Finding correspondence between datasets about the past, particularly historical texts and archaeological remains, has the potential to tell wonderfully nuanced and satisfying stories. However, the cases of Gorm's and Egil's reburials are the exceptions, rather than the rule. A final example—and cautionary tale—drawn from Iceland illustrates the tendency of scholars to want to find correspondences, but also how further interdisciplinary study can set the record straight.

Nineteenth-century investigations of a runestone in a graveyard at the farmstead of Borg in Borgarfjörður suggested that the stone was a marker for the saga hero Kjartan Olafsson. *Laxdæla Saga* recalls, "Thorstein Egilsson had had a church built at Borg. He moved Kjartan's body home to his place and Kjartan was buried at Borg."[114] When the British traveler W. G. Collingwood visited Borg in the 1890s, he made the following observation: "in the churchyard is the grave of Kjartan, so named by an ancient tradition confirmed by the runic stone that lies on it, the only one in Iceland: bearing the words carved by some medieval hand, HIAR HVILA HALUR KIARTAN OLAFSSON—'Here sleeps the hero, Kjartan, son of Olaf'" (Figure 4.10).[115] More careful fieldwork has shown that this was far from the only runestone in Iceland, and that the form of the stone belonged to a series of runic grave markers made from oblong prismatic basalt columns. These stones, dating 1300–1700, postdate the Viking Age by several hundred years.[116] Further study of the runes showed that Collingwood's reading was incorrect, and heavily influenced by the saga story and allure of identifying the grave. The extent of Collingwood's—and his Icelandic antiquarian co-author Jón

Figure 4.10 Collingwood's drawing of the runestone that marked what he believed to be Kjartan's grave in the churchyard at Borg in Iceland. The identification of archaeological remains with saga heroes such as Kjartan from *Laxdæla Saga* exemplifies the allure of direct correspondence between text and archaeology that was particularly common in the Antiquarian Period.
Source: Collingwood and Stefánsson 1899: 59

Stefánsson's—imagination is revealed by the most recent reading of the runes, which have now been dated to the fifteenth century: "*her huiler halur hranason*" ("here rests Hallur Hranason").[117] I sometimes joked with visitors to the Hrísbrú excavation that only a plaque with Egil's name on it would prove that the grave under the chancel of the Hrísbrú church was the saga hero's grave. In the case of the Borg cemetery, it was a mistaken translation of a plaque and the influence of a saga story that tied the grave to Kjartan. Such correspondences are enticing, but it is encouraging that over time, data-driven and careful interdisciplinary study was able to reassess the veracity of these connections and reveal the truth about the past.

5

Political Centralization in Denmark

The Viking State

Foreign and native texts about Viking Age Scandinavia mention kings often and confidently envision these kings as the rulers of vast geographical areas. The nature of the power of these kings and the political organization of their societies are the focus of this chapter. The use of "king" implies the presence of a state. In the Middle Ages, however, the title of "king" has several meanings and encompasses individuals of varying degrees of political power. For instance, some Scandinavian leaders are called "sea-kings" because they possess economic and military power without any substantial geographic area to rule. The personal nature of the power wielded by the early Viking Age Scandinavian kings bears closer resemblance to the type of power possessed by leaders called chiefs in the anthropological literature, which has long sought to establish cross-culturally comparable schemata of political organization.

Introducing a few classic anthropological systems will help frame this discussion. The most widely used typologies are those proposed in the 1960s by ethnographers Elman Service (band, tribe, chiefdom, state) and Morton Fried (egalitarian, rank, stratified).[1] Typologies create somewhat arbitrary breaks in the social variation that constitutes a continuum of human societies from the most organizationally simple to the most organizationally complex, and leave out important nuances in specific social dynamics.[2] Typologies, however, are useful analytical tools that allow scholars to conceptualize variation and to conduct comparative analyses of different societies.

The nature of the power of Scandinavian kings and the organization of the individual polities changed over the course of the Viking Age. At the beginning of the Viking Age, leadership was characterized by personal power (as discussed in Chapter 3). Although personal power could be achieved by an individual leader, it was to a large degree inherited ("ascribed," in anthropological terms) through a class structure that appears to have been in place by the beginning of the Viking Age. The formation of the proper Scandinavian states—from the anthropological perspective—took place in the Viking Age. This resulted from a fundamental alteration in the nature of royal power and the hierarchical structure, by which power shifted along a continuum from persuasive power toward power that was coercive. The territorial flux of the Viking Age stabilized into three

Age of Wolf and Wind. Davide Zori, Oxford University Press. © Oxford University Press 2024.
DOI: 10.1093/oso/9780190916060.003.0005

large kingdoms that would persist and become the modern states of Denmark, Norway, and Sweden. These nations continue to look to Viking Age roots for their origins as well as for each of their respective Golden Ages.

The changes in the political organization of the Viking Age help explain the end of the Viking Age itself. A focus on personal wealth and power derived from raiding, trading, and foreign conquests abroad shifted to that of territorial power in the homelands and wealth extraction from domestic production and exchange. By the end of the Viking Age, the kings and elite in Scandinavia also relied on the uniform ideological system of Christianity. Christianity offered a class of elite administrators trained in record keeping. Payments for ecclesiastical services and public gifts to churches provided new revenue streams for centralizing wealth. In 1103/1104, just after the end of the Viking Age, the Church tithe provided an ideologically acceptable tax that could be extracted in addition to older levies and royal fees. The Church was also self-organizing in the diocesan structure accepted and sponsored by late Viking Age kings. Through the dioceses and beginnings of parish organization, the Church crystalized territorial divisions across the Scandinavian realms and offered a new stability to the secular political organization.

The shift to Christianity and the accompanying imposition of the Church administrative structure is the major—but not the only—component of the influence of continental Europe on Viking Age Scandinavia. When the Viking Age began, Scandinavia would not have been considered part of "Europe" per se. The cultural area of Europe was ideologically defined by belonging to "*Christianitas*." With Christianity, a number of other integrative relationships emerged between Scandinavians and other Europeans. This was particularly the case for the elite, as Christianity was the pan-elite ideology of the European kingdoms. Entrance into the political structure of wider Europe required the adoption of Christianity, after which Scandinavian royals quickly began to integrate, intermarry, and interact on the international political stage with rulers of the countries to the south, east, and west of Scandinavia.

To examine closely the trajectory of one of these Viking polities, this chapter focuses on the emergence of the state in Denmark. A key starting point is that the ethnic group known as the Danes should be understood separately from the organization of the polity that came to be called Denmark. The first mention of a group of people called Dani appears in *Getica*, written by Jordanes, a sixth-century Gothic historian working in Byzantium.[3] Jordanes believed that the Dani lived on Sjælland and Scania in the Migration Period. A separate ethnic group, the Jutes, inhabited the Jutland peninsula and some Jutes migrated to Britain in the fifth to sixth century. By the early Viking Age, Danes dominated the modern area of Denmark, as well as modern-day Scania and the northern part of Germany to the north of the Eider River.

The Danes of the early Viking Age were only marginally unified in a broad political and administrative sense. A general Danish ethnicity united the inhabitants of this region, at least in the eyes of foreign observers and writers. In wars with neighbors, the Danes from all or most of the regions within what would become Denmark could unite to fight as a group. At the same time, however, regional chieftains operated independently in raiding and trading activities and appear to have led sub-ethnic groups that were tied to specific geographically defined areas, such as individual islands or regions of Jutland. Chieftains controlled the assemblies, where feuds were settled, and laws were passed (see Chapter 1). These assemblies also elected and approved kings. The tug-of-war between centralizing royal power and the corporate power of the chieftains is one of the key arenas of state formation in this period.

Divergent ideas of when precisely Denmark emerged as a unified "kingdom" have been proposed. Some scholars see a very early unification of the Danish kingdom in the sixth century, well before the beginning of the Viking Age. Others have proposed that despite mentions of Danish kings in contemporary foreign and later Scandinavian texts, the political unification of Denmark as a state only occurred toward the end of the tenth century.[4] I will argue for this latter position. The polity of Denmark, characterized by a centralized bureaucratic and administrative structure and a supporting ideological framework, came into place in the late tenth century. The state emerging in the late 900s then saw greater consolidation, particularly around 1000. Once the Christian Danish state was in place in the second half of the eleventh century, the Viking Age can truly be said to be over.

Texts and Runestones

Foreign texts from neighboring Christianized peoples provide insight into the nature of power in Viking Age Denmark. Annals from the Frankish realm name kings and describe confrontations, negotiations, and peace deals between Franks and Danes. The view is always from the very top of the hierarchy, although occasionally we glimpse sub-rulers, chieftains, and co-kings, as well as internal power struggles that suggest the presence of multiple "kings" (see list of kings in Table 5.1 and Figure 5.1). Native Danish chronicles written in Latin emerge in the twelfth century. These sources as well as sagas from Iceland based on skaldic poetry and oral traditions are highly entertaining narratives focusing on the role of kings. These later sources—focused on the personal accomplishments of kings—stress the antiquity of the Scandinavian kingdoms. Special attention will be paid in this chapter to the Danish runestones, as they are the only native contemporary textual evidence for the majority of the Viking Age, at least until the eleventh century, when a few documents and inscriptions on coins appear.

Table 5.1 List of Viking Age Danish kings that are known historically, along with the dates of their reigns.

Sigfred	c. 770s–790s
Godfred	c. 800
Hemming	c. 811–812
Harald "Klak"	c. 812–814
Sons of Godfred	c. 814–820s
Horik I	c. 827–850s
Horik II	late 850s–860s
Sigfred and Halfdan	c. 873
Gnupa and Gyrd (Olafsson?)	934
Gorm "the Old" (Knutsson?)	c. 936–c. 958
Harald "Bluetooth" Gormsson	c. 958–986
Svein "Forkbeard" Haraldsson	986–1014
Harald Sveinsson	1014–1018
Knut "the Great" Sveinsson	1018–1035
Hardaknut Knutsson	1035–1042
Magnus "the Good" Olafsson	1042–1047
Svein Estridsen/Astridarson/Ulfsson	1047–1074
Harald "the Whetstone" Sveinsson	1074–1080
Knut "the Saint" Sveinsson	1080–1086

Note: Gaps exist between the reigns of the earliest kings, who may have just been kings of part of Denmark, most likely southern Jutland, as they appear mostly in Frankish/German texts. The dates of reigns become increasingly secure over time, especially after Harald Bluetooth. Some legendary kings of dubious historical veracity are omitted, such as Ragnar Lodbrok.

Foreign Contemporary Views: Travelers, Annals, Missionaries, and Bishops

The foreign sources on Viking Age Denmark focus on the interactions of Christian Europeans with the Danes through missionary journeys, war, diplomacy, and to a lesser extent, trade. The sources were almost all written in Latin and were all compiled for purposes other than to describe the conditions in Denmark. For instance, Frankish annals focus on the actions of Frankish kings, and the saints' lives point toward the holiness and sacrifices of the saints, while

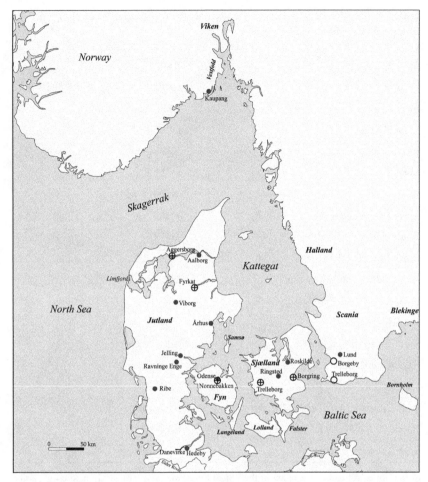

Figure 5.1 Map of Viking Age Denmark. Circles with crosses indicate locations of Trelleborg-type fortresses, while the open circles show locations of possible Trelleborg-fortresses.
Source: map by author

the histories written about the Ottonian emperors or the Archbishopric of Hamburg-Bremen glorify and moralize about the accomplishments of German kings and archbishops. At times, Denmark serves as a canvas and Danes (mostly Danish kings) as actors that help to make the authors' overarching points. Nevertheless, we occasionally glimpse social conditions in Denmark or clues about the nature of royal power.

To begin with geography, we can turn to two travel accounts by a Norwegian and an Anglo-Saxon merchant that are preserved in an Anglo-Saxon translation of Orosius' *History of the World* from just before 900.[5] These two accounts, which include the first historical mention of the political unit of Denmark, describe travel to and from the main Danish port of Hedeby.[6] In describing sailing routes, they also indicate which islands and areas were part of "Denmark." For instance, when the Norwegian Othere (Óttar) sails south from Sciringesheal (probably Kaupang) in the Viken region of Norway to the Danish port of að Hæþum (Hedeby), he "had Denmark on the port [left, east] side and open seas on the starboard [right, west] for the first three days; and then for two days before he reached Hedeby he had Jutland, Silland [south Jutland], and numerous islands on the starboard side. . . . And on the port side he had for two days the islands that belong to Denmark."[7] Othere considers the lands that were initially on his port (east) side to be part of Denmark. These lands would encompass Scania and Halland, the two coastal and westernmost provinces in modern Sweden (see Figure 5.1). He also considered Jutland and the islands through which he passed on the starboard and port sides as part of Denmark. This is confirmed by the Anglo-Saxon traveler, Wulfstan, who sailed east from Hedeby and includes the islands of Langeland, Lolland, and Falster, as well Scania, as part of Denmark.[8] East of Scania, Wulfstan describes Blekinge as belonging to the Swedes and the island of Bornholm as having its own king.[9] Othere and Wulfstan give us a rough but relatively consistent view of what was considered Denmark around 900. A short Anglo-Saxon scribal addition to Orosius' work explains that Denmark was divided between North Danes who lived on the Danish islands and the South Danes who lived on Jutland. A mention of South Danes is also included on a tenth-century runestone on the island of Lolland, which groups South Danes with other foreigners.[10] In spite of the apparent existence of Denmark as a recognized geographical unit, there were notably distinct types of Danes within this area.

Annals from the Frankish realms, compiled year-by-year in the kings' courts, provide the most reliable foreign source of information about Denmark, particularly for the ninth century. The *Royal Frankish Annals* (RFA, *Annales regni Francorum*), covering the years 741–829, provide a Frankish courtly view of the Danes in a period when they were faced with the expansionist policies of Charlemagne (reign, 768–814), the Frankish Empire's most powerful ruler. The *Annals of St. Bertin* (AB, *Annales Bertiniani*) continue the annual entries in the royal court annals from 830 to 882 with a focus on western Francia, while the *Annals of Fulda* (AF, *Annales Fuldenses*) cover the years 830–901 with a focus on eastern Francia. Somewhat surprisingly, these annals appear rather free of direct royal interference or propaganda, although they are of course rife with pro-Frankish biases.

Danish kings appear in the annals just before 800. In the beginning of the 800s, the kings of Denmark send envoys to make agreements and exchange gifts with

Frankish kings at their general assemblies. For instance, the Danish King Sigfred sent his emissaries to one of Charlemagne's assemblies in 782 at the river Lippe.[11] The Danish kings appear to have had representatives at these assemblies routinely by the 830s. We do not, however, get any insight into the geographical area ruled by these Danish kings, and often there are clearly multiple kings ruling different parts of the Danish territory at the same time. Internal in-fighting between rival Danish kings was rampant, especially in the years between 804 and 829. Thereafter, at least in the Frankish annals, we hear less about the Danish kings and more about Viking chieftains who raid along the rivers of Francia. A few times the leaders of these Viking groups are called "kings" or "princes" by the annals, but they do not appear to have possessed a definable geographic region and function instead like the leaders of other Viking raiding parties.

One Danish king of the ninth century, King Godfred, stands out among the rest because of his extensive appearances in the Frankish sources, his brashness in confronting Charlemagne, and his power to mobilize his population for war and public works. He is the only Danish king mentioned by Einhard and Notker the Stammerer, Charlemagne's two biographers.[12] According to Einhard, Godfred extracted tribute from the Slavic Obodrites who lived on the southern Baltic shore east of Denmark and thought of Frisia and Saxony as being under his rule. Einhard thought little of Godfred's threats to attack the Franks and considered them to be empty threats. Even this most powerful Danish king of the ninth century fell prey to internal rivalries and was murdered by either his own son or a follower.[13] The annals give more specifics. In 804, Godfred amassed his fleet and cavalry at his kingdom's border at Schleswig (Hedeby) and refused to show up at one of Charlemagne's assemblies.[14] In 808, Godfred invaded the Slavic lands, making the Obodrites tributary and forcibly transferring merchants from the Slavic port of Reric to Schleswig (Hedeby) so he could more effectively extract tax revenue from the merchants. In the same year, Godfred fortified his southern border by building a rampart from the Baltic Sea to the North Sea.[15] This fortification must be the Danevirke rampart (addressed below), which has been rebuilt many times on Denmark's southern border. Charlemagne appears to have taken the threat seriously because he built a fort and established a Frankish garrison on the south side of the Elbe River that formed the border between Denmark and Francia. In 810, Godfred invaded Frisia with a large fleet and forced the Frisians to pay a tribute of 100 pounds of silver.[16] In response, Charlemagne raised a large army, but before the tensions came to a head, Godfred was murdered.

Hemming, Godfred's nephew and successor, was quick to seek peace. The following year, twelve Danish chieftains and twelve Frankish nobles met at the Eider River to make a cooperative agreement. Much has been made of the fact that one of the Danes was called Osfrid from Scania.[17] This might seem to suggest that Scania was associated with the Danish kingdom already in the early ninth century; however, it might also indicate the opposite. Since Osfrid is the only person given a geographical homeland in the list of twelve men, it may in fact indicate that he was considered a foreigner, being from beyond the royal realm of Denmark. The answer is unclear. In any case, the presumed ethnic unity of these twelve Danes does not necessitate their shared allegiance to a single united and politically stable Danish kingdom.

When Hemming died the following year, royal power disintegrated into unstable kingships lasting only a few years, often with several kings ruling simultaneously. In 812, two rivals, Sigfred and Anulo, died fighting for the kingdom, after which the kingdom was co-ruled by Anulo's brothers, Harald ("Klak") and Reginfred. Harald and Reginfred launched a campaign against Vestfold in the Viken region of Norway, which RFA recounts "was located in the furthest northwestern part of their kingdom . . . whose leaders and people refused to submit to them."[18] This indicates that the area of Viken was claimed although not easily possessed by the Danish kings. This situation continued throughout the Viking Age. This particular campaign was supposedly successful, but when the kings returned, they were immediately overthrown by the unnamed and unnumbered sons of Godfred. After an unsuccessful attempt to wrest back the kingdom, Harald sought help in Francia and became Charlemagne's vassal. Harald renewed this vassal relationship in 826, when he was given land in Frisia and received baptism at the hands of Charlemagne's successor, Louis the Pious. This is perhaps the best example of a Carolingian strategy meant to stoke Scandinavian factionalism and disrupt the Danish kingdom by sponsoring royal rivals like Harald. On two occasions, Charlemagne provided Harald with Saxon and allied Obrodrite armies for unsuccessful attempts to reclaim the Danish throne by force.[19] With the support of Charlemagne and Louis the Pious, Harald did manage to gain a contentious shared kingship with the sons of Godfred from 821 to 828. Presumably, Harald would have owed allegiance to the Frankish king during this period.[20]

The quick successions, frequent sharing of the kingship, and Frankish interference appear to have weakened the Danish kingdom; at least, the formidable entity glimpsed during the time of Godfred disappears from view. A rumor of a planned attack on Saxony by the sons of Godfred caused enough concern for Louis the Pious that he responded by levying troops. But the rumor was just that and the Danish kings would not threaten Europe for over a hundred years. Instead, the threat came from Viking collectives led by shifting alliances of chieftains, whose goal was wealth extraction through looting, ransoming, and tribute rather than conquest.[21] Raids—said to be by Danes but explicitly not led by kings—started to be common in 820 when Vikings landed in Flanders, in the mouth of the Seine, and in Aquitaine. The *Annals of St. Bertin* and *Annals of Fulda* give the impression that the Danish kings were not players in these Viking ventures. Instead, the leaders were sea-borne warlords that often established themselves in fortified bases and islands along the main Frankish rivers (e.g., Seine, Loire, Somme, Weser, and Rhine). When the Viking collectives began to seriously damage Francia, the Danish King Horik—the last remaining son of Godfred—in fact disowned their piratical activities, sending envoys to Louis the Pious in 836 to declare that he had not supported the Viking attacks. Later that year, King Horik claimed to have caught and killed the guilty Vikings. For his efforts, Horik also requested that Louis pay him a reward for killing those Vikings.[22]

After the death of Louis the Pious and the split of the Carolingian Empire into three separate kingdoms, Horik must have sensed opportunity because he led a raid up the Elbe River to Hamburg in 845. But he was just one of many Danish warlords taking advantage of the situation; during the same year other Danish Viking groups laid waste to Seine River communities all the way up to Paris, while still others ravaged Aquitaine. The military potential of Denmark was clearly not under the control of the king.[23] This fact was underscored when in 847, all three kings of the Frankish kingdoms—Charles the Bald from West Francia, Lothar from Lotharingia (the central Frankish kingdom), and Louis the German from East Francia—sent envoys to Horik, asking him to restrain the Danish Viking attacks and threatening a coordinated attack on Denmark if he did not comply. But the Danish king did not have the power to control the Vikings. Later that year, a Viking group attacked Aquitaine, laying siege to Bordeaux, while another group took possession of the important port site of Dorestad. Increasingly, the chieftains leading Viking expeditions returned to Denmark to claim parts of the realm, which is exactly what Horik's nephews did upon their return from Frisia in 850. In 854, the *Annals of St. Bertin* reports that a battle lasting three days resulted in "the killing of Horik and the other kings who were with him."[24] The splintering of royal authority at the hands of Viking chieftains only intensified through the remainder of the *Annals of St. Bertin* and *Fulda*, and we hear less and less about Danish kings actually ruling in Denmark in the years leading up to 900.[25]

The Latin *Life of St. Anskar* by the German archbishop Rimbert provides an additional glimpse of ninth-century Danish politics from the life of a missionary who, in contrast to the annalists, spent time in Denmark.[26] Emperor Louis the Pious sent Anskar "the Apostle of the North" (801–865) north into Jutland with the exiled King Harald Klak to spread Christianity. Although centered on the pious deeds of Anskar, this source sheds light on power relations in Denmark as Anskar sought permission and protection from the kings of the Danes. Harald Klak, Anskar's first Danish protector, is described as a "king over some of the Danes" who had been exiled by "other kings of the same province."[27] Once in Denmark, Anskar logically focused on the main trading centers, where foreign

Christian merchants would make natural friends and where converts might be found more easily. In the late 820s, Harald Klak helped him to establish a Christian school for children, probably in Hedeby.[28] On a later trip to Denmark, he gained permission from King Horik, who is described as "sole monarch of the kingdom of the Danes," to build Denmark's first church in the emporium of Hedeby (c. 850).[29] After the fall of Horik, pagan magnates, including one who is described as the chieftain (Latin *comes* or count) of Hedeby, temporarily persuade King Horik II to close the church.[30] Horik II soon reversed his decision and allowed Anskar to reopen his church at Hedeby and build another church in Ribe (c. 860).[31] The general picture of multiple kings and frequent battles for succession is consistent with the information from the Frankish Annals. The *Life of St. Anskar* also importantly underscores the close relationship between the early Scandinavian towns and royal power, as well as the alliance that the Church sought with this royal power from the beginning.

From just before 900 until 934, there is a dearth of foreign sources on Denmark. Mentions of the Danish homeland then reappear in the East Frankish-German chronicles with a renewed series of border conflicts between the Danish Kings and the East Frankish (German) kingdom beginning in 934. These tenth-century relations between the East Frankish kingdom and the Danes are recounted by chroniclers Widukind of Corvey, who was a Saxon monk in a royal monastery, and Thietmar of Merseberg, a politically savvy bishop. Widukind's *Deeds of the Saxons* (*Res gestae Saxonicae*), completed around 973, is a deep history of the Saxon people with a focus on the political and military affairs of the East Frankish kingdom in the mid-tenth century.[32] Thietmar's *Chronicon*, completed in 1018, provides a narrative history focused on the deeds of the German kings/ emperors from 908 until 1018. Thietmar uses Widukind's work for the early to mid-tenth century, but is then increasingly original in the narrative of the last decades of the tenth and the first decades of the eleventh century.[33]

Widukind and Thietmar record numerous wars between Denmark and the German Empire to the south. These wars look like more than just border skirmishes, and although they do not use the term Denmark, they do depict the Danes as united under one king. The nature of royal power is obscure, as are the geographic boundaries of the Danish king's power beyond Jutland. The wars included attacks launched both by the Germans and the Danes. When the Germans invaded Denmark, they did not proceed beyond Jutland, being concerned primarily with the border fortifications and the rich emporium of Hedeby. The first significant tenth-century conflict came in 934, when the German King Henry Fowler attacked the Danes in retaliation for a Danish raid on Frisia.[34] Henry's victory led to a payment of tribute and conversion to Christianity by the Danish king, Gnupa. Both Widukind and Thietmar tell a story of the conversion of the Danish King Harald (Bluetooth) by a missionary named Poppo.[35] Widukind adds that Harald "ordered all of his subjects to re-ject idols, and gave all due honor to the priests and servants of God."[36] If this conversion in the late 960s was an attempt to stave off military aggression from Germany by removing the ideological justification, it did not work. Less than a decade later, the German King Otto II, who had by now been crowned Holy Roman Emperor, attacked Schleswig (Hedeby) in 974 and defeated the "rebel-lious" Danes who Thietmar says had taken up arms at the ditch built to defend their homeland (surely, Danevirke).[37] An addition in one of the manuscripts of Thietmar's *Chronicon*, stating that the emperor built an *urbs* (probably a for-tress but maybe fortifications in a town) with a garrison on the border, raises the possibility that the Germans retained possession of the southern portion of Denmark, including Hedeby.[38] The Danes took advantage of Otto II's death in 983 to reconquer the *urbs* (fortress or town), which Thietmar says the em-peror had "secured against the Danes with a wall and garrison."[39] The cessa-tion of wars thereafter correlates with Denmark's integration into Western Christendom.

At the very end of the Viking Age, circa 1076, the German cleric Adam of Bremen wrote a history of the Archbishopric of Hamburg-Bremen that includes a description of the Scandinavian lands in the missionary sphere of Hamburg-Bremen. Adam's primary goal was the glorification of the Hamburg-Bremen archbishops and their role in the Christianization of Scandinavia. Nevertheless, his work remains an invaluable source for the conditions at the end of the Viking Age.[40] The reliability of the text owes much to the fact that one of Adam's sources was the Danish King Svein Estridsen (reign 1047–1074), who was apparently Adam's friend.[41] For the ninth century, Adam relies on the annals and reiterates much information treated more thoroughly in them, while going through a sketch of the succession of kings: Godfred's threats toward Charlemagne—Hemming—battles between Sigfred and Anulo that led to coregency of Reginfred and Harald (Klak)—Harald's exile by sons of Godfred—and the gifting of parts of Frisia to various Danish factions.[42] Relying on *Vita Anskarii*, Adam also reiterates that King Horik built the first church in Denmark in Schleswig and that Anskar built the land's second church in Ribe with the permission of Horik the Younger (son of the previous Horik). Adam confirms the idea of multiple simultaneously active Danish kings, stating "there were also other kings of the Danes and the Northmen, who brutalized Gaul with piratical attacks at this time."[43] Adam completes his historical review by stating that after the reign of King Arnulf of East Francia (d. 899), he could find no further written sources about the Danish kings, which he assumes is because "the Northmen and Danes were pursued by King Arnulf with heated battle until they were destroyed."[44] Adam proceeded by stating that the remainder of his information relies on King Svein Estridsen's knowledge of his forefathers.

Svein told Adam that a king named Olaf from Sweden took the Danish kingdom by force in the early tenth century. After Olaf, his sons Gurd and Chnuba inherited the kingdom.[45] Adam suspected the existence of other un-named kings who ruled simultaneously. According to Svein, Sigeric ruled after Gurd and Chnuba, followed by the violent takeover by a Viking coming from Norway (or Normandy): Hardaknut Sveinsson (nicknamed "Gorm").[46] Adam says it is this Gorm who ruled in 934 when King Henry Fowler invaded. This contrasts with Widukind, who thought Chnuba was king at that time. Adam makes another likely mistake in attributing the next German invasion of Denmark to Otto I rather than Otto II. He claims that Otto I was responding to the murder of Frankish officials and Saxon inhabitants of Schleswig and that his invasion reached the northern tip of Jutland. As a result, Harald Gormsson, his wife Gunnhild, and their son, Svein, agreed to be baptized and the Danish realm became subject to Otto's overlordship. After this victory, the Archbishopric of Hamburg-Bremen was able to consecrate the first bishops in Denmark at Schleswig/Hedeby, Ribe, and Aarhus.[47] These towns are all on Jutland, suggesting that the Danish realm was centered in Jutland at this time.

Adam holds up Harald as an ideal Christian king who Christianized his people and "filled the whole north with preachers and churches."[48] He suggests that Harald died a martyr's death in a civil war with his son, Svein Forkbeard. After fleeing Denmark, Harald died in the Slavic lands at the town of Jumne be-fore being brought back for burial in the church he built in Roskilde on Sjælland, after which miracles were noted at his grave.[49] Adam says that Svein reverted to paganism and as divine punishment suffered domination by Swedish kings that is otherwise undocumented in other sources. Adam notes that Harald extended his control over the Norwegians and that Svein was able to maintain this control through his reign after defeating the Norwegian King Olaf Tryggvason.[50] Adam also quickly recounts the conquests of England by Svein Forkbeard and his son Knut recorded in detail in English sources (see Chapter 2).[51] Although we are not provided with details of Svein's administration, the Danish kingdom appears increasingly united, as evidenced by Harald's church building and his burial on Sjælland (away from his original power center on Jutland) and Svein's royal inva-sion of England.

Adam reveals more about state organization in his treatment of Knut, who introduced his own English bishops to Denmark, placing them throughout the realm in Scania, Fyn, and Sjælland, that is, well beyond the traditional three bishoprics on Jutland. Adam sees this as a betrayal of the Archbishopric of Hamburg-Bremen, but it was probably a shrewd move by Knut to solidify his administrative power in Denmark and free his kingdom from the archbishopric's substantial influence. Knut entered firmly into the arena of the European Christian kings when he and Emperor Conrad II—who became public allies

and seemingly also personal friends—made a treaty that reaffirmed the traditional border at the Eider River. They sealed the agreement with the marriage
of Knut's daughter Gunhild to Conrad's son Henry.[52] Knut established his three
sons as sub-kings over his three realms: Harald in England, Svein in Norway,
and Hardaknut in Denmark. Knut's empire disintegrated after his death, and
after the death of his sons the kingdom of England reverted to an English king,
while King Magnus of Norway briefly established control over both Norway
and Denmark. Svein Estridsen—Adam's friend and Knut's nephew—appears
in the narrative as a champion of Denmark who resists Magnus and wins back
Denmark and later also Norway. Svein is also said to have contemplated an invasion of England, but he resisted because the English king governed so justly and
because Svein preferred peace and tribute from England.[53] This is an exceedingly
pro-Svein narrative, as can be seen by comparison with the stories preserved in
later Danish accounts and the Icelandic sagas. Adam does not hide, however,
that Svein was dominated for a time by the Norwegian King Harald, who often
raided in Denmark. Striking at the heart of Denmark, Harald even burned the
church in Aarhus and sacked the rich town of Schleswig.[54] Though frequently on
the losing side, Svein held the Danish realm, probably because of the substantial
and growing state administration present in Denmark. For instance, Adam notes
Svein's reorganization of the Danish bishoprics, which expanded their number
to eight: Schleswig, Ribe, Aarhus, Viborg, Wendila/Wendssyssel, Fyn, Sjælland,
Lund, and Dalby.[55] Svein's efforts at reorganization included direct correspondence with the pope to establish an archbishopric in Denmark, which would
have further solidified his independence from the Archbishopric of Hamburg-
Bremen.[56] In this venture, Svein was not successful and Scandinavia would have
to wait until 1101 for the Archbishopric of Lund to be established. In Adam's
final description of the lands of Scandinavia, he provides ethnographic information, presumably told to him by Svein. He says, significantly, that Sjælland had a
number of Vikings who paid tribute to the Danish king for the license to conduct
pirate raids on the surrounding "barbarians" (presumably non-Christian Slavs
and other pagans). This was a new and unprecedented level of royal control over
Viking activities. Although Adam says that these Vikings occasionally targeted
their own people, the noteworthy aspect here is that the Vikings knew that it was
now the Danish king who held the monopoly on force.

Later Danish Legends and Histories: Sven Aggesen and Saxo Grammaticus

Two native Danish sources—Sven Aggesen's *Brevis Historia Regum Dacie*
(*A Short History of the Danish Kings*, c. 1188) and Saxo Grammaticus's *Gesta*

Danorum (*Deeds of the Danes*, written over many years until c. 1218)—offer reflective narratives that combine traditional Danish stories with material from the Icelandic saga tradition and the narratives of *Adam of Bremen* and *Vita Anskarii*.[57] These Danish sources re-centered the narratives around heroic Danish accomplishments. One of the primary goals of the Danish authors, who were both religiously trained historians writing in Latin, was to project back in time the greatness and permanence of Denmark and the Danish kings. Although they contain a great deal of tradition that complements foreign textual sources, this agenda means that they cannot be trusted to accurately reflect the scale and extent of power wielded by Danish Viking Age kings from the late eighth to mid-eleventh century. On the one hand, since they are written in Latin, and are thus unanchored to the Viking Age skaldic poems that guide the sagas, these sources are less reliable than the Icelandic sources. On the other hand, the Danish sources provide an opportunity to approach the evolution of the Viking Age state from a native Danish vantage point that is different from the perspective of the foreign sources and from the Icelandic sources that are the focus of the following section. In the following sections, then, we will explore how the German, Danish, and Icelandic sources confirm, contradict, and complement one another in their view of the formation of the state in Denmark.

Saxo's *Gesta* is many times longer and much more complex than Sven's *Historia*, a fact recognized by Sven, who knew Saxo and self-consciously expected "his successor" to fill many of the gaps left in his own narrative.[58] For the kings predating Christianity, both narratives are highly creative works that attempt to order legends and tales circulating in their diverse sources. During the pre-Christian period, gods, dragons, and giants move freely in and out of the narratives, and the authors arrive at very divergent chronologies for the Danish kings (Figure 5.2). The goal is certainly not historical accuracy, especially before the arrival of Christianity, which provides a significant chronological and cultural break for both clerical writers.

Saxo's *Gesta* consists of sixteen books. The first seven are too fantastical for the gleaning of historical information. The first historical king in Saxo's work is Godfred, who—just as in the Frankish sources—resists Charlemagne's aggression, attacks the Frisians, and dies by the hands of a trusted retainer.[59] Saxo's account omits mention of Godfred's founding of Hedeby and the construction of the Danevirke. After Godfred, Saxo's account becomes historically confused, so that there is some correspondence in the names that appear in the Frankish sources, but less so in the actions of kings. At other times, Saxo finds solutions to lacunae in the series of kings, by for instance creatively dealing with the chaotic ninth century in Denmark by inserting the tales of the semi-legendary Ragnar Lodbrok and his sons. These Ragnar legends are absent from Sven Aggesen's *Historia*. In general, though, Saxo agrees with the Frankish observation of the

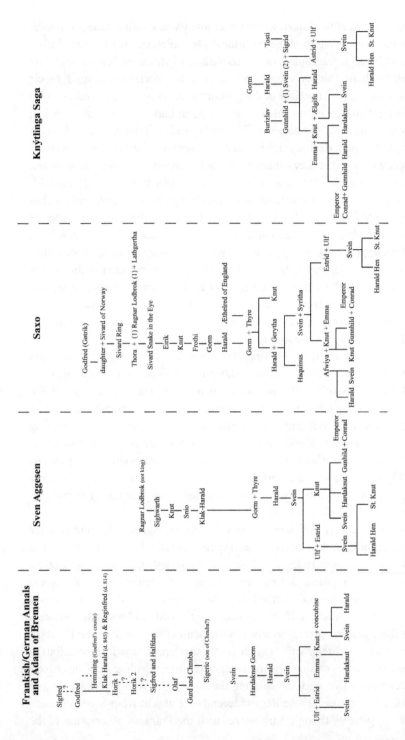

Figure 5.2 Genealogies of Danish Kings according to (1) Frankish/German Annals and Adam of Bremen, (2) the twelfth-century Danish Historian Sven Aggesen, (3) the twelfth- to thirteenth-century Danish historian Saxo Grammaticus, and (3) *Knýtlinga Saga*, the Icelandic saga about the Danish dynasty. The sources tend to agree on the kings once the Jelling dynasty begins with (Hardaknut) Gorm, although lesser inconsistencies in parentage do persist.

Source: graphic by author

plural nature of early Danish kingship. He describes, for instance, separate kings over Jutland and islands of eastern Denmark.[60]

Saxo and Sven's stories of Danish kings begin to align and provide a somewhat more historically reliable narrative starting with Gorm and his son Harald Bluetooth. Both authors think rather poorly of Gorm—Sven calls him an indulgent "sluggard," while Saxo blames him for intolerance toward Christians—but both suggest that Denmark was saved by his wife, Thyre. Sven tells how Thyre saved Denmark from German interference and masterminded the original construction of the Danevirke fortification. In his narrative, Thyre falsely promises to marry the German emperor, and while she stalls the proceedings, she diverts three successive years of Danish tribute meant for Otto toward the construction of the Danevirke.[61] This origin story of the Danevirke mistakenly places its original construction later than recounted in the foreign annals. Saxo also credits Thyre with the construction of Danevirke, but places this construction after Otto's invasion of Denmark, in the reign of Harald.[62]

Underlying these stories is the fame of a small runestone at the royal site of Jelling, upon which Thyre is called "Denmark's betterment (or adornment)," a phrase that Sven Aggesen translates into Latin and uses explicitly twice in his narrative (decus datiae from tanmarkur bot; see runestone section below).[63] The runestone was raised by her husband Gorm, indicating that Saxo was mistaken in thinking that Gorm predeceased Thyre. A further example of the interaction of the twelfth-century narratives with archaeological remains from this period include the tradition that Harald Bluetooth had his parents buried in matching grave mounds at Jelling. Archaeological excavation has revealed this tradition to be partially true (see below and Chapter 4). Both authors give more information about the important Jelling site. Sven recalls that the burial mounds were close to the king's residence at Jelling. Archaeologists have only recently come to understand this to be true, changing the interpretation of Jelling from a mortuary site to a palace complex with royal burials (see more below).

The significant labor involved in the creation of the Jelling site may be behind the story in both Sven and Saxo's narratives of Harald Bluetooth's single-minded and tyrannical use of Danish labor for his own building projects. In both accounts, Harald has his army haul an immense rock to Jelling to be placed atop Thyre's burial mound. This unreasonable labor demand leads to widespread dissent and a successful rebellion, led by Svein Forkbeard. Sven also blames the conversion to Christianity for creating discontent, while Saxo goes further in describing Svein's rebellion as a pagan backlash. A major value in the twelfth-century sources is that they transmit the Danish tradition that Harald Bluetooth pushed the Danes to unprecedented political centralization with massive labor demands and Christian conversion, both of which were unpopular.

According to Danish tradition, Harald's reign also saw expansion of Danish power to the southern Viken region of Norway around the Oslofjord and to the southern shores of the Baltic. Harald interferes in Norwegian rivalries, supporting Harald Greycloak against Hakon the Good, with the final goal of entrenching his overlordship and extracting tribute from Norway. Harald also asserts overlordship over a group of Danish Vikings settled in the trading site of Jomsborg/Wolin in modern-day Poland.[64] These so-called Jomsvikings have their own semi-legendary saga that recounts stories of their exploits in the Baltic and their role as Harald's shock troops against the Norwegians. After Harald is wounded in his civil war with his son Svein, he flees to Jomsborg before dying and ultimately being returned to Roskilde for burial in a Christian church. Saxo, who calls Harald "master of Sclavia," explains that the Danish Vikings from Jomsborg "covered the waters of the north with the continual destruction of sea-farers. This contributed to the supremacy of the Danes more than any soldiering by land."[65] These would have been risky but useful allies for a Danish king and speak to Harald's sweeping ambitions: the endgame of controlling southern Norway and the southern shores of the Baltic may well have been royal Danish domination of the profitable regional sea-based trade and exchange networks that connected the Atlantic Ocean and the Baltic Sea.

Svein Forkbeard's reign, which is famous in history primarily for his conquest of England, is given mixed reviews by Sven and Saxo, who spend much time discussing how he was taken prisoner and ransomed by Vikings. In fact, Svein Forkbeard might have felt the negative effects of the royal alliance with the Jomsborg pirates, as both Sven Aggesen and Saxo describe his kidnapping at the hands of the Jomsvikings. Saxo's account styles Svein Forkbeard's time in captivity as divine punishment for his rebellion against his Christian father. Svein's defeat of the Norwegians and invasion of England is entirely omitted by Sven Aggesen and given shorter shrift by Saxo than Adam of Bremen and the sagas (see Chapter 2 for Svein´s invasion of England).

Knut, the son of Svein Forkbeard, is credited with expanding the Danish empire, but the accounts of Sven Aggesen and Saxo add little new material, and the foreign sources and the Old Norse sagas are more informative. Sven Aggesen, however, did produce a document called *The Law of Retainers* (*Lex Castrensis*), which purports to be a list of laws established by Knut to govern his diverse and international personal army. Saxo relies on Sven's law and both authors have a great deal to say about these laws. Most scholars today feel that these laws reveal much more about twelfth-century military organization than they do about eleventh-century Danish political organization. Although the expansive details, for instance, about seating arrangements and the feeding of horses are not likely to be original to Knut's reign, the document does record the memory of a period when the new Danish empire had to accommodate international troops with clear laws and rules for how the king governed court proceedings. We are also left with the impression that Knut had a larger and more professional army than any previous Danish king. Although probably an exaggeration, Saxo says that Knut had a professional force of six thousand men in sixty ships.[66] He goes on to say that in the inactive winter months, this army was dispersed to barracks and paid a monthly wage.[67] The text's historicity is dubious, but even in its twelfth-century distorted form, it may preserve the memory of the first Danish king to oversee a state-level military organization.

Sagas: Traditions Maintained and Transformed in Iceland

The saga traditions concerning the Danish kings are preserved primarily in the narratives about Norwegian kings, most notably in Snorri Sturluson's *Heimskringla* (c. 1230).[68] As discussed in Chapter 3, Snorri's long work centers on the saga about King Olaf the Saint but stretches back into stories of legendary ninth-century Norwegian kings and forward until 1177. A shorter saga modeled on *Heimskringla* but centered on the life of the Danish St. Knut was written by Snorri's nephew, Olaf Thordarson, who stayed at the Danish court of King Valdemar in 1240–1241. *Knýtlinga Saga* is split into three sections: (1) the Danish kings from Harald Bluetooth to St. Knut (the great nephew of Knut the Great), (2) St. Knut's reign, and (3) the kings after St. Knut. The central section concerns the saint whose reign is addressed at the end of this chapter. What concerns us here is the first part, which addresses St. Knut's ancestors. Although *Knýtlinga Saga* focuses on the Danish kings, *Heimskringla* has much more to say about the Danish kings before St. Knut and includes a greater number of skaldic poems, which anchor the prose in poetry from the Viking Age.

The skaldic poems are especially valuable because they were mostly composed in the Viking Age by poets who lived at the kings' courts. These skaldic poems, which focus on battles and praise-worthy leadership qualities, often provide a narrative structure for the saga stories. Skaldic poems preserved in Iceland are much richer in detail about the Norwegian kings and earls because Viking Age Icelanders more frequently joined the retinues of Norwegian kings and because the thirteenth-century saga writers found themselves in the Norwegian kingdom's sphere of political influence. An exception is the substantial corpus of poems about Knut the Great, whose unprecedented power over a broad empire drew warriors (and warrior poets) from across the north.

In general, the sagas report the same order of kings—starting with Gorm—as do the Frankish and Danish sources (Gorm—Harald—Svein—Harald—Knut the Great—Hardaknut—Svein—Harald—St. Knut; see Figure 5.2). In addition, they offer a different look into the political development of the Viking Age, albeit one still centered on kings, earls, and chieftains. The sagas' main contribution to our understanding of the Danish kingdom's emergence comes from the details provided about Danish interactions with Norwegian kings. This section focuses on the more reliable material preserved in poetic form within these sagas, supplemented by the prose saga narratives that exemplify aspects of Danish power structure in the face of conflicts with Norwegians. In contrast to the foreign sources that offer external views of Denmark and the twelfth-century Danish clerically educated chroniclers who wrote in Latin from the perspective of the Church, the skaldic poems present glimpses of Danish politics from the ideological viewpoint of Viking Age kings.

From the earliest reference to the Danish kings in the sagas, the focus of the action is their attempt to control the Viken region of southern Norway, located around the Oslofjord. Like the accounts given by the Danish twelfth-century chroniclers, the sagas suggest that this region was often tributary to Denmark, but also that this was often hotly contested. When Danish kings were strong, this region was tributary or even considered part of Denmark, whereas when Norwegian kings were ascendant, then the region was firmly part of Norway. The Gorm of the sagas is described as king of Denmark, but it is only with his son Harald Bluetooth (in the mid-tenth century, by saga chronology) that the Danish domination of the Viken region is recorded. Frequently, the Danish king allied with the Earls of Lade (Hlaðir), based in the Trondelag region of coastal Norway that lies north of the large western fjords facing the Atlantic Ocean. In Norway, the Earls of Lade were second only in power to the upstart Norwegian kings, who, starting with Harald Fairhair, aimed to unite Norway. The goals of the Earls and the Danish kings therefore often coincided in their desire to curtail Norwegian royal power. The Earls of Lade were often very willing, for example, to allow Danish control of the Viken region and to pay tribute from that region's resources.

In the sagas, this pattern begins when Earl Hakon Sigurdsson of Lade stays at Harald Bluetooth's court in Denmark, and they hatch a plan to overthrow the Norwegian King Harald Greycloak Eiriksson. Hakon states his proposition in *Heimskringla*: "I will then become your earl and confirm that by oaths; and with your support I will conquer Norway for you and hold it thereafter under your overlordship and pay tribute to you."[69] The skaldic poem, *Vellekla* (*Lack of Gold*), composed by the Icelander Einar Helgason in praise of Hakon, follows this story and confirms the result:

> Under the earl lies now
> all the land of Norway
> north of Vik[en]; so widely
> wields his power Hakon.[70]

The region of Viken (referred to in the sagas as Vík) of course went to Harald Bluetooth. Hakon's oath to Harald Bluetooth included an obligation to help defend Denmark. When Otto II of Germany threatened to invade Denmark, Harald summoned Hakon and a Norwegian contingent to fight on the southern border. The sagas attribute Otto's aggression to a demand for Harald to convert to Christianity, which is inconsistent with the chronology from the foreign sources, which have a thirteen-year gap between the Danish conversion in the 960s and the German invasion in 973. That Hakon answered Harald's call and fought at the Danevirke rampart is recounted by the saga narrative and supported by another stanza in *Vellekla*:

> And toward winter would the
> wealth-dispensing Danish
> folk-king test the troth of
> tough-minded Earl Hakon
> when the breastwork's builder
> bade the doughty fighter
> guard the goodly ramparts
> 'gainst the Saxons' onrush.[71]

The "breastwork" in this stanza is probably Danevirke, which the saga says Harald reinforced, but it is tempting also to connect this reference to Harald's larger defensive building projects in Denmark (see below on the Trelleborg fortresses). After his conversion, the sagas relate that Harald sent Danish bishops to southern Norway to shore up his power. This is but the first instance of a strategy by which the Danish kings employed Danish priests and bishops to support Danish interests in Norway, whether it was to sustain administration or to sow discontent.[72] Hakon refused Christianity and appears to have renounced his tribute obligations, causing renewed hostilities with Harald Bluetooth.[73]

During the reign of Svein Forkbeard and after Earl Hakon's death, the aspiring King Olaf Tryggvasson took power in all Norway, including the Viken region. The familiar pattern repeated itself, however, as Svein Forkbeard allied himself with Earl Hakon's sons (Earl Svein and his brother Eirik) and the Swedish king to defeat the Norwegian king in a great sea battle in 1000.[74] Norway was again divided, and the Danish king took direct control over the Viken region. The repeating pattern continued as the Norwegian King St. Olaf Haraldsson retook the Viken region in the 1010s, only to be ousted by King Knut the Great in 1028 with the help of Earl Hakon Eiriksson (the grandson of the Hakon who allied with Harald Bluetooth).[75]

The sagas suggest that Knut the Great tightened royal control, probably with the help of resources, revenues, and administrators from England. Even

Knut's ousting of St. Olaf seems to have been accomplished mostly through promises of financial rewards to Norwegian chieftains rather than open battle. The sagas and skaldic poems repeatedly describe how Knut bought Norwegian supporters with his wealth.[76] In 1030, however, Knut forewent the usual pattern of having a Norwegian earl function as regent when he installed his young son, Svein Knutsson, as sub-ruler over Norway. His rule was unpopular with Norwegians, and we get a sense that this was because of harsh "Danish-style" laws that drew more power and money toward the king than had previously been acceptable in Norway. Svein Knutsson's laws are said to have included novel ways to funnel wealth to the king, such as changes to inheritance laws that made the king the inheritor of assets possessed by murderers and outlaws. A series of taxes on every farmer—the *vinartoddi* tax on agricultural produce and the *rykkjató* tax on measures of raw textiles— were introduced. In addition, every seventh male had to equip one warrior for the Danish army and share in the building of warships.[77] The historicity of these specifics is unverifiable, but the memory of more systematic control of agricultural produce and weapons of war under Knut's rule is consistent with other written sources.

Upon Knut's death, the Norwegian kings gained the upper hand for a few decades and began raiding extensively in Denmark. His sons who ruled Norway (Svein) and England (Harald) soon died in quick succession, leaving Knut's third son, Hardaknut, who had inherited Denmark, to hold the empire together. Hardaknut moved his court to England—the most valuable and most organized portion of the kingdom—leaving Norway to Magnus the Good, son of St. Olaf. After Hardaknut's death, Magnus asserted kingship over Denmark as well. His rule in Denmark was always contested by Knut's nephew, Svein Astridarson/Estridsen, who also claimed the Danish throne.[78] During Svein Astridarson's early years of rule, up to 1050, Denmark was repeatedly ravaged by King Magnus and his uncle Harald "the Hardruler" Sigurdsson, who himself assumed Norwegian kingship after Magnus. Skaldic poems recall the sacking of the major Danish port sites of Aarhus ("hard was the hail-of-darts, their homecoming, at Árós") and Hedeby ("Burned down was at both ends . . . by Harald's valiant henchmen Heithabýr [Hedeby] alto- gether").[79] A key point, however, is that in spite of apparent Norwegian dom- inance for a few decades, the Norwegian kings could never truly consolidate their rule over Denmark. In this depiction, the sagas agree with the Danish chroniclers Saxo and Sven Aggesen. Svein Astridarson's early reign reads like a series of defeats and the saga authors seem to wonder how he actually held on to Denmark. They offer some explanations, such as the final stanza in the Icelandic skald Thorleik the Handsome's praise poem to Svein, preserved in *Knýtlinga Saga*:

Those who vied with Svein
often put themselves at risk;
three rulers gained little
while striving for victory.
Yet the friend of farmers [Svein] has held, battle-strong,
all the land of the Jutes from border to border
and Denmark, too;
he is a clever king.[80]

This stanza's three rulers who warred—ultimately unsuccessfully—against Svein are the two Norwegian kings, Magnus and Harald, and the Swedish King Steinkel, who also tried to take advantage of the apparent weakness of the Danish kingdom. The prose of *Knýtlinga Saga* further explains Svein's success in spite of repeated losses on the battlefield: "no other Danish king has been so beloved by all of the people."[81] Svein's success, however, is probably due to the administrative strength that had been built in Denmark since the reign of Harald Bluetooth. In Svein's reign, the Danish state could not so easily be broken or mastered, especially by Norwegian kings who had not yet solidified their own state-level society in Norway.

The sagas hint at the changes in Denmark from the view of the kings. In the next section, the runestones spread across the Danish landscape will reveal a contemporary view of those changes, not just from the perspective of the kings' poets, but also from the viewpoint of local chieftains and administrators.

The Runestone Evidence

Well over 200 runestones are known from Viking Age Denmark, including the regions of Scania and Halland (now in Sweden) and Schleswig (now in Germany).[82] The inscriptions are typically short, but the stones have a broad spatial dispersal across the Danish landscape and record claims to land and leadership roles. The stones, which are the only substantial native primary sources from the Viking Age, shed substantial light on the social structure and political organization. Their placement in the landscape has in a little less than half of the stones been stable since the Viking Age, meaning that their distribution across Denmark can be examined for temporal and geographical trends.[83] The distribution of runestones across the landscape reflects a combination of factors, including where people lived, the availability of usable stone, and most importantly for our consideration, the politics of power negotiation. Temporal variations in their use, discernible through rune form, language, style, and decoration, allow us to see changes to claims on local power. At the same time, associations with particular sites and personages known from later written sources shed light on royal power and international conflicts.[84]

The placement of runestones in the landscape indicates that they were meant to be visible in prominent locations and along travel routes and that they were often associated with "special sites" such as assembly sites, burial mounds, and magnate farms.[85] Written in formulas on the runestones, curses and warnings against desecrating, moving, or reusing stones clearly indicate that the monuments were seen as visual and material manifestations of local power.[86] Perhaps one of the best examples that the raising of runestones was largely about highlighting inheritance rights can be read on the Gunderup 1 stone. This stone explicitly states that a man is inheriting wealth from his stepfather: "Toki raised these stones and made this monument in memory of Ebbi, his kinsman-by-marriage, a good þegn, and Tofa, his mother. Both of them lie in this mound. Ebbi granted Toki his wealth after himself."[87] The runestones and their texts are claims to property and inheritance, as well as expressions of social relations, between both living and dead and the living and the living.[88] In a sense, they were the modern American-style billboards of the Viking Age. They were meant to be seen and meant to be read.[89]

Local Power on Runestones

Runestone inscriptions sometimes articulate titles of social roles for the person that the stones commemorate. Although these titles are not easy to interpret and they vary over time and are not mutually exclusive, they can yield information about political organization. Some titles—especially *þegn* and *dreng*—have been connected to royal power, but this connection is difficult to uphold because of the scarcity of our sources. Both titles were clearly ones of praise and prestige. Especially *þegn* clearly refers to a chieftain with political and economic power, and late in the Viking Age a *þegn* was probably someone who had a role in royal administration. The Glavendrup runestone from circa 900 to 950 commemorating the man Alli includes multiple titles that are left in bold italics here:

> Ragnhild raised this stone after Alli the Pale, *goði* [*priest*] of the sanctuary, honorable **þegn** [*chieftain*] of the *lið* [*warrior band*]. Alli's sons made these memorials after their father and his wife after her husband. And Soti carved these runes after his **dróttin** [*lord*]. Thor hallow these runes. May he become an outcast who harms this stone or drags it away to commemorate someone else.[90]

The titles *þegn* and *goði* indicate that Alli was a local chieftain. Þegn indicates a role of political and military leadership over a group of followers. The goði title is known from later Icelandic sources as a secular chieftain, but the root of the word goði (god) indicates that they had a priest-like role as the head of local pre-Christian worship and sacrifice in the Viking Age.[91] The goði role as religious specialist encompassed ideological and likely political power over a territory or group of people, as indicated by the text of two runestones also from Fyn in which a man named Roulv is called "Nura goði" (goði of the people of the nes). The nes is likely the peninsula of Helnæs, upon which the stones were raised.[92] The word *dróttin* on the Glavendrup stone indicates that the þegn Alli was the lord of Soti, who was probably a warrior in Alli's *lið* (a group of warrior followers attached to a chieftain). Membership in a chieftain's lið was considered honorable in the Viking warrior ethos and is commemorated on several other runestones, such as the Sjørring Stone, on which Asa commemorates her husband with the primary designation as "Finulv's hemþegi (follower)."[93] Here the term hemþegi (literally "home-dweller") means a warrior who is part of a chieftain's household, serving as part of his retinue or lið.

The Glavendrup runestone was placed at the prow of a 60-meter-long stone ship setting atop a low mound (Figure 5.3). The stern end of the ship setting culminates on a Bronze Age barrow. The stone itself had special significance dating back to the Bronze Age, as indicated by multiple so-called skålgruber (bowl-shaped holes with symbolic and ritual functions).[94] The monument's message of power and inheritance is evident visually, as the text places the inheritor literally at the center of the text. The first word of the text, which appears in one of the central vertical rune rows read from bottom to top, is the name of the raiser, Ragnhild. Moreover, her name appears in larger runic letters than the rest of the runes in the inscription.[95] This same Ragnhild had earlier raised a stone on Sjælland and therefore seems to have come to Fyn to marry Alli, evidencing marriage alliances between the upper class across geographical areas and, in this case, islands.[96]

The titles on runestones, as well as the patron-client relationships articulated in the runestone texts, paint a picture of a chiefly society in which reciprocal relationships of personal loyalty structured society. This social structure was co-opted into royal administration in the late Viking Age.

Royal Power on Runestones: The Jelling Runestones

The two Jelling runestones, the most famous runestones in Scandinavia, are explicitly tied to royal power. The stones are positioned in the middle of a royal center. The smaller of the two stones, erected by King Gorm the Old, includes the first runic mention of the polity of Denmark. This smaller stone also signals the initiation of major symbolic monumental construction at the royal site of Jelling (the archaeological evidence for which is discussed below). The smaller stone, which was originally probably placed at the prow of the world's largest ship setting, reads: "King Gorm made these monuments in memory of Thyre, his

Figure 5.3 The Glavendrup monument and runestone. A widow, Ragnhild, raised this runestone at the tip of a large setting of standing stones made to look like a ship. The message commemorates her husband described simultaneously as a *þegn* (chieftain), a *dróttin* (lord), and a *goði* (a leader in his pre-Christian worship community).

Source: photos by author

wife, Denmark's betterment."[97] The larger stone also directly mentions Denmark and is often called "Denmark's birth certificate" because the runic text proclaims the unification of Denmark: "King Harald commanded these memorials made to Gorm, his father, and to Thyre, his mother. That Harald who won for himself all of Denmark and Norway and made the Danes Christian" (Figure 5.4).[98] The use of "all of Denmark" purposefully indicates that the land considered Denmark was not fully unified before. The impressive large three-sided Jelling stone follows a less common tradition in that Harald Bluetooth raised the monument for himself, rather than in commemoration of dead relatives. King Harald had himself placed center-stage in the text, such that the name Harald is the first word in both the first and the last horizontal line of the text side of the stone, while Denmark (tanmaurk) is the last word on that side.[99]

Many aspects of the large Jelling runestone suggest that Harald had raised a runestone that was qualitatively different from those seen before, with the intention of projecting novel messages both to the population of Denmark and to visitors to the royal site. The stone, which is the world's largest runestone, must have been the largest stone in the region and would have required substantial effort to transport.[100] It is covered by ornamentation on all three sides, with images that blend Christianity with native language, runic letters, and artistic references. The text is unusual in that it is organized in horizontal bands, one of only two such stones in Denmark, in a probable visual reference to the Christian European texts written in horizontal lines in manuscripts.[101] The monument includes echoes of the past with the use of purposefully archaic language and specific ornamentation such as a serpent that recalls the serpent on his father Gorm's runestone for Thyre.[102] The single runestone, then, does what the overall Jelling monument also does, which is to wed the political messaging of the old pagan Scandinavian past with the new Christian messaging.

Harald's son, Svein, is not mentioned on the stones from Jelling, but his role as military leader of the Danes is notably memorialized on stones connected to wars with the German Holy Roman Empire. Three runestones are presumably connected to the Danish reconquest of Hedeby from the German Empire, recorded in continental texts as taking place in 983. One of these, Aarhus 1, identifies Amund, who died fighting at Hedeby. The other two provide greater detail in memorializing two of Svein Forkbeard's fallen followers who also died fighting at Hedeby, presumably when the Danes besieged and reconquered the town from the Germans.[103] Hedeby 1 states "Thorulf raised this stone, Svein's **hemþegi**, in memory of Eirik, his **félagi**, who died when **drengs** besieged Hedeby; and he was a captain, a very good **dreng**."[104] From one of Svein's personal household warriors to one of his fallen comrades, this stone gives key insight into the royal warrior bands surrounding kings. They considered themselves *félagar* (sg. *félagi*) or partners in a presumably profitable common

Figure 5.4 The Large Jelling Stone, the largest runestone in the world, was the centerpiece of Harald Bluetooth's monumental restructuring of the royal site of Jelling. One side (top in figure) contains the main part of the runic text, a second side (left) shows a lion and serpent, while the third side (right) depicts Denmark's only runestone crucifix.

Source: photos by Roberto Fortuna, National Museum of Denmark (CC-BY-SA)

endeavor, such as war or trade. The root of the word félagi is *fé*, meaning wealth and originally meaning wealth measured in livestock. *Dreng* has been explained as an official title linked to the king, but recent scholarship has stressed that it seems more likely simply to be a designation of commendation, especially used for young men who had showed accomplishment (e.g., bravery, loyalty, skill) in the engagement of praiseworthy communal activities, such as war.[105] Typically drengs seem to have belonged to a félagi, such as a lið, as evidenced by the common association of these words in the runic inscriptions, especially from the period after Christianization.

The link to royal power is even more explicitly made in the Hedeby 2 stone, found beside a burial mound lying along the major road leading north from Hedeby: "King Svein placed the stone in memory of Skardi, his hemþegi, who had journeyed westward, but who then died at Hedeby."[106] This stone, placed in a prominent place and probably beside the dead warrior's grave mound, highlights Skardi's praiseworthy accomplishments, including voyages westward (most likely raids in England) and his death in Svein's service in the victorious attack on Hedeby. But importantly, King Svein places himself center stage here and explicitly uses his title of king on this stone, a title absent from the inscription on Hedeby 1. In terms of examinations of social power and state formation, these Hedeby stones show that the late tenth-century kings still operated with the same basic personal military bands as local chieftains attested on the Glavendrup stone. Simultaneously, the title of king was being explicitly used—at least by the king himself, when erecting runestones.

Several stones post-dating the Hedeby stones also commemorate warriors who fell in wars led by kings. Although the specific battles are less clear, these stones strongly suggest that rulers called kings were leading larger regional polities into wars with one another. One common refrain is that a warrior died "when kings fought." The most famous is Aarhus 3, which states that "Gunnulf and Audgaut and Aslak and Hrolf raised this stone in memory of Ful, their félagi (partner), who died when kings fought."[107] Presumably, the Viking Age audience would have understood to which unnamed battle this stone referred. One common suggestion is that the reference is to the famous Battle of Svold from the sagas, which took place around 1000. At Svold, Svein Forkbeard, aided by Jarl Eirik of Lade and Olof Skötkonung from Sweden, defeated the upstart Norwegian King Olaf Tryggvason. The story is good, but the correspondence is dubious.

Runestones as Monuments of Social Stress and Political Change
The Danish Viking Age runestones can be divided into four typological groups that, broadly speaking, follow one another chronologically: (1) Helnæs Type (720–800), (2) Gørlev Type (800–900), (3) Pre-Conversion Type (900–970),

and (4) Post-Jelling Type (c. 970–1025).[108] The vast majority of the stones were erected in the decades before and after conversion.

The runestones are monuments of power erected strategically at times of change, such as when new people, new power, or new modes of land ownership are introduced. The proliferation of runestones in specific areas at particular times could therefore be indicators of internal social change and the ongoing negotiation of the centralization of power. Once the new form of power was entrenched, runestones might then have become less necessary. In this conceptualization, runestones would be erected primarily by either new power wielders given land grants by an overlord or by a traditional power wielder who took on new and expanded powers. In both cases, the new powers would benefit from the public legitimization projected through statements such as those made on runestones.

The earliest stones of the Helnæs and Gørlev types from the eighth and ninth centuries are dispersed across the fertile areas of central Denmark, concentrating in East Central Jutland, Fyn, and Sjælland. Randsborg suggested that this distribution might be associated with the emergence of an early centralized Danish kingdom centered on Fyn (Figure 5.5).[109] This polity need not necessarily be called a kingdom, and certainly not THE Danish kingdom. It is perhaps safer to say that the distribution of stones indicates a general centralization of power.[110] In any case, "royal" power cannot be detected on the early stones from the 700s and 800s, and none of the power-wielders use the name king (konungr) on the stones.[111] In fact, the names and titles of the power-wielders provide an example of contradiction between the continental texts about Denmark and the runestones. The specific names we read in the texts do not appear on the runestones, and their political titles of rulership are different.[112]

The tenth-century Pre-Conversion Type stones appear with greater frequency in Jutland, possibly indicating increased centralization in Jutland and, in particular, a shift of the center of political power in Denmark to Jutland (Figure 5.6). This would correspond with the flourishing of the Jutlandic towns of Hedeby, Ribe, and Aarhus, as well as the emergence of Jelling as the political center of the Jelling Dynasty at the end of this period. As discussed further below, the runestones from the 900s until the conversion under Harald Bluetooth have a similar geographical distribution as the contemporaneous rich cavalry chamber graves, providing us with correspondence between runestones and a specific grave assemblage associated with the centralization of macro-regional political power.

Attempts have also been made to create further confirmation of emergent kings by linking runestones, archaeology, and the Frankish written sources. For example, the Ladby ship burial, which is among the very richest of the tenth-century chamber graves, has been connected with the person named Gnupa known from runestones Hedeby 2 and 4, and with king Chnuba, who Widukind

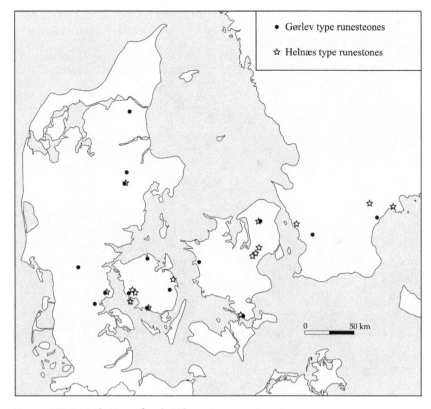

Figure 5.5 Distribution of early Viking Age runestone types across Denmark: Helnæs Type (720–800) and Gørlev Type (800–900). The concentration of stones on Fyn, east central Jutland, and to a lesser extent Sjælland may indicate political centralizing efforts in these areas during the eighth and ninth centuries.
Source: map by author

of Corvey says was forced into baptism in 934. The effort to make these links seeks an unattainable level of confirmation. The Frankish sources are invaluable, but we should give priority to the runestones, which are situated in the landscape, and therefore more likely to reflect local conditions in Denmark.

The post-Jelling runestones are by far the most abundant, numbering over a hundred stones. After the Jelling runestones, the practice of erecting runestones became more common across Denmark and into southwestern (Danish) Sweden. To an extent, this proliferation follows the elite trend established by the Danish king at Jelling, but other factors were at work too. The new runestones signal the institutionalization of what appears to be a new type of leadership associated with the Jelling Dynasty's control over the various regions of Denmark.

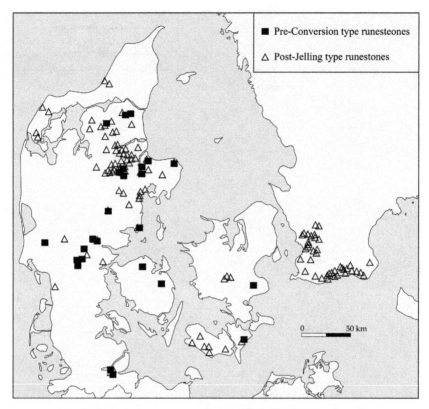

Figure 5.6 Distribution of runestones from the tenth and early eleventh centuries: Pre-Conversion Type (900–970) and Post-Jelling Type (970–1025). The distribution of these stones at the margins of the Danish Kingdom suggests that power was particularly contested in these areas as the Danish state extended tighter control.

Source: map by author

The post-Jelling stones seem to follow the spread of royal power to the final peripheries of the emergent Danish state into northeast Jutland and Scania. They were likely erected in the reigns of Svein and Knut the Great. King Svein's name appears on two of the Jutland stones, while Knut appears on a single stone from Scania.[113] The proliferation of stones in these two regions indicates that the new Christianized elite had a particular need to justify their new power in those specific regions. Following this interpretation, the struggle between the new royally sanctioned administrative elite and the traditional chieftains was the most contentious in Jutland and Scania. The late tenth-century post-Jelling stones often stress warrior ethos and praise death in battle. This has been interpreted as indicating times of war associated with state formation.[114]

Right after 1000, the post-Jelling stones begin carrying overt Christian symbology or language, such as the expression "God help his/her soul" and crosses as decoration or as small symbols separating words. These features might be expected as a new Christian aristocracy established itself in roles of political and ideological power.[115] Some stones were explicitly tied to Christian good works, such as bridge-building and sometimes even construction of churches. For instance, the fragmented text on Lund 2 from Scania declares that "Toki had this church built and . . ."[116] These runestones fused a traditional medium with Christian ideas and symbols to make statements about novel relations of power, replacing those made previously in lavish pagan burials—such as the chamber graves of the mid-tenth century—that were no longer acceptable in Christian death.

The early kings of the Jelling dynasty—Gorm, Harald, and Svein—are all mentioned on runestones in Denmark. But Knut the Great is not mentioned on any stone in Denmark, except a single stone in Scania. This is particularly noteworthy, as several stones in central Sweden mention men who joined Knut in England and "took his payment" there.[117] By Knut's time, therefore, the runestone fashion seems to have largely disappeared in Denmark. The fading of the runestones is at least partially connected with the stabilization of the new forms of local power within the framework of the Danish state. The fashion continued and picked up pace in central Sweden, where state formation pressures were then ramping up. In the end, the erection of new runestones virtually ceased in the eleventh century as the stresses of state formation dissipated and claims to landownership and the creation of written social memory shifted to the state-allied Christian bureaucracy of bishops, churches, and monasteries.[118]

Archaeology

Archaeological evidence of the power structures in late eighth- to eleventh-century Denmark appears in rural settlements, urban trading centers, treasure hoards, burial assemblages, and monumental state-driven constructions. The archaeological evidence from these datasets indicates a transformation of society in the late tenth and eleventh centuries that resulted from a state-driven centralization of economic, political, military, and ideological power.

Villages: Economic Transformation

The Viking Age settlement pattern is dictated in part by local variations in geology and concomitant differences in agricultural practices. A major difference in the soils of Denmark resulted from whether an area was covered by glaciers during the last Ice Age. The soils of the Danish islands—including Fyn, Sjælland, Falster, and Lolland—are glacial moraine soils rich in clay and nutrients left behind by glacial coverage during the last Ice Age. By contrast, the glaciers of the last Ice Age did not extend into western Jutland and as a result, the soils there derive from the previous glacial maximum. These soils, particularly in the western and central parts, are sandy and less fertile than the island soils. As a result, Viking Age agriculture on the islands focused on grain cultivation, whereas cattle farming was dominant in Jutland. This appears to have resulted in larger and more stable villages on the islands and in Scania. In contrast, the cattle-dependent villages of Jutland were smaller and shifted their position in the landscape more frequently.[119]

The inhabitants of Danish villages—whether in Jutland or on the islands—subsisted on mixed agriculture of cereals (mostly barley, rye, and oats) together with animal husbandry (mostly cattle, but also sheep and goats). Relic plowed fields, such as the Lindholm Høje field buried in drifting sand in the eleventh century, show crops were planted on man-made ridges about 1 m wide and 25 cm high, separated by furrows for water drainage.[120] Palaeobotanical and pollen samples from rural sites confirm the presence of the major grain crops, but also attest to other food plants such as cabbage, strawberries, mustard, honey, and bog myrtle for flavoring beer.[121] Local environmental conditions dictated the animal meat focus, such that the central parts of Denmark (Fyn and Sjælland and eastern Jutland) focused on pig husbandry, while sheep and cattle were more dominant in the sandy open lands of western Jutland. The rural villages in general have a higher ratio of sheep to cattle and pig, while the opposite is true for urban areas, suggesting that the meat animals such as cattle and pig were transported there for sale and subsequent consumption.[122] The villages appear self-sufficient but were linked into the trade and exchange network of the Viking Age, as indicated by imports recovered from village excavations. Non-local goods included soapstone vessels and schist whetstones from Norway, basalt quern stones from the Rhineland, and glass beads from the Mediterranean.[123] These imports were probably mostly acquired in exchange for surplus agricultural products.

The excavation of the Jutlandic village of Vorbasse has contributed greatly to our understanding of the makeup and temporal changes of Danish Viking Age villages. Vorbasse shifted position slightly through time, such that eight phases of the village have been recognized. The eight phases date from the first century BC to the eleventh century AD, after which the village stabilized in its final medieval position and stopped moving around in the landscape.[124] The discovery of fence boundaries between individual farms permits the definition of the number of farms and the buildings within each farm unit. The farm units were organized on either side of a central road running through the village. Each farm unit has the appearance of intended self-sufficiency. Remarkably, the village was relatively stable in size across all eight of its phases, always encompassing between six and eight farms.

Within Vorbasse phase 7, dating to roughly 700–1000, each farm unit included one large longhouse that was split between a human habitation area and a byre area for animals. Cohabitation of humans and animals under a single longhouse roof has a long tradition in Scandinavia. The stall dividers have been identified in many of the Vorbasse longhouses, allowing estimation of the maximum cattle capacity for each house, such that the early Vorbasse houses have room for around twenty cattle. Also within each farm unit were a series of subsidiary buildings and pit houses that functioned as workshops, storage facilities, and additional houses, probably inhabited by workers or slaves. Significantly, each farmstead had its own well, indicating significant investment in subsistence independence for each farm. So, although the village coherence itself suggests communal cooperation, the fences, separate storage facilities, and independent wells indicate a social convention of conspicuous economic autonomy.

Excavations of other villages, especially in Jutland, suggest that the Vorbasse is relatively characteristic of Viking Age Danish villages, both in terms of size and in the division of villages into separate homesteads that comprised larger longhouses, smaller houses/workshops, and pit houses. Some interesting variation in village layout demonstrates their adaptability. For example, the village of Sædding in eastern Jutland had a centrally positioned open public plaza, like a village square, measuring 120 x 25 m, around which the houses of the village were oriented. Nearly 200 separate buildings have been mapped, including 75 sunken-feature buildings or pit houses with relatively square dimensions (2.5–5.5 x 2–4.75 m). Like Vorbasse, Sædding has shown a pattern of large houses with curved walls, straight gable-ends, and roofs supported by two rows of internal posts, surrounded by smaller agricultural and subsidiary buildings. Here, the absence of fences and boundary ditches makes the farmstead units difficult to discern and complicates conclusions about how many farms existed at one time. Another village at Trabjerg in western Jutland, inhabited from 725 to 1050, also appears to have a central public plaza. In general, the same types of houses were found here as elsewhere, but at Trabjerg the houses displayed greater stylistic variation, with, for instance, some houses having bowed long walls and others having straight walls.

Toward the end of the Viking Age a major settlement change took place in which villages stabilized within the landscape and stopped shifting location, as seen above with the Vorbasse village that ceased its translocation in the eleventh century.[125] Why exactly earlier villages shifted so much across the landscape is not well understood, but it most likely relates to maximizing land fertility, as some fields became exhausted and highly fertile grazing areas were converted for cultivation. This stabilization represents a break or discontinuity with a longstanding settlement pattern that is likely associated with a combination of changing farming practices, political changes, and a new planning of most villages.[126]

The stabilization of villages may correspond to improvements in agricultural technology, most notably the replacement of the simple ard plow with the heavy, wheeled moldboard plow, the arrival of which is evidenced by deep furrows dating to around 1000. The moldboard plow was already used in northern Germany by the first century AD, so some economic or social factors must have militated against an earlier adoption of this technology in Denmark. The new plow needed increased cooperation among farmers because pulling the plow required six to eight draft animals. Perhaps the arrival of the plow had to await village reorganization and a shift from square to long narrow fields because of the difficulty in turning the large plow. This presents a bit of a chicken-and-egg problem, as it is still unclear whether the arrival of the moldboard plow caused the stabilization of the settlements or whether the stabilization of villages allowed for the use of the new plow.

The re-planning and stabilization of the villages might also reflect new ownership or at least a reformed management of the villages. In the context of the state formation processes occurring around 1000, it is likely that the stabilization of villages was forced or at least encouraged by increasingly powerful kings and elites who sought to maximize agricultural production that could be taxed. Stable villages were easier to control and to monitor and might also facilitate military organization and recruitment of the military levy, in which each farm and each village presumably contributed according to population.[127]

Just before the villages stabilized, another important change occurred within the structure of villages: the emergence of magnate farms that stand out from the standard farms within villages. Magnate farms or manors with central place functions had been a feature of the Danish landscape since before the beginning of the Viking Age.[128] What may be different here is the appearance of qualitatively larger farms within the village settlements themselves, and which seem to have links to a central power. In the eighth and final Viking Age phase of the Vorbasse village, one of the farms dramatically distinguished itself from the others in terms of size. This new farm area—as indicated by the surrounding fence—measured 215 x 160 m, while the contemporary farms in the village encompassed a much smaller area of about 80 x 80 m. These larger village farms indicate increased economic and social differentiation within the villages that may ultimately derive at least in part from connections to the king.

Contemporaneously, the main houses within the Danish villages changed character, adopting the same novel form as the Trelleborg-type houses that were built within the late tenth-century royal fortresses (discussed below). The

Trelleborg-type house, in which the animal byre disappeared from the habitation buildings and external buttresses were used instead of internal lines of posts to support the roof, appears to have originated with the upper classes. This house type certainly existed in rural sites, especially in eastern Denmark, before it was adopted as the standard house form in the fortresses in the late 970s to early 980s. Subsequently, the Trelleborg house type spread as an elite fashion to the rural villages. This propagation of the Trelleborg house type also occurred in places where it had not previously been used in western Denmark, including especially Jutland. For instance, in the final Viking Age phase at Vorbasse, all the main farmhouses were constructed in the Trelleborg style. Also, at the village of Omgård, the houses shifted to Trelleborg-type houses in the late tenth to early eleventh century. At Trabjerg, on the other hand, only some of the building owners adopted the new style, while others retained the old house style with internal rows of posts supporting the roof. Nonetheless, the widespread adoption of the Trelleborg-style house indicates the attraction and influence of the Danish state and an increased degree of integration and ideological unity among the elite.

Population growth and the resultant pressure on economic production have often been seen as a, if not *the*, underlying impetus for increased centralization and the appearance of state-level societies. The same is true of Viking Age Denmark, with scholars attempting to locate the period of this population growth.[129] The population may have increased in the centuries leading up to the Viking Age with an expanded focus on rye over barley cultivation, but it is telling that the ratio of cultivated to forest lands appears to have been virtually unchanged from AD 100 until 800.[130] While the beginning of the Viking Age is not characterized by a clear expansion of population or settlement, a series of new place names, most notably -*thorpe* names, do appear just after 1000 and until 1200. Across Denmark, the new -thorpe settlements (with endings in -*rup*, -*strup* and -*drup* such as in Kirkerup, Kastrup, Perstorp) were founded in marginal areas.[131] For instance, the -thorpes are situated generally on soils that are sandier than the more clay- and silt-rich loams of the older Iron Age farms.[132] There are 3,500 -thorpe settlements in Denmark; these new settlements in all likelihood accommodated a population undergoing expansion beginning around 1000.

The stabilization of villages, the appearance of larger magnate farms within villages, the adoption of a uniform style of elite house construction, and the expansion of the -thorpe settlements—all of which began around 1000—signal a major change in the settlement landscape of Denmark. The correspondence of these factors indicates a shift in the rural economy and represents a hierarchy that could be harnessed and might even have been fostered by the emergence of the administratively capable Danish state.

From Emporia to Towns: Urban Transformation

The first towns in Scandinavia appeared in the Viking Age. In the half century or so leading up to the start of the Viking Age, seasonal markets developed at a few places, such as Ribe, in Denmark. But it was not until the Viking Age that true towns evolved, providing centralized, regular markets. These towns emerged as central nodes in the long-distance trade networks of Northern Europe and linked the agricultural hinterlands into the wider Viking Age trade network. Agricultural products from the hinterland supported manufacturing at increasing scales within towns while merchants imported foreign (mostly prestige) goods and exported local products. From the start, chieftains and nascent kings played a role in establishing, encouraging, and protecting these markets. The early towns, therefore, also functioned as centers for regional administration, and those leaders who controlled access to these sites had potential for increasing their wealth and power.

These trading centers underwent a major transformation in the Viking Age from externally oriented emporia to internally oriented towns. The early emporia were located on the borders of polities and had a distinctly international character, in terms of both the inhabitants—traders and crafts-people—and the goods of exchange. In contrast, the many increasingly urbanized sites that appeared around 1000 were anchored in regional trade within Denmark. These new urban centers, as well as the earlier emporia, were fortified with high ramparts in the second half of the tenth century or around 1000, indicating both a perceived need for defense that transformed towns into fortifications and the consolidation of royal power into a state-level society capable of organizing large public works across the Danish kingdom.[133]

The two main early Viking Age trading centers in Denmark were Ribe and Hedeby, both situated in southern Jutland. Ribe, which appears to be the earliest, was located on the west coast of Jutland and thus oriented toward trade across the North Sea, while Hedeby, located on the east coast of Jutland, was directed east toward trade with the Baltic Sea zone. Geographically, both sites have easy access to the sea, but are located on waterways that would protect them from direct assaults from the sea.

Ribe, Denmark's first urban site, was situated about 7 km up the Ribe River, behind coastal islands that lent protection and far enough inland to allow easy access to the hinterland. The site dates back to the first decade of the 700s, well before the start of the Viking Age, when Ribe was the northernmost of a handful of emporia situated on either side of the English Channel.[134] The earliest houses appear to be inhabited for shorter periods, perhaps by self-organizing merchants or by renters who leased their houses for a few years.[135] More enduring houses inhabited by permanent residents appeared by the mid-700s. By then a planned settlement of about fifty similar-shaped plots had been laid out in a zone stretching 70 x 220 m along the south side of the Ribe River, and a symbolic moat was dug to surround the site. Perhaps from the beginning, but certainly by mid-700s, political leadership played a role in the organization and regulation of the site. Coins minted in Ribe in the eighth century are the earliest known coins made in Scandinavia. Evidence of craft manufacture includes metalworking, bronze-casting, and bead-making workshops.[136] Specialization in manufacture can be seen in production of standardized personal adornments meant for the Scandinavian cultural market, with goods such as oval brooches found commonly in middle- and upper-class Scandinavian female graves.[137] Although early imported goods were primarily high value prestige goods, evidence of some bulkier imports have been found at Ribe. For instance, already in the ninth century, large amounts of heavy schist for whetstones were imported to the Ribe emporium from Norway, mostly from the area of Trondelag.[138] Ribe continued to thrive in its original location into the tenth century, after which the urban settlement was reorganized and appears to shift onto the south side of the Ribe River where an early church and Christian graveyard have been found beside the current cathedral.

Hedeby was the largest trading center in the Viking Age. It spanned from the late eighth century until its abandonment in the mid-eleventh century, at which point the trade and administrative functions shifted to the recently established town of Schleswig, farther toward the Baltic Sea on the Schlei fjord.[139] Situated at a strategic point on the narrowest part of the Jutland peninsula and along the major north-south road (Hærvejen or the Army Road; also sometimes called the Ox Road), Hedeby existed already in the eighth century as a small, unorganized settlement at the inner reaches of the Schlei fjord, 40 km from the Baltic Sea. Soon after 800, the settlement shifted slightly to the north and assumed a planned layout with rectangular plots and urban-style rectangular houses (c. 5 x 10 m) facing streets. This regulated plan suggests organization by a local ruler, if not a king. The plots housed craftspeople who produced luxury goods, such as bronze and silver jewelry and glass and amber beads.[140] The protected harbor featured a wide jetty upon which goods were exchanged.[141] The site showed widespread import of luxuries, but also more utilitarian products, such as schist for whetstones from western Norway and reindeer antler for comb-making from the Norwegian Arctic.[142] Exports from Hedeby reached the far corners of the Viking world.[143] Evidence of exchange in the form of weights and scales have been found, as well as local coins minted in Hedeby from the ninth century, emulating coins from Dorestad, the major Frisian emporium directed toward North Sea trade (see section below on coinage). In the tenth century, the site saw significant expansion, and by the second half of the tenth century, the 1,300-meter-long semi-circular rampart surrounding Hedeby was built, mostly likely concurrently with the so-called Connecting Wall (dendrochronologically dated to 968 and 951–961) that connected the rampart around Hedeby with the Danevirke fortification network marking the southern extent of the Danish realm (see discussion of Danevirke below).[144] The fortification extended out into the water in the form of rows of posts restricting the access to the harbor. To the south of the semicircular wall, another wall, the Fore Wall, may also have been added at the same time in the second half of the tenth century.

The number of urban sites in Denmark increased dramatically in the late tenth and early eleventh century. The urban character of these sites developed out of extant smaller settlements or as in the case of Odense and Viborg, probably from cult and assembly sites. Most of these new towns had been secondary trading villages located on the major land travel routes and on streams and fjords with access to the sea. These trading sites were probably encouraged, if not directly established, by local magnates in the eighth or ninth centuries and served regional trade, linking the agricultural hinterland with the larger emporia, like Ribe and Hedeby, and from there the wider Viking world. The wealth of these secondary trading sites served as a source of power for local elites, whose wealth would have attracted the attention of the king as Danish royal power became more entrenched in the tenth century. In the late tenth century and early eleventh century, these sites were restructured with regular urban plots, formalized streets, and monumental Christian architecture, and enclosed by large fortification walls. These new urban sites are mentioned in documents, particularly related to the establishment of the dioceses of Denmark in 1060. By this time, the state institutions of power were in place. The new towns with roles in state and Church administration include Aarhus (Aros), Odense, Viborg, Lund, and Roskilde.

Aros (Árós), meaning "lagoon in a river mouth," was an ideal ship-landing site.[145] Its location, about halfway up the east side of the Jutland peninsula, was strategic for shipping. As Adam of Bremen indicates, from Aros one could either proceed farther down the coast of Jutland to Hedeby/Schleswig or cross Kattegat to Odense on Fyn or Roskilde on Sjælland. Evidence of a trading village with pit houses and small dwelling houses measuring 5 x 10 m located beside the river appeared in the late eighth century, at which time a substantial cemetery lay behind the settlement.[146] The site is first mentioned in 948 as a bishopric, so the town must have been in place before then. Although excavation is complicated by the fact that Viking Age Aros lies below the modern city center of Aarhus (Denmark's second largest city), a rampart enclosing 4–5 hectares was built in 934, and a number of pit house workshops from the tenth century have been documented. By 1100 a church and churchyard had been constructed over the older pagan burial ground.[147] Five runestones in the city also link the site to the tenth century. Coins minted here in 1040 by King Hardaknut provide a link to royal power, as does a thirteenth-century document indicating that Aarhus was a royal property. The late eleventh-century crypt of the Church of Our Lady made from tuff stone blocks shows substantial investment in Christian church infrastructure. Such stone church buildings are the first major public architecture inside the ramparts of the Viking Age towns. Their presence provides another indication of the growing institutionalization of state power, allied with the new ideological system of Christianity.

Viborg, or Vé-bjarg, meaning "enclosure or hill of the sacred place," was an assembly site located at the northern culmination of the major overland north-south road through Jutland, the Army Road.[148] Viborg was Jutland's main assembly site, and post–Viking Age texts indicate that the power-wielders of Jutland met here to elect or confirm kings. Such assemblies would have attracted large numbers of people from across Jutland and resulted in large markets. Traces of a dispersed tenth-century village have been found on a hill in central Viborg. This village was reorganized into the form of a town in the mid-eleventh century, possibly associated with or immediately following King Knut the Great's establishment of a mint in the town around 1018. At that time, the old village road was paved with stone and equal-sized plots were laid out along the road. Houses for permanent habitation lined the street, while workshops were situated behind the houses.[149] The link to ecclesiastical power is indicated by several early stone churches in the town and the establishment of a bishopric in the mid-eleventh century.[150]

Although it did not become a bishopric, Aalborg in northern Jutland offers another example of a secondary trading site becoming a royally controlled town around 1000.[151] Aalborg was situated beside a natural ship-landing where the river Østerå runs into the south side of the Limfjord, through which ships could traverse across the northern part of Jutland in the Viking Age. Initially a small trading village existed here, linking the hinterland to the wider exchange network. The character of the settlement was transformed around 1000, when uniform plots surrounded by ditches appeared (980), the wooden St. Clemens church was built (1000), and the town's main road was laid out (1000–1050). Soon afterward, King Hardaknut (1035–1043) minted the first coins in Aalborg. Hardaknut's silver coins have his name on the obverse and the name of the English minter (Alric) followed by the town's name "Alabu" (meaning, probably, "fortified settlement at the meeting place of water courses").[152]

Odense, or Óðins-vé, meaning "Odin's Holy Place," lies at the point where intersecting land travel routes crossing Fyn meet the Odense River that leads out through Odense Fjord to Kattegat. The place name indicates a pre-Christian holy site, while written sources tell that Odense was the site of Fyn's main assembly. Excavations in the town center yielded settlement evidence, such as clusters of pit houses, several longhouses, and workshops, dating back to the eighth and ninth centuries. The interpretation of this evidence, obtained as it was from small excavations across the overlying modern city, is difficult, with some archaeologists suggesting that it shows a proto-urban site developing already as early as the eighth century.[153] Others urge caution.[154] Before major expansion around 1000, the settlement's buildings and internal organization are consistent with a substantial village located where the overland route across Fyn intersects with the Odense River. In any case, no unambiguous evidence of trade activities in the form of hacksilver, imported goods, or urban-style housing can be connected to this phase of Odense.[155] A connection to royal power in Odense is first indicated by the construction of a royal circular fort around 980 (addressed below). The town of Odense probably expanded in the shadow of this circular fort, and by 988, the first mention of the town of Odense names it as the site of a bishopric.[156] Less than a hundred years later, King Knut the Saint was martyred in the wooden Church of St. Alban, right across the river from the remains of the circular fort. Subsequently, a large stone church was built close by to house the relics of Denmark's first saint.

Roskilde, located at the southern end of the long Roskilde Fjord extending deep into Sjælland, appears also to have grown quickly under royal sponsorship in the late tenth and early eleventh centuries.[157] Harald Bluetooth was said to have built a church in which he was subsequently buried after his death in circa 986. Harald's Church of the Holy Trinity was the predecessor of Denmark's first stone church (c. 1026), which would become the cathedral that has since been the primary burial place of the royal Danish family.[158] A second stone church was built in Roskilde around 1040, revealing substantial royal investment in Roskilde and the close ties between the Church and the growing state power. These Romanesque stone churches, like the stone churches in Aarhus and Odense, are monumental architectural indications of integration of Denmark's kings into the European Christian pan-elite ideology.

Lund, the main town of Swedish Denmark and the site of the eventual first Archbishopric of Scandinavia established in 1104, yields little settlement evidence before 1000.[159] A cemetery excavated in Lund indicates that a settlement of at least village-size existed by around 1000. The oldest houses, dated to around 1020, have the same form as the elite, late tenth-century Trelleborg-type houses, with three rooms, a central fireplace, and buttressing posts outside of the houses' bow-sided walls.[160] The presence of these classic Trelleborg-type houses links Lund to royal Danish power already in the early eleventh century. The site was leveled by a possibly intentional flooding event around 1050, after which it was restructured in a more regular and dense urban style with regular house plots divided by fences. The Trelleborg-type houses were replaced by smaller, urban-style houses, some with corner ovens and evidence of craft production found inside. A large 25-meter-long stave church was built in the town center in this period.[161] The town became the location of a major mint under Knut the Great. The coins minted in Lund show a connection with Knut's English realm, many being stamped with names of English moneyers who had been transplanted to the town. The significant restructuring of the buildings and layout, followed by church construction and minting of Knut's currency, are clear indications of royal power. The first Danish document from 1085 records a gift from King Knut the Saint to Lund's church. This same document also states that the people of Lund paid a land-tax to the king, suggesting the same was the case for other contemporary Danish towns. Lund is the only town in late-Viking Age Denmark that was not linked to a waterway. The town is clearly associated rather to the internal administration of Scania, much more so than international trade.

To conclude, the earliest urban centers in Denmark—Ribe and Hedeby—were from the start tied to long-distance international trade that spread across the northern European world. These emporia, located on the borders of the nascent Danish state, had a far more international and multi-ethnic character than did the later towns that would grow up in the late Viking Age. These later towns—probably Aarhus and Odense, definitely Viborg and Aalborg, and especially Roskilde and Lund—were from the start of their fluorescence fostered by the increasingly powerful Danish state, in combination with the spread of Christian Church infrastructure manifested in large church construction and the minting of coins (Tables 5.2–5.4). The seat of the bishops and the large cathedral churches were urban. These later towns engaged in international trade, but were directed internally, to regional trade, and especially internal administration on behalf of the increasingly centralized Danish state. In the later tenth century, the urban centers were fortified with ramparts. The king served as the towns' patron (as indicated in trade-agreement documents), protector (as shown by the rampart construction), and ideological head (as seen in the coinage). From at least the tenth century, the king received custom dues and first rights on choice imports, and by the early eleventh century more regular taxes may have been introduced. The division of Denmark into dioceses in 1060 further signaled the cementation of a new system of rulership, less personal and more institutionalized. The Church fostered increased trade with Christian neighbors to the south, while Church feast days offered predictable market days aligned with the rest of European Christianity.

The Emergence of Coinage and the Transformation of Exchange

The means of exchange were transformed over the course of the Viking Age. Although simple coins, known as sceattas, do appear to have been used from

Table 5.2 Known mints established in Denmark by the eleventh century.

Location	First King to Mint	Date Established	Pre-Royal Coinage
Aarhus	Hardaknut	1020s	
Lund	Svein Forkbeard	c. 1020	
Viborg	Knut the Great	c. 1020	
Roskilde	Knut the Great	c. 1020	
Aalborg	Knut the Great	1020s	
Odense	Knut the Great	1044–1050	
Hedeby/Schleswig	Harald Bluetooth	970s	x
Ribe	Knut the Great	c. 1020	x
Ørbæk*	Knut the Great	c. 1020	
Slagelse*	Knut the Great	c. 1020	
Ringsted	Knut the Great	c. 1020	
Gori*	Hardaknut	1020s	

Note: The coins minted in early emporia were not explicitly connected with a known king; these early mints are indicated in the column to the far right. After 1000, Lund was the main Danish mint, followed by Roskilde. Locations indicated with a * might not have been towns. The location of Gori is unknown, but probably is somewhere in Scania, based on similarities of the Gori coins with those of Lund.

Table 5.3 Bishoprics established in Denmark by the end of the eleventh century based on written texts, primarily Adam of Bremen's *History of the Bishops of Hamburg*.

Location	Date First Attested
Aarhus	948
Ribe	948
Schleswig	948
Odense	988
Roskilde	c. 1020
Viborg	1060
Lund	1060
Børglum (Vendsyssel)	1060
Dalby	1060 (only until 1066)

Note: The earliest bishoprics—Ribe, Aarhus, Schleswig—saw at best inconsistent presence of foreign bishops from Hamburg-Bremen until after Denmark's conversion to Christianity around 965.

Table 5.4 Known stone churches in Denmark by the end of the eleventh century. Stone churches were an urban phenomenon, manifesting simultaneously the alliance between the Danish state and the Church and the entry of Denmark into the Christian European pan-ethnic elite ideological system.

Town	Name	Date
Roskilde	Holy Trinity/Roskilde Cathedral	1026
Roskilde	St. Clemens/St. Jørgensbjerg	c. 1040
Aarhus	St. Nicholas/Church of Our Lady	second half of eleventh
Odense	St. Knut's Church	c. 1095

Source: Roskilde (Roesdahl 1982: 83–84), Aarhus (Roesdahl 1982: 80), Odense (Runge and Henriksen 2018).

the earliest period of the emporia, most exchange was conducted through barter or by use of weighed silver bullion. The earliest native Danish coinage probably appeared in Ribe in the first half to the eighth century, although these Wodan-monster sceattas are thought by some to be Frisian imports (Figure 5.7, row 1 A).[162] The sceattas (sg. sceat) were small silver pennies weighing about a gram and without any text on the obverse or reverse. From the start, they were international in nature, meant for exchange between the so-called wics of the seventh and eighth centuries that were located on both sides of the English Channel.[163] Coins of the Wodan-monster type were used extensively in Ribe in the eighth century. A crucial point of debate is whether these coins, which are found in England, Frisia, and southern Denmark, were minted in Ribe or whether they appear there because of Ribe's inclusion in the eighth-century wic-based trading network. The coins are "silent" (i.e., they are only pictorial and bear no inscriptions), making their origin particularly difficult to provenience. If minted in Denmark, then it could signal a significant involvement—and control—over local trade by a Danish ruler in southern Denmark. The variety in the appearance of sceattas suggests to some that the minting process was decentralized, with a limited involvement and possibly no control by a central authority. However, Metcalf has pointed out that the majority of the sceattas found in Ribe are of the Wodan-monster type, which he believes were minted locally. He argues that the prevalence of this coin type indicates that a centralized authority, or king, enforced the use of the Wodan-monster coinage minted in Ribe in the town's market zone. Recent research has documented that 85 percent of the sceattas found in Ribe were of this type, supporting this suggestion.[164] The Wodan-monster sceattas of the eighth century do not, however, appear to have been used even in the hinterland of Ribe,

1,

2, (a)   (b)

3,

4,

5,

6, (a)   (b)

and did not spread to parts of Denmark beyond southwestern Jutland.[165] As such, the royal power, if it in fact controlled this coinage, did not extend—at least commercially—beyond this zone.

Coins continued to be minted in Ribe and Hedeby in the ninth century. A modified Wodan-monster coinage was by then certainly minted in Denmark, while other coins appear that are clearly inspired by and in most cases directly modeled on Frankish coins, particularly the Dorestad coins. Sometimes Danish minters even imitating in distorted forms the word "Dorestad" or "Carolus" (i.e., Charlemagne) on the coins. At other times, Danish minters made iconographic changes, stressing Scandinavian identity with Viking-style houses and sailing ships (Figure 5.7, row 2 B). The image of the ship itself was also inspired by Frankish examples, although the ship takes on a Scandinavian appearance in the Danish coins.[166] Relatively few of these ninth-century coins were minted, and minting of coins may have nearly disappeared in the late ninth and early tenth century, in favor of bullion exchange and use of foreign coins. The few known early and mid-tenth-century Danish coins continued to imitate Carolingian coins.

The ninth- and early tenth-century Danish coins existed parallel to a system still dominated by direct barter and/or use of weighed silver bullion. A general transition from barter to measured weights of silver has been suggested around 880, based on the appearance of standardized weights, cut pieces of silver, and scales in Hedeby around that time.[167] The Danish treasure hoards show this transition from the ninth century, when hoards were dominated by complete objects (used in barter) to the tenth-century appearance of increased amounts of hacksilver (used as measured weight).

Only in the late tenth and early eleventh century do the percentages of whole coins markedly increase to levels suggesting an exchange system operating on a widely accepted Danish coinage with predetermined and royally sanctioned values.[168] The first efforts at a "national" coinage occurred with Harald Bluetooth, who from about 975 to 995 minted large quantities of coins with crosses and

---

Figure 5.7 Danish Viking Age Coins. 1. Ribe Wotan/monster sceatta, eighth century; 2. Hedeby coins, ninth and tenth centuries; 3. Harald Bluetooth coin imitating Byzantine coins of Christ enthroned with cross; 4. Svein Forkbeard coin from a Danish mint with Svein called Rex; 5. Knut the Great coin calling him king of Denmark; 6. (a) Svein Estridsen coin imitating an Anglo-Saxon model for the cross and a Byzantine model for the saint holding a banner, (b) St. Knut seated with sword and shield, minted in Jutland in years before 1086.

Source: 1: American Numismatic Society, 0000.999.622; 2a, 3, 5, and 6a: © The Trustees of the British Museum; 2b: Werner Karrasch, © The Viking Ship Museum, Denmark; 4: Ola Myrin, Historiska museet/ National Historical Museums, Sweden (CC BY 4.0); 6b: courtesy of Thomas Guntzelnick Poulsen

faces or masks seen from the front, potentially inspired by Byzantine coinage (Figure 5.7, row 3). The overt Christian symbol on these coins, found at sites across Denmark and along the southern shore of the Baltic Sea, was part of Harald's ideological propaganda linking royal power and public declarations of conversion to Christianity.[169] Contemporaneously, large numbers of coins of the same weight as Harald's cross-type coin were also struck at Hedeby, suggesting coordination of standardized coin weights.

A further expansion of royal coinages and ideological messaging came in the eleventh century during the reign of Svein Forkbeard. Coins minted in his name emulated Anglo-Saxon coinage, using the cross on one side and a ruler in profile on the other, complete with Latin inscriptions around the margins that included the king's name and that of the mint (Figure 5.7, row 4). This general form continued after Svein and marks the integration of the Danish exchange system into the wider European model, based ultimately on late-Roman coinage. From the turn of the millennium, citizen buy-in to the royal control of the economic system was also manifest in the increased ratio of minted coins to hacksilver and ingots found in hoards. Coinage from this point forward served as both a centrally guaranteed means of exchange and a means of disseminating royal propaganda. Foreign coins continued to circulate in Denmark in the early eleventh century but with a virtual disappearance of non-local currency sometime around 1080, possibly reflecting a ban on use of foreign coinage by the king (Harald Hen, 1074–1080) that would have been in line with such bans in other European kingdoms.[170] Already by the end of the reign of Svein Estridsen (1019–1076), however, foreign coins appear to have been mostly absent from internal circulation in Denmark.

Monumental Constructions and Royal Power

Monumental construction across the Danish landscape—including ramparts, canals, sea barriers, bridges, burial mounds, and fortresses—bear witness to large-scale cooperative efforts that required massive labor mobilization. This labor mobilization necessitated a significant central authority. Early examples of monumental construction, and therefore also centralized authority, occur mainly in southern and central Jutland. These earlier projects, beginning just before the onset of the Viking Age, testify to the existence of a strong regional polity. Country-wide projects requiring state-level organization, however, appear only in the late tenth century.

Canals, Sea Barriers, and Bridges

One of the absolute earliest indications of substantial political power in early Denmark is the Kanhave canal, which was dug across the island of Samsø in the early eighth century. The island lies in Kattegat, along one of the key maritime travel routes that led past the Danish islands east of Jutland. Ships followed this route when traveling from the Atlantic Ocean or Norway to Hedeby and on into the Baltic Sea. Three sea passages are available through the Danish islands: (1) through the Little Belt between Jutland and Fyn, (2) through the Big Belt between Fyn and Sjælland, and (3) through Øresund between Sjælland and Scania (Figure 5.1). Samsø controlled the entrances from the north into the first two of these waterways. Samsø is 29 km long in its roughly north-south orientation, but narrow from east to west, with a minimal width of about 1 km. The Kanhave canal was dug across this narrowest point. The canal was 11 m wide and had a depth of about 1.5 m, allowing for passage of Viking-style boats and ships. The sides of the canal were lined with three inclining horizontal planks positioned edge-to-edge. The planks were held into place by large wooden pegs penetrating into the earth, as well as sloping posts positioned every 3 m along the canal's length. Dendrochronology dates the canal to between 726 and 729.

An economic function for the Kanhave canal does not make sense, because the small size of the island would not have seriously delayed merchant traffic. Instead, the canal must have had a military function in allowing ships to efficiently control the waterways on both sides of the island. The canal connects an excellent natural harbor, Stafnsfjord, on the eastern side of the island, with the sea on the west side. A hill on a small island in the Stafnsfjord harbor, Hjortholm, permits views of the waterways on both sides of the island. Whoever built the canal had substantial resources and could mobilize the labor needed for the initial construction and the frequent upkeep. It is therefore more likely that the canal was built by a petty-king rather than a pirate group—at least as far as those two can be considered different. Interestingly, Samsø has been a possession of the Danish king for as long as property rights can be traced in the texts. Whoever the builder was, the canal represents an early signature of what was at least a regionally centralized power, and evidence of a significant attempt to control trade and travel through Danish waters.

Sea barriers blocking or restricting access to important harbors and trading sites were used throughout the Viking Age. They show significant investment of effort in protecting ports of trade. Sea barriers have for example been found in several places in the Schlei Fjord, where they served to restrict access to Hedeby. Only people who knew the watercourse would be able to approach without trouble. In some cases, barriers appear to have been useful in defending bays where regional fleets levied by chieftains or kings could be mustered. In the most famous sea barrier, access to Roskilde was blocked at some point in the eleventh century by the purposeful scuttling of four ships in the Peberrende channel of the Roskilde Fjord.[171] The ships, which were filled with stone, reinforced one another, while posts and bundles of brush were added to strengthen the barricade.

The blocking of Roskilde has been connected with efforts, possibly by the Danish king Svein Estridsen, to block the frequent raids by the Norwegian King Harald Hardrada described in texts like *Heimskringla*. In general, the sea barriers represent significant communal effort, but could have been coordinated by regional leaders without necessitating state-level royal coordination.

Established roads existed in Denmark since the initiation of a settled landscape in the Neolithic period. The roads of the Viking Age continued to follow the earlier pattern, keeping to dry land and routes that minimized the need to cross marshes and rivers. The first true bridges, as opposed to built-up ford crossings, appear in the Viking Age. The known bridges, however, all come from the late Viking Age, possibly in association with increases in royal power and the arrival of Christianity. Often these wooden bridges, such as the one at Risby in southern Sjælland, are preceded by fords. The Risby bridge was about 70 m long and 2.5 m wide, supported by pairs of square vertical posts and angled buttresses. A stone-lined paved road leading up to and covering the earliest phase of the bridge has been radiocarbon dated to the early eleventh century.[172]

The most impressive Viking Age bridge was built in circa 979 to cross the Vejle River Valley and lead travelers to the royal site of Jelling, located 10 km to the north. Almost 1 km in length and 5.5 m wide, the bridge made a strong statement of royal power that would have been seen (and used) by those approaching Jelling from the south, including representatives of the German emperor. A system of around 400 wooden frames supported the bridge. Each separate support frame, separated by 2.4 m, was made up of four vertical posts and two angled posts. In total, this amounted to 1,700 vertical posts and 800 angled posts. The road approaching the bridge on either side was paved, and, to ease transport, it was cut into the steep northern slope of the river valley. The labor investment needed for this road and bridge system was on par with the massive Trelleborg fortresses (see below), and similarly, the bridge was only used for a short time since it does not appear to have been repaired. The bridge improved travel along the north-south Army Road running up the spine of Jutland and would have been useful for royal military mobility. The bridge would have also facilitated control of land travel and possibly lent itself to the charging of a royal bridge toll.[173]

Border Fortification: The Danevirke Ramparts

The earliest and one of the most impressive archaeological manifestations of power in Viking Age Denmark is a series of interconnected bank-and-ditch ramparts that extends for about 32 km across the narrow southern part of the Jutland peninsula between the Baltic Sea and the marshlands bordering the North Sea.[174] The series of ramparts primarily defend a 6-kilometer-wide stretch of passable higher ground called the Isthmus of Schleswig, which extends between the swamplands of the Treene and Rheide Rivers in the west and the Schlei

Fjord in the east (Figure 5.8). The defensive earthwork marks the southern extent of the Danish kingdom and comprises at least eight accumulative phases in which centralized authority mobilized large labor forces to construct, enlarge, and maintain this impressive public work.[175] Recent radiocarbon dating results from a 5-kilometer-long turf portion of the Main Rampart have pushed the earliest construction date back to the fifth to sixth century, while remains of an even earlier earthen wall lie beneath. The first of three broad Viking Age phases consisted of a complete refortification of the Main Rampart, with the construction of a rampart with a fieldstone core dating to the decades preceding 800.[176] The stone core was covered in earth and the rampart faced with horizontal timbers held in place by vertical timbers every 2 m. A ditch with a U-shaped profile, from which the earth had been removed to build the rampart, lined the external side of the wall.

Excavations in 2010 revealed a gateway in the Main Rampart and the remains of a 3.5-meter-wide section of Jutland's main thoroughfare, the Army Road.[177]

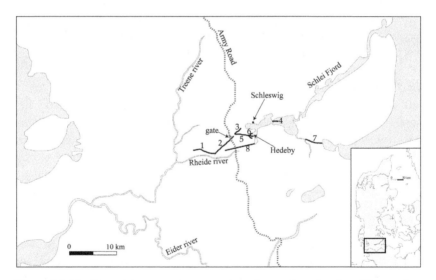

Figure 5.8 The Danevirke rampart system along the southern border of Denmark. The multi-phased system dates back at least to the fifth to sixth century. The Viking Age constructions can be grouped into three phases (numbers in the following match the numbers on map). (**I**) **Late eighth century**: (1) Crooked Rampart, (2) Main Rampart, (3) North Rampart, (4) East Rampart, (7) Reesholm wall; (**II**) **Mid-tenth century**: (5) Connecting Rampart and (6) Semi-Circular Rampart added and North Rampart abandoned; (**III**) **Late tenth century**: (8) Kovirke Rampart added.

Source: map by author

The eighth-century phase also includes construction of the Crooked Rampart and the North Rampart, which extended to the west and north from the Main Rampart. A similarly constructed and probably contemporary rampart (East Rampart) defends 3.3 km of access to the Svansen peninsula, which extends to the south of Schlei Fjord.[178] Finally, a partially offshore wall was built across the Reesholm Headland to defend a shallow crossing point of the Schlei Fjord.[179]

The second major Viking Age phase consisted of a restructuring of the main series of walls and the addition of the 3.5-kilometer-long Connecting Wall that united the Danevirke ramparts with the semi-circular rampart around Hedeby, which appears to date to this same period. These additions, dating to the 960s, comprised a tall rampart (c. 3 m high) with a wooden palisade at its top.[180] The third and probably the last major Viking Age phase of construction, dating to the late tenth century, included the addition of a strikingly straight rampart (Kovirke), spanning the 6.5 km from Selk Nor (just south of Hedeby) to the marshes of the Reine River. This defensive line, which lies separate and south of the rest of the Danevirke system, consisted of a V-shaped ditch and rampart lined externally with wood and wooden buttressing posts. This last phase, with its straight course, was most likely built in the same period and with a similar regimented design as the Trelleborg forts; this connection is bolstered by the fact that both share the V-shaped ditch features in their defenses.

The Jelling Palace Complex

In the center of Jutland along the north-south trade axis, the Army Road, lies the sleepy village of Jelling that once was the monumental political center of the tenth-century nascent Danish state. Jelling is centrally located in east-central Jutland, facilitating quick travel overland to the main centers in Jutland and via the Vejle river into Kattegat and on to the Danish islands.[181] The political importance of the site has been known for centuries, beginning with antiquarian examination of the two monumental mounds, known as Gorm and Thyre's mounds. The declaration on one of the three sides of the large runestone located between these two mounds that Harald had "won for himself all of Denmark and Norway and made the Danes Christian" has been taken as a sort of birth certificate for the modern nation-state of Denmark (see discussion of runestones above). The second side of this runestone, bearing the earliest surviving native image of Christ in Scandinavia, graces the inside cover of Danish passports, while the ornate pagan beast on the third side of the stone appears in the top right corner of each passport page. Jelling thus looms large as a source of important symbols of Danish national identity and legitimacy.

Jelling was also of immense political importance in the tenth century, and research in the past ten years has shown the site to be even more impressive and complex than originally suspected. Whereas earlier models of site function

focused exclusively on an impressive burial landscape refashioned and spectacularly Christianized by Harald Bluetooth (see Chapter 4), new research has shown
the site to be a fortified palace complex incorporating both domestic structures
and royal ritual messaging.

The tenth-century palace complex was built in successive and cumulative stages
in a landscape that had been of political importance since the Bronze Age. Probably
the first Viking Age phase of this site was the construction of a massive—by far the
largest in Scandinavia—stone ship setting measuring 350 m in length and dating
to the late first half of the tenth century. The setting was aligned such that its central
long axis bisects a Bronze Age burial mound, which sits at the center of the ship
setting. The setting literally and figuratively incorporated the ritual and political
power embodied in the Bronze Age barrow. The ship setting with the mound at
its center probably served as a political assembly place, as has been suggested for
other mound and stone setting combinations in pre-Christian Scandinavia.[182] The
mound provided a vantage point from which a large gathering could be addressed
and in all likelihood also incorporated the idea of ancestral wisdom and legitimization afforded by the ancient burial mounds.[183] That Gorm the Old (reign
c. 936–958) may have built the ship setting gains some support from the smaller
of the two Jelling runestones, which was likely positioned at the prow of the setting. The stone reads "King Gorm made these monuments in memory of Thyre,
his wife, Denmark's betterment" (see discussion of runestone above).[184] Gorm may
also have built a recently discovered large hall located just south of the Bronze Age
barrow. The discovery of this hall necessitated expanding the interpretation of the
site from a mortuary site to a palace complex with a king's residence.

After the initial monumental ship setting, a second phase of the Jelling
monuments saw the construction of a large burial mound (65 m wide and 8.5
m high) over the Bronze Age barrow. This occurred in 958–959.[185] The dating
would fit a scenario in which King Harald Bluetooth built this mound for his
father, Gorm. Shortly thereafter, a large palisade in a parallelogram shape with
sides measuring 360 m in length was built to precisely encompass the ship setting. The formidable palisade, which has been estimated to be over 2 m tall based
on the sizes of the postholes, had gateways at least in the north and south sides.
The height of the palisade restricted view of the monuments within, as well as
any political undertakings occurring there, until visitors passed through one of
the gateways. In the northeast corner of the palisade, excavations have unearthed
a series of three regularly spaced longhouses of the Trelleborg-type running parallel to the palisade walls. It seems likely that similar houses will be found along
the insides of all four of the palisade walls. The king's warriors and visitors could
have inhabited these houses. Together with the older longhouse centrally located
in the middle of the ship setting, these residences give a clear impression of the
site as a palace complex.

The third phase at Jelling saw a thorough restructuring and Christianization of the palace complex. A second large mound (77 m wide and 11 m high) was built on top of the southern part of the ship setting, partially destroying or at least covering the earlier pagan monument. Mounds are in general considered pagan, but excavations of the South Mound showed no sign of burials, although they did uncover ingenious timber framing within the mound designed to give the mound a uniform rounded appearance.[186] This mound could have been a transitional pagan-Christian monument, as it was soon followed by Harald's clearly Christian runestone that was placed exactly between the two large mounds. Finally, Gorm's old hall was demolished, and a large timber church was built over it, co-opting and simultaneously erasing the pagan hall, which had previously served as both political and ceremonial center. As described in greater detail in Chapter 4, the body of Gorm was then retroactively Christianized and re-entombed in front of the church altar. Fascinatingly, this also served to rebury Gorm beneath the floor of his old longhouse.

Sometime before 1000, the palisade at Jelling burned, and major monumental refashioning at the site ended. The power of the Jelling political center—as represented by the king's hall within the sacred space demarcated by the ship setting and palisade—diffused across the Danish landscape to multiple domiciles, often within new royally supported towns or back to the traditional assembly sites such as Viborg and Odense. The burial place of kings moved to the churches in Roskilde and Ringsted on Sjælland, where the Danish royals have since been buried. The flurry of monumental constructions completed at Jelling by the end of the tenth century—all vividly symbolic and overtly political—were meant to show the populace and chieftains of Denmark that a new and more powerful monarchy had arrived. The political messaging worked and the unity of Denmark under a powerful monarch was not subsequently in doubt. In this way, the cessation of construction on a massive scale at places like Jelling and the Trelleborg forts (see below) should not be interpreted as a sign of decentralization; instead, it indicates the success of a monarchy that had established control and no longer needed to make such grandiose statements.

Circular Trelleborg Fortresses: Military Transformation

The circular fortresses built in Denmark from about 975 to 980 are one of the marvels of Viking archaeology. Dating firmly within the last decade of Harald Bluetooth's reign (c. 958–986), they are the clearest and most geographically extensive evidence of the transformed nature of royal power at the end of the tenth century. This system of forts extending across Denmark constitutes a massive public-works project integral to the royal militarization of the kingdom (Figure 5.1). This same militarization is seen in the runestones, in the fortifications of towns, in the Jelling palisade, and in the unbending straightness of the Kovirke section of the Danevirke rampart system. Equally remarkable is the fact that the fortresses are completely unattested in any of the contemporary or even later written sources, highlighting the importance of the physical archaeological record.

The Trelleborg fortresses have perfectly circular wood-clad ramparts with an internal timber support system and four gates aligned with the four cardinal points of the compass. Two planked axial streets join opposite gates in straight lines that meet in the center to form four right angles. The streets thereby divide the fortresses into four equal-sized quadrants. Four of these forts—Trelleborg, Aggersborg, Fyrkat, and Nonnebakken—are universally accepted as belonging to the classic "Trelleborg type" fortresses built in the years immediately before 980 (Figure 5.9).[187] These four fortresses also share the structural similarity of being surrounded by V-shaped moats. Of these, all but Nonnebakken have evidence of distinct Trelleborg-type longhouses positioned perpendicularly to form house-squares within each of the fortress quadrants.[188] A probable fifth fortress at Borgring has a timber-clad rampart and four gates oriented in the cardinal directions, although no internal wooden structure and no internal organization is apparent.[189]

In addition to the overall layout and internal elements, there is striking uniformity in the massive dimensions of the various Trelleborg fortresses. Fyrkat in Jutland, Nonnebakken on Fyn, and Borgring on Sjælland have ramparts with an internal diameter measuring about 120 m, while the largest fortress of Aggersborg has a diameter that is precisely double at 240 m. Trelleborg varies from the group with a diameter of 136 m. Each of the fortresses would have required massive labor and resource mobilization. The Museum at Trelleborg estimates that the construction of the fort at Trelleborg would have required the wood resources of 8,000 oak trunks, the equivalent of 85 hectares of a modern Danish forest.[190] Two wood samples from the Aggersborg rampart were revealed to be fir (*Pinus* sp.) and spruce (*Picea* sp.), which may point to import of building materials from Norway.[191]

Four additional fortresses in what is now Sweden and Norway have been suggested as Trelleborg-type fortresses of the late tenth century. Two fortresses in Scania—Borgeby and a second fort also named Trelleborg—are possibly connected to the Trelleborg system, but they deviate from the Danish examples with less geometric accuracy in the ramparts, no apparent internal organization, U-shaped external ditches, pre-existing fort phases dating back to earlier periods, and only imprecise dating evidence tying their second phases to the late 970s to early 980s (see Table 5.5 for comparison of main shared features of the fortresses).[192] Two additional sites have been suggested—in northern Scania at Helsingborg and southern Norway at Rygge—based on an attempt to find fortresses in the remaining parts of the medieval Danish kingdom. Although

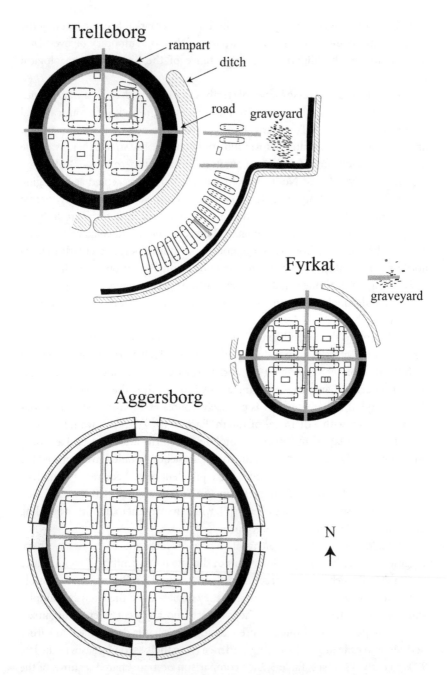

Figure 5.9 The Trelleborg-type fortresses: Trelleborg, Fyrkat, and Aggersborg. The fortresses show an unprecedented precision in construction and organization that signal the arrival of the state in Denmark. For scale, the diameter of Fyrkat measures 120 m, while the diameter of Aggersborg is exactly double at 240 m.

Source: map by author

Table 5.5 Seven late tenth-century circular fortresses in the Danish kingdom that may be classified as "Trelleborg-type fortresses." The top four in the table (Trelleborg, Fyrkat, Aggersborg, and Nonnebakken) are the traditionally accepted Trelleborg-type forts. Nonnebakken may not share the same internal organization, although the location of the fort within the city of Odense has made this determination as yet impossible. The Scanian Trelleborg and Borgeby have yielded the right date, but their construction appears different. Borgring, the last of these to be discovered (in 2014), also seems to lack the internal quadrants and longhouses organized in squares. This on the other hand may also be the case for Nonnebakken.

	Date (^{d} = dendrodate; ^{a} = by artifacts, ^{c} = by ^{14}C)	Diameter	Four Gates in Cardinal Directions	Axial Streets	Houses Squared in Quadrants	House Length (m)	V-Shaped Ditch
Trelleborg	980/981[d]	136	Yes	Yes	Yes	29.4	Yes
Fyrkat	975[d]	120	Yes	Yes	Yes	28.4	Yes
Aggersborg	late-900s [a]	240	Yes	Yes	Yes	32	Yes
Nonnebakken	post-967[d]	120	Yes	?	?	?	Yes
Borgring	post-966[d]	123	Yes	?	?	?	No
Trelleborg in Scania	late-900s[c]	c. 116	Yes (but offset by 20°)	No	No	?	No
Borgeby	late-900s[a]	c. 150	?	?	No	?	No

Note: See review of the fortresses' similarities and differences with particular focus on rampart construction in Sindbæk 2014: 184–197. Dendrodates are reported from Trelleborg (Christensen 1981), Fyrkat (Christensen 2014: 425), Aggersborg (Roesdahl and Sindbæk 2014), Nonnebakken (Jensen and Sørensen 1989). See also Roesdahl and Sindbæk (2014: 203–208) for a review of the dating of the fortresses and a suggestion for the succession of the building of the fortresses starting with Aggersborg, then Fyrkat, followed by Nonnebakken, Trelleborg, and Borgeby. But see some discrepancies in building order suggested in the same volume by Sindbæk (2014: 193).

these last two proposed forts would fit the distribution nicely and incorporate the Oslo Fjord area of Norway, which was under some form of Danish control in the 970s, evidence of fortresses here has not been archaeologically verified.

An overview of the relative confidence in these seven forts being tied to the same unified, state-financed fort system can be understood in the following five levels:

1. **Clear unified plan**: Trelleborg, Fyrkat, Aggersborg
2. **Almost certainly part of unified plan**: Nonnebakken, Borgring
3. **Probable part of unified plan**: Borgeby
4. **Possible part of unified plan**: Trelleborg in Scania
5. **Unverified**: Helsingborg and Rygge

The houses found in three of the fortresses—Trelleborg, Fyrkat, and Aggersborg—all have the same shape, size, and internal divisions. Each of the houses was divided into three sections with one large central room and two smaller gable rooms. The precision of the measurements is exemplified by the houses from Trelleborg, which average 29.42 m in length with a maximum deviation of 0.7 percent.[193] In the center of some of the quadrants, a small central building was added. The basic pattern for the Danish forts included four quadrants with four houses in each quadrant (sixteen total), but at Aggersborg, each of the four quadrants was further split into three quadrants, bringing the total house count to forty-eight. Within the fortresses, not all houses show evidence of habitation. The presence of fireplaces typically only in the houses along the axial streets suggests that the fortresses were not always inhabited to maximum capacity. A small resident force seems to have guarded these fortresses, with the potential to call in surrounding populations for defense in times of need.

The equal-sized longhouses organized in a regular pattern have the distinctive appearance of barracks. The self-contained groups of houses in each of the fortresses' quadrants must reflect some aspect of the organization and/or mobilization of the Danish army in the tenth century. According to the written sources (both the Danish royal chroniclers and Icelandic sagas), the Danish kings of the tenth and eleventh centuries would not have had a permanent standing army, but rather a core of loyal bodyguards known as the *hirð/lið* that could be supplemented in times of crises or foreign campaigns by calling up the general levy.[194] The division of the quadrants and the longhouses in the Danish circular forts were probably meant to house different regional groups of the recruited levy. The levy recruitment system in tenth-century Denmark depended on regional chiefs gathering their constituents for royal service. The quadrants could have been meant to house a regional force, with each of the separate houses meant to be occupied by local chieftains and their constituents.

As discussed above, the longhouses within the Trelleborg fortresses match contemporary houses at aristocratic manors such as Omgård and late Viking Age elite houses from villages such as Vorbasse. Significantly, the Trelleborg fortresses show no indication of housing stratification that would support the existence of any kind of hierarchical military structure or a place of residence for the king. The best candidates for a special hall in the fortresses of Fyrkat and Trelleborg are a house in each with a limestone-lined hearth.[195] If the king did visit, which he likely did, then these halls would be the best candidates for royal housing. In general, the apparent equality among the houses and quadrants could be attributed to a symbolic equality among regional chieftains as well as an equality among the attached warriors that would have arrived with each chieftain.

The faunal remains, artifacts, and human burials found in the fortresses and within the cemeteries of Trelleborg and Fyrkat (the only two fortresses with identified cemeteries) show indications of elite and warrior inhabitants, but in addition, reveal an underlying typical population structure. Beyond the elite-style houses themselves, the faunal bone assemblage from Trelleborg has a higher ratio of cattle and pig bones to sheep than do rural sites, indicating that the inhabitants of the fortress were accorded a certain status and provisioned with choice meat.[196] Other indications of elite culture include riding equipment and even something as small as a bone from a probable hunting-falcon, recovered at Trelleborg.[197] Evidence of trade includes weights and scales from Trelleborg and Fyrkat, while craft production in the form of blacksmithing, comb production, and spinning and weaving are found at all of the excavated fortresses. The latter activities, witnessed by spindle whorls and loom weights, are often connected with female presence. The presence of women is indicated in the cemeteries, which contain both female and children's graves in addition to those of men. Setting aside for the moment the obvious issue that men can weave too, and women have been shown to be warriors, it does appear that the permanent warrior inhabitants of the fortresses had their families with them.

Weapons were more common in the fortresses than at rural village sites. Weapons are generally rare in rural villages but are more common in elite sites like the Tissø manor. The twenty-eight arrowheads found at Aggersborg indicate a military presence, although it is unclear how many of these may belong to an elite manor that was leveled to construct the fortress.[198] The Trelleborg excavations yielded sixty-six arrowheads. The significant numbers found in the external portions of the rampart, combined with evidence of burning, may evidence a battle that raged here.[199] The Trelleborg cemetery contains evidence of at least one weapon death, as well as three mass graves.[200] The most remarkable mass grave held ten young adult individuals (mostly twenty to forty years old) with their arms around each other's necks as brothers-in-arms. One of these individuals had his leg severed above the knee, with no evidence of healing, suggesting he obtained the wound in battle and subsequently died. Elite burial is seen at both Trelleborg in the form of an elaborately decorated axe and at Fyrkat where a rich female wagon burial parallels other graves of the highest social standing across tenth-century Denmark (see below). The Fyrkat wagon burial and the character of the cemeteries at Fyrkat and Trelleborg in general are interesting in that they appear more pagan than Christian. This is perhaps unexpected, considering Harald Bluetooth's explicit conversion to Christianity. In the early phases, this state-sponsored Christianity was probably tolerant of religious diversity, and the fortresses must have held a mixed-faith population.

Diversity is also shown in the foreign things and foreign people found within this otherwise clearly Danish fortress system. Analyses of pottery forms, food remains, and skeletal material from the fortresses suggest international connections that probably relate to a purposeful strategy of rulership. Staple foods imported from overseas must have been rare, but evidence from the Fyrkat fortress excavation suggests that large quantities of rye grains with dimensions larger than the typical Danish rye were imported from Eastern Europe.[201] Isotopic analysis of the skeletons from the cemetery at Trelleborg also suggests that warriors from abroad were included among the king's warriors who lived, fought, and died in the fortress.[202] The connection with Eastern Europe for both food and people within these forts is notable and indicates the international connections of the Danish kings, as well as the likely use of these foreign contacts to maintain control over the local Danish population. The analogy to private forces of foreigners seen in other medieval cultures, most notably the Scandinavian Varangian Guard of the Byzantine emperor, suggests that the strategy of engaging non-locals in the nascent establishment of a monopoly of force was employed by the Danish kings.

These circular fortresses were a new phenomenon in Scandinavia, representing a system meant to be monumental and impressive in scale and in which each fort was designed to control or serve one particular region.[203] The primary point regarding the Trelleborg fortresses is that they were manifestations of a new type of state power, capable of organizing a unified construction project requiring massive labor mobilization across the geographical area identified with the subsequent medieval kingdom of Denmark. This conclusion is the same, whether the two fortresses in Scania—Borgeby and Trelleborg in Sweden—are included in the group. The inclusion of the Scanian fortresses would certainly change the area across which the state power of the king was backed by fortresses, as would the potential inclusions of the proposed Helsingborg and Rygge forts, but it would not change the character of that state power. The interpretation of the function of the Trelleborg fortresses within the emergent Danish state is a fascinating and complex question that we will return to at the end of the chapter, as an example of attempts to combine archaeological data and texts without any one-to-one correspondence. The datasets cannot confirm or contradict one another, but rather must be put in dialogue so that they complement one another. As suggested at the top of this section, this is a fascinating example because the Trelleborg fortresses, which as a group constitute the largest communal investment in public works in the Viking Age, have gone completely unmentioned in any extant historical texts. Archaeologists have instead used indirect evidence from texts to provide the historical context for these fortresses, while the fortresses themselves represent such profound statements of political domination that historians cannot ignore the broad historical significance encapsulated in the archaeology of these sites.

Stone Churches
The centralization of the Danish state in the late tenth century relied on Christian institutions that required the Christianization of death and worship in towns and politically significant localities in the rural landscape. The earliest churches in Denmark mentioned in the written sources were built in towns. None of these have been identified archaeologically. The earliest excavated churches were built of wood and are found in more rural areas associated with sites of ritual prominence in the pre-Christian period. For instance, the church at Jelling was located in the center of the primary royal site and immediately atop the foundations of an earlier large hall within a symbolic ship setting. The ritual activities previously performed in the king's hall and within the ship setting were now transferred to the church. Another early church at Hørning, dating to around 1060, was built over a leveled burial mound containing a high-status female burial assemblage in a chamber grave from around 950.[204] The purposeful destruction of the mound signaled the new religion's victory over the old. At the same time, however, the builders of the church incorporated the rich woman within the new ritual space. They left the chamber grave untouched, organizing the church construction so that the grave remained safely below the church floor. In this way, the retroactive Christianization of a venerable ancestor was achieved, albeit in a slightly different way than, for instance, the exhumation of Gorm at Jelling described above and in Chapter 4.

   In the eleventh century, during the reign of Knut the Great, a new monumental type of stone church appeared. These were constructed in calcareous tuff. The first recorded stone church was commissioned by Knut's sister in Roskilde, with the intent of replacing their grandfather's wooden church of the Holy Trinity. Archaeological evidence of a later phase of this church, dating to around 1080, has been found below the current Roskilde Cathedral. Excavations of St. Clement's Church in Roskilde revealed the town's second stone church, dating to around 1040 and showing the spread of this stone church style, probably by royal initiative.[205] The royal connection is made more plausible as the church style of St. Clement's Church is akin to contemporaneous Anglo-Saxon churches. The kings of Denmark at this time—Knut the Great and Hardaknut—were also kings of England and emulated and adopted both clerics and church styles from the institutionalized English Church. Subsequently, Svein Estridsen may have overseen the proliferation of this style of stone churches in towns across Denmark, in conjunction with his new division of the country into dioceses centered on these towns and churches, where the king often installed English bishops.[206]

Around 1100, stone churches appeared also in the countryside. One such church is the large stone church at Ravnkilde in northern Jutland, dating to the late 1000s. The church was built close to a grave mound, and a runestone (Ravnkilde 1) found inside the church was reused as the raised sill of the door of the main entrance with the text facing up.[207] The runestone, presumably connected with the earlier burial mound, was likely moved into this visible and symbolic position in the church in order to tie the new Christian ideological power of the church to the old power of the mound and the runestone's claim on the landscape. The runestone reads: "Qzurr *landhirðir* (estate-manager), Køgir's son, carved these runes in memory of his *dróttin* (female lord) Asbod."[208] The ritual bowl-shaped indentations that cover the back of the runestone date to the Bronze Age and testify to an even earlier manifestation of the ritual power embedded in this object and the broader local landscape. By placing this stone in a highly visible location in the doorway of the church, this embedded power was literally built into the fabric of the new religious and aristocratic symbol of the stone church. Across the Danish landscape, these early Christian stone churches were instruments of state formation that show the proliferation of a royally sanctioned and powerfully visible manifestation of a new ideological system tying the countryside to the towns and to the king.

Graves: Ideological Transformation

Viking Age graves in Denmark, spanning from the pagan to the Christian periods, evince key temporal trends. The pre-Christian graves contain significant diversity, while the coming of Christianity brought simplicity and uniformity, as discussed in Chapter 4. Even before conversion to Christianity, however, the average Danish Viking Age graves were simpler and generally materially poorer than the graves from Sweden and Norway. This is not because the Danish population was poorer than the Norwegian or Swedish counterparts. Instead, even prior to the Viking Age, Danes had been more influenced by their Christian neighbors to the south.[209] Denmark was after all the only Scandinavian land that shared a border with a Christian state. As indicated by the written sources, Christian missionary activity was earlier and more forceful in Denmark than elsewhere. The Carolingian Empire, followed by the German Holy Roman Empire, had also politically pressured Danish Viking leaders to accept Christian ideas and at times even personal Christianization (if only sometimes as nominal *prima signatio*, or "first signing" with the cross as a sort of preliminary baptism). The empire had, for instance, given support to exiled Danish kings, such as Harald Klak, in exchange for loyalty and acceptance of Christianity. As a result, some aspects of presumably pagan graves from the ninth and tenth centuries share characteristics with Christian graves, such as an absence of grave goods and an east-west orientation.

A relatively more stratified and socially stable society in Denmark, as compared with Norway and Sweden, has also been suggested as a factor in the general simplicity of Danish graves from the ninth and tenth centuries. This draws on the idea that rich graves indicate hierarchies in flux, in which new power-wielders need to make public claims to their status. This parallels arguments made using the runestone evidence discussed above. In fact, one particular period during the late tenth century, in which the elite chose to be buried in rich martial-themed chamber graves, corresponds temporally with the proliferation of runestones praising martial prowess.

Two widespread changes, indicating major shifts in social structure and the institutionalization of power, will be pursued in the next two sections. The first is an emergence of a group of distinctly wealthy chamber graves in the mid-to late tenth century, indicative of the development of a new state-level elite that needed to legitimize claims to power and authority. The second is the late tenth- to early eleventh-century co-option of the social statements made during burial within the state-allied Christian Church.

Pre-Christian Graves and the Emergence of New Status Signaling in the Tenth Century

The eighth- to ninth-century grave assemblage from Denmark is relatively meager, and most graves appear rather simple.[210] We know more about the tenth century, partially because the increased number of objects in graves makes them more prone to accidental and archaeological discovery. In the tenth century, evidence of separation of elite and commoner cemeteries appears. The burials of a presumed village at Stengade on the island of Langeland illustrate this point. Eighty-five simple graves containing the village commoners were part of a large cemetery called Stengade II, whereas the wealthier graves were found in the separate and smaller cemetery of Stengade I.[211]

The appearance of distinctive and wealthy tenth-century chamber graves signals the emergence of a new type of elite burial.[212] The self-conscious expenditure of wealth and display of status suggests that these are new elites who need to solidify their status locally. The similarity and wide geographical distribution of these graves indicate an elite with ties to the central state. Scholars have suggested that these were vassals of the expansionist Jelling Dynasty, granted new powers across the borderlands of the Danish state.[213] The new wealth appears both in male and female graves. Both contain elite modes of transportation, presumably meant to convey them in an appropriate manner to the afterlife. The male graves were furnished with horses and riding equipment, while the females were placed in wagon bodies.

The most dramatic new appearance was a series of male graves representing the deceased as wealthy mounted warriors (Figure 5.10).[214] These cavalry graves typically contain a standardized set of furnishings and martial equipment, including a horse (or horses), riding gear with stirrups, a dog, swords, lances,

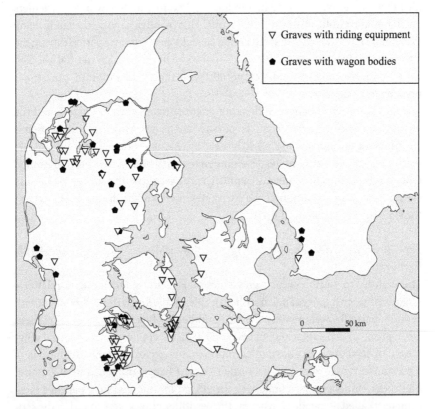

Figure 5.10 Rich graves from the late tenth century that were interred with either military-style riding equipment or wagon cart bodies. The appearance of these graves across Denmark suggests a newly empowered elite signaling their novel power within the emergent Danish state.

Source: map by author

and other weapons. The stirrups in these graves suggest combat in the saddle. Equipment for lavish feasting also characterizes these graves, which are furnished with standardized bronze platters and bronze-trimmed buckets for alcoholic drink. The stress on martial power is especially noteworthy, as the inclusion of weapons in Viking Age Danish graves was relatively rare from the eighth to the early tenth centuries.[215] Another male martial-type grave includes ceremonial axes. These were less overtly martial than the cavalry graves, but still likely indicated an official role within the state administration. A particularly beautiful axe with silver inlay was found in a grave at Mammen, while a similar axe was recovered from the cemetery of the royal fortress of Fyrkat, further linking the axe burial rite to royal administration.[216]

Female graves in the same wealth class as the male cavalry burials are often accompanied by wagons, or at least the bodies of wagons, since the wheels are sometimes missing (Figure 5.10).[217] These four-wheeled wagon bodies were sometimes employed as coffins in graves, such as in burials 4 and 20 at Fyrkat, the grave under the Hørning church, and five chamber graves from Thumby-Bienebek near Hedeby.[218] These graves can contain other components of the driving-gear, including horse harness bows, such as those from Søllested on Fyn and Elstrup on Als.[219] Some of these graves also include feasting equipment comparable to, but distinct from, that recovered in the male equestrian graves. For instance, Fyrkat 4 and one of the Thumby-Bienebek graves contained pairs of drinking horns, while a number of the wagon graves, including the Hørning grave and two of the Thumby-Bienebek graves, contained buckets and bronze platters similar to those in the male equestrian burials.[220] The dress of the females in these burials is sumptuous, sometimes with silk and textiles woven with silver and gold threads. Notably, however, they rarely contain oval tortoise brooches, which are the classic female Viking Age dress ornament used in pairs to hold up the straps of an outer tunic. This shift could be interpreted as a new dress style that looked toward styles to the south in Europe.[221] The burials in carts are therefore simultaneously looking back toward a pagan past, when vehicles of transport to the next world were common, as well as outward as women in Scandinavia strove to emulate the rich and powerful Christian classes of Europe.

The uniformity of the male cavalry equipment and the female wagon burials shows that these individuals would have had similarly impressive gear, at least in death and presumably also in life. Similarities in metalwork included in various graves also suggest that the same craftsmen, probably working in the kings' workshops, made many of the objects. The objects—such as the swords, stirrups, and feasting equipment—might then have been royal gifts to new vassals, marking their position as the king's men and a new martial elite.

The distribution of these wealthy graves across the landscape manifests patterning that likely reveals key nodes in the administration of the nascent

Danish kingdom (Figure 5.10). The central part of Jutland, around Jelling, is devoid of these rich graves: cavalry, axe, and cart graves are simply absent from this Danish heartland. Randsborg argues instead that the wealthy graves cluster around the borderlands of the expanding state in a pattern that is similar to the distribution of the circular Trelleborg fortresses.[222] This may indicate a semi-feudal scenario for these cavalry graves, in which the buried individuals had received new land rights and standardized military equipment in exchange for military obligations and local administrative duties. The cavalry graves are sometimes found within cemeteries, while elsewhere (especially in Jutland) they were emplaced in preexisting and prominently visible barrows, serving to embed them in the local landscape. In both cases, they stand out as novel statements of state-affiliated power within the previous burial landscape.

Christian Burial in Parish Churchyards

As described above, the first churches in Denmark were made of wood. These were followed in the late eleventh century by stone churches. Both church types seem to have appeared first in royally sponsored towns.[223] In the early eleventh century, Christian cemeteries were laid out around the new parish churches; many of these continue to be used today. Recovery of Viking Age Christian graves, given the active nature of these cemeteries, is rare. Two notable exceptions are the early Christian graveyard at the seasonal production and trade site of Sebbersund on the Limfjord waterway, and the early Christian burial ground in the town of Lund.[224] These sites exemplify, respectively, rural and urban graves from the earliest Christian period. Together with the examples of the Jelling and Hørning churches, they illustrate how burial was re-centered around churches in different ways, sometimes incorporating earlier graves, sometimes incorporating earlier modes of burial, but always restructuring the burial community around the new ideological and administrative center represented by the church.

Excavations at Sebbersund revealed a 40 x 40 m graveyard bounded by ditches and with a wooden church at its center. The church was a simple nave and chancel building, evidenced only by post holes and an absence of burials in the middle of the graveyard. Of the 468 graves excavated at Sebbersund, twenty were interred in boats, referencing earlier burial traditions in which boats were conceived as modes of transport to the next world (see Chapter 4). As in many early Christian graveyards in Scandinavia, the populations were divided across the space by age, gender, and status. Women were interred mostly to the north of the church, while men were buried south of the church. This significant reorganization of gender-based inhumation was not universal. One woman buried in a stone coffin on the south (male) side of the church and close to the church wall shows that she was accorded status in new ways within the Christian ritual practice.[225] Like the re-burial of Gorm under the altar at Jelling, high-status burial was now accorded to people by proximity to the church and more specifically to the central ritual performed at the altar.

The wooden church and churchyard at Sebbersund were established in the early eleventh century and continued to be used into the early twelfth century. In the late eleventh century, a granite church was constructed on a high point above the wooden church, and burials began to be interred around the new church. Interestingly, the churches and the graveyards were therefore in use contemporaneously at the end of the eleventh century. Perhaps the wooden church at Sebbersund was erected and controlled by a regional chieftain who aligned himself quickly with the new religion. The new granite church, which took an appearance and style similar to the late eleventh-century royal-sponsored stone churches in towns, might then represent increased royal interference in ritual practice and church organization at Sebbersund.

In the urban fabric of royally sponsored towns, such as Lund, which emerged around 1000, the hand of the king was felt from the beginning. The two stone churches in Roskilde, which have been documented archaeologically, were according to written sources sponsored by Knut the Great's sister. Both texts and the archaeological evidence suggest they were built with the help of master builders from Knut's English realm. The royal family already had invested in church burial as a symbol of royal power and connection to the Christian God, as indicated by the transfer of Gorm to the Jelling church. Subsequently all kings were buried in churches, including Harald and Svein in Roskilde, Knut in Winchester, and St. Knut in Odense. Large-scale excavations at the Trinitatis (Holy Trinity) church in Lund have unearthed traces of a wooden church and a large cemetery with thousands of graves, dated dendrochronologically to as early as the early 990s. This date falls within the reign of Svein Forkbeard, who is said in written sources to have built a church in Lund.[226] Status in burial is seen here too, with the elite being buried close to the church in nicely made coffins. Poorer segments of society were placed in graves located at the outskirts of the cemetery and buried in makeshift coffins, such as re-used rough wooden troughs that were sometimes too small for the deceased. A stone church replaced the wooden one by around 1020. An empty grave was found in front of the altar of the old wooden church. It is possible that the person, a royal personage surely, who had been buried in this grave was exhumed and moved into the new stone church. Some have suggested that this may have been the grave of Svein Forkbeard, said in the *Encomium Emmae* to have been buried in the Holy Trinity Church, albeit the one in Roskilde. In any case, the royal hand has been distinguished in the choir of the stone church, which is modeled on the church in Winchester, England, the eventual burial church of King Knut the Great.

Complementarity of Datasets from Late Tenth-Century Denmark: The Case of the Trelleborg Fortresses

Thinking about the function of the Trelleborg fortresses offers us an interesting chance to explore a form of indirect complementarity between archaeology and written sources. The fortresses are probably the single greatest material indication of the emergence of a centralized state with the power to coordinate massive building projects across Denmark. Together, they certainly represent the largest public works project carried out by a king during the Viking Age. Yet they are not mentioned in any contemporary runestone or any foreign texts, or even in post–Viking Age saga traditions. Seeking confirmation of datasets is therefore impossible. Pursuing the contradiction of sources is also impossible in absence of evidence from texts, even if the dramatic archaeological evidence paired with the absence of textual mention might sow some distrust in our written sources. So how might interdisciplinarity work in this case?

One solution is to build separate yet mutually supporting scaffolds of interpretation, especially relying on the archaeological character of the fortresses, modern dating sciences, historical sources, and careful consideration of the geographical positioning of the fortresses. The crucial linchpin in these interpretations is that modern sciences have allowed precise dendrochronological dating of the fortresses. Without these precision dates, the historical context would be too broad to allow an understanding of the specific state preoccupations that led to the fortresses' construction. Simultaneously, only in light of the specific historical context can the archaeological evidence from the fortresses—site distribution, architecture, and artifact and ecofact analyses—be employed to shed light on the nature and the outcomes of royal power in the reign of a specific king.

After their initial discovery, the forts were thought to be training camps and staging points for King Svein Forkbeard's attacks on England.[227] This interpretation was guided especially by the Anglo-Saxon sources that document Svein's attacks from 1002 until 1013 when he conquered all of England. This interpretation seemed to successfully wed the historical narrative with the military nature of the fortresses, but it was wrong precisely because the dating was not yet exact enough to pinpoint the right historical context for the interpretation of the archaeology. The dendrochronological dating of the fortresses to between 975 and 980 pushed back the dates and placed their construction twenty years before the invasion of England began, and instead within the historical reign of Svein's father, Harald Bluetooth. The forts also did not appear to have ever been repaired, suggesting that the forts may have been abandoned before 1000, or at least soon thereafter.[228]

Re-focusing the historical microscope on the 970s and 980s, the large Jelling runestone reveals that Harald's reign was preoccupied with the internal considerations of consolidating power within the Danish realm, while converting the people to Christianity and extending power over parts of Norway. Beyond Denmark, continental texts suggest that Harald's main concern was defending against political pressure and invasions from the German Holy Roman Empire to the south, rather than invading England. These German texts of course foreground relationships with the German Empire, but Danish chroniclers—Sven Aggesen and Saxo Grammaticus—also highlight the relationship with Germany. The Icelandic sagas concerning the Norwegian kings provide some balance, focusing on Harald's efforts to make the Norwegian kingdom tributary and bring under his control the Viken region around the Oslo Fjord.

With the first dendrochronological evidence in the late 1970s that the fortresses were actually built around 980, scholars reinterpreted the archaeological evidence in light of Harald Bluetooth's preoccupations and therefore re-centered their understanding of the fortresses around internal politics. Scholars such as Else Roesdahl saw the forts as "fortresses of coercion," or strongholds meant to control both the people of Denmark and local travel routes.[229] With a focus on the interior of the country, they could function as "normal royal estates" and were ascribed a multiplicity of functions related to internal politics, such as the nexuses of tolls and customs, minting of coins, maintenance of law and order, protection of state revenue, royally controlled craft production, and bases from which to launch military attacks.[230] In 1980, Klavs Randsborg, who saw the fortresses in light of state formation, observed that the fortresses formed a "belt of defenses" around the Danish state, with Jelling at its center.[231] He suggested that the fortresses were directed against outside invasion and to control border provinces of the nascent Danish state. He also observed that their location corresponds with the location of cavalry graves from the late tenth century, which he interpreted as the graves of new pro-Jelling dynasty elites governing these outlying provinces (see above). He argued that they were likely designed to function much like the English King Alfred's fortified burhs, which helped Wessex effectively defend against the late ninth-century Viking incursions (see Chapter 2).

These were important corrections, but the story benefits from an even closer look at the historical events. After the erection of the large Jelling stone, Harald's reign saw the German invasion of Denmark in 974, during which the Holy Roman Empire probably gained control of Hedeby, the greatest trading emporium in Denmark and a significant source of royal tolls. The recent dendrochronological dating of the Aggersborg fortress to circa 975 means that construction of the fortresses began immediately after this attack, strongly suggesting that the fortresses should be seen as reactive and defensive responses to German aggression.[232] The construction of the fortresses is in fact sandwiched between the date of the German invasion in 974 and 983, when the Danes reconquered Hedeby, pushed the Germans back across the Danevirke, and raided Hamburg. The Danevirke system was refortified with the addition of the Kovirke rampart around this time, and the Danish reconquest of the region provides the most likely specific historic moment for such a construction. The Trelleborg fortresses were all in existence at the time of the battle at Hedeby and the raid on Hamburg, but we cannot know whether soldiers stationed there participated in these Danish military successes.

Turning to their positioning in the landscape, the forts are strategically located throughout the Viking Age kingdom of Denmark. Their location within the Danish realm indicates that the Trelleborg fortresses were not designed as a perimeter defense and should not be seen as an attempt to deter an enemy, especially because of their invisibility from the shoreline. Rather, they seem purposefully distant from Denmark's main external threat, the German Ottonian Empire. The fortresses are defensive both in their fortified character and position in the landscape. They were situated away from the shore and along smaller rivers that precluded the mass advance of an attacking fleet. The distance from the shore also allowed time for advance warning by sentries stationed at the mouths of the rivers.

Yet the forts are not only meant to defend against attacks. They seem purposefully positioned to facilitate control of major trade routes. The forts are all directed toward controlling the Kattegat Sea, through which sea-borne trade from the Baltic Sea to the Atlantic Ocean had to pass. For example, Trelleborg and Nonnebakken are well placed to control the trade from the Baltic Sea that passes between Fyn and Sjælland. Borgring and Borgeby would have controlled similar travel through Øresund between Sjælland and Scania. Aggersborg is ideally positioned to control the trade from Kattegat through the Limfjord inland sea, which was particularly busy because of the treacherous seas in Skagerak north of the Jutland peninsula. The sheer size of Aggersborg, which is large enough to hold perhaps all the warriors from Trelleborg, Fyrkat, and Nonnebakken together, however, indicates that it held some special role in the fortress system. The Limfjord was frequently attacked by Norwegian raiders and was especially often used as a calm-watered staging point for Danish fleets in the late Viking Age, such as those of the two King Knuts discussed in the next section. Harald's Jelling runestone claims that his control over Norway had been regained (probably in the early 960s), while the written sources, most explicitly the Icelandic sagas, recount that Harald may have lost this overlordship in the later years of his reign. Aggersborg therefore is probably directed toward maintenance of control, or even the reconquest, of southern Norway.

Seeking complementarity between the fortresses and the specific historical events in the 970s and 980s, Roesdahl and Sindbæk have recently arrived at the similar conclusion that the fortresses were responses to the crisis of military pressure from the German Empire under Otto I (912–973) and Otto II (973–983). They propose that the primary function of the fortresses was as defensible storage depots for surplus food and as local stations from which to mobilize military responses. As they stress from the artifactual record, other activities took place in the fortresses as well, such as trading, craft production, and possibly even coin minting, but these were secondary to the defensive military and supply considerations. The overall character of the fortresses is that of military barracks meant to house fighters in uniform buildings modeled on rural high-status houses. These buildings were in all likelihood meant to house the retinues of local chieftains, who saw themselves as equals to one another. As such, the houses and internal layout of the fortresses reveal no hierarchical organization. The absence of archaeological evidence for a single command center could be interpreted as a failure to impose a strict military hierarchy on the independent regional leaders. There is no doubt that the king ordered the construction of these fortresses, however, and their ingenious design instantiated a new royally dictated structuring of local chieftains in the pursuit of war that continued to employ the traditional vocabulary of chieftainly independence.

These points are mostly made by Roesdahl and Sindbæk, and I would deviate from their understanding only in challenging their conclusion about the importance of these fortresses for royal power. They say that "the fortresses made possible the increase of royal control of the sources of the Danish Kingdom and Norway," but follow this with "but they were not tools in the unification of the Danish Kingdom."[233] Here I would disagree in a fundamental way that revolves around the meaning of the "the unification of the Danish Kingdom." This is more than just a semantic issue. If unification is perceived as ceasing with the recognition of a single king throughout Denmark, then perhaps they are right. But if unification is a process toward the formation of a state, as I have argued in this chapter, then these fortresses play a key role. These fortresses are the first clear signal that the "Danish Kingdom" has become a state-level society with royal control over local administration and labor mobilization. Possibly most importantly, they indicate the virtual monopoly of force by one ruler within the country. This monopoly of legitimate force is a key feature in classic definitions of a state-level society.[234] Archaeologically, large-scale organization and distribution of contemporary and typologically similar barracks is a classic material correlate of such state power. The Trelleborg fortresses, with the elite-style houses that are meant to hold warriors from across the country, represent such barracks. Harald Bluetooth had these fortresses built in a time of crisis as a response to a military threat and invasion from the south; however, as a result he projected a novel level of state power across the Danish landscape.

If the fortresses, although unmentioned in the written sources, were instrumental in uniting Denmark under Harald's reign and in the reconquest of Hedeby and southern Norway, it is difficult to understand why they were not maintained and were instead abandoned perhaps just a few years after their construction.

We may seek an explanation again in the texts, which tell of Svein overthrowing his father Harald in a civil war. The massive labor mobilization that Harald had used to build the fortresses, as well as the other major monumental works such as the Ravninge Enge bridge, the Jelling palace complex, and the new phase of Danevirke, amounted to a kingdom-wide forced-labor project unlike any that had ever taken place in Denmark. On this very point, the written sources may retain an echo of Harald's coercive power and the Danish people's dissatisfaction with the mandated labor required to build the fortresses. The two Danish twelfth-century chroniclers—Sven Aggesen and Saxo Grammaticus—both mention that Harald forced the Danes to haul an immense stone across the Jutlandic landscape to grace his mother's burial mound at Jelling.[235] This labor may be a reference to the large-scale construction projects at Jelling (the monumental palisade and the burial mounds) or nearby at Ravninge Enge bridge. Perhaps more obviously, it might refer to the erection of the large Jelling runestone, although the transfer of this stone from its source would require much less labor. I would rather see this stone-dragging story as a more all-encompassing metaphor for Harald's unprecedented mobilization of labor, including the construction of the Trelleborg fortresses, which would have touched every part of Denmark. In this light, the monumental fortresses were likely the greatest symbol of Harald's coercive power. It may have been necessary, then, for them to be abandoned if Svein was to consolidate his power with the Danish elite and general populace. Harald's reign, as seen particularly in the archaeological evidence of state power, was the turning point in the creation of the Danish state. Although other historical trajectories were possible thereafter, the mobilization of labor and centralization of power internally in Denmark had solidified.

The Culmination of State Formation: A Tale of Two Knuts

As the Viking Age drew to a close, two King Knuts embody the major transformations in institutionalized power that took place in eleventh-century Denmark. The first Knut—Knut the Great—created an empire by incorporating England, Denmark, Norway, and large parts of Sweden. The second Knut—Saint Knut—ruled a different Denmark and found himself limited in his ambitions for overseas conquest by a realm that was increasingly Europeanized, Christianized, and inward-looking for the sources of power. The story of these two kings—as told from the perspective of historical sources and archaeological evidence—is enriched by the exponential increase in the available written sources for the mid- and late eleventh century. Although texts are more plentiful, their availability is still problematic because of their respective selectivity. Knut the Great established his court in England and rarely visited Denmark. His reign in England is well known from Anglo-Saxon texts, and skaldic poets praise his accomplishments, but we know much less about Knut the Great's Denmark. Insights into the reign of St. Knut, whose donation to the Cathedral in Lund is the earliest written document in Denmark, are difficult for different reasons. The plethora of historical sources written after St. Knut's death are very much focused on the attempt to style him as a royal saint for the Danish Church. As we will see, archaeology provides a useful corrective and complementary source to tell the stories of two of the last Danish Viking Age kings.

Knut the Great: King of Denmark and England

Knut, the second son of Svein Forkbeard, had joined his father in his conquest of England in 1013 and was left as the leader of the Danish invasion after Svein's sudden death. He returned to Denmark, where his older brother Harald Sveinsson was now king, and raised an army for another invasion. Knut's army was drawn from across Scandinavia, with Jarl Hakon of Trondelag and Thorkel the Tall (probably from Scania) joining with their own followers (the story of the invasion and Knut's England is treated in Chapter 2). His conquest of England and subsequent paying of his warriors, commemorated on runestones in Denmark and as far away as central Sweden, was a quintessential Viking endeavor. Knut was a Viking king, a second son, who carved out a new kingdom for himself. He came to rule an empire when his brother Harald died, and Knut became king of both Denmark and England. Over the course of his reign, both Knut and Denmark would be transformed: Knut would become a Christian European king, while the Danish state would become a Christian European bureaucracy.

A key aspect of state formation is representation of the ideology of rulership. Knut's reign shows an ideology of rulership that harkens back to the traditional Scandinavian values of rulership, while simultaneously looking toward new Christian models. Skaldic poets reciting praise poems in Old Norse at Knut's court in England show Knut as a profoundly Scandinavian ruler with traditional Viking ideals. Hallvard Hareksblesi's *Knútsdrápa* (*Praise Poem for Knut*), for instance, relies on a complex understanding of Scandinavian history and Norse mythology to style Knut as a traditional Viking king:

> Knut, you let the hard-byrnied ships
> resound forward to Fljot [in England];
> the famous guardian of the lightnings of battle [=swords]
> sailed, battle-bold over the sea.
> Noble strengthener of the sea horse [=ship] of Ull [=shield],
> You bound your fleet

to Ælla's family inheritance [England],
and rejoiced the seagull of the Valkyrie [=raven].[236]

The reference to Ælla—the ninth-century king of Northumbria—makes Knut the heir of the Viking Great Army that conquered Northumbria and conjures images of the Ivar the Boneless, who brutally murdered King Ælla (see Chapter 2). The kennings using the god Ull, Valkyries, and the ravens who arrive with the Valkyries to feast on the dead show Knut's and his court's taste for pagan Scandinavian imagery. These complex poems, recited in Old Norse, show that the Scandinavian language must have been understood by a large portion of Knut's English court, giving the sense of a multi-ethnic, if not purely Viking, group of warriors and retainers. Art produced in Knut's court also mirrors Scandinavian elite tastes, as is readily evidenced in the St. Paul tombstone decorated with a twisting and tendrilled beast in the eleventh-century Scandinavian Ringerike style (Figure 2.10).

Although Knut was at heart a Scandinavian king, he ruled a Christian empire with its center of gravity in southern England. Here Knut engaged strong traditions of kingship that allied with the Christian Church and looked toward continental Europe. After his conquest of England, Knut had needed to stress his rule in the Christian model to be accepted as king.[237] For instance, after his final victory over the English King Edmund at Ashingdon (see Chapter 2), Knut took possession of the relics of St. Wendreda that had been carried into battle by the English. Knut kept the expensive jewel-covered gold reliquary intact for years until he could present it with the saints' relics to the archbishop of Canterbury.[238]

Knut transposed his Christian ideology of rulership along with the intertwined Anglo-Saxon bureaucracy onto his Danish kingdom. The emergence of a bureaucracy during the reign of Knut in Denmark was deeply influenced by the English system. The written sources, from Adam of Bremen to the Danish chroniclers to the saga writers, all recount that Knut brought English clerics to Denmark to help organize the Danish Church and support his own Christian administration of the kingdom. Glazed English pottery found in early eleventh-century domestic layers in the new urban centers of Lund, Roskilde, and Viborg suggest an influx of English people during the time of Knut.[239] The transfer of English bureaucracy to administer Denmark is especially evident in Knut's English (Anglo-Saxon/Anglo-Danish) moneyers, who minted his new coins (e.g., Figure 5.7, row 5 A).

In fact, coinage offers an instructive example of Knut's ideology of kingship, as it combines visual representation of rulership and tangible economic benefits. Knut the Great's economic and ideological restructuring of Denmark is exemplified by the systematic proliferation of a new network of mints across the Danish realm. The mint in Lund predated his reign, but by the end of the

1020s, Knut extended the minting of coins to every region of Denmark: Roskilde (northern Sjælland), Ringsted (central Sjælland), Slagelse (western Sjælland), Ørbæk (Fyn), Hedeby (southern Jutland), Ribe (western Jutland), Aarhus (eastern Jutland), Viborg (central Jutland), Aalborg (northern Jutland).[240] The redistribution of Knut's main mints to internal areas of the kingdom, far beyond the major international exchange centers, suggests that royal propaganda was a key function. The coinage also represents salary paid by the ruler, infusing his imagery into the local economy, and furthermore assisting in payment of state-imposed taxes.[241]

The adoption of Christian European style coinage in Denmark was institution-alized during the reign of Knut the Great. There are at least two phases of coinage minted under Knut. The first phase, beginning around 1018, was based on heavy Anglo-Saxon pennies (1.4 grams) with the cross on one side and the king's por-trait on the other.[242] In this phase, Knut imported Anglo-Saxon minters from England. For example, English moneyers struck their names, including Ælfwine, Godwine, and Leofwine, on coins minted at Lund during Knut's reign.[243] The name Leofwine was also found inscribed on a small English-style pencase used for record keeping and excavated at Lund in layers dating to the first half of the eleventh century.[244]

In the second phase, beginning in the late 1020s, Knut expanded and systematized the production of coinage. New, lighter weight standards (1 gram in eastern Denmark and 0.75 grams in western Denmark) were introduced that deviated from the Anglo-Saxon exemplars. In this phase, having reasserted his power in Denmark after the battle of Helgå, the coinage represents a firm as-sertion of royal power with a more distinctly Danish national identity and the addition of his son's name, Hardaknut, to some coins.[245] Knut's coinage was never an exclusive coinage in Denmark, and English and German coins con-tinued to circulate. His royal coinage did bring substantial revenues, however, and perhaps more importantly, it placed Danish royal coins in people's hands across the country, and especially in towns, thereby making clear claims to a royal monopoly on the means of exchange. In their wide distribution, these coins also broadly disseminated a visual representation of Knut's ideological justifica-tion of rulership with the pairing of his image and name on the obverse and the Christian cross on the reverse.

Knut's Christian ideology of rulership is underscored late in his reign by his trips abroad, as described in his own letters, skaldic poetry, and in contempo-rary Church iconography. When Knut went to Rome as one of only two chosen witnesses to participate in the Pope's coronation of the German Emperor Conrad II, he did so as a thoroughly European and Christian king.[246] As discussed in Chapter 2, his own words written back to the English people in his 1027 letter appear to reveal a very devout man, but also show a very savvy king. He styled his trip to Rome as a religious pilgrimage undertaken for the good of his subjects, consistent with the contemporary models of Christian rulership in which the king was the chosen intermediary between God and his people. The letter expresses how he had long vowed to God to make this journey, stating explicitly that he had provided for protection and toll exemptions for both Danes and Englishmen traveling to Rome on pilgrimage.

Also, at home in his own court in England, the traditional Norse praise poetry recited by his skalds took a turn later in his life to underscore his Christian kingship more so than his Viking prowess. These poems show a new and direct alignment between Knut and God.[247] In his *Knútsdrápa* (c. 1027), Sighvat Thordarson signals that Knut's power flows from God by repeatedly employing the phrase "Knut is under Heaven."[248] The same point is made more explicit by Hallvard in his *Knútsdrápa*: "There is not under the earth-tree [Yggdrasil] a ruler closer to the lord of monks [=God] than you."[249] Knut is seen also to be an ideal king, modeled on divine kingship. In his *Hofuðlausn* (*Head Ransom*, c. 1027), Thorarin Loftunga praises Knut by drawing a parallel between Knut's and God's rule: "Knut protects the land as the guardian of Byzantium [=God] protects the heavenly kingdom."[250]

The praise of a ruler by the comparative juxtaposition of a king's rule and that of the Christian God was new to skaldic poetry. Skaldic poetry typically praises kings for success in warfare as a manifestation of the favor of the gods. These skaldic poems from late in Knut's reign, which praise him for peaceful all-encompassing kingship, indicate a realignment of rulership along Christian ideals. Where traditional skaldic verses suggest that divine sanction of kingship is lost with losses in battle, these verses from Knut's court in the late 1020s suggest that Knut possesses a peaceful authority stabilized by God's choosing.[251]

Finally, a confraternity book, *Liber Vitae*, produced circa 1031 in Winchester to record patrons and visitors includes a page showing an image of Knut and Queen Emma in their roles as Christian rulers (Figure 5.11). As generous Christian rulers, they are seen donating a massive gold cross to the Winchester church. In return, the king and queen receive the regalia of rulership from angels who point toward the enthroned Christ as the source of their power to rule. As an indication of his role as defender of the realm—and perhaps also as Viking conqueror—Knut touches the hilt of his sword.

Knut was born and raised in Denmark, went on Viking raids and voyages of conquest to England in his youth, and through his successes became king of Denmark, England, and Norway. Perhaps the most successful Viking of the Viking Age, he ended his life in Winchester, England, and was remembered as a most pious Christian ruler. As king, he retained the martial ethos of his Scandinavian heritage, but tempered it with ideals of Christian kingship, becoming the first Viking king to enter fully into the political theater of the upper

Figure 5.11 A page from the *Liber Vitae* Winchester manuscript (c. 1031) showing King Knut and Queen Emma donating a golden cross to the Winchester church, while receiving the regalia of kingship from angels pointing towards Christ, the source of earthly authority.

Source: British Library, New Minster Liber Vitae, shelfmark Stowe MS 944

echelons of the Christian European royalty. Yet, Knut's empire would not out-last Knut himself. After his death in 1035, his empire split. His son Hardaknut by Emma of Normandy inherited Denmark (reign 1035–1042), while his son Harold Harefoot by Ælfgifu of Northampton succeeded to the throne in England (reign 1035–1040), and the Norwegian son of St. Olaf, Magnus the Good, took Norway (reign 1035–1047). After Harold Harefoot's early death, Hardaknut briefly reunited Denmark and England from 1040 to 1042, but after his death, the Edward the Confessor succeeded to the throne in England. The institutions of the state that Knut had strengthened in Denmark, however, remained a key legacy that provided internal cohesion and strength that aided future Danish kings, like Svein Estridsen, who as we have seen above held the kingdom together even under sustained assaults from King Harald Hardrada of Norway. Knut's other legacy of a North Sea empire that included England also underlay Harald Hardrada's failed invasion of England in 1066. Danish ambitions to reestablish Knut's North Sea empire also persisted and would be rekindled by Knut's name-sake and great nephew, Knut the Saint, in perhaps the last gasp of the Viking Age.

St. Knut: Failed Viking Plans, Successful Hagiography, and the End of the Viking Age

In in the old crypt of St. Knut's Cathedral in Odense, two wooden casket-like shrines hold the skeletons of two brothers whose mortal wounds are still vis-ible (Figure 5.12). One of these two skeletons is the remains of arguably the last Viking king of Denmark, who as a transitional figure would also become the first Danish saint.

Like his great-uncle before him, St. Knut had ambitions to conquer England. In 1085, Knut summoned the country's fleet to assemble at the Limfjord. When Knut delayed his own arrival to deal with trouble at the kingdom's southern border, the men of the fleet returned home for harvest in late summer. In re-taliation, the king levied a fine on his people for returning home without royal permission, causing a revolt. Knut fled to Odense, where he barricaded himself and sought sanctuary in the wooden Church of St. Alban. This church housed the relics of the English saint that Knut himself had brought home from England. The rebels broke into the church and killed Knut, his brother Benedikt, and sev-enteen of Knut's hirðmen who stood by his side. Soon after, miracles were re-ported. In 1095, the clerics of St. Alban's Church in Odense exhumed Knut's body from his grave at their church and placed it in a stone sarcophagus in the crypt of the new St. Knut Church (a process called *elevatio*). In 1101, he was canonized as a saint and moved again in a formal *translatio* ceremony, this time into a gilded shrine at the church's high altar.

Figure 5.12 St. Knut statue in front of Odense's St. Knut Cathedral, which was begun shortly after Knut's martyrdom. In the crypt, Knut's bones, which show evidence of violent death, still lie enshrined in a twelfth-century decorated casket beside the bones of his brother Benedict.

Source: photos by author

Knut's story is told in some of the earliest written records composed in Denmark and revisited by the twelfth-century Danish chroniclers and in the Icelandic *Knýtlinga Saga*. The earliest sources—known as the Odense Literature—were written in Odense in the community of Anglo-Saxon clerics associated with a Benedictine monastery and the St. Alban's Church in which Knut was martyred.[252] The authors, some of whom had been eyewitnesses to the events of Knut's martyrdom, elevation, and translation, aimed to show ahead of his canonization that Knut had all the necessary makings of a saint. To do so, they praised Knut's just and pious rule as a king and described his martyrdom with parallels to Christ's own martyrdom. Two of the three earliest anonymous texts—a commemorative plaque (*Tabula Othiensis*, "The Odense Tablet") and a poetic plaque (*Epitaphium*, "The Epitaph")—were short inscriptions on metal tablets buried with King Knut in his shrine at the time of his translation in 1101. These tablets were moved several times with the body of Knut after the Protestant Reformation, but they were fortunately transcribed before being lost in the late seventeenth century when the shrines of Knut and Benedikt were also looted and deprived of their bejeweled decoration. A third source, the first hagiographical text (*Passio S. Kanuti regis et martiris*, "The Passion of Saint Knut, King and Martyr"), may even predate the two tablets placed in his shrine.[253] The final form of the Odense Literature's hagiographical production is the English cleric Ælnoth's longer *Gesta*

(*History*).[254] Neither *Tabula* nor *Epitaphium* even mention Knut's planned invasion of England, which appears to have been a direct catalyst for the Danish rebellion. In aiming single-mindedly to show Knut in a positive and pious light, the longer compositions of the Odense Literature—*Passio* and Ælnoth's *Gesta*—state that Knut's motivation for his invasion of England was the liberation of the English people from the impious Norman tyranny that had been instated after William the Conqueror's conquest of England in 1066. The *Passio* adds that, through his planned Danish invasion, Knut sought the spiritual restoration of his Danish soldiers, while Ælnoth specifically relates that the English asked for Knut's assistance. The Odense Literature also had to explain how the rebellion was an unjust assault on the king and therefore an assault on God's natural order. The *Tabula* tersely states that Knut was martyred because of his "zeal for the Christian religion and just actions."[255] The king was meant to be strong in ordering society, according to God's law. *Passio* and Ælnoth make similar statements and draw parallels to the biblical figures of Moses and David but spend little time offering any details. None of the documents mention Knut's punitive fines for the fleet's abandonment of his planned English invasion. *Passio* simply blames the devil's intrigue, while Ælnoth removes any blame from Knut by disassociating the royal fines from the failed invasion and ascribing blame to Knut's greedy royal agents, who he says tampered with weights and scales for their own benefit.

The Odense Literature describes Knut's martyrdom with direct parallels to the death of Christ in the medieval tradition of *imitatio Christi* (imitation of Christ). All four sources state that Knut was killed after confessing his sins in front of the altar. Like Christ he was stabbed in the side by a lance, and taking up the final position of Christ, Knut outstretched his arms to form a cross with his body. *Tabula* notes that, like Christ, he died on the week's sixth day (Friday). *Epitaphium*, *Passio*, and Ælnoth add that, like Christ, Knut was betrayed by a Judas-like traitor who had been his follower.[256] As he is assailed in the church, Knut also asks for a drink of water from his attackers, which is temporarily granted, but thwarted just as Christ is mocked when the Roman soldiers offer him only a sponge of vinegar. All sources also agree on the unlikely point that Knut refused to defend himself, also in imitation of Christ. *Passio* and Ælnoth stress that he wanted to avoid holding weapons at the moment of his death to make it clear that he valued his immortal soul more than his mortal body.

There is not much of the classic Viking left in the Knut we find in the Odense Literature. For that, we must turn to the later Danish chroniclers and the sagas. Sven Aggesen and Saxo Grammaticus both ascribe more satisfying political motives to Knut's planned invasion of England and admit that Knut retaliated for his army's desertion by levying harsh fines on the people. Saxo describes how the harshness of these fines, exacerbated by greedy royal agents and tax collectors, led to the beginnings of the revolt in the impoverished province of Vendsyssel in northern Jutland, precisely because they had trouble paying the excessive cost.

Behind the people's discontent lay strict royal law enforcement and favoritism shown toward the Church and bishops over lay magnates. We see Knut's favoring of the Church clearly in a donation letter to the Cathedral of Lund in 1085.[257] But the Danish narrative tradition tells us little else about the apparently oppressive power wielded by Knut.

A memory of this oppressive power may, however, be seen in Knýtlinga saga's careful description of a conflict that Knut had with Egil Ragnarsson, a powerful magnate from southern Jutland sent to govern twelve royal farms on the island of Bornholm. Tasked with defending an island far from direct royal oversight, Egil establishes himself as a classic Viking petty king, engaging in frequent summer raids and subsequent redistribution of wealth to a large group of supporters. When Egil's retinue balloons, he further increases raiding to redistribute ever-increasing amounts of wealth. King Knut takes this badly because, as the saga says, he had forbidden "looting and plundering."[258] Knut confronts Egil, stating, "You have taken up a bad habit in becoming a Viking raider. That is a heathen way of life and I have made it illegal."[259] Knut then reveals what is perhaps a greater reason for his discontent: "I've also been told that you have been keeping large numbers of men around you as if you were a king."[260] When Knut dismisses Egil from his service, Egil refuses to leave Bornholm and continues to surround himself with a large retinue of Vikings. After Egil, who is now called Blood-Egil for having drunk human blood, robs a royally sponsored Norwegian merchant ship, the Norwegian king asks Knut to interfere. With both internal order to keep and his international reputation to uphold, Knut imprisons Egil and asks his magnates—some of whom have kinship ties to Egil—how he should punish Egil's wickedness. In old Viking fashion, Egil's kinsmen offer blood money to save him, but Knut says he will not curb his Christian justice for bribery or friend-ship alliances, insisting that Egil's killings deserve an eye-for-an-eye-style jus-tice. He has Egil hanged on the gallows, while to deal with Egil's Vikings (called a "gang of ruffians"), he orders "some put to death, some maimed, and others banished from his country."[261] In this story, Knut is intolerant of sub-kings and employs his monopoly of military might to eliminate those who would challenge his power. Viking raiding led by local lords is not tolerated unless sanctioned by the king. Royal justice is also of a different nature than earlier in the Viking Age. Knut's justice is public, with state mandated punishments of imprisonment and execution, rather than the earlier privatized justice system where offenses were managed with monetary compensation and outlawry. Overlying Knut's jus-tice system is a Christian ideological justification and demonization of heathen practices. Knýtlinga Saga is of course a late source, but the general components in this story of royal justice and suppression of local magnates are the types of activ-ities that transformed royal power in Denmark, and, in the case of Knut, also the factors that contributed to the revolt that left him martyred.

A view of Knut's novel royal power can also be seen by returning to the important economic and ideological realm of royal coinage. Hoards from St. Knut's time show that the kings of Denmark had made much progress since the days of Knut the Great in establishing a monopoly on the means of exchange. Knut the Great had established a network of royal mints, but the proliferation of German and English coins in contemporary hoards in Denmark shows that the king had not yet established an exclusive Danish coinage. In contrast, nearly all the coins in hoards from St. Knut's reign are Danish. St. Knut used his royal monopoly of coinage to help finance his rule and provide legitimacy for royal actions. For instance, it appears that he made monetary alterations to his currency in 1085 in order to raise money in the year leading up to his planned invasion of England. Specifically, in Jutland, Knut issued a large quantity of a new coin type featuring the king in a warlike pose, holding a sword and shield (see Figure 5.7, row 6 B). The silver content in these coins was purposefully debased so that the king could distribute the coins for the same price, while expending less of his own silver.[262] Knut's debasement of the coins to finance war was a strategy pursued by high medieval kings in general, but novel in Denmark and only possible with royal mastery over a bounded kingdom paired with his monopoly on an exclusively Danish coinage.

Returning to our earliest sources from Odense, what can be drawn from these texts about Knut's reign? Does the apparent single-minded goal of glorifying the saintly nature of Knut for the purpose of sanctification and veneration make the examination of correspondence with archaeological evidence unfruitful? After all, these texts distort the key political motives of Knut's planned invasion of England, as well as the cause of the rebellion, in order to avoid casting any negative light on Knut's hagiographical narrative. At the most basic level, the early texts give us confidence that an invasion had been planned and a rebellion did take place. But more than that, when we examine the details and context of the events described in the Odense Literature, we find a surprising level of confirmation between specific points in the texts and the archaeological evidence from the churches of St. Alban and St. Knut. *Passio* and Ælnoth's *Gesta* both describe Knut's martyrdom in a wooden church, and two phases of such a wooden church have been found below the old stone Church of St. Alban that lies less than 100 m west of St. Knut's Cathedral.[263] The first phase was built in the early eleventh century. The second phase of the wooden church may have been built after the partial destruction of the church described in Knut's martyrdom story. On the *Tabula*, this church is described as a basilica, a term reserved for a bishop's cathedral, but the existence of a bishopric centered on the wooden Church of St. Alban was not at all certain. In 2015, however, the existence of a bishopric was supported by archaeological evidence when archaeologists discovered a bishop's grave in a stone sarcophagus placed in a venerable position beneath the floor of the wooden church.[264] The grave contained a valuable Eucharist set made up of a silver cup and a plate depicting the hand of God and the inscription "*dextera domini fecit virtutem amen*" ("God's right hand has brought victory, Amen").[265]

More correspondence between the historical and archaeological records was revealed through recent study of the shrines that contain the remains of St. Knut and his brother, Benedikt. Dendrochronological dating of three samples from Knut's shrine revealed that the shrine was made of wood felled after circa 1025, 1072, and 1074, while the decorative elements point to the late eleventh or early twelfth century, consistent with the stories reporting that the gilded wooden shrine was made when Knut's bones were moved to the altar after his canonization in 1101.[266] Identification of metal fragments and empty jewel settings on the shrines also parallel the gilded metal and gemstones described in the texts. Ælnoth tells that Knut's widow, Adela, who had remarried Count Roger of Apulia in Italy, sent gifts including valuable saffron-yellow silk textiles to wrap and adorn Knut's remains. Dye analyses of the textiles from Knut's grave, including a silk pillow with repeated bird and cross motifs, indicate production probably in Byzantium during the eighth or ninth century and use of yellow dye. The dye and decoration are consistent with the description of the gifts from Adela in southern Italy, where Byzantine silks would have been readily available to the elite.[267]

The bones of Knut and Benedikt themselves tell a story that is generally consistent with the textual accounts. Considering the value of medieval relics and the multiple disappearances and reappearances of these relics in St. Knut's Cathedral, it is reasonable to question whether these bones in fact belong to Knut and Benedikt. Three separate forensic studies of the bones confirm that these were adult men who had engaged in vigorous physical activity.[268] The presumed bones of Knut were from an older man, between thirty and forty, while the bones of Benedikt were from a younger man between eighteen and twenty-five.[269] Both men had unhealed weapon wounds. From this study comes perhaps the most surprising archaeological confirmation of the Odense Literature. In what was commonly interpreted as hagiographical fiction, Knut was said to have received martyrdom by being pierced in his side by a lance while lying prone on the ground. Computed tomography (CT) scanning of Knut's bones in 2008 revealed that his sacrum (the bony structure connecting the vertebral column to the pelvis) had been pierced from the front by a sharp metal object. Such a wound is consistent with a spear or lance wound entering a prone body through the abdomen and lodging into the sacrum.[270] The presumed bones of Benedikt exhibited a slice wound to the top of the left femur from an edged weapon, likely a sword. The wound did not heal and is consistent with the sources that describe his death by weapon wounds.[271] Before we proclaim an unprecedented degree of archaeological confirmation, it is well worth noting that the written accounts are not themselves always consistent, such that the archaeological evidence shows one version of the story to be wrong while seeming to vindicate another. For instance, Ælnoth, in an attempt to make Benedikt saintlier, has him dismembered and chopped to pieces by the rebel mob.[272] This part of the Ælnoth's story cannot be true if Benedikt's mostly intact bones are allowed to bear witness.

Like the previous Knut, St. Knut grew up in Denmark, joined Viking raids to England in his youth, and returned to Denmark with wealth and fame from Viking successes abroad.[273] He was, until then at least, a Viking in all the senses of the word. It is not so surprising that when he felt he had the opportunity, he attempted a conquest of England, just as his great-uncle and great-grandfather had both achieved. He never launched his invasion of England, and no Danish monarch would attempt to do so after him. St. Knut met a different death from his forefathers, and if the stories of his refusal to bear weapons to defend himself can be believed, he met a very un-Viking death. Knut's legacy for Denmark came mostly after his death, as illustrated by the early texts of the Odense Literature and the collections of songs and lectures meant to be recited during masses in praise of St. Knut. In becoming Denmark's first saint, he strengthened the link between Church and state in Denmark. After achieving sainthood for his brother, King Eirik (reign 1095–1103) soon received permission to establish a Danish archbishopric, freeing the Danish Church from domination by Hamburg-Bremen. The high medieval state of Denmark was taking shape. As such, Knut posthumously ushered in the end of Viking Age Denmark. Tellingly, the author of *Knýtlinga Saga* offers no Viking-style skaldic praise poems about St. Knut. Instead, Knut's songs of martyrdom and divine favor would be sung by Benedictine monks in procession through Odense each year on his feast day.

6

Into Marginal North Atlantic Environments

Viking Colonization of Iceland

On one hand, the discovery, exploration, and settlement of the North Atlantic islands—the Faroes, Iceland, and Greenland—were an extension of other ocean-crossing movements of Viking Age Scandinavians. On the other hand, the processes, motivations, and end results were very different, primarily because these islands were as yet unmarked by human settlement. In the North Atlantic islands, the Norse—as the diasporic Viking Age Scandinavians in the North Atlantic are called—encountered no substantial populations and found pristine environments that were unaltered by humans. The motivations for Norse expansion onto the North Atlantic islands were also different from those driving incursions into Europe and the British Isles; raiding and trading were absent, since there were no people there to raid or with which to trade. From the outset, the Norse came to the North Atlantic islands to settle and to farm. In other parts of Europe, Scandinavian settlers had complex encounters and interactions with local populations, as described in Chapter 2 for Anglo-Saxon England. By contrast, the dynamic interactions on the northern Atlantic islands were with new and highly challenging environments. These northerly, remote, and unsettled landscapes imposed constraints on traditional Scandinavian subsistence and political economies, at the same time as they offered immense opportunities. Interacting with the local environment and with one another, the migrants colonizing the North Atlantic islands developed a new culture related to, but distinct from, the society of mainland Scandinavia. This new migrant society is visible above all in Iceland, where textual and archaeological sources combine to give a vivid picture of a Viking society transplanted yet undergoing significant remodeling in light of local environmental and socioeconomic pressures.

This chapter focuses on the migration experiences in Iceland and on the resultant diasporic society that developed from the rapid settlement of the island in the mid- to late ninth century. The Icelandic colony was the largest and most historically important of the Viking North Atlantic communities (Figure 6.1). We also know much more about the settlement of Iceland than any other Norse settlements of the North Atlantic islands. High-quality textual, archaeological,

Age of Wolf and Wind. Davide Zori, Oxford University Press. © Oxford University Press 2024.
DOI: 10.1093/oso/9780190916060.003.0006

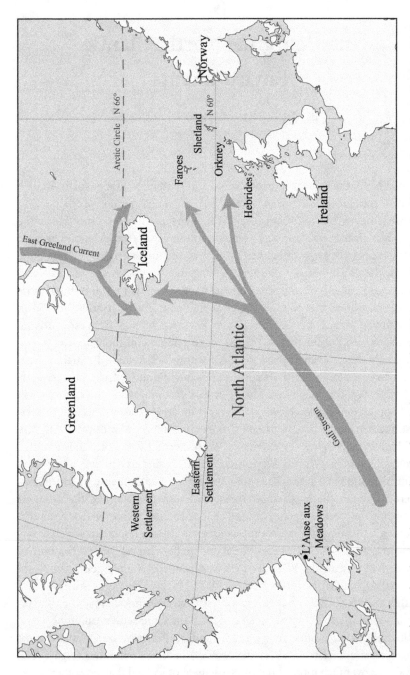

Figure 6.1 The North Atlantic, showing the islands settled as part of the Viking Age Scandinavian diaspora beginning in the late eighth century and reaching the shores of North America by circa 1000. *Source: map by author*

and environmental data provide complementary insights into the human impact on this northern environment and the development of the newly emerging
society. We will follow the Viking story in Iceland from initial settlement until
around 1100, drawing on the sagas produced during what has been called "the
Long Viking Age" of the North Atlantic.[1] The power of the Christian Church
became institutionalized at this time as indicated by the formalization of the
tithe system in 1097. However, the essentially Viking Age socio-political system
did not come to an end in Iceland until 1264, when the council of chieftains at
the Icelandic Althing accepted the overlordship of the Norwegian king and became part of the Norwegian state. At that point, the Viking Age Icelandic laws
preserved in *Grágás* (compiled in 1117–1118 from orally preserved laws) were
replaced with Norwegian laws, and local administration was placed in the hands
of Norwegian state representatives.

   We will focus on three issues concerning the processes of migration and
the subsequent developments for the Norse community in Iceland: (1) the
motivations for migration, (2) the social structure of the settlement, and (3) the
adaptation of Viking Age society to the Icelandic environment. In exploring
these key issues, we will engage the themes of correspondence, complementarity,
and contradiction in the available data sets that derive from written sources, archaeology, and the sciences of geology, botany, palynology, and genetics. In the
final section, two case studies explicitly integrate these distinct data sources to
shed further light on the identity/ethnicity of the Icelandic settlers and the emergence and evolution of the settlement structure of the Mosfell Valley in southwest Iceland.

Migration and Diaspora Society

The Norse migration into the North Atlantic resulted in a diaspora, creating a
series of colonies that looked back to Scandinavia—mostly Norway—for their
shared historical identity. For the Scandinavian diaspora in the North Atlantic,
the connectedness to the homeland faded after the end of the Viking Age but
never really disappeared in Iceland, even after the end of the Long Viking Age.[2]

   Diaspora is a useful concept that recognizes a consciousness—on the
part of both the community and the individual social actors—of the cultural
connections between the homeland and places to which people have migrated.
The social groups of a diaspora persist in orienting themselves in regard to specific values, practices, and identities of the homeland, creating a "continuity
across time and space" between diasporic communities and their places of origin.[3] Diasporic communities emphasize and even accentuate features of the
homeland in ways that signal these persistent connections.

In the case of the diasporic communities of Iceland, one way that this manifested was in the enhanced cultural creativity and productivity that generated the enormous corpus of saga literature dating to the Long Viking Age.[4] In Iceland, poetic and saga composition—both oral and later written— provided both the cultural connection to the Scandinavian homelands and a mechanism by which those connections were maintained. Already in the Viking Age, kings and earls of Northern Europe recognized that Icelandic skaldic poets and storytellers were particularly skillful at accurately recounting the memories of the Viking Age past, even beyond Iceland. The new colonial identity of the Viking North Atlantic was self-confidently Norse, but each of the island groups— Shetland, Orkneys, Faroes, Iceland, and Greenland—also developed a separate identity within the overarching Norse ethnicity. A shared language, along with a consciousness of the connectedness this entailed, was a vital component of this common ethnicity. Icelanders writing in the twelfth and thirteenth centuries, soon after the end of the Viking Age, still thought that Icelanders, Faroese, Norwegians, Danes, and Swedes spoke the same language, which they called *dǫnsk tungu* (Danish tongue). The linguistic foundation of shared ethnicity is borne out in the Icelandic *Grágás* law code, which specifies that a requirement for full inheritance rights and participation in the Icelandic legal system was speaking *dǫnsk tungu*.[5] The strong relationship among enfranchisement, language, and shared ethnicity, however, does not mean that differences between these islands and emergent Scandinavian countries were not recognized. For instance, *Grágás* has specific laws for who was allowed to prosecute court cases for the killing of foreigners, with special privileges being giving to Danes, Swedes, and Norwegians.[6]

The diasporic communities of the Viking North Atlantic share much with what sociologist Richard Tomasson has termed "fragment new societies," which came into being through distant transmarine migration.[7] Fragment societies, like diasporic communities, look to the connection with and seek the goodwill of the homelands. At the same time, fragment societies differ from those that are diasporic in that they need to create a unifying myth that separates the new society from its place of origin.[8] The sagas, which contain Iceland's founding myth, evidence how these forces seem to pull in directions that are diametrically opposed. Two broad examples will illustrate the point. The most defining characteristic of the government established in Viking Age Iceland was the absence of a king—a conscious decision taken in direct defiance of the prevailing governmental system in the Scandinavian homelands. On the other hand, the sagas often refer to foreigners in relation to the conceptual geographical location of Norway, rather than Iceland. Irishmen were Westmen, in spite of the fact that Ireland is not west but east of Iceland, and Germans were Southmen, although Germany is found due south of Scandinavia, but not of Iceland. The homeland remained the conceptual center from which socio-geographic directions were gauged.

In Iceland's history, Tomasson saw "structural and cultural continuities" and a "persistent concern with these continuities—the results of the society's isolation, small size, homogeneity, and unique literary tradition."[9] In addition to the saga tradition, the legal code was another cultural focus that emerged for the diasporic community in Iceland. This emphasis on the law is shared by other new fragment societies that experience attenuation of kin groups as a result of overseas migration.[10] When establishing their legal system, the Icelanders explicitly drew on the legal traditions of their homelands: in 930, the Icelanders sent a representative to Norway to retrieve the laws of Gulathing in Norway. This concern with the law, however, was also implicated in the Icelanders' efforts to distinguish themselves from the societies they had left behind in the homelands. Specifically, the Icelanders nostalgically harkened back to a Nordic social past, seeking to maintain the old laws of Viking Age Scandinavia that had existed before the onset of state formation and the appearance of overbearing kings.

The Icelanders marked their connections to the homelands through a shared language, the fluorescence, and ultimate transformation of a long-standing oral tradition to a body of saga literature, and the participation in the conservative, chieftain-based Scandinavian legal tradition. At the same time, these were the arenas in which the people of Iceland consciously acted to construct a society that was distinct from what had come to characterize the homeland.

Dating the Settlement of Iceland by Interdisciplinary Means

Pinpointing the date of the migration to Iceland is essential to situate the process in its historical context. As a starting point to the discussion of the Norse experience in Iceland, this section seeks correspondence among the textual, archaeological, tephrochronological, and palynological record in the dating of the settlement of the island. A range of texts—of both Old Norse and other European origins—help to date the beginning of settlement and to delineate its pace and progress through time. The native Icelandic texts *Íslendingabók* (*The Book of Icelanders*, c. 1125) and *Landnámabók* (*The Book of Settlements*, c. mid-1200s, based on an earlier, no longer extant version from the early twelfth century) have as explicit goals the description of the settlement of Iceland.[11] The texts consistently place the Norse settlement of Iceland around 870. Ari "the Learned" Thorgilsson (1068–1133) wrote in his *Íslendingabók* that Iceland was settled at the time "when Ivar, son of Ragnar Lodbrok, caused St. Edmund, the English King, to be killed; and that was 870 years after the birth of Christ according to what is written in his saga."[12] *Íslendingabók* states that the first permanent settler, the Norwegian Ingolf Arnason, "first went to Iceland when Harald Fairhair was sixteen years old, and for a second time a few years later; he settled south in Reykjavík" (Figure 6.2).[13] Accordingly, Ingolf made his first voyage to Iceland in the late 860s and his second voyage and permanent settlement around 870.[14] Norwegian sources supporting the timing of Icelandic settlement include texts in Latin from the 1170–1180s, such as *Historia Norwegiæ* by an anonymous monk and *Historia de Antiquitate Regum Norwagiensium* by the Benedictine monk Theodoricus.

Archaeological dating methods used in Iceland incorporate radiocarbon dating and tephrochronology, as well as typologies of buildings and artifacts. These methods attribute the earliest Norse structures and anthropogenic changes to the environment to the same date range suggested by the written sources. In spite of controversial radiocarbon dates from the Westman Islands (*Vestmannaeyjar*) off the southern coast of Iceland, which date the earliest occupation there to the eighth century, the total suite of radiocarbon dates from Iceland consistently support post-870 settlement of the island.[15] The house and artifact types of the earliest settlers are consistent with ninth- to tenth-century archaeological remains found in the Norse homelands and colonies. For example, the earliest Icelanders constructed bow-sided houses from turf, stone, and wood. This architectural style is known from the ninth- to tenth-century northwestern

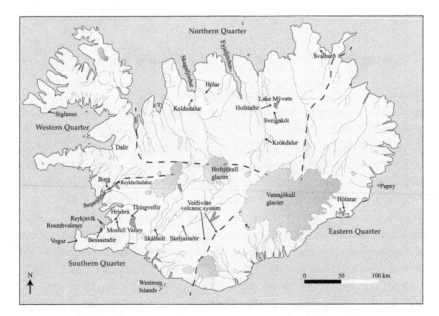

Figure 6.2 Map of Viking Age Iceland.
Source: map by author

Norway (e.g., Oma in Rogaland), the Scottish Isles (e.g., Underhoull in Shetland, and Brough of Birsay and Udal, both in Orkney) and the Faroes Islands (e.g., Kvívík and Toftanes).[16] With the exception of a few apparent heirloom objects, the artifacts found at the earliest Icelandic sites are also comparable to ninth- to tenth-century finds from Scandinavia and the British Isles.[17]

Iceland, a volcanic island lying on the Mid-Atlantic Ridge, sees frequent volcanic eruptions that deposit tephra layers across the island. Using comparative analyses of ice cores from Greenland, these layers are now datable to within a few years of when the eruption occurred. The tephra layers thus provide stratigraphic horizons with absolute dates, a technique known as tephrochronology.[18] Especially in the lowlands, where post-settlement erosion has buried Viking Age remains, these tephra layers provide clear and unmistakable dating horizons. The tephra layers vary by region, but the majority of Iceland has some manifestation of a recognizable tephra layer called the Landnám Tephra, which derives from an eruption from the Veiðivötn volcanic system that occurred in 877±1.[19]

The settlers' use of turf cut from wetlands for building materials resulted in volcanic tephra layers becoming incorporated into the walls of buildings. The walls of the earliest buildings typically contain the Landnám Tephra, confirming a post-877 construction date. In a few instances, indications of pre-877 structures have been found where the in situ Landnám Tephra lies atop cultural constructions. The only widely accepted case is a wall fragment found in association with an otherwise post-877 Scandinavian-style house in downtown Reykjavík.[20]

Very few other indications of settlement predate the 877-tephra layer. For instance, pollen studies, which rely on lake and bog cores that contain sequences of tephra layers, show anthropogenic vegetation change occurring overwhelmingly after 870, with only few exceptions pre-dating 870. The birch forest decreased markedly at the time of settlement.[21] Pollen signals of imported plants that were useful to settlers are an even more convincing indication of human arrival. The appearance of barley pollen (*Hordeum vulgare*), a plant not native to Iceland, also indicates the arrival of human settlement.[22] Barley pollen has been registered just below the Landnám Tephra at Hrísbrú in southwest Iceland and in Reykjavík, suggesting that these areas may have been settled slightly before 870.[23] Other bioindicators of the Norse colonization include accidental "hitchhikers," such as the dung beetle (*Aphodius lapponum*), which also appear in soil samples at the end of the ninth century.[24]

All sources agree that the settlement of Iceland began in the late ninth century, shortly before 870, and then progressed rather quickly so that people were living in nearly all habitable areas of the island by the mid-tenth century. The motivations that drove this rapid settlement process are explored in the next section through the written sources.

Push and Pull Factors of the Migration to Iceland

Anthropologists have used a variety of models to help understand why people decide to leave their homeland and migrate to new places. There is risk in migration, and in general, people will not choose to move unless they believe conditions in their new homes stand to be substantially better than their lot in their old homes. This fundamental logic underlying the motivations for migration can be divided into negative "push" factors and positive "pull" factors.[25] Push factors incentivize people to leave their homes; classic examples are warfare (threats to life), lack of economic opportunity (threats to subsistence), and political/ideological oppression (threats to lifestyle). Pull factors encompass the opportunities available in the new lands; examples include peaceful existence (safety), economic opportunities (land availability, profitable work), and freedom from oppression (ability to control lifestyle and influence political organization).

Pull Factors: Land, Trade Goods, and Information Transmission

Iceland was one of the final large habitable areas of the globe to be settled by humans. The most obvious pull factor for the Viking Age settlement of Iceland was the discovery of this large uninhabited island with significant expanses of land suitable for cultivation and grazing. Iceland would have seemed more attractive in the late ninth and tenth centuries than in later centuries because of the climatic amelioration known as the Medieval Warm Period (c. 900–1250), when average temperatures in the North Atlantic were approximately one degree Celsius (1.8° Fahrenheit) higher than they are today.[26] Even independent of any population pressure, this anthropogenically unaltered landscape would have been a draw for Viking Age Scandinavians who were used to seeking wealth, land, and prestige from overseas journeys and settlement.

Ari's Íslendingabók is considered the most trusted source on the migration because of his careful attention to chronology and articulation of the sources from which he draws the main storylines of his text. Yet his account is sparse and obscures details, for instance seeing the key immigrants to Iceland coming only from Norway. Landnámabók is a messier text made up of collections of local oral traditions from various parts of Iceland, and accumulated in the twelfth to thirteenth centuries, over multiple generations. Landnámabók records the names of about 430 settlers and about 600 farms, and provides at least a general idea of the location and extent of the land claimed by settlers (Figure 6.3). Although the sagas and Landnámabók sometimes contradict each other, indicating the existence of different independent traditions, they agree in the general depiction of the settlement.

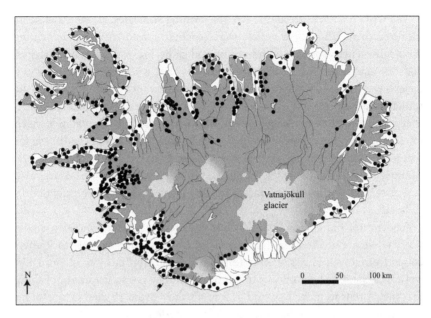

Figure 6.3 Farm sites of the original settlers of Iceland according to *Landnámabók*. The settlers chose farm sites close to the coast, in the lowlands, and sheltered in low valleys. The highlands and mountains (land over 200 m above sea level is shown in gray) were devoid of settlements.
Source: map by author

Landnámabók includes traditions about the phases of discovery that preceded the permanent settlement, including memories about the explorers' first impressions. The initial explorers' observations were impactful in spreading the news of the new land's potentials and limitations.[27] One version of *Landnámabók* holds that Naddod "the Viking" discovered Iceland after his ship was blown off course while sailing to the Faroes Islands. Naddod praised the land, which he named Snowland. Significantly, the terse record of Naddod's discovery relates how he and his men "climbed a high mountain in the East Fjords and surveyed widely in all directions, looking for smoke or any other sign that the land was inhabited, but they saw nothing."[28] The land was free for the taking. Thereafter, a man called Gardar the Swede set out explicitly to explore the newly discovered island. Following the logic of sea-based exploration, Gardar circumnavigated the land to prove it was an island, after which he named it Garðarshólm (Gardar's Island) and returned to Norway full of its praise. Floki Vilgerdarson, nicknamed Raven Floki, was the first to attempt to permanently settle the island, but his effort failed because he neglected to collect enough hay for the winter. Floki returned to Norway and gave the island the less than favorable name Iceland, which has stuck since then.

The written sources stress the settlers' farming strategies, as later Icelanders idealized them. The Norse settlers were sedentary pastoralists supplementing their subsistence economy with hunting and gathering, especially of fish, eggs, and sea mammals. Ari Thorgilsson indicates that when the settlers arrived, Iceland was "covered with woodland between the mountains and the sea."[29] The settlers removed much of this tree cover to provide pasturage for their cattle, sheep, goats, and horses. These animals, which co-evolved with humans at much lower latitudes, do not thrive unaided in Iceland, or in most of Scandinavia for that matter. As a result, the settlers were obliged to harvest and store hay in the summer to keep livestock alive in the winter. Hay was the most basic resource and also became the limiting factor of subsistence and wealth production in Iceland.

Evidence of the natural abundance of wild food resources, but also a cautionary tale about the great importance of keeping your animal stock alive, comes from Raven Floki's attempt to settle in Breiðafjörður ("Broad Fjord") in western Iceland: "The fjord was full of fish, and they got so involved in fishing that they forgot to make hay, and as a result their livestock died of starvation during the winter."[30] In spite of Raven Floki's experience, the hayfields of Iceland were favorably remembered by one of Floki's men, Thorolf, who recounted that "butter dripped from every blade of grass in the land they had found."[31] The imagery used by Thorolf combines the essential resources for survival: lush grass and milk products from the animals that fed on grass and hay.

The primacy of the "farming hypothesis," in which the settlers to Iceland were attracted by the available land suitable for Norse settled pastoralism, has been challenged. An alternative "trade hypothesis" sees at least the early exploration phase of the settlement as driven by the acquisition of products—specifically, walrus ivory—intended for the increasingly globalized market of the Viking Age.[32] A similar explanation has been offered for the late tenth-century settlement of Greenland, which has been described as a "market-driven economic strategy" underlain by desire for the acquisition of luxury goods for the European market.[33] Iceland had more to offer Norse settlers than the hunting grounds in Greenland or the hunting grounds *cum* tribute extraction zones in Arctic Norway. Nevertheless, this trade motivation hypothesis gains some support from place names that include walrus elements, such as Rosmhvalanes (Walrus peninsula) in southwest Iceland. Walrus tusks have also been found in middens and buildings from the earliest period of the Reykjavík settlement, which, according to the written sources, was the first permanent settlement in Iceland.[34]

It is notable, however, that the walrus colonies did not last, and the settlements founded by the colonizers of Iceland were not clustered around these types of marine resources. Instead, the farmsteads were dispersed and organized to maximize productivity for a sedentary pastoralist adaptation relying on cattle and sheep. Early exploration may have been partially motivated by the acquisition of animal products like walrus tusks that would be profitable in the widespread Viking Age trading network. However, this did not sustain the large diaspora that populated the Faroes Islands, Iceland, and the fjords of southwestern Greenland. The more significant and sustained pull factor was available land.

Written sources, radiocarbon dating, material-culture typologies, tephrochronology, and palynology agree that the settlement began after 850, with the clearest evidence for a large-scale migration coming after 870. The written sources, including *Landnámabók* and *Íslendingabók*, suggest that when the Scandinavians arrived around 870, a small number of Irish monks were already there living in isolated places on the Icelandic coast. According to the texts, these monks departed quickly once the Scandinavians arrived. If Irish priests reached Iceland by the dawn of the Viking Age, circa 790, news must have spread quickly to Celtic and Scandinavian communities living in Ireland and the northern British Isles. This has led scholars to voice surprise that Iceland was not settled earlier.[35] If knowledge of the island's existence preceded 870, the push-pull factors must have changed to tip the scale in favor of migrating to the open land after 870. Once substantial migration began, information trickling back to the Scandinavian homelands and other colonies became a steady stream. With increasingly reliable information about the conditions in the new land, the risk of migration would have decreased. Increasing quality and quantity of information created a positive feedback loop encouraging growing immigration to Iceland.

Push Factors: Declining Opportunities in Europe and State Formation in Norway

Key historical push factors encouraged the Viking Age Scandinavians to leave their homelands and homes in Western Europe to settle the North Atlantic. The two most important push factors were waning opportunities for Viking activities in the British Isles and state-formation processes in the homelands. Population pressure—the most standard push factor used to explain migration—has not been documented for the early Viking Age. Rather, the population increased toward the end of the Viking Age, when migrations ceased and villages in Scandinavia stabilized into their medieval pattern.[36] In fact, Ari Thorgilsson suggests the opposite, that is, an emptying Norwegian landscape: "And then a great number of people migrated out here from Norway so that King Harald banned it because he thought that his lands would become depopulated. Thereafter, they agreed that everyone who moved from there to here should pay the king five ounces [of silver] unless they were exempt."[37] King Harald's imposition of additional costs on emigration was one factor militating against the pulls of immigration.

In wider European political context, however, increasingly effective armed resistance to Viking incursions in England, Ireland, and the Frankish lands in the late ninth century pushed the Scandinavians to seek other and more peaceful opportunities in the North Atlantic. Two of the three early explorers—Naddod and Floki—are called great Vikings (*víkingr mikill*) in *Landnámabók*, lending some credence to the idea that retired Viking raiders, who had perhaps heard stories of Iceland in the Celtic portions of the British Isles, were instrumental in the island's settlement.[38] After these exploratory journeys, the sagas tell of Scandinavians in Ireland and the British Isles who seek to settle permanently after the opportunity for raiding lessened. In Ireland, Irish kings had begun to counteract the Viking incursions, and in 902, they expelled the Vikings from their primary power center in Dublin.[39] These setbacks for the Vikings help explain the frequent trajectory of immigration documented in the sagas, in which Scandinavians come to Iceland via the Celtic areas of the British Isles. In the late 870s, the Viking Great Army in England also reached a standstill in the wars with King Alfred's kingdom of Wessex, which had been strengthened with a system of fortified settlements, a more mobile army, and a new fleet.[40] In the wake of Alfred's defensive improvements, the leaders of the Viking Great Army settled and distributed land to their leading followers in the area that became the Danelaw. In this context, members of the Viking Great Army, particularly those of lesser rank unlikely to have been well endowed with land, may have sought land elsewhere.

The opportunities for raiding in continental Western Europe were also lessening. The Frankish military, which had been organized to mobilize large offensive campaigns under Charlemagne, underwent significant reorganization. The changes stressed local defensive positions and fortified bridges to block Viking access to the numerous navigable rivers of Western Europe. Local Frankish rulers—such as Odo of Paris and Baldwin II of Flanders, whose marriage to Alfred the Great's daughter created "an anti-Viking alliance"—prioritized local defense and fortification against Viking incursions.[41] A local duke, Arnulf of Carinthia, gained power in the East Frankish kingdom and decisively defeated the Vikings at the Battle of Leuven in 891. Even in the typically weak polity of Brittany, the Bretons defeated the Vikings in 890.[42] Potentials for Viking raiding in Francia were further curtailed after the Frankish King Charles the Simple granted Normandy as a fief to the Viking Hrolf (or Rollo) in 911, in exchange for his agreement to repel other Vikings and defend the Seine River that gave access to Paris.[43] The regionalization of power in Francia and militarization of local elites who lived within fortified centers have been seen as contributing to the emergence of feudalism.[44] Whether or not the Vikings sowed the seeds of feudalism, these systemic changes in Francia made Viking raiding a more risky endeavor.

According to the written sources, the most important push factors from Norway, the place of origin of most of the settlers, were associated with Harald Fairhair's (c. 885–930) efforts to centralize Norway under one king. He imposed land taxes on formerly free farmers and claimed ultimate ownership of property that farmers had previously controlled as *oðal* or family-owned hereditary land. The increased tax burden left ninth-century Norwegians with added expenses without any additional production capabilities.[45] Harald allegedly imposed a new political hierarchy, with regional *jarls* (earls) overseeing local *hersir* (military leaders) who led army regiments, collected taxes, and administered the king's justice locally. The new system disenfranchised former local chieftains and landowners. The sagas record many ancestors' violent clashes with the Norwegian king over land ownership. Norwegian households had choices, but for many of them, emigration to Iceland was an attractive option.

In this text-based understanding, the colonization of Iceland was not a centrally planned venture. Instead, independent farmers and petty chieftains financed their own voyages, bringing along with them attached household members and slaves.[46] The first permanent settler, Ingolf Arnarson, was also a raider, but his ultimate motivation for immigrating to Iceland was not lack of raiding opportunity, but conflict with a jarl in Norway. As a result of this clash, *Landnámabók* says that Ingolf and his sworn brother Leif were forced to hand over all their possessions to the earl; "and thereafter the sworn brothers prepared a large ship that they owned and set out to look for the land that Raven Floki had found and that was called Iceland."[47]

The texts also inform us that King Harald attempted to extend his power over the North Atlantic colonies. According to saga traditions, Harald successfully extended his authority over the Orkneys, Hebrides, Shetland, and the Faroes, but his efforts in Iceland were more half-hearted. He encouraged Uni, the son of Gardar the Swede, to conquer Iceland. In return, Harald would make him Jarl of Iceland. Harald does not seem to have provided Uni any real support, and the plot failed as soon as other settlers discovered Uni's plans.[48] Iceland was too distant for the Norwegian king to gain effective control over the island. Subsequent Norwegian kings were to influence events there, such as the conversion of the island to Christianity in 1000, but Iceland remained independent from Norway until 1264.

The push factors stemming from the centralization of power in Norway—and probably other areas of Scandinavia as well—is further illuminated with a few examples from saga narratives of immigration. *Eyrbyggja Saga* begins, as most Family Sagas, in Norway before the decision to immigrate had been made. *Eyrbyggja Saga* tells of Thorolf Mostur-Beard, a popular chieftain on the island of Mostur, located off Norway's western coast. Thorolf had sheltered a man outlawed by King Harald because of his resistance to the king's claims to his ancestral farm.

Harald now claimed Thorolf's estates as well and demanded that he hand himself over to the king's stewards. The weighty decision left Thorolf to consult the gods: "Thorolf Mostur-Beard held a great sacrificial feast and asked his beloved friend Thor [the god] whether he should come to terms with the king or emigrate from the land to seek his destiny elsewhere."[49] Thorolf's process of evaluating his options brings us back to the key role of information as a migration pull. The saga sets up this decision in previous sentences by revealing the circulating information of the day: "This was ten years after Ingolf Arnarson had sailed to settle Iceland, and his voyage was talked about by everyone because those who had returned from Iceland said that the quality of the land was good."[50] In this case, the god Thor suggests emigration.

The pull and push factors that led to the immigration to Iceland combined in new ways in the late ninth and early tenth centuries. Eventually the pull of available land in Iceland would be lessened as the best land, and then all usable land, was claimed. *Grettir's Saga* tells of Onund Tree-Foot, a powerful Viking who stayed in Norway to fight King Harald at the famous Battle of Hafrsfjord. He arrives in Iceland after much of the good land has been settled and is offered a marginal land claim centered on a snow-covered mountain. When Onund sees his new land, he composes a poetic immigrant lament:

> While the ship careens ahead,
> life goes adrift for a man
> whose spears were always honed;
> my power, my estates have foundered.
> My lands and my many kinsfolk
> I fled, and now a new blow:
> what use the bargain, if I quit
> my fields to buy Cold Back?[51]

As for push factors, Harald's centralization efforts—which appear to have been an early and ultimately only partially successful manifestation of state formation processes that matured in the late tenth century—were at least partially scaled back after his death. Viking opportunities reemerged in the British Isles, particularly in the late tenth and early eleventh centuries. Immigration to Iceland ultimately stopped, in light of the changing calculus of push and pull factors.

The Settlement of Iceland According to the Written Sources

After the Norse discovery of Iceland and a brief period of exploration, the expansion to Iceland shifted to permanent colonization. Reconstruction of the Norse settlement and habitation of Iceland has largely depended on written sources, including sagas and historical works like *Landnámabók* and *Íslendingabók*. These texts provide details of immense value, but these details must be evaluated in terms of the limitations imposed by the fact that they are based on oral traditions written down in the twelfth and thirteenth centuries, several centuries after the events of Icelandic settlement.

Depictions of an Ideal New Society: Chieftain-Based Settlement

The texts—including *Landnámabók*, *Íslendingabók*, the sagas, and *Grágás*— still provide the dominant model for the social and political structure of early Iceland. These texts depict Norse Iceland as a decentralized, stratified society made up of chiefs, free farmers, attached laborers, and slaves. This classic view of early Icelandic social structure stresses the leaders of the colonizing population—chieftains and rich farmers from Norway—as the dominant forces in establishing the new political order.[52] These people, mostly men but also some women, led expeditions with one or several ships that contained their families, loyal followers, and often slaves. Upon arrival in Iceland, they claimed large tracts of land and gifted land to their followers. This is borne out in *Landnámabók*, where the most successful settlers such as Ingolf Arnarson in Reykjavík, Helgi the Lean in Eyjafjörður, Skallagrim (Bald-Grim) in Borgarfjörður, and the female settler Aud the Deep Minded in Dalir claimed massive land areas for themselves (Figure 6.4). Helgi the Lean, for instance, claimed all of Eyjafjörður, an area that encompassed 450 separate farms in the eighteenth century.

The written sources suggest that the settlement of Iceland was rapid and geographically extensive. In *Íslendingabók*, Ari the Learned writes that the island was "fully settled" ("albyggt") by 930, when Icelanders established the Althing parliament.[53] Much debate has centered on what Ari meant by "fully settled." This preoccupation began as early as the Middle Ages. Already in the thirteenth century, *Landnámabók* interprets Ari's words to mean that the land was densely settled: "Learned men say that the land [Iceland] was fully settled in sixty years, so that no more settlements were made thereafter."[54] Another possibility is that Ari meant that settlers had claimed all land that was considered viable. Since land claims were extensive, with the initial settlers claiming whole fjords and districts, this would not necessarily indicate that the land had reached anything close to carrying capacity.

The first settlers established a form of extensive farmsteading. In this system, primary farmers founded large central farms and then divided their land among supporters, who established a series of small satellite farms that often specialized in utilizing particular resources within the larger territory.[55] Dividing farms

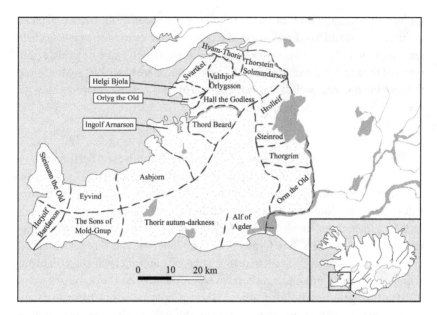

Figure 6.4 Map of the land claims of the *landnámsmenn* who settled within Ingolf Arnarson's original land claim (shown with dotted texturing). The settlers who received land from Ingolf constructed a regional kin-based alliance network.
Source: map by author; borders of land claims after Júlíusson et al. 1991: 39.

among supporters also assured the first settlers a political support network in their chiefly competitions with neighboring high-status settlers. The right of the *landnámsmenn* (land-takers) to claim enormous pieces of land was increasingly restricted as the colonization process proceeded. According to *Landnámabók*, the Norwegian king helped to negotiate an agreement whereby no man could claim an area larger than he and his crew could carry fire over in a single day.[56] By this time, however, early settlers had redistributed many of their large land claims to their followers and kin, creating politically powerful families with broad allegiance networks.

The settlement organization of the *landnámsmaðr* (land-taker) Skallagrim Kveldulfsson as described in *Egil's Saga* illustrates this settlement model of extensive farmsteading.[57] Skallagrim distributed his large land claim to followers and dependents, keeping direct control over a number of farms while exerting indirect control over others. Besides his own main farm at Borg, Skallagrim retained direct control over five farms run by dependent settlers. He established Álftanes (Swan Promontory) to take advantage of marine and coastal resources, such as fishing, seal hunting, and sea-bird fowling. He established the farm called Akrar (Grain Fields) to cultivate grain crops. Grísartunga (Pig

Promontory) focused on highland summer pasturage, and Einubrekkur specialized in salmon-fishing in the river Gljúfrá. He sets up his ironworking close to the wood resources at Raufarnes (originally Rauðanes or Red-Iron Ore Promontory). In general, Skallagrim gave a higher degree of independence to his followers whose farms he managed only indirectly. In return for a greater degree of economic independence, the men running these farms owed their political allegiance to Skallagrim.

Political Organization

In 930, Icelanders established the Althing, an island-wide governing body that met for two weeks around the summer solstice on the plains of Thingvellir (Figure 6.5). Due to the emigrating Norwegian free-farmers' concerns with maintaining household autonomy, the Icelanders established a legal system that functioned without a king or any form of executive power.[58] A Lawspeaker mediated the yearly Althing and recited one-third of the laws every year, but had no executive power. The Althing had a legislative branch called the Lögretta and a judicial branch that made decisions concerning disputes and conflicts. Enforcement of these decisions was, however, a private matter. This led to a feuding society mediated by the chieftains (goðar, sg. goði) who themselves profited by taking advantage of the judicial system.[59]

In 960, court reforms to the Althing divided the island into four quarters and gave each quarter a separate court at the Althing. Each quarter contained three spring assemblies (várþing), and each spring assembly was led by three goðar. Each quarter had nine chieftaincies (goðorð). The goðar did not possess territorial dominion over certain areas. Their political power was rather personal and based on the loyalty and strength of their supporters. Free farmers had the liberty to choose which goði to support as long as that goði lived within the same quarter of the island (Figure 6.6). Since chieftains could share a single chieftaincy or own several, the number of chieftains often varied, while in theory the number of chieftaincies remained constant. Since the northern quarter contained four major fjords, it received a fourth spring assembly to facilitate travel to the assembly meetings (Figure 6.7). To maintain political balance, each of the other quarters was given three extra chieftaincies. The total number of chieftaincies in Iceland therefore became forty-eight, and they all sat on the Lögretta legislative body, supported by two advisors each. When Iceland was Christianized, the island's two bishops—established at Skálholt (1056) and Hólar (1106)—received a seat on the Lögretta as well. This picture of Icelandic political organization is depicted in the Grágás laws, and to a high degree, this system seems to have worked in practice.

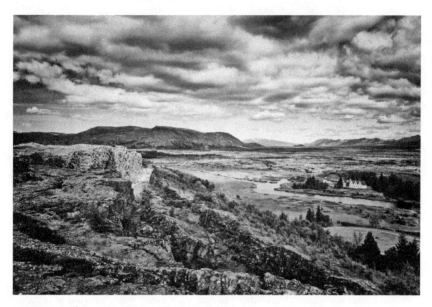

Figure 6.5 Thingvellir (Thing Plains) is a distinctive and tectonically active geographic zone in southwest Iceland where the North American and European plates pull away from each other. Here the chieftains and their supporters from across Iceland met every year for a week in the beginning of June to resolve disputes, agree on laws, and exchange goods and information.
Source: photo by Pétur Reynisson

By the end of the Viking Age and certainly by the end of the twelfth century, chieftaincies, which could be traded, bought, or sold, were centralizing into the hands of a few families that were solidifying political control as an emergent aristocracy. Among these families, the most powerful were the Sturlungar in the north and west, the Haukdælir and Oddaverjar in the south, and the Svinafellingar in the east.[60] These families competed for territorial control and support of local leaders in increasingly violent confrontations. The *Sturlunga Sagas* vividly portray intensification of conflict and a change in warfare that occurred during the thirteenth century. For the first time, these sagas recount instances of armed bands destroying farms to weaken the economic base of rival chieftains. The Icelandic political system was undergoing the processes of state formation. In 1258, a member of the newly emerging aristocracy was named Earl of Iceland by the Norwegian king, in exchange for his promise to extract tribute from Icelanders for the king.[61] Any autochthonous social evolution came to an end in 1262 as Icelanders at the Althing officially bent to the will of the Norwegian king and accepted incorporation into the kingdom of Norway. With this, a Viking Age political organization, which had persisted in Iceland for over a century after the close of the Viking Age, came to an end.

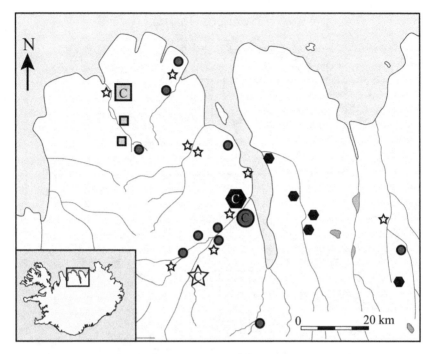

Figure 6.6 Four chieftains (large symbols) and their supporters (small matching symbols) in Eyjafjörður, c. 1190. As the map illustrates, Icelandic chieftains were not territorial overlords in the Viking Age. Rather, their power relied on personal loyalties from supporters that often lived scattered among other potential chieftains.
Source: map by author based on Byock 1988: 115 and Haywood 1995: 92

Archaeology and Environmental Science: Character of the Settlement of Iceland

The initial settlement or *landnám* period was formative for the trajectory of Icelandic society. The first settlers had a dramatic "founders' effect" on the environment, as well as on the emergent social structure. Since the data on the Icelandic Viking Age—textual, archaeological, and environmental—is of such high resolution, Iceland provides the clearest window into Norse economic strategies and efforts in environmental management of the Scandinavian North Atlantic diaspora. This section focuses on archaeological and environmental research on this founder's effect, which has dramatically enriched the account provided by the sagas and other written documents. The Norse impacts on the island's ecosystem were dramatic, but so too were the effects that the challenging Icelandic environment had on the Norse settlers' efforts to adapt their traditional Scandinavian lifestyle to the North Atlantic.

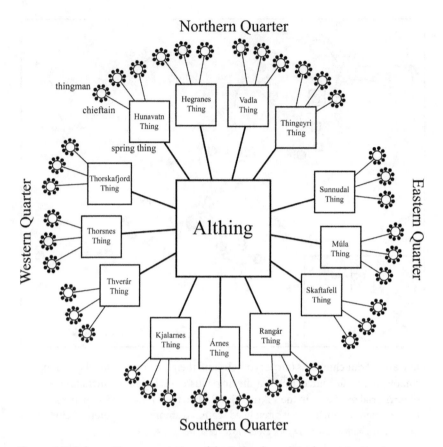

Northern Quarter

thingman

chieftain

Hunavatn Thing

Hegranes Thing

Vadla Thing

Thingeyri Thing

spring thing

Thorskafjord Thing

Sunnudal Thing

Western Quarter

Thorsnes Thing

Althing

Múla Thing

Eastern Quarter

Thverár Thing

Skaftafell Thing

Kjalarnes Thing

Árnes Thing

Rangár Thing

Southern Quarter

Figure 6.7 Schematic representation of the Icelandic political organization in the Viking Age after 930, when the Icelandic chieftains established the Althing at Thingvellir. At the center is the legislative body of the Althing parliamentary assembly of chieftains. The assemblies—Althing and regional assemblies—are shown as squares, while circles indicate individual chieftains (large circles) and supporters (black circles). Originally, each quarter had three spring assemblies (*várthing*) that served as the regional meeting place for three chieftains and their supporters. In 965, a fourth assembly with three additional chieftains was added to the Northern Quarter.
Source: schematic representation by author based on Byock 2001: 180

Settlement Impact on the Environment

Viking Age Iceland provides a case study for evaluating the impacts of human settlement on previously unoccupied landscapes. The comprehensive settlement had dramatic impacts on the fragile Icelandic environment. Substantial portions of the low-highlands became denuded and uninhabitable, the birch forests in the lowlands all but disappeared, and the resource that may have been partially responsible for drawing settlers to the island—the walrus colonies—vanished. Norse domesticated grazing animals were destructive to the native vegetation.[62] The settlers added to the environmental destruction wrought by their animals by deliberately burning woods to create pastureland and felling trees to fuel iron production.[63] Studies of pollen samples show that the native birch forests quickly began to vanish in most coastal regions with the arrival of the Norse settlers.[64] Soil studies aided by tephrochronology show cultural overuse of the landscape, causing detrimental erosion and landscape deterioration.[65] After the end of the Viking Age, the Little Ice Age (beginning c. 1300) caused further problems, as shortening growing seasons stressed the grasslands that were already being overgrazed.[66] The Norse were clearly not model stewards of their new island landscape. This perspective was maintained in most research from the 1980s until the early 2000s, which offered the Norse colonies of Iceland, Greenland, and Newfoundland as examples of human resistance to environmentally adaptive socio-economic change and the effects of short-sighted strategies of self-interest on the part of aggrandizing chiefs and stubborn bishops.[67]

Although the bulk of scholarship has stressed the destructive impacts of the Norse settlement, recent work has begun to provide nuance to the picture with more hard evidence of resilience and adaptability. These studies have tempered the destructive image of the Norse settlers by indicating ways in which they managed their resources more carefully than previously assumed. Norse resource management has been interpreted in several arenas, including birch forests, wild animals, and domesticated animals. Woodland management has been suggested by geoarchaeological study in Mývatnssveit and with palynological research in Borgarfjörður and in the Mosfell Valley.[68] Norse management of wild animal resources, specifically of water fowl, has been detected through the zooarchaeological study of egg shells in Mývatnssveit.[69] Even the relative decline of goats and pigs in comparison to sheep over time, which has long been recognized in the zooarchaeological assemblages, can be interpreted to give more positive agency to Norse settlers. Scholars now credit early Icelanders with consciously managing the proportional composition to favor sheep over goats and pigs in response to their increasing familiarity with the Icelandic environment.[70]

In long-term perspective, the Norse settlement of Iceland was a success story.[71] After encountering a challenging marginal environment, the early Icelanders made changes necessary to adapt to their environment, leading to their ultimate survival and the persistence of human settlement on the island. Icelanders, the inheritors of the Viking Age colony, have created a wealthy and successful society, despite the challenges posed by the sub-arctic ecosystem.

Settlement and Adaptation to the Icelandic Environment

Archaeology is amending, nuancing, and expanding the traditional text-based narrative for the establishment and evolution of early Icelandic social order.[72] The *Landnámabók* record of settled farms provides an excellent starting point, but the circa 600 named farmsteads it contains are only a fraction of the total number of Viking Age farms in early Iceland. This fact is apparent from Ari's *Íslendingabók*, in which he states that a census taken by Bishop Gizur Isleifsson in 1096—right at the close of the Viking Age—recorded 4,560 land-owning farmers.[73] Furthermore, although reference to modern place names often allows for farms named in *Landnámabók* to be located on the landscape, this reveals little about the life on these farms. In the end, the available texts provide an excellent starting point, but generating new information depends on archaeological fieldwork and combination of available sources, including scientific examination of samples from cultural material and natural deposits dating to the Viking Age. Contributions of archaeology and its associated environmental sciences have been particularly felt in the arena of settlement patterns, individual household comparisons, and the abandonment of farmsteads. Combining data from these lines of inquiry fleshes out the stories of how the Norse adapted to the unfamiliar and unoccupied Icelandic environment.

Pollen studies that trace the vegetation of the island by examining soil profiles extracted from bogs and lakes are consistent with *Íslendingabók* assertion that the first settlers found woods covering much of the lowland between the sea and the mountains. These pollen studies show that the woods were largely made up of downy and dwarf birch (*Betula pubescens* and *Betula nana*) and dwarf willow (*Salix herbacea*). The woods were a valuable resource for fuel, but the trees were too small for ship-building and for large structural elements in buildings, although archaeological analysis of wood from within early Icelandic houses shows the use of birch in smaller structural elements, such as internal wooden paneling.[74] Larger timbers had to be imported or recovered on the beaches onto which driftwood from larger trees, such as Siberian larch (*Larix sibirica*), was deposited by circumpolar ocean currents.[75] Driftwood was often used for the larger timbers, such as the central roof-supporting pillars in Viking Age Icelandic houses. The internal structural framework of the Viking Age Icelandic house was wooden, but the external walls and roofs were made of turf. The settlers constructed their house walls from strips and blocks of wetland turf that had a dense root mat. Although dry sod could also be used, the wetland turf was better for insulation and had the advantage of being a lightweight construction material when dry. Those Scandinavian settlers who emigrated from the northern portion of western Norway would have had experience with turf construction, and early Icelanders ubiquitously adopted this form of house construction because it was widely available and provided good insulation against the northern North Atlantic weather.

Although the woods were a valuable resource, the Norse farmsteads required open grazing lands of sedge and grass to support an agro-pastoral lifestyle. To achieve this end, settlers either cleared land, typically by burning standing trees, or they established their first farms farther inland by the foothills that were devoid of trees.[76] Computer modeling of deforestation has shown that only large-scale efforts to transform the landscape into grazing lands—a process that continued well into the tenth century—could have had as dramatic of an effect on the landscape as what is observed palynologically and archaeologically.[77] As the landscape changed with deforestation, the sites farther inland, which were now exposed to snow for longer periods of the winter, lost their advantageous settlement status.

Archaeological surveys and excavations have confirmed that Viking Age Icelandic settlements followed the dispersed settlement pattern of isolated farmsteads that persisted into pre-modern Iceland. The exception may be the very early days of settlement, a period that required cooperation between settlers. Archaeological correlates of such early multi-household cooperation have been found at Herjólfsdalur, Hvítárholt, and Bessastaðir where two or more contemporaneous longhouses occupy the same site.[78] Beyond the cooperation necessary to establish human habitation in Iceland, farms worked optimally if widely spaced across the landscape. This was intimately related to the fact that the Norse practiced an extensive form of settled but transhumant pastoralism, whereby herds were taken up into the highlands for grazing in the summer in order to spare the lowland pasturage for collection and storage for winter fodder. Sheep were allowed to graze freely while cattle were kept at shielings (temporary summer farms or dairy stations) where they could be milked regularly and managed more closely. These shielings appear frequently in the sagas, and archaeological excavations have confirmed their character as seasonally occupied small farms.[79] The sagas often recall lower-status individuals managing the cattle at shielings and transporting milk and milk products back to the main farm. The medieval law codes, such as Grágás, include regulations for where shielings could be built. Archaeological surveys of shielings have shown that they generally lie about 2 km from their mother farms, although some may lie as far as 15 km away.[80] The artifact assemblage from these sites is materially poor compared with assemblages from permanent farms, which may just be a factor of their temporary habitation, but could also reflect the comparatively lower status of individuals living at shielings during the summer months.

Current research is now focused on understanding the principles of settlement and evidence of social stratification in early Iceland. One strategy often applied is to use data about later medieval conditions and work backward to the Viking Age. Vésteinsson and colleagues used such data—post-medieval property values, shapes/sizes of farmlands, and presence of early churches on farmsteads—to propose a three-tiered settlement hierarchy of large complex, large simple, and planned settlements that has proved very influential.[81] This model sees inequality and social hierarchies, including non-landowning tenant farms, as embedded in the initial settlement process. Models such as this—built on data separate from the archaeological record—are consequently amenable to testing with archaeological fieldwork.

A key contribution of such archaeological work is to provide the time-depth and missing temporal control needed to discern when and in what order farms were established. This temporal resolution is emerging from pairing regional settlement surveys with strategic sub-surface testing and larger open-area excavations of individual sites. Multiple projects now incorporate such multi-scalar regional work in areas such as Mývatnssveit, Mosfell Valley, Reykholtsdalur, and Skagafjörður.[82] In Skagafjörður, the Skagafjörður Archaeological Settlement Survey (SASS) examined the entirety of the land claimed by the initial settler Ulfljot and showed that there was a direct correlation between those farms that were settled first and those that grew to be the largest in the later Viking Age.[83] Here, the twenty-eight settlers recorded in the written sources claimed land averaging 61.5 km^2, which is exponentially greater than the 3.7 km^2 average size of historical farms documented in the same area.[84] The early settlers had an advantage over the late-comers that derived from their claim to large portions of land that they subsequently redistributed to relatives, household members, and followers. The advantage of being first to claim land may have further incentivized rapid settlement of Iceland, as it appears that settlers able to muster the means to immigrate to Iceland could achieve both lasting, multi-generational economic wealth and political power. If this is true, then it is imaginable that the promise of political power for ambitious would-be chieftains should be added to the economic "pull" of available land.

In their work in Skagafjörður, SASS used geophysics, coring, and excavation to collect data on three variables: farmstead location, farmstead establishment date, and farmstead size at the close of the Viking Age. The landscape was settled rapidly, with four farms established before 930. However, the settlement rate peaked between 930 and 1000, during which time the landscape between the first farms filled in with at least six additional farms.[85] According to SASS, these smaller tenth-century farms do not exhibit institutionalized hierarchy or land tenancy but should rather be interpreted as divisions from the estates among multiple family heirs. The next phase occurred in the eleventh century, coincident with the conversion to Christianity. At this time, SASS sees the emergence of tenant farmers who worked property owned by landlords, manifesting on the landscape as the establishment of six new and significantly smaller (tenant) farms located close to large earlier (landowner) farms.[86] This conclusion significantly disagrees with the model proposed by Vésteinsson and his colleagues about the emergence of tenancy already in the early stages of settlement. The issue is important because on it hinges the nature of power in Viking Age Iceland: whether it was dictated by personal loyalties as, for instance, suggested by the chiefly allegiance map generated from the sagas (Figure 6.6), or whether a manorial system of land tenancy, in which powerful farmers owned the productive lands of other lesser farmers, was in place from the settlement's beginnings. Another possibility is that there were regional differences in social organization within Iceland, with the transition to land tenancy varying in timing.

Archaeological and palaeoecological data from other areas of Iceland show differential adaptations to local conditions. Studies of particularly marginal areas of the already marginal Icelandic environment provide perhaps the best illustration of how the settlement process varied locally. One example is Svalbarðstunga, a part of northeast Iceland particularly exposed to the hyperborean Arctic waters from the East Greenland Current flowing along northern Iceland (Figure 6.1).[87] Archaeological studies of Svalbarðstunga add data to textual accounts of late-arriving settlers, exemplified above by Onund Tree-Foot's poetic lament over his unproductive land claim at Kaldbak in the West Fjords. Multi-disciplinary investigation of farms in this region demonstrates that the large primary settlement of Svalbarð was settled right around the traditional 930 date associated with the closure of the settlement process, according to *Íslendingabók*. The filling of the landscape with farms then took place over the ensuing decades. Three farms that were later dominated by the Svalbarð farm were established across the landscape, stretching from the Hjálmarvík farm on the coast, to the Kúða farmstead approximately 12 km inland. At Hjálmarvík, analysis of pollen profiles revealed a dramatic increase in *Poaceae* (grass) pollen associated with the emergence of grazing lands around 960. Also, at Kúða, peat bog samples showed dramatic increases in seeds of the weed *Stellaria media* (chickweed) around 960, which is consistent with purposeful fertilization of agricultural fields. The marginal and relatively high-altitude inland farm of Kúða (120 m above sea level) was then abandoned circa 1190. Similar semi-highland farms were abandoned in other areas by the thirteenth to fourteenth century. The farmstead of Kúða was subsequently reoccupied after the end of the Viking Age in circa 1500, at a time when the climate would have been comparatively colder. These examples demonstrate the shifting nature of Icelandic settlement, as inhabitants struggled to make a living off land at the edge of the Arctic Circle.

Households
The economy of Iceland centered on the household as the productive unit. The farms that have been excavated are generally consistent with the saga descriptions

of farmstead organization. A central longhouse served as the living quarters for the farmer's family, as well as the extended family and attached farmstead workers, both slaves and free farmhands (Figure 6.8). Around the farm stretched the homefield, typically protected from grazing domesticates by a homefield wall constructed of turf or a combination of stone and turf. Positioned within the homefield were ancillary structures such as byres for stabling animals, smithies, and private churches (after conversion to Christianity). In addition, archaeological excavations have uncovered multiple ancillary structures of unidentifiable function for which parallels cannot be drawn from texts.[88]

Relative to other parts of the Viking world, especially beyond the Scandinavian homelands, a large number of Viking Age houses have been excavated in Iceland. Excavations of individual households have revealed relatively self-sufficient and uniformly organized farmsteads. Houses followed the internal organization of Viking Age Scandinavian houses, usually with three rooms, each divided into three aisles. Two rows of load-bearing posts located between the aisles supported the heavy turf roof. The floors were usually earthen, except the side aisles in the central hall, which were frequently raised and covered with planks. These side aisles served as benches and also as beds in the night (Figure 6.9). Collapsed roofs and toppled house walls often cover and preserve individual features

Figure 6.8 Turf longhouse reconstruction based on a tenth-century house excavated at Eiríksstaðir, a farm named after Eirik the Red. Turf houses such as this were well-suited to the Icelandic environment. This modestly sized house of a free farmer can be contrasted with larger chieftain's houses, such as that excavated at Hrísbrú (see Figure 3.8 and 6.9 and comparisons in Chapter 3).
Source: photo by author

Figure 6.9 The Hrísbrú longhouse during excavation, looking west across the central room. Post holes for roof-supporting posts are visible between the central aisle and the raised side aisles where people would have worked and slept. A large fireplace appears in the middle of the room.
Source: Mosfell Archaeological Project

within the archaeologically examined longhouses. One example is impressions of barrels found in parts of the houses that appear to have been used for food storage. According to the sagas and recent Icelandic practices, these barrels would have contained sour whey (i.e., the liquid remaining after milk is curdled and strained) in which meat was preserved.

Within the uniformity in houses, however, social status differences can be observed. Archaeological excavations show variations in house size, construction technique, and farm layout, all details that are difficult to glean from saga accounts. Artifact assemblages are another key indicator of differences in social status, although excavated Icelandic houses appear poor when compared to contemporary Scandinavian find assemblages, even for houses like Hofstaðir, which all indications suggest is a high-status house.[89]

The farmstead excavations have not just revealed structures, features, and artifacts, but also recovered ecofacts like plant material, seeds of grain, and insect exoskeletons that allow new understandings of households and comparisons of household assemblages. Increasingly careful sampling methods have seen the collection of seeds, bone fragments, and micro-artifacts not recovered in earlier excavations during the twentieth century. Geochemical analyses of earthen and ash floors and soil micromorphological studies of floor stratigraphy illuminate specialized activity areas within buildings and across sites. Such studies have helped to identify zones of the houses used, for instance, to stable animals and process wool.[90] Examinations of parasites recovered in Norse buildings reveal the presence of specific animals, the health of the resident human population, and economic activities.[91] Large numbers of fleece louse (*Damalinia ovis*) and sheep ked (*Melophagus ovinus*) recovered in specific rooms, for instance, have been used to suggest wool processing, which is otherwise difficult to detect archaeologically.[92]

New methods of archaeological sampling within houses paired with, for instance, pollen sampling close to the farmstead allow us to approach the agency of individuals and families in pursuing subsistence, political, and ideological goals. For instance, we have seen in Chapter 3 that comparisons of house size, zooarchaeological remains, macrofossils, finds assemblages, and pollen records revealed how the chieftain household at Hrísbrú mobilized their subsistence base for political reasons, such as the production of beef and beer for consumption during politically charged feasting.[93] Pollen records and plow marks indicate that barley was cultivated on a limited scale across Iceland, while barley consumption is evident by the increasing numbers of charred seeds recovered from houses and middens.[94] The limited distribution of barley pollen suggests that grain was probably never a major food source, but did become a prestige crop indicative of high status.[95]

Farmstead Abandonment

Although the Icelandic settlements were generally stable, many of the initial farms were either moved or abandoned altogether. Sometimes the Norse settlers moved their farms only a short distance. The SASS settlement surveys in Skagafjörður suggest farm relocation was common at the end of the tenth century.[96] The farms appear to have moved from lower areas to slightly higher elevations, although the farm buildings themselves shifted only a few hundred meters. Explanations for this apparently systemic settlement change vary. Climate changes could have made the landscape wetter, requiring relocations to higher, dryer land. Reorganizations of farmstead economies could have triggered social transformations that required living in differently organized homes, easier to build anew than to reconfigure the preexisting one. Or possibly the changing of homes was ideologically motivated, as newly Christianized people felt it necessary to sever associations with a house where pagan practices had taken place.

About one-fourth of the farms mentioned in *Landnámabók* were later deserted.[97] Farmstead abandonment has been seen as the result of destructive Norse agriculture or of bad judgment, but can equally be seen as part of an essential process of learning from and adapting to a challenging environment. The desertion of farms does not have a single cause. Environmental destruction of highland vegetation from overgrazing and forest clearance for iron production made some sites uninhabitable for the Norse pastoral economy.[98] In other cases, Norse settlers—basing their site choices on their knowledge of environmental conditions from their homelands—initially chose unviable settlement sites that were either too high in elevation or too far inland.[99] Later Norse settlements were relocated away from denuded landscapes, clustering more densely in coastal plains, valleys, and bays. Marginal upland sites were sometimes completely abandoned and other times used as summer grazing farms or shielings.[100]

In the 1970s, evidence of this abandonment process was identified through study of soil profiles from the now-deserted highland valley of Krókadalur and other marginal zones across northern Iceland.[101] These studies suggested that human errors in initial landscape assessments led to deforestation and overgrazing, which in turn caused anthropogenic soil erosion. This erosion deprived the land of its economic viability and led to abandonment by the eleventh to twelfth centuries, even before the added climatic challenges posed by the cooling effects of the Little Ice Age (c. 1300–1850).

Recent research following the trends of stressing Norse resource management and rational decision-making has called the 1970s evaluation into question. For example, reevaluation of the Krókadalur farms suggests that the settlers expanded into the valley from Mývatn in a second wave of settlement in the mid- to late tenth century, after the 930 date when the island was supposedly "fully settled."[102] In this light, the occupation of at least some of the marginal regions such as Krókadalur now appears as a rational choice in a more gradually filling island landscape. The authors of the most recent study suggest a very different interpretation of the Krókadalur evidence, namely that owners of large farms in the lowlands bought and vacated the Krókadalur farms in order to use the land to graze increasing numbers of sheep and extract wood and iron resources.[103] This reevaluation, which foregrounds complex micro-regional socio-economic decision-making, cautions against environmentally deterministic models for the abandonment of farms in marginal lands.

Interpretations of when and why farmsteads were abandoned have shifted away from simple environmentally deterministic explanations. Mounting evidence indicates that settlement choices in Iceland were the product of a complex calculus of environmental, economic, social, and ideological factors. The complexities of their entanglements are increasingly coming to light through interdisciplinary fieldwork.

Trade: Long Distance Prestige Good Exchange and Local Bulk Exchange
Overseas exchange was important to Viking Age Icelandic society, but more for the maintenance of cultural connectedness with Europe and the acquisition

of prestige goods than for subsistence survival. As might be expected, archaeological excavations of Icelandic houses reveal more about what was imported
to Iceland than what was exported. The available texts suggest that homespun
sheep's wool called *vaðmál* was an important export good from Iceland during
the Viking Age, and that this bulk trade expanded especially after the close of
the Viking Age.[104] Within Iceland, vaðmál was used as the standard unit of value
throughout the medieval period and up until the eighteenth century.[105] In the
Viking Age, the most valuable exports from Iceland were wild-animal products,
such as walrus tusks or seal skins, or the wild animals themselves, like arctic fox
and white falcons. Walrus—discussed above as a potential pull factor for the initial immigration to Iceland—were valuable primarily for the ivory from their
tusks. The hunting of walrus and value placed on walrus tusks for interregional
exchange has been extrapolated from the early Icelandic houses of Aðalstræti
and Vogur, where walrus bones were found placed into house walls as hunting
trophies.[106] Both of these sites were built early in the settlement process and are
located in southwest Iceland close to place names that indicate the previous existence of walrus colonies.

The *Grágás* law book specifies that grain, linen, timber, wax, and tar were
the products most essential for Icelanders to import.[107] Unfortunately, most
of these are difficult to detect with any regularity in the archaeological record.
Nevertheless, Icelandic dependence on grain import from Norway has even
been held up as an underlying cause of the loss of Icelandic independence to
the Norwegian monarchy.[108] Icelanders did not need it for subsistence, but as
we saw in Chapter 3, grain was a prestige good used for beer production aimed
at chiefly feasts.[109] Some imported everyday goods are more visible archaeologically, such as for instance stone schist from Norway, used to fashion whetstones
for sharpening iron blades.[110] Luxury objects of non-ferrous metals—bronze,
copper, lead—all had to be imported. Such metals are found regularly at archaeological sites, although they become less prevalent over time. This likely tracks
a decline of wealth over the course of the Viking Age, but also suggests that
many of these objects might have been brought over as part of the original settlement package. Glass, found especially in the form of decorative beads, was
also imported, often from areas far beyond Scandinavia. For instance, among the
large corpus of glass beads found in the Hrísbrú household were four dark glass
beads with decorative sun or eye motifs. These were originally produced in the
area east of the Caspian Sea.[111] Such objects—probably acquired in Scandinavia
through trade—would have carried significant status in Iceland.

Household excavations, combined with isotopic studies of human skeletal
remains, provide evidence of regional exchange within Viking Age Iceland.
Although the farms were essentially self-sufficient, regional trade in fish has
been documented between coastal producer farms and inland farms in northern

Iceland. For instance, the coastal chieftain's farm of Siglunes yielded a prepon-
derance of cranial cod fish bones over post-cranial bones, suggesting that cod
were being butchered (i.e., the heads removed) at the site but the meat consumed
elsewhere. The reverse pattern, showing higher proportions of post-cranial cod
bones and many fewer cranial elements, is documented in farms in the Mývatn
area, which is located circa 70 km from the sea. The Mývatn evidence shows
that marine fish was traded to these inland sites after having been cleaned elsewhere.[112] Isotopic studies of human remains from the pre-Christian and post-
Christian Viking Age support the existence of regional exchange in fish. One
example is provided by the inland cemetery of Skeljastaðir, located circa 60 km
from the south coast of Iceland, where individuals buried there consumed a diet
that was at least partially marine-based.[113]

Interdisciplinary Integration: Icelandic Ethnicity and the Settlement Structure

This final section takes up two critical issues for understanding the formation
of Viking Age Icelandic society: the ethnic diversity/unity of the settlers and the
socio-political structure of the initial Icelandic settlements. Both these cases
have engendered significant scholarly debate, and both require full integration of
the available datasets if we hope to make progress in our understanding. First, by
allowing traditional historical and archaeological evidence to be complemented
with scientific analyses, we will unravel the genetic, linguistic, and cultural identity of the Viking Age settlers who colonized Iceland. Behind a cultural and
linguistic uniformity lie complex geographical origins and a genetic diversity.
Second, complementarity of data sets—textual, archaeological, and scientific—
will be sought at a regional level to shed light on the settlement process. Here, our
understanding of stable place names still used in a valley landscape in southwest
Iceland provides a model of settlement hierarchy that can be tested and nuanced
with archaeological evidence, saga studies, and environmental sciences.

Ethnicity and Population Diversity in Viking Age Iceland: Texts, Archaeology, Isotopes, and Genetics

Ascertaining the origin of Iceland's settlers is important for reconstructing cultural history, but also for questions of post-settlement identity negotiation and
the creation of an Icelandic identity. The origin and ethnicity of the settlers of
Iceland can be approached through written sources, archaeological remains,
isotopic analyses, and genetic studies. These sources agree that the population

consisted of mostly (though not exclusively) Norse settlers from Norway and the Scandinavian colonies in the British Isles. In general, recent genetic studies support a multi-ethnic origin of the Icelandic settlers. However, the texts and the genetics diverge in the proportions of settler origins. A different picture is provided by the archaeological record, which has yielded the material correlates of a relatively uniform identity that is culturally Norse and religiously Norse pagan.

The identity of their ancestors was fundamentally important to later medieval Icelanders, to the point that the author of the Þórðarbók version of Landnámabók states: "It is often said that writing about the settlements is irrelevant learning, but we think we can all the better meet the criticism of foreigners when they accuse us of being descended from slaves or scoundrels, if we know for certain the truth about our ancestry."[114] Landnámabók and the sagas stress the Norwegian origin, particularly for the high-status land-claiming settlers. These texts are colored by the Icelandic foundation myth, which emphasizes the freedom-seeking ideals of independent-minded farmers and big men from the western coast of Norway. However, many saga characters are also from other areas of Northern Europe. Ulfljot, for instance, who brought the model laws to Iceland, as well as Glam, the shepherd-turned-monster in Grettir's Saga, are both Swedes. One settler in Landnámabók is said to have had a Flemish mother and a father from Götaland in Sweden. Even on the famous Vínland journeys to North America, one German and two Scots were among the voyagers. Celtic peoples are particularly common in the texts, often identified by Celtic names including Kjartan, Kodran, and Njal. Such names also appear in place names of farms and geographical features in Iceland.

The Irish monk Dicuil, writing De Mensura Orbis Terrae in West Francia around 825, speaks of a few Irish monks living in a place called Thule that is probably Iceland. Place names including the element pap—the Norse papi draws from the Irish pabba, which in turn derives from the Latin papa meaning "father"—support an Irish presence on the island.[115] Ari the Learned's Íslendingabók recalls that early settlers encountered these papar, but that the monks left quickly. Ari uses their Irish Christian material culture, such as bells, croziers, and books, as part of the proof for their previous presence on the island. Following Ari's tantalizing material evidence, scholars—including Kristján Eldjárn, who comprehensively searched the island of Papey—have looked meticulously for signs of the papar, but no convincing evidence has yet been found.[116] Ultimately, it appears that the Irish monks had no distinguishable effect on the natural environment, did not contribute to the settler population, and had no impact on the subsequent social developments on the island.

Archaeological approaches to ethnicity in Viking Age Iceland have had limited success in recognizing overt displays of ethnicity beyond the ubiquitous Norwegian pagan identity visible in burial practices, house styles, and artifact types. Some Celtic-style objects, such as the characteristic Hiberno-Norse bronze ring pins, are found in graves, but always in Scandinavian style burials and in association with typically Scandinavian objects.[117] The suggestion that circular cemetery enclosure walls or turf churches as opposed to timber churches might represent Irish Christian influence from the time of settlement does not appear to be consistent with the growing dataset of early Icelandic churches.[118] More promising is the study of fragments of preserved textiles from pre-Christian burials in Iceland that exhibit some technical styles for spinning and weaving that can be linked with Celtic traditions, possibly brought to Iceland by women from the British Isles.[119] But even these stylistic influences from the British Isles were embedded within the dominant Scandinavian traditions of textile production, dress, and pagan burial. In light of the diaspora model discussed above, this persistence in reproducing the dominant culture of the Norwegian homeland is unsurprising. Given the textual evidence for individuals that were not from Norway, however, the ubiquity of these stylistic elements suggests that the settlers were making purposeful material statements of uniformity in their new Icelandic identity. Seen from the perspective of a new fragment society, individual differences may have been glossed over in favor of the outward trappings of cultural unity.

The presence of ethnically Slavic peoples in Iceland is not attested in the written sources, but has been suggested on the basis of pit houses in the archaeological record.[120] Pit houses are found across the Scandinavian and Northern European world, and are also sometimes the earliest houses found clustered at Icelandic Settlement Period (870–930) sites such as Bessastaðir, Hvítárholt, Stóraborg, and Hofstaðir.[121] Urbańczyk argues that such houses are indications of Slavic ethnicity, while Vésteinsson argues that only the site of Sveigakót is a likely representative of the Slavic cultural model because the pit houses there were inhabited well beyond the first settlement phase and into the tenth century.[122] In Vésteinsson's view, these pit houses are therefore purposeful statements of identity made by people who did not conform to the dominant Norse cultural tradition of bow-sided and three-aisled longhouses. To him, the most parsimonious explanation is that they were built and inhabited by unfree Slavs who had been settled in Iceland against their will.

Urbańczyk and Vésteinsson usefully remind us that the archaeology of structures as well as artifacts can provide insight into questions of ethnicity, and furthermore underscore archaeology's potential to add nuance to the story provided by texts. Their specific suggestions concerning pit houses remain unconvincing, however, because these building types are not unique to Slavic regions. Without additional artifact evidence indicative of Slavic identity and without associated human skeletal material for isotopic studies of tooth enamel—which have been shown to be effective in distinguishing people who grew up in Slavic lands from people who grew up in the Scandinavian countries—this remains a hypothesis in need of further material support.[123] It seems more likely that pit houses had multiple purposes, including use as weaving rooms and storage buildings.[124] Pit houses also appear to have characterized the earliest habitation phase at some sites precisely because they could be built quickly and expediently.[125] The relatively impoverished people who built the pit houses at Sveigakót may have had a range of different reasons—including, but certainly not limited to, ethnicity—for choosing to live in a pit house for longer than other settlers. Excavations of Viking Age houses and buildings in Iceland have shown differences in choices of construction methods. Although drawing from common traditions under the umbrella of broader cultural uniformity, these choices result in significant variations in the social space of early Icelandic farmsteads.

Where archaeology has fewer answers, isotopic and genetic analyses have been successful in documenting diversity among the Viking Age inhabitants of Iceland. Isotope studies, mostly strontium ($^{87}Sr/^{86}Sr$), are effective in determining whether individuals grew up in locations other than Iceland. However, these studies are limited to the first generation of immigrants, as subsequent generations would have incorporated the island's isotopic signature into their bones. An examination of ninety skeletons from thirty-six pagan grave sites (presumably predating the adoption of Christianity in 1000) and two early Christian graveyards indicated that 14.4 percent of the sample had grown up elsewhere.[126] This study permitted only a broad suggestion for the homelands of the people tested, primarily Ireland, the Hebrides, and western Scandinavia. This aligns with the areas of origin for early Icelandic populations indicated by the written sources. Studies of the strontium isotopes in the enamel of teeth of individuals buried at the early Christian cemetery at Hrísbrú—dating to the late tenth to early eleventh century and therefore representing a later period than the pagan graves discussed above—indicate that all individuals lived in Iceland during their childhood, when the teeth were forming.[127]

Perhaps the strongest evidence for the multi-ethnic origin of Icelanders is provided by genetic studies of the mitochondrial DNA of contemporary female Icelanders, Y-chromosome data from contemporary Icelandic males, as well as ancient DNA (aDNA) from early Icelandic burials.[128] The modern DNA studies indicate that over 50 percent of the mitochondrial DNA (mtDNA) of modern Icelanders is comparable to modern populations of the British Isles, while the contribution of mtDNA from Scandinavia to Iceland is somewhat less, at 37.5 percent.[129] By contrast, the Y-chromosome data suggest that over 80 percent of males in Iceland today descend from immigrants from Scandinavia.[130] These studies are consistent with saga accounts of Viking men taking Celtic women to Iceland. The DNA evidence, however, suggests a larger proportion of non-Scandinavian women than is depicted in the texts. Genetic studies employing contemporary individuals as proxies of the original settlers are complicated by potential post-Viking Age population migrations. However, studies of aDNA appear to confirm the general statistics for ethnic origins of Icelanders provided by the modern DNA studies.[131] Adding to the ethnic diversity, identification in the modern population of mtDNA haplogroup C1—a haplogroup not found in Europe, but common among North American native populations—has led geneticists to theorize that the Vínland voyages may have led to the migration of one or more individuals from the New World to Iceland.[132]

The overlapping, yet divergent views of ethnic identity and geographical origins of early Icelanders bring to the fore the recognition that ethnicity in the Middle Ages was more fluid than indicated in traditional historical narratives.[133] The active process of ethnogenesis—the formation of a new ethnic identity—in Iceland can be seen in the archaeological record as early Icelanders purposefully chose to replicate Norse material culture, both in their homes and in their burials. The resolution of the ethnogenesis process can be gleaned from the sagas and texts like *Íslendingabók* and *Landnámabók*, which accept in varying degrees contributions of non-Scandinavians, but see the colonization process as organized, planned, and executed by free Norwegians. Both data sets mask the extent of the ethnic diversity involved in the migration process, as revealed by the genetics research. Archaeological excavation of additional Viking Age sites, closer study of artifact assemblages, and especially isotopic and aDNA analyses of Settlement Period human remains hold promise to reveal more about the origins of the early Icelanders and the processes involved in the subsequent formation of a new Icelandic identity.

The Mosfell Valley: An Interdisciplinary Case Study of Settlement Structure

The nature of the settlement of Iceland had lasting effects on the society that developed in Iceland. The initial settlers claimed large swathes of land and used their power over that land to reinforce kinship networks and create economic dependence and political indebtedness. The founders of the new society also determined the political trajectory that saw the founding of regional assemblies and a single, politically unifying Althing. As we saw in the previous section, the settlers also made choices about which culture and language was prioritized in the newly settled land. They created a new Icelandic ethnicity, and generations later the sagas reinforced this "foundation myth" of their own origins. The economic and social background of this system and new identity was the network of individual farms that spread across the Icelandic landscape.

The Mosfell Valley in southwest Iceland offers an excellent case study of the settlement of Iceland and the subsequent formation of an organization of farms. The interdisciplinary sources for the study of this valley are rich and include textual data, place names, archaeological survey, subsurface testing, palynology, and extensive excavations conducted at the chieftain's farmstead at Hrísbrú.[134] Chapter 3 presented the Hrísbrú house and the patterns of elite feasting visible in the archaeological and ecological record, while Chapter 4 examined local syncretization of paganism and Christianity within the Hrísbrú burial ground during the process of Christian conversion. Now we will see how this chieftain's farm fits into the wider Viking Age settlement landscape of the valley.

According to *Landnámabók*, Skeggjastaðir was the valley's first farm, established by and named after the valley's original settler, Thord Skeggi. The Icelandic sagas identify one additional site, Mosfell, as a chieftain's farmstead that was in existence before 1000. *Egil's Saga*, *Gunnlaug's Saga Serpent-Tongue*, and *Hallfred's Saga* identify the Mosfell farm as the seat of the Mosfell Valley chieftains (Mosfellsdælingar) and the center of power in the region, while *Egil's Saga* mentions the existence of a farm named Hrísbrú.[135] Two additional farms appear in sources pre-dating 1400, meaning that five farms in this valley are recorded in medieval texts: Skeggjastaðir, Mosfell, Hrísbrú, Helgadalur, and Hraðastaðir.[136] Place-name studies, archaeology, and palynology provide data for a much clearer understanding of the emergence of this Viking Age valley community.

Scandinavian place name scholars have developed a body of theory that uses place-name types in the reconstruction of settlement order and social ranking. Place names can be broadly divided into two types: topographical names and habitative names. Topographical names (or nature names) describe a topographical feature, almost always a natural feature, but sometimes and more rarely a man-made feature. Habitative names (or culture names) denote inhabited places, such as farms, villages, and enclosures. In the Norse expansion into the North Atlantic, the first farms established in an area almost always take their name from the prominent topographical features, typically those visible from the sea.[137] Secondary settlements frequently contain habitative generic suffixes. A common habitative suffix that appears across the Viking North Atlantic colonies and in the Mosfell region is -staðir.[138] Since the -staðir place name suffix went out of style in the eleventh century, the North Atlantic -staðir names can be securely dated to the Viking Age.[139] Viking Age Icelanders used the -staðir suffix for secondary farms established in areas inside the borders of the primary settlement farms.[140] The personal name commonly preceding the -staðir suffix could be either the name of the landowner or the name of the farm's occupant/ tenant. In fact, the term -staðir meant "land parts," and the usage of the plural form *staðir* rather than the singular *staðr* probably reflects the existence of several divided parts from each original farm.[141] Tertiary farms have less prestigious names derived from other settlement names or from smaller natural or man-made landscape features. These farms are more difficult to ascribe any clear date range but can tentatively be dated sequentially as established after the secondary settlements.

Employing these place-name principles, we can create a model of the primary, secondary, and tertiary farmsteads in the Mosfell Valley and then test this model with reference to local textual, archaeological, and palynological evidence (Figure 6.10). According to the model derived from place names, the primary farms in the valley are those with macro-topographical names: Mosfell ("Moss Mountain"), Leirvogstunga (or Tunga ["Promontory"] in the earliest documents), and Helgadalur ("Holy Valley"). The place name model predicts that the farm named Mosfell was the first. The mountain called Mosfell is the valley's most distinctive landmark, prominently visible from the sea and rising from lowlands on all sides.[142] The Mosfell farm lies at the foot of the mountain's southern slope. Strong supporting evidence that Mosfell is the region's primary farm is provided by the inclusion of Mosfell as the appellative base in nearly all regional place names, including Mosfellsdalur (Mosfell Valley), Mosfellsveit (Mosfell Region), and Mosfellsheiði (Mosfell Heath).

The stability of Icelandic farms suggests that the original Mosfell farm would lie in the same place as the current farm called Mosfell. However, written sources indicate that the original Mosfell farm moved from the current site of the farm Hrísbrú to its present position.[143] When the main farm moved, the place name Mosfell moved with it. The name Hrísbrú was then given to a new farm established at the location of the old farm. *Egil's Saga* provides a clue to the date of the relocation of the Mosfell farm by stating that the church connected to the main farmstead was moved when the priest Skapti Thorarinsson lived at Mosfell. The same Skapti is recorded in *Prestatal*, a list of important Icelandic priests from 1143.[144]

Archaeological research corroborates the suggested shift of the old farm from an original location at modern-day Hrísbrú to modern-day Mosfell, circa 100 m to the east. Excavations at Hrísbrú unearthed a chiefly farmstead, including a large longhouse, an early church and Christian graveyard, and a pre-Christian cremation burial that have been addressed in Chapters 3 and 4. The house excavated at Hrísbrú is a Viking Age longhouse built between 877 and 920/934, partially rebuilt after 920/934, and abandoned in the eleventh century (Figure 6.9).[145] The length of the house, at almost 30 m, is among the longest excavated in Iceland. The number of imported glass beads is greater than the assemblages from inside any other Viking Age house in Iceland. The recovery of a large number of barley seeds and high ratios of cattle to caprine bones suggest that the chieftains occupying the house hosted expensive feasts.[146] The presence of an early church from circa 1000 at the farmstead is consistent with expectations

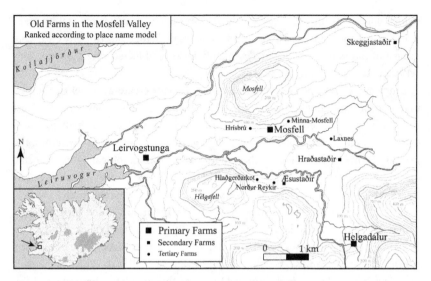

Figure 6.10 The Mosfell Valley with primary, secondary, and tertiary farms as suggested by the place-name model. Textual and archaeological testing of this model largely confirmed its accuracy. However, hints from *Egil's Saga* suggested the original Mosfell farm was located at Hrísbrú. This was confirmed with archaeological excavation. In the twelfth century, the Mosfell farm changed locations and the old farm site was renamed Hrísbrú. The secondary sites split from one of the primary sites—most likely Mosfell—in the tenth or early eleventh century. The tertiary sites that cluster on the northern and southern slopes of the valley were products of the gradual intensification of agricultural production.
Source: map by author

of higher-status households, which quickly realized and utilized the potential ideological power of Christianity.[147] By contrast, archaeological research at the current Mosfell farm revealed a farmstead and church that predate 1500, but no evidence of a Viking Age farm.[148] The combined evidence from place names, sagas, and archaeological excavations agree that the farm located at Hrísbrú occupied the top of the settlement hierarchy as the most successful, and in all likelihood the earliest, farm in the valley.

The second primary farm according to the place-name model is Leirvogstunga (Tidal-flats-bay-promontory). Originally simply called Tunga (Promontory), this farm takes its name from the prominent spit of land jutting out into the sea at the western mouth of the Mosfell Valley. The site is not mentioned in any medieval texts predating 1400, but archaeological excavations at Leirvogstunga documented a farmstead of substantial size, inhabited continuously throughout the Viking and medieval periods.[149] The presence of Landnám Tephra in structural turf blocks suggests that these turf features were built not long after the Landnám Tephra fell in 877±1. The most significant element of the oldest farmstead is the remains of the turf homefield wall surrounding the old farm buildings. The Medieval Tephra Layer from 1226 was identified above this wall, meaning that the wall was constructed prior to this date. The excavators interpreted this farm as a medium-sized holding of intermediary status, probably belonging to a free landowning farmer.[150]

The third primary farm according to the place name model is Helgadalur (Holy Valley), a farmstead that carries the name of a subsidiary valley extending south from the Mosfell Valley. The site is not mentioned in the texts until the end of the fourteenth century. Systematic archaeological coring across a ridge of accumulated cultural material at Helgadalur, however, demonstrated that human settlement began very soon after the Landnám Tephra fell in 877.[151] Charcoal of cultural origin within an anthropogenic deposit was found immediately above a lens of in-situ Landnám Tephra. Examination of an eroding slope of a streambank south of the cultural ridge revealed deposits including mixed midden with charcoal, bone, peat ash, and re-deposited turf blocks containing multiple Landnám Tephra layers. The inclusion of substantial amounts of Landnám Tephra in turf blocks suggests a Viking Age date for portions of this mixed deposit. Small charcoal fragments immediately above the Landnám Tephra in one of the modern drainage trenches to the north provide additional evidence for the substantial nature of this early occupation.

The secondary farms proposed for the Mosfell Valley by the place-name model are Skeggjastaðir, Hraðastaðir, and Æsustaðir, which all employ the habitative suffix -staðir preceded by a personal name. These farms are evenly spaced across the landscape. Systematic archaeological coring at Skeggjastaðir discovered a Viking Age farmstead.[152] The farm is situated near the edge of a steep gully through which a small tributary stream flows from south to north down to the river Leirvogsá. This placement is ideal for access to fresh water. The subsurface survey recovered evidence of a large occupation area, including remains of turf walls, and peat ash midden layers. The medieval date of these farmstead remains is evidenced by the Katla Tephra from 1500, which lies atop the occupation layers in many of the core samples. The turf walls found beneath the Katla Tephra contained large amounts of Landnám Tephra (877), suggesting an early post-settlement date for the construction of the walls.

At Hraðastaðir and Æsustaðir, sub-surface archaeological coring was unable to establish the antiquity of the farms. A closer look at the intersection of the historical landscape, oral traditions, and the early texts, however, sheds more light. *Landnámabók* does not explicitly mention the farms of Hraðastaðir or Æsustaðir, but it does mention a man from the Mosfell area named Thorbjorn Hradason (Hraðason, or "son of Hraði"). If this tradition is true, then perhaps

Thorbjorn's father, Hraði, founded Hraðastaðir (Hraði's Farm). A local oral tradition dating back to at least the end of the eighteenth century may corroborate the antiquity of Hraðastaðir. This oral tradition holds that a low mound at
the bottom of the valley is called Hraðaleiði or "Hraði's burial mound."[153] The
Hraðaleiði mound, which is distinct in the landscape, lies precisely at the intersection of the traditional boundaries of the Mosfell, Hraðastaðir, and Æsustaðir
farms (Figure 6.11). Pagan burial mounds often lie prominently positioned
on old farm boundaries.[154] The correspondence of farm boundaries and the
Hraðaleiði mound suggests two possible conclusions. The mound is either a genuine pagan burial or a very old oral tradition that was co-opted into the valley's
land division. The Hraðaleiði mound suggests that the nineteenth-century farm
boundaries in this area may correspond with the original farm boundaries established during the early settlement of the valley before the conversion to
Christianity in 1000. This evidence suggests that the three farms sharing this

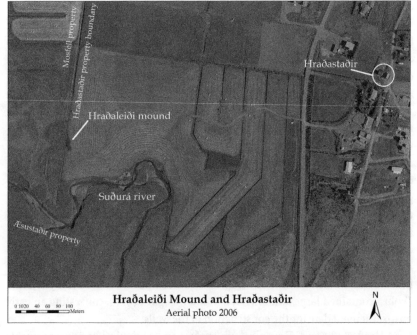

Figure 6.11 Aerial photograph showing the location of the Hraðaleiði mound at the
intersection of the traditional boundaries of the Mosfell, Hraðastaðir, and Æsustaðir
farms. The placement is consistent with the placement of Icelandic pagan burial
mounds on the boundaries of farms, outside of cultivated fields, and in prominent
places in the landscape.

Source: map by author

boundary intersect—Hrísbrú/Mosfell, Hraðastaðir, and Æsustaðir—were established prior to 1000.

The tertiary farms as proposed by the place-name model are Hrísbrú, Laxnes, Minna-Mosfell, Norður Reykir, and Hlaðgerðakot. Of these farms, only Hrísbrú showed any archaeological evidence of habitation before the end of the Viking Age. This is consistent with the absence of these farms in texts about the Viking Age. Except for Hrísbrú (because of the farmstead shift from Hrísbrú to Mosfell), this evidence is also consistent with the place-name model.

The complementarity of the sources allows for a general picture of the Viking Age settlement of the valley. Generally, the stratification of these farms, as suggested by the place names, is supported by the textual focus on the chiefly farm at Mosfell and by the archaeological evidence of wealth recovered by the Hrísbrú excavations. Archaeological surveys and excavations indicate that settlers established at least four farms—Hrísbrú/Old Mosfell, Leirvogstunga, Helgadalur, and Skeggjastaðir—during the early settlement history in the Mosfell Valley. This is three more than the number of farms indicated by the texts. The archaeology agrees with the place-name model that predicted that Mosfell was the first farm in the valley, and that settlers founded subsequent early settlements at Leirvogstunga, Helgadalur, and Skeggjastaðir. The archaeology also supports the view from the textual sources that the chiefly establishment and the farm name was moved from the current Hrísbrú site to present-day location of the Mosfell farm during the twelfth century.

Recent palynological research at the farms in the Mosfell Valley indicates that the primary and secondary farms were founded before the end of the Viking Age.[155] Early evidence for habitation, starting just after 870, was found at all three primary farms. Furthermore, and confirming the social hierarchy suggested by place names and archaeological excavation, only the lands of the Old Mosfell/Hrísbrú farm show evidence of barley cultivation. As discussed in Chapter 3, this was the preserve of the elite in Iceland, a consequence of its intimate relationship to politically motivated feasting. The other primary farms—Helgadalur and Leirvogstunga—along with the secondary farms show no grain cultivation, but do exhibit changes in flora (e.g., expansion of grazing lands) between 870 and 1100. By contrast, the tertiary farms yielded no evidence of changes in the local farm flora in the Viking Age.

The distribution of the earliest farms suggests an economic logic in their placement, one that may reflect chiefly design in settling supporters in specific areas to take advantage of local resources. The paramount site, Hrísbrú/Old Mosfell, is located on the northern side of the valley, which receives the most sunshine at this northerly latitude. The sunny south-facing slopes of the mountain support the widest dry hay meadow in the valley. The farm is positioned prominently at the mouth of the valley, maximizing visibility and access to low wetlands for cattle-grazing.

The agency in the placement of the additional farms is difficult to determine, but the evidence fits a model whereby the farm locations resulted from
a chiefly design of the primary settler. Following this model, the primary settler at Hrísbrú/Old Mosfell established supporters at economically intensifiable
locations in the valley. The three primary farms, Hrísbrú/Old Mosfell,
Leirvogstunga, and Helgadalur, are evenly distributed across the landscape,
maximizing distance between the farms within the productive areas of the
valley. Leirvogstunga and Helgadalur may also have had specialized functions
or roles in the valley's earliest cultural landscape. Specifically, the placement of
Leirvogstunga is oriented toward maritime resources and possibly connected to
the monitoring of ocean-going trade and travel, whereas the place name "Holy
Valley" suggests Helgadalur held special ritual or religious importance. The three
secondary -staðir farms are distributed evenly across the valley landscape, filling
available locations between the primary farms. Their locations therefore appear
to be predicated on the availability of grazing land and the maximization of settlement spacing on the landscape.

The textual, place-name, and archaeological evidence for the Mosfell Valley
was rarely contradictory. The discrepancy in the location of the first settlement
site provides the clearest example. But in this contradiction, we access a richer
story. *Landnámabók* holds that the valley's first settler, Thord Skeggi, lived at
Skeggjastaðir. Place-name evidence, on the other hand, suggests that the Mosfell
farm was the first settlement and that the farm names with -staðir suffixes, like
Skeggjastaðir, were secondary settlements. The archaeological record showed
Hrísbrú to be the most likely candidate for the primary site in the valley with the
excavation of a high-status farmstead and the earliest datable evidence of human
habitation.

Conclusions

The case of the Mosfell Valley exemplifies the potential, complexities, and future promise of data-driven interdisciplinary approaches. The *Landnámabók*
tradition about the Mosfell Valley must have lost the memory of the first settler's
farmstead. To compensate for this loss, the creators of this tradition reimagined
the settlement history by connecting the place name Skeggjastaðir with the primary residence of the imputed first settler, Skeggi. The ability to cross-check
and modify imprecision derived from the oral traditions that inform the sagas
is one of the strengths of interdisciplinary research on the Viking Age. Only reference back to the textual record, however, could explain the incongruity between the archaeological findings and the place-name evidence in the Mosfell
Valley. Without the medieval texts indicating that the place name Mosfell shifted

from the location of the Hrísbrú farm to the current position of the Mosfell farm in the twelfth century, the archaeological and place-name evidence would have appeared to be in direct contradiction.

The complementary evidence from texts, archaeology, and place names shows the dynamic nature of the Scandinavian society created in Iceland. Diaspora societies typically emerge in relation to host cultures. In Iceland—as well as in Greenland and the Faroes—there was no host culture. The diasporic host can instead be conceived of as being the sub-arctic environment. The members of the new society defined themselves in relationship to the new nature, adapting their subsistence, economics, and even politics to the new environment. Viking-style houses were built of insulative turf blocks from the wetlands, peat was burned for fuel, and the cattle-herding preference gave way to transhumant sheep-herding. The absence of a host population left Viking Age Icelandic society free to evolve independently as a "New Society." A period of ethnogenesis for Icelanders emphasized Scandinavian, and particularly Norwegian, heritage to the point that the population contributions of the British Isles became nearly invisible in the material signals of identity. The island defined the geographic extent of Icelandic culture, while the dramatic landscape of the mid-Atlantic ridge provided the political center for a decentralized polity split according to island quarters and subdivided with respect to the land's deep fjords. In their new identity, early Icelanders still strove for the maintenance of diasporic relationships with the homelands. The continued relationship relied on material and information exchanges across the Atlantic Ocean as well as the recounting of common poems and saga stories. Even seemingly subsistence-oriented imports, such as a grain, tied the Icelanders to Viking Age Scandinavian cultural practices of cereal cultivators, bread eaters, and beer drinkers. Subsistence in a Scandinavian fashion with grain fields and feasts of beer and beef became the preserve of the Icelandic elite. The early settlers signaled their pagan Scandinavian identity for instance in burials adorned with bronze brooches, glass beads, inlaid swords, and at times also Arabic silver. After conversion to Christianity, other imports, such as wax for candles and wine for church services, were imported by the new church-based elites. The import of these goods became increasingly difficult as the Viking Age wound down and fewer ships carrying migrants, goods, and information crossed the Atlantic Ocean. The Icelandic society increasingly looked inward, as the Viking Age drew to a close.

7

Stories of Vínland

The End of the Viking Horizon

The subject matter of this penultimate chapter allows us to focus squarely on the essential methodological questions presented in the introduction. The Viking voyages west and south beyond Greenland occupy a space in Viking Studies between legend and history. The journeys are evidenced in written sources and the archaeological record. The timespan of the primary voyages appears to have been short, beginning sometime shortly before 1000 and drawing to a close less than fifty years later. Among the written sources, the sagas provide the fullest narrative about the voyages and record the existence of only one or two settlements. Later texts track efforts to visit places mentioned in the sagas but mention no additional settlements or attempts at colonizing the lands beyond Greenland. Only one site has been verified archaeologically: L'Anse aux Meadows, located on the auspiciously named island of Newfoundland (Figure 7.1). Before the archaeological site was discovered, the opinion of scholars about the voyages depended on their beliefs about the veracity of the saga accounts: some viewed the voyages as fantastical fictional tales, while others considered the sagas to be credible accounts of historical journeys. The archaeological discovery of L'Anse aux Meadows dramatically changed this situation.

A large body of scholarship has attempted to harmonize the places mentioned in the sagas with North American geography and the single New World Viking archaeological site at L'Anse aux Meadows. Most commonly, scholars have assigned this archaeological site to one of the Vínland settlements remembered in the sagas. Is it possible, however, that L'Anse aux Meadows is instead a short-lived and ultimately unsuccessful attempt at colonization of the New World *not* recorded in the sagas? L'Anse aux Meadows presents a clear example of scholars seeking a very specific level of confirmation of the sagas from archaeological evidence. Taking a wider perspective, the archaeological site has indeed confirmed the basic saga narrative that Viking Age Scandinavians reached the New World. How detailed can the correspondence be? To press further, do we know more now from the combination of sagas and archaeology than from either of them taken independently? Finally, are there contradictions between the texts and the archaeology, or even between individual texts? Since the written sources are few

Age of Wolf and Wind. Davide Zori, Oxford University Press. © Oxford University Press 2024.
DOI: 10.1093/oso/9780190916060.003.0007

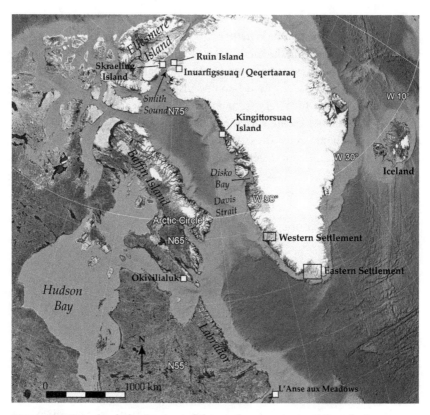

Figure 7.1 Greenland, the Arctic, and the northeastern coast of Canada. In Greenland, the Norse established two main settlement clusters, known as the Eastern and Western Settlements. A third settlement cluster, the Middle Settlement, was established between the two. All the voyages to Vínland departed from Eirik the Red's farm, Brattahlíð, in the Eastern Settlement. L'Anse aux Meadows, on the northern tip of Newfoundland, is the only undisputed Norse Viking Age site in North America.

Source: map by author

in number for the Scandinavian exploration and settlement in North America, there is room to delve deep into these questions in this chapter.

Legends in Text

Only a handful of texts preserve the memory of the Vínland voyages. The key sources are Adam of Bremen's *Gesta Hammaburgensis* (c. 1076) written in northern Germany, and *Íslendingabók* (1122–1133), Landnámabók (c.

1150–1250), the Icelandic annals, *Greenlanders' Saga*, and *Eirik the Red's Saga*, all written in Iceland. Whether or not we find credible the details in these texts, it is clear that the medieval Icelanders, Greenlanders, Danes, and Germans who told these stories and wrote these texts all believed that these voyages had taken place. The difference in geographical origin and genre among these texts, which vary from annals to historical works to sagas, amplify the significance of their agreement in the existence, geographical position, and main characteristics of Vínland. Although the texts agree on the broadest scale, significant differences exist, especially within the elaborated saga narratives.

The Sagas about Vínland: Greenlanders' Saga and Eirik the Red's Saga

The most detailed accounts of the voyages to Vínland are found in two Icelandic sagas. The similarities between the sagas suggest their origins in a similar oral tradition predating the written form. Although the shared elements do not in themselves necessitate their historicity, it does at least render it plausible that the sagas retain a core of factual memories concerning the voyages. The importance of these sagas for the Vínland question warrants a closer look at the textual traditions, the manuscripts in which they are preserved, and the relationship between the two sagas.

Eirik's Saga is preserved in two manuscripts, *Hauksbók* (c. 1302–1310) and *Skálholtsbók* (first half of the 1400s). Both manuscript versions derive from the same text that was probably written sometime after 1262 but before 1302. This shared written ancestral text was presumably based on another original text written in the first half of the 1200s.[1] *Hauksbók* appears to be closer to the original text, although it includes many purposeful emendations by the editor, such as changes to landscape descriptions and sailing directions.[2] In the analysis that follows, this chapter employs primarily the standard version of *Hauksbók*, while also highlighting how the variances between the two manuscripts sometimes subtly change the interpretation of the text.[3]

Greenlanders' Saga is preserved in only one manuscript, *Flateyjarbók* (1387–1394), where it is found divided in two parts and inserted into a longer saga about Olaf Tryggvason, the Christianizing Norwegian king.[4] Such insertions often result in editorial truncations or elaborations of the text. In this case, the original opening of *Greenlanders' Saga* appears to be missing and is instead replaced within the larger saga by material copied from the Icelandic *Book of Settlements* (*Landnámabók*) concerning Eirik the Red and the settlement of Greenland. Most scholars believe that an older written version of *Greenlanders' Saga* existed that could date back to the early thirteenth century, while others believe that the saga was only written down in the early fourteenth century.[5]

The two versions of *Eirik's Saga* and the insertion of *Greenlanders' Saga* into the saga about King Olaf provide useful reminders of the creative and varied ways that written text was used in medieval Iceland. The editorializing and alteration of saga texts show that written text is far from static and not necessarily more fixed in form or content than oral traditions. Refocusing on the audience of the written and oral texts helps to place textual variation in its social context. If the audience can be assumed to have been familiar with the basic storylines of sagas like the story of the exploration of Vínland, it would explain why and how sagas could be truncated or expanded upon without losing the audience. The well-known saga stories were meant to both entertain and to function as repositories of historical memory that also provided education on social norms and reinforced cultural values. Within this framework, different versions of the saga could easily highlight particular aspects and characters. Carol Clover discussed this underlying story framework as the "immanent whole" that existed as basic knowledge in the minds of the audience.[6] Even if the story within the saga were not told in its entirety, the audience could fill in the blanks because they had previously heard parts or all of the sagas before. Clover has discussed the potential fission and fusion effect this could have on sagas in their oral phase. This could result in longer or shorter sagas, and different foci on one character or the other, depending on the audience. The use of *Greenlanders' Saga* in *Flateyjarbók* demonstrates that the written versions of sagas, much like Clover's oral sagas, could just as easily be carved up or reassembled for use in larger or smaller works.

In the case of the Vínland sagas, Gísli Sigurðsson has argued that the two written sagas derive from separate oral traditions that maintain memories about historical events. Sigurðsson summarizes, "in many respects their narratives tell the same story, but they also differ on a large number of points, making them particularly interesting for any discussion of the interconnections linking the sagas, oral tradition, and the external historical reality."[7] Much disagreement still exists, as is evident in Sverrir Jakobsson's assertion that "the compatibility of the account given in the sagas is far from great, except for a few basic facts."[8] An obvious subjective interpretive distance separates Sigurðsson's and Jakobsson's opinions about the sagas. The next pages explore the substance and implications of the shared facts that both Sigurðsson and Jakobsson recognize within the sagas. The stories in the two sagas share traditions about the voyages, a common cast of characters, and even a handful of specific similar scenes. The differences between the sagas indicate significant divergence between the two narratives, especially in individual actions, and in some cases in specific characters. These differences do not, however, change the general impression of the voyages, the lands they encountered, or the natives that they met. Without any additional support from other sources, however, even the great correspondence between the sagas would not necessarily mean that the events should be judged as historical facts. They should be considered as separate data sets, but as unlikely as it might seem, the commonalities in the stories could have emerged in a very early oral phase of the saga before it split into the two separate written sagas that we have preserved today. For this reason, it is helpful to hold up the sagas against the evidence of the Vínland voyages from other medieval texts and the archaeological data.

The narratives about the voyages presented in the two sagas include a wide array of fundamental correspondences in a series of basic points, including similar protagonists, motives for exploration, sailing directions, timescale, and characteristics of the new lands. They both record long voyages from the Eastern Settlement in Greenland to multiple lands lying to the west and south. The most northerly of these lands is characterized by towering mountains, glaciers, and large slabs of rock. To the south is a forested and hilly landscape that, although potentially useful for timber, does not have the grasslands or resources conducive to Norse settlement. Still farther south lies a land that had both ample meadows for cattle and other flora—like grapes and self-sown wheat—that would be attractive to Norse settlers. In both sagas, these lands were first discovered by sailors accidentally blown off course on their way to Greenland. The lands are explored, and, subsequently, an attempt is made to permanently settle the southernmost of these newly discovered lands. In both sagas, the date range of these voyages—circa 986 to 1020—is the same. The saga protagonists—many of whom appear to be historical people—are also mostly the same. The children of Eirik the Red, for instance, feature prominently in the expeditions and Eirik the Red's farm is the primary point of departure from Greenland (Table 7.1). In both sagas, the southernmost of the new lands is inhabited by natives, whom the Norse called Skrælings. The etymology of the word *Skræling* (plural, Skrælingjar) is unclear, but probably originally meant something like "animal pelt wearers," or possibly "screamers."[9] These natives were unfamiliar with European weapons and large European domesticated animals. The interaction between the Norse and Skrælings included attempts at non-verbal communication, trading European-specific goods for animal skins, and open hostilities. Both sagas relate that the attempted colony failed, and the Norse returned to Greenland and Iceland, with conflict with the natives given as the primary reason for abandoning the colony.

The correspondences paint a consistent general sociological picture of the voyages and contain several direct chronological, character, and event correspondences that originate in a common story. That common story could date back to original events, or the stories could have diverged from one another at some later time between 1020 and the early 1200s, when both these sagas were committed to parchment. We do not know when the story traditions diverged

Table 7.1 Voyages to Vínland according the sagas: Settlers and their settlements

Greenlanders' Saga	Eirik's Saga	Settlements Built or Visited
1. Bjarni Herjolfsson		accidental landfall, does not disembark
	1. Leif Eiriksson	accidental landfall, short stay only
2. Leif Eiriksson		Leif's Booths
3. Thorvald Eiriksson		Leif's Booths
4. Thorstein Eiriksson		failed trip
	2. Thorstein Eiriksson	failed trip
5. Karlsefni and Gudrid		Leif's Booths
	3. Karlsefni and Gudrid (including Thorvald and Freydis)	Straumfjörð and Hóp
6. Freydis, Helgi, and Finnbogi		Leif's Booths

Note: Greenlanders' Saga records six separate voyages to Vínland. *Eirik's Saga* discusses only three voyages. The sagas also use different names for the settlements. *Greenlanders' Saga* mentions only one site, Leif's Booths, while *Eirik's Saga* has the Norse establish two settlements: Straumfjörð and Hóp. The many similarities between the sagas include the names of the primary leaders of the voyages.

from the common ancestor story, but it must have been substantially before 1200 because of key differences that exist between the sagas. These variations in the sagas suggest that the common tradition spent considerable time in the oral phase of saga transmission, prior to the emergence of the two written sagas.

Both saga variants retain Icelandic traditions about voyages made primarily from the Greenland colony. The end of both sagas provides clues about who told these stories. Both sagas end with a treatment of the descendants of Gudrid and Thorfinn Karlsefni, who lead the last voyage in *Eirik's Saga* and the penultimate voyage in *Greenlanders' Saga*. Both sagas describe these characters in a very positive light. Most scholars believe that so much attention is lavished on Gudrid and Karlsefni in both sagas because they are ancestors of three twelfth-century bishops that the saga authors wished to glorify. However, some have suggested that *Greenlanders' Saga* preserves an oral tradition held by Greenlanders, while *Eirik's Saga* reflects a tradition that had spent a longer phase of oral transmission in Iceland.[10] This line of reasoning holds that Karlsefni's Icelandic descendants highlight his Vínland voyage in *Eirik's Saga* and ascribe actions to him that were undertaken by Leif (a Greenlander) in the *Greenlanders' Saga* version.

Separate oral traditions can explain many of the differences. One example is the name of a relatively minor character who is married to Thorstein the Black in the Western Settlement. In *Greenlanders' Saga* her name is Grimhild, while *Eirik's Saga* calls her Sigrid. Other differences are more likely due to authorial preference and contemporary political considerations. For instance, in *Eirik's Saga*, Gudrid and Karlsefni end their lives on a farm named Reynines in Skagafjörður in northern Iceland. *Greenlanders' Saga* agrees that they moved to Skagafjörður but locates their farm at the nearby Glaumbær. The preference for one farm over the other could relate to later medieval inhabitants of these farms, who wanted to chart their heritage back to Gudrid and Karlsefni. Þorláksson suggests, for instance, that *Eirik's Saga* is correct, and that *Greenlanders' Saga* shifted Gudrid and Karlsefni's residence to flatter the powerful fourteenth-century chieftains who lived at Glaumbær.[11] Furthermore, *Greenlanders' Saga* has Gudrid become a nun at Glaumbær after Karlsefni's death. There does not appear to have been a nunnery at Glaumbær, but one was founded in the late thirteenth century at Reynines. In Þorláksson's view, *Greenlanders' Saga* is hereby also not-so-subtly suggesting that Glaumbær is a more appropriate place for a socially powerful nunnery than Reynines. Such textual alterations (or preferences) can reveal much about politics in thirteenth- and fourteenth-century Iceland. But we also cannot rule out that the two saga authors simply and honestly disagreed about where Gudrid and Karlsefni spent their final days. Whatever the case may be, these sorts of differences are rather minor in the grander narrative of the Viking Age explorations of the lands beyond Greenland. The broader descriptions of these voyages and lands are unlikely to be affected in the same way by political rivalries in post–Viking Age Iceland.

A major point of contention in past scholarship is the attempt to determine which of the two sagas offers truer or better information. Traditional thinking held that the older a saga was, the more reliable it would be. Here too there is disagreement about which saga is older and whether either of them borrowed material from the other. Jón Jóhannesson believed *Greenlanders' Saga* predated *Eirik's Saga* and that the latter was at least partially derivative of the former.[12] But Helgi Þorláksson has argued that *Greenlanders' Saga* was written later and that although it was recorded "more or less in its unprocessed oral form" from independent oral stories, it relied in a few cases on a version of *Eirik's Saga* that had been written down earlier.[13]

Reconciling the different numbers of voyages recorded in the two sagas has always proved a challenge to demonstrating historicity. *Greenlanders' Saga* recalls a total of six trips to Vínland, whereas *Eirik's Saga* remembers only three. Some see the six voyages in *Greenlanders' Saga* as being closer to reality than the compressed version of the three voyages preserved in *Eirik's Saga*.[14] Helge Ingstad, following Jóhannesson's view, thought that the material in *Greenlanders' Saga* was more accurate, while discounting *Eirik's Saga* as a derivative product, molded and corrupted by literary borrowings from the European medieval tradition.[15] When he sought Vínland in North America, he therefore trusted *Greenlanders' Saga*. Others feel that the greater descriptive detail provided in *Eirik's Saga* for Karlsefni's voyage rings truer.[16] In light of this logic, for instance, Jónas Kristjánsson and colleagues followed *Eirik's Saga* in their search for Vínland.[17]

A third position, focusing on the idea of two independent oral traditions, seeks to use both sagas as repositories of historical information about the individual voyages. This position seeks to reconcile the divergent information from the two sagas as results of processes in oral storytelling. One possibility is that *Eirik's Saga* could have combined the six voyages from *Greenlanders' Saga* into three more extensive expeditions.[18] Possibly the other voyages had been forgotten. Another view sees *Eirik's Saga* as focused on telling fuller stories of two particular voyages while still recognizing that other voyages were also taken. This position assumes that the saga author and the saga audience knew about the other voyages even if they were not recounted in the saga. And indeed, there is some evidence that the author of *Eirik's Saga* knew about some of the additional voyages undertaken in *Greenlanders' Saga*. Most convincingly, Karlsefni and Gudrid discover a ship's keel on a peninsula two days south of Markland, which they subsequently name Kjalarnes (Keel Promontory).[19] The discovery of wreckage from a Viking ship— in a place where Norsemen had ostensibly never been—makes no sense unless the audience already knew of an earlier voyage that involved a shipwreck, which is exactly what is described as occurring during Thorvald's voyage in *Greenlanders' Saga*. *Greenlanders' Saga* states that Thorvald stands the keel upright on the stormy headland and gives the landmark a name: "Now I want that we raise up the keel of the ship on this promontory and call it Kjalarnes."[20]

The assumption that both sagas contain different complementary stories has allowed scholars such as Gísli Sigurðsson to use information from both sagas together to reconstruct a more complete narrative.[21] Sigurðsson explains that his method capitalizes on the complementary stories and prioritizes information that provides the fuller account: "*Grœnlendinga saga* has more to say about the voyages of Leif and Thorvald Eiriksson, while in *Eiríks saga rauða* the center of interest lies in the expedition of Thorfinn Karlsefni and Gudrid, about which *Grœnlendinga saga* says comparatively little."[22] Prioritizing information from each saga where the description is more complete allows Sigurðsson for instance to conclude that there were at least three settlements in Vínland: Leifsbúðir (Leif's Booths), Hóp (Tidal Lagoon), and Straumfjörð (Tide-Fjord or Current-Fjord). Leif's Booths is the only site recorded in *Greenlanders' Saga*, whereas Hóp and Straumfjörð appear in *Eirik's Saga*. However, if the voyages recorded in *Eirik's Saga* need to be reconciled with the voyages in *Greenlanders' Saga*, then we are left with only two sites. Following this logic, Birgitta Wallace believes that Leifsbúðir in *Greenlanders' Saga* is the equivalent of Straumfjörð in *Eirik's Saga*, leaving only two rather than three settlements.[23] In essence, the question is: what is more likely, that the two sagas use different names for the same site, or that they remember distinct efforts at establishing different settlements? Both positions accept that each saga has a core of historicity and can provide information about the Vínland voyages. However, they reach different conclusions about key aspects of the Vínland settlement because of contrasting views about how the two saga narratives relate to each other. Scholarship based on the sagas alone would appear to be at an impasse.

Adam of Bremen: Memory Transfer to Europe

Aside from the two sagas, several other medieval texts mention Vínland. At least three of these sources predate the written sagas by over a century. Although the mentions of Vínland are short and the sources post-date the presumed events of the Vínland exploration, they provide key details that allow us to address the possibility that they independently confirm stories circulating about Vínland in the Viking Age.

The earliest datable mention of Vínland comes not from the North Atlantic but from northern Germany. Adam of Bremen wrote his *History of the Bishops of Hamburg* (*Gesta Hammaburgensis Ecclesiae Pontificum*) in the early 1070s and finished circa 1076, perhaps sixty years after the last Vínland voyage recorded in the sagas would have occurred. Adam received his information from the Danish King Svein Estridsen in 1068 or 1069.[24] The mention is short but provides a rough idea of the geographical position and an explanation of the place names as based on the lands' useful natural resources. Recounting the king's stories about the lands beyond Greenland, Adam says:

> He spoke also of yet another island of the many found in that ocean [the North Atlantic]. It is called Vínland because vines producing excellent wine grow wild there. That unsown crops also abound on that island we have ascertained not from fabulous reports but from the trustworthy relation of the Danes. Beyond that island, he said, no habitable land is found in that ocean, but every place beyond it is full of impenetrable ice and intense darkness.[25]

This short quotation makes up the entirety of what Adam says about Vínland. Without other texts concerning Vínland, this mention could be easily dismissed as fanciful. The mention of freely available wine and grain sounds like an idyllic land. Those who view Vínland of the sagas as a fictive place of literary fancy have proposed that medieval authors drew inspiration from Classical legends of the Fortunate Isles that also appeared in Irish legends of the Fair Isles, and that Christian mythologizing explains the presence of the two products necessary for the Christian communion—wine and bread—symbolizing the blood and body of Christ.[26] It is important to remember, however, that people traveled and carried stories freely in the interconnected North Atlantic World at the twilight of the Viking Age. The sagas describe how even the people who were supposedly involved in the voyages to Vínland subsequently traveled to Scandinavia and further into Europe. For instance, Gudrid goes on pilgrimage to Rome. Before his death, her husband Karlsefni travels to Norway and there interacts with traders from farther afield. Karlsefni sells a costly and mysterious item called a *húsasnotra* made of a type of wood called *mǫsurr* (probably burlwood) from Vínland to a merchant from Bremen.[27] The transfer of such an exotic object must have involved the telling of the story of that object's origin. If this event indeed took place, the *húsasnotra* would have materialized the memory of the Vínland voyages. Karlsefni or other merchants and travelers from Greenland and Iceland undoubtedly would have passed along stories of new lands beyond Greenland when they traded in Europe. Intermediaries like the merchant from Bremen would have further disseminated those stories at harbors and courts of kings, like King Svein of Denmark, who we know told the story of Vínland to Adam of Bremen.

Other Icelandic Sources: Historical Works and Icelandic Annals

An independent mention of Vínland in historical sources from Iceland is found in Ari Thorgilsson's *Íslendingabók* (*Book of the Icelanders*), compiled between 1122 and 1133. Ari only mentions Vínland to help explain the nature of the archaeological remains of earlier Dorset houses that Eirik the Red found in Greenland when he was planning his colony. In Ari's words: "They found abandoned human dwellings in both in the Eastern and the Western Settlements, as well as pieces of skin boats and stone tools from which it can be seen that the people who had been there were those same people who lived in Vínland and whom the Greenlanders call Skrælings."[28] The mention of Vínland is circumstantial and used here as a common reference point to explain the abandoned Greenlandic (probably Dorset Culture) pre-Norse houses. Ari's analogy reveals that among twelfth-century Icelanders, Vínland was widely known as a geographic reality, and the voyages—including details concerning the natives of Vínland—were considered historical fact.

The Icelandic *Landnámabók* (*Book of Settlements*, c. 1150–1250), which recounts the settlement of Iceland, also includes material concerning the Greenland colony and further exploration from that colony.[29] *Landnámabók*, for instance, relates the story of Greenland's settlement, which is also told in a similar way in the beginning of *Eirik's Saga*. It also mentions Vínland twice, calling the land "Vínland the Good" (*Vínland hið góða*).[30] *Landnámabók* treats Vínland in much the same way as does *Íslendingabók*: tangentially, but as an accepted reality in discussions of other lands and the achievements of historically known people. The first mention indicates that Vínland is located six days sailing distance west from Ireland.[31] The second mention is embedded in a long genealogy in one version of *Landnámabók*, in which Thorfinn Karlsefni is mentioned as "the one who found Vínland" and "the father of Snorri."[32] Although the extended genealogies of Karlsefni in *Landnámabók* and *Eirik's Saga* have some discrepancies that could be attributable to separate oral traditions, the association of Thorfinn Karlsefni with Vínland and with his son, Snorri, are convincingly consistent.

The Icelandic annals include two brief mentions of the lands documented in the sagas about the Vínland voyages. The first from 1121 states that the bishop of Greenland, Eirik Upsi, sailed out in search of Vínland. This entry is preserved in multiple manuscripts that all read simply "Bishop Eirik sought Vínland."[33] The annals do not relate anything about the journey's outcome, nor even the bishop's motivation for undertaking the journey in the first place. The second entry, for the year 1347, states: "there came also a ship from Greenland, smaller in size than small Icelandic trading vessels. It came into the outer Stream-firth. It was without an anchor. There were seventeen men on board, and they had sailed to Markland, but had afterwards been driven here by storms at sea."[34] The record of this strange ship from Markland is also preserved in multiple manuscripts. The ship appears to be a trading vessel, but unfortunately, we can only guess at its cargo. In general, the Icelandic annals are very short and sparse with information even about Greenland, so we can assume these two events were known and discussed widely to warrant their inclusion in the annals. The main value of these two short mentions is twofold. First, the mentions indicate a clear persistence of the belief in the historicity of the stories about Vínland. Second, they indicate that these lands were still considered economically worthwhile to visit.

Intertextuality

Two specific examples of intertextuality will show how the available texts provide an interlacing network of information about the Vínland voyages. Because most of the written sources are probably based ultimately on the same group of stories that were told about Vínland, it is probably not justifiable to treat them as completely independent data sets. But since the stories vary significantly, it is fair to say that where they *do* converge, they provide a measure of independent confirmation. It is also clear in reading the sources that none of them seeks to be a comprehensive discussion or treatment of the events of the Vínland voyages. All the sources, except perhaps Adam of Bremen, imply that the audience knows more about Vínland than what is being said overtly. As such, these texts provide individual windows into a much larger Vínland narrative that medieval Icelanders were aware of, but that we will never be able to fully reconstruct. Sometimes the views from these windows overlap, and when they do, we have some measure of confirmation. Other times sources leave out specific events or voyages or geographical description, but we should not interpret these omissions as contradicting sources that do make fuller descriptions. The dance of interpretation is not easy, and more ink has been spilled over the Vínland question than any other in Viking Studies. This section seeks intertextual correlation and disagreement between our sources concerning two key issues: the value, both economically and socially, of undertaking voyages to the southwest of Greenland, and the nature of the encounters with the natives in these new lands.

Why Go to Vínland? Resource Extraction, Colonization, and Renown
The Vínland voyages were the ultimate extension of Viking expansion and colonization in the North Atlantic. The Scandinavian Viking Age expansion in the North Atlantic targeted resources, especially in the initial phases, but more than anything else, it was aimed at permanent settlement of available land. The unifying cultural experiences and shared motivations of colonization lay within the minds of the Norse explorers who first reached the shores of North America. But Vínland was also something different: it offered milder environments than Greenland and Iceland and products that were unavailable elsewhere in the North Atlantic. The texts, especially the sagas, give a detailed account of the resources that the Norse valued in Vínland.

The oldest source, Adam of Bremen's *History of the Bishops of Hamburg*, extols the remarkable aspects of the newly discovered land: wild grain and wild grapes suitable for making wine. The name of the land itself, Vínland (Wine Land), shows the primacy of this main product in the minds of the explorers and in the collective memory of the medieval storytellers. This resource-focused naming of the land was also practiced by Leif's father in his naming of Greenland, for the grazing potential of the land. After Bjarni Herjolfsson's initial discovery of the lands beyond Greenland, *Greenlanders' Saga* also portrays Leif's exploration as resource-centered. For instance, in the first land, Helluland (Stone-slab Land), the saga reports that there was "no grass" and that the land was "like a single flat slab of stone all the way from the sea to the glaciers."[35] The saga declares, "this land seemed to them useless."[36] In the second land, Leif declares "the virtues of this land will give it name and it will be called Markland (Forest Land)."[37] For an island like Greenland, barren of native forests or trees, wood was an valuable resource. As the Icelandic annal entry from 1347 indicates, Norse Greenlanders continued to visit Markland for resource extraction for centuries afterward. Finally, Leif makes landfall in a land to the south of Markland, which is subsequently called Vínland. Here he encounters grass covered in dew that was sweeter than any they had ever tasted.[38] For sedentary pastoralists, this would sound like an ideal landscape for grazing livestock. Leif and his crew initially build temporary shelters in the form of booths (búðir), but quickly decide to make a more permanent base, building "large houses" (hús mikil) by a freshwater stream that runs from a lake to the ocean and is filled with salmon.[39] Remaining there for some months, they find that the weather is so mild that livestock can graze outside all through the winter. This can be contrasted to the situation in Greenland and Iceland, where cattle had to be provisioned with hay to survive winters when forage was snow-covered.

After finishing their housing preparations, Leif organizes two groups to further explore the land. One group stays with the houses while the other explores as far as they can while still being able to return in the evenings. On one of these daily exploratory ventures, Leif's German crewmember, Tyrkir, returns home with news of grapes and grapevines. At this point, the saga makes clear that Leif's voyage is also—and perhaps primarily—an expedition aimed at resource extraction. Leif divides the work of his crew into two tasks: harvesting grapes and felling trees. After loading their ships with these goods, they returned to Greenland, having named this last land for its primary resource, wine-producing grapes.[40]

In *Greenlanders' Saga*, the third Vínland voyage, which was made by Leif's brother Thorvald, is explicitly made because Thorvald felt that "the land had been inadequately explored."[41] Thorvald returns to Leif's Booths (Leifsbúðir) in Vínland and spends one summer exploring by sea to the west along the coast and the second summer exploring along the coast to the east.[42] Thorvald finds an idyllic spot for a permanent farm, but after his untimely death at the hands of natives, his crew loads "grapes and grapevines" (vínber og vínvið) onto the ships and returns to Greenland.[43]

The next trip to Vínland detailed in *Greenlanders' Saga* also has the dual motives of resource extraction and the possible establishment of a permanent settlement. At the start of this voyage, led by Thorfinn Karlsefni, explorers make an agreement to divide equally among themselves any valuable resources that they find. The crew that Karlsefni organizes includes sixty men and five women, a gender division probably reflective of resource extraction goals rather than the foundation of a permanent settlement.[44] Perhaps the intention was for some to stay behind in Vínland while others returned to Greenland with the valuables. In any case, the saga informs us of their intentions directly: "they brought all sorts of livestock with them because they wanted to settle in the land if they could."[45] The conditional voice in the saga narrative is noteworthy and fits well with the

Viking spirit of opportunism: permanent settlement if possible and resource extraction if not. Upon arriving back at the Leif's Booth's site in Vínland, the crew begins the work of collecting the rich natural resources: "Karlsefni had trees felled and hewn to load aboard his ship, laying the timber on a large boulder to dry."[46] The saga continues, "they had all the resources of the land . . .including grapes, all kinds of fish and game."[47] The fish and game named here were immensely useful supplements to Norse subsistence and would surely have raised the prospects of permanent settlement in the minds of the saga audience. These hopes are abruptly dashed in the saga's next sentence, with the arrival of the natives. After the encounter with the natives, addressed further in the section below, Karlsefni's crew opts for resource extraction rather than permanent settlement. The saga says, "now they prepared for their journey and took with them a large quantity of the land's resources: grapevines, berries [grapes], and animal skin products."[48] The skins were acquired largely from trade with natives, although in the long term, the potential hostilities appear to have outweighed the advantages of potential trade. Concerning the value of the products, the saga relates Karlsefni's trading voyage back to Norway: "men say that no ship departing from Greenland was ever loaded with a more valuable cargo than this one captained by Karlsefni."[49] His cargo likely included the combined products of Greenland and Vínland. As related above, he certainly received a healthy price of half a mark of gold for his Vínlandic burlwood ship prow.

The final voyage in *Greenlanders' Saga*, led by Freydis Eiriksdottir and two Icelandic brothers, begins with an agreement to split the profits between the two parties. Immediately prior to their departure, the saga tells us that Greenland was buzzing with talk of organizing another trip to Vínland, "because the voyage seemed to bring both wealth and honor."[50] This explicit statement of motivations for the final Vínland voyage references the financial benefits but also draws attention to the social capital gained by undertaking these trips. Although harder to quantify, it must have been substantial. It is also noteworthy that Karlsefni's encounter with the natives at Leif's Booths does not deter further voyages. In fact, Freydis' group encounters no natives, despite spending an entire winter in Vínland. When Freydis' group does leave Vínland, the saga tells us that they loaded the ship "with all the resources they could gather," but it does not articulate the precise products, perhaps because, at this stage in the saga, the products of Vínland have been made clear on multiple occasions.[51]

Eirik's Saga recounts very similar motives for the Vínland voyages, although it only records two separate journeys. Leif Eiriksson's accidental discovery of Vínland includes a description of the land that highlights its valuable resources: "self-sown wheat and grapevines grew there. Also, there were trees, called *mǫsurr* [burl-bearing trees, possibly maple]. They took samples of all of these products."[52] The saga adds that some of the trees were so large that they could be used for building houses.[53] This description corroborates the two main products—grain and grapevines—referenced in *Greenlanders' Saga*, while also underscoring the value of large construction timbers unavailable in Greenland and Iceland.

The second trip failed to reach the destination, but the third and final voyage to Vínland recorded in *Eirik's Saga* provides the most detailed description of the lands on the way to and around Vínland (see voyages in Table 7.1). The voyage set out with 140 people in three ships under the leadership of Thorfinn Karlsefni. As in *Greenlanders' Saga*, the text explicitly states that "they brought all sorts of livestock with them."[54] Karlsefni's group travels across the ocean to the Bear Islands (presumably named for polar bears) before traveling south to Helluland (Slab-Land), which is characterized by flat slabs of stone, as described also in *Greenlanders' Saga*. Traveling farther south, they find Markland (Forest-Land), which is, as in *Greenlanders' Saga*, characterized by extensive forests of large trees. *Eirik's Saga* adds that the land has many animals. Sailing on past peninsulas, inlets, and a long beach that they call Furðustrandir (Wonder Beaches), they go ashore to explore the land. Here they discover the same resources described by Leif: self-sown wheat and grapes. They settle in for the winter with their livestock at a place called Straumfjörð (Tide-fjord), where they find a series of wild food resources, particularly birds, a beached whale, and eggs so plentiful that they had to be careful to not step on them.[55] The two *Eirik's Saga* manuscripts diverge slightly here in the description of the landscape. The *Hauksbók* manuscript is terser, while *Skálholtsbók* elaborates that "the grass grew tall" and "their livestock improved."[56] Both manuscripts agree, however, that the group prioritized exploration over food procurement, that they suffer a harsh winter, and that the group's efforts at hunting and fishing fail. Overall, both manuscripts of *Eirik's Saga* agree that the fruits of the land at Straumfjörð do not provide nearly as idyllic an existence as does the landscape around Leif's Booths described in *Greenlanders' Saga*.

In the spring, the group splits in three, one staying at Straumfjörð, a second sailing west, and a third sailing south along the eastern coast of the land. Karlsefni leads the voyage south along the east coast, settling in and building temporary dwellings (*búðir*) beside a lake with a freshwater stream leading into a lagoon.[57] The place, which they call Hóp (Tidal Lagoon), has self-sown wheat in the lowlands, grapevines in the hills, deer in the forest, and "every stream there was filled with fish."[58] Karlsefni's crew returns to Straumfjörð, where quarrels break out among the Norsemen because "the men who had no women tried to take those of the married men."[59] Significantly, although the resources are the same as those mentioned in *Greenlanders' Saga*, *Eirik's Saga* does not explicitly specify that any of these resources were brought back to Greenland. This is a substantial difference indicative of distinct aims between the two sagas: resource exploitation in *Greenlanders' Saga* and permanent settlement in *Eirik's Saga*.

Native Encounters

Succinct confirmation of the saga narrative describing the meeting between Norsemen and North American natives is found in *Íslendingabók*. The author of *Íslendingabók* argues, based on the remains of skin boats and stone tools found in Greenland, that the previous inhabitants of Greenland used the same material culture as the inhabitants of Vínland. The author concludes that they were "the same kind of people," which he calls Skrælings.[60] What is meant by "the same kind of people" is less clear, but certainly the author assumes that similar material culture is an indication of similar racial phenotypes. The author of *Íslendingabók* tacitly assumes that the audience knows the stories of the Vínland voyages but says no more. Besides a very short mention in *Eyrbyggja Saga* of an Icelander who died in a battle with the Skrælings, only *Greenlanders' Saga* and *Eirik's Saga* relate anything further about the natives of Vínland and the interactions that resulted from their meeting with the Norse explorers.

Greenlanders' Saga and *Eirik's Saga* tell comparable but distinct stories. In *Greenlanders' Saga*, the Norse travelers encounter natives during two of six expeditions: during the third voyage led by Thorvald Eiriksson and the fifth voyage led by Karlsefni. *Eirik's Saga*, which discusses only three voyages altogether, records a native encounter during the third voyage, led by Karlsefni. The first encounter in *Greenlanders' Saga* is violent and disturbing from our modern perspective. While searching for a place to build his farm east of Leif's original settlement, Thorvald comes across three skin boats with three men under each boat.[61] The Norsemen catch and kill eight of the men for no apparent reason, while the last of the natives manages to escape in one of the boats. The Norsemen then see some hill-shaped features farther up the fjord and assume them to be native settlements.

After some time, the natives, which the text calls Skrælings, counterattack in "a vast number of skin boats" from which they shoot arrows, one of which wounds and kills Thorvald.[62] This encounter is not recorded in *Eirik's Saga*. In *Eirik's Saga*, Thorvald does not lead his own voyage, but takes part in the last voyage with Karlsefni, during which Thorvald's death is still attributed to an arrow shot. The *Eirik's Saga* narrative replaces Thorvald's native attackers with a one-legged man, a stock character in the learned medieval Latin tradition that traces its origins to Pliny's *Natural History* from the first century AD.

In both sagas, the main encounters between Vikings and native North Americans happen in the voyage led by Karlsefni and Gudrid. Their voyage was a multi-year settlement effort, including men, women, and livestock. In *Greenlanders' Saga*, the encounter with natives occurs in the second summer at Leif's original settlement, Leif's Booths. A group of native males have a chance encounter with Norse cattle during which they become frightened of a bellowing bull. The natives flee toward the Norse houses but are physically prevented from entering by Karlsefni's men. The saga informs us that they could not understand each other's language. Somewhat surprisingly in what would appear to be a rather precarious situation, however, the natives offer animal skins for trade. Karlsefni forbids the trade of weapons to the natives, but offers various milk-products instead, which the natives readily accept. The saga states: "the trading resulted in the Skrælings carrying away their purchases in their stomachs."[63] Although the exchange seemingly goes well, Karlsefni nonetheless builds a palisade around the settlement. A few months later, before the second winter, the natives return in greater numbers, wishing again to trade. Karlsefni tells his men only to offer the same milk products as before, which the natives seem to accept, and they respond by throwing their packs with animal skins over the palisade. This time, however, things turn badly as one of Karlsefni's men kills a native who the saga says was trying to take Norse weapons. The natives flee, leaving behind their trade goods. Believing the natives will now attack in large numbers, Karlsefni takes his men to a chosen battlefield, leading the way with the bull that had previously frightened the natives. Many natives die in the ensuing battle before a strange event takes place, in which one of the natives picks up a Norse iron axe and strikes one of his companions, who falls over dead. The leader of the natives then examines the axe and throws it far out into the sea. Thereafter the natives flee. Karlsefni and his group stay through the winter, but decide to return to Greenland in the summer, presumably—but not explicitly—because of the escalating issues with the natives.

Greenlanders' Saga offers little detail regarding the natives' physical appearance and does not seem to be negatively predisposed toward their appearance. The leader who throws away the axe is described as "tall and handsome."[64] A native woman is also described during the second trading encounter. While the Norse women bring out the food products for trade, a native woman approaches Gudrid, who sits cradling her young son. The native female is described as "a rather short woman in a black dress with a ribbon in her light brown hair. She was pale and so big-eyed that such big eyes had never been seen in a human head."[65] This interaction between Norse and native women also includes a fascinating, albeit short-lived, attempt at verbal communication. The native woman is curious, asking Gudrid, "What is your name?" Gudrid answers, "my name is Gudrid, what is yours?" Whereupon the native woman responds, "My name is Gudrid."[66] A loud noise and the outbreak of battle breaks off the interaction between the two women. This scene has always been considered strange because of the name duplication, but also because the saga has already informed us that neither group could understand the other's language. A likely explanation is that the scene records a memory of a first encounter upon which the native woman simply repeated Gudrid's words, including her name.[67]

Eirik's Saga tells of native encounters that share many basic similarities with Greenlanders' Saga but contains interesting specifics and key differences in the narrative. As noted above, the main encounters take place during the voyage led by Karlsefni in both sagas. In Greenlanders' Saga the native encounters take place at Leif's Booth, whereas Eirik's Saga sets the encounters in a place called Hóp (Tidal Pool), a site newly founded by Karlsefni and his partner Snorri Thorbrandsson. After a short while at Hóp, Karlsefni's crew sees a group of people in nine skin boats waving wooden poles "sunwise."[68] They read this as a sign of peace and return a Norse sign of peace by raising a white shield. This initial non-verbal communication seemingly goes well and is certainly more positive than the first encounter Thorvald has with the natives in Greenlanders' Saga. At this point, Eirik's Saga provides a physiological description of the natives: "they were dark and grim-looking men and had bad hair on their heads. They were big-eyed and broad-cheeked."[69] In this ascription of physical qualities, Eirik's Saga is more negative than Greenlanders' Saga, whether recording initial impressions or retro-spectively imbuing the native people with unfavorable associations.

Karlsefni's group winters at Hóp. Some time later, the natives return in great numbers of hide boats, again waving poles sunwise as a sign of peace. As in Greenlanders' Saga, a phase of mutually beneficial trading takes place. The natives offer animal skins and in return request red cloth and weapons. As in Greenlanders' Saga, the Norse leaders forbid the trade of weapons. During the trading, and in a clear echo of Greenlanders' Saga, Karlsefni's bull appears and bellows loudly, scaring the natives and causing them to flee in their boats. After three weeks, the natives return, this time offering bellicose signs that include shrieking loudly and waving their poles counter-sunwise. The Norse take up red shields and begin battle against the natives, described as possessing more advanced weapons of war than the group documented in Greenlanders' Saga. In Eirik's Saga, the natives go into battle with "warslings," usually translated as catapults, but they were more likely hand slings.[70] They also wield poles with a large round object on the end, described as "about the size of a sheep's gut and really black in color."[71] When launched from the poles, the object makes a threatening noise as it hits the ground, striking fear into Karlsefni's men. The men flee and are chastised for unmanly behavior by Freydis Eiriksdottir, who is pregnant and cannot move fast enough to escape the natives. Instead, Freydis picks up the sword of a fallen Norseman, Thorbrand Snorrason, who had been killed by a stone projectile. In a strange moment, Freydis turns to face the natives, removes one of her breasts from her dress, and slaps it on the sword. This terrifies the natives, who turn and run. The saga says that the battle resulted in the death of two Norsemen and many natives. The saga then relates a direct parallel to the story of the iron axe in Greenlanders' Saga. The natives find the iron axe next to a second, although unnamed, dead Norseman. They try the axe first on a tree and find it cuts very well. When one of them strikes at a rock, however, the axe breaks. Thinking that a weapon that breaks on a stone is rather worthless, the native throws it away.

At this stage, the saga gives an explicit statement of why the Norsemen abandon their camp: "Karlsefni's group now realized that, despite the land's excellent qualities, they would live in fear and be under constant threat of attack from the natives."[72] On the return trip, Karlsefni has two further confrontations with natives. The first seems to echo Thorvald's first encounter in *Greenlanders' Saga*. They find five natives sleeping in skins along the shore and without any discussion, the Norsemen kill them. The second encounter on the return voyage occurs in Markland, where they meet five natives—perhaps a family—including a bearded man, two women, and two boys. Karlsefni's crew capture and abduct the two boys, subsequently teaching them the Norse language and baptizing them into Christianity. What happens to these boys is unclear, but the saga leads us to believe that they return with the crew to Greenland, where they tell stories of their homeland and the strange neighboring lands where people dress in white clothes, walk around with poles, and wave banners.[73]

A third saga, *Eyrbyggja Saga*, mentions conflict with natives in Vínland as part of Karlsefni's voyage. In relating the fate of one of the saga's characters, *Eyrbyggja Saga* states, "and Snorri went to Vínland the Good with Karlsefni; they fought with the Skrælings in Vínland and there Snorri Thorbrandsson was killed, the bravest of men."[74] This mention occurs in passing while the saga outlines the genealogy of another saga character. This same Snorri Thorbrandsson is mentioned in *Eirik's Saga* as Karlsefni's partner, but he does not appear in *Greenlanders' Saga*.[75] *Eirik's Saga* tells that two of Karlsefni's men died fighting the Skrælings, and among those two dead, only Thorbrand Snorrason is named. This intertextual connection provides a good example of an inconsistency grounded in a broader textual confirmation. Both texts—*Eirik's Saga* and *Eyrbyggja Saga*—record the death of an Icelandic man in conflicts with natives during Karlsefni's journey to Vínland. The two names—Snorri Thorbrandsson and Thorbrand Snorrason—reverse the order of first name and last name patronymic.[76] They could be the names of a father and son pair who both died in Vínland, although this seems unlikely. Rather one or the other is probably a misremembering (or mis-recording) of the fallen Icelander's name.

This confusion over the Snorri Thorbrandsson/Thorbrand Snorrason issue is borne out by a closer look at variations within the original manuscripts of *Eyrbyggja Saga*. One version of the saga derives from the fourteenth-century Vatnshyrna vellum manuscript, which burned in 1728 and has come down to us in two seventeenth-century copies: V_1 and V_2. A second version of the saga derives from the fourteenth-century Wolfenbüttel vellum manuscript (W). Both V_2 and W name the dead man as Snorri Thorbrandsson, and this is followed by the standard Icelandic edited version of the saga and all English translations.[77] However, the V_1

variant of the Vatnshyrna manuscript uses the phrase "Þorbrandr, sonr Snorra" (Thorbrand, Snorri's son), giving the dead man an identity consistent with the name given in *Eirik's Saga*. Delving deeper, we know the identities of the copyists of the V_1 and V_2 version of the sagas. V_1 was transcribed by a learned priest named Ketill Jörundarson (1603–1670), while V_2 was copied by a man named Asgeir Jonsson in Copenhagen in the years 1686–1688.[78] It is unclear which version accurately transcribes the name given in the now-lost original Vatnshyrna manuscript, although the correspondence between V_2 and W versions seems to favor Snorri Thorbrandsson. This would mean that in his V_1 version, Ketill may have tried to correct the name to match the name written in *Eirik's Saga*. Whether either *Eirik's Saga* or *Eyrbyggja Saga* is historically accurate is impossible to say.

In this manuscript comparison, we have reached the limits of seeking specific intertextual confirmation. The Snorri Thorbrandsson/Thorbrand Snorrason disagreement provides another reminder of how the texts continued to change, with post-medieval copyists sometimes trying to correct what they perceived as inconsistencies or errors. The fact that *Eirik's Saga* and *Eyrbyggja Saga* relate essentially the same story of conflict and death in a New World cross-cultural encounter but reverse first and last names of a single character is precisely the minor variation we should expect as traditions are retold in oral form and transcribed into multiple versions in the written form.

Drawing conclusions about the Norse and native encounters from our texts, we can start with the most obvious: they happened. The description of the material culture of the native Vínland inhabitants provided by *Íslendingabók* is echoed in multiple sagas. The natives use skin boats and stone weapons and tools. The two sagas add direct parallel stories of the natives being unfamiliar with iron and discarding an iron axe after unsuccessfully attempting to use it. *Greenlanders' Saga*, *Eirik's Saga*, and *Eyrbyggja Saga* all agree that the Norsemen clashed violently with the natives and that deaths occurred on both sides. *Greenlanders' Saga* and *Eirik's Saga* also record attempts at non-verbal and verbal communication, as well as peaceful trading of animal skins for novel Norse products (milk products from domesticates in *Greenlanders' Saga* and woven red cloth in *Eirik's Saga*). Both sagas explicitly state that the natives desired iron weapons, but that the Norse leaders felt it was dangerous to provide the natives with these weapons and therefore forbade it.

Shifting beyond generalities to specific people, the sagas agree that the main conflicts occurred during Karlsefni's voyage and that these major clashes erupted after failed trading attempts. The sagas also mostly agree on the Norsemen who died on the Vínland voyages. The only named death in *Greenlanders' Saga* is that of Thorvald Eiriksson, who also dies in *Eirik's Saga*, although the sagas disagree about which voyage he was on. *Eirik's Saga's* only other named death, Snorri Thorbrandsson, has a distorted echo in the only line of *Eyrbyggja Saga* that mentions Vínland and the death of Thorbrand Snorrason. Despite some considerable differences then, the saga evidence does provide a consistent view of the Vínland voyages that we can use as an independent data set when interpreting the archaeological evidence.

Legends Made Reality through Archaeology

The search for material traces of Norse voyages to the Americas has long engaged European, Canadian, and American scholars, to say nothing of the public fascination with pursuit of evidence that Vikings "discovered" America. Based on the sailing directions and lands described in the sagas, specialists and enthusiasts alike have proposed numerous different locations for Norse settlements. The uniting factor among these scholars is the belief that the sagas provide geographical information that can be fruitfully compared with the modern landscape to identify Viking Age Scandinavian sites in North America.

By the early to mid-twentieth century, two geographical zones had emerged as the leading candidates for Vínland: a northerly one centered on Newfoundland and a southerly one focused on New England. Scholarly disagreement concerning these two zones revolved around the interpretation of the word "Vínland." Some, who followed Sven Söderberg's suggestion that the "i" in Vínland should be short (Vin-land), meaning "pastureland" rather than "wineland" (Vín-land with a long i), found ample justification for this pastureland translation in the grasslands of northern Newfoundland. This interpretation held that the grapes described in the sagas were a fiction added because of a misreading of the word. Those who believed that the saga authors retained a legitimate tradition about the presence of wild grapes (and not pastureland or other wild berries) favored a southerly location centered in New England and stretching as far south as New York. Other theories proposed areas in-between, such as Nova Scotia and New Brunswick. Periodically, large monuments, such as some interesting stones found around Pistolet Bay in Newfoundland or the Newport Tower in Rhode Island (which turned out to be a historically documented windmill), have been attributed to the Vikings.[79] But none held up to serious scrutiny—that is, until the discoveries made by Helge and Anne-Stine Ingstad.

Helge and Anne-Stine Ingstad: Testing the Legend

Helge Ingstad, a Norwegian explorer who had spent much of his life among the peoples of the circumpolar regions, felt that if he sailed along the same route as the Norse explorers, he would recognize the landforms described in the sagas. He especially felt confident that he could identify landscapes that would be attractive to the Scandinavian sedentary pastoral farmers of the North Atlantic. Ingstad also put great stock in a document known as the Skálholt Map, which was drawn by the Icelander Sigurd Stefánsson in circa 1570. The map depicts Vínland as a peninsula extending north, which to Ingstad looked like the northern finger of Newfoundland (Figure 7.2). When he arrived at the northern tip of Newfoundland, the landscape of L'Anse aux Meadows drew his attention because he felt that the wide grasslands there would have been particularly attractive to Norsemen looking for pasturelands (Figure 7.3).

When Ingstad, accompanied by his daughter Benedicte, went ashore in the village of L'Anse aux Meadows in 1961, he was not the first researcher to believe that L'Anse aux Meadows could be a Viking landing site, nor was he even the first Scandinavian who had asked the local population about old ruins. The Newfoundlander William Munn had suggested in 1914 that Leif first stepped ashore at L'Anse aux Meadows, and that this was the place where *Greenlanders' Saga* recorded Leif tasting the sweet dew on the grass. Subsequently, in 1955, the Dane Jørgen Medlegaard visited the area, including L'Anse aux Meadows, but decided to target his excavations in Pistolet Bay at Wester Brook.[80] Six years later, when Ingstad asked the people from the local fishing village of L'Anse aux Meadows whether they had seen any old ruins, a man named George Decker showed him a series of grass covered hillocks to the west of the village. These ruins faced the Bay of Epaves and had the characteristics of collapsed Norse turf houses. In the 1960s, Ingstad and his archaeologist wife, Anne-Stine, carried out excavations at the site and discovered a series of Norse structures and artifacts, including a distinctively Viking-style bronze ring pin, that beyond any doubt established the site as the first—and still only—Viking Age Scandinavian site in North America.

The Wider Landscape Setting of L'Anse aux Meadows

The natural setting of the L'Anse aux Meadows site includes many features that would have been attractive to Norse explorers and potential settlers. The Norse site sits on the tip of the finger-like and northernmost extension of the island of Newfoundland. This northern tip of Newfoundland is separated from the coast of mainland Labrador by the circa 50-kilometer-wide Strait of Belle Isle. In the middle of the strait lies the small island of Belle Isle. Seafarers proceeding south along the coast of Baffin Island and Labrador would have been helped along by the south-flowing Labrador Current until they arrived at Belle Isle, where they would have found themselves for the first time with land on both sides of their ship. Crossing over east to Belle Isle and then on to Newfoundland would have brought them into a series of bays and coves. It is in one of these inlets, Epaves

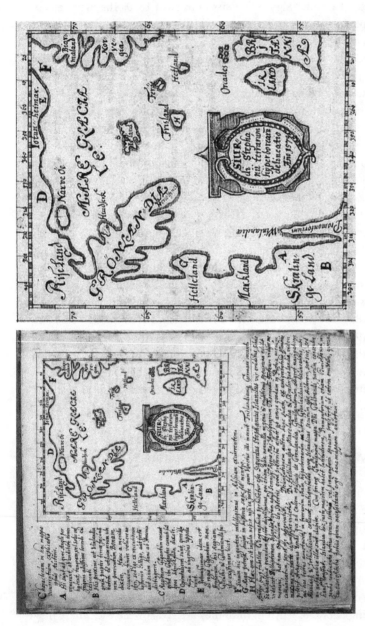

Figure 7.2 The Skálholt Map from c. 1590. The Map tries to reconcile the stories of the Norse voyages with the post-Columbian explorations of North America. The capital letters on the map each have corresponding Latin text. The letter B locates Vinland, which is described as follows: "B: Next to these [the Skrælings] lies Vinland, which has been called The Good because of its good soil and abundance of other good things. Men from our country thought that this land was bounded by the ocean in the south, but as a result of more recent [scholars'] information I have come to the conclusion that it is separated from America by a sound or a bay."

Source: Det Kongelige Bibliotek, Denmark (public domain). Translation by Helge Ingstad 1985: 324

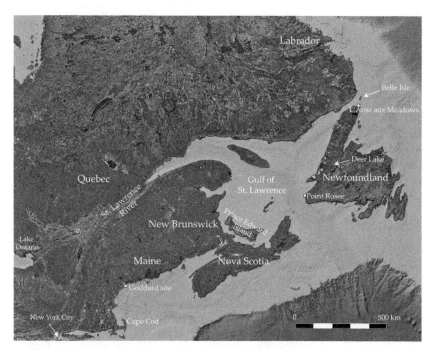

Figure 7.3 The Gulf of St. Lawrence and surrounding lands.
Source: map by author

Bay, that the Norse built their settlement. Epaves Bay, a shallow bay just west of L'Anse aux Meadows, offered the Norse a place to beach their ships. A small stream, Black Duck Brook, flows northwest from a nearby pond into Epaves Bay. Landscape reconstruction has shown that in the Viking Age, the water level was almost 1 m higher, meaning that Viking ships could have been pulled partially up the stream. Despite the positive attributes of Epaves Bay, however, the site is very exposed to storms; other bays farther east offer better shelter. Likely, the explorers preferred to build their exploratory settlement close to the strait of Belle Isle so that they could monitor possible passersby. Building in this location would have ensured its visibility so that the site itself could be found again on return trips.

The landscape had other attractive features. Freshwater from the stream was essential, while the grasslands around the site offered fodder to animals, if, in fact, the Norse brought domesticated animals. Off-shore islands, such as Belle Isle, might also have been used for grazing livestock. The explorers built their structures just above the beach on an elevated relic beach terrace. On either side of the terrace, peat bogs offered access to peat for fuel and presented readily available turf necessary for building the large turf buildings.

The construction of the large permanent turf structures would have taken at least several months, representing a significant investment on the part of the inhabitants. The structures, which were roofed and boasted central hearths and thick insulating turf walls, were suitable for permanent and year-round habitation. At a minimum, the builders intended this to be a permanent multi-year base for exploration and resource extraction in the new land. The site would have been relatively easy to find on return journeys. Additionally, because of the unique landscape as seen from the sea when journeying south along Labrador, the location of the turf houses could have been described to other Norsemen in Greenland interested in exploring Vínland, extracting its resources, or making an attempt at permanent settlement.

Archaeology of L'Anse aux Meadows

The location and especially the layout of the Norse settlement of L'Anse aux Meadows are atypical for Viking Age settlements in the North Atlantic. The unusual character can be attributed to the role that the site had as an exploratory base camp, rather than a standard farming settlement. L'Anse aux Meadows instead exhibits preference for accessibility from a long-distance travel route and cooperation among an unusually large number of inhabitants.

The L'Anse aux Meadows settlement comprises eight turf buildings organized into three separate but coordinated complexes (Figure 7.4). Each of the three complexes is centered on a large longhouse for habitation, with one or more smaller ancillary hut-like structures constructed alongside each longhouse. The groupings likely represent three social divisions, probably three ship's crews and/or family groups. This type of clustering is unusual in the North Atlantic. To date, it has only been documented in Iceland at a handful of sites dating to the very early phases of the settlement of the island. There, house clustering appears to have been a cooperative strategy employed during the phase of exploration and the initial efforts at settling new lands. In Iceland, the settlers quickly dispersed across the landscape, shifting to a settlement pattern composed of widely separated farmstead complexes made up of a single longhouse and associated smaller buildings and byres for animals.

The L'Anse aux Meadows site shows signs of a short, albeit probably multi-year, habitation dating to the first decades of the 1000s.[81] The middens at the site were thin, much thinner than typical Viking Age middens in the North Atlantic area, indicating a relatively short-lived occupation. Because of the site's uniqueness and the importance of establishing a precise chronology, partially driven by desires to link the site to the sagas, many radiocarbon dates have been obtained for L'Anse aux Meadows: a total of 148 samples site-wide with about

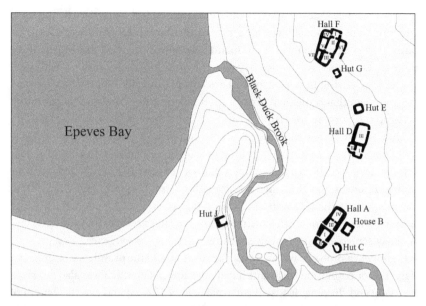

Figure 7.4 L'Anse aux Meadows, the only verified Norse site in North America. The cluster of three large halls with ancillary structures is unusual for Norse North Atlantic sites and characterizes the exploratory phase of Norse settlement expansion. The three halls might suggest three ships or at least three separate social groups.

Source: map by author based on Wallace 2000: 210 and 2006: 88

50 of these relating to the Norse habitation phase. Results were skewed by the presence of old carbon in many of the samples. The most accurate dates were obtained from seven samples from young branches and twigs, and these have a mean calibrated intercept of 1014 and a range between 990 and 1050. The date range obtained from radiocarbon dating is consistent with the dating estimates from artifact typologies of objects recovered in the excavations, such as a bronze ring-pin, a soapstone spindle whorl, a glass bead, and a quartzite whetstone for needles. The ring pin in particular can be closely dated to between circa 925 and 1025, while the rest of the objects belong typologically to the Viking Age in the North Atlantic.[82] It is also notable that features of the long houses—specifically the turf walls built directly on the ground without stone footings—are typical of the Viking Age in the North Atlantic.

Although a modest quantity of objects and work debitage was recovered across the site, L'Anse aux Meadows is relatively artifact poor. This likely indexes the short habitation and orderly abandonment of the site, rather than serving as any indication of the status of the occupants. Moreover, the artifacts provide further evidence that the site was different from typical Norse farms. The most common finds are not objects that typify regular farm life, but rather relate to industrial work, specifically iron production, woodworking, and ship repair. These three types of work are divided between the three longhouse clusters, with each cluster specializing in one of the three activities. This division of labor bolsters the argument that settlement organization reflects a high degree of cooperation between the Norse residents.

One of the three building clusters—complex A-B-C—consists of three buildings used for living and working quarters (see Figure 7.4). Hall A had an external length of 29 m, with an internal floor space of 102 m^2 divided into four rooms. Rooms I and II formed a unit, with central fireplaces and wide, raised benches within the side aisles indicating that the spaces functioned as living/sleeping quarters. Room III, which had two separate entrances from Rooms I and II, likely served as a small-scale smithing workshop, as evidenced by a possible forge fire pit, a probable wooden base for an anvil, and the prevalence of smithing slag. A door connected this smithing area to Room IV, which was also designed for living and sleeping. House B (internal area of 17.5 m^2 and external length of 7.9 m), which is located beside Hall A, served both as living quarters and possibly a place for roasting bog ore. These activities left behind a 26-centimeter-thick and 65-centimeter-wide deposit of mixed ash, charcoal, and roasted ore beside a central hearth where two large stone boulders used to crush the roasted ore were recovered. A small building, Hut C, was positioned just outside the southwest door of House A. The small size (7.5 m^2 floor space) and a central fireplace indicate that this modest hut was probably used as low-status living quarters.

The second building cluster—Complex D-E—consisted of a longhouse (Hall D, 20 m in external length with 88.36 m^2 floor space) and a small ancillary building (Hut E). Hall D, the smallest of the three halls, had one main living and sleeping room (Room III) and two work rooms. The three rooms were essentially three separate structures abutting each other that each had separate roofs and individual external entrances, while only the smaller rooms were connected internally by a door. Absence of activity-related artifacts suggests Room I was a storage room. Room II was used for carpentry, as evidenced by the woodworking debris spilling out of the doorway and into the adjacent bog, which fortunately preserved the wood in water-logged deposits. Hut E (13.65 m^2 floor space) was probably a working space, as indicated by a store of nineteen fist-sized cobbles of the type used both as net sinkers and for weighing down the yarn on a vertical loom.

The third building cluster—Complex F-G—encompassed the site's largest longhouse (Hall F, 160 m^2 floor space) and an ancillary building (Hut G, 7.76 m^2). Hall F had seven separate rooms, five of which were connected by internal doors. A sixth room (Room VII) was accessible only from the outside, as was a lean-to addition (Room VI) built onto the east side of the hall. Rooms I, II, and III, which were all equipped with central fireplaces and benches along the walls, served as living/sleeping spaces. Room II was located at the heart of the building with no external entrances and had a long (2.25 m) fireplace in the center and wooden paneling along the inside of the walls. The cut iron ship nails known as clench bolts found in and around the open-gabled shed added to the east side of Hall F suggest that this area was used for boat repair, while the size of the shed (c. 7 m long and 3 m wide) suggests that the boat (or boats) repaired here was a small craft rather than a large ocean-going vessel.

In addition to the three clusters, a single building (Hut J) used for iron production was located across the stream.[83] Excavators found a stone anvil and a furnace for smelting iron inside this structure. The furnace was formed by stone slabs set on end in a square, forming a box that was then sealed with smaller stones and clay. Holes at the front of the furnace allowed for insertion of bellows used to raise the temperature of the charcoal fuel and iron ore. The charcoal was produced a short distance from this building, where a charcoal pit was found.[84] Bog ore was readily available along the nearby stream. Evidence suggests that iron production was only carried out once at this site. Wallace suggests that anywhere between 3 and 5 kg of iron was produced, and that this production episode was targeted at nails and clench bolts for ship repair. Over eighty nail fragments were recovered at the site, but only one intact nail. This intact nail had a sulfur content that was higher than all analyzed nail fragments. This higher sulfur content matched that of the local iron ore, indicating that local ore was used to produce this new nail.[85] Approximately 100–200 nails could have been produced with the 3 to 5 kg of iron smelted here, which indicates that the others likely found use in repairs to the vessels in which the Norsemen had arrived. Residue from iron smithing, probably of nails, was also found in Hut J as well as House A, while the actual ship repair took place in the lean-to of Hall F.[86]

While iron was produced locally, other objects show connections to the wider Viking world and provide some indication of where the site's inhabitants might have traveled. One of the most diagnostic Viking Age finds recovered from the site was the bronze ring pin. The style of this pin originates from the Viking-Celtic cultural area around the Irish Sea. It became common in the North Atlantic in the tenth to eleventh centuries and has been found at sites in the Faroes, Iceland, and Greenland.[87] This object supports the general conclusion that the people at L'Anse aux Meadows were part of the North Atlantic Viking Age diaspora. Unfortunately, most of the other objects, such as the soapstone spindle whorl and the glass bead, are common throughout the Viking North Atlantic and are therefore neither as geographically nor as temporally diagnostic as the ring pin. Instead, approaches using archaeological sciences were needed to move beyond the style of the artifacts and gain insight into their provenience.

An innovative geochemical study of ten jasper strike-a-lights found at L'Anse aux Meadows revealed the source from which the stones were acquired. The Norse used these stones to start fires by striking the stone with iron to make sparks. Instrumental Neutron Activation Analysis (INAA) was employed to identify trace elements in the jasper at L'Anse aux Meadows, as well as in potential sources of jasper in the North Atlantic. The geochemical signatures of the jasper from L'Anse aux Meadows were then compared with the signatures from the jasper samples taken from the potential source sites. The study revealed that five of the jasper fragments came from Iceland, while four came from Greenland, and one derived from a source in Newfoundland about 250 km to the south. The results connect the population at L'Anse aux Meadows directly with Iceland and Greenland. The mundane character of these artifacts means that they likely stayed in the possession of the people who initially acquired them. The spatial distribution of these strike-a-light fragments across the site may therefore help us understand the social groupings and geographical origins of these groups. Halls A and D yielded only jasper from Iceland, suggesting that these halls may have been inhabited by people—perhaps two ship's crews—from Iceland. Hall F contained both Icelandic and Greenlandic jasper, suggesting that Greenlanders and Icelanders shared the largest hall at the site. The piece of Newfoundlandic jasper indicates exploration and resource extraction farther to the south.[88]

Searching for Additional Archaeological Evidence

Archaeological evidence of the Norse exploration of North America has been sought in Scandinavian colonies throughout the North Atlantic and widely in the Americas. Very little verifiable archaeological evidence has been encountered. Back in Greenland, only one native North American arrowhead has been recovered in the many excavations of Norse sites on the island. Aside from the indisputable evidence of the settlement at L'Anse aux Meadows, no other Norse settlements in North America have been found. The best evidence comes from loose finds of Norse material culture in sites in northern Canada. South of L'Anse aux Meadows, a single Norse object has been found at a Native American site. The search for such sites and Viking visitors has resulted in many false starts, forgeries, and fruitless field seasons.

Native North American Material Culture in Greenland
Only a single piece of verifiable North American Native material culture has been found in the Norse layers in Greenland. A chert arrowhead matching types used by Native peoples in Labrador and Newfoundland between 1000 and 1500 was found eroding out of the Christian graveyard at the farm of Sandnes

in the Western Settlement.[89] Because it was not found in any particular grave, the dating and context of this projectile point are impossible to establish with any greater accuracy. The reason that it was deposited in a graveyard is equally obscure. An exciting narrative might have the projectile point lodged in a Norseman who had voyaged to Markland, joined battle with natives, and then returned to the Western Settlement—either dead or alive—for final Christian burial at Sandnes.[90] The saga story of Thorvald Eiriksson's death by a native arrow in the New World and the intent of his brother Thorstein to bring him back for proper burial could be held up as a possible analog. Alternatively, the arrowhead may have been a souvenir brought back from a voyage, and subsequently either purposefully deposited in a grave or lost accidentally in the graveyard. However it arrived in Greenland, this projectile point remains a tantalizing allusion to the transport of New World materials throughout the North Atlantic.

Loose Finds in Native American Sites
Norse material culture has been found in a number of pre-Columbian Native American sites. These materials provide credible and scientifically document-able evidence of contacts between native groups and Norse Viking Age and me-dieval populations. These sites are almost exclusively located in the circumpolar region, north of the arctic circle (65° N). Objects that are identifiable as Norse— or at the very least, European—are primarily worked iron, the exogenous origins confirmed by the fact that iron was not produced in pre-Columbian North America except in rare cases when meteoric iron was used. These iron objects are primarily nails and ship rivets. Wooden objects or fragments of objects that are diagnostically Norse have also been found, like components of barrels and ship timbers. Finally, some figurative art found in Native settlements may depict Norse people.

Archaeological evidence indicates interaction between Norse and indige-nous circumpolar peoples—Thule and probably Dorset populations—in north-western Greenland and in northeastern Canada.[91] In the far north, a voyage of less than 50 km across Smith Sound separates Greenland and Ellesmere Island in northeastern Canada. Norse objects have been found at indigenous sites on ei-ther side of Smith Sound (Figure 7.1).[92] A substantial number of Norse artifacts have been found at Thule sites on Skraeling Island (Canada) and Ruin Island (Greenland) from around 1300. The Skraeling Island site yielded over fifty probable Norse artifacts, including iron objects like ship rivets, knife and spear blades, and a piece of chain mail, as well as smelted copper. The Ruin Island site yielded similar objects, including an iron spear blade, a lump of chain mail, and smelted copper. The similarity and concentration of these finds, combined with the multiple ship rivets from Skraeling Island, indicate that they might have been salvaged from a single Norse shipwreck.[93]

Alternatively, other and somewhat more domestic finds in this zone might indicate trading interactions involving all three population groups: Norse, Dorset, and Thule. For instance, evidence of interaction between Norse and a remnant Dorset population was extrapolated from the leg of a bronze cooking pot found in a thirteenth-century Dorset house at Qeqertaaraq, located in northern Greenland.[94] A Thule (Proto-Inuit) house at the nearby Greenlandic site of Inuarfissuaq yielded imports of both Dorset-style decorated walrus tusks and Norse iron. One interesting suggestion holds that members of the newly arrived and highly mobile Thule culture served as intermediaries between Dorset walrus hunters and the Norse.[95] Another concentration of Norse finds—including whetstones, cordage, and worked wood—has been found in Dorset sites on the south coast of Baffin Island.[96] The Norse origins of some of these findings are still controversial: recent analysis of spun yarn at Dorset and Thule sites, for instance, suggests that the yarn fragments thought to be Norse imports derive instead from an independent indigenous tradition.[97]

One of the most evocative finds is a small figurine discovered on the house floor of a thirteenth-century Thule structure at Okivilialuk, located on the south coast of Baffin Island. The figurine appears to depict a Norseman (Figure 7.5).[98] The featureless face is a common Thule style; but the dress has provoked scholarly excitement. The figure wears an ankle-length robe with pleats and a yoked hood. The tunic is open in the front from the waist down. A cross hanging from the figure's neck, like an amulet, completes the picture of a Christian European—possibly Greenlandic—visitor. The figure does not appear threatening and wields no weapons. The Thule house where the figurine was found was constructed with a roof of whale ribs, reminding us that the hunter-gatherer Thule-controlled sea-mammal resources would have been of great interest to Norse traders. In particular, walrus ivory could have generated extraordinary profits in mainland Europe. The items found in the Thule settlements, coupled with the depiction of the Okivilialuk Figurine, suggest peaceful trade. Ivory is the most likely resource that would make such a trading voyage to Baffin Island and the Canadian Arctic worthwhile for the Norse Greenlanders.

Farther south, in Labrador, the trail of Norse contact goes cold. Whereas the islands of Ellesmere and Baffin were valued for trade in ivory, Labrador would probably have offered primarily wood, an increasingly valuable construction material for the Greenlandic Norse. Gathering construction wood would not require contact with native peoples, and in fact probably would have been better accomplished without any native encounter. An absence of valuable native-controlled trade goods in this area may account for why there is little archaeological evidence of exchange between Norsemen and Native Americans in native sites in Labrador.

Figure 7.5 The Okivilialuk Figurine, depicting a person seemingly dressed in European style clothes and wearing a cross pendant, was found in a thirteenth-century Thule house on the southern coast of Baffin Island.
Source: Canadian Museum of History, KeDq-7:325

Far to the south, the most tantalizing of all the Norse finds outside of L'Anse aux Meadows is a Norwegian penny that was found in 1957 by an amateur archaeologist working at a Native American site called Goddard on Penobscot Bay in Maine.[99] It was not until 1978 that it was correctly identified as a Norwegian coin minted in the reign of Olaf the Peaceful between 1065 and 1080 (Figure 7.6).[100] Unlike the objects described above from Thule and late-Dorset sites, which are clearly of European origin but not diagnostic of a precise time period, this object has an unassailable chronological origin in the Viking Age, albeit the very end of the period. The coin was perforated at the top and probably worn as a necklace. The coin does not mean that Norsemen necessarily came to Maine. Rather, the coin probably arrived at the Goddard site through down-the-line trade. This possibility is reinforced by the fact that subsequent professional

Figure 7.6 A Norwegian penny from the reign of Olaf the Peaceful (1065–1080) found at the Native North American site of Goddard on the coast of Maine.
Source: Collections of the Maine State Museum (72.73.1/ME 30.42.1)

archaeological work at the Goddard site has not yielded any further Norse objects. Excavations at Goddard also recovered hundreds of Ramah chert flakes from northern Labrador and a reutilized Dorset tool imported from Labrador or Newfoundland. The Goddard site, which has turned out to be the largest coastal site in Maine from 900 to 1500, was a trading hub for goods from up and down the Eastern Seaboard—including a coin possibly obtained from the Norse by Dorset traders.

But the Goddard Penny has its problems too. Some—such as anthropologist Edmund Carpenter—have suggested that the coin may have been planted. This assertion is based on distrust of the amateur archaeologist, Guy Mellgren, who found the penny. He was known to have an interest in pre-Columbian interactions between Europeans and Native Americans, as well as a part-time job at an auction house where he could have obtained access to Norse coins.[101] In a thorough review of the coin evidence, however, the Norwegian numismatist Svein Gullbekk demonstrates that no Olaf the Peaceful coins of this type (a variant of class N) were sold from known Norwegian hoards or single finds prior to the 1957 find-date.[102] Gullbekk's close inspection also found that the Goddard Penny has the type of extensive wear found on loose finds, as opposed to the more limited wear usually found on coins from hoards, which typically appear on auction.[103] The evidence leans strongly toward the coin being genuine, although the case remains admittedly unsolved or, as Carpenter says, "not proven."[104]

Strange Runes and Rune Stones in Strange Places
Potentially the earliest written mention of Vínland—predating Adam of Bremen's work—comes from a now-lost runic inscription from Hønen in Norway.[105] Significant doubt exists about the veracity of the stone and also about the interpretations of the inscription.[106] But if it was indeed a real epitaph for a deceased voyager to Vínland, it is dramatic. The text, which was dated to circa 1050, has been reconstructed in different ways, but might have read as follows:

> ... They came out and over wide expanses, and needing cloth to dry themselves in and food, away towards Vínland, up into the ice in the uninhabited land. Evil can take away luck, so that one dies early.[107]

The reference to Vínland (written as UINLAT on the stone) is controversial, but the mention of the "uninhabited land" (*úbygd*) is more secure, as it is typically used in other texts to refer to the uninhabited regions of Greenland. The latter allusion is credible since both texts and archaeological evidence indicate that Norsemen traveled to the northern parts of western Greenland, well beyond the walrus hunting grounds around Disko Bay, known to the Norse as Norðsetr (Figure 7.1).

A more secure runic inscription was found on a stone within one of three Norse-style cairns built atop a mountain on Kingittorsuaq Island at 73 degrees north, just over 1,000 km north of the Western Settlement and 1,500 km north of the Eastern Settlement (Figure 7.7). The text, which appears to date from the twelfth to the fifteenth centuries, is clear and reads: "Erling Sighvatsson and Bjarni Thordarson and Eindridi Oddsson on the Saturday before the minor Rogation Day [25 April] piled these cairns and rode . . ."[108] The cairns were likely set up in a visible location to help guide future voyages to the northern hunting grounds. Regarding the question of Vínland, the Kingittorsuaq stone provides material proof that Greenlanders traveled far from their two main settlements in southwest Greenland. These travels would have taken them through the narrowest point (c. 320 km wide) on the Davis Strait that separates Greenland from Baffin Island. From there, the mountains of Baffin Island can be seen only a short distance from the Greenlandic shore. On a short journey into the open sea, which the Norsemen would have made to hunt the walrus that gathered in the bottleneck of the strait, they would have seen the mountains of Davis Point on Baffin Island.[109]

A substantial number of stones with Scandinavian-style runic inscriptions have been reported over the past two centuries in North America. However, none of these inscriptions appear to be genuine. These stones range in find

Figure 7.7 The Kingittorsuaq Runestone found on Kingittorsuaq Island, far to the north of the Western Settlement in Greenland. The stone was left within a cairn atop a mountain, probably by a Norse hunter in the thirteenth century.
Source: photo by Lennart Larsen; National Museum of Denmark (CC-BY-SA

location from Spirit Pond, Maine, to Heavener, Oklahoma. Most of these finds, like the Heavener Stone, were never really considered believable by the academic community. Others, like the Spirit Pond Stones found in 1971, took more effort to be proven fraudulent. Often it was the alphabet, the grammar, and the vocabulary that gave the stones away as hoaxes. As famous linguist Einar Haugen put it about the Spirit Pond Stones, the runes were a few Norse words that stood "out like a sore thumb in a sea of gibberish."[110]

The most famous, elaborate, and impactful runestone hoax was the so-called Kensington Runestone (Figure 7.8). In 1898, a Swedish immigrant named Olof Ohman reported finding this stone beneath some tree roots on his land in Minnesota.[111] The stone had a rather long inscription:

> 8 Goths and 22 Norwegians on an exploration journey from Vínland to the west. We had camp by 2 skerries one day's journey north from this stone. We were out to fish. One day after we came home we found 10 men red of blood and dead. AVM [Ave Maria] save us from evil. We have 10 men by the sea to look after our ships 14 day's travel from this island. [in the year] 1362.[112]

Popular interest and a decision by the Smithsonian Museum to display the stone between 1948 and 1953 resulted in some acceptance of its veracity within the academic community.[113] The Smithsonian press release from 1948 called the

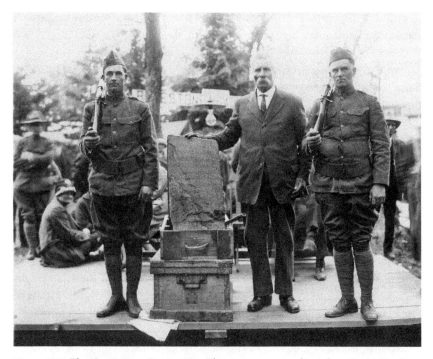

Figure 7.8 The Kensington Runestone. The stone generated much excitement when it was unveiled in 1898 as it suggested that Scandinavians had been to Minnesota during the fourteenth century. In the end, it turned out to be a forgery made by the Swedish immigrant Olof Ohman (seen here next to the stone at a carnival near Kensington) and his friend.
Source: Minnesota Historical Society

Kensington Stone ". . . one of the most significant historical objects ever found in the New World."[114]

From the outset, however, most rune specialists considered the stone a fraud. Their verdict was based on a series of reasons, including the use of improper runic numbers, the lack of patina on the runes, and modernisms in the "Old Norse" language, such as the lack of medieval noun cases and verb conjugations. Scholars looking into Ohman's life found that he had knowledge of runes and that some of the runes on the Kensington Stone were of a nineteenth-century type used in the Swedish province of Dalecarlia, from which his mother had emigrated.[115] In the end, Olof Ohman's neighbor, John Gran, admitted on tape that Olof and a friend had composed the text and that he and Olof chiseled the runes and buried the stone under a tree as a prank.[116] Funny. Even so, the runestone still has its academic supporters, is displayed in the local museum, and is alive in popular culture.[117] You can even view Olof's story

as a musical, "Runestone! The Rock Musical," which sets his internal struggle with
the accusations against him to pop, rock, and Viking metal.[118]

Scientific Approaches and Space Archaeology: Investigations at Point Rosee
Since the Ingstads first proved that Viking Age Scandinavians did indeed reach
the eastern shores of the New World, amateur researchers, members of the interested public, and academics from a diverse range of disciplines have been
searching for a second Norse site in North America. The vastness and complexity of the geography of northeastern Canada and New England, with the
countless bays, inlets, and islands, has made looking for the second Viking site
in the Americas a task comparable to looking for a needle in a haystack. Helge
Ingstad found L'Anse aux Meadows by following the directions of the sagas and
his own intuition as a mariner. This approach narrows the search, but repeated
attempts at duplicating Helge's success have proved futile. Fortunately, new
Scientific methods of remote sensing using satellite imagery are revolutionizing
the possibilities of searching broadly for the relatively small sites that might
have been established by the Norse in North America. Now the vast coastline of
Canada and New England can be surveyed from a computer, in the comfort of a
high-tech lab.

Recently, Sarah Parcak, one of the harbingers of the use of satellite remote
sensing in archaeology, turned her methods to the search for Norse sites in the
North Atlantic. I was in Italy in the summer of 2016 when Sarah Parcak and her
research partner, Greg Mumford, emailed me for a phone conversation about
joining their project in Newfoundland. I had seen a ninety-minute special on
BBC/PBS featuring their work in Newfoundland during the previous summer.[119]
This preliminary work had discovered what appeared to be a second Viking
Age Norse site in North America. Sarah and Greg's offer of contributing to
uncovering such a site was too good to pass up. One month later, I was excavating
an 8x1 m trench at Point Rosee, located on the southern tip of Newfoundland.

Satellite remote sensing relies on the fact that subsurface structures, such as
longhouses and pit features, can affect vegetation health on the surface, resulting
in crop marks that mirror the sub-surface features. This principle has been used
to find sites across the globe with pedestrian and aerial surveys, but the availability of satellite images has revolutionized the field. Furthermore, satellite imagery now captures multiple light spectra, including infrared, which penetrate
the surface to show plant health patterns invisible to the naked eye. This imagery
is still expensive, so it is necessary to use free imagery to start. Parcak's team
began with Google Earth, identifying sixty potential sites in Newfoundland, before using high-resolution aerial photographs to further narrow their search to
six sites. Purchasing multispectral satellite imagery at this stage narrowed the list
to two final candidates. The most promising was Point Rosee on the southwestern

tip of Newfoundland, where the satellite imagery showed what appeared to be outlines of longhouse-sized structures inside a characteristic-looking farmstead boundary wall. Parcak's team then conducted a magnetometry survey on the ground, which revealed magnetic anomalies consistent with the satellite data. The next step was to "ground truth" the remote sensing with excavation.[120]

The first season of excavation, which was featured in the 2015 BBC documentary, found a feature that looked like a turf wall and a possible iron roasting feature. Metallographic analysis revealed that the microstructure of iron-rich samples from the feature appeared consistent with roasted iron. Viking Age iron production involved roasting the iron ore to remove moisture before it was placed in the furnace for smelting. Radiocarbon dates from below the ground surface were also consistent with a possible Viking Age habitation. After the first season, the excavation area opened to assess the possible turf feature needed to be expanded in order to confidently ascertain whether the feature was in fact a man-made wall or just a naturally occurring anomaly. We needed to open a larger exposure of the possible turf features to see the edges of the potential wall and ideally find objects that could be connected to medieval Europeans. Just a single iron nail would go a long way.

The site of Point Rosee situated on the southwestern tip of Newfoundland made sense as a location for a Norse site. In many ways it mirrors the position of the site at L'Anse aux Meadows and could be a jumping-off point to cross the Gulf of St. Lawrence. To the south of the Gulf of St. Lawrence lay the lands that many considered to be the Vínland of the sagas (see below). The sea cliffs below the site were a bit problematic, as there was nowhere nearby to safely pull up a Viking ship. Norsemen conducting reconnaissance for resource exploitation or attempting the initial phases of settlement would typically have chosen a site with an easily accessible beach, stream, or lagoon. Point Rosee does not fit that description and is rather exposed to the sea and potential storms. However, if there was indeed a rich iron-bearing bog source, perhaps this explained the site choice.

Also brought in to help with the excavations of the potential Norse site was an archaeologist from Newfoundland, Blair Temple, and Karen Milek and Óskar Sveinbjarnarson, with whom I had previously worked on excavations in Iceland. From the outset, the results were not encouraging. The putative turf feature kept going in all directions and did not look like a wall. In another unit, I sectioned a similar turf-like feature that had shown up in the magnetometry data and saw only one layer of banded strata. By contrast, a turf wall should have stacked layers of turf in the wall, such that the banded layers should be repeated at least once. Sectioning the original feature that was thought to be a wall showed that it too contained no stacked turfs. Equally problematic was the iron roasting feature. Around the possible iron roasting pit, chunks of iron spread out across the site, more suggestive of a naturally occurring iron-rich deposit than anthropogenic evidence of iron production. After two weeks of digging, we also had not a single man-made artifact to show. There was no convincing evidence of a Norse site.

In terms of the archaeology, in the end we came up empty-handed at Point Rosee. But that is science. Part of what is so striking about the experience is the attention that the site received internationally before it could be conclusively evaluated and verified. This was the allure of the Vikings at work, and more particularly the promise of discovery of their farthest-flung outpost. It would have provided further vindication for the sagas that speak of exploration beyond a single base camp, especially *Eirik's Saga*, which mentions more than one habitation site. When looking back on the work at Point Rosee, the main value in the project is the novel method of survey with satellite imagery that Parcak's team brought to the search for Norse sites in the Americas. More sites will likely be found. And when they are, they will probably be discovered with the increasingly sophisticated application of satellite imagery and new scientific survey methods.

What Does the Correspondence between Text and Archaeology Mean?

Without the archaeological discoveries at L'Anse aux Meadows, the Vínland sagas might still be considered complete literary fabrications. Simultaneously, without the sagas, the archaeological discoveries are unlikely to have been made. Even if they had been made, the site would have remained enigmatic.[121] The discovery of L'Anse aux Meadows, probably more than any other archaeological find, allowed scholars to uphold the historicity of the Icelandic sagas.

The Ingstads' use of the sagas to discover the L'Anse aux Meadows site provided substantial vindication for using these texts to identify sites. This has had important implications for subsequent attempts to identify additional Norse sites, such that the sagas have been the starting point of each of these efforts. In Mats Larsson's opinion, "constructing theories based on analysis of the sagas and using those theories in search for physical traces of the Norsemen is the only possible recourse if we do not want to give up completely or wait for new discoveries by mere chance."[122] Fortunately, new technologies—most obviously the satellite imagery used by Parcak's team to identify potential Norse structures—open avenues for research that do not take the sagas as a necessary starting point.

The Vínland sagas tell stories of amazing voyages beyond the known Viking world. They are occasionally, as with the reference to the one-legged man, soaked in literary inventions and borrowings from a High Medieval Christian worldview. Yet, archaeology now seems to have verified the basic facts of the Vínland sagas, although, as we will see, there is still significant disagreement about to what extent L'Anse aux Meadows site can be equated with any of the specific sites mentioned in the sagas. If the seemingly fantastical Vínland sagas show a high degree of correspondence with the archaeological discoveries, would that not then justify assumptions about the historicity of other less fantastic sagas, such as those about Icelandic chieftains and farmers in Iceland? After all, the thirteenth-century Icelandic saga authors were much closer conceptually to those Icelandic farmers than to the explorers of Vínland. However, what are the limits of the correspondence between the sagas and archaeology? This section explores this question through three topics—the location of Vínland, the identity of the natives, and the presence of livestock—where a high level of specific correspondence has been sought between the written sources and the geographical and archaeological realities.

Location: Where Is Vínland?

The temptation to try to locate Vínland and the Norse settlement sites on the modern geographical map has enticed countless authors to weigh in on the matter. Significantly, the number of suggestions is staggering, and nearly no two scholars agree.[123]

Most scholars who accept the stories as historical fact believe that Helluland is Baffin Island and Markland is some portion—the southern part or the entirety—of Labrador.[124] *Greenlanders' Saga* says that Helluland has glaciers and no glaciers exist in Labrador south of Baffin Island.[125] This limits Helluland to Baffin Island, if the sagas are to be trusted at all. The sagas agree that Markland is characterized by forests. The tree line in coastal Canada lies at N 58°, meaning that northern Labrador is north of the tree line.[126] Substantial forests do not begin until south of N 55°.[127] This should be considered the northern extent of Markland. In general, there is direct correspondence between the saga lands and the geographical realities of the North Atlantic coast of Canada. More major disagreements emerge in locating Vínland, which has been positioned anywhere from southern Labrador to New York City.[128]

To determine the geographical positions of the places mentioned in the sagas, authors have used sailing directions and sailing durations, combined with descriptions of geographical features, natural resources, and native populations. Sailing directions in the sagas are generally consistent with geographical realities of traveling between Greenland and the eastern coast of Canada. After being blown off course, the initial discoverers of the new lands all travel from south to north to return to Greenland. *Greenlanders' Saga* relates that Bjarni keeps the land to his port (left) side as he sails north from the first hilly wooded land to a flat wooded landscape. He then catches a wind blowing from the southwest (taking his ship northeast) until he and his crew arrive at a large island with high mountains topped by a glacier. Importantly, from this land they turn their stern toward the shore (west) and sail out to sea (east) with the same wind (from the southwest), which strengthens and brings them to Greenland. The travels here are clearly from south/southwest to north/northeast. The newly discovered lands therefore lie south and west of Greenland.[129]

Distances are difficult to determine from the saga narratives. Distance estimates have been calculated by combining the travel durations in the sagas with the speeds achieved by contemporary Viking ship reconstructions. The sagas recount durations of sailing in days (*dægr*), but it is not clear whether this refers to a twelve- or a twenty-four-hour period.[130] In *Greenlanders' Saga*, for instance, Bjarni's ship sails for two days between the hilly wooded land to the flat wooded land, then for three days from the flat wooded land to the mountainous island, and finally for four days from the mountainous island to Greenland. If this information is taken literally, the combined sailing time of Bjarni's voyage was nine days or 216 hours. The estimated maximum speed of a Viking ship under optimal wind conditions, such as those described on Bjarni's journey from the mountainous island to Greenland, was around 15 knots (24 km/h). This means the absolute maximum distance traveled by Bjarni was 6,048 km, which far exceeds the circa 2,800 km that separate Greenland from Newfoundland, for instance.[131] But we have no way of knowing the speed of these Viking ships on these particular voyages, and we cannot be confident of the twelve- versus twenty-four-hour day. Therefore, the reality is that the durations given in the sagas do not help us a great deal in pinpointing precisely where subsequent voyages would set up base camps. The directions and distances are, however, at least consistent with the voyages from Greenland to landscapes in Canada that would match the descriptions of the lands mentioned in the sagas.

One particular passage in *Greenlanders' Saga* in which Leif observes the height of the sun in midwinter has received intensive examination because of the belief that it might reveal the latitude of Vínland. The sentence reads: "The days and nights were more equal in length than in Greenland or Iceland; the sun reached southeast [*eyktar stað*] and southwest [*dagmála stað*] in the middle of the winter [*skammdegi*]."[132] Even if we assume the statement to be an accurate observation of the sun's position at mid-winter that was maintained through the oral tradition, there is still disagreement about the meaning of the terms *eyktar stað*, *dagmála stað*, and *skammdegi*. The conceptions of time in medieval Iceland add another complication.[133] Optimists have held that the meaning defines a time of sunrise and sunset precisely at winter solstice and that *eyktar stað* and *dagmála stað* refer to specific times, around 3–3:30 in the afternoon, and 9 in the morning.[134] But these descriptions may be referring just to the position of the sun rather than time. The term *skammdegi* means "short days" or "middle of the winter," rather than precisely the winter solstice. Even if the optimist's view is accepted, estimates of latitude vary between 31° N and 58° N, placing Vínland anywhere between southern Labrador and the US state of Georgia.[135] The range is too broad to be useful.[136]

The most credible attempts to locate Vínland rely on the correspondence among the medieval texts, pre-modern and modern botanical observations, and archaeological discoveries at L'Anse aux Meadows. The presence of grapevines and wild wheat in Vínland is attested in the name itself, in Adam of Bremen's account, in the sagas, and in the Icelandic historical sources. Traveling south-southwest of Greenland, the first region with both grapes and wild wheat lies south of the Gulf of St. Lawrence, in New Brunswick and Quebec. The wild grapevine *Vitis riparia* (riverbank-grape) is the most likely candidate for a grape-bearing vine and may be the only native grape species in Canada.[137] This grape was recorded by early explorers of the sixteenth to eighteenth centuries along rivers and estuaries south of the Gulf of St. Lawrence.[138] The most likely candidate for the self-sown grain along the northeastern coast of North America is wild rye (*Elymus virginicus*), which grows around the Gulf of St. Lawrence, in Nova Scotia, as well as along Newfoundland's southwestern coast.[139]

Botanical remains preserved in the wet deposits at the L'Anse aux Meadows site indicate travel and resource extraction from areas to the south, including the region south of the Gulf of St. Lawrence. Most significantly, three butternuts (*Juglans cinerea*, a type of wild walnut) and one carved piece of butternut burl wood were found among the carpentry debris close to complex D-E. Since butternuts do not and did not grow north of northern New Brunswick and the mouth of the St. Lawrence River, their presence here strongly suggests that the Norse explored these more southerly areas and brought resources back to L'Anse aux Meadows.[140] Butternuts are probably not the types of goods obtained through trade, nor is transport by birds likely. Butternuts grow in ecological zones in New Brunswick that also have wild grapes and wild rye.[141] This means that the people who lived at L'Anse aux Meadows traveled to and collected re-sources from precisely the geographical regions that would have had the major natural resources described in the sagas. Birgitta Wallace suggests that "whoever picked the butternuts found at L'Anse aux Meadows could hardly have avoided seeing grapevines."[142] The archaeological evidence therefore provides a proxy correspondence with the saga narratives of exploration in areas with grapes, even though the products of grapes (grape seeds or vines) and grains of wild rye have not been recovered at L'Anse aux Meadows. In addition, the collection of burl wood itself from this same area and its subsequent recovery at the L'Anse aux Meadows site provide an archaeological correlate of the trade and production of artifacts in burl wood documented in the sagas.

Other botanical remains corroborate exploration and resource gathering within Newfoundland. In the Norse levels of the bog excavation, five pin cherry pits (*Prunus pensylvanica*) were also recovered. The closest modern growth of pin cherries lies 160 km to the south of L'Anse aux Meadows. Some of the discarded wooden artifacts found in the bog also showed import of wood from farther south in Newfoundland. For instance, a barrel lid was made of eastern white cedar (*Thuja occidentalis*), a tree that does not grow north of the Deer Lake area (see Figure 7.3).[143]

The saga descriptions of animal species have also been used to bolster the identification of Vínland. The sagas describe a beached whale (probably a finback whale), flatfish (possibly halibut), salmon, and deer (or caribou, or even moose).[144] The various ungulate species and whales are too widespread along the eastern seaboard to be useful. Salmon, as a cold-water fish, might define a southern limit to the possible locations of Vínland. Catherine Carlson has argued that absence of salmon bones from native archaeological sites in New England shows that the warmer climate meant that there were no salmon in the rivers south of northern Maine around 1000.[145] Her conclusions, however, have been challenged recently on the basis of preservation, sampling problems, and absence of salmon bones from archaeological sites during other periods where salmon is known to have been plentiful.[146] This leaves the best faunal constraint of Vínland's location in some doubt.

Descriptions of the Native American groups encountered in the sagas have been used to narrow down the location of Vínland. Conversely, geographical estimations of Vínland's presumed location have also been used in attempts to identify the native groups encountered by the Norsemen. It should be added that the other historical texts say nothing about the Skrælings, beyond their existence. The assumptions therefore start compounding upon one another and can become circular. The textual descriptions indicate higher population densities among the native groups than existed among the circumpolar Thule or Dorset peoples, setting a northern limit for Vínland. The native groups' material cultures have also been used to set a southern limit of Vínland. The native boats were made of skin (*húðkeipar*), while dugout canoes were the primary boat types used south of central Maine.[147] Native groups south of southern Maine around 1000 also tended to cultivate corn (maize). The sagas do not mention this crop, although there is reference to a wooden structure that the Norsemen interpret as a grain storage shed (*kornhjalmr*), which could point toward cereal-plant utilization and possibly cultivation of domesticated crops.[148] This hut reference is too uncertain, however, while the absence of the mention of maize is a very weak indicator that the native groups encountered were limited to hunter-gatherer subsistence strategies.

Saga accounts of the natural resources of Vínland (grapes, self-sown wheat) combined with archaeology and botanical research (butternuts, burlwood) strongly suggest a position of Vínland south of the Gulf of St. Lawrence. The saga descriptions of Skræling material culture (specifically skin boats) and the fauna in Vínland (presence of salmon) weakly suggest a southern limit of Vínland in central Maine. A distinction should be made clear here. The northern limit is made stronger by the direct interdisciplinary correspondence among text, archaeology, and botany. The southern limit relies more strongly on the saga observations.

The effort to locate the specific sites in and around the Vínland of the sagas suffers from a problem of scale. Just how far were these explorers able and willing to sail? Innovative efforts have been made to return to sailing directions to create cumulative mental maps that combine the various directions and different lands considered in both sagas.[149] Yet, the travel durations provided by the sagas leave room for varying interpretation (e.g., twelve- or twenty-four-hour "days"). Different estimates of travel speeds combined with changes in wind conditions add additional variables to geographical precision.

It may in the end be impossible to locate the Vínland sites from the sagas with much precision. There are too many possible locations that could be made to fit the variable interpretations of the saga texts. Too many beaches, too many islands, too many bays, and too many lagoons. We will have to hope for further archaeological discoveries. It is clear, however, that L'Anse aux Meadows is not in Vínland. Birgitta Wallace is probably right in calling it a "gateway to Vínland."[150] For the broad area encompassing Vínland, the most logical location would be the closest place to the south of Labrador that has the key resources of wild grain, wild grapes, and butternut trees. This would be the southern shores of the St. Lawrence Bay.

At the same time, we cannot be sure that the L'Anse aux Meadows site is any of the three sites mentioned in the sagas (Leif's Booths in *Greenlanders' Saga*; Straumfjörð and Hóp in *Eirik's Saga*). Wallace makes a good case for it having the same function and role as Straumfjörð. In the saga geography, however, the key characteristic of Straumfjörð is that it is a fjord. L'Anse aux Meadows does not lie on a fjord. We have reached the limit of correspondence in this case.

Who Were the Natives Met by the Norsemen?

Approaching this question requires a number of assumptions built on a foundation of combined text and archaeology. First, we have to believe that the Norsemen who went on the Vínland voyages around 1000 met indigenous Native American peoples south of the circumpolar regions. This encounter is a central component of the written accounts—both the sagas and Icelandic historical sources—but archaeological evidence does not provide unequivocal and direct corresponding evidence. None of the objects at L'Anse aux Meadows necessitate direct contact and neither do the two chert arrowheads in Norse sites in Greenland. The objects from Thule and Dorset sites from the circumpolar region suggest some face-to-face interaction, but these all substantially post-date the 1000 threshold by several centuries. Even the Goddard Penny is more likely to have arrived in Maine by down-the-line trade than by direct, firsthand transport by the Norse.

One way to approach this question is by looking at the archaeological cultures present along the eastern coast of North America around 1000. In northern Labrador, Norsemen would have encountered circumpolar Dorset people, who lived in small bands and relied on seal and caribou. In southern Labrador, they would have encountered ancestral Innu, hunter-gatherers who lived in more densely populated habitation sites. The Innu relied primarily on products of the forest during the winter and the abundant wildlife along the coastal estuaries during the summer. In Newfoundland, Norsemen would have encountered ancestral Beothuk peoples, who shared many cultural features with their Innu neighbors in Labrador.

Around 1000, no natives lived at L'Anse aux Meadows. Contemporary ancestral Beothuk native sites have been identified at Bird Cove and Port aux Choix just over 150 km to the southwest.[151] The Norse might have met these or similar groups in Newfoundland. But since northern Newfoundland was sparsely populated, it is conceivable that they did not encounter natives there. To place the Norse beyond northern Newfoundland, we must rely on conclusions about the location of Vínland addressed in the previous section.

Can we use the physical and cultural descriptions of the natives in the sagas to identify which native groups were encountered? This probably pushes the limits of correspondence too far. The physical characteristics of the Skrælings include such generalities as short stature (but also sometimes tall), large eyes, and broad-cheeked. These might be interpreted as being consistent with phenotypes of both circumpolar and North American natives. On the other hand, the descriptions also document the natives as dark and grim looking with bad hair, which reminds us that these are biased and ethnocentric accounts. The saga accounts tell us at least as much about the prejudices of the Norse, as they do about the physical appearance of the peoples they encountered in North America.[152] The phenotypic characteristics cannot be used to specify native groups beyond a generalized non-European categorization.

Other cultural characteristics of the Skrælings are a bit more helpful. The descriptions that are most helpful are the accounts of conflicts around the Hóp settlement in *Eiriks' Saga* and Leif's Booths in *Greenlanders' Saga*. The sagas concur about the basic material culture of the natives. They had a stone-age technology, used skin boats, and lived in villages, and their economy included hunting and trading with the animal products of the forest, but probably not maize agriculture. If these general descriptions are accurate, then they would most closely approximate archaeologically known native cultures living between central Maine and Labrador. Attempts to correlate some of the stranger weapons only described in *Eiriks' Saga*, such as the catapult-like slings or the sheep-gut sized projectile on a pole, with archaeological evidence or ethnographic accounts have been unsuccessful but are an important reminder that the complex material culture of Native North Americans could become the stuff of Norse legend.[153] Ethnographic research in particular helps make the story in *Eirik's Saga* appear less fantastic. But since these ethnographies describe native groups some 800 years after the Norse-Skræling contact, they are of limited utility in establishing a correlation between the text and the observed weapons.

The Norse themselves did not distinguish between Skrælings that lived in the various lands west of Iceland, including Greenland, Markland, and Vínland. Trying to do so using only the sagas—themselves written records of oral memories transmitted over centuries—without direct archaeological evidence for contact, is beyond the limits of any reasonable cross-dataset verification. The archaeological evidence from northern Greenland and Baffin Island offers interesting future work, but so far, all evidence post-dates the Viking Age.

Genetic research might offer a new avenue for exploring the question of native/Norse interaction. Recent research identified a mtDNA haplogroup in Iceland that is not found in Europe but is common among Native American populations.[154] This suggests that at least one Native American woman (or possibly the female child of a Norse male and native female union) journeyed to Iceland, contributing her mtDNA to her Icelandic descendants. Additional genetic research might tell a story that complements *Eiriks' Saga*'s story of the two native children who Karlsefni brought back from Markland.

If we return to just the saga evidence, the issue of the scale of the voyages returns. Are the natives at Hóp and Leif's Booths the same or distinct groups? They share basic characteristics but differ significantly in technology, with the Hóp natives wielding slings or catapults and projectile objects launched from poles. What about the natives who were seen by Thorvald, who were the only ones to have drying huts presumed to be for grain? Seeking further correlations and answers to these questions might be possible, but only with additional archaeological evidence from either Native North American sites or new Norse sites in North America.

Did the Norse Bring Livestock?

This may seem like a rather specific question, but the implications are critical for understanding the intention of the Viking Age expeditions to North America. If the explorers brought livestock, they likely had designs to stay and settle. The sagas, as has been discussed, state clearly that livestock were on board the ships. They recount that the conditions in Vínland were excellent for livestock, so good in fact that they could be left outside to graze during the winter. The *Skálholtsbók* version of *Eirik's Saga* informs us that Karlsefni's livestock thrived at Straumfjörð, while a scene with a bull scaring the natives appears in both sagas. The sagas thus agree that the Norse brought livestock and that permanent settlement was a goal, if not the primary goal, of the voyages.

The absence of archaeological evidence for European domesticated livestock comes close to contradicting the sagas. A particularly noteworthy aspect of the settlement at L'Anse aux Meadows is that animal byres have not been found, despite widespread archaeological efforts to locate them.[155] This might indicate absence of livestock, at least cattle, that traditionally were sheltered over the winter. The question remains, however, whether this was necessary—or rather thought to be necessary by the Norsemen—in light of the mild temperatures. The sagas directly suggest that byres were not thought necessary.

The animal bones found at L'Anse aux Meadows also seem to indicate the absence of domesticated livestock. The short habitation of the site limited the amount of food debris that has been recovered, while the acidic soils at the site militated against the preservation of animal bone. Significantly, however, all of the analyzed faunal bones, numbering in the hundreds, were identified as belonging to wild animals, mostly seal and some whale.[156] This means that the archaeology provides no indication of the presence of any domesticated animals at the site. Perhaps they brought no animals. Or perhaps they brought livestock only to provide milk products, while relying on wild animal species for meat.

For livestock, the archaeological evidence clearly does not confirm the sagas, and the evidence might even be seen as contradictory. There may have been, however, livestock that either were not eaten or whose skeletal remains were not recovered, possibly because of adverse preservation conditions. The absence of evidence calls for some caution and should not be taken for evidence of absence. The archaeological evidence does not directly contradict this detail from the sagas. It does, however, make their presence much less certain.

Conclusion: Does It Still Come Down to Belief?

Archaeology has confirmed that Viking Age Scandinavians reached lands to the southwest of Greenland. Archaeology provides good support for the saga accounts that they arrived in lands with wild grapes and self-sown wheat. The two datasets agree on the combined Greenlandic and Icelandic participants and on the general size of the voyaging groups. The archaeological evidence so far seems to contradict the saga stories about Norse livestock being present on the Vínland voyages. Archaeology and the sagas complement each other in very specific ways to create a uniquely interdisciplinary narrative. Modern science also provides potentially complementary data, as in the case of the apparent North American mtDNA haplogroup found in Iceland. The archaeologically vindicated sagas tell a story of Native Americans brought back to Greenland, and DNA suggests Native Americans may have traveled on to Iceland. With increasing interreliance among multiple lines of evidence, the interdisciplinary narratives become increasingly probable.

At some point in scholarly narratives about Vínland, however, the academic objectivity frequently breaks down, and we see how the personal preferences and beliefs of the individual writers come to the fore. Much disagreement has been voiced about the historicity of various characters and places in the Vínland sagas. Erik Wahlgren, for instance, opens his discussion of the Vínland voyages, by saying, "Bjarni Herjólfsson of the *Saga of the Greenlanders*—I think he was real—was a youngish merchant with his own *knǫrr* or merchant ship."[157] In a keynote lecture at a conference celebrating the 1,000 years since the discovery of Vínland, the famous historian Magnus Magnusson stated, "for my own part, for what it's worth, 'Vínland the Good' smacks much more of a wistful concept than a geographical reality." His suspicion was that it "never existed as an actual place."[158] Magnusson's suspicion has no more or less evidence than Wahlgren's feeling that Bjarni was a real person.

If we return to the discussion of the Hønen stone, we find similar statements revealing personal wishes and feelings gaining the upper hand over sober academic conclusions. Taylor in an otherwise disinterested article shifts into the first person when the question turns toward the possible interpretation of the runes that could spell Vínland or windcold (probably Greenland): "Nonetheless, I am disappointed. Try as I may, I can see neither *Vínland* nor *windcold* here, and I suspect both Bugge and Olsen of seeing what they want to see."[159]

With the Goddard Penny too, a key component was whether scholars believed Guy Mellgren to be telling the truth about the coin. The coin is obviously real. In this case, Carpenter tries to juxtapose enough circumstantial evidence to cast doubt on Mellgren's actions. Carpenter opens his critical work by citing a passage of Hjalmar Holand's 1956 book that suggests Thorvald Eiriksson would have sailed by Mt. Desert Island in Maine.[160] He points out that the Goddard site is just a few kilometers away. Carpenter finishes his opening argument by asking, "am I alone in finding such a coincidence remarkable?"[161] In Gullbekk's ingenious demonstration that the coin cannot have come from Norwegian collections, he still turns to a personal conclusion: "based on the numismatic and archaeological evidence, I am inclined to believe that this was a genuine find."[162]

Perhaps more so in the study of Vínland than in any other realm of Viking Studies, the scholarship is marked by polarized optimism and skepticism. These, as I can attest from my own experience, even alternate within the single scholar. This was also felt by Sarah Parcak as our season at Point Rosee drew to a close and reporters came to interview the group: "This is a difficult site. I keep flipping my hats. I'm a skeptical scientist, but you have to be an optimist to be an archaeologist. I mean, scraping bits of soil for hours at a time under the hot sun. If you're not an optimist, you're in the wrong field."[163] Perhaps Sarah is right. Doubt of preliminary results—especially if deriving from one dataset—is healthy academic practice. If so, then skepticism about broad conclusions drawn from a single dataset provides a powerful argument for interdisciplinarity and a rigorous method of cross-checking correspondences, confirmations, and contradictions.

8

Conclusion

Fenrir howls loudly at gates of Hel,
the chains will break, and the wolf run free.
I have great wisdom, I see far into the future,
to Ragnarok, the doom of the gods.

Brothers will fight and kill one another,
cousins will violate kinship bonds,
hard times on the earth, an age of adultery,
axe age, sword age, shields are shattered,
wind age, wolf age, before the world sinks,
men will not spare each other.[1]

An age of wolf and wind, foreseen in the poem *Prophecy of the Seeress* (*Vǫluspá*) as a figurative expression of the turbulent time immediately preceding Ragnarok, is also a fitting metaphor the for the historical Viking Age. It was the time when the old world of the pagan gods ended, and traditional behavioral norms faded with the arrival of Christianity. The wolf, associated with Odin because it stalked battlegrounds feeding on the dead, is a predatory creature. In the mythic present, Odin's two wolves, Geri and Freki ("Ravenous" and "Greedy"), roam the world, seeking to satiate their hunger. Like wolves, the Vikings were predatorial, traveling widely and beyond the confines of the world known to contemporary Europeans. In the pre-Christian period, many Vikings may have yearned for the battlefield, which offered the promise of riches and renown as well as the possibility of an afterlife of war and feasting with Odin. Several sagas recall berserker groups known as wolf-warriors (*Ulfheðnar*), who went into battle donning wolf skins. Wolves were animal symbols of the transition to the next world, and therein lies a fundamental connection of the wolf to Odin, the god of dead warriors. At Ragnarok, wolves play a catalytic role in the end of this world and the transition leading to the rebirth of a new one. The most famous wolf in Norse mythology, the Fenris Wolf, kills Odin, while two other monstrous wolves swallow the sun and the moon.

Wind, an image of turbulence, is appropriate for the Viking Age that saw many changes: in economics, in the emergence of towns, in the formation of the state-level political orders, and in the transition of religions. Perhaps the most defining

Age of Wolf and Wind. Davide Zori, Oxford University Press. © Oxford University Press 2024.
DOI: 10.1093/oso/9780190916060.003.0008

characteristic of Viking Age Scandinavians, sea-borne travel aboard sailing ships, depended on the wind. A good wind could mean survival, successful migration, and glory, while a bad wind or lack of wind might bring failure, poverty, and death. The Viking ship is the clearest and most enduring symbol of the Viking Age. The ship was the catalyst of the age, allowing the movement of unprecedented numbers of Scandinavians beyond their homelands for raiding, trading, and migration. These Viking Age voyagers brought wealth back to Scandinavia, and through intensified contact with other cultures, they also brought home new ideas that helped to reshape the economic, political, and ideological systems in Scandinavia. Abroad, the movement of people had lasting impacts on the world, as the Vikings embedded themselves in new homelands, creating new hybridized cultures in places like the Danelaw and extending colonies into the vast North Atlantic region, still today inhabited by people who see themselves as Scandinavian.

Contemporary fascination with the Vikings is at least partially built on a combination of ideas about the heroism, violence, danger, and unfamiliar character of Viking Age Scandinavians. Current political analyses of potentially threatening and unfamiliar population groups—ranging from political movements and peaceful migrants to terrorists—are often framed as providing answers to two key questions: "Who are they, and what do they want?"[2] This book has sought to contribute a range of answers to these questions for the Vikings by looking at them in a new way, through an interdisciplinary lens. They were migrants, often thought of as strange, and they certainly committed acts of terror on peoples they met on their voyages. Summing up the answers is not so easy, of course, as they would not have been the same for all Norse peoples at the time. We might begin answering the first question by reiterating that not all Viking Age Scandinavians were *víkings*—that is, seaborne raiders—and not all *víkings* were Scandinavians. As we have seen, many of the people we have encountered—who lived in Scandinavian forts and towns or boarded Viking ships—were born outside of Scandinavia. Part of the answer to the first question, therefore, is that they were a motley crew. The dead Vikings who were executed at Ridgeway Hill in England appear to have been mostly Scandinavians, but also included people born and raised on the southern coast of the Baltic Sea (Germany or Poland), as did the warriors within the Trelleborg fortress in Denmark that was a key lynchpin in the late tenth-century formation of the Danish state. These are important correctives to views of Viking uniformity, but they are not really that surprising, as both voluntary and involuntary population movements are defining characteristics of human societies throughout history. What is different in the Viking Age is the unprecedented scale of the movement of Scandinavians beyond their borders—one that has not been seen since in Scandinavia. Supporting this dynamic period of movement was an unparalleled glorification of Scandinavian voyagers, who were commemorated at home with monumental runestones and through poems and sagas that exalted their exploits.

The characteristic dynamism of the Viking Age is also clearly visible in dramatic societal changes that occurred in the Scandinavian homelands. Right at the start of the Viking Age, the overseas ventures required mobilization of whole communities and reorganization of local economies to build and outfit ships. Demand for wool for sails and homespun sailing suits led to an expansion of grazing lands for sheep, documented for instance in pollen records in Norwegian fjords. This "textile revolution" was accomplished on farms and by the spinning and weaving labor of women.[3] The flow of wealth and engagement with overseas communities saw the concomitant rise of urban trading centers in Scandinavia. By the end of the Viking Age, the proliferation of urban centers within Scandinavia had changed the settled landscape and the organization of production and exchange, at both the local and the regional level. Especially within the network of urban production and trade, the means of exchange shifted from bartered goods and silver bullion to coinage backed by kings. On the political level, the period saw the emergence of three separate states: Denmark, Norway, and Sweden. In the beginning of the Viking Age, state-level political organization did not exist, but it had emerged by its end. Service to the king and taxation became facts of life. This political shift went hand in hand with an ideological shift from pre-Christian to Christian religion. By 1100, the monuments of the state and the Church dominated the new Scandinavian urban centers, as they did in much of the rest of medieval Western Europe.

One of the most important changes over the course of the Viking Age is that the people of Scandinavia became more like their Christian neighbors, while the people of the three emerging Scandinavian countries became less like one another. With the adoption of Christianity, there was a diminution of the distinctiveness of the Scandinavians from the Franks, Anglo-Saxons, Germans, and Slavs. With the Christian Church came a pan-European class of educated clerics and the adoption of Latin as the language of the record-keepers of the state. Saxo Grammaticus, for example, wrote his *History of the Danes* (*Gesta Danorum*) in Latin, translating many Old Norse/Old Danish legends and poems. As the Scandinavian kings of the nascent states of Denmark, Norway, and Sweden cultivated innovations in statecraft and religious organization, they also fostered the internal differences among the peoples of these three future nations. Danes became people of the kingdom of Denmark, Norwegians became people of the kingdom of Norway, and Swedes became the people of the kingdom of Sweden. The first mention of Denmark, rather than Danes, appears on a runestone at the royal site of Jelling, likely erected in the mid-tenth century, when the Danish kings were making dramatic efforts to consolidate the kingdom. Regional differences, dialects, and local cultural practices persisted, but macro-identities and political allegiances were increasingly organized in terms of the three medieval states.

This pattern is also discernable in the Scandinavian languages. From Greenland to Gotland, Scandinavians spoke a mutually intelligible language, Old Norse, from the beginning of the Viking Age until the end. Interregional travels likely encouraged this mutual intelligibility, while the common language in turn facilitated economic, social, and political cooperation. Local dialects—typically grouped into Old West Norse spoken in Norway and the North Atlantic colonies and Old East Norse spoken in Denmark and Sweden—diverged after the end of the Viking Age into separate languages, decreasing the mutual intelligibility and further reifying the Scandinavian national identities.

The second question that we might ask of the Vikings—what do they want?—is an even more difficult question. Again, they clearly did not all want the same thing. Peoples' personal identities, age, gender, social standing, and beliefs all yielded complex constellations of motivations. The Viking Age king might want to centralize power, a farmer might work primarily for a good harvest, and a slave yearn above all else for his or her freedom. But can we say anything in general about the overarching desires that motivated Viking Age Scandinavians: was there a zeitgeist of the Viking Age? One might say that when free enough to take the initiative, the Vikings were opportunists, as perhaps most people are in most periods of history, simply seeking to better their conditions. But especially in their overseas endeavors—facilitated by new ship technology and driven by an ideology that encouraged worldly deeds—they were the ultimate opportunists. They sought new wealth abroad at an unprecedented scale, and through a combination of strategies that included expansionist settlement, warfare, and trade. So where were the opportunities? They found these new opportunities in exploiting the weak and fragmented polities in Western Europe, in rerouting trade between the Arab and Byzantine worlds and Western Europe through the Northern Arc, and in settling the uninhabited islands of the North Atlantic.

The seaborne movement of Scandinavian people beyond their homelands impacted Eurasia tremendously. Through exploiting military weaknesses and/ or political fragmentation, they created the Danelaw in England, catalyzed urbanism in Ireland, and established the polity of Normandy in northern France. The search for products for international trade, such as walrus ivory, may have spurred Scandinavian explorers farther into the North Atlantic, but it was then the availability of free productive lands that sustained the development of the Norse colonies of the North Atlantic. In the east, the search for silver and lucrative markets to sell slaves and furs brought the Scandinavians to the Black and Caspian Seas and into direct contact with the powerful empires centered in Constantinople and Baghdad. Seeking to dominate the trade that connected these imperial capitals with Western Europe through the Baltic Sea, they established fortified trading hubs on the Dnieper River, eventually founding the Rus dynasty of Novgorod and Kyiv. The desire for wealth acquisition drove them to escalate raiding activity, bringing brutality and fear to communities that were accessible from the sea and rivers of Europe. There was a violence and a horror to the Viking Age that should not be glossed over. Fortune-seeking Viking raids involved unprovoked slaughter, enslavement, destruction of economic resources, violation of sacred sites, and devastation of communities. A significant part of the Viking interregional trade revolved around the human beings acquired through violent surprise attacks on communities from Ireland to the river basins of the Dnieper and the Volga. The intersection of raiding and trading remains an understudied aspect of the Viking Age economy. Even in the settlement in new Scandinavian communities abroad—as in Danelaw and the Scottish Isles—the very real possibility of campaigns of ethnic cleansing remains.

People's desires in the ideological realm were guided by belief systems that were in flux throughout the Viking Age. In its first two centuries, most Scandinavians shared a pre-Christian worldview that was variable across the Scandinavian cultural area but based in common myths, beliefs, and rituals. Pre-Christian graves offer us an idealized view of individuals, one that typically encompasses both the self-image of the deceased and the perspective of those who buried the dead. The proliferation of objects in graves that stress the consumption and presentation of food and drink show that the ability to lavishly host friends, supporters, and rivals loomed large in people's minds. The prominence of the accoutrements and products of the feast in both male and female graves suggests that feasting in the afterlife was a desire for a wide spectrum of society. Gender roles were often strictly represented in graves, revealing, for example, how female identity was tied to the household and to spinning and weaving. Graves containing men outfitted for battle echo the militaristic ethos and fatalism that is so prominently featured in the written sources. In the afterlife, as in life, battle was expected. Yet, Viking Age graves also show us the complexity of individual identities and a degree of fluidity, as demonstrated by the genetic research showing that one of the quintessential Viking warriors buried at Birka was in fact a biological female. We do not know to what extent the Birka warrior woman determined how she was arrayed in her grave, but this representation surely lies at the intersection of her own desires in life and the hopes that her kin and friends had for her in the afterlife.

As the Viking Age came to an end, so did the old pre-Christian worldview and belief in the old Æsir gods. The highly variable pre-Christian burial traditions, which tell such vivid and individualized stories, were replaced with simpler and more uniform Christian burials in churchyards. Only dwindling numbers of believers in the old faith remained in regional pockets, mostly in Sweden. As the divinity of the old gods faded, aspects of their power persisted in local folklore and folk magic, evidenced, for example, in runic inscriptions seeking Odin's help to find lost things.[4] Publicly, the ideological goals of Scandinavians became more closely aligned with the rest of Christian Europe, and while regional Christian culture was colored by their local native traditions, as seen in the beautiful Norwegian stave churches, the beliefs and motivations of the Scandinavians became less distinct. So too, at the end of the Viking Age, their possibilities and desires to voyage far beyond their shores were transformed dramatically. Kings, such as the Norwegian Sigurd Jerusalem-Farer (reign 1103–1130) and the Danish Eirik the Good (reign 1095–1103), still set out with armies on overseas voyages, but they would do so under the banner of Crusade.

***

This book has also been about creating methodological voyages through the Viking world by building a new framework for approaching the data that underlies our understanding of the Vikings and their age. The Viking Age in Scandinavia is one of those fascinating periods of history in which nearly no contemporary written sources were created by the Scandinavians themselves. The short runic inscriptions found on objects and standing stones are the exception. To this we can add the nearly always hostile records written by their Christian European neighbors and a few Muslim travelers. Proto-historic periods, like the Viking Age, offer fertile ground for the archaeological record to redefine our understanding of past people's lives. Over the past century, archaeology has done this, revolutionizing popular perceptions by shining new light on daily lives and stressing especially the economic and commercial complexity of Scandinavian society. Archaeological excavations at farmsteads and in burgeoning towns have provided a corrective that underscores the peaceful and productive aspects of daily life. At this level, life for Scandinavians in the eighth to eleventh centuries looks similar to the lives of other peoples in Europe in the same period. Despite scholarly trends focusing on these peaceful "Vikings," however, archaeology has simultaneously and steadily brought to light evidence of the uniqueness of the Scandinavians. The pre-Christian cult buildings or temples are an excellent example. Scholarly fashion had begun to distrust their existence, as narrated in the written sources. Over the last two decades, however, archaeologists have found such temples across the Viking world and documented a range of ritual behavior that includes both the bloody sacrifices described in the written sources and also much complexity that is not included in the sources. Importantly, for instance, archaeology has shown great variation in these cultic structures and their associated rituals, such that temporal and regional differences can now be appreciated.

The flowering of scientific techniques applied to archaeological materials and relic landscapes has resulted in a second revolution in our understanding of the

Viking Age. For instance, isotope analysis of human bones has provided insight into human diets and health, revealing differences in consumption patterns related to status, age, and gender. Isotope analysis has also shed light on the voyages people made during their lifetimes and shown the diverse regional origins of social groups that cooperated in raids, mutual defense, and communal urban living. New genetics research has opened the door to greater understanding of Scandinavian interactions and intermarriage/interbreeding with the population groups they encountered beyond their homelands, showing for instance variable composition in settlement populations for the different islands of the North Atlantic. Revolutions in dating sciences—particularly dendrochronology, tephrochronology, and refined radiocarbon dating with Bayesian statistics—have enabled the narrowing of age ranges for archaeological sites to within single years, in turn permitting closer comparisons with dates from historical sources. Improvements in sampling techniques now allow the study of microscopic refuse, plants, seeds, and insects from archaeological sites. Widespread application of non-destructive geophysical methods, including ground penetrating radar and magnetometry, have discovered and mapped countless sites, while even more recent use of satellite imagery and drones bearing cameras and LiDAR (Light Detection and Ranging) antennas are producing landscape models of previously unimaginable detail. These techniques are discovering small sites, but also large ones—such as ship burials and lost fortresses—that still remain buried beneath the fields and forests of the Viking world.[5]

Armed with scientific tools to combine with historical and archaeological methods, we are better equipped than ever before to come to know the people who lived during the Viking Age. The case studies in this book have highlighted the importance of a critical, interdisciplinary approach for achieving this understanding. Each discipline offers different data sets for deciphering the past. When the independent data sets extracted from the written sources, archaeology, and scientific testing are analyzed independently and then juxtaposed, new arenas for analysis emerge. The encounters between the data sets result in confirmation, contradiction, and complementarity. The cases we have explored in this book provide a plethora of examples of these "three Cs."

The temptation to seek confirmation of historical events or connections to known people of the past in objects and structures is probably universal. The exhilaration of an unearthed relic connecting us to past individuals is palpable, and this is surely one of the underlying reasons that historical sources have often dictated both the objectives and interpretation of archaeological research. Early archaeological work in places such as Iceland, where the historical truth of the sagas was a central position of early antiquarian researchers, was guided by some improbable assumptions about the likelihood that ruins or burial mounds visible in the landscape should correspond with saga characters. Archaeology was not yet valued as an independent means for investigating the past. As it emerged as a separate discipline, many archaeologists shied away from seeking direct confirmation between historical sources and archaeological evidence. But now, with archaeology on equal footing with history, we can again, and with greater critical rigor, ask questions such as, "might the empty grave under the Hrísbrú church in Iceland be the emptied grave of the saga hero Egil Skallagrimsson?" or "Could the bones of a murdered man lying in the crypt of St. Knut's Cathedral in Odense show evidence that these are St. Knut's remains and that he was killed in the manner described in texts about his martyrdom?" It is very possible that the answer to both these questions is "yes," and that is both exciting and important for our understanding of the historical value of written sources about the Viking Age. But when the written sources, archaeological evidence, and scientific analyses confirm one another on a broader societal scale, the impacts on our understanding of the past are even more significant. For example, the historical sources, archaeological remains, and pollen records all agree that Scandinavians first settled Iceland around 870 and that the available land was quickly claimed. Farther west, the discovery of L'Anse aux Meadows confirmed that Viking Age Scandinavians reached and temporarily lived in the lands southwest of Greenland in North America, while analysis of the whetstones found at the site confirmed that the travelers came from both Iceland and Greenland. For the Viking Age in general, confirmation among the sources is found broadly on the societal scale, but much more rarely at the scale of historical particulars regarding people and events.

In contrast, examples of direct contradiction among the sources are plentiful for historical details but rarer at the broader societal scale. Individual written sources contradict one another frequently at the level of historical particulars, such as dates, names, and events. At the most basic level, names of people associated with events can be confounded. For example, Adam of Bremen mixed up his chronology when he wrote that Emperor Otto I invaded Denmark and conquered Hedeby, while the contemporary *Deeds of the Saxons* by Widukind of Corvey informs that the conquest occurred under Emperor Otto II. Some apparent contradictions in texts might be omissions. For instance, in the stories about the Vínland voyages, *Eirik's Saga* recounts three voyages, while *Greenlanders' Saga* recalls six. *Eirik's Saga* might simply have omitted some voyages from its narrative, and as discussed in the previous chapter, there is some evidence for this. But even so, we are still left with contradictions concerning the specific individuals who undertook each journey and even the identity of the person who first discovered the new lands—was it Bjarni Herjolfsson or Leif Eiriksson? If we consider the archaeological evidence, the excavations at L'Anse aux Meadows have confirmed that Scandinavians reached the New World around the year 1000, but there are apparent contradictions as well. The site at L'Anse aux Meadows shows no evidence of livestock, for instance, while both sagas discuss the presence of cattle. But perhaps the absence of archaeological evidence for livestock is not evidence of their absence. Concerning the date of the site, new analyses of excavated material have introduced a possible chronological contradiction with the historical sources. A recently identified cosmic ray event that caused a global upsurge in atmospheric ^{14}C in the year 993 has allowed precise dating of wood samples found at L'Anse aux Meadows. A suite of radiocarbon dates identified this carbon anomaly in tree rings of three wood samples felled with iron tools. Counting the tree rings between the carbon anomaly from 993 and the external bark of the samples revealed that the trees were felled in 1021.[6] In broad terms, this date is consistent with the voyages described in the sagas, but the exact 1021 date is over a decade later than the chronological range suggested by the sagas, circa 995–1010. If L'Anse aux Meadows is indeed one of the sites mentioned in the sagas, which seems probable, then the firm 1021 date might suggest that the saga chronology is mistaken, or that Norse occupation continued longer than suggested by the sagas. Alternatively, the new dates might be seen as complementary to the written sources, indicating that the Norse continued to visit L'Anse aux Meadows sporadically after the last voyages described in the sagas. Only further research at L'Anse aux Meadows will clarify these questions. Exploring the apparent contradictions among the sources helps to fine tune our understanding and reveals where written sources may have been mistaken, confused, or misunderstood by previous researchers, or where archaeologists might have made incorrect interpretations based on the archaeological record, which is inevitably always incomplete.

The complementarity of sources is arguably the most fruitful of the encounters among the written sources, archaeology, and science. At a general level, much of our fundamental knowledge about the Viking Age is built on complementarity. For instance, we would clearly know very little about Norse mythology without Snorri's *Prose Edda* and the compilation of poems preserved in the *Poetic Edda*. Both sources are Icelandic, but the distribution of Viking Age art with recognizable scenes from mythology, such as Thor's fishing trip to catch the Midgard Serpent, indicate the widespread knowledge of these myths. Countless Thor's hammer pendants unearthed in archaeological excavations show the pervasive veneration of the god across the Viking world. Returning then to our scaffolding of complementary sources, we would have no hope of understanding the rich belief system that lay behind such small personal objects of adornment without the myths preserved in writing. Grand political narratives, such as the formation of the Scandinavian states, are only comprehensible through the complementary use of texts, archaeology, and science. For instance, broadly speaking, the rise of the state in Denmark in the late tenth century finds corresponding evidence in all of our sources. But it is in exploring the complementarity of the sources that we gain access to the nuances, regional variations, and individuals involved in these processes. The written sources and the larger of the two runestones at Jelling speak of King Harald Bluetooth, the expansionist and Christianizing king who united all of Denmark. Archaeology reveals a uniform style of cavalry burials and a flurry of runestones in corresponding zones, bringing to light the operation of local elites making claims to local power and landownership within this new state-level political system. The system of Trelleborg fortresses, which are not mentioned in the written sources or on the runestones, offer perhaps the clearest signs of state-level efforts at monopolizing military power. Studies of isotopes from individuals buried at Trelleborg testify to the diversity of the people who were drawn to inhabit these royal forts. Finally, although the written sources do not mention the forts, precise dating offered by dendrochronology allows the fortresses to be placed in a specific historical context at the end of the reign of Harald Bluetooth. In sum, using complementary sources to build a scaffold of interpretation allows us to tell richer and more convincing stories than have ever been told before.

This book has advocated for an optimistic methodological approach that directly seeks encounters among text, archaeology, and scientific analyses with the goal of maximizing integration and exploration of the interplay among the various data sources. Past approaches, especially of saga skeptics and archaeologists rightly seeking to liberate their discipline from the role of playing second fiddle to historians, have focused on the risks of combining these data sets. These risks are now well understood, and it is time we moved past them to a position recognizing that *more* integration and collaboration, not less, is necessary if we are to maximize our understanding of the complexity, variability, and foreignness of the Viking world.

Notes

Chapter 1

1. "Ecce trecentis et quianquaginta ferme/ annis quod nos nostrique patres huius pulcherrime patrie incole fuimus et numquam talis terror prius apparuit in Brittannia ueluti modo a pagana gente perpessi sumus, nec eiusmodi nauigium fieri posse putabatur. Ecce ecclesia sancti Cuðberhti sacerdotum Dei sanguine aspersa, omnibus spoliata ornamentis, locus cunctis in Brittania uenerabilior, paganis gentibus datur ad depredandum." The translation here as the rest of the translations in the book are my own unless otherwise noted (Latin letter edition in Chase 1975: 53–54). This letter to King Æthelred of Northumbria was one of five that Alcuin sent to correspondents in England, including to the bishop of Lindisfarne.
2. Gilbert et al. 2017
3. Dudo tells the story of Hastein's capture of Luni in chapter 2 of his *Historia Normannorum* (Christiansen 1998; a Latin edition and a good translation by Felice Lifshitz is also available at https://sourcebooks.fordham.edu/source/dudo-stquentin-gesta-transcription-lifshitz.asp).
4. See e.g., Bisson 2009: 43–63.
5. Price et al. 2016; Price 2020: 275–277.
6. Rus was likely a self-prescribed name by Scandinavians who engaged in trading on the Russian rivers. The modern Finnish name for Sweden, Routsi, still retains the same root.
7. The cultural significance of the concept of oath is underscored by the existence of a goddess with the same name, Vár, who took vengeance on oath-breakers (Lindow 2001: 312).
8. Recent analysis of graffiti in Hagia Sophia has even revealed multiple depictions of what appear to be Viking-style ships (Jarman 2021: 254, 270–272; Thomov 2014).
9. Blöndal and Benedikz 2007.
10. Christiansen 2002.
11. For Bookprose see e.g., Nordal 1958 and Clover 1982; for an early articulation of the Freeprose position see e.g., Jónsson 1907, 1921.
12. Lord 1960; Vansina 1985.
13. Rubin 1995.
14. Byock 1982; Kellogg 1988; Lönnroth 1971; G. Sigurðsson 2004.
15. Ingstad and Ingstad 2001; Byock et al. 2005.
16. See e.g., Byock 1982, 1988, 2001; Miller 1990; Durrenberger 1992; J. V. Sigurðsson 1999; G. Sigurðsson 2004.
17. See e.g., the Ramsund stone in Sweden; a cross at Halton in Lancashire, England (Bailey 1980: fig. 15); and four Manx crosses found at Jurby (119), Malew (120), Andreas (121), and Maughold (122) on the Isle of Man, most of which date to the tenth century (Wilson 2008: 82–84, figs. 40–42).
18. For reviews of the myths, rights, and roles of women in Scandinavian societies of the Viking Age and medieval period, see Jesch 1991 (especially strong on the runic inscriptions), Jochens 1995 (particularly excellent on the sagas), and Friðriksdóttir 2020 (the most up-to-date feminist analysis of the Old Norse written sources and archaeological evidence for the myths and realities of women's lives in the Viking world).

19. See e.g., Young 1992 for a discussion of tyranny of the text in medieval archaeology and Papadopoulos 1999 for Classical archaeology.

20. I draw many fundamental principles from Anders Andrén's (1998) work on the relationship between archaeology and text in which he, for instance, advocates for separate analyses of textual and archaeological datasets before they are combined in scholarship. He analyses the new contexts for interpretation that arise from the encounters between text and archaeology. The three "Cs" used in this book (correspondence, contradiction, and complementarity) are my own but build on Andrén's three categories of encounter: *identification correspondence* (occurs when an object or occurrence mentioned in text is identified in the archaeological record), *correspondence correlation* (occurs when patterns identified in the texts are identified as corresponding to patterns in the archaeological record), and *contrast or negative correspondence* (identified when realities portrayed in texts directly contrast with what is gathered from the archaeological record).

21. For example, such overview coverage is excellently provided in Logan 1983 (third edition 2005), Jones 1968 (second edition 1984), and Roesdahl 1992 (third edition 2018). For a more up-to-date introduction that delves deeper into the Viking worldview, I highly recommend Neil Price's *Children of Ash and Elm: A History of the Vikings* (2020).

22. Milek 2012 and especially Hayeur Smith 2020: 19–23 for discussion of semi-subterranean weaving huts, called dyngjur (dyngja, sg.), as spaces of female work and empowerment.

23. Visits to Hedeby described in written sources include those by the Frankish missionary St. Anskar in the early ninth century, the Anglo-Saxon merchant Wulfstan in the late ninth century, and Al-Tartushi, the merchant/geographer/spy from Muslim Córdoba.

24. The Kvalsund ship was long thought to date to the end of the seventh century, but recent dating by dendrochronology revised this date to 780–800, placing it much closer in time to the Oseberg ship (Nordeide et al. 2020).

25. Jochens 1995: 142; Cartwright 2015; Hayeur Smith 2020: 6–8.

26. For Viking ships see especially the works of Ole Crumlin-Pedersen 1997 and 2002. See also Williams 2014.

27. A text by the Muslim traveler on the Volga, who observes the burial rituals of a chieftain describes the sacrifice of a young female slave said to be accompanying the chieftain to the next world. This harrowing description is given particular attention in Chapter 4.

28. Codex Wormianus, probably written around 1350 in the Benedictine monastery of Þingeyraklaustur in northwestern Iceland. The codex also contains a version of Snorri Sturluson's *Prose Edda*, which tells us much of what we know about Norse mythology. The Old Norse version of the text used for the following is Bray 1908 (other editions available on http://heimskringla.no). For a full translation see Larrington 2014 or Crawford 2015.

29. "var kalfr soðinn krása beztr" (Bray 1908: 208). Bray's edition and Guðni Jónsson's edition of *Rígsþula* on http://heimskringla.no transpose the food eaten at the free-farmer household based on Sophus Bugge's (1867) suggestions because it is very unfortunately missing from Codex Wormianus. Other editions and the modern translations by Larrington 2014 and Crawford 2015 omit this line, although Hollander 1962 includes it.

30. "Auþ nam skipta, öllum veita: meiþmar ok mösma, mara svangrifja; hringum hreytti, hjó sundr baug" (Bray 1908: 213).

31. He is referred to as "Kinr Ungr" (young kin), which if combined is very close to the Old Norse word for king, konungr (Lindow 2001: 261).

32. "kjóli at ríða, egg at kenna, undir rjúfa" (Bray 1908: 216).

33. Here I draw from Michael Mann's (1986) work on the sources of social power.

34. Zachrisson 1994; Sanmark 2017: 85.

35. On Füsing overlooking the fjord entrance to Hedeby see Dobat 2010 and 2022; on Huseby interpreted as the legendary Skiringssal (Skíringssalr) overlooking Kaupang see Skre 2007.

36. Skre 2007: 229–241.

37. For discussion of the Huseby/Husaby place name see Christensen et al. 2016.

38. I treat the story of King Knut's martyrdom in detail in Chapter 5 about the formation of the state in Denmark.

39. Sanmark 2017: 48, drawing on runestone numbers from Sawyer 2002.

40. See Sanmark 2017, who divides assemblies into three groups, (1) top-level, (2) regional, and (3) local. The regional things in her typology are not found everywhere.

41. The sacral nature of at least some kings is suggested by names of early kings that refer to fertility. Several legendary kings, for instance, were named Fróði ("the fruitful/wise one"). Stories of various Fróðis, including one named Peace-Fróði, are told for instance by the Icelander Snorri Sturluson in his *Ynglinga Saga* (Hollander 1962) and by the Danish Saxo Grammaticus in Book 5 of *Gesta Danorum* (Davidson and Fisher 1996).

42. The story of the sacrifice of Dómaldi is told in several sources, including Snorri's *Ynglinga Saga*, the earlier Latin *Historia Norwegiæ* (Kunin and Phelpstead 2001), and in poetic form in the skaldic poem *Ynglingatal*, which enumerates the legendary kings of the Ynglinga family who ruled in central Sweden and later migrated to Norway (http://heimskringla.no).

43. Sanmark 2017: 37.

44. Sanmark 2017: 86–89.

45. Sanmark 2017: 63–64, 77, 89–91.

46. Sanmark 2017: 78.

47. "Iarlabanki let ræisa stæin þenn[a] at sik kvikvan, ok þingstað þenna gærði, ok æinn atti allt hu[n]dari þetta" (U 212). This and other runic inscriptions can be found in the Scandinavian Runic-text Data, which is now available online and for download at https://rundata.info/.

48. Ellis Davidson 1988: 58–68; Lindow 2001: 35; Lucas and McGovern 2007.

49. Ellis Davidson 1988: 58; Lindow 2001: 34–35.

50. The stories retold in the following paragraphs are drawn from Snorri's *Prose Edda* and the *Poetic Edda*. I draw also from insights from Ellis Davidson 1964 and 1988; Dubois 1999; and Lindow 2001. For translations of the *Prose Edda* see Faulkes 1987 and Byock 2005. For translations of the *Poetic Edda* see Hollander 1962; Larrington 2014; Crawford 2015.

51. "Vęit ek, at ek hekk | vindga męiði á | nætr allar níu, | gęiri undaðr | ok gefinn Óðni, | sjalfr sjalfum mér . . ." *Hávamál*, stanza 138 (Guðni Jónsson's edition on http://heimskringla.no).

52. Hel is the personification of an older conception of the underworld in which Hel is a place underground instead of a person (Lindow 2001: 172).

53. "Sól tér sortna, | sígr fold í mar, | hverfa af himni | heiðar stjörnur; | geisar eimi ok aldrnari, | leikr hár hiti | við himin sjalfan" (translation by Byock 2005: 75).

Chapter 2

1. Brown 2003.

2. "iii scipu Norðmanna of Hereðaldande, ⁊ þa se gerefa þærto rad, ⁊ he wolde drifan to ðes cininges tune þy he nyste hwæt hi wæron, ⁊ hine man ofsloh þa ðæt wæron þa erestan scipu deniscra manna þe Anelcynnes land gesohton" (Peterborough Manuscript E [787] edited by Irvine [2004: 41] is used here and generally throughout the book. The ⁊, the "Tironian *et*," is the

standard annotation used for the Old English "and" coordinating conjunction. The year given in brackets in footnotes is the year listed in the manuscript, which is often off by a few years and has been corrected in the text of this book and generally in most translation of the *Anglo-Saxon Chronicle*. Translation by Swanton 1998: 55).

3. "⁊ þa hæðenan on Norðhymbrum hergodon ⁊ Ecgferðes mynster æt Donemuþe berefodon, ⁊ þær heora heretogena sum ofslægen wearð, ⁊ eac heora scipu sume þurh oferweder wurdon tobrocene, ⁊ heora feala þær adruncon, ⁊ sume cuce to þam stæðe comon, ⁊ þa man sona ofsloh æt ðære ea muðan" (MS E [794], Irvine 2004: 41; translation by Swanton 1998: 57).

4. See Danish Viking activity on the northern borders of the Carolingian Empire in the early ninth century in the *Royal Frankish Annals*, which also records contemporaneous Viking exploits to Ireland and Scotland (Scholz 1970: 83–122). See also historical outline in Jones 1984.

5. For example, the Peterborough Manuscript relates that in 837 (840) the thirty-three shiploads of Danes fought against an Ealdorman named Wulfheard at Southampton, before fighting another Ealdorman named Æthelhelm in Portland. Æthelhelm was killed in the battle and the *Chronicle* says that "the Danish had possession of the place of slaughter" (Swanton 1998: 63).

6. ". . . hi to anum gecyrdon . . ." (MS E [835], Irvine 2004: 45; translation by Swanton 1998: 63).

7. Peterborough Manuscript E; Swanton 1998: 64.

8. The arrival of the Great Summer Army is recorded in the *Anglo-Saxon Chronicle* (Swanton 1998: 72–73) and by Asser (Keynes and Lapidge 1983: 80).

9. ". . . þa comon hi to Medeshamstede [original name of Petersborough], beorndon ⁊ bræcon, slogon abbot ⁊ munecas ⁊ eall þet hi þær fundon, macedon hit þa þet ær wæs ful rice, þa hit wearð to nan þing" (MS E [870], Irvine 2004: 48; translation by Swanton 1998: 71).

10. Irvine 2004: 48–49.

11. ". . . him georo wære swa hwilce dæge swa hi hit habban woldon ⁊ he geare wære mid him sylfum ⁊ mid eallum þam þe him gelæstan wolden to þæs heres þærfe" (MS E [874], Irvine 2004: 50; translation by Swanton 1998: 73). Ceolwulf II of Mercia (reign 874–879), traditionally seen as a puppet king of the Vikings, appears to be more complex and savvier politically than previously thought. The Watlington Hoard found in 2015 in Oxfordshire includes several examples of a coins showing Alfred the Great and Ceolwulf II sitting side by side in a Classical style known as "Two Emperors," suggesting that the two rulers established an alliance that may have been part of a strategy to resist the Viking incursions (Williams and Naylor 2016). However, Ceolwulf II goes unheralded in the historical record from which he disappears, while Alfred and the subsequent kings of Wessex go on to conquer Mercia and eventually unite England.

12. "þy gear Healfdene Norðanhymbra land gedældle, ⁊ hergende weron ⁊ heora tiligende wæron" (MS E [876], Irvine 2004: 45; translation in Swanton 1998: 74–75).

13. Swanton 1998: 77.

14. The battle, the agreement, and Guthrum's baptism are recorded in the *Anglos-Saxon Chronicle* (Swanton 1998: 77), while it is Asser, King Alfred's biographer, who adds that it was King Alfred who "raised him from the font of baptism, receiving him as his adoptive son" (Keynes and Lapidge 1983: 85).

15. ". . . gesæt þet land ⁊ gedælde . . ." (MS E [880], Irvine 2004: 45; translation in Swanton [1998: 74–75]).

16. Preserved in both an Anglo-Saxon and a Latin manuscript from the reign of Alfred, the treaty probably dates to the mid- to late 880s after Alfred reconquered London in 886 and before Guthrum's death in 890.

17. ". . . tofor se here sum on Eastengle, sum on Norðhymbre, ⁊ þa þe feohlease wæron him þær scipu begeaton ⁊ suþ ofer sæ foran to Signe" (MS B [897], my translation).

18. In 897 Alfred built "many" long-ships, some with more than sixty oars to oppose Viking sea-based raiders.

19. See Hill 1969 for texts of all seven known versions of the *Burghal Hidage*, which show some inconsistencies but together list thirty-three separate burhs; see also Hill and Rumble 1996 and a translation in Keynes and Lapidge 1983: 193–194.

20. The location of the Battle of Brunanburh is much debated, but it probably took place in northern England and possibly on the Wirral Peninsula where we find the only Brunanburh (Bruna's Stronghold) place name in Britain (see Williams 2017: 284–287).

21. The Brunanburh poem appears in the *Anglo-Saxon Chronicle* in the entry for 937 (translation Alexander 1991: 96).

22. The victory at the Battle of Brunanburh was used to legitimize the Wessex dynasty. It was the first poem incorporated into the *Anglo-Saxon Chronicle*, itself a historical tool employed to legitimize the Wessex dynasty.

23. Alexander 1991: 99.

24. The *Battle of Maldon* poem appears in the *Anglo-Saxon Chronicle* in the entry for 991 (translated by Alexander 1991: 103 with my modifications).

25. Alexander 1991: 103 with minor modifications.

26. See Chapter 5 on state formation in Denmark.

27. Latin letter in Liebermann 1903: 276–277; full English translation in Trow 2005: 193.

28. Translation by Crossley-Holland 1984: 30; Old English version in Liebermann 1903: 273. Knut's letter is preserved in the York Gospels, and some parts of his letter appear to have been edited by Archbishop Wulfstan of York in whose possession this manuscript was brought to York in cicra 1020. See Early English Laws Project, which is publishing high-quality manuscript scans, transcriptions, and translations: http://www.earlyenglishlaws.ac.uk/.

29. Data from Scandinavian Runic-text Database created by the Rundata Project: http://www.nordiska.uu.se/forskn/samnord.htm. Throughout this book, unless otherwise stated, I have used the runic inscription from the Rundata database in the normalized Old Norse form.

30. Runestone U241: "En Danr ok Húskarl ok Sveinn létu rétta stein eptir Ulfrík, fôðurfôður sinn. Hann hafði á Englandi tvau gjald tekit. Guð hjalpi þeira feðga sálu ok Guðs móðir" (Rundata database).

31. Runestone N184: "Arnsteinn reisti stein þenna eptir Bjór, son sinn. Sá varð dauðr í liði, þá's Knútr sótti England. Einn er Guð" (Rundata database).

32. Runestone U344: En Ulfr hefir á Englandi þrjú gjald tekit. Þat var fyrsta þat's Tosti ga[l]t. Þá [galt] Þorketill. Þá galt Knútr" (Rundata database).

33. Adapted and modified from Rundata: "Ástráðr ok Hildu[ng]r/Hildv[íg]r/Hildu[lf]r reistu stein þenna ept Fraða/Freða, frænda sinn sinn, en hann var þá feikn(?) vera, en hann varð dauðr á Svíþjóðu ok var fyrstr(?) í(?) Friggis(?) liði(?) þá allir víkingar)" (normalized Norse from the Scaldic.org database of *The Skaldic Project*, an international effort to edit the Old Norse/Old Icelandic skaldic poetry). Translation based on Moltke, 1976: 150–151. See also Imer and Fortuna 2016: 74 and 75.

34. Runestone SÖ179: "Tóla lét reisa stein þenna at son sinn Harald, bróður Ingvars. Þeir fóru drengila fjarri at gulli ok austarla erni gáfu, dóu sunnarla á Serklandi" (Rundata database).

35. Kjartanson 2002. *Ingvar's Saga* is preserved in a late Icelandic copy (probably early 15th century) that appears to be a translation of an original Latin text written by the monk Odd Snorrason at the Benedictine monastery of Þingeyrar in northern Iceland. The Icelandic version explicitly cites three oral sources, including a merchant who heard the story at the Swedish king's court. Three Icelandic annals (*Annales regii*, *Lögmanns annáll* and *Flateyjarbók* annals) mention Ingvar's death in 1041.

36. ". . . herjuðu um sumarit víða um Suðreyjar ok Skotlandsfjǫrðu ok áttu margar orrostur, ok reyndisk Gunnlaugr inn hraustasti ok inn vaskasti drengr ok inn harðasti karlmaðr, hvar sem þeir kómu" (*ÍF* 3: 99).

37. "En er Þórólfr var á tvítugs aldri, þá bjósk han í hernað; fekk Kveld-Úlfr honum langskip. Til þeirar ferðar réðusk synir Berðlu-Kára, Eyvindr ok Ǫlvir,—þeir hǫfðu lið mikit ok annat langskip,—ok fóru um sumarit í víking ok ǫfluðu sér fjár ok hǫfðu hlutskipti mikit. Þat var nǫkkur sumur, er þeir lágu í víking, en váru heima um vetrum med feðrum sínum. Hafði Þórólfr heim marga dýrgripi ok fœrði fǫður sínum ok móður; var þá bæði gott til fjár ok mannvirðingar" (ÍF 2: 5–6).
38. The Battle of Hafrsfjord was traditionally dated to 872, however more recent scholarship places the battle sometime in the 880s (see Lincoln 2014).
39. In the medieval period, *Ragnar Lodbrok's Saga* was thought of as one of the legendary sagas, as is evident in the organization of the Ny kgl. Saml. 1824b 4 manuscript (c. 1400), in which *Ragnar Lodbrok's Saga* follows immediately after the *Saga of the Volsungs*. See Waggoner 2009, especially introduction pp. xiii–xvii.
40. "Gnyðja mundu nú grísir, ef þeir vissi, hvat inn gamli þyldi" (*Ragnars saga loðbrókar* ch. 15, Guðni Jónsson's editions of *Ragnar's Saga* and other Sagas of Ancient Times (Fornaldur sögur) are available online at https://www.snerpa.is/net/index.html).
41. "fjár ok ágætis" (*Ragnars saga loðbrókar* ch. 7).
42. "En þar sem þeir berjast við menn, fá þeir meira hlut ok fá sér nú bæði mikit lið ok fé" (*Ragnars saga loðbrókar* ch. 7).
43. "Spari manngi röf Rínar / ef röskva vill hermenn, / verr samir horskum hilmi / hringa fjöld en drengja" (*Ragnars saga loðbrókar* ch. 15; translation by Waggoner 2009: 28).
44. "[Þórólfr] lét þar á bera skreið ok húðir ok vǫru ljósa; þar lét hann ok fylgja grávǫru mikla ok aðra skinnavǫru, þá er hann hafði haft af fjalli, ok var þat fé stórmikit. Skipi því lét hann Þorgils gjallanda halda vestr til Englands at kaupa sér klæði ok ǫnnur fǫng, þau er hann þurfti. Heldu þeir skipi því suðr með landi ok síðan í haf ok kómu fram á Englandi, fengu þar góða kaupstefnu, hlóðu skipit með hveiti ok hunangi, víni ok klæðum, ok heldu aptr um haustit" (ÍF 2: 42).
45. "Áleifr of kom jǫfri, | ótt vas víg, á bak flótta, | þingharðan frák þengil | þann, en felldi annan; | glapstígu lét gnóga | Goðrekr á mó troðna; | jǫrð spenr Engla skerðir | Alfgeirs und sik halfa" (ÍF 2: 131, translation by Pálsson and Edwards 1976: 119).
46. "því at þat var þá mikill siðr, bæði med kaupmǫnnum ok þeim mǫnnum, er á mála gengu með kristnum mǫnnum" (ÍF 2: 128).
47. Richards 2004: 26. After this statement, Richards does go on to chart evidence of Viking raids through hoards, fortifications, cemeteries, and stray finds.
48. Raffield et al. 2017. The threat to reliquaries and the saintly contents of the shrines was well known to monks, such as the monks of Iona. As recorded in the *Annals of Ulster* for 878 where the monks sent the shrine of Colum Cille to Ireland "to escape the foreigners."
49. Heen-Pettersen and Murray 2018.
50. Lowe 2008: 151–156.
51. Murray 2015.
52. Murray 2015.
53. Heen-Pettersen and Murray 2018.
54. Kershaw 2014: 155–156.
55. Archibald 2013; Kershaw 2014: 155.
56. Project leader Jane Kershaw's blog: http://vikingmetalwork.blogspot.com/ (accessed August 7, 2018).
57. von Heijne 2011.
58. Gullbekk 2011: 177; Eldjárn 1948.
59. Lamm 2007.
60. Jankoviak 2016: 118; Lamm 2007.

61. Östergren 2011, esp. 328–330; Lamm 2007.
62. Graham-Campbell 2013.
63. Williams and Ager 2010.
64. Williams and Ager 2010: 15.
65. Williams and Ager 2010: 17.
66. Martin Goldberg's presentations of the hoard on National Museums Scotland website (accessed August 6, 2018): https://www.nms.ac.uk/explore-our-collections/stories/scottish-history-and-archaeology/galloway-hoard.
67. Owen 2015.
68. Snorri Sturluson explains in *Heimskringla* that pre-Christian peoples often buried objects in the ground so that they could use them in the afterlife (see Chapter 4).
69. Hadley and Richards 2021: 81.
70. At least two and probably all four of the monumental crosses had been deliberately toppled and then smashed. The majority of the 223 fragments of these crosses that were found strayed within the destruction layer of the monastery belonged to monumental cross D, which had recently been completed and was erected at the southwestern edge of the monastery facing the sea (Carver 2016: 99, 127, 146).
71. Carver 2016: 146–148.
72. Carver 2016: 160; see also Williams 2017: 52–58.
73. Carver 2016: 146–155.
74. Carver 2016: 53.
75. Carver 2016: 155–156, 161.
76. Carver 2016: 160–161.
77. On Cronky ny Merriu see Wilson 2008: 93–95; on Camp de Péran see Price 1989: 55–60.
78. Swanton 1998: 72.
79. Swanton 1998: 72.
80. Mercian kings buried at Repton include Æthelbald (d. 757) for whom the mausoleum crypt may have been built, Wiglaf (d. 840), and Wigstan (d. 849). Biddle and Kjølbye-Biddle 1992: 36.
81. Biddle and Kjølbye-Biddle 1992: 37.
82. Biddle and Kjølbye-Biddle 2001: 84.
83. On the Viking graves from Repton see Biddle and Kjølbye-Biddle 2001; Jarman 2021: 18–41; and Hadley and Richards 2021: 146–163.
84. Biddle and Kjølbye-Biddle 2001: 66.
85. Biddle and Kjølbye-Biddle 2001: 66; Jarman 2021: 18–29.
86. Jarman 2021: 30.
87. Jarman et al. 2018; Jarman 2021: 30–36; Hadley and Richards 2021: 155–161.
88. Jarman 2021: 37–41.
89. Biddle and Kjølbye-Biddle 2001: 81–84.
90. Biddle and Kjølbye-Biddle 2001: 82.
91. Richards et al. 2004; Hadley and Richards 2021: 163–172.
92. Jarman 2018.
93. For the very preliminary evidence from Foremark see Jarman 2021: 66–67, 83, 85; and Hadley and Richards 2021: 115–116. To indicate the connection between the three sites, they have collectively referred to it as the "Repton/Foremark/Heath Wood complex" (Hadley and Richards 2021: 172).
94. Raffield 2013 reviews the archaeological evidence for Viking bases in Britain and finds that few have been verified and no apparent uniformity in camp form or layout existed.

95. Swanton 1998: 72
96. Portable Antiquities Scheme database accessible at https://finds.org.uk/database.
97. On Torksey see Hadley et al. 2016 and Hadley and Richards 2021.
98. Hadley et al. 2016: 50.
99. Hadley et al. 2016: 48; Hadley and Richards 2021: 101–102.
100. Hadley and Richards 2021: 96–97.
101. Hadley et al. 2016: 43–44.
102. Hadley and Richards 2021: 106–107.
103. Hadley and Richards 2021: 108.
104. Hadley et al. 2016: 56–57.
105. Williams 2015; Williams 2020; Hadley and Richards 2021.
106. Swanton 1998: 72, 74.
107. Williams 2015: 99.
108. Hadley et al. 2016: 31–32. Torksey means literally Tork's Island (Hadley and Richards 2021: 93).
109. Hadley et al. 2016: 31.
110. Hadley and Richards 117–140. One such site, Cottom, located just over 20 km east of York, shows evidence of being looted by Vikings in the 870s, before being abandoned, and then reinhabited by Scandinavian settlers (Hadley and Richards 2021: 178–185).
111. Buckberry et al. 2014.
112. Chenery et al. 2014.
113. The sex was determined to be male in forty-seven of the skeletons, while no biological females were identified (Loe et al. 2014: 53).
114. Loe et al. 2014; Abrams 2014: 15.
115. Arcini 2005; Loe et al. 2014: 212.
116. Loe et al. 2014: 153, 212–213.
117. Evans et al. 2018.
118. Sawyer 1962: 202–203.
119. Wormald 1982: 147–148.
120. See e.g., Ashby's (2015: 92) call for the need of considering human agency and the "social element" of raids more explicitly.
121. "He namque gentes. petulanti nimium luxu exardescentes. feminasque quamplurimas singulari turpitudine stuprantes commiscendo. illinc soboles innumeras obscenas inliciti conubii commixtione patrando generant. Hi postquam adoleuerint rerum possessionibus contra patres. auosque aut sepius inter se ferociter obiurgati fuerint exuberantes; atque terram quam incolunt habitare non sufficientes. collecta sorte multitudine pubescentium. uae terrae moritu in externa regna extruduntur nationum. ut acquirant sibi praeliando regna. quibus uiuere possint pace perpetua" (*Historia Normannorum*, ch. 2; Latin edition by Lifshitz (1998) available online at https://sourcebooks.fordham.edu/source/dudu-stquentin-gesta-transcript ion-lifshitz.asp; translation by Christiansen 1998: 15–17.
122. See e.g., Myhre 2000 on early Viking Age in Norway.
123. Sawyer 1997: 3–8.
124. Barrett 2008 and Ashby 2015; see Wicker 1998 on female infanticide and Raffield et al. 2016 on polygamy and concubinage.
125. Raffield et al. 2017.
126. Raffield et al. 2017.
127. Sigurðsson 2011: 71.
128. "Haraldr konungr eignaðisk í hverju fylki óðul ǫll ok allt land, byggt ok óbyggt, ok jafnvel sjóinn ok vǫtnin, ok skyldu allir búendr vera hans leiglendingar, svá þeir, er á mǫrkina ortu, ok

saltkarlarnir ok allir veiðimenn, bæði á sjó ok landi, þá váru allir þeir honum lýðskyldir. En af þessi áþján flýðu margir menn af landi á brott, ok byggðusk þá margar auðnir víða, bæði austr í Jamtaland ok Helsingjaland ok Vestrlǫnd, Suðreyjar, Dyflinnar skíði, Írland, Norðmandí á Vallandi, Katanes á Skotlandi, Orkneyjar ok Hjaltland, Færeyjar. Ok í þann tíma fannsk Ísland" (*ÍF* 2: 11–12).

129. See Chapter 5 on state formation in Denmark.

130. Sindbæk 2011a, who is followed by others, including Ashby 2015.

131. E.g., Barrett 2008; Sindbæk 2011a; Ashby 2015; Raffield et al. 2016; Raffield et al. 2017; for an early statement on collections of bridewealth as an explanation of Gotlandic hoards, see Burström 1993.

132. Sindbæk 2011a.

133. Ashby 2015.

134. Heen-Pettersen and Murray 2018: 57, untanned animal skin found adhering to the object suggested its use as a cloak fastener.

135. Brink 2008, 2012, and 2021; Raffield 2018.

136. Raffield 2018.

137. Although see Brink 2012 and Raffield 2018.

138. Sindbæk 2011a.

139. Myhre 2000; for the beginning of the Viking Age see Hadley 2006: 18.

140. Wormald 1982: 144–148.

141. "Dęyr fé, dęyja frændr, dęyr sjalfr hit sama; ęn orðstírr dęyr aldrigi hvęims sér góðan getr" (Jónsson 1932: 34). *Hávamál* is preserved in the Icelandic *Codex Regius* manuscript dating to the thirteenth century.

142. "Hjoggum vér með hjörvi. | Hitt lægir mik, jafnan | at Baldrs föður bekki | búna veitk at sumblum; | drekkum bjór af bragði | ór bjúgviðum hausa; | sýtira drengr við dauða | dýrs at Fjölnis húsum; | eigi kemk með æðru | orð til Viðris hallar" (*Krákumál* verse 25; Guðni Jónsson and Bjarni Vilhjálmsson's edition [1943–1944], which is available online at http://www.heims kringla.no; translation by Waggoner 2009: 82). The poem consists of the last words of the Viking hero Ragnar Lodbrok as he lies dying in King Ælla of Northumbria's snake pit.

143. "Nortmannia propter asperitatem montium sive propter frigus intemperatum sterilissima est omnium regionum, solis apta pecoribus . . . Itaque rei familiaris inopia coacti, totum mundum circumeunt et pyraticis raptibus amplissimam terrarum facultatem reportant domum, penuriam suae regionis tali modo sustinentes . . . didicerunt iam pacem et veritatem diligere, paupertate sua contenti esse . . ." (*Gesta Hammaburgensis Ecclesiae Pontificum*, book 4, ch. 31; Latin edition in Schmeidler 1917: 264–265; translation by Tschan in Tschan and Reuter 2002: 211).

144. "Ecce populus ille pyraticus, a quo totas olim Galliarum et Germaniae provincias legimus depopulatas, suis nunc finibus contentus est, dicens cum apostolo: 'Non habemus hic manentem civitatem, sed futuram inquirimus'" (*Gesta Hammaburgensis Ecclesiae Pontificum*, book 4, ch. 44; Schmeidler 1917: 280; translation by Tschan in Tschan and Reuter 2002: 2002: 223).

145. Christiansen 1997.

146. Fellows-Jensen 2008: 396–399; Graham-Campbell and Batey 1998; Crawford 1995 (ed.).

147. On Balladoole see Wilson 2008: 28–46. On Scar see Owen and Dalland 2000.

148. Hall 2000: 148; Raffield 2016: 311.

149. Townend 2014: 100–112.

150. Richards 2004: 63.

151. Richards 2004: 63.

152. Townend 2002; Townend 2014.
153. Richards 2004: 60.
154. Fellows-Jensen 2008: 392.
155. Richards 2004: 61.
156. Townend 2014: 104–105; but see Brink 2008; Raffield 2018.
157. Richards 2004: 55.
158. These objects are frequently dress items and jewelry. See Kershaw 2013; Hadley and Richards 196–197.
159. Kershaw and Røyrvik 2016: 1678–1679.
160. Cooke 2016.
161. Wilson 2008: 28–46.
162. Jesch 2015: 183–190.
163. Jesch 2015: 185.
164. H. Williams 2016a; H. Williams 2016b; Richards 2004: 221–224; Walton 1954.
165. Over fifty of the hogback monuments are decorated with such end-beasts (Richards 2004: 221).
166. Townend 2014: 14.
167. H. Williams 2016a with a graphical depiction of these material citations in his Figure 5.
168. The style of the serpent bears resemblance to the late tenth-century Jelling style of art, which takes its name from the royal site of Jelling in Denmark (Townend 2014: 2).
169. Townend 2014: 1–5.
170. Ibn Fadlan's account of Viking Rus has the chieftain seated in a chair and several burials from Birka show evidence of the dead having been seated with their weapons leaning against them or placed around them.
171. Solmerca is used in the Kirkdale inscription, while the Old Byland stone uses huscarl (Jesch 2001: 238–239 and 2015: 184).
172. Jesch 2015: 183–187.
173. "Skjǫldungr, vannt und skildi; skœru verk, inn sterki; fekk blóðtrani bráðir; brúnar Assatúnum. Vátt, en valfall þótti; verðung, jǫfurr, sverði; nær fyr norðan stóru; nafn gnógt Danaskóga" (translation from Poole 1987: 275 and M. Townend 2012: 767; accessible on website of *The Skaldic Project*: http://skaldic.abdn.ac.uk).
174. See Chapter 5 on state formation in Denmark.
175. "Kom á fylki; farlyst, þeims bar; hervíg í hug; hafanda staf; Rauf ræsir af; Rúms veg suman; kærr keisara; klúss Pétrúsi" (http://skaldic.abdn.ac.uk).
176. Corpus of Anglo-Saxon Sculpture (http://www.ascorpus.ac.uk/catvol4.php?pageNum_urls= 80); Jesch 2015: 187.
177. Corpus of Anglo-Saxon Sculpture (http://www.ascorpus.ac.uk/catvol4.php?pageNum_u rls=80).
178. Townend 2014: 9–10.
179. *History of St. Cuthbert*, Johnson South 2002: 53.
180. Johnson South 2002: 53.
181. Johnson South 2002: 53.
182. Hadley 2006: 39–40; the monks of St. Cuthbert came in large part to control the lands between the Tees and the Tyne rivers (see Figure 2.1).
183. Kershaw 2017.
184. Blackburn 2005; Blackburn 2006.
185. Maltsberger 2018.
186. Townend 2014: 47.
187. Kershaw 2017: 184; Mainman and Rogers 2000: 2478, 2559–2564.

188. Skre 2008.
189. Townend (2014: 47) describes these coins as characterized by "independence, innovativeness, and vigour."
190. Blackburn 2005.
191. Townend 2014: 71–72.
192. Sawyer 1962.
193. Hadley 2006: 130.
194. Kershaw and Røyrvik 2016: 1678–1679.
195. Hadley 2006: 6.
196. Wirral and Lancashire Project published in Bowden et al. 2008, Turi 2015, and Harding, Jobling, and Turi 2010. The People of Britain Project published in Leslie et al. 2015 and reinterpreted in Kershaw and Røyrvik 2016.
197. Goodacre et al. 2005; Jorgensen et al. 2004.
198. New research suggests that in rare cases there can be transmission of paternal mitochondria to the offspring, who then harbor mitochondria from both the mother and the father (Luo et al. 2018). The infrequency of this occurrence coupled with greater quantity of maternal mitochondria means that mtDNA is a reliable source of information about maternal ancestry.
199. Griffiths and Harding 2015; Griffiths 2015; Harding, Jobling, and Turi 2010. Hoards of Scandinavian character include those found at Meols, Crosby, and Cuerdale.
200. Bowden et al. 2008: 302.
201. Bowden et al. 2008: 302–303; Turi 2015: 174.
202. Turi 2015: 174–175.
203. Goodacre et al. 132–133; Capelli et al 2003.
204. Capelli et al. (2003: 983) conclude, "Our evaluation of the Danish and Anglo-Saxon source populations, however, shows that the contributions of these groups are unlikely to be distinguishable by using the resolution available in our analyses."
205. Leslie et al. 2015: 313.
206. Leslie et al. 2015: 311.
207. Leslie et al. 2015: 313.
208. Leslie et al. 205: 313.
209. See Chapters 6 and 7 on North Atlantic migrations.

Chapter 3

1. Hayden 2014.
2. Gurevich 1985: 227, Roesdahl 1998: 44–45.
3. E.g., Pálsson 2016.
4. Mauss 1990: 75 (1924 in French; 1954 first English translation).
5. Mauss 1990, especially 37, 41, 74. The potlatches or gift-giving feasts of the native tribes of the American Pacific Northwest provide the classic example of competitive wealth destruction during feasts (Mauss 1990: 33–46).
6. Hayden 2001.
7. Dietler 2001: 67. Ritual in this sense is not necessarily religious or sacred and can be based on secular ceremony.
8. Dietler and Hayden 2001: 3–4.

9. See Pálsson's (2016: 60–65) thorough discussion of the term *veizla*.
10. Mauss 1990; Dietler 1996.
11. Citations from Dietler 2001: 66.
12. Dietler 2001: 76–82. Dietler (1996) previously referred to this feast type as the "entrepreneurial feast."
13. E.g., Clarke 2001; Wiessner 2001; Adams 2004.
14. Rosenswig 2007: 21–22.
15. Dietler 1996: 96–97.
16. E.g., Clarke 2001: 155.
17. "sicut mos est inter barbarous, ad confirmandum pactum federis opulentum convivium habetur vicissim per VIII dies" (*Gesta Hammaburgensis Ecclesiae Pontificum*, book 3, ch. 18; Schmeidler 1917: 161; translation by Tschan in Tschan and Reuter 2002: 130).
18. Lunde and Stone 2012.
19. The Eddic poetry, which also forms a key foundation for Snorri's work, is preserved primarily in the *Codex Regius* manuscript and to a lesser degree in other manuscripts such as *Hauksbók* and *Flateyjarbók* (see Chapter 1).
20. "Mjök er auðkennt, | þeim er til Óðins koma | salkynni at séa; | sköftum er rann reft, | skjöldum er salr þakiðr, | brynjum um bekki strát" (*Grímnismál* stanza 9, Guðni Jónsson's edition from www.heimskringla.no is used for all quotations from the Eddic poetry in this chapter; translation by Crawford 2015: 62).
21. The etymology of Einherjar is unclear, but should most likely be connected to battle-frenzied warriors devoted to Odin who have no fear of fighting alone.
22. "Fimm hundruð golfa | ok umb fjórum tögum, | svá hygg ek Bilskirrni með bugum; | ranna þeira, | er ek reft vita, | míns veit ek mest magar" (*Grimnismál* 24; translation by Crawford 2015: 65).
23. "fleska bezt" *Grimnismál* stanza 18. The name Sæhrímnir translates to something like "sooty sea-beast" (Lindow 2001: 262). The *hrím-* portion of the name refers to the soot that remains on a cooking pot.
24. "En aldri er svá mikill mannfjöldi í Valhöll, at eigi má þeim endast flesk galtar þess, er Sæhrímnir heitir." *Gylfaginning* chapter 38, Guðni Jónsson's edition from www.heimskringla.no is used for all quotations of the *Prose Edda*; translation by Byock (2005: 46–47).
25. "skapker fylla | hon skal ins skíra mjaðar; | kná-at sú veig vanask" (*Grimnismál* 25; translation by Crawford 2015: 65).
26. "Undarliga spyrr þú nú, at Alföðr mun bjóða til sín konungum eða jörlum eða öðrum ríkismönnum ok myni gefa þeim vatn at drekka" (*Gylfaginning* chapter 39; translation by Byock 2005: 48).
27. "er dýrt mundi þykkjast kaupa vatnsdrykkinn, ef eigi væri betra fagnaðar þangat at vitja" (*Gylfaginning* chapter 39; translation by Byock 2005: 48).
28. "..at mér horn beri Skeggjöld ok Skögul . . . þær bera Einherjum öl" (*Grimnismál* 36). "They bring my horn, my Valkyries . . . they bring the Einherjar beer" (translation by Crawford [2015: 67]).
29. In the poem *Alvíssmál* (Sayings of All-Wise), Thor asks a wise dwarf a series of questions about the world. One concerns the names for the "seed that is grown in the earth." Alvís explains that humans call it barley, that giants refer to it as "good eating," and that the elves call it "things to make beer from." Barley, as even the giants know, is good eating, but the wise elves can be trusted to understand that the highest value of the grain is in producing beer.(*Alvíssmál* 31–32; Crawford 2015: 139).
30. *Skáldskaparmál* 24 (Byock 2005: 87).
31. *Skáldskaparmál* 39 (Byock 2005: 114). Snorri recommends aspiring poets use suffixes -selja (giver) and -log (disposer) in combination with the alcohol provided, whether beer, ale, wine, or mead.

32. "... hví Freyja skal skenkja honum sem at gildi ása" (*Skáldskaparmál* 24; translation by Byock 2005: 87). Thor's first question is who invited Hrungnir to Valhalla.

33. "*mjöðrann*" (*Atlakviða* 9, describing Gunnar's hall), "*ölskálir*" (*Atlakviða* 34, describing Atilla's multiple halls and *Hamðismál* 23 on the Gothic king Jörmunrekk's hall), "*halir ölreifir*" (*Hamðismál* 18 on Jörmunrekk's hall).

34. "Land sáu þeir Atla | ok liðskjalfar djúpa, | Bikka greppar standa | á borg inni háu, | sal of suðrþjóðum | sleginn sessmeiðum, | bundnum röndum, | bleikum skjöldum, | dafar darraðar; | en þar drakk Atli | vín í valhöllu, ..." (*Atlakviða* 14; translation by Crawford 2015: 297).

35. "rastar djúpan" (*Hymiskviða* 5; translation by Crawford 2015: 92).

36. "Hvern létu þeir | höfði skemmra | ok á seyði | síðan báru; | át Sifjar verr, | áðr sofa gengi, | einn með öllu.

   öxn tvá Hymis (*Hymiskviða* 14–15; translation by Crawford 2015: 94).

37. In the poem *Þrymskviða* 24, Thor also consumes extraordinary quantities of feasting products at a wedding feast hosted by the giant Thrym. Disguised as the goddess Freyja, Thor eats a whole ox and drinks three kegs of mead.

38. "'Mörg veit ek mæti | mér gengin frá, | er ek kálki sé | ór knéum hrundit;" karl orð of kvað: | 'knákat ek segja | aftr ævagi, | þú ert, ölðr, of heitt." " *Hymiskviða* (translation by Crawford 2015: 98).

39. "en véar hverjan | vel skulu drekka | ölðr at Ægis | eitt hörmeitið" (*Hymiskviða* 39; translation by Crawford 2015: 99).

40. Mauss 1990: 82.

41. "Er-a svá gótt | sem gótt kveða | öl alda sona, | því at færa veit, | er fleira drekkr | síns til geðs gumi" (*Hávamál* 12; translation by Crawford 2015: 19).

42. "Ölr ek varð, | varð ofrölvi | at ins fróða Fjalars; | því er ölðr bazt, | at aftr of heimtir | hverr sitt geð gumi" (*Hávamál* 14; translation by Crawford 2015: 19).

43. "Haldi-t maðr á keri, | drekki þó at hófi mjöð, | mæli þarft eða þegi, | ókynnis þess | vár þik engi maðr, | at þú gangir snemma at sofa" (*Hávamál* 19; translation by Crawford 2015: 19).

44. "Söngr ok öl | hefr seggjum verit | mörgum at móðtrega, | sumum at bana, | sumum at bölstöfum; | fjölð er, þat er fira tregr" (*Sigdrífumál* 30; translation by Crawford 2015: 258).

45. The story is told in the *Gylfaginning* portion of Snorri's *Prose Edda*, chapter 46.

46. The poem provides one of the earliest datable depictions Valhalla (Lindow 2001: 105–106). The battle took place at Stainmore, northern Yorkshire.

47. "Hvat es þat drauma |, es ek hugðumk fyr dag lítlu | Valhöll ryðja | fyr vegnu folki? | Vakða ek einherja, | bað ek upp rísa | bekki at stráa, | borðker at leyðra, | valkyrjur vín bera, | sem vísi komi" (*Eiríksmál* from *Fagrskinna* manuscript, edited by Fulk 2012: 1003. This first stanza also appears in *Skáldskaparmál*).

48. The three main compendia—*Heimskringla*, *Morkinskinna*, and *Fagrskinna*—were written in the early 1200s, probably between 1220 and 1230. They chart Norwegian kingship from its origins until 1177 (Pálsson 2016: 51; Whaley 1991). I primarily use *Heimskringla*, the best of these compilations.

49. Pálsson 2016: 117. Viðar Pálsson primarily discusses these political bonds as existing in the saga world rather than in the Viking Age. He sees them more as a reflection of thirteenth-century realities and thirteenth-century perceptions of the Viking Age.

50. "... bœir stórir ok kornhlǫður stórar, naut mǫrg ok sauðir" (*ÍF* 27: 108).

51. "'Þat vilda ek, at nesit væri þetta allt sáit hvert sumar, er út gengr í vatnit ...' Mikit korn mætti þar á standa" (*ÍF* 27: 108).

52. "Þá er þær gengi til vats, skyldu þær standa sem þykkst umhverfis vatnit" (*ÍF* 27: 108).

53. "'Húskarla ... Þat vilda ek, at þeir æti at einu máli kýr Hálfdanar, broður míns' ... 'Hér muntu konung upp fœða, móðir' " (*ÍF* 27: 108).

54. "Thiggia kná med gulli glöð | gotna ferð at ræsi miöd. | Drekka lætr han vseit at sín | silfri skenkt it fagra vín" (*Háttatal* 91; edition and translation by Faulkes 1987: 216 with my modifications).

55. "thar er hilmir drekkr . . ." (*Háttatal* 87; translation by Faulkes 1987: 215).

56. "Seimthverrir fefr seima | seimörr lidi beima. | Hringmildan spyr ek hringum | hringskemmi brott stinga. | Baugstökkvir fremr baugum | bauggrimmr hiarar drauga. | Vidr gullbroti gulli / gullhættr skada fullan" (*Háttatal* 47; edition and translation by Faulkes 1987: 194–195).

57. Hollander 1964: 288–289.

58. "Búa hilmis sal hjǫlmum | hirðmenn, þeirs svan grenna, | hér sék, bens, ok brynjum, | beggja kost á veggjum. | Því á ungr konungr engi, | ygglaust es þat, dyggra | húsbúnaði at hrósa. | Hǫll es dýr með ǫllu" (*ÍF* 27: 140–141; translation by Hollander 1964: 338–339).

59. Hollander 1964: 18–19.

60. Hollander 1964: 15.

61. "tvær nausíður digrar ok feitar" (*ÍF* 26: 314).

62. "því at þeir hugðu allir, at svá myndi vera sem áðr var mælt, at vinátta væri með jarli ok Þorkatli" (*ÍF* 27: 166).

63. Hollander 1964: 424–425.

64. "Þar var siðvenja í þann tíma, þar er erfi skyldi gera eptir konunga eða jarla, þá skyldi sá, er gerði ok til arfs skyldi leiða, sitja á skǫrinni fyrir hásætinu allt þar til, er inn væri borit full, þat er kallat var bragafull, skyldi sá þá standa upp í móti bragafulli ok strengja heit, drekka af fullit síðan, síðan skyldi hann leiða í hásæti, þat sem átti faðir hans. Var hann þá kominn til arfs alls eptir hann" (*ÍF* 26: 66; translation by Hollander 1964: 39 with my amendments).

65. The saga states, "Hann skyldi erfa Harald, fǫður sinn" (*ÍF* 26: 273), which carries a dual meaning that "He intended to honor his father, Harald, with a funerary feast" and that "He intended to enter into his inheritance from Harald, his father." The two meanings are inextricably and ritually linked.

66. "in stœrstu horn af inum sterkasta drykk" (*ÍF* 26: 274).

67. "Varð þat allfrægt víða um lǫnd" (*ÍF* 26: 275). Making vows of allied action and sealing the vows with a drink at feasts was relatively common. Another example in *St. Olaf's Saga* has five kings of the Heiðmörk region of Norway vow communal action against that king in such a setting (Hollander 1964: 310–311).

68. "Þá skyldi blóta í móti vetri til árs, en at miðjum vetri blóta til gróðrar, it þriðja at sumri, þat var sigrblót" (*ÍF* 26: 20).

69. The etymology of *jól* is unclear, although it may be connected to sacrifices to Odin as one of his nicknames is Jólnir. On beer brewing see Gunnell (2005: 125–126), who also observes that the eleventh-century Norwegian Gulathing law book made the brewing of beer at Christmas mandatory.

70. "Furðu mikit torrek lætr faðir þinn sér at, er ek tók vist nǫkkura frá honum í vetr, en ek mun þér þat launa með feginsǫgu. Faðir þinn er nú dauðr, ok skaltu heim fara. Muntu þá fá ríki þat allt, er hann hefir átt, ok þar með skaltu eignask allan Nóreg" (*ÍF* 26: 92).

71. "Þar var ok drepin alls konar smali ok svá hross, en blóð þat allt, er þar kom af, þá var kallat hlaut, ok hlautbollar þat, er blóð þat stóð í, ok hlautteinar, þat var svá gǫrt sem stǫkklar, með því skyldi rjóða stallana ǫllu saman ok svá veggi hofsins útan ok innan ok svá støkkva á mennina, en slátr skyldi sjóða til mannfagnaðar" (*ÍF* 26: 167–168; translation by Hollander 1964: 107).

72. "Haft maðr ask né eskis | afspring með sér þingat | fésæranda at fœra fats" (*ÍF* 26: 168; translation by Hollander 1964: 107).

73. *ÍF* 26: 171–172.

74. "Hvirfingsdrykkjur" (*ÍF* 27: 178).

75. "til gleði gott at drekka mǫrgum saman" (*ÍF* 27: 179).

76. *ÍF* 27: 179–181.

77. "... reisti fyrst kirkjur á sjálfs síns hǫfuðbólum, ok felldi blót ok blótdrykkjur, ok lét í stað koma í vild við lýðinn hǫtíðardrykkjur jól ok páskar, Jóansmessu mungát, ok haustǫl at Míkjálsmessu" (Driscol 2008: 30, 32). Terry Gunnell (2005: 123) notes that this is also consistent with advice given by Pope Gregory the Great in 601 that pagan festivals and ritual structures be adapted into the new Christian religion.

78. Hollander 1964: 366.

79. "glaðr við ǫl, drykkjumaðr mikill" (*ÍF* 28: 202).

80. "'Ek vil ... nǫkkurar eignir þiggja, er liggja nær kaupstǫðum þeim, er þér, herra, eruð vanir at sitja ok taka jólaveizlur'" (*ÍF* 28: 197). This Skuli was the great-grandfather of the Earl Skuli with whom Snorri, the author of *Heimskringla*, spent time as part of his retinue in Norway.

81. By 1135 Orderic Vitalis identified the six most important towns (*civitates*) of the Norwegian kingdom as Niðarós (Kaupangur), Björgvin (Bergen), Túnsborg, Oslo, Sarpsborg (Borg), and Konungshella (Pálsson 2016: 110–111). These same sites are centers of royal power mentioned as King Olaf the Peaceful's favored places to winter.

82. "Þat var siðr forn í Nóregi, at konungs hásæti var á miðjum langpalli. Var ǫl um eld borit. En Óláfr konungr lét fyrst gera sitt hásæti á hápalli um þvera stofu ... Um daga Óláfs konungs hófusk mjǫk kaupstaðir í Nóregi, en sumir settusk at upphafi ... Óláfr konungr lét setja Miklagildi í Niðarósi ok mǫrg ǫnnur í kaupstǫðum, en áðr váru þar hvirfingsdrykkjur ... Á dǫgum Óláfs konungs hófusk skytningar ok leizludrykkjur í kaupstǫðum. Ok þá tóku menn upp sundrgørðir, hǫfpu drambhosur lerkaðar at beini ... ok þá hǫfpu menn dragkyrtla ... Mǫrg ǫnnur sundrgørð var þá. Óláfr konungr hafði þá hirðsiðu, at hann lét standa fyrir borði sínu skutilsveina ok skenkja sér með borðkerum ok svá ǫllum tignum mǫnnum, þeim er at hans borði sátu. Hann hafði kertisveina, þá er kertum heldu fyrir borði hans ok jafnmǫrgum sem tignir menn sátu upp. Þar var ok stallarastóll útar frá trápizu, er stallarar sátu á ok aðrir gœðingar ok horfðu innar í mót hásæti. Haraldr konungr ok aðrir konungar fyrir honum váru vanir at drekka af dýrahornum ok bera ǫl ór ǫndugi um eld ok drekka minni á þann, er honum sýndisk" (*ÍF* 28: 204–206; translation by Hollander 1964: 664–665 with my modifications).

83. Hayden 2014: 248–251; see also Kobishchanow 1987 for work comparing Norse and other European medieval itinerant feasts with a series of ethnographic and historical examples.

84. See e.g., Pálsson 2016; see also Gautier 2009 and Roach 2011.

85. See examples in Pálsson 2016: 71.

86. *ÍF* 29: 65; the *St. Olaf's Saga* portion of *Heimskringla* states that it was customary for kings to survey the region of Uppland with sixty or seventy men, "but never with more than a hundred men" ("en aldri meirr en hundrað manna") (*ÍF* 27: 49).

87. *Morkinskinna* in *ÍF* 24: 9.

88. *ÍF* 27: 101–104.

89. "Eiríkr konungr ok hans menn hǫfðu ǫll forn ker ok svá horn ok þó gyllt ok allvel búin, en Haraldr konungr ok hans menn hǫfðu ǫll ný ker ok horn ok búin ǫll með gulli, váru þau ǫll líkuð ok skyggð sem gler. Drykkr var hvárrtveggi inn bezti" (*ÍF* 26: 110; translation by Hollander 1964: 71 with my modifications).

90. "Hví skiptir þú svá fagnaði með okkr Haraldi konungi, at hann skyldi hafa af ǫllu inn betra hlut? Ok veiztu, at þú ert minn maðr" (*ÍF* 26: 111).

91. "En þar er þú minntir mik, at ek væra þinn maðr, þá veit ek hitt eigi síðr, at þú ert minn maðr" (*ÍF* 26: 111).

92. "En bœndr kjósa hinn kost heldr, at búa konungi veizlur þá stund alla, er han þurfti, til þess, ok tók konungr þann kost, at hann fór um land at veizlum með sumt lið sitt, en sumt gætti skipa hans" (*ÍF* 26: 334–335).

93. "vist ok drykk" (*ÍF* 27: 53).
94. "skyldum ok skǫttum" (*ÍF* 28: 162). For Harald on feasting tour see *ÍF* 28: 102.
95. "Nú es of verk, þaus vísi, | vandmælt, svát af standisk, | auðan plóg at eiga | Upplendingum kenndi" (*ÍF* 28: 167; translation by Magnusson and Pálsson 1966: 129).
96. See e.g., Pálsson 2016: 110. Itinerancy continued to a lesser extent as exemplified in the *Heimskringla* account of the feasting tour of two co-kings, Eystein and Sigurd, in Uppland around 1120 (Hollander 1964: 702).
97. See Chapter 6.
98. ". . . skal ek launa þér liðsemðina með heimboði ok vingjǫfum" (*ÍF* 8: 27).
99. "en þat er heimilt þeim, er fara vilja með mér; hinum er ok leyfiligt eptir at vera, er þat vilja" (*ÍF* 8: 36).
100. "margir búnir at fara með Ingimundi, þeir er mikils váru virðir, bæði bœndr ok lausir menn" (*ÍF* 8: 36).
101. *ÍF* 8: 89.
102. "efni váru gnóg, en fé eigi sparat" (*ÍF* 5: 9).
103. "þá er auðveldast at afla allra tilfanga" (*ÍF* 5: 11).
104. "Bjǫrn kveð ek at þessu, bróður minn, ok Helga ok aðra frændr mína ok vini; bólstað þenna með slíkum búnaði, sem nú megu þér sjá, sel ek í hendr Óláfi, frænda mínum, til eignar ok forráða" (*ÍF* 5: 12).
105. "Óláfr feilan tók þá við búi í Hvammi ok allri fjárvarðveizlu at ráði þeira frænda sinna, er hann hǫfðu heim sótt" (*ÍF* 5: 13).
106. "Mun ek ok nú til þess bjóðask í sumar á þingi at bjóða mǫnnum til boðs þessa; mun ek leggja fram kostnað at þriðjungi til veizlunnar" (*ÍF* 5: 73).
107. " 'eru hér nú margir menn, frændr hans ok vinir. Nú er þat vili brœðra minna, at ek bjóða yðr til erfis eptir Hǫskold, fǫður várn, ǫllum goðorðsmǫnnum, því at þeir munu flestir inir gildari menn, er í tengðum váru bundnir við hann; skal ok því lýsa, at engi skal gjafalaust á brott fara inna meiri manna. Þar með viljum vér bjóða bœndum hverjum, er þiggja vill, sælum ok veslum; skal sœkja hálfsmánaðar veizlu á Hǫskuldsstaði, þá er tíu vikur eru til vetrar' " (*ÍF* 5: 74).
108. "ok fengu þeir brœðr mikinn sóma, ok var Óláfr mest fyrirmaðr" (*ÍF* 5: 74–75).
109. "Þeim fannsk fátt um ok þótti œrit mikit við haft" (*ÍF* 5: 74).
110. "er sá kallaðr æ minni maðr, er ǫðrum fóstrar barn" (*ÍF* 5: 75).
111. "Þat var siðvenja þeira Gunnars ok Njáls, at sinn vetr þá hvárr heimboð at ǫðrum ok vetrgrið fyrir vináttu sakir" (*ÍF* 12: 90).
112. "Ok svá var dátt með þeim ǫllum, at engum þótti ráð ráðit, nema þeir réði allir um. Bjó Hǫskuldr í Ossabœ lengi svá, at hvárir studdu annarra sœmð, ok váru synir Njáls í ferðum með Hǫskuldi. Svá var ákaft um vináttu þeira, at hvárir buðu ǫðrum heim hvert haust ok gáfu stórgafar" (*ÍF* 12: 247–248).
113. "Vinátta var ok mikil með þeim Óláfi ok Ósvífri ok jafnan heimboð" (*ÍF* 5: 112).
114. "Skilðusk eptir þat með engri blíðu" (*ÍF* 5: 135).
115. On the importance of seating arrangements and the potential for contested seating generate discord, see Miller 2014: 51–58.
116. "Takask nú af heimboðin" (*ÍF* 5: 144).
117. Dietler 1996: 96–97.
118. "Sámr setti bú á Aðalbóli eptir Hrafnkel, ok síðan efnir hann veizlu virðuliga ok býðr til ǫllum þeim, sem verit hǫfðu þingmenn hans. Sámr býzk til at vera yfirmaðr þeira í stað Hrafnkels. Menn játuðusk undir þat ok hugðu þó enn misjafnt til" (*ÍF* 11: 123).
119. Pálsson (2016: 184) believes these patron client feasts to be very rare and finds most of the feasts in the Norse world to have been diacritic feasts between leaders of equal or near-equal

status. As stated in the introduction to this chapter, I believe that the visibility of the elite-only feasts is an artifact of the saga genre, which focuses on kings, chieftains, and the richest farmers.

120. "Guðmundr helt boð fjǫlmennt eitt sinn á Mǫðruvǫllum, ok var Halli þar, sem at hverju boði ǫðru, því er Guðmundr helt" (ÍF 9: 238).

121. "Hann var því vanr at fara norðr um heruð á várit ok hitta þingmenn sína ok rœða um heraðsstjórn ok skipa málum með mǫnnum. Ok stóð þeim af því hallæri mikit, er hǫfðu lítt áðr skipat til búa sinna. Hann reið opt með þrjá tigu manna ok víða sat sjau nætr ok hafði jafnmarga hesta" (ÍF 10: 117).

122. Lindqvist 1941 and 1942 are still the major publications of this corpus.

123. Ney 2012: 81. Additional examples of the welcoming scene continue to be identified with new techniques in photography, such as RTI (Reflectance Transformation Imaging), and 3-D Scanning (see e.g., Oehrl 2012: 92–96 and Oehrl 2019).

124. Lindqvist 1942: 96; Lindqvist 1941: figures 176 and 178. The Levide Kyrka stone postdates 1000. The inscription invokes the help of God for a married couple: ". . . son, who his father's . . . on one of them. That was(?) . . . God (help) this married couple's souls" (. . . sonr, sem síns fǫðu[r] . . . á ein. Þat var . . . Guð sálu þeira hjóna) (Rundata database).

125. In his Skáldskaparmál, Snorri Sturluson explains that, in poetics, women can be referred to by the "ale or wine or other drink that she serves or gives, also by ale vessels . . ." (Faulkes 1987: 94). For further discussion see Helmbrecht (2012: 83–87).

126. Lindqvist 1941: figures 106figures 118 and and 119; Lindqvist 1942: 110.

127. See Chapter 5 for more on power signaling with runestones in Denmark.

128. DR 248/DK Sj 35. Imer 2016: 108–109, 112–113, 270. The short text reads "Gunnvaldr's stone, Hróaldr's son, reciter/skald of Salhaugar." "Gunnvalds stæinn, sonaR Hróalds, þulaR á Salhaugum" (www.runer.ku.dk).

129. DR NOR1988;5. Translation from Imer 2016: 124. Rundata normalizes the portion of the text as follows: ". . . Véfriðr/Véfrøðr gerði . . . ept . . . fǫður. Kolfinnr/Gullfinnr fal/fals teitirúnar ok ævinrúnar . . ."

130. N 247. "[Ǫ]lhúsmenn reistu stein þenna eptir "Skarða, en þeir drukku [e]rfi hansI" (www.runedata.info).

131. Sawyer 2000: 101–102, 178–181.

132. DR 291. "Tonna setti stein þenna eptir Bram, bónda sinn, ok Ásgautr, sonr hans. Han var beztr búmanna ok mildastr matar" (Rundata database).

133. Imer 2016: 222–223, 244, 335.

134. Sm 44. "Vémundr setti stein þenna . . . bróður sinn,[Sve]in, mil[dan við] sinna [ok] A matar góðan, í orðlofi allra m[ikl]u."

135. The details of the Ladby burial in the following paragraphs are drawn primarily from Sørensen 2001: 58–120.

136. Sørensen 2001: 61.

137. Sørensen 2001: 64.

138. The following paragraphs about Oseberg are based primarily on the original publications by Brøgger et al. 1917 and 1928, and updated with Holck 2006 on skeletal analysis, Gansum and Risan 1999 on the mound stratigraphy, and Bill and Daly 2012 on dendrochronological dating. The grave goods are detailed in Grieg 1928.

139. Grieg 1928.

140. Herschend 2000.

141. Grieg 1928: 146–148.

142. The two women had similar $\delta^{13}C$ values, measured at −21.6‰ for the older woman and −21.0‰ for the younger woman (Holck 2006). On the use of the ratios of the stable isotopes ^{13}C

to ^{12}C (conventionally reported as δ^{13}C) in human bone collagen to identify marine vs. terrestrial diets, see Schwarcz and Schoeninger 1991. In general, terrestrial plants and animals that derive most of their carbon from atmospheric CO_2 have depleted levels of ^{13}C relative to marine organisms, which primarily derive carbon from the photosynthetic activity of phytoplankton.

143. Bill and Daly 2012.
144. Harris et al. 2017.
145. See Arents and Eisenschmidt 2010 and Eisenschmidt 2011 on Hedeby. There are wealthy graves in the nascent towns and emporia, such as the large ship burial at Hedeby and the wealthy chamber graves in Birka (see Chapter 4).
146. Runestone U Sl95. "Öl gott" (Rundata database).
147. Pluskowski 2010.
148. Isaksson 2003: 275; see also Isaksson 2000.
149. McCormick 2009: 406.
150. Sundt 1865.
151. Grønnesby 2016.
152. Bukkemoen 2016: 124–126.
153. Bukkemoen 2016.
154. Rundkvist 2011 suggests that it is so ingrained in Scandinavian research that it is difficult to argue that a particular site is an elite settlement unless a hall building has been found.
155. This section on Helgö draws primarily on Clarke and Lamm 2017, as well as new analyses by Frölund and Göthberg 2011; Göthberg 2015. For a comparison with sites such as Tissø see Jørgensen 2009; for early identification of the hall building on BG 2: Terrace 1 see Herschend 1995, although the original excavator had already suggested the site as a setting for political feasting (Holmqvist 1957: 107).
156. This assemblage makes up 95 percent of the glass excavated from the eight building groups and six cemeteries excavated on Helgö (Clarke and Lamm 2017: 51).
157. Building Group 2: Terrace 4.
158. Clarke and Lamm 2017: 60.
159. Lisbjerg (Jeppesen 2004), Erritsø (Ravn et al. 2019), Toftegård (Tornbjerg 1998), Tissø (Jørgensen 2009, 2010, 2013, 2014), Järrestad (Söderberg 2003, 2005).
160. The information concerning Tissø is drawn from Jørgensen 2009, 2010, 2013, 2014
161. "Hann hafði jóladrykkju at Helgafelli, ok var þar fjǫlmenni mikit, ok með ǫllu hafði hann mikla rausn þann vetr, en Guðrún latti þess ekki ok sagði til þess fé nýtt vera, at menn miklaði sik af, ok þat mundi ok á framreitum, er Guðrúnu skyldi til fá um alla stórmennsku" (ÍF 5: 217).
162. For more on the Mosfell Archaeological Project excavations, see Byock et al. 2005 and Zori and Byock 2014. Earlier statements about the hall at Hrísbrú are found in Zori et al. 2013, Byock and Zori 2013, and Byock and Zori 2014. The evidence for feasting has been presented in Zori et al. 2013; Zori et al. 2014 focuses on the evidence from excavated animal bones.
163. Byock et al. 2015; Byock and Zori 2017.
164. Carstens 2015: 23.
165. The narrower position was first theorized by Frands Herschend (1993), who proposed that a hall should exhibit the following five characteristics: (1) be located on a large farm, (2) show efforts to minimize the numbers of room-supporting posts, (3) have a special/central position on the farm, (4) have a fireplace without evidence of cooking or craft production, and (5) include special artifacts. I would agree to all these characteristics except #4. Carstens 2015 provides a recent revision of Herschend's proposal; see Tonning et al. 2020 for a recent application of Herschend's position that halls are not dwellings.

166. The narrow definition of the hall is also problematic, in my view, because it confounds non-domestic cult buildings with halls.

167. Lucas 2009: 376.

168. Orri Vésteinsson (2004: 74–75) has proposed ranking Icelandic longhouses into low, middle, and high status according to three parameters: house size, prestige-good presence, and mention in historical sources. By his criteria, the Hrísbrú longhouse ranks among the highest status farms in Viking Age Iceland.

169. The Hofstaðir excavations that took place from 1991 to 2002 are comprehensively published in Lucas 2009.

170. Lucas 2009: 116.

171. Lucas 2009: 390, 394. This interpretation has been questioned (see e.g., Sindbæk 2011b) and the unusual beam slots may also simply be supports for a wooden covering of the raised side aisles.

172. For instance, Gudrun Osvifsdottir's fourth wedding in *Laxdæla Saga*, which she hosts herself, had approximately 160 guests (*ÍF* 5: 201), while Hallgerd's (Gunnar's future wife) first wedding in *Njal's Saga* to the nouveau-riche and ill-fated Thorvald Osvifsson had no fewer than a 120 guests (*ÍF* 12: 32).

173. *ÍF* 12: 186. See Chapter 6.

174. "risuligr" (*ÍF* 5: 67).

175. "Þat sumar lét Óláfr gera eldhús í Hjaðarholti, meira ok betra en menn hefði fyrr sét. Váru þar markaðar ágætligar sǫgur á þilviðinum ok svá á ræfrinu; var þat svá vel smíðat, at þá þótti miklu skrautligra, er eigi váru tjǫldin uppi" (*ÍF* 5: 79).

176. "Þar hykk sigrunni svinnum sylgs valkyrjur fylgja heilags tafns ok hrafna" (*Skáldskaparmál* 14; translation by Faulkes 1998: 68).

177. "Þótti Óláfr vaxit hafa af þessi veizlu" (*ÍF* 5: 79).

178. Zori et al. 2013.

179. My discussion of the Hofstaðir cattle is based on Lucas and McGovern 2007 and McGovern 2009.

180. See fuller treatment of faunal remains from Hrísbrú in Zori et al. 2013 and Zori et al. 2014.

181. McGovern 2009: 331–332; Vésteinsson et al. 2002: 108–109.

182. Vésteinsson et al. 2002: 108–109; McGovern 1980 and 1985.

183. The wetlands were a valuable resource for the Viking Age settlers of Iceland, particularly because of the availability of sedge that could be collected and stored for winter fodder.

184. Perdikaris 1999.

185. The original pollen study by Hallsdóttir 1987 has now been supplemented by many more (see e.g. Erlendsson et al. 2006 and 2014). Probable ard plow furrows were noted in the excavations at Ingiríðarstaðir, Þegjandadalur (Hreiðarsdóttir and Roberts 2009).

186. Drying kilns have been found at for instance Leikjagata in Reykjavík (Mooney and Guðmundsdóttir 2020) and at the farms of Gröf (Friðriksson 1959) and Bergþórshvol (Friðriksson 1960) along the south coast. See Mooney and Guðmundsdóttir 2020 for review of finds.

187. Sveinbjarnardóttir et al. 2007.

188. A letter from Pope Celestine III in 1194 authorizes the archbishop of Norway to export grain to Iceland (*Diplomatarium Islandicum*, Sigurðsson 1857: 291–295).

189. See for instance *The Tale of Ale-Hood* (*Ölkofra þáttr, ÍF* 11), in which Ale-Hood brews and sells beer at the annual Icelandic Althing.

190. "'. . . mér þykki uggligt, þá er þér komið annars staðar, at þat flytisk, at þér hafið engi jól verri haft en þessi, er nú koma, ok Eiríkr inn rauði veitti yðr í Brattahlíð á Grœnlandi.' 'Þat mun eigi

svá fara, bóndi,' segir Karlsefni. 'Vér hǫfum á skipi váru bæði malt ok korn, ok hafið þar af slíkt, er þér vilið, ok gerið veizlu svá stórmannliga, sem yðr líkar fyrir því' " (ÍF 4: 220).

191. Lucas 2009: 78–79.
192. Guðmundsson 2009: 332 and 334.
193. Pollen research on Hrísbrú and the wider Mosfell Valley is presented in Zori et al. 2013, Erlendsson et al. 2014, and Riddell et al. 2018.
194. Riddell et al. 2018.
195. The so-called *Sturlunga Sagas* and *Bishops' Sagas* cover this period.

Chapter 4

1. Metcalf and Huntington 1992.
2. van Gennep 1960.
3. van Gennep 1960: 11 and 21.
4. Scholars of the Vikings (see e.g., Roesdahl 1998; Jones 1984) generally identify the Rus (Rusiyyah) with Scandinavians engaged in raids, trade, and tribute extraction along the Dnieper and Volga Rivers. For a cautionary voice about Rus identity, see Montgomery 2000, who also provides a translation of the section of Ibn Fadlan's text regarding the Rusiyyah. The *Russian Primary Chronicle* relates that the Rus were a sub-group of the larger ethnic group that it calls Varangians. The *Chronicle* tells that the Varangian Rus were invited in 860/862 to govern the Slavic tribes of western Russia (Cross and Shrebowitz-Wetzor 1953: 59).
5. Zori et al. 2013.
6. Lunde and Stone 2012: 49.
7. Lunde and Stone 2012: 51.
8. The funerary feast was a central arena for reinforcing—ritually and legally—the rights of inheritors. The Old Norse noun "funerary feast" (*erfi*) is directly related to the words for "inheritance" (*afr*) and "heir" (*arfi*). The connection derives from the social tradition that the inheritor had the duty and honor of throwing the funerary feast—in fact, the verb for "to throw a funerary feast" was *erfa* (see Grønvik 1982 for a detailed etymological argument for the connection between the institutions of inheritance and funerary feasting).
9. Lunde and Stone 2012: 51.
10. Lunde and Stone 2012: 52.
11. Lunde and Stone 2012: 52.
12. See Eriksen 2013 on thresholds.
13. Lunde and Stone 2012: 52.
14. Metcalf and Huntington (1992: 35) note that for both sacrifice and secondary burials "objects must be destroyed in this world in order that they may pass to the next."
15. Lunde and Stone 2012: 54.
16. Hertz 1960.
17. Lunde and Stone 2012: 54.
18. Snorri Sturluson might have been partially influenced by Christian views of heaven and hell in this binary reading of the fate of the Viking dead. However, this is not certain, and Snorri leaves more room for other fates than is allowed in Christian cosmology.
19. " . . . at alla dauða menn skyldi brenna ok bera á bál með þeim eign þeira. Sagði hann svá, at með þvílíkum auðœfum skyldi hverr koma til Valhallar sem hann hafði á bál . . ." (ÍF 26: 20). In *Ynglinga Saga*, Snorri tried to explain the origins of the pagan Scandinavian gods as being

legendary kings that were later thought of as gods. This was a common tradition for medieval Christian authors when explicating polytheistic beliefs in general. Known as euhemerism (from the Greek Euhemerus of Messene, who wrote similarly about Zeus), this approach, which divested pagan gods of their deity, let Christian authors like Snorri justify writing about the old gods (Lindow 2021: 103–120).

20. "Þat var trúa þeira, at því hæra sem reykinn lagði í loptit upp, at því háleitari væri sá í himninum, er brennuna átti, ok þess auðgari er meira fé brann með honum" (*ÍF* 26: 22–23).

21. "In fyrsta ǫld er kǫlluð brunaǫld. Þá skyldi brenna alla dauða menn ok reisa eptir bautasteina, en síðan er Freyr hafði heygðr verit at Uppsǫlum, þá gerðu margir hǫfðingjar eigi síðr hauga en bautasteina til minningar um frændr sína. En síðan er Danr inn mikilláti, Danakonungr, lét sér haug gera ok bauð at bera sik þannig dauðan med konungsskrúði ok herbúnaði ok hest hans við ǫllu sǫðulreiði ok mikit fé annat ok hans ættmenn gerðu margir svá síðan, ok hófsk þar haugsǫld i Danmǫrku, en lengi síðan helzk brunaǫld med Svíum ok Norðmǫnnum" (*ÍF* 26: 4–5; translation by Hollander 1964: 3–4 with my modifications).

22. "Hann andaðist þann sama morgun í lýsing, ok var lagðr í haug at heiðnum sið" (Jónsson's 1904 edition from *Flateyjarbók* is rare but available at www.heimskringla.no).

23. " . . . var lagðr Skalla-Grímr í skip ok róit með hann út til Digraness. Lét Egill þar gera haug á framanverðu nesinu; var þar í lagðr Skalla-Grímr ok hestr hans ok vápn hans ok smíðartól; ekki er þess getit, at lausfé væri lagt í haug hjá honum" (*ÍF* 2: 175).

24. *ÍF* 26: 23–25.

25. "Sá atburðr varð at Hlíðarenda, at smalamaðr ok griðkona ráku fé hjá haugi Gunnars; þeim þótti Gunnarr vera kátr ok kveða í hauginum" (*ÍF* 12:192).

26. "Þeim sýndisk haugrinn opinn, ok hafði Gunnarr snúizk í hauginum ok sá í móti tunglinu . . . Þeir sá at Gunnarr var kátligr ok með gleðimóti miklu" (*ÍF* 12: 193).

27. "Heldr kvazk hjálmi faldinn / hjǫþilju sjá vilja / vættidraugr en vægja, / val-Freyju stafr, deyja" (*ÍF* 12: 193; translation by Cook 2001: 130).

28. "Þat var eitt kveld um haustit at suðamaðr Þorsteins fór at fé fyrir norðan Helgafell; hann sá, at fjallit lauksk upp norðan; hann sá inn í fjallit elda stóra ok heyrði þangat mikinn glaum ok hornaskvǫl; ok er hann hlýddi, ef hann næmi nǫkkur orðaskil, heryði hann, at þar var heilsat Þorsteini þorskabít ok fǫrunautum hans ok mælt, at hann skal sitja í ǫndvegi gegnt feðr sínum" (*ÍF* 4: 19; translation by Quinn 1997: 138). *Hornasvǫl*—the word that Quinn translates as feasting—is a drinking bout using drinking horns or literally, the noise made with drinking horns.

29. Turner 1969: 95.

30. van Gennep 1960: 160.

31. "Brá hann þá saxinu ok hjó hǫfuð af Glámi ok setti þat við þjó honum . . . Fóru þeir þá til ok brenndu Glám at kǫldum kolum. Eptir þat báru þeir ǫsku hans í eina hít ok grófu þar niðr, sem sízt váru fjárhagar eða mannavegir" (*ÍF* 7: 122; translation by Byock 2009: 102).

32. "var þar myrkt ok þeygi þefgott. Leitask hann nú fyrir, hversu háttat var. Hann fann hestbein, ok síðan drap hann sér við stólbrúðir ok fann, at þar sat maðr á stóli. Þar var fé mikit í gulli ok silfri borit saman ok einn kistill settr undir fœtr honum, fullr af silfri" (*ÍF* 7: 57–58; translation by Byock 2009: 52).

33. " . . . var gripit til hans fast" (*ÍF* 7: 58; translation by Byock 2009: 52).

34. "fyrr skalk hǫgg við hǫggvi, / hjaldrstœrir, þér gjalda" (*ÍF* 13: 455; translation by Taylor 1997: 443).

35. "Nú hafðir þú þat ráðit, Þorsteinn, er helzt til, ok mundi eigi hlýtt hafa ella" (*ÍF* 13: 455; translation by Taylor 1997: 443).

36. Price 2008.

37. Stylegar 2007: 88.
38. Schetelig 1912; Sjovold 1974.
39. Ramskou 1950.
40. For Ingleby see Chapter 3 and Richards et al. 2004; for Salme see Price et al. 2016; for Trelleborg-type cemetery see Roesdahl 1977 and also later in this chapter.
41. Callmer 1991.
42. Callmer 1994; Price 2008.
43. Eldjárn 2000 reports no cremations, but see Byock and Zori 2014.
44. Sikora 2003; Leifsson 2012.
45. Pederson 1997; see Chapter 5.
46. Sørensen 2001: 62–63; as discussed in Chapter 3.
47. Leifsson 2012: 186.
48. Leifsson 2012: 186.
49. Eldjárn 2000: 4.
50. Leifsson 2012: 191–192.
51. Cooke 2016.
52. Cooke 2016.
53. For beach markets in the Irish Sea see Griffiths 2010: 110–118.
54. Ramskou 1954 and Ramskou 1976.
55. See, e.g., Roberts and Hreiðarsdóttir 2013 for such features revealed through excavation in northern Iceland.
56. Hedeby appears to have had the largest number of burials of the three towns, probably reflecting the fact that this was the largest of the Scandinavian early towns. The six Hedeby cemeteries have an estimated 10,000 graves (Steuer 1974: 19) that extend both outside and inside the town rampart. The Hedeby graves have only recently been carefully examined (see Eisenschmidt 2011, and especially Arents and Eisenschmidt 2010), and the graves contain few grave goods, which makes drawing insights into images of death more difficult. A notable exception is a rich boat grave in which the burial chamber was dug below the ship (Müller-Wille 1976).
57. Stylegar 2007: 66–68.
58. Stylegar 2007.
59. Stylegar 2007: 87.
60. Stylegar 2007: 77.
61. Stylegar 2007: 77.
62. Ambrosiani 2008: 97–98; Wigh 2001: 17.
63. Wigh 2001: 17.
64. Gräslund 1980: 86.
65. Gräslund 1980: 50–62; all grave numbers and statistics from Birka in this section draw from Gräslund's comprehensive 1980 publication of the Birka graves.
66. Gräslund 1980: 67–71.
67. Gräslund 1980: 55–58; for rivets (alternatively called clench bolts) found in graves that suggest the presence of pieces of boats, see, e.g., Zori 2007.
68. Linderholm et al. 2008.
69. Gräslund 1980: 67–71.
70. Brønsted 1965: 299.
71. Else Roesdahl (1998: 154 and republished in 2018: 162) used an illustration of this grave in her excellent textbook, *The Vikings* to exemplify the quintessential male Viking burial with the caption's opening line reading, "rich male grave from Birka."
72. Hedenstierna-Jonsson et al. 2017.

73. Linderholm et al. 2008.
74. Naumann et al. 2014.
75. Price 2008: 267.
76. Brøgger and Shetelig 1928.
77. Eriksen 2015: 89; Gardeła 2016: 188.
78. Gansum and Oestigaard 2004.
79. Wilson 2008: 28–35; Griffiths 2010: 81–83.
80. See Griffiths 2010: 83 for a statement on the ritual variations between the Rus and the Ballateare sacrifices.
81. Gansum and Risan 1999.
82. Klevnäs 2016: 460.
83. On breaking open burial mounds to eliminate the dangerous dead see Gardeła 2013; for an argument on monument destruction to mark transitions in power, see Bill and Daly 2012; and on monument re-fashioning to reconnect with ancestors, see Klevnäs 2016.
84. Gardeła 2013: 114.
85. Bill and Daly 2012.
86. Bill and Daly 2012: 815–816.
87. Bill and Daly 2012: 818–822.
88. Klevnäs 2016: 458.
89. "þat fekk ek aldri af feðr mínum, meðan hann lifði" (ÍF 7: 60; translation by Byock 2009: 53).
90. The transliterated rune text reads: "Haraldr kunungR bað gørva kumbl þósi æft Gorm, faður sinn, ok æft Þórvī, mõður sīna, sā Haraldr es sēR vann Danmǫrk alla ok Norveg ok dani gærði krīstna" (my translation from runestone DR 42 in Danish National Museum database, http://runer.ku.dk). The monuments at Jelling, including the messages on the runestones, are discussed further in Chapter 5 on the emergence of the state in Denmark.
91. Jochens 1999; the Christianization of Iceland is further treated in Chapter 6.
92. See, e.g., the Christians and the Christian church in Kjalnesinga saga (ÍF 14).
93. Eisenschmidt 2011: 97–100.
94. Similar items with Christian motifs have also been found in some Birka graves, where arguments have been put forth about blending of ritual traditions. It is also possible that some of the graves at Birka, particularly the simple inhumation graves inside the ramparts, are Christian. Here too, however, we are missing the other elements of Christian burial complexes: churches and cemetery walls.
95. Roesdahl 2004a.
96. Price 2002: 149–157, 185–186.
97. Roesdahl 2004a.
98. See Chapter 5 for more on the evidence of Christianization in Denmark.
99. Vésteinsson 2000a; Kristjánsdóttir 2004; Byock et al. 2005; Byock and Zori 2013; Zoëga 2014.
100. Zoëga 2014: 33.
101. On retroactive Christianization beyond Scandinavia see, e.g., Geary 1994: 37.
102. Zori 2007.
103. "GõrmR kunungR gærði kumbl þósi æft Þórvī, kunu sīna, DanmarkaR bōt" (runestone DR 41; Danish National Museum database at http://runer.ku.dk).
104. Krogh and Leth-Larsen 2007.
105. In Danish: "Kong Gorm højsat 959 og siden gravlagt her."
106. Randsborg 2008.

107. "Egill tók sótt eptir um haustit, þá er hann leiddi til bana. En er hann var andaðr, þá lét Grímr fœra Egil í klæði góð; síðan lét hann flytja hann ofan í Tjaldanes ok gera þar haug, ok var Egill þar í lagðr ok vápn hans ok klæði" (ÍF 2: 298).

108. "Grímr at Mosfelli var skírðr, þá er kristni var í lǫg leidd á Íslandi; hann lét þar kirkju gera. En þat er sǫgn manna, at Þórdís hafi látit flytja Egil til kirkju, ok er þat til jartegna, at síðan er kirkja var gǫr at Mosfelli, en ofan tekin at Hrísbrú sú kirkja, er Grímr hafði gera látit, þá var þar grafinn kirkjugarðr. En undir altarisstaðnum, þá fundusk mannabein; þau váru miklu meiri en annarra manna bein. Þykkjask menn þat vita af sǫgn gamalla manna, at mundi verit hafa bein Egils. Þar var þá Skapti prestr Þórarinsson, vitr maðr ... Bein Egils váru lǫgð niðr í útanverðum kirkjugarði at Mosfelli" (ÍF 2: 298–299).

109. The Icelandic law book *Grágás* states that all human remains from a graveyard that is being abandoned must be moved to consecrated ground at another church (Dennis et al. 1980, 1995; Jóhannesson 1974: 168).

110. For an alternate interpretation of the passage concerning the movement of Egil's bones see Tulinius 2004, who argues that the author of *Egil's Saga* invented this story in ironic imitation of a saint's *translatio*.

111. Byock et al. 2005; Byock and Zori 2014.

112. Erlandson et al. 2014.

113. For alternative interpretations of the Jelling monuments and the identity of the persons responsible for their construction see, e.g., Anderson 1996; Staecker 2005; and Randsborg 2008.

114. "Þorsteinn Egilsson hafði gera látit kirkju at Borg. Hann flutti lík Kjartans heim með sér, ok var Kjartan at Borg grafinn" (ÍF 5: 158).

115. Collingwood 1899: 59.

116. Bæksted 1942; Bjarnason 1972.

117. Snædal 2002.

Chapter 5

1. Service 1962; Fried 1967.

2. Feinman and Neitzel 1984.

3. See *Getica* chapter 3; English translation in Mierow 1908.

4. For the position of an early Danish kingdom see Ulf Näsman (2000, 2006) summarizing the ideas and results of the "Fra Stamme til stat i Danmark" project. For an early articulation of Danish state formation in the late tenth century see Randsborg 1980.

5. The translation of Orosius' work was traditionally thought to have been the work of Alfred, but the evidence is circumstantial at best. The work does, however, fall in the period of Alfred's reign. A parallel Old English/translation version of the text is available in Godden 2016.

6. Othere's account is also the first to mention the name Hedeby (að Hæðum = at the heathers).

7. "þa wæs him on þæt bæcbord Denamearc, and on þæt steorbord widsæ þry dagas; and þa, twegen dagas ær he to Hæþum come, him wæs on þæt steorbord Gotland, and Sillende, and iglanda fela ... And hym wæs ða twegen dagas on ðæt bæcbord þa igland þe in Denemearce hyrað" (Godden 2016: 42–44).

8. "on the port side of him were Langeland, Lolland, Falster, and Scania, and those lands belong to Denmark" ("... on bæcbord him wæs Langaland and Læland and Falster and Sconeg, and þas land eall hyrað to Denemearcan") (Godden 2016: 44).

9. Godden 2016: 44.

10. Randsborg 1980: 17.

11. Scholz 1970: 59.

12. Translations of both biographies in Thorpe 1969: 68, 157–158. Einhard was a contemporary, advisor, and friend of Charlemagne, while Notker wrote in the late 880s for Charlemagne's grandson, Emperor Charles the Fat.

13. Einhard says a follower; Notker reports it was his own son.

14. Scholz 1970: 83–84.

15. Scholz 1970: 88–89.

16. RFA reports that the fleet consisted of 200 ships (Scholz 1970: 91–92).

17. Scholz 1970: 93.

18. "quae regio ultima regni eorum inter spetentrionem et occidentem sita . . . cuius principes ac populus eis subici recusabant" (Kurze 1895: 138).

19. Scholz 1970: 99, 106.

20. Scholz 1970: 119; Harald continued to be entangled with the Frankish kings during the 830s. In 840, he supported Lothar, the son of Louis the Pious, against his father and was given further lands in Frisia. Eventually, everyone seems to have doubted his loyalties and Harald was executed in 852 (Reuter 1992: 32–33).

21. The *Annals of St. Bertin* explain that the larger Viking expeditions such as that which burned Paris in 960 consisted of separate *solidatates*, which should be understood as brotherhoods bonded by oaths of mutual benefit (Nelson 1991: 96).

22. Nelson 1991: 35.

23. These Viking activities are noted both in AB (Nelson 1991: 60–62) and in AF (Reuter 1992: 23).

24. "Orico [Horik] rege et ceteris cum eo interfectis regibus" (Waitz 1883: 45); the same civil war is reported in AF (Reuter 1992: 36).

25. For instance, a Viking named Godfred is referred to as king in the 880s in the *Annals of Fulda*, but he is indistinguishable in activities from other Viking leaders, except that, like Harald Klak before him, he became a vassal of Frankish kings and was granted land in Frisia.

26. Waitz 1884.

27. "Herioldus quidam rex, qui partem tenebat Danorum, ab aliis ipsius provintiae regibus odio et inimicitia conventus, regno suo explulsus sit" (Waitz 1884: 26). See English translation in Robinson 1921.

28. Waitz 1884: 30.

29. "solus monarchiam regni tenebat Danorum" (Waitz 1884: 52).

30. Waitz 1884: 63.

31. Waitz 1884: 63–64.

32. Bachrach and Bachrach 2014: xiii–xvii, xxix–xxx.

33. Warner 2001: 3, 62.

34. Bachrach and Bachrach 2014: 58.

35. Bachrach and Bachrach 2014: 139–140; Warner 2001: 101–102.

36. ". . . idola respuenda subiectis gentibus imperat, Dei sacerdotibus et ministris honorem debitum deinde prestitit" (Hirsch and Lohmann 1935: 141; translation by Bachrach and Bachrach 2014: 140).

37. Holtzmann 1935: 102–104; Warner 2001:131. Widukind only mentions the threat of this war, but his account cuts off before the German invasion in 974. The account here relies on Thietmar.

38. Holtzmann 1935: 104. The addition is found in the Corvey Manuscript but is absent from the otherwise primary Dresden Manuscript (on the manuscripts see Warner 2001: 62–63).

39. ". . . quam imperator contra Danos opera ac residio firmavit . . ." (Holtzmann 1935: 128, translation by Warner 2001: 146). As noted by Warner (2001: 64), Thietmar's use of *urbs* is inconsistent

and variable to the degree that he uses the term to describe sites ranging from commercial centers to temporarily garrisoned fortresses.

40. Tschan and Reuter 2002: xi
41. Adam's other main sources were early missionary biographies, which gave preference over annals or chronicles (Tschan and Reuter xxix).
42. Tschan and Reuter 2002: 20–26.
43. "Erant et alii reges Danorum vel Nortmannorum, qui piraticis exursionibus eo tempore Galliam veabant" (Adam of Bremen chapter 39; Migne 1853: 486).
44. "Nortmanni vel Dani tunc ab Arnulfo rege gravibus præliis usque ad internicionem deleti sunt" (Migne 1853: 492).
45. Tschan and Reuter 2002: 44.
46. Tschan and Reuter 2002: 47.
47. Tschan and Reuter 2002: 56–57.
48. "totum septentrionem ecclesiis et prædicatoribus replevit" (Migne 1853: 520).
49. Tschan and Reuter 2002: 72–73.
50. Tschan and Reuter 2002: 70.
51. Tschan and Reuter 2002: 90–91.
52. Tschan and Reuter 2002: 100.
53. Tschan and Reuter 2002: 123.
54. Tschan and Reuter 2002: 124.
55. Tschan and Reuter 2002: 135, 182–183, 188, 191.
56. Tschan and Reuter 2002: 140.
57. On Sven Aggesen's work see introduction in Christiansen 1992. On Saxo see introduction and commentary in Davidson and Fisher 1996.
58. Christiansen 1992: 55–60.
59. Davidson and Fisher 1996: 270–273.
60. Saxo describes these kingdoms as "insignificant" because of their "smallness" (Davidson and Fisher 1996: 279).
61. Christiansen 1992: 55–60.
62. Christiansen 1980: 6.
63. Christiansen 1992: 56, 59.
64. Called *Iulinum* by Saxo, Hynnisbrugh by Sven Aggesen, *Iumne* by Adam of Bremen, and Jómsborg in the sagas. The site is located in modern Poland on an island in the estuary of the Oder River.
65. Christiansen 1980: 6.
66. Sven Aggesen says 3,000 men.
67. Barracks (Latin: *contubernii*); Christiansen 1980: 36–37.
68. Other works on the Norwegian kings that are earlier than Snorri's but also less developed include *Morkinskinna* (c. 1220, covering years 1025 to 1157), *Fagrskinna* (c.1220, covering the period from the ninth century until 1177), and a few more synoptic versions in Latin, most notably Theodoricus Monichus' *Historia de Antiquitate Regum Norwagiensium* (c. 1180, covering the period from the mid-ninth century to 1130).
69. "Vil ek þá gerask yðvarr jarl ok binda þat svardǫgum ok vinna Nóreg undir yðr með yðrum styrk, halda þá síðan landinu undir yðvart ríki ok gjalda yðr skatta . . ." (*ÍF* 26: 238).
70. "Nú liggr allt und jarli | ímunborðs fyr norðan | veðrgœðis stendr víða | Vík, Hǫkunar ríki" (*ÍF* 26: 242; translation by Hollander 1964: 155 with my amendments in brackets and removing accents).

71. "Ok við frost at freista | fémildr konungr vildi | myrk- Hlóðynjar -markar | morðalfs, þess's kom norðan, | þás valserkjar virki | veðrhirði bað stirðan | fyr hlym-Njǫrðum hurða | Hagbarða gramr varða" (ÍF 26: 256–257; translation by Hollander 1964: 165).

72. For instance, to prepare the ground for his conquest, Knut the Great sent the Danish bishop Sigurd to Norway to help a rebellion against the Norwegian King Olaf the Saint (ÍF 26: 371).

73. ÍF 26: 298–299 and 302; both *Heimskringla* and *Knýtlinga Saga* claim that Harald's renewed attacks on Hakon's Norway were due to Hakon's refusal to accept Christianity.

74. ÍF 26: 371–372; Hollander 1964: 244. The sagas say the battle took place at Svold Island in the Baltic Sea while Adam of Bremen says the battle took place in the Øresund strait between Denmark and Scania.

75. See Thorarin Loftunga's poem *Tögdrápa* (Skaldic Project database and Hollander 1964: 463) that tells how Knut sailed to Norway, was elected king there without a battle, and thereafter appointed Hakon as regent.

76. On this point, Saxo Grammaticus agrees that Knut "bought" Norway.

77. Hollander 1964: 525.

78. Svein is known by his matronymic because he derived his claim to the throne through his mother Astrid (Ástríðr), who was Knut the Great's sister. In Modern Danish his name is rendered Sven Estridsen. His father's name was Úlfr, so he is sometimes also called Svein Úlfsson in the sagas.

79. Magnus' raid of Árós/Aarhus is described by skald Thjodolf (Hollander 1964: 566); Harald's sack of Hedeby is described by skald Stuf (Hollander 1964: 604).

80. "Hætt hafa sér, þeirs sóttu | Sveins fundar til, stundum; | lítt hefr þeim at þreyta | þrimr bragningum hagnat. | Þó hefr hauldvinr haldit | — hanns snjallr konungr — allri | Jóta grund með endum | ógnstarkr ok Danmǫrku" (Skaldic Project online database; for translations see Gade 2009: 313–322 and Pálsson and Edwards 1986: 47 on which mine is based).

81. "eigi hefir einhverr Danakonunga ástsælli verit of ǫllu landsfólkinu" (ÍF 35: 136).

82. The database for Danish runes consulted here is available from the Danish National Museum online at http://runer.ku.dk; unless otherwise noted all Danish runestone texts are from this database and all translations are my own. Imer 2016 is a recent treatment of the whole Danish corpus. The groundbreaking work that brought the Danish material together was *Danmarks runeinskrifter* by Jacobsen and Molke (1942). This is the basis of all subsequent work including the digital database and the standard numbering system that uses the prefix DR.

83. For an argument on the representative distribution of the runestones across the Danish landscape (because of their immobility in the landscape and variable distribution pattern through time) see Randsborg 1980: 29–31.

84. For dating of runestones see Imer 2014.

85. Nielsen 2005.

86. The Björketorp stone (DR 360) has a good example at the end of its inscription: "Unceasingly plagued by shame (unmanliness) and visited by sorcery, death will be the one who breaks this (the monument). I prophesy destruction" (original from Danish National Museum database: "Argiu hermalausR {utiAR} weladauþe, saR þat brytR. Uþarba spa").

87. 143. "Tōki ræisþi stæina þessi ok gærði kumbl þausi æft Apa/Æbba, māg sinn, þegn gōðan, ok Tōfu, mōður sīna. Þau ligg[i]a bǣþi ī þæim haugi. Api/Æbbi unni Tōka fēaR sīns æft sik" (Danish National Museum database; Imer 2016: 142).

88. See Lund 2020 for a focus on the social relationships; see Sawyer 1988 and 2000 for focus on property and inheritance; see Randsborg 1980 for focus on social offices in geographical space.

89. This general idea of messaging suggests a substantial portion of the population would be able to read these messages.

90. Runestone DK 209. The transcription from runes into Old Norse reads, "Ragnhildr satti stæin þannsi æft Alla Sǫlva, **goða** vīa, **liðs** hæiðverðan **þegn**. Alla syniR gærðu kumbl þausi æft faður sinn ok hans kona æft ver sinn. En Sōti rēst rūnaR þessi æft **drōttin** sinn. Þōrr vīgi þessi rūnaR. At rǣdda(?) sā verði es stæin þannsi ælti(?) eða æft annan dragi." Words bolded in this text are titles discussed in the main text. (Danish National Museum database; see also Imer 2016: 56; Roesdahl 1982: 26.

91. The title goði appears on three Danish runestones: Glavendrup, Flemløse 1 (DR 192), and Helnæs (DR 190) (Imer 2016: 114).

92. The term *nuRA* is debated, but the association with the ness of Helnæs is still the most logical (Imer 2016: 116).

93. Runestone DR 155: "Āsa satti stēn þannsi æftiR Ōmunda, ver sinn, es vaR hēmþegi Finnulfs" (Danish National Museum database).

94. Imer 2016: 56–57, 148–149, 151.

95. Imer 2016: 68.

96. Randsborg 1980: 16.

97. Runestone DR 41: "GōrmR kunungR gærði kumbl þōsi æft Þōrvī, kunu sīna, DanmarkaR bōt" (Danish National Museum database). On the probable original location of the stone, see Imer 2016: 137.

98. Runestone DR 42: "Haraldr kunungR bað gørva kumbl þōsi æft Gorm, faður sinn, ok æft Þōrvī, mōður sīna, sā Haraldr es sēR vann Danmǫrk alla ok Norveg ok dani gærði krīstna" (Danish National Museum database).

99. Imer 2016: 81.

100. Imer 2016: 81.

101. Imer 2016: 64.

102. On language style, the stone for instance uses the old-fashioned þausi instead of þusi for the demonstrative pronoun "these" (see Imer 2016: 174).

103. Roesdahl 1982: 145.

104. Runestone DR 1: "Þōr[u]lf[R] rēsþi stēn þannsi, hēmþegi Svēns, æftiR Ērīk, fēlaga sinn, es varð dōðr, þā drængiaR sātu um Hēðabȳ; en hann vas stȳrimannr, drængR harða gōðr" (Danish National Museum database).

105. See Imer 2016: 207, 209.

106. Runestone DR 3: "Svēnn kunungR satti stēn øftiR Skarða, sinn hēmþega, es vas farinn vestr, en nū varð dōðr at Hēðabȳ" (Danish National Museum database).

107. Runestone DR 66: "GunnulfR ok Øðgotr ok Āslākr ok RōlfR rēsþu stēn þannsi æftiR Fūl, fēlaga sinn, eR varð . . . dōðr, þā kunungaR barðusk" (Danish National Museum database).

108. Different typologies have been constructed. I follow Imer's (2014) revised typology, which is based on but varies from the traditional typology employed in *Danmarks runeinskrifter* (DR). The DR typology also had four phases but grouped the H and G Types together into one group, whereas it split the tenth-century inscriptions into Pre-Jelling and Jelling types.

109. Randsborg 1980: 31–33.

110. See e.g., Imer 2016: 112.

111. The first use of the word for king (*konungr*) is found on the Haddeby 4 stone (runestone DR 4) dated to 935–950 because of the presumed connection with a German victory over King Gnupa in 934 described by Widukind of Corvey (see above). On use of konungr see Imer 2016: 113, 154. The stone reads: "Asfrid, Odinkar's daughter, made this monument in memory of King Sigtrygg, her son and Gnupa's. Gorm carved the runes" (Āsfrīðr gærði kumbl þausi, dōttiR Ōðinkaurs, æft Sigtrygg kunung, sun sinn ok Gnūpu. GōrmR ræist rūnaR) (Danish National Museum database).

112. See Imer 2016: 131.
113. Randsborg 1980: 35.
114. Imer 2016: 277.
115. Imer 2016: 252.
116. Runestone DR 315: "Tōki lēt kirkiu gørva ok ..." (Danish National Museum database).
117. Imer 2014: 170; Nielsen 1970: 43.
118. But see Imer 2016: 298–318 on runestones in the late tenth century and into the eleventh century, specifically on the island of Bornholm. The late stones from Bornholm indicate a late arrival of Christianity and state power to the island and therefore also fit the general trend seen in the rest of Denmark whereby the proliferation of runestones occurs contemporaneously with Christianization and centralization.
119. Thurston 2001: 44; Callmer 1986: 204.
120. The ridges where crops were planted at Lindholm Høje.
121. Hald et al. 2020.
122. Randsborg 1980: 56–57.
123. Roesdahl 1982: 67.
124. The current village of Vorbasse has a Romanesque church of granite ashlar construction indicating the village's presence in the current location by the twelfth and thirteenth centuries (Roesdahl 1982: 54).
125. Roesdahl 1982: 52.
126. Randsborg 1980: 68.
127. Randsborg 1980: 69.
128. For example, Lejre in Sjælland, Gudme on Fyn, and Uppåkra in Scania.
129. Randsborg (1980:53) for instance states, "It is clear that the entire Viking Age experienced a growth in population, but it is equally clear that this development started much earlier than the political evolution leading to the formation of the state of Denmark at the close of the tenth century ... though we are not able to connect the onset of population growth with a particular social development."
130. Randsborg 1980: 50–54, 168.
131. A significant debate revolves around the issue of -thorpe settlements (see the classic view presented here and upheld by analysis conducted by Hedemand et al. 2003 as well as alternative views by Porsmose 1981 based on villages on Fyn).
132. Hedemand et al. 2003.
133. For innovative recent re-dating of Ribe ramparts see Croix et al. 2019, who also suggest a major effort to fortify Danish sites in the late tenth century.
134. Kieffer-Olsen 2008; Feveile and Jensen 2000; Croix 2015; Sindbæk 2022a
135. Croix et al. 2022: 49–50; Sindbæk 2022b: 435–443.
136. See Croix, Neiß and Sindbæk 2019 for an example of a non-ferrous metal workshop from Ribe and the role of craft production in organizing early emporia.
137. Roesdahl 1982: 78; see Croix, Neiß and Sindbæk 2019 for evidence of a workshop casting copper alloy decorative objects including possible Odin mask strap ends.
138. Baug et al. 2019.
139. Hilberg 2016; Hedeby and Schleswig appear to have coexisted during the late tenth and early eleventh century, during which period functions gradually shifted to the episcopal town of Schleswig.
140. See Hilberg 2009 for an overview of archaeological evidence from Hedeby excavations, metal-detector campaigns, and geophysics surveys.
141. Kalmring 2010, 2011.

142. See Resi 1990 on whetstones and Ashby et al. 2015 on reindeer antler.

143. Hilberg and Kalmring 2014 for imports from Hedeby found in Iceland.

144. Dendrochronology dates reported in Roesdahl 1982: 145.

145. Skov 2005: 15–39.

146. Skov 2005: 16–22.

147. Skov 2008: 220–222.

148. Nielsen 1968; Hjermind 2008.

149. Roesdahl 1980: 81.

150. Hjermind 2008: 188.

151. Møller 2008.

152. Møller 2008: 203–204.

153. Runge and Henriksen 2018.

154. Ulriksen et al. 2014.

155. Runge and Henriksen 2018: 17–18, 61.

156. Runge and Henriksen 2018.

157. Ulriksen 2008; Ulriksen et al. 2014.

158. The early stone cathedral is dated by textual reference to its construction by Estrid, sister of Knut the Great.

159. Hervén 2008.

160. The oldest of these houses had these dimensions 5.5 x 21 m.

161. Mårtensson 1976: 116; Roesdahl 1982: 82.

162. Malmer (2007) favors a Frisian origin. Others, particularly Danish researchers following Metcalf (1996), see the abundance of Wodan-monster sceattas in the eighth-century layers at Ribe as an indication that they were minted in Ribe (see e.g., Mosgaard and Kastholm 2014: 104).

163. The wics included Hamwic, London (Lundenwic), and Ipswich in England and Quentovic (France), Dorestad (Netherlands), Domburg (Netherlands), and Ribe on the Continent.

164. Feveile 2019.

165. Metcalf 1996: 404–408.

166. Malmer 2007: 16–18; Moesgaard and Kastholm 2014: 104–105.

167. Malmer 2007.

168. Randsborg 1980: 139.

169. Randsborg 1980: 151–161; these coins, potentially the first mass-produced coinage from Denmark, have been found for instance at Harald's ring fortress at Trelleborg, which may even have served as a mint location.

170. Roesdahl 1982: 93–94.

171. Crumlin-Pedersen 2002.

172. Roesdahl 1982: 45–47; Jørgensen 1977: 42–51.

173. On Ravninge Enge bridge see especially Ramskou 1981 and Jørgensen 1997; and also Randsborg 1980: 77, Roesdahl 1982: 47–49, and Christensen 2003 (for problematizing of the dendrochronology date, which Christensen believes can only be established as between c. 980 and c. 1010).

174. Anderson 2004; Dobat 2008; Tummuscheit and Witte 2018 and 2019.

175. Tummuscheit and Witte 2018: 69.

176. This phase had been previously dated by dendrochronology to 737, but recent excavations suggest that this dendrochronological dating pertains rather to a minor rebuilding of the earlier wall phase (Tummuscheit and Witte 2018: 71–72).

177. Tummuscheit and Witte 2018: 72–73.

178. Major phases and dating follow Tummuscheit and Witte 2019. See Anderson 2004 and Dobat 2008 for older and alternative phasing.

179. Ramparts on the peninsula worked in tandem with a log box-frame wall extending into the fjord (Dobat 2008: 40).

180. Roesdahl 1982: 141–146.

181. Randsborg 1980: 77.

182. See e.g., Sanmark 2017.

183. E.g., King Gautrek from the legendary *Hrolfs saga Gautrekssonar* spends a great deal of time sitting on his wife's burial mound (Jónsson and Vilhjálmsson 1943–1994: 43–151).

184. Runestone DR 41: "GōrmR kunungR gærði kumbl þōsi æft Þōrvī, kunu sīna, DanmarkaR bōt" (Danish National Museum database).

185. On dating see Krogh and Leth-Larsen 2007 and Chapter 4.

186. Dyggve 1948.

187. The fortress at the site of Trelleborg (literally, "Slave-fortress") was the first to be excavated, starting in the late 1930s (Nørlund 1948). This site has become the type site, giving name both to the Trelleborg Fortresses and to the distinctive Trelleborg-style longhouses, which were first excavated here. For the most updated and comprehensive statements on each of these fortresses see the following publications: Trelleborg (Nørlund 1948; Nielsen 1990), Fyrkat (Olsen and Schmidt 1977; Roesdahl 1977), Aggersborg (Roesdahl et al. 2014), Nonnebakken (Runge 2018; Runge and Henriksen 2018).

188. Runge 2018; Nonnebakken does have a plank-paved road running along the inside of the rampart as do Trelleborg, Fyrkat, and Aggersborg.

189. Goodchild et al. 2017; Christensen et al. 2018; excavations have also not uncovered a circular street inside the ramparts, which has been found at the four other Trelleborg fortresses.

190. S. Anderson 1996. Estimates for Aggersborg at 3,000 trees and 40 hectares of woodland are smaller in part because of a slighter rampart and the suggestion that house walls there were made with branches and wattle and daub construction (see Sindbæk 2014: 174, 181–183).

191. Pedersen and Roesdahl 2014: 423; Dobat and Roesdahl 2014: 211.

192. Trelleborg in Scania (Jacobsson et al. 1995; Oleson 2000); Borgeby (Svanberg 2000).

193. S. Andersen 1996; the lengths of the houses were slightly different in each fort.

194. Skaaning 1992

195. Randsborg 1980: 101

196. Randsborg 1980: 101–102.

197. On riding equipment see Nørlund 1948; Roesdahl 1977; Pedersen and Roesdahl 2014: 306–311; On falcon bone see Degerbøl 1948: 263.

198. Pedersen and Roesdahl 2014: 302–305. The presence of an elite manor underneath the Aggersborg fortress might link the site to royal power even before the construction of the fortress. Conversely, it may also signal the royal destruction of old aristocratic power at the moment of the fortresses' construction.

199. Nørlund 1948.

200. Nørlund 1948: 105–114; Price et al. 2011.

201. Helbæk 1977: 1–9, 39.

202. Dobat 2009; Price et al. 2011.

203. Roesdahl 1982: 154.

204. Krogh and Voss 1961.

205. On stone churches in Roskilde see Ulriksen 2008 and Ulriksen et al. 2014.

206. Examples include the stone churches in Slagelse, Ringsted, and Aarhus (Roesdahl 1982: 182–183, 221).

207. Imer 2016: 143.
208. DR 134: "Assurr landhirþiR, Køgis(?) sun, rēst rūnaR þessi at Ās[b]ōð/Ās[m]ōð drōttning" (Danish National Museum database). See discussion in Imer 2016: 143–145.
209. Roesdahl 1982: 167.
210. Roesdahl 1982: 40.
211. Roesdahl 1982: 169.
212. Randsborg 1980: 126–133, Pedersen 1997, and especially Pedersen 2014a and Pedersen 2014b.
213. E.g., Randsborg 1980: 126–133.
214. The horsemen graves appear to all be males (Roesdahl 1982: 42), however, recent reevaluations of the biological sex of warrior graves, e.g., the Birka warrior woman (Hedenstierna-Jonson et al. 2017), could cast some doubt on this generalization.
215. Randsborg 1980: 126.
216. Roesdahl 1977.
217. Pedersen 2014a: 209–221. See especially table of all these burials in Pedersen 2014a: 212–213.
218. Pedersen 2014a: 212–223, 214 (Hørning); Roesdahl 1977: 83, 91, and 148; Roesdahl 1982: 43.
219. Roesdahl 1982: 43.
220. Roesdahl 1977: 92; Pedersen 2014a: 215.
221. Randsborg 1980: 131.
222. Randsborg 1980: 127.
223. Thaastrup-Leth 2004; Roesdahl 2004.
224. For Sebbersund see Birkedahl and Johansen 1995, Birkedahl 2000, and Nielsen 2008; for Lund see Cinthio 2002, Cinthio 2004, and Arcini et al. 2018.
225. Nielsen 2008: 137–138.
226. Cinthio 2002 and 2004; Arcini et al. 2018.
227. First articulated by Nørlund (1948) for Trelleborg and then extended to the other forts.
228. Roesdahl and Sindbæk (2014: 385) suggest that the fortresses may even have been decommissioned before the raids on England in the 990s, leaving them functional only for ten to fifteen years. The absence of artifacts dating to around 1000 or later suggests to them that Aggersborg was certainly abandoned before 1000 (Roesdahl and Sindbæk 2014: 203).
229. Roesdahl 1982: 155.
230. Roesdahl 1982: 153.
231. Randsborg 1980: 99.
232. Roesdahl and Sindbæk 2014b.
233. Roesdahl and Sindbæk 2014b: 413.
234. See classic statement in Weber 1946.
235. Christiansen 1980: 12 and 1992: 61.
236. "Knútr lézt framm til Fljóta, (frægr leið vǫrðr of ægi) heiptsnarr (hildar leiptra) harðbrynjuð skip dynja; Ullar lézt við Ellu ættleifð ok mô reifðir sverðmans snyrtiherðir sundviggs flota bundit" (Frank 1994: 120).
237. Following Anglo-Saxon tradition, Knut still needed to be elected king by an assembly (witena-gemot) of Anglo-Saxon nobles, which he called in London in 1016.
238. Bolton 2017: 87–89; the story is told in *Liber Eliensis* about the monks of Ely.
239. Bolton 2017: 139; see also Christensen et al. 1994; Roesdahl 2007.
240. Metcalf 1999: 395–397; Becker 1981: 119–121; to these, Knut's son Hardaknut added the mint in Odense before 1050.
241. Randsborg 1980: 80.
242. Jonsson 1994: 223; the initial English prototype was the so-called Last Small Cross type of Æthelred II.

243. Bolton 2017: 142–144; the English moneyers were not just limited to Lund as the Anglo-Saxon name Beortred was struck on coins from Slagelse on Sjælland.
244. Okasha 1984.
245. Metcalf 1999: 424, who hesitatingly suggests this possibility.
246. Bolton (2017: 158–171) argues that Knut was also a key mediator in the succession of Conrad II, which would further elevate his status as a political player on the continental scale.
247. Frank 1994; Bolton 2017: 189–191.
248. "Knútr vas und himnum" (Townend 2012; Skaldic Project database).
249. "Esat und jarðar hǫslu . . . munka valdi mæringr an þú næri" (Frank 1994: 120–121).
250. Frank 1994: 116; Bolton 2017: 190.
251. Bolton 2017: 189–191.
252. Gertz 1907; Hope 2019.
253. Parallel Latin and Danish version of *Tabula Othiensis*, *Epitaphium* and *Passio* in Gertz 1907.
254. Latin and English versions of Ælnoth's *Gesta* in Marchlewski 2012 (the full title is *Gesta Swenomagni regis et filiorum eius et passio gloriosissimi Canuti regis et martyris*).
255. "pro zelo christiane relifiounis et iusticie operibus" (Gertz 1907: 2).
256. *Epitaphium* leaves nothing to guesswork: "Traditus a propio sicut deus ipse ministro" ("Betrayed by his own man, like God himself") (Gertz 1907: 24).
257. Hansen 2019.
258. "rán ok óspekð" (*ÍF* 35: 157).
259. "Þar tekr þú illt ráð upp, er þú gerir þik at víkingi. Er þat heiðinni háttr" (*ÍF* 35: 157).
260. "Þat er mér ok sagt, at þú hafir fjǫlmenni um þik sem konungar . . ." (*ÍF* 35: 157).
261. "Óaldarflokki"; "Suma lét hann drepa, en suma meiða, suma rak hann ór landi í brott" (*ÍF* 35: 162).
262. Poulsen 2019: 57.
263. Christensen and Bjerregaard 2017; Bjerregaard 2019: 34–38.
264. Bjerregaard et al. 2017; Bjerregaard 2019.
265. A quote from the book of psalms (Bjerregaard et al. 2017: 109).
266. The dendrochronology samples did not include the outer rings, meaning that the last years of tree growth could not be counted (Bjerregaard 2019: 32).
267. Krag 2017 and 2019. The yellow dye from Persian Berries (Ramnus family) likely arrived in Byzantium along the Silk Road.
268. Tkocz and Jensen 1986; Rasmussen et al. 1997; Leth and Boldsen 2009.
269. The estimates vary in the three studies, for instance the skeleton thought to be Knut was aged as thirty to fifty-five (by Tkocz and Jensen 1986), thirty-five to forty-five (by Rasmussen et al. 1997), and twenty-seven to thirty-eight (by Leth and Boldsen 2009).
270. Bjerregaard 2019: 29.
271. Bjerregaard 2019: 29.
272. Marchlewski 2012: 205.
273. The *Anglo-Saxon Chronicle* records Knut's participation in raids in England in 1069–1070 and 1075 that resulted in looting along the Thames River and Humber estuary and at religious sites like St. Peter's Minster in York (Swanton 1998: 204–206, 211–212).

Chapter 6

1. Jesch 2015.
2. There is a huge literature on diaspora in anthropology. Often, diasporic communities have to be defined in relation to a homeland that has been left, but simultaneously in opposition to the

host society where the diasporic community has been newly established. Some of the emphasis and accentuation of the features drawn from the homeland are adopted precisely because they both establish and preserve an identity distinct from the host society. For the use of diaspora for Viking Age North Atlantic colonies, see Jesch 2015, especially pages 3 and 81.

3. Jesch 2015: 56.

4. Jesch 2015: 79.

5. Egerton 1848: xiv; Jesch 2015: 76.

6. *Grágás* states, "If foreigners are killed here in the country, Danish or Swedish or Norwegian, then in the case of these three kingdoms that share our language the suit lies with the kinsmen of the dead man if they are here in the country. But cases for killing foreigners from all lands other than those with the languages I just told may be prosecuted here on grounds of kinship by nobody except father or son or brother, and only these if they themselves had previously acknowledged the kinship here in the country" (Dennis, Foote and Perkins, 1980: 160). This law shows both that the Scandinavian countries were distinguished from one another and that the language of those three countries and Iceland was considered to be the same.

7. Tomasson 1980: 3–8.

8. Byock 2001: 22–24.

9. Tomasson 1980: ix–x.

10. Tomasson 1980: 12–13.

11. Rafnsson 1999.

12. "... es Ívarr Ragnarssonr loðbrókar lét drepa Eadmund enn Helga Englakonung; en þat vas sjau tegum [vetra] ens níunda hundraðs eptir burð Krists, at því es ritit es í sǫgu hans" (ÍF 1: 4).

13. "... fœri first þaðan til Íslands, þá es Haraldr enn hárfagri vas sextán vetra gamall, en í annat sinn fám vetrum síðarr; hann byggði suðr í Reykjavík" (ÍF 1: 5).

14. Jóhannesson 1974: 14–15.

15. See Hermanns-Auðardóttir 1991 for a presentation of the evidence for an early settlement of the Westman Islands.

16. For northwestern Norway see Skre 1996, for the Scottish Isles see Graham-Campbell and Batey 1998: 155–178, and for the Faroes Islands see Arge 2014.

17. Graham-Campbell 1980.

18. Grönvold et al. 1995.

19. Schmid et al. 2017.

20. Vésteinsson 2006.

21. See Hallsdóttir 1987 on the decline in birch pollen at the time of settlement. However, see Erlendsson and Edwards 2009 for presentation of evidence that there was some natural decline in birch forests already before the Viking Age settlement of Iceland.

22. Guðmundsson 1996.

23. See Erlendsson et al. 2014 for Hrísbrú; see Hallsdóttir 1996 for Reykjavík.

24. Buckland 2000.

25. Lee 1966; Anthony 1990.

26. Dugmore, Borthwick, et al. 2007; Dugmore, Keller, et al. 2007: 14; Mann et al. 2009. Estimates vary on the beginning and end of the Medieval Warm Period, and variations also existed regionally across the Europe and the North Atlantic. The Medieval Warm Period was followed closely by the start of the Little Ice Age (c. 1300–1850).

27. *Landnámabók*, first written down in the early twelfth century, is now preserved in three thirteenth- to fifteenth-century manuscripts known as *Sturlubók*, *Hauksbók*, and *Melabók*. These manuscripts largely correspond to one another but do vary in some details that are due to variations in oral traditions and choices made by the compilers of each.

28. *Sturlubók* manuscript: "Þeir gengu up í Austfjǫrðum á fjall eitt hátt ok sásk um víða, ef þeir sæi reyki eða nǫkkur líkindi til þess, at landit væri byggt, ok sá þeir þat ekki" (*ÍF* 1: 35).
29. "... viði vaxit á miðli fjalls ok fjǫru" (*ÍF* 1: 5).
30. "Þá var fjǫrðrinn fullr af veiðiskap, ok gáðu þeir eigi fyrir veiðum at fá heyjanna, ok dó allt kvikfé þeira um vetrinn" (*ÍF* 1: 38).
31. "... drjúpa smǫr af hverju strái á landinu, því er þeir hǫfðu fundit" (*ÍF* 1: 38).
32. Pierce 2009; Frei et al. 2015.
33. Keller 2010.
34. Pierce 2009; Einarsson 2011; Frei et al. 2015.
35. Jones 1984: 271.
36. Myhre 2000; Barrett 2008: 673–674; see also Chapter 5 for evidence from Denmark
37. "En þá varð fǫr manna mikil mjǫk út hingat ýr Norvegi til þess unz konungrinn Haraldr bannaði, af því at hónum þótti landauðn nema. Þá sættusk þeir á þat, at hverr maðr skyldi gjalda konungi fimm aura, sá es eigi væri frá því skiliðr ok þaðan fœri hingat" (*ÍF* 1: 5–6).
38. Jones 1984: 272–273.
39. The *Annals of Ulster* for 902: "The heathens were driven from Ireland, i.e., from the fortress of Áth Cliath, by Mael Finnia son of Flannacán with the men of Brega and by Cerball son of Muiricán, with the Laigan; and they abandoned a good number of their ships and escaped half dead after they had been wounded and broken" (Somerville and McDonald 2014: 246).
40. See Chapter 2.
41. Dunbabin 1985: 37–43.
42. Jones 1986: 46.
43. Dunbabin 1985: 78–82.
44. Bloch 1961: 39–59; Dunbabin 1985: 42–43.
45. Durrenberger 1992.
46. Byock 2001: 7–8.
47. "En þeir fóstbrœðr bjǫggu skip mikit, er þeir áttu, ok fóru at leita lands þess, er Hrafna-Flóki hafði fundit ok þá var Ísland kallat" (*ÍF* 1: 41).
48. *ÍF* 1: 299–300.
49. "Þórólfr Mostrarskegg fekk at blóti miklu ok gekk til fréttar við Þór, ástvin sinn, hvárt hann skyldi sættask við konung eða fara af landi brott ok leita sér annarra forlaga" (*ÍF* 4: 7).
50. "Þat var tíu vetrum síðar en Ingólfr Arnarson hafði farit at byggja Ísland, ok var sú ferð allfræg orðin, því at þeir men, er kómu af Íslandi, sǫgðu þar góða landakosti" (*ÍF* 4: 7).
51. "Réttum gengr, en ranga | rinnr sæfarinn, ævi, | fákr, um fold ok ríki | fleinhvessanda þessum; | hefk lǫnd ok fjǫld frænda | flýt, en hit es nýjast, | krǫpp eru kaup, ef hreppik | Kaldbak, en ek læt akra" (*ÍF* 7: 22; skaldic poem translated by Russell Poole in Byock 2009: 23).
52. E.g., Rafnsson 1999: 118.
53. *ÍF* 1: 9.
54. "Svá segja fróðir menn, at landit yrði albyggt á sex tigum vetra, svá at eigi hefir siðan orðit fjǫlbyggðra..." (*ÍF* 1: 396).
55. Karlsson 2000: 15; Sigurðsson et al. 2005: 128.
56. Benediktsson 1968: 335, 337.
57. Nordal 1933: 72–79.
58. Tomasson 1980: 14–17; Byock 2001: 82–83.
59. Byock 2001.
60. Sveinsson 1953: 10–12; Karlsson 2000: 72–78.
61. Jóhannesson 1974: 271–272.
62. Amorosi 1989; McGovern 1990; Amorosi et al. 1997.

63. Amorosi et al. 1997; for felling trees for fuel for iron production see especially Smith 1995.
64. Hallsdóttir 1987; Lawson et al. 2007.
65. E.g., Dugmore and Buckland 1991; Sveinbjarnardóttir 1992; and Dugmore et al. 2009.
66. Amorosi et al. 1997: 497–498.
67. See e.g., McGovern 1980.
68. See Simpson et al. 2003 on geoarchaeological study in Mývatnssveit; see Erlendsson et al. 2012 and Erlendsson et al. 2014 for palynological research in Borgarfjörður and in the Mosfell Valley.
69. McGovern et al. 2006.
70. McGovern et al. 2007.
71. See e.g., Diamond 2005.
72. E.g., Vésteinsson et al. 2002, Sveinbjarnardóttir et al. 2008, and Helgason 2009.
73. Byock 2001: 254 and Grønlie 2006: 11.
74. For instance, charred paneling found inside the Hrísbrú longhouse in the Mosfell Valley was identified as birch.
75. The importance of driftwood can be read for instance in medieval church charters, such as the one from the Viðey monastery that listed the rights to collect driftage from specific beaches along with other valuable possessions and privileges.
76. Deforestation of Iceland appears to have been multifactorial, caused by overgrazing, and cutting down trees for iron production and house construction, but possibly most importantly by burning to create grazing land for livestock. Deforestation led to severe erosion of the light Icelandic volcanic soils and prevented forests from redeveloping (Hallsdóttir 1987; McGovern et al. 1988; Smith 1995; Amorosi et al. 1997; Byock 2001). The settlement of early farms in various regions farther inland than seems logical based on the post-deforestation landscape has been suggested for multiple farms across the island, such as Skeggjastaðir in Mosfell Valley (Bjarnason and Sigurðsson 2005) and Kúða in Svalbarðstunga (Roy et al. 2017).
77. Trbojević 2016.
78. Vésteinsson 1998: 12–14.
79. Lucas 2009; Zori and Byock 2014; Kupiec and Milek 2015.
80. Kupiec and Milek 2015: 107–108.
81. Vésteinsson et al. 2002: 117.
82. On Mývatnssveit see McGovern et al. 2007; on Mosfell Valley see Byock et al. 2005; on Reykholtsdalur see Sveinbjarnardóttir et al. 2008; on Skagafjörður see Steinberg and Bolender 2004 and Zoëga 2014. See also Carter 2015 for use of coring to date settlements.
83. For the Skagafjörður Archaeological Settlement Survey, see Steinberg et al. 2016; Bolender et al. 2011.
84. Bolender 2015: 155.
85. Steinberg et al. 2016: 397, 399–400; only 20 percent of the farms in the surveyed region had been established before 930 (Bolender 2015: 162, 164).
86. Bolender 2007: 402.
87. Roy et al. 2017.
88. See for example the ancillary structures at Vatnsfjörður (Edvardsson and McGovern 2005; Mikołajczyk and Milek 2016).
89. Batey 2011 and Hansen et al. 2014; see Chapter 3 and later in this chapter for more on Hofstaðir.
90. Milek and Roberts 2013; Milek et al. 2014.
91. Forbes et al. 2013.
92. Buckland 2000.

93. Zori et al. 2013.
94. Trigg et al. 2009; Guðmundsson et al. 2012; Zori et al. 2013.
95. Zori et al. 2013.
96. Bolender et al. 2011.
97. Jóhannesson 1974: 33.
98. Dugmore and Buckland 1991; Sveinbjarnardóttir 1992.
99. Jóhannesson 1974: 32.
100. Sveinbjarnardóttir 1992.
101. Þórarinson 1977.
102. Vésteinsson et al. 2014.
103. Vésteinsson et al. 2014: 58, 62–65.
104. Gelsinger 1981: 12; Hayeur Smith 2020.
105. Þorláksson 1992; Byock 2001: 44–45; Hayeur Smith 2015; Hayeur Smith 2020.
106. Smiarowski et al. 2017; on Vogur, Bjarni Einarsson, personal communication.
107. Gelsinger 1981: 14.
108. Gelsinger 1981.
109. Durrenberger 1992; Zori et al. 2013.
110. Hansen et al. 2014.
111. Callmer 1977; Hreiðarsdóttir 2014; Byock and Zori 2014.
112. Smiarowski et al. 2017. The bulk trade in fish remained regional until after the close of the Viking Age and took off during the thirteenth century as documented in the emergence of larger trading sites, like Gásir in northern Iceland, that show clear evidence of fish production for export as part of the zooarchaeological profile of the site.
113. Price and Gestsdóttir 2006.
114. Pálsson and Edwards 1972: 6.
115. Jóhannesson 1974: 5–7.
116. Eldjárn 1989.
117. For examples of Hiberno-Norse ring pins see Vésteinsson 2000b: 172.
118. Kristjánsdóttir 2004 argues for Irish influence. For a counterargument and examples of other early Icelandic churches see Zoëga 2014: 45.
119. Specifically, Viking Age Norwegian Norse textiles were typically made from wool spun only clockwise (Z-spun), resulting in so called ZZ-spun cloth (i.e., clockwise spun wool both in the vertical warp strands and horizontal weft strands on the loom). ZZ-spun textiles were also the norm in Iceland in the Viking Age, but some of the early Icelandic cloth shows wool spun in both clockwise and counterclockwise (S-spun) directions, a cultural tradition that may have been brought from the British Isles (Hayeur Smith 2020: 34–53).
120. Urbańczyk 2012.
121. Vésteinsson 1998.
122. Urbańczyk 2002; Vésteinsson 2010.
123. Price et al. 2012.
124. Milek 2012.
125. Einarsson 1995.
126. Price and Gestsdóttir 2006.
127. Walker et al. 2012; Grimes et al. 2014.
128. For mitochondrial DNA of contemporary female Icelanders see Helgason et al. 2001 and Helgason, Sigurðardóttir, Gulcher et al. 2000; for Y-chromosome data from contemporary Icelandic males see Helgason, Sigurðardóttir, Nicholson et al. 2000; for aDNA from early Icelandic burials see Helgason et al. 2009.

129. Helgason et al. 2001.
130. Helgason et al. 2000.
131. Helgason et al. 2009.
132. Ebenesersdóttir et al. 2011.
133. Geary 2003.
134. By the Mosfell Archaeological Project (MAP).
135. For background on the Mosfellsdælingar chieftains see Byock and Zori 2014; Byock 2014; Zori 2010.
136. Helgadalur and Hraðastaðir first appear in a charter from 1395 of the lands owned by the Viðey monastery, situated on an island in the bay west of the Mosfell Valley. *Diplomatarium Islandicum*, vol. 3: 598.
137. Kruse 2004: 105.
138. Kruse 2004: 104; see also Gammeltoft 2001.
139. Olsen 1971: 36–39.
140. Sigmundsson 1979: 238–248.
141. Sigmundsson 1979: 241–243.
142. The first element (Mos-) refers to the green vegetation that would have covered the mountain when the Viking Age settlers first arrived. See Kålund 1877: 47.
143. Grímsson 1886. See also Thórðarson 2014 and Byock 2014 for more on movement of the Mosfell farm. The movement of farms and the name of the farm was not uncommon (see Jóhannesson 1974: 33).
144. Byock et al. 2005.
145. Landnám Tephra (877±1) in all walls of the house indicates that it was built after 877. A thin black tephra layer, which is either the Katla-R Tephra from 920 or the Eldgjá Tephra from 934, was found only in a section of repaired walls, indicating that the original house was built before that tephra fell (Zori 2010; Byock and Zori 2014).
146. See Chapter 3; see also Zori et al. 2013; see Zori et al. 2014 for a presentation of the faunal material from the Hrísbrú excavation.
147. See Chapter 4.
148. Earle et al. 1995.
149. Pálsdóttir and Hansson 2008.
150. Pálsdóttir and Hansson 2008.
151. Zori 2010 and 2014.
152. Byock and Zori 2009.
153. The mound is discussed as a pagan burial in 1817 by the priest Markús Siguðsson (see Rafnsson 1983; Stefánsdóttir et al. 2006: 57).
154. Fríðriksson 2009: 9–21.
155. Riddell et al. 2018.

Chapter 7

1. Sigurðsson 2004: 265; Jakobsson 2012: 496; Halldórsson 2001: 40–46.
2. See Þorláksson (2001: 73–75) for more information on the editor of the manuscript, Haukur Erlendsson, and the specific changes that he made.
3. The standard edited version of the sagas about Vínland cited in this chapter are found in *Íslenzk fornrit*, volume 4, edited by Einar Ólafur Sveinsson and Matthías Þórðarsson (1935).

Their edition uses the *Hauksbók* manuscript (AM 544, 4to) for *Eirik's Saga* and *Flateyjarbók* for *Greenlanders' Saga*. As in other chapters, the translations of the texts in this chapter are my own unless otherwise stated. *Skálholtsbók* has been used for most previous translations.

4. The insertion into *Óláfs saga Tryggvasonar hin mesta* (*The Greatest Saga of Olaf Tryggvason*) makes sense particularly in light of Leif's Christianizing role in Greenland assigned to him in the saga by King Olaf. *Greenlanders' Saga* is split in two parts within the larger *Óláfs saga Tryggvasonar hin mesta*, such that the first part of *Greenlanders' Saga* (chapter 1) appears forty chapters before the second part (chapters 2–8). Although the two parts are typically considered part of one united saga, the issue remains somewhat unresolved (see e.g., Larrington 2004: 93).

5. See Jóhannesson (1956) for an early date of *Greenlanders' Saga* (c. 1200). For an argument for the late recording of *Greenlanders' Saga*, see Þorláksson 2001: 66–67.

6. See Clover 1985:293–294 and 1986: 34–39. Clover (1986: 34) summarizes her view of the immanent saga: "[b]riefly stated, it is that a whole saga existed at the preliterary stage not as a performed but as an immanent or potential entity, a collectively envisaged 'whole' to which performed parts of þættir [short stories] of various sizes and shapes were understood to belong, no matter what the sequence or the frequency of their presentation." Although Clover doubts whether whole sagas were told in oral tradition, others including Anderson (1964) and Byock (1982) believe that repeated thematic elements and saga macrostructural similarities suggest that long prose sagas could have and probably did exist also in oral form.

7. Sigurðsson 2004: 266.

8. Jakobsson 2012: 497.

9. The root of the word Skræling is probably *skrá*, meaning "dried skin." It might also be derived from *skrækja*, meaning "to yell or scream."

10. Gathorne-Hardy 1921: 139; Gray 1930; Merrill 1935. Ingstad (2001: 63) shares the view that the account in *Greenlanders' Saga* preserves a Greenlandic as opposed to an Icelandic tradition, and this view, in part, means that he believes in the greater historicity of the straightforward descriptions of the Vínland voyages preserved in that saga.

11. Þorláksson 2001: 67–70.

12. Jóhannesson 1962.

13. Þorláksson 2001: 66–67.

14. E.g., Ingstad 1985; Ingstad and Ingstad 2001.

15. Ingstad 1985; Ingstad and Ingstad 2001.

16. E.g., Kristjánsson et al. 2012.

17. Kristjánsson et al. 2012.

18. Jóhannesson 1962; Wallace 2006.

19. *ÍF* 4: 223.

20. "Nú vil ek, at vér reisim hér upp kjǫlinn á nesinu ok kallim Kjalarnes" (*ÍF* 4: 255).

21. Sigurðsson 2004: 283–284 and Sigurðsson 2008: xxxii–xxxiii.

22. Sigurðsson 2004: 284.

23. Wallace 2009.

24. Reuter 2002; see also Sigurðsson 2004: 264. On Svein Estridsen/Astridarson (r. 1047–1076) see Chapter 5.

25. "Preterea unam adhuc insulam recitavit a multis in eo repertam oceano, quae dicitur Winland, eo quod ibi vites sponte nascantur, vinum optimum ferentes. Nam et fruges ibi non seminatas habundare non fabulosa opinione, sed certa comperimus relatione Danorum. Post quam insulam, ait, terra non invenitur habitabilis in illo oceano, sed omnia, quae ultra sunt, glacie intolerabili ac caligine inmensa plena sunt" (*Gesta Hammaburgensis Ecclesiae Pontificum*, book 4, ch. 39; Schmeidler 1917: 275; translation by Tschan in Tschan and Reuter 2002: 219).

26. Nansen (1911) proposed that the stories of Vínland were fantastical stories based on Classical poets like Plutarch and appearing in Isidore of Seville that came into the Irish legends of an ideal land that lay to the west. Vínland the Good in this theory was essentially the Norse translation of the Fortunate Isles. This theory was rejected by most scholars in the early twentieth century (see e.g., discussion in Merrill 1935: 40–41), but has since then appeared as a possibility in many recent works, especially those that view the voyages as being more legendary than historical.

27. The identification of *mǫsurr* wood has been contentious. Sometimes translated as maple wood (see e.g., Magnusson and Pálsson 1965: 71 and Hollander 1964: 596), while at other times translated as generic burl wood. Burl wood is a deformed outgrowth from a tree, caused by an injury, fungus, virus, or other stressor. The deformed grains and knots provide a visually striking material for carved woodwork. In an indication of the potential value of such carved objects, in the *Saga of Harald Sigurðarson*, King Harald the Hard Ruler gives a gift of a *mǫsurr* bowl to Thorir of Steig, who had conferred the Norwegian crown on Harald on behalf of a national assembly. The gift was afterwards passed down in the family as a prized heirloom (*ÍF* 28: 101).

28. "Þeir fundu þar manna vistir bæði austr ok vestr á landi ok keiplabrot ok steinsmíði þat es af því má skilja, at þar hafði þess konor þjóð farit, es Vínland hefir byggt ok Grœnlendingar kalla Skrælinga" (*ÍF* 1: 13–14).

29. See Chapter 6 on the settlement of Iceland and *Landnámabók*; the material in *Landnámabók* began to be compiled from oral tradition and possibly shorter writings around 1150, while additional material was added until around 1250.

30. The same expression is used in the *Hauksbók* version of *Eirik's Saga* but not in the *Skálholtsbók* version.

31. *Landnámabók* uses the dative phrase "nær Vínlandi enu góða" (close to Vínland the Good) to explain the location of a semi-mythical land named Hvítramannaland (Land of the White People) (*ÍF* 1: 162).

32. In the *Hauksbók* version of *Landnámabók*: ". . . Karlsefnis, er fann Vínland hit góða, fǫður Snorra . . . " (". . . Karlsefni, who found Vínland the Good, father of Snorri . . ."; *ÍF* 1: 241). This phrase is omitted in the other main manuscript version of *Landnámabók*, called *Sturlubók*.

33. The manuscripts include *Flateyjarbók* (with Annals completed before 1395), AM 420 B, 4to—Lewman's Annals, Royal Library of Copenhagen, No. 2087, 4to—Annales reggii. See Reeves et al. 1906.

34. The manuscripts that preserve this entry include AM 420 a, 450 (*Elder Skálholt Annals*) and *Flateyarbók* Annals. See Reeves et al. 1906.

35. ". . . eigi gras . . . sem ein hella væri allt til jǫklanna frá sjónum" (*ÍF* 4: 249).

36. ". . . sýndisk þeim þat land vera gœðalaust" (*ÍF* 4: 249).

37. "Af kostum skal þessu landi nafn gefa ok kalla Markland" (*ÍF* 4: 250).

38. *ÍF* 4: 250.

39. *ÍF* 4: 251.

40. *ÍF* 4: 252–253.

41. ". . . of óvíða kannat hafa verit landit" (*ÍF* 4: 254).

42. *ÍF* 4: 255.

43. *ÍF* 4: 257.

44. *ÍF* 4: 261.

45. "Þeir hǫfðu með sér alls konar fénað, því at þeir ætluðu at byggja landit, ef þeir mætti þat" (*ÍF* 4: 261).

46. "Karlsefni lét fella viðu ok telgja til skips síns ok lagði viðinn á bjarg eitt til þurrkunar" (*ÍF* 4: 261).

47. "Þeir hǫfðu ǫll gœði af landkostum, þeim er þar váru, bæði af vínberjum ok alls konar veiðum ok gœðum" (*ÍF* 4: 261).

48. "Nú búa þeir ferð sína ok hǫfðu þaðan mǫrg gœði í vínviði ok berjum and skinnavǫru" (ÍF 4: 264).

49. "er þat mál manna, at eigi mundi auðgara skip gengit hafa af Grœnlandi en þat, er hann stýrði" (ÍF 4: 267).

50. "... því at sú ferð þykkir bæði góð til fjár og virðingar" (ÍF 4: 264).

51. "... með þeim ǫllum gœðum, er þau máttu til fá ..." (ÍF 4: 267).

52. "Váru þar hveitiakrar sjálfsánir ok vínviðr vaxinn. Þar váru þau tré, er mǫsurr heita, ok hǫfðu þeir af þessu ǫllu nǫkkur merki" (ÍF 4: 211).

53. ÍF 4: 211.

54. "Þeir hǫfðu með sér alls konar fénað" (ÍF 4: 224).

55. ÍF 4: 224.

56. ÍF 4: 224; translation of Skálholtsbók version by Kunz 2008: 42.

57. ÍF 4: 227.

58. "Hverr lœkr var þar fullr af fiskum" (ÍF 4: 227).

59. "... vildu þeir, er ókvæntir váru, sœkja til í hendr þeim, sem kvæntir váru ..." (ÍF 4: 233).

60. "... þess konar þjóð ..." (ÍF 1: 13).

61. The word used for the skin boat is "húðkeipr" (ÍF 4: 255). Íslendingabók employs a different word with the same root to say skin boat fragment (keiplabrot). The masculine noun keipull is a Norse loan word related to the English coble (a small boat used in northeastern England), which in turn derives from the Latin caupulus, meaning a light boat.

62. "ótal húðkeipa" (literally, uncountable skin boats; ÍF 4: 256).

63. "Nú var sú kaupfǫr Skrælinga, at þeir báru sinn varning í brott í mǫgum sínum ..." (ÍF 4: 262).

64. "... mikill ok vænn ..." (ÍF 4: 263).

65. "... kona í svǫrtum námkyrtli, heldr lág, ok hafði dregil um hǫfuð ok ljósjǫrp á hár, fǫlleit ok mjǫk eygð, svá at eigi hafði jafnmikil augu sét í einum mannshausi" (ÍF 4: 262).

66. The verbal exchange is as follows: "'Hvat heitir þú?' segir hon. "'Ek heiti Guðríðr; eða hvert er þitt heiti?' 'Ek heiti Guðríðr,' segir hon" (ÍF 4: 263).

67. ÍF 4: 263, footnote 1.

68. The word used for skin boats, húðkeipa, is the same as in Greenlanders' Saga. The poles that the natives wave sunwise (sólarsinnis) are described as being like the poles that the Norse use to thresh grain (ÍF 4: 227).

69. "Þeir váru svartir men ok illiligir ok hǫfðu illt hár á hǫfði; þeir váru mjǫk eygðir ok breiðir í kinnum" (ÍF 4: 227).

70. "valslǫngur" (ÍF 4: 228). The Icelandic editors of the saga suggest that these were "handslǫngur" (hand-slings) and not "valslǫngur" (catapults) (ÍF 4: 228–229, footnote 3).

71. "... nær til at jafna sem sauðarvǫmb, ok helzt blán at lit ..." (ÍF 4: 229).

72. "Þeir Karlsefni þóttusk nú sjá, þótt þar væri landskostir góðir, at þar myndi jafnan ótti ok ófriðr á liggja af þeim, er fyrir bjuggu" (ÍF 4: 230).

73. An editorial note by the saga author suggests that people believed this land was the Land of the White Men, a mythical land also mentioned in Landnámabók as located six days sail west of Ireland.

74. "En Snorri fór til Vínlands ins góða með Karlsefni; er þeir bǫrðusk við Skrælinga þar á Vínlandi, þá fell þar Snorri Þorbrandsson, inn rǫskvasti maðr" (ÍF 4: 135).

75. ÍF 4: 219.

76. A person's last name was constructed by adding -son or -daughter to the first name of the father. So, Thorbrandsson is literally "the son of Thorbrand" and Snorrason is "the son of Snorri."

77. Old Icelandic version: Eyrbyggja Saga in ÍF 4 by Sveinsson and Þórðarson 1935; see English translation, for example, in Pálsson and Edwards 1989.

78. See analysis and parallel presentation of manuscript fragments of *Eyrbyggja Saga* in Scott 2003.
79. Mallery (1951) thought Vínland was to be found in Newfoundland and centered his work on Parker Brook in Pistolet Bay, where he recovered the supposed Viking stones that were later shown to be natural (see discussion in Wallace 2006: 29).
80. Munn 1914; Medelgaard 1961; Wallace 2006: 29
81. However, for a suggestion that the Greenlanders continued to visit this site for hundreds of years, see Ledger et al. 2019. They base their suggestion on the dating of a cultural layer containing dung and European-type insects. The data is intriguing but at this point is still preliminary, and further work is needed.
82. On dating the site, see Nydal 1985; Wallace 2006: 70–73; for more recent application of Bayesian modeling to radiocarbon dates see Ledger et al. 2019.
83. Eldjárn 1985: 97–103; Wallace 2006: 59–63.
84. Eldjárn 1985: 103–104.
85. Wallace 2006: 63.
86. Wallace 2006: 59–63.
87. Wallace 2006: 70.
88. Smith 2000: 217.
89. Roussell 1936: 106; Sutherland 2000: 239.
90. Seaver 2000: 275.
91. The Dorset were a Paleo-Eskimo culture existing in the arctic regions of North America and in Greenland from about 500 until the 1300s, when they were mostly displaced by the Thule (proto-Inuit) culture that spread across the Arctic with the cooling temperatures of the Little Ice Age.
92. See overview in Sutherland 2008.
93. Especially the rings on the chain mail are thought to derive from the same original mail coat (Schledermann and McCullough 2003: 193). For a detailed list of the finds (many found within Thule-Proto-Inuit houses) from Skraeling Island and Ruin Island, see Schledermann and McCullough 2003; for an earlier statement see Schledermann 1980.
94. Appelt and Gulløv 2009: 311.
95. Appelt and Gulløv 2009; although see Park 2008, who does not see enough evidence for direct interaction between Norse and Dorset peoples.
96. Sutherland 2009.
97. Hayeur Smith et al. 2018.
98. Sabo and Sabo 1978; Magnusson 2000: 160. However, see Hayeur Smith et al. 2018, who report on recent radiocarbon-dating of cloth fragments from the Okivilialuk site that yielded fifteenth- to sixteenth-century dates. This raises the possibility that the Thule house and the figurine were mistakenly dated to the thirteenth century. If this is the case, then the figurine could represent post-Columbian European visitors, such as members of the historically attested mining expedition of 1576–1578.
99. Cox 2000: 206–207; Carpenter 2003; Gullbekk 2017.
100. The coin was first identified as an English penny from the reign of Stephen (1135–1154).
101. Carpenter (2003) concluded that the coin could not be proven to come from the Goddard site; Gullbekk (2017) on the other hand considers it to be genuine.
102. Gullbekk 2017: 2–4. The University of Oslo only sold exact duplicates (from the same die) of coins from each hoard. The Goddard coin does not match any of the coins from the Norwegian hoards, and therefore it would not have been sold on the public market.
103. Gullbekk 2017: 5.
104. Carpenter 2003: 18.

105. The Hønen stone was 126 cm long, 21 cm wide, and 10.5 cm thick. The stone was broken and the beginning of the inscription was never found. After the original discovery in 1816, the inscription was sketched in 1823, but the stone itself disappeared sometime between 1825 and 1838 and has not been recovered. Even the original sketch itself has disappeared, but not before a runic scholar from the museum of Bergen made a copy of the sketch. All subsequent writings have therefore been based on a copy of the inscription sketch. This series of events warrants approaching this text with apprehension (see Olsen 1951: 23–68; Taylor 1976; Wahlgren 1986: 73–74).

106. E.g., Taylor 1976.

107. Translation from Wahlgren 1986: 74. In the runic text Vínland is written as UINLAT while the "uninhabited land," written as UBUKT = ON úbygd, could possibly refer to unsettled parts of Greenland or the Canadian Arctic.

108. "Erlingr Sigvatssonr ok Bjarni Þórðarsonr og Eindriði Oddsson laugardaginn fyrir gangdag hlóðu varða þessa ok ryðu" (Rundata database, stone GR1; six unknown runes follow the last decipherable word).

109. Seaver 2000: 271–272.

110. Haugen 1974: 59.

111. Wallace and Fitzhugh 2000: 380–382.

112. Wallace and Fitzhugh 2000: 381.

113. The Danish ethnologist, William Thalbitzer (1951), who was commissioned by the Smithsonian, deemed the stone authentic.

114. Wallace and Fitzhugh 2000: 382.

115. Wahlgren 1958.

116. Wallace and Fitzhugh 2000: 383.

117. See Kehoe 2005 for a recent book that is sympathetic to the possibility that the Kensington Stone might be genuine.

118. Play by Mark Jensen and staged in St. Paul. https://www.brainerddispatch.com/entertainm ent/theater/950387-Playwright-brings-hometown-feel-to-Kensington-Runestone-musical-being-staged-in-St.-Paul.

119. *The Vikings Unearthed*. BBC/PBS Nova. April 6, 2016.

120. For Parcak's own account of the work at Point Rosee, see Parcak 2019: 67–86.

121. Wahlgren 1986: 27. Without the discovery of the L'Anse aux Meadows site, Nansen's (1911) view that the stories were reflections of the myths of the Fortunate Isles would have been more commonly accepted.

122. Larsson 1992: 306.

123. See a chart of scholars and their ideas about the location of Helluland, Markland, and Vínland in Sigurðsson 2000: 233.

124. Although see Larsson 1992 for an argument for Helluland being Labrador and Markland being Newfoundland.

125. Larsson 1992: 320.

126. The coastal tree line lies at Napaktok Bay. See Elliott and Short 1979; Lemus-Lauzon et al. 2016.

127. Wallace 2000: 228–229.

128. Much less realistically, areas to the south of New York, such as Virginia and even Florida, have been suggested. These suggestions are widely disregarded.

129. Although see e.g., Jakobsson (2012: 496–498), who problematizes particularly the nearly universal scholarly assumption that Vínland lay to the west of Greenland. He reads the saga as only directing voyagers to the south. South would indeed have been the primary direction of a journey to Vínland. However, based on the directional information in the beginning of

Greenlanders' Saga it is also clear, for instance, that Bjarni Herjolfsson sails east at the end of his return journey from Vínland to Greenland.

130. Merrill 1935: 44; Kristjánson et al. 2014 favor a twelve-hour day.

131. This distance (2,800 km) calculates a sailing route from Brattahlíð (home of Leif Eiríksson) to the L'Anse aux Meadows outpost that first brought the mariners north to cross over to the Baffin Islands. If they continued south across the Gulf of St. Lawrence to Prince Edward Island, then the journey would have entailed crossing at least 3,700 km of ocean.

132. "Meira var þar janfdœgri en á Grœnlandi eða Íslandi; sól hafði þar eyktar stað ok dagmála stað um skammdegi" (*ÍF* 4: 251).

133. Vilhjálmsson (2001: 112), who translates *eyktar stað* and *dagmála stað* as southeast and southwest, believes, for instance, that it is an anachronism to translate precise time for these observations.

134. Sveinsson and Þórðarson (1935) believe this indicates a position south of N 50° (*ÍF*: 251, note 2).

135. Vilhjálmsson 2001; Sigurðsson 2005: 280

136. Bergþórsson (2000: 161–165) views the latitude as consistent with the position of L'Anse aux Meadows.

137. Larsson (1992) believes *Vitis riparia* (riverbank-grape) to be the only native grape species in Canada, while Wallace (2003: 229) cites the eighteenth-century Finnish explorer Peter Kalm (1972), who recorded the larger fox grape (*Vitia labrusca*) and frost grape (*Vitis valpina*) along the Saint Lawrence Estuary in Quebec.

138. Some debate remains about whether these grapes were also found in Nova Scotia. Larsson (1992: 311–313) argues that grapes were present there based on the accounts of the seventeenth-century explorers Nicolas Denys (1908) and Samuel de Champlain (1922). Larsson supports this observation by noting that the current northern limit of the grape runs through southern Nova Scotia. However, Wallace (2003: 228–229) argues that these accounts are flawed and that the grapes present today in Nova Scotia were introduced recently. This debate reveals the challenges of using eye-witness accounts of the historical presence of plant species to seek correlation between the sagas and archaeological evidence.

139. Larsson 1992.

140. Wallace 2006: 58–59.

141. Larsson 1992: 314.

142. Wallace 203: 229.

143. Wallace 2006: 119.

144. For discussion of translation of dýr (deer/animal) see Wallace 2000: 229–230.

145. Carlson 1992 and 1996; Sigurðsson 2005: 281.

146. Jane et al. 2014.

147. Larsson 1992: 308.

148. "... kornhjálm af tré ..." (*Greenlanders' Saga*, *ÍF* 4: 255).

149. Sigurðsson 2005: 300–301.

150. Wallace 1991.

151. McAleese 2003: 356.

152. For the value of these sagas for understanding the mentality and worldview of later medieval Icelanders, see Jakobsson 2001 and 2012.

153. Wallace 2000: 231.

154. Ebenesersdóttir et al. 2011.

155. Wallace 2006 and 2009.

156. Wallace 2006: 117.

157. Wahlgren 1986: 91.
158. Magnusson 2003: 94.
159. Taylor 1976: 4. Bugge interpreted the text as reading Vínland and Olsen as windcold, which probably refers to Greenland.
160. Holand 1956.
161. Carpenter 2003: 5.
162. Gullbekk 2017: 6.
163. CBC News, September 12, 2016: https://www.cbc.ca/news/canada/newfoundland-labrador/viking-dig-point-rosee-newfoundland-2016-1.3751129.

Chapter 8

1. "Geyr nú Garmr mjök fyr Gnipahelli, | festr mun slitna, en freki renna; | fjölð veit ek fræða, fram sé ek lengra | um ragna rök römm sigtíva. | Bræðr munu berjask ok at bönum verðask, | munu systrungar sifjum spilla; | hart er í heimi, hórdómr mikill, | skeggöld, skalmöld, skildir ro klofnir, | vindöld, vargöld, áðr veröld steypisk; |mun engi maðr öðrum þyrma" (Vǫluspá, stanzas 44–45, Guðni Jónson's edition, available online at https://heimskringla.no).

2. E.g., the BBC news article "Proud Boys and Antifa: Who Are They and What Do They Want?" (September 20, 2020); the article in The Independent Review by James Payne (2008, vol. 3) "What Do the Terrorists Want?"; the Forbes article "What Do Immigrants Want and How Do They Get It?" (January 20, 2020).

3. Cartwright 2015: 160; see especially, Hayeur Smith 2020: 4–8 and 12–24.

4. Lindow 2021: 140.

5. For instance, use of ground penetrating radar (GPR) revealed a ship burial under flat ground at Gjellestad in Norway (Gustavsen et al. 2020), while LiDAR mapping revealed a likely Trelleborg-type fortress at Borgring (Goodchild et al. 2017).

6. Kuitems et al. 2022.

Bibliography

Abrams, Lesley. 2014. Historical Background. In *"Given to the Ground": A Viking Age Mass Grave on Ridgway Hill, Weymouth*, edited by Louise Loe, Angela Boyle, Helen Webb, and David Score, 10–16. Oxford: Berforts Information Press.

Adams, Ron L. 2004. An Ethnoarchaeological Study of Feasting in Sulawesi, Indonesia. *Journal of Anthropological Archaeology* 23:56–78.

Alexander, Michael. 1991. *The Earliest English Poems*. London: Penguin.

Ambrosiani, Björn. 2008. Birka. In *The Viking World*, edited by Stefan Brink and Neil Price, 94–100. London: Routledge.

Amorosi, Thomas. 1989. Contributions to the Zooarchaeology of Iceland: Some Preliminary Notes. In *The Anthropology of Iceland*, edited by E. Paul Durrenberger and Gísli Pálsson, 203–227. Iowa City: University of Iowa Press.

Amorosi, Thomas, and Thomas McGovern. 1995. A Preliminary Report of an Archaeofauna from Granastaðir, Eyjafjarðarsýsla, Northern Iceland. In *The Settlement of Iceland: a Critical Approach*, edited by Bjarni F. Einarsson, 181–194. Reykjavík: Hið íslenska bókmenntafélag.

Amorosi, Thomas, Paul Buckland, Andrew Dugmore, Jón Ingimundarson, and Thomas McGovern. 1997. Raiding the Landscape: Human Impact in the Scandinavian North Atlantic. *Human Ecology* 25 (3):491–518.

Andersen, Harald. 1996. The Graves of the Jelling Dynasty. *Acta Archaeologica* 66:281–300.

Andersen, H. Hellmuth. 2004. *Til hele rigets værn. Danevirkes arkæologi og historie*. Højbjerg: Moesgård Museum & Wormianum.

Andersen, Steen Wulff. 1996. *The Viking Fortress of Trelleborg*. Slagelse: Museet ved Trelleborg Press.

Anthony, David W. 1990. Migration in Archeology: The Baby and the Bathwater. *American Anthropologist* 92 (4):895–914.

Appelt, Martin, and Hans Christian Gulløv. 2009. Tunit, Norsemen, and Inuit in Thirteenth-Century Northwest Greenland—Dorset between the Devil and the Deep Sea. In *The Northern World, AD 900–1400*, edited by Herbert Maschner, Owen Mason, and Robert McGhee, 300–320. Salt Lake City: University of Utah Press.

Archibald, Marion. 2013. Testing. In *The Cuerdale Hoard and related Viking-Age Silver and Gold from Britain and Ireland in the British Museum*, edited by James Graham-Campbell, 51–64. London: The British Museum.

Arcini, Caroline. 2005. The Vikings Bare Their Filed Teeth. *American Journal of Physical Anthropology* 128:727–733.

Arcini, Caroline Ahlström, T. Douglas Price, Bengt Jacobsson, Maria Cinthio, Leena Drenzel, Bibiana Agustí Farjas, and Jonny Karlsson. 2018. *The Viking Age: A Time of Many Faces*. Oxford: Oxbow Books.

Arents, Ute, and Silke Eisenschmidt. 2010. *Die Gräber von Haithabu*. Neumünster Wachholtz Verlag.

Arge, Símun V. 2014. Viking Faroes: Settlement, Paleoeconomy, and Chronology. *Journal of the North Atlantic* 7:1–17.

Ashby, Steven P. 2015. What Really Caused the Viking Age? The Social Content of Raiding and Exploration. *Archaeological Dialogues* 22 (1):89–106.

Ashby, Steven P., Ashley N. Coutu, and Søren M. Sindbæk. 2015. Urban Networks and Arctic Outlands: Craft Specialists and Reindeer Antler in Viking Towns. *European Journal of Archaeology* 18 (4):679–704.

Bachrach, Bernard S., and David S. Bachrach, eds. and trans. 2014. *Widukind of Corvey: Deeds of the Saxons*. Washington, DC: Catholic University of America Press.

Bailey, Richard. 1980. *Viking Age Sculpture in Northern England*. London: Collins.

Barrett, James. 2008. What Caused the Viking Age? *Antiquity* 82:671–685.

Batey, Colleen. 2011. Hofstaðir: Does the Artefact Assemblage Reflect Its Special Status? In *Viking Settlements and Viking Society. Papers from the Proceedings of the Sixteenth Viking Congress*, edited by Svavar Sigmundsson, 18–30. Reykjavík: Hið íslenzka fornleifafélag and University of Iceland Press.

Baug, Irene, Dagfinn Skre, Tom Heldal, and Øystein J. Jansen. 2019. The Beginning of the Viking Age in the West. *Journal of Maritime Archaeology* 14:43–80.

Becker, C. J. 1981. The Coinages of Harthacnut and Magnus the Good at Lund, c. 1040–1046. In *Studies in Northern Coinages of the Eleventh Century*, edited by C. J. Becker, 119–175. Copenhagen: Det Kongelige Danske Videnskabernes Selskab.

Beckett, Francis. 1924. *Danmarks Kunst I: Oldtiden og den Ældre Middelader*. Copenhagen: Koppel.

Benediktsson, Jakob, ed. 1968. *Íslendingabók, Landnámabók, Íslenzk fornrit 1*. Reykjavík: Hið íslenzka fornritafélag.

Bergþórsson, Páll. 2000. *The Wineland Millennium: Saga and Evidence*. Reykjavík: Mál og Menning.

Biddle, Martin, and Birthe Kjølbye-Biddle. 1992. Repton and the Vikings. *Antiquity* 66 (250):36–51.

Biddle, Martin, and Birthe Kjølbye-Biddle. 2001. Repton and the "Great Heathen Army," 873–4. In *Vikings and the Danelaw: Select Papers from the Proceedings of the Thirteenth Viking Congress, Nottingham and York, 21–30 August 1997*, edited by James Graham-Campbell, 45–96. Oxford: Oxbow.

Bill, Jan, and Aoife Daly. 2012. The Plundering of the Ship Graves from Oseberg and Gokstad: An Example of Power Politics? *Antiquity* 86: 808–824.

Birkedahl, Peter. 2000. Sebbersund—en Handelsplads med Trækirke ved Limfjorden—Forbindelser til Norge. In *Havn og handel i 1000 år: Karmøyseminaret 1997*, 31–40. Stavanger: Dreyer Bok.

Birkedahl, Peter, and Erik Johansen. 1995. The Sebbersund Boat-graves. In *The Ship as Symbol in Prehistoric and Medieval Scandinavia*, edited by Ole Crumlin-Pedersen and Birgitte Munch Thye, 160–164. Copenhagen: Publications for the National Museum.

Bisson, Thomas N. 2009. *The Crisis of the Twelfth Century: Power, Lordship, and the Origins of European Government*. Princeton, NJ: Princeton University Press.

Bjarnason, Bjarki, and Magnús Guðmundsson. 2005. *Mosfellsbær: Saga Byggðar í 1100 Ár*. Reykjavík: Pjaxi.

Bjarnason, Einar. 1972. Rúnasteinar og Mannfræði. *Árbók hins íslenzka fornleifafélags* 1971:46–73.

Bjerregaard, Mikael Manøe. 2019. The Archaeological Sources on the Killing and Enshrining of King Cnut IV. In *Life and cult of Cnut the Holy: The first royal saint of Denmark*, edited by Steffen Hope, Mikael Manøe Bjerregaard, Anne Hedeager Krag, and Mads Runge, 26–41. Odense: Odense Bys Museer and University Press of Southern Denmark.

Bjerregaard, Mikael Manøe, Jakob Tue Christensen, and Jesper Hansen. 2017. Bispegraven i Skt. Albani Kirke. In *Knuds Odense—Vikingernes by*, edited by Mads Runge and Jesper Hansen, 107–115. Odense: Forlaget Odense Bys Museer.

Blackburn, Mark. 2005. Currency under the Vikings. Part 1: Guthrum and the Earliest Danelaw Coinages. *British Numismatic Journal* 75 (3):18–46.

Blackburn, Mark. 2006. Currency under the Vikings. Part 2: The Two Scandinavian Kingdoms of the Danelaw, c. 895–954. *British Numismatic Journal* 76 (2):204–229.

Bloch, Marc. 1961. *Feudal Society*, Vol. 1: *The Growth of Ties of Dependence*. Translated by L. A. Manyon. Chicago: University of Chicago Press.

Blöndal, Sigfús, and Benedikt Benedikz. 2007. *Varangians of Byzantium*. Cambridge: Cambridge University Press.

Bolender, Douglas J. 2007. House, Land, and Labor in a Frontier Landscape: The Norse Colonization of Iceland. In *The Durable House: House Society Models in Archaeology*, edited by Jr. Robin A. Beck, 400–421. Carbondale: Southern Illinois University Press.

Bolender, Douglas J. 2015. From Surplus Land to Surplus Production in the Viking Age Settlement of Iceland. In *Surplus: The Politics of Production and the Strategies of Everyday Life*, edited by Christopher T. Morehart and Kristin De Lucia, 153–174. Boulder: University Press of Colorado.

Bolender, Douglas, John Steinberg, and Brian Damiata. 2011. Farmstead Reorganization at the End of the Viking Age: Results of the Skagafjörður Archaeological Settlement Survey. *Archaeologia Islandica* 9:77–101.

Bolton, Timothy. 2017. *Cnut the Great*. New Haven, CT: Yale University Press.

Bowden, Georgina R., Patricia Balaresque, Turi E. King, Ziff Hansen, Andrew C. Lee, Giles Pergl-Wilson, Emma Hurley, Stephen J. Roberts, Patrick Waite, Judith Jesch, Abigail L. Jones, Mark G. Thomas, Stephen E. Harding, and Mark A. Jobling. 2008. Excavating Past Population Structures by Surname-Based Sampling: The Genetic Legacy of the Vikings in Northwest England. *Molecular Biology and Evolution* 25 (2):301–309.

Bray, Olive. 1908. *The Elder or Poetic Edda. Part I. The Mythological Poems*. London: The Viking Club.

Brink, Stefan. 2008. Slavery in the Viking Age. In *The Viking World*, edited by Stefan Brink and Neil Price, 49–56. New York: Routledge.

Brink, Stefan. 2012. *Vikingarnas slavar: Sen nordiska träldomen under yngre järnåldern och äldsta medeltid*. Stockholm: Atlantis.

Brink, Stefan. 2021. *Thraldom: A History of Slavery in the Viking Age*. New York: Oxford University Press.

Brøgger, Anton Wilhelm, Hjalmar Falk, and Haakan Schetelig. 1917. *Osebergfundet, Bind I*. Kristiania: Universitetets Oldsaksamling.

Brøgger, Anton Wilhelm, and Haakan Schetelig. 1928. *Osebergfundet, Bind II*. Oslo: Universitetets Oldsaksamling.

Brønsted, Johannes. 1965. *The Vikings*. Translated by Kalle Skov. Harmondsworth: Penguin Books.

Brown, Michelle P. 2003. *The Lindisfarne Gospels: Society, Spirituality, and the Scribe*. Toronto: University of Toronto Press.

Buckberry, Jo, Janet Montgomery, Jacqueline Towers, Gundula Müldner, Malin Holst, Jane Evans, Andrew Gledhill, Naomi Neale, and Julia Lee-Thorp. 2014. Finding Vikings in the Danelaw. *Oxford Journal of Archaeology* 33 (4):413–434.

Buckland, Paul C. 2000. The North Atlantic Environment. In *Vikings: The North Atlantic Saga*, edited by William W. Fitzhugh and Elisabeth I. Ward, 146–153. Washington, DC: Smithsonian Institution Press.

Bugge, Sophus. 1867. *Norrœn fornkvœði*. Christiania: P.T. Mallings Forlagsboghandel.

Bukkemoen, Grethe Bjørkan. 2016. Cooking and Feasting: Changes in Food Practice in the Iron Age. In *Agrarian Life of the North 2000 BC–AD 1000: Studies in Rural Settlement and Farming in Norway*, edited by Frode Iversen and Håkan Petersson, 117–131. Kristiansand: Portal Books.

Burström, Mats. 1993. Silver as Bridewealth: An Interpretation of Viking Age Silver Hoards on Gotland, Sweden. *Current Swedish Archaeology* 1:33–37.

Byock, Jesse. 1982. *Feud in the Icelandic Saga*. Berkeley: University of California Press.

Byock, Jesse. 1988. *Medieval Iceland: Society, Sagas and Power*. Berkeley: University of California Press.

Byock, Jesse. 2001. *Viking Age Iceland*. London: Penguin Books.

Byock, Jesse, ed. and trans. 2005. *The Prose Edda: Norse Mythology*. London: Penguin Books.

Byock, Jesse, ed. and trans. 2009. *Grettir's Saga*: Oxford University Press.

Byock, Jesse. 2014. The Mosfell Archaeological Project: Archaeology, Sagas and History. In *Viking Age Archaeology in Iceland: Mosfell Archaeological Project*, edited by Davide Zori and Jesse Byock, 27–44. Turnhout: Brepols Publishers.

Byock, Jesse, Phillip Walker, Jon Erlandson, Per Holck, Davide Zori, Magnús Guðmundsson, and Mark Tveskov. 2005. A Viking-age Valley in Iceland: The Mosfell Archaeological Project. *Medieval Archaeology* 49: 195–218.

Byock, Jesse, and Davide Zori. 2009. *Farmstead Survey in the Mosfell Valley: Mosfell Archaeological Project, 2009*. Reykjavík: Unpublished report submitted to Fornleifavernd Ríkisins, Iceland.

Byock, Jesse, and Davide Zori. 2013. Viking Archaeology, Sagas, and Interdisciplinary Research in Iceland's Mosfell Valley. *Backdirt: Annual Review of the Cotsen Institute of Archaeology at UCLA* 2013:120–137.

Byock, Jesse, and Davide Zori. 2014. Introduction to Viking Age Archaeology in Iceland's Mosfell Valley. In *Viking Age Archaeology in Iceland: Mosfell Archaeological Project*, edited by Davide Zori and Jesse Byock, 1–18. Turnhout: Brepols Publishers.

Byock, Jesse, Davide Zori, Claus von Carnap-Bornheim, Sven Kalmring, Dennis Wilken, Tina Wunderlich, Wolfgang Rabbel, Ralph Schneider, David Höft, Steven Shema, and Klaus Schwarzer. 2015. A Viking Age Harbor and Its Hinterland in Iceland: The Leiruvogur Harbor Research Project (DFG SPP 1630). In *Häfen im 1. Millenium A.D.–Bauliche Konzepte, herrschaftliche und religiöse Einflüsse*, edited by Thomas Schmidts and Martin Vucetic, 289–312. Mainz: Verlag des Römisch-Germanischen Zentralmuseums.

Byock, Jesse, and Davide Zori. 2017. Predictive Models and Historical Sources for Finding a North Atlantic Port: The Leiruvogur Harbour at the Mouth of Iceland's Mosfell Valley. In *Häfen im 1. Millennium AD: Standortbedingungen, Entwicklungsmodelle und ökonomische Vernetzung*, edited by Sven Kalmring and Lukas Werther, 137–157. Mainz: Romano-Germanic Central Museum Press (RGZM).

Bæksted, Anders. 1942. *Islands Runeindskrifter*. Copenhagen: Ejnar Munksgaard.

Callmer, Johan. 1977. *Trade Beads and Bead Trade in Scandinavia, ca. 800–1000 AD*. Bonn: Rudolf Habelt Verlag.

Callmer, Johan. 1986. To Stay or to Move: Some Aspects of Settlement Dynamics in Southern Sweden. *Meddelanden från Lunds Universitets Historiska Museum* 1985–1986:167–208.

Callmer, Johan. 1991. Territory and Dominion in Late Iron Age Southern Scandinavia. In *Regions and Reflections. In Honour of Märta Strömberg*, edited by Kristina Jennbert, Lars Larsson, Rolf Petré, and Bozena Wyszomirska-Werbart, 257–273. Stockholm: Almqvist & Wiksell International.

Callmer, Johan. 1994. The Clay Paw Rite of the Åland Islands and Central Russia: A Symbol in Action. *Current Swedish Archaeology* 2:13–46.

Capelli, Cristian, Nicola Redhead, Julia K. Abernethy, Fiona Gratrix, James F. Wilson, Torolf Moen, Tor Hervig, Martin Richards, Michael P.H. Stumpf, Peter A. Underhill, Paul Bradshaw, Alom Shaha, Wales, Mark G. Thomas, Neal Bradman, and David B. Goldstein. 2003. A Y Chromosome Census of the British Isles. *Current Biology* 13:979–984.

Carlson, Catherine C. 1992. The Atlantic Salmon in New England Prehistory and History: Social and Environmental Implications. PhD dissertation, University of Massachusetts-Amherst.

Carlson, Catherine C. 1996. The [In]Significance of Atlantic Salmon. *Federal Archaeology* 8 (3/4):22–30.

Carpenter, Edmund. 2003. *Norse Penny*. New York: The Rock Foundation.

Carstens, Lydia. 2015. Powerful Space: The Iron-Age Hall and Its Development during the Viking Age. In *Viking Worlds: Things, Spaces, and Movement*, edited by Unn Pedersen Marianne Hem Eriksen, Bernt Rundberget, Irmelin Axelsen, and Heidi Lund Berg, 12–27. Oxford: Oxbow Books.

Carter, Tara. 2015. *Iceland's Networked Society: Revealing How the Global Affairs of the Viking Age Created New Forms of Social Complexity*. Leiden: Brill.

Cartwright, Ben. Making the Cloth That Binds Us: The Role of Textile Production in Producing Viking-Age Identities. In *Viking Worlds: Things, Spaces, and Movement*, edited by Marianne Hem Eriksen, Unn Pedersen, Bernt Rundberget, Irmelin Axelsen, and Heidi Lund Berg, 160–178. Oxford: Oxbow Books, 2015.

Carver, Martin. 2016. *Portmahomack: Monastery of the Picts*. Edinburgh: Edinburgh University Press.

Champlain, Samuel de. 1922. *The Works of Samuel Champlain*, Vol. 1. Toronto: The Champlain Society.

Chase, Colin, ed. 1975. *Two Alcuin Letter-Books, Toronto Medieval Latin Texts*. Toronto: Pontifical Institute of Mediaeval Studies.

Chenery, Carolyn A., Jane A. Evans, David Score, Angela Boyle, and Simon R. Chenery. 2014. A Boatload of Vikings? *Journal of the North Atlantic* 7:43–53.

Christensen, Jakob Tue, and Mikael Manøe Bjerregaard. 2017. Skt. Albani Kirke og Kirkegård. In *Knuds Odense—Vikingernes by*, edited by Mads Runge and Jesper Hansen, 117–127. Odense: Forlaget Odense Bys Museer.

Christensen, Jonas, Nanna Holm, Maja K. Schultz, Søren M. Sindbæk, and Jens Ulriksen. 2018. The Borgring Project 2016–2018. In *The Fortified Viking Age: 36th Interdisciplinary Viking Symposium in Odense, May 17th, 2017*, edited by Jesper Hansen and Mette Bruus, 60–68. Odense: University Press of Southern Denmark.

Christensen, Kjeld. 1981. Oversigt over samtlige dendrokronologiske prøver fra Trelleborg, Hejninge sogn, Slagelse herred, Sorø amt. Unpublished Report, The National Museum of Denmark.

Christensen, Kjeld. 2003. Ravning-broens alder—En af Danmarks sikreste dendrokronologiske dateringer? *KUML: Årbog for Jysk Arkæologisk Selskab* 2003:213–226.

Christensen, Kjeld. 2014. Appendix 6: Dendrochronological Dating of Wood Samples from Fyrkat. In *Aggersborg: The Viking-Age Settlement and Fortress*, edited by Else Roesdahl, Søren M. Sindbæk, Anne Pedersen, and David M. Wilson, 425. Moesgaard: Jutland Archaeological Society and The National Museum of Denmark.

Christensen, Lisbeth Eilersgaard, Thorsten Lemm, and Anne Pedersen, eds. 2016. *Husebyer: Status Quo, Open Questions and Perspectives*. Copenhagen: National Museum.

Christensen, Tom, Anne-Christine Larsen, Stefan Larsson, and Alan Vince. 1994. Early Glazed Ware from Denmark. *Medieval Ceramics* 18:67–76.

Christiansen, Eric, ed. and trans. 1980. *Saxo Grammaticus. Danorum Regum Heroumque Historia, Books X–XVI*. Oxford: British Archaeological Reports.

Christiansen, Eric, ed. and trans. 1992. *The Works of Sven Aggesen: Twelfth-Century Danish Historian*. London: Viking Society for Northern Research.

Christiansen, Eric. 1997. *The Northern Crusades*. London: Penguin.

Christiansen, Eric, ed. and trans. 1998. *Dudo of St Quentin: History of the Normans*. Woodbridge: Boydell.

Christiansen, Eric. 2002. *The Norsemen in the Viking Age*. Oxford: Blackwell Publishers.

Cinthio, Maria. 2002. *De Första Stadsborna: Medeltida Graver och Människor i Lund*. Stockholm: Brutus Östlings Bokförlag.

Cinthio, Maria. 2004. Trinitatiskyrkan, Gravarna och de förste Lundboarna. In *Kristendommen i Danmark før 1050. Et symposium i Roskilde den 5–7 februar 2003*, edited by Niels Lund, 159–173. Roskilde: Roskilde Museums Forlag.

Clarke, Helen, and Kristina Lamm. 2017. *Helgö Revisited: A New Look at the Excavated Evidence for Helgö, Central Sweden*. Schleswig: Stiftung-Schleswig-Holsteinische Landesmuseen Scholss Gottorf Zentrum für Baltische und Skandinavische Archäeologie.

Clarke, Michael J. 2001. Akha feasting: an ethnoarchaeological perspective. In *Feasts: Archaeological and Ethnographic Perspectives on Food, Politics, and Power*, edited by Michael Dietler and Brian Hayden, 144–167. Washington, DC: Smithsonian Institution Press.

Clover, Carol. 1982. *The Medieval Saga*: Cornell University Press.

Collingwood, W. G., and Jón Stefánsson. 1899. *A Pilgrimage to the Saga-Steads of Iceland*. Ulverston: W. Holmes.

Cook, Robert, trans. 2001. *Njal's Saga*. London: Penguin Books.

Cooke, Siobhan. 2016. Trading Identities: Alternative Interpretations of Viking Horse Remains in Scotland. A Pierowall Perspective. *Papers from the Institute of Archaeology* 26 (1):1–15.

Cox, Steven L. 2000. A Norse Penny from Maine. In *Vikings: The North Atlantic Saga*, edited by William W. Fitzhugh and Elisabeth I. Ward, 206–207. Washington, DC: Smithsonian Institution Press.

Crawford, Barbara, ed. 1995. *Scandinavian Settlement in Northern Britain: Thirteen Studies of Place-Names in Their Historical Context*. London: Leicester University Press.

Crawford, Jackson, ed. and trans. 2015. *The Poetic Edda: Stories of the Norse Gods and Heroes*. Indianapolis: Hackett Publishing Company, Inc.

Croix, Sarah. 2015. Permanency in Early Medieval Emporia: Reassessing Ribe. *European Journal of Archaeology* 18 (3):497–523.

Croix, Sarah, Olav Elias Gundersen, Søren M. Kristiansen, Jesper Olsen, Søren M. Sindbæk, and Morten Søvsø. 2019. Dating Earthwork Fortifications: Integrating Five Dating Methods in Viking-age Ribe, Denmark. *Journal of Archaeological Science: Reports* 26:1–11.

Croix, Sarah, Michael Neiß, and Søren M. Sindbæk. 2019. The réseau opératoire of Urbanization: Craft Collaborations and Organization in an Early Medieval Workshop in Ribe, Denmark. *Cambridge Archaeological Journal* 29 (2):345–364.

Croix, Sarah, Pieterjan Deckers, Claus Feveile, Maria Knudsen, Sarah Skytte Qvistgaard, Søren M. Sindbæk, and Barbora Wouters. 2022. Excavation atlas. In *Northern Emporium*, Vol. 1: *The Making of Viking-age Ribe*, edited by Søren M. Sindbæk, 49–217. Mosgaard: Jutland Archaeological Society.

Cross, Samuel Hazzard, and Olgerd P. Shrebowitz-Wetzor. 1953. *The Russian Primary Chronicle: Laurentian Text*. Cambridge: Medieval Academy of America.

Crossley-Holland, Kevin. 1984. *The Anglo-Saxon World: An Anthology*. Oxford: Oxford University Press.

Crumlin-Pedersen, Ole. 1997. *Viking-Age Ships and Shipbuilding in Hedeby/Haithabu and Schleswig*. Ships and Boats of the North, Vol. 2. Schleswig and Roskilde: Viking Ship Museum.

Crumlin-Pedersen, Ole. 2002. *The Skuldelev Ships 1: Topography, Archaeology, History, Conservation and Display*. Roskilde: Viking Ship Museum and the National Museum of Denmark.

Davidson, Hilda Ellis. 1964. *Gods and Myths of Northern Europe*. London: Pelican Books.

Davidson, Hilda Ellis. 1988. *Myths and Symbols in Pagan Europe: Early Scandinavian and Celtic religions*. Syracuse: Syracuse University Press.

Davidson, Hilda Ellis, and Peter Fisher, eds. and trans. 1996. *Saxo Grammaticus: The History of the Danes, Books I–IX*. Woodbridge: Boydell & Brewer.

Degerbøl, Magnus. 1948. Dyreknogler fra Vikingeborgen "Trelleborg." In *Trelleborg*, edited by Poul Nørlund, 241–264. Copenhagen: Det Kongelige Nordiske Oldskriftselskab.

Dennis, Andrew, Peter Foote, and Richard Perkins, eds. and trans. 1980. *Laws of Early Iceland: Grágás I*. Winnipeg: University of Manitoba Press.

Dennis, Andrew, Peter Foote, and Richard Perkins, eds. and trans. 1995. *Laws of Early Iceland: Grágás II*. Winnipeg: University of Manitoba Press.

Denys, Nicolas. 1908. *The Description and Natural History of the Coasts of North America (Acadia)*. Toronto: The Champlain Society.

Diamond, Jared. 2005. *Collapse: How Societies Choose to Fail or Succeed*. London: Penguin.

Dietler, Michael. 1996. Feasts and Commensal Politics in the Political Economy: Food, Power, and Status in Prehistoric Europe. In *Food and the Status Quest*, edited by Polly Wiessner and Wulf Schiefenhövel, 87–125. Oxford: Berghahn Books.

Dietler, Michael. 2001. Theorizing the Feast: Rituals of Consumption, Commensal Politics, and Power in African Contexts. In *Feasts: Archaeological and Ethnographic Perspectives on Food, Politics, and Power*, edited by Michael Dietler and Brian Hayden, 65–114. Washington, DC: Smithsonian Institution Press.

Dietler, Michael, and Brian Hayden. 2001. Digesting the Feast—Good to Eat, Good to Drink, Good to Think: An Introduction. In *Feasts: Archaeological and Ethnographic Perspectives on Food, Politics, and Power*, edited by Michael Dietler and Brian Hayden, 1–22. Washington, DC: Smithsonian Institution Press.

Diplomatarium Islandicum: Íslenzkt fornbréfasafn. 1857–1915. 16 volumes. Copenhagen and Reykjavík: S. L. Möller and Hið íslenzka bókmenntafélag.

Dobat, Andres Siegfried. 2008. Danevirke Revisited: An Investigation into Military and Socio-political Organisation in South Scandinavia (c. AD 700 to 1100). *Medieval Archaeology* 52 (1):27–67.

Dobat, Andres Siegfried. 2009. The State and the Strangers: The Role of External Forces in a Process of State Formation in Viking-Age South Scandinavia (c. AD 900–1050). *Viking and Medieval Scandinavia* 5:65–104.

Dobat, Andres Siegfried. 2010. *Füsing: Ein Frühmittelalterlicher Zentalplats im Umfeld von Haithabu/ Schleswig. Bericht über die Ergebnisse der Prospektionen 2003–2005*. Neumünster: Wachholtz Verlag.

Dobat, Andres Siegfried. 2022. Finding Sliesthorp? The Viking Age Settlement at Füsing. *Danish Journal of Archaeology* 11:1–22.

Dobat, Andres, and Else Roesdahl. 2014. Remains of Building Materials and Larger Objects. In *Aggersborg: The Viking-Age Settlement and Fortress*, edited by Else Roesdahl, Søren M. Sindbæk, Anne Pedersen, and David M. Wilson, 211–213. Moesgaard: Jutland Archaeological Society and The National Museum of Denmark.

Driscoll, M. J., ed. 2008. *Ágrip af Nóregskonungasǫgum*. 2nd ed. London: Viking Society for Northern Research.

DuBois, Thomas A. 1999. *Nordic Religions in the Viking Age*. Philadelphia: University of Pennsylvania Press.

Dugmore, Andrew, and Paul Buckland. 1991. Tephrochronology and Late Holocene Soil Erosion in South Iceland. In *Environmental Change in Iceland: Past and Present*, edited by Judith K. Maizels and Chris Caseldine, 147–159. Dordrecht: Kluwer Academic Press.

Dugmore, Andrew J., Douglas M. Borthwick, Mike J. Church, Alastair Dawson, Kevin J. Edwards, Christian Keller, Paul Mayewski, Thomas H. McGovern, Kerry-Anne Mairs, and Guðrún Sveinbjarnardóttir. 2007. The Role of Climate in Settlement and Landscape Change in the North Atlantic Islands: An Assessment of Cumulative Deviations in High-Resolution Proxy Climate Records. *Human Ecology* 35:169–178.

Dugmore, Andrew J., Christian Keller, and Thomas H. McGovern. 2007. Norse Greenland Settlement: Reflections on Climate Change, Trade, and the Contrasting Fates of Human Settlements in the North Atlantic Islands. *Artic Anthropology* 44 (1):12–36.

Dugmore, Andrew J., Gudrún Gísladóttir, Ian A. Simpson, and Anthony Newton. 2009. Conceptual Models of 1200 Years of Icelandic Soil Erosion Reconstructed Using Tephrochronology. *Journal of the North Atlantic* 2:1–18.

Dunbabin, Jean. 1985. *France in the Making 843–1180*: Oxford: Oxford University Press.

Durrenberger, E. Paul. 1992. *The Dynamics of Medieval Iceland: Political Economy and Literature*. Iowa City: University of Iowa Press.

Dyggve, Ejnar. 1948. The Royal Barrows at Jelling Excavations Made in 1941, 1942 and 1947, and Finds and Findings Resulting Therefrom. *Antiquity* 22 (88):190–197.

Earle, Timothy, Jesse Byock, Phillip Walker, and Sigurður Bergsteinsson. 1995. *Mosfell Archaeological Project 1995 Field Season*. Reykjavík: Unpublished report submitted to Fornleifavernd Ríkisins.

Ebenesersdóttir, Sigríður Sunna, Ásgeir Sigurðsson, Federico Sánchez-Quinto, Carles Lalueza-Fox, Kári Stefánsson, and Agnar Helgason. 2011. A New Subclade of mtDNA Haplogroup C1 Found in Icelanders: Evidence of Pre-Columbian Contact? *American Journal of Physical Anthropology* 144:92–99.

Edvardsson, Ragnar, and Thomas H. McGovern. 2005. Archaeological Investigations at Vatnsfjörður. *Archaeologia Islandica* 4:16–30.

Egerton, Francis. 1848. *Guide to Northern Archaeology by the Royal Society of Northern Antiquaries of Copenhagen*. James Bain: London.

Einarsson, Bjarni F. 1995. *The Settlement of Iceland: A Critical Approach*. Reykjavík: Hið íslenska bókmenntafélag.

Einarsson, Bjarni F. 2011. Róum við í selinn, rostungs út á melinn. Um rostunga við Íslandsstrendur. In *Fjöruskeljar. Afmælisrit til heiðurs Jónínu Hafsteinsdóttur sjötugri 29. Mars 2011*, edited by G. Kvaran, H. J. Ámundason and S. Sigmundsson, 31–52. Reykjavík: Mal og Menning.

Eldjárn, Kristján. 1948. Gaulverjabær-fundet og nogle mindre islandske møntfund fra vikingetiden. *Nordisk Numismatisk Årsskrift* 1948:39–62.

Eldjárn, Kristján. 1985. Investigations. In *The Norse Discovery of America*, Vol. 1, edited by Anne Stine Ingstad, 97–108. Oslo: Universitetsforlaget.

Eldjárn, Kristján. 1989. Papey. Fornleifarannsóknir 1967–1981. *Árbók hins íslenzka fornleifafélags* 1988:35–188.

Eldjárn, Kristján. 2000. *Kuml og Haugfé úr Heiðnum Sið á Íslandi*, edited by Adolf Friðriksson. 2nd ed. Reykjavík: Mál og Menning. Original edition, 1956.

Eisenschmidt, Silke. 2011. The Viking Age Graves from Hedeby. In *Viking Settlements and Viking Society. Papers from the Proceedings of the Sixteenth Viking Congress, Reykjavík and Reykholt*,

16–23 August 2009, edited by Svavar Sigmundsson, 83–102. Reykjavík: Hið íslenzka fornleifafélag and University of Iceland Press.

Elliott, Deborah L., and Susan K. Short. 1979. The Northern Limit of Trees in Labrador: A Discussion. *Artic* 32 (3):201–206.

Erlandson, Jon M., Jesse Byock, and Davide Zori. 2014. Egill's Grave? Archaeology and Egils Saga at Kirkjuhóll, Hrísbrú. In *Viking Age Archaeology in Iceland: Mosfell Archaeological Project*, edited by Davide Zori and Jesse Byock, 45–53. Turnhout: Brepols Publishers.

Erlendsson, Egill, and Kevin J. Edwards. 2009. The Timing and Causes of the Final Presettlement Expansion of Betula Pubescens in Iceland. *The Holocene* 19 (7):1083–1091.

Erlendsson, Egill, Kevin J. Edwards, Ian Lawson, and Orri Vésteinsson. 2006. Can There Be a Correspondence between Icelandic Palynological and Settlement Evidence? In *Dynamics of Northern Societies*, edited by Jette Arneborg and Bjarne Grønnow, 347–353. Copenhagen: National Museum of Denmark.

Erlendsson, Egill, Kim Vickers, Frederick Gathorne-Hardy, Joanna Bending, Björg Gunnarsdóttir, Guðrún Gísladóttir, and Kevin J. Edwards. 2012. Late-Holocene Environmental History of the Reykholt Area, Borgarfjörður, Western Iceland. In *From Nature to Script: Reykholt, Environment, Centre and Manuscript Making*, edited by Helgi Þorláksson and Þóra Björg Sigurðardóttir, 17–47. Reykholt: Snorrastofa.

Erlendsson, Egill, Kevin J. Edwards, and Guðrún Gísladóttir. 2014. Landscape Change, Land Use, and Occupation Patterns Inferred from Two Palaeoenvironmental Datasets from the Mosfell Valley, SW Iceland. In *Viking Archaeology in Iceland: Mosfell Archaeological Project*, edited by Davide Zori and Jesse Byock, 181–192. Turnhout: Brepols.

Eriksen, Marianne Hem. 2013. Doors to the Dead: The Power of Doorways and Thresholds in Viking Age Scandinavia. *Archaeological Dialogues* 20:187–214.

Eriksen, Marianne Hem. 2015. Portals to the Past: An Archaeology of Doorways, Dwellings, and Ritual Practice in Late Iron Age Scandinavia. PhD dissertation, University of Oslo.

Evans, J. A., V. Pashley, C. A. Chenery, L. Loe, and S. R. Chenery. 2018. Lead Isotope Analysis of Tooth Enamel from a Viking Age Mass Grave in Southern Britain and the Constraints it Places on the Origin of the Individuals. *Archaeometry* 60 (4):859–869.

Faulkes, Anthony, ed. and trans. 1987. *Edda*. London: Everyman.

Faulkes, Anthony, ed. and trans. 1998. *Skáldskaparmál 1. Introduction, Text and Notes*. London: Viking Society for Northern Research.

Feinman, Gary and Jill Neitzel. 1984. Too Many Types: An Overview of Sedentary Prestate Societies in the Americas. *Advances in Archaeological Method and Theory* 7:39–102.

Fellows-Jensen, Gillian. 2008. Scandinavian Place Names in the British Isles. In *The Viking World*, edited by Stefan Brink and Neil Price, 391–400. New York: Routledge.

Feveile, Claus. 2019. Sceattas i Sydskandinavien—fra ekspanderende frisere til kontrollerende kongemagt. *By, marsk og geest: Kulturhistorisk tidsskrift for Sydvestjylland* 31:21–43.

Feveile, Claus, and Stig Jensen. 2000. Ribe in the 8th and 9th Century: A Contribution to the Archaeological Chronology of North Western Europe. *Act Archaeologia* 71:9–24.

Forbes, Véronique, Frédéric Dussault, and Allison Bainc. 2013. Contributions of Ectoparasite Studies in Archaeology with Two Examples from the North Atlantic Region. *International Journal of Paleopathology* 3:158–164.

Frank, Roberta. 1994. King Cnut in the Verse of his Skalds. In *The Reign of Cnut: King of England, Denmark, and Norway*, edited by Alexander Rumble, 106–124. London: Leicester University Press.

Frei, Karin M., Ashley N. Coutu, Konrad Smiarowski, Ramona Harrison, Christian K. Madsen, Jette Arneborg, Robert Frei, Gardar Guðmundsson, Søren M. Sindbæk, James Woollett, Steven Hartman, Megan Hicks, and Thomas H. McGovern. 2015. Was It for Walrus? Viking Age Settlement and Medieval Walrus Ivory Trade in Iceland and Greenland. *World Archaeology* 47 (3):439–466.

Friðriksdóttir, Jóhanna Katrín. 2020. *Valkyrie: The Women of the Viking World*. London: Bloomsbury Academic.

Friðriksson, Adolf. 2009. Social and Symbolic Landscapes in Late Iron Age Iceland. *Archaeologia Islandica* 7:9–21.

Friðriksson, Sturla. 1959. Korn frá Gröf í Öræfum. *Árbók hins Íslenzka Fornleifafélags* 1959: 88–91.

Friðriksson, Sturla. 1960. Jurtaleifar frá Bergþórshvoli á söguöld. *Árbók hins Íslenzka Fornleifafélags* 1960: 64–75.

Fried, Morton. 1967. *The Evolution of Political Society: An Essay in Political Anthropology*: Random House, Inc.

Frölund, Per, and Hans Göthberg. 2011. Helgö, stolphål blir hus. En arkeologisk byggnadsanalys av terrass I och III inom husgrupp 2 på Helgö. *Upplandsmuseets rapporter* 2011:22.

Gade, Kari Ellen. 2009. Þorleikr fagri, Flokkr about Sveinn Úlfsson. In *Poetry from the Kings' Sagas 2: From c. 1035 to c. 1300. Skaldic Poetry of the Scandinavian Middle Ages 2*, edited by Kari Ellen Gade, 313–322. Turnhout: Brepols.

Gammeltoft, Peder. 2001. *The Place-Name Element Bólstaðr in the North Atlantic Area*. Copenhagen: C.A. Reitzels Forlag A/S.

Gansum, Terje, and Terje Oestigaard. 2004. The Ritual Stratigraphy of Monuments that Matter. *European Journal of Archaeology* 7 (1):61–79.

Gansum, Terje, and Thomas Risan. 1999. Oseberghaugen—en stratigrafisk historie. *Vestfoldminne* 1998/1999:60–72.

Gardeła, Leszek. 2013. The Dangerous Dead? Rethinking Viking-Age Deviant Burials. In *Conversions: Looking for Ideological Change in the Early Middle Ages*, edited by Leszek Słupecki and Rudolf Simek, 99–136. Vienna: Fassbaender.

Gardeła, Leszek. 2016. Worshipping the Dead: Viking Age Cemeteries as Cult Sites? In *Germanische Kultorte: Vergleichende, historische und rezeptionsgeschichtliche Zugänge*, edited by Matthias Egeler, 169–205. Munich: Herbert Utz Verlag.

Gathorne-Hardy, Frederick. 1921. *The Norse Discoverers of America*. Oxford: Clarendon Press.

Gautier, Alban. 2009. Hospitality in pre-viking Anglo-Saxon England. *Early Medieval Europe* 17 (1):23–44.

Geary, Patrick. 1994. The Uses of Archaeological Sources for Religious and Cultural History. In *Living with the Dead in the Middle Ages*, edited by Patrick Geary, 30–45. Ithaca, NY: Cornell University Press.

Geary, Patrick. 2003. *The Myth of Nations: The Medieval Origins of Europe*. Princeton, NJ: Princeton University Press.

Gelsinger, Bruce. 1981. *Icelandic Enterprise: Commerce and Economy in the Middle Ages*. Columbia, SC: University of South Carolina Press.

Gertz, Martin Clarentius, ed. 1907. *Knud den Helliges Martyrhistorie: Særlig efter de tre ældste kilder*. Copenhagen: Universitetsbogtrykkeri.

Gilbert, Edmund, Seamus O'Reilly, Michael Merrigan, Darren McGettigan, Anne M. Molloy, Lawrence C. Brody, Walter Bodmer, Katarzyna Hutnik, Sean Ennis, Daniel J. Lawson, James F. Wilson, and Gianpiero L. Cavalleri. 2017. The Irish DNA Atlas: Revealing Fine-Scale Population Structure and History within Ireland. *Scientific Reports* 7 (1):1–11.

Godden, Malcolm R., ed. 2016. *The Old English History of the World: An Anglo-Saxon Rewriting of Orosius*. Cambridge, MA: Harvard University Press.

Goodacre, S., A. Helgason, J. Nicholson, L. Southam, L. Ferguson, E. Hickey, E. Vega, K. Stefánsson, R. Ward, and B. Sykes. 2005. Genetic Evidence for a Family-based Scandinavian Settlement of Shetland and Orkney during the Viking Periods. *Heredity* 95:129–135.

Goodchild, Helen, Nanna Holm, and Søren M. Sindbæk. 2017. Borgring: the discovery of a Viking Age ring fortress. *Antiquity* 91 (358):1027–1042.

Göthberg, Hans. 2015. Hus på Helgö. Arkeologisk analys av byggnader på terrass V och VI inom husgrupp 2 på Helgö. *Upplandsmuseets rapporter* 2015:22.

Graham-Campbell, James. 1980. *Viking Artefacts: A Select Catalogue*. London: British Museum Publications Ltd.

Graham-Campbell, James, and Colleen Batey. 1998. *Vikings in Scotland: An Archaeological Survey*. Edinburgh: Edinburgh University Press.

Graham-Campbell, James. 2013. *The Cuerdale Hoard and Related Viking-Age Silver and Gold from Britain and Ireland in the British Museum*. London: The British Museum.

Gräslund, Anne-Sofie. 1980. *Birka IV The Burial Customs: A Study of the Graves on Björkö*. Stockholm: Almqvist & Wiksell International.

Gray, Edward F. 1930. *Leif Eriksson Discoverer of America: A.D. 1003*. New York: Oxford University Press.

Grieg, Sigurd. 1928. *Osebergfundet, Bind II*, edited by Anton Wilhelm Brøgger and Haakan Schetelig, 1–286. Oslo: Universitetets Oldsaksamling.

Griffiths, David. 2010. *Vikings of the Irish Sea*. Stroud: The History Press.

Griffiths, David. 2015. A Brief History and Archaeology of Viking Activity in North-West England. In *In Search of Vikings: Interdisciplinary Approaches to the Scandinavian Heritage of North-West England*, edited by Stephen E. Harding, David Griffiths, and Elizabeth Royles, 33–49. Boca Raton: CRC Press.

Griffiths, David, and Stephen E. Harding. 2015. Interdisciplinary Approaches to the Scandinavian Heritage of North-West England. In *In Search of Vikings: Interdisciplinary Approaches to the Scandinavian Heritage of North-West England* edited by Stephen E. Harding, David Griffiths, and Elizabeth Royles, 1–31. Boca Raton: CRC Press.

Grimes, Vaughan, Benjamin T. Fuller, and Eric J. Guiry. 2014. Reconstructing Diets and Origins of Vikings at Hrísbrú, Mosfell Valley, Iceland: The Carbon, Nitrogen and Strontium Isotope Evidence. In *Viking Age Archaeology in Iceland: Mosfell Archaeological Project*, edited by Davide Zori and Jesse Byock, 105–116. Turnhout: Brepols Publishers.

Grímsson, Magnús. 1886 [1861]. Athugasemdir við Egils sögu Skallagrímssonar. In *Safn til sögu Íslands og íslenzkra bókmennta að fornu og nýju II*, 251–276. Copenhagen: Hið íslenzka bókmenntafélag.

Grønlie, Siân. 2006. *Íslendingabók, Kristni Saga: The Book of the Icelanders, The Story of the Conversion*. London: Viking Society for Northern Research.

Grønnesby, Geir. 2016. Hot Rocks! Beer Brewing on Viking and Medieval Age Farms in Trondelag. In *Agrarian Life of the North 2000 BC–AD 1000: Studies in Rural Settlement and Farming in Norway*, edited by Frode Iversen and Håkan Petersson, 133–149. Kristiansand: Portal Books.

Grønvik, Ottar. 1982. *The Words for "Heir", "Inheritance", and "Funeral Feast", in eEarly Germanic: An Etymological Study of ON arfr m, arfi m, erfi n, erfa vb and the Corresponding Words in the Other Old Germanic Dialects*. Oslo and Irving-on-Hudson, NY: Columbia University Press.

Grönvold, Karl, Níels Óskarsson, Sigfús Johnsen, Henrik Clausen, Claus Hammer, Gerard Bond, and Edouard Bard. 1995. Ash Layers from Iceland in the Greenland GRIP Ice Core Correlated with Oceanic and Land Sediments. *Earth and Planetary Science Letters* 135:149–155.

Guðmundsson, Garðar. 1996. Gathering and Processing of Lyme-grass (Elymus arenarius L.) in Iceland: An Ethnohistorical Account. *Vegetation History and Archaeobotany* 5:13–23.

Guðmundsson, Garðar. 2009. The Plant Remains. In *Hofstaðir: Excavations of a Viking Age Feasting Hall in North-Eastern Iceland*, edited by Gavin Lucas, 322–334. Reykjavík: Fornleifastofnun Íslands.

Guðmundsson, Garðar, Guðrún Sveinbjarnardóttir, and Gordon Hillman. 2012. Charred Remains of Grains and Seeds from the Medieval High-status Farm Site of Reykholt in Western Iceland. *Environmental Archaeology* 17 (2):111–117.

Gullbekk, Svein H. 2011. Money and Its Use in the Saga Society: Silver, Coins and Commodity Money. In *Viking Settlements and Viking Society. Papers from the Proceedings of the Sixteenth Viking Congress, Reykjavík and Reykholt, 16th–23rd August 2009*, edited by Svavar Sigmundsson, 176–188. Reykjavík: University of Iceland Press.

Gullbekk, Svein H. 2017. The Norse Penny Reconsidered: The Goddard Coin—Hoax or Genuine? *Journal of the North Atlantic* 33:1–8.

Gunnell, Terry. 2005. The Season of the Dísir: The Winter Nights and the Dísablót in early Medieval Scandinavian Belief. *Cosmos* 16:117–149.

Gurevich, Aaron. 1985. *Categories of Medieval Culture*. London: Routledge & Kegan Paul.

Hadley, Dawn M. 2006. *The Vikings in England: Settlement, Society and Culture.* Manchester: Manchester University Press.

Hadley, Dawn M., and Julian D. Richards. 2021. *The Viking Great Army and the Making of England.* London and New York: Thames & Hudson.

Hadley, Dawn M., Julian D. Richards, Hannah Brown, Diana Mahoney Swales Elizabeth Craig-Atkins, Gareth Perry, Samantha Stein, and Andrew Woods. 2016. The Winter Camp of the Viking Great Army, AD 872-3, Torksey, Lincolnshire. *The Antiquaries Journal* 96:23-67.

Hald, Mette Marie, Betina Magnussen, Liv Appel, Jakob Tue Christensen, Camilla Haarby Hansen, Peter Steen Henriksen, Jesper Langkilde, Kristoffer Buck Pedersen, Allan Dørup Knudsen, and Morten Fischer Mortensen. 2020. Fragments of Meals in Eastern Denmark from the Viking Age to the Renaissance: New Evidence from Organic Remains in Latrines. *Journal of Archaeological Science: Reports* 31:1-21.

Hall, Richard A. 2000. Scandinavian Settlement in England—the Archaeological Evidence. *Acta Archaeologica* 71:147-157.

Halldórsson, Ólafur. 2001. The Vínland Sagas. In *Approaches to Vínland,* edited by Andrew Wawn and Þórunn Sigurðardóttir, 39-51. Reykjavík: Sigurður Nordal Institute.

Hallsdóttir, Margrét. 1987. *Pollen Analytical Studies of Human Influence on Vegetation in Relation to the Landnám tephra layer in Southwest Iceland.* Lund: Lund University.

Hallsdóttir, Margrét. 1996. Fjógreining. Fjókorn sem heimildir um landámið. In *Um landnám á Íslandi: Fjórtán erindi,* edited by Guðrún Ása Grímsdóttir, 123-134. Reykjavík: Vísindafélag íslendinga.

Hansen, Jesper. 2019. King Cnut's Donation Letter and Settlement Structure in Denmark, 1085: New Perspectives on an Old Document. In *Life and Cult of Cnut the Holy: The First Royal Saint of Denmark,* edited by Steffen Hope, Mikael Manøe Bjerregaard, Anne Hedeager Krag, and Mads Runge, 60-80. Odense: Odense Bys Museer and University Press of Southern Denmark.

Hansen, Sigrid Cecilie Juel. 2011. The Icelandic Whetsone Material—An Overview of Recent Research. *Archaeologia Islandica* 9:65-76.

Hansen, Sigrid Cecilie Juel, Davide Zori, and Jesse Byock. 2014. Artefacts from the Viking Age Longhouse at Hrísbrú. In *Viking Age Archaeology in Iceland: Mosfell Archaeological Project,* edited by Davide Zori and Jesse Byock, 117-133. Turnhout: Brepols Publishers.

Harding, Stephen E., Mark Jobling, and Turi King. 2010. *Viking DNA: The Wirral and West Lancashire Project.* Boca Raton: CRC Press.

Harris, Oliver J. T., Hannah Cobb, Colleen E. Batey, Janet Montgomery, Julia Beaumont, Héléna Gray, Paul Murtagh, and Phil Richardson. 2017. Assembling Places and Persons: A Tenth-century Viking Boat Burial from Swordle Bay on the Ardnamurchan Peninsula, Western Scotland. *Antiquity* 91 (355):191-206.

Haugen, Einar. 1974. The Rune Stones of Spirit Pond, Maine. *Visible Language* 8 (1):33-64.

Hayden, Brian. 2001. Fabulous Feasts: A Prolegomenon to the Importance of Feasting. In *Feasts: Archaeological and Ethnographic Perspectives on Food, Politics, and Power,* edited by Michael Dietler and Brian Hayden, 23-64. Washington, DC: Smithsonian Institution Press.

Hayden, Brian. 2014. *The Power of Feasts: From Prehistory to the Present.* Cambridge: Cambridge University Press.

Hayeur Smith, Michèle. 2015. Weaving Wealth: Cloth and Trade in Viking Age and Medieval Iceland. In *Textiles and the Medieval Economy: Production, Trade, and Consumption of Textiles, 8th-16th Centuries,* edited by Angela Ling Huang and Carsten Jahnke, 23-40. Oxford: Oxbow.

Hayeur Smith, Michèle. *The Valkyries' Loom: The Archaeology of Cloth Production and Female Power in the North Atlantic.* Gainesville: University Press of Florida, 2020.

Hayeur Smith, Michèle, Kevin P. Smith, and Gørill Nilsen. 2018. Dorset, Norse, or Thule? Technological Transfers, Marine Mammal Contamination, and AMS Dating of Spun Yarn and Textiles from the Eastern Canadian Arctic. *Journal of Archaeological Science* 96:162-174.

Hedemand, Laura, Peder Dam, Johnny Grandjean, and Gøgsig Jakobsen. 2003. De danske torp-landsbyers jordbundsforhold. In *Nordiske torp-navne: Rapport fra NORNAs 31. Symposium i Jaruplund 25.–28. april 2002*, edited by Peder Gammeltoft and Bent Jørgensen, 95–108. Uppsala: NORNA-förlaget.

Hedenstierna-Jonson, Charlotte, Anna Kjellström, Torun Zachrisson, Maja Krzewińska, Veronica Sobrado, Neil Price, Torsten Günther, Mattias Jakobsson, Anders Götherström, and Jan Storå. 2017. A Female Viking Warrior Confirmed by Genomics. *American Journal of Physical Anthropology* 164:853–860.

Heen-Pettersen, Aina, and Griffin Murray. 2018. An Insular Reliquary from Melhus: The Significance of Insular Ecclesiastical Material in Early Viking-Age Norway. *Medieval Archaeology* 62 (1):53–82.

Helbæk, Hans. 1977. The Fyrkat Grain: A Geographical and Chronological Study of Rye. In *Fyrkat: En jysk vikingeborg. I. Borgen og Bebyggelsen*, edited by Olaf Olsen and Holger Schmidt, excurs 1–39. Copenhagen: H.J. Lynge og Søn.

Helgason, Agnar, Sigrún Sigurðardóttir, Jeffrey R. Gulcher, Ryk Ward, and Kári Stefánsson. 2000. mtDNA and the Origin of the Icelanders: Deciphering Signals of Recent Population History. *The American Journal of Human Genetics* 66 (3):999–1016.

Helgason, Agnar, Sigrún Sigurðardóttir, Jayne Nicholson, Bryan Sykes, Emmeline W. Hill, Daniel G. Bradley, Vidar Bosnes, Jeffery R. Gulcher, Ryk Ward, and Kári Stefánsson. 2000. Estimating Scandinavian and Gaelic Ancestry in the Male Settlers of Iceland. *American Journal of Human Genetics* 67:697–717.

Helgason, Agnar, Eileen Hickey, Sara Goodacre, Vidar Bosnes, Kári Stefánsson, Ryk Ward, and Bryan Sykes. 2001. mtDNA and the Islands of the North Atlantic: Estimating the Proportions of Norse and Gaelic Ancestry. *American Journal of Human Genetics* 68:723–737.

Helgason, Agnar, Carles Lalueza-Fox, Shyamali Ghosh, Sigrún Sigurðardóttir, Maria Lourdes Sampietro, Elena Gigli, Adam Baker, Jaume Bertranpetit, Lilja Árnardóttir, Unnur Þorsteinsdóttir, and Kári Stefánsson. 2009. Sequences from First Settlers Reveal Rapid Evolution in Icelandic mtDNA Pool. *Plos Genetics* 5 (1):1–10.

Helgason, Sigurjón. 2009. Hvernig Byggðist Ytrihreppur?: um landnám og mótun byggðar í Hrunamannahreppi. *Árbók Hins Íslenzka Fornleifafélags* 2008–2009:143–176.

Helmbrecht, Michaela. 2012. "A Man's World": The Imagery of the Group C and D Picture Stones. In *Gotland's Picture Stones: Bearers of an Enigmatic Legacy*, edited by Maria Herlin Karnell, 83–90. Visby: Gotland Museum.

Hermanns-Auðardóttir, Margrét. 1991. The Early Settlement of Iceland: Results Based on Excavations of a Merovingian and Viking Farm Site at Herjólfsdalur in the Westman Islands, Iceland. *Norwegian Archaeological Review* 24:1–9.

Herschend, Frands. 1993. The Origin of the Hall in Southern Scandinavia. *TOR* 25: 175–199.

Herschend, Frands. 1995. Hus på Helgö. *Fornvännen* 90 (4): 221–228.

Herschend, Frands. 2000. Ship Grave Hall Passage: The Oseberg Monument as Compound Meaning. In *Old Norse Myths, Literature and Society. Proceedings of the 11th International Saga Conference 2–7 July 2000*, edited by Geraldine Barnes and Margaret Clunies Ross, 142–151. University of Sydney.

Hertz, Robert. 1960 [orig. 1907]. A contribution to the Collective Representation of Death. In *Death and the Right Hand*, 29–87. Glencoe: Free Press.

Hervén, Conny Johansson. 2008. Den tidiga medeltidens Lund—vems var egentligen staden? In *De første 200 årene—nytt blikk på 27 skandinaviske middelalderbyer*, edited by Ingvild Øye and Hans Andersson Gitte Hansen, 259–275. Bergen: Universitetet i Bergen.

Hilberg, Volker. 2009. Hedeby in Wulfstan's Days: A Danish Emporium of the Viking Age between East and West. In *Wulfstan's Voyage: The Baltic Sea region in the early Viking Age as seen from shipboard*, edited by Anton Englert and Athena Trakadas, 79–113. Roskilde: The Viking Ship Museum.

Hilberg, Volker. 2016. Hedeby's Demise in the Late Viking Age and the Shift to Schleswig. In *New Aspects on Viking-age Urbanism c. AD 750–1100*, edited by Lena Holmquist, Sven Kalmring, and Charlotte Hedenstierna-Jonson, 63–80. Stockholm: Archaeological Research Laboratory, Stockholm University.

Hilberg, Volker, and Sven Kalmring. 2014. Viking Age Hedeby and Its Relations with Iceland and the North Atlantic: Communication, Long-distance Trade and Production. In *Viking Archaeology in Iceland: Mosfell Archaeological Project*, edited by Davide Zori and Jesse Byock, 221–245. Turnhout: Brepols Publishers.

Hill, David. 1969. The Burghal Hidage: The Establishment of a Text. *Medieval Archaeology* 13:84–92.

Hill, David, and Alexander R. Rumble, eds. 1996. *The Defence of Wessex: The Burghal Hidage and Anglo-Saxon Fortifications*. Manchester: Manchester University Press.

Hirsch, Paul, and H.-E. Lohmann, eds. 1935. *Widukindi Monachi Corbeiensis Rerum Gestarum Saxonicarum*. Monumenta Germaniae historica, Scriptores rerum Germanicarum in usum scholarum 60. Hannover: Impensis Bibliopolii Hahniani.

Hjermind, Jesper. 2008. Theatrum Urbis Vibergensis 1000–1150. In *De første 200 årene—nytt blikk på 27 skandinaviske middelalderbyer*, edited by Gitte Hansen, Ingvild Øye and Hans Andersson, 181–193. Bergen: Universitetet i Bergen.

Holand, Hjalmar R. 1956. *Explorations in American Before Columbus*. New York: Twayne.

Holck, Per. 2006. The Oseberg Ship Burial, Norway: New Thoughts on the Skeletons from the Grave Mound. *European Journal of Archaeology* 9 (2–3):185–210.

Hollander, Lee M, trans. 1962. *The Poetic Edda*. Translated by L. M. Hollander. Austin: University of Texas Press.

Hollander, Lee M., trans. 1964. *Heimskringla*. Austin: University of Texas Press.

Holmqvist, Wilhelm. 1957. Gårdsanläggningar från yngre järnåldern från Helgö (Lillön), Ekerö socken i Mälaren. *Fornvännen* 52:97–115.

Holtzmann, Robert, ed. 1935. *Thietmari Merseburgensis Episcopi Chronicon*. Monumenta Germaniae Historica, Scriptores rerum Germanicarum Nova Series 9. Berlin: Weidmannsche Büchhandlung.

Hope, Steffen. 2019. The Odense literature and the early liturgy of St Cnut Rex. In *Life and cult of Cnut the Holy: The first royal saint of Denmark*, edited by Steffen Hope, Mikael Manøe Bjerregaard, Anne Hedeager Krag, and Mads Runge, 100–117. Odense: Odense Bys Museer and University Press of Southern Denmark.

Hreiðarsdóttir, Elín. 2014. Beads from Hrísbrú and Their Wider Icelandic Context. In *Viking Archaeology in Iceland: Mosfell Archaeological Project*, edited by Davide Zori and Jesse Byock, 135–141. Turnhout: Brepols Publishers.

Hreiðarsdóttir, Elín Ósk, and Howell Roberts. 2009. Þögnin rofin: Fysrtu niðurstöður rannsókna á eyðibyggð á Þegjandadal. *Árbók Þingeyinga* 2009:5–24.

ÍF = Íslenzk Fornrit series, 1933– (the standard publication series of Old Norse/Icelandic texts, especially the sagas). Reykjavík: Hið íslenzka fornritafélag.

ÍF 1 = *Íslendingabók, Landnámabók*. Jakob Benediktsson, ed. 1968.

ÍF 2 = *Egils saga Skallagrímssonar*. Sigurður Nordal, ed. 1933.

ÍF 3 = *Borgfirðinga sögur: Hœnsa-Þóris saga, Gunnlaugs saga ormstungu, Bjarnar saga Hítdœlakappa, Heiðarvíga saga, Gísls þáttr Illugasonar*. Sigurður Nordal and Guðni Jónsson, eds. 1938.

ÍF 4 = *Eyrbyggja saga, Brands þáttr örva, Eiríks saga rauða, Grœnlendinga saga, Grœnlendinga þáttr*. Einar Ól. Sveinsson and Matthías Þórðarson, eds. 1935.

ÍF 5 = *Laxdæla saga, Halldórs þættir Snorrasonar, Stúfs þáttr*. Einar Ól. Sveinsson, ed. 1934.

ÍF 6 = *Vestfirðinga sögur: Gísla saga Súrssonar, Fóstbrœðra saga, Þáttr Þormóðar, Hávarðar saga Ísfirðings, Auðunar þáttr vestfirzka, Þorvarðar þáttr krákunefs*. Björn K. Þórólfsson and Guðni Jónsson, eds. 1943.

ÍF 7 = *Grettis saga Ásmundarsonar, Bandamanna saga, Odds þáttr Ófeigssonar*. Guðni Jónsson, ed. 1936.

ÍF 8 = *Vatnsdœla saga, Hallfreðar saga, Kormáks saga, Hrómundar þáttr halta, Hrafns þáttr Guðrúnarsonar*. Einar Ól. Sveinsson, ed. 1939.

ÍF 9 = *Eyfirðinga Sögur: Víga-glúms saga, Ǫgmundar þáttr dytts, Þorvalds þáttr tasalda, Svarfdæla saga, Þorleifs þáttr jarlsskálds, Valla-Ljóts saga, Sneglu-Halla þáttr, Þorgríms þáttr Hallasonar*. Jónas Kristjánsson, ed. 1956.

ÍF 10 = *Ljósvetninga saga, Reykdœla saga, Hreiðars þáttr*. Björn Sigfússon, ed. 1940.

ÍF 11 = *Austfirðinga sögur: Þorsteins saga hvíta, Vápnfirðinga saga, Þorsteins þáttr stangarhöggs, Hrafnkels saga Freysgoði, Droplaugarsona saga, Ölkofra þáttr, Gunnars þáttr Þiðrandabana, Fljótsdæla saga, Þorsteins saga Síðu-Hallssonar, Draumr Þorsteins Síðu-Hallssonar, Þorsteins þáttr Austfirðings, Þorsteins þáttr sögufróða, Gull-Ásu-Þórðar þáttr.* Jón Jóhannesson, ed. 1950.

ÍF 12 = *Brennu-Njáls saga.* Einar Ól. Sveinsson, ed. 1954.

ÍF 13 = *Harðar saga, Bárðar saga, Þorskfirðinga saga, Flóamanna saga, Þórarins þáttr Nefjólfssonar, Þorsteins þáttr uxafóts, Egils þáttr Síðu-Hallssonar, Orms þáttr Stórólfssonar, Þorsteins þáttr tjaldstæðings, Þorsteins þáttr forvitna, Bergbúa þáttr, Kumlbúa þáttr, Stjörnu-Odda draumr.* Þórhallur Vilmundarson and Bjarni Vilhjálmsson, eds. 1991.

ÍF 14 = *Kjalnesinga saga, Jökuls þáttr Búasonar, Víglundar saga, Króka-Refs saga, Þórðar saga hreðu, Finnboga saga, Gunnars saga Keldugnúpsfífls.* Jóhannes Halldórsson, ed. 1959.

ÍF 26 = *Heimskringla I: Ynglinga saga, Hálfdanar saga svarta, Haralds saga ins hárfagra, Hákonar saga góða, Haralds saga gráfeldar, Ólafs saga Tryggvasonar.* Bjarni Aðalbjarnarson, ed. 1942.

ÍF 27 = *Heimskringla II: Ólafs saga helga.* Bjarni Aðalbjarnarson, ed. 1945.

ÍF 28 = *Heimskringla III: Magnúss saga góða, Haralds saga Sigurðarsonar, Ólafs saga kyrra, Magnúss saga berfœtts, Magnússona saga, Magnúss saga blinda ok Haralds gilla, Haraldssona saga, Hákonar saga Herðibreiðs, Magnúss saga Erlingssonar.* Bjarni Aðalbjarnarson, ed. 1951.

ÍF 29 = *Ágrip af Nóregskonunga sögum, Fagrskinna.* Bjarni Einarsson, ed. 1985.

ÍF 34 = *Orkneyinga saga, Legenda de sancto Magno, Magnúss saga skemmri, Magnúss saga lengri, Helga þáttr ok Úlfs.* Finnbogi Guðmundsson, ed. 1965.

ÍF 35 = *Danakonunga sögur: Skjöldunga saga, Knýtlinga saga, Ágrip af sögu Danakonunga.* Bjarni Guðnason, ed. 1982.

Imer, Lisbeth M. 2014. The Danish Runestones: When and Where? *Danish Journal of Archaeology* 3 (2):164–174.

Imer, Lisbeth M. 2016. *Danmarks Runesten: En Fortælling.* Copenhagen: Nationalmuseet and Gyldendal.

Ingstad, Helge. 1985. *The Norse Discovery of America*, Vol. 2. Oslo: Norwegian University Press.

Ingstad, Helge, and Anne Stine Ingstad. 2001. *The Viking Discovery of America: The Excavation of a Norse Settlement in L'Anse aux Meadows, Newfoundland.* New York: Checkmark Books.

Irvine, Susan, ed. 2004. *The Anglo Saxon Chronicle*, Vol. 7: *MS E.* Cambridge: D. S. Brewer.

Isaksson, Sven. 2000. *Food and Rank in Early Medieval Time.* Stockholm: The Archaeological Research Laboratory, Stockholm University.

Isaksson, Sven. 2003. Vild vikings vivre: Om en tidigmedeltida matkultur. *Fornvännen* 98 (4):271–288.

Jacobsen, Lis, and Erik Moltke. 1942. *Danmarks Runeindskrifter.* Copenhagen: Ejnar Munksgaards Forlag.

Jacobsson, Bengt, Eje Arén, and K Arne Blom. 1995. *Trelleborgen: en av Harald Blåtands danska ringborgar.* Trelleborg: Trelleborgs kommun.

Jakobsson, Sverrir. 2001. Black Men and Malignant-looking: The Place of the Indigenous Peoples of North America in the Icelandic World View. In *Approaches to Vínland*, edited by Andrew Wawn and Þórunn Sigurðardóttir, 88–104. Reykjavík: Sigurður Nordal Institute.

Jakobsson, Sverrir. 2012. Vínland and Wishful Thinking: Medieval and Modern Fantasies. *Canadian Journal of History* 47:493–514.

Jane, Stephen F., Keith H. Nislow, and Andrew R. Whiteley. 2014. The Use (and Misuse) of Archaeological Salmon Data to Infer Historical Abundance in North America with a Focus on New England. *Reviews in Fish Biology and Fisheries* 24:943–954.

Jankowiak, Marek. 2016. Byzantine Coins in Viking-Age Northern Lands. In *Byzantium and the Viking World*, edited by Fedir Androshchuk, Jonathan Shepard, and Monica White, 117–139. Uppsala: Uppsala University.

Jarman, Cat. 2018. The "Great Army" at Repton and the New Archaeology of Viking Campaigns. *The SAA Archaeological Record* 18 (3):19–22.

Jarman, Cat. 2021. *River Kings: The Vikings from Scandinavia to the Silk Roads.* London: William Collins.

Jarman, Catrine L., Martin Biddle, Tom Higham, and Christopher Bronk Ramsey. 2018. The Viking Great Army in England: New Dates from the Repton Charnel. *Antiquity* 92 (361):183–199.

Jensen, Nils M., and Jens Sørensen. 1989. En ny brik til udforskningen af Nonnebakke-anlægget i Odense. *Fynske Minder* 1989:77–84.

Jeppesen, Jens. 2004. Stormandsgården ved Lisbjerg kirke: Nye undersøgelser. *KUML: Årbog for Jysk Arkæologisk Selskab* 2004:161–180.

Jesch, Judith. 1991. *Women in the Viking Age.* Woodbridge: Boydell & Brewer.

Jesch, Judith. 2001. Skaldic Verse in Scandinavian England. In *Vikings and the Danelaw: Papers from the Proceedings of the Thirteenth Viking Congress, Nottingham and York, 21–30 August 1997*, edited by James Graham-Campbell, Richard Hall, Judith Jesch, and David Parsons, 313–325. Oxford: Oxbow Books.

Jesch, Judith. 2015. *The Viking Diaspora.* New York: Routledge.

Jochens, Jenny. 1995. *Women in Old Norse Society.* Ithaca, NY: Cornell University Press.

Jochens, Jenny. 1999. Late and Peaceful: Iceland's Conversion through Arbitration in 1000. *Speculum* 74 (3):621–655.

Jóhannesson, Jón. 1962. The Date of the Composition of the *Saga of the Greenlanders. Saga-Book* 16 (1):54–66.

Jóhannesson, Jón. 1974. *A History of the Old Icelandic Commonwealth.* Translated by Haraldur Bessason. Winnipeg: University of Manitoba Press.

Johnson South, Ted, ed. 2002. *Historia de Sancto Cuthberto: A History of Saint Cuthbert and a Record of His Patrimony.* Woodbridge: D.S. Brewer.

Jones, Gwyn. 1984. *A History of the Vikings.* Oxford: Oxford University Press.

Jones, Gwyn. 1986. *The Norse Atlantic Saga: Being the Norse Voyages of Discovery and Settlement to Iceland, Greenland, and North America.* 2nd ed. Oxford University Press. Original edition, 1964.

Jonsson, Kenneth. 1994. The Coinage of Cnut. In *The Reign of Cnut: King of England, Denmark, and Norway*, edited by Alexander Rumble, 193–230. London: Leicester University Press.

Jónsson, Þorleifr. 1904. *Fjörutíu íslendinga-þættir.* Reykjavík: Sigurður Kristjánsson.

Jónsson, Finnur. 1907. *Den Islandske Litteraturs Historie Tilligemed den Oldnorske.* Copenhagen: G. E. C. Gad.

Jónsson, Finnur. 1921. *Norsk-Islandsk Kultur- og Sprogforhold i 9. og 10. Årh.* Copenhagen: Det Kgl. Danske Videnskabernes Selskab. Historisk-filologiske Meddelelser 3/2. Bianco Lunos.

Jónsson, Finnur, ed. 1932. *De Gamle Eddadigte.* Copenhagen: Gads.

Jónsson, Guðni, and Bjarni Vilhjálmsson, eds. 1943–1944. *Fornaldarsögur Norðurlanda*, Vol. 3. Reykjavík: Forni.

Jørgensen, Lars. 2009. Pre-Christian Cult at Aristocratic Residences and Settlement Complexes in Southern Scandinavia in the 3rd–10th centuries AD. In *Glaube, Kult und Herrschaft Phänomene des Religiösen im 1. ahrtausend n. Chr. in Mittel- und Nordeuropa*, edited by Uta von Freeden, Herwig Friesinger and Egon Wamers, 329–354. Bonn: Dr. Rudolf Habelt GmbH.

Jørgensen, Lars. 2010. Gudme and Tissø. Two magnates' complexes in Denmark from the 3rd to the 11th century AD. In *Trade and Communication Networks of the First Millennium AD in the northern part of Central Europe: Central Places, Beach Markets, Landing Places and Trading Centres*, edited by Babette Ludowici, Hauke Jöns, Sunhild Kleingärtner, Jonathan Scheschkewitz, and Matthias Hardt, 273–286. Hannover: Niedersächsisches Landesmuseum.

Jørgensen, Lars. 2013. Vikingetidens kongsgård ved Tissø. Kult-, samlings- og markedsplads gennem 500 år. In *Menneskers veje—kulturhistoriske essays i 100-året for Kalundborg Museum*, edited by L. Pedersen, 125–144. Kalundborg: Kalundborg Museum.

Jørgensen, Lars. 2014. Norse Religion and Ritual Sites in Scandinavia in the 6th–11th Century. In *Die Wikinger und das Fränkische Reich: Identitäten zwischen Konfrontation und Annäherung*, edited by Kerstin P. Hofmann, Hermann Kamp, and Matthias Wemhoff, 239–264. Paderborn: Wilhelm Fink.

Jørgensen, Mogens Schou. 1977. Risby-vejene: Veje over Risby Å fra stenalder til vikingetid. *Nationalmuseets Arbejdsmark* 1977:42–51.

Jørgensen, Mogens Schou. 1997. Vikingetidsbroen i Ravning Enge—nye undersøgelser. *Nationalmuseets Arbejdsmark* 1997:74–87.

Jorgensen, Tove H., Henriette N. Buttenschön, August G. Wang, Thomas D. Als, Anders D. Børglum, and Henrik Ewald. 2004. The Origin of the Isolated Population of the Faroe Islands Investigated Using Y Chromosomal Markers. *Human Genetics* 115:19–28.

Júlíusson, Árni Daníel, Jón Ólafur Ísberg, and Helgi Skúli Kjartansson, eds. 1991. *Íslenskur Sögu Atlas 1: frá Öndverðu til 18. Aldar.* Reykjavík: Iðunn.

Kalmring, Sven. 2010. *Der Hafen von Haithabu.* Neumünster: Wachholtz.

Kalmring, Sven. 2011. The Harbour of Hedeby. In *Viking Settlements and Viking Society: Papers from the Proceedings of the Sixteenth Viking Congress,* edited by Svavar Sigmundsson, 245–259. Reykjavík: Hið íslenzka fornleifafélag & University of Iceland Press.

Karlsson, Gunnar. 2000. *The History of Iceland.* Minneapolis: University of Minnesota Press.

Kålund, Kristian. 1877. *Bidrag til en Historisk Topografisk Beskrivelse af Island: I. Syd- og Vest-Fjærdingerne.* Copenhagen: Gyldendalske Boghandel.

Kehoe, Alice Beck. 2005. *The Kensington Runestone: Approaching a Research Question Holistically.* Long Grove, IL: Waveland Press.

Keller, Christian. 2010. Furs, Fish, and Ivory: Medieval Norsemen at the Arctic Fringe. *Journal of the North Atlantic* 3:1–23.

Kellogg, Robert. 1988. *A Concordance to Eddic Poetry.* East Lansing: Michigan State University Press.

Kershaw, Jane. 2013. *Viking Identities: Scandinavian Jewellery in England.* Oxford: Oxford University Press.

Kershaw, Jane. 2014. Viking Age Silver in North-West England: Hoards and Single Finds. In *In Search of Vikings: Interdisciplinary Approaches to the Scandinavian Heritage of North-West England,* edited by Stephen E. Harding, David Griffiths, and Elizabeth Royles, 149–164. Boca Raton: CRC Press.

Kershaw, Jane. 2017. An Early Medieval Dual-Currency Economy: Bullion and Coin in the Danelaw. *Antiquity* 91 (355):173–190.

Kershaw, Jane, and Ellen C. Røyrvik. 2016. The "People of the British Isles" Project and Viking Settlement in England. *Antiquity* 90 (354):1670–1680.

Keynes, Simon, and Michael Lapidge, eds. and trans. 1983. *Alfred the Great: Asser's Life of King Alfred and Other Contemporary Sources.* London: Penguin.

Kieffer-Olsen, Jakob. 2008. Ribe—de første par hundrede år. In *De første 200 årene—nytt blikk på 27 skandinaviske middelalderbyer,* edited by Hans Andersson, Gitte Hansen, and Ingvild Øye, 155–164. Bergen: Universitetet i Bergen.

King, Turi. 2015. What Can Genetics Tell Us about the Vikings in Wirral and Lancashire? In *In Search of Vikings: Interdisciplinary Approaches to the Scandinavian Heritage of North-West England,* edited by David Griffiths and Elizabeth Royles Stephen E. Harding, 165–178. Boca Raton: CRC Press.

Kjartansson, Helgi Skúli. 2002. From the Frying Pan of Oral Tradition into the Fire of Saga Writing: The Precarious Survival of Historical Fact in the Saga of Yngvar the Far-Traveller. Sagas and Societies. International Conference at Borgarnes, Iceland, September 5–9, 2002.

Klevnäs, Alison Margaret. 2016. "Imbued with the Essence of the Owner": Personhood and Possessions in the Reopening and Reworking of Viking-Age Burials. *European Journal of Archaeology* 19 (3):456–476.

Kobishchanow, Yurii M. 1987. The Phenomenon of Gafol and Its Transformation. In *Early State Dynamics,* edited by Henri Claessen and Pieter Van de Velde, 108–128. Leiden: Brill.

Krag, Anne Hedeager. 2017. Tekstilerne i krypten: byzantinsk or orientalsk silke. In *Knuds Odense-Vikingernes by,* edited by Mads Runge and Jesper Hansen, 79–83. Odense: Forlaget Odense Bys Museer.

Krag, Anne Hedeager. 2019. Oriental and Byzantine Silks in St Cnut's Reliquary Shrine. In *Life and Cult of Cnut the Holy: The First Royal Saint of Denmark,* edited by Steffen Hope, Mikael Manøe Bjerregaard, Anne Hedeager Krag, and Mads Runge, 42–49. Odense: Odense Bys Museer and University Press of Southern Denmark.

Kristjánsdóttir, Steinunn. 2004. *The Awakening of Christianity in Iceland: Discovery of a Timber Church and Graveyard at Þórarinsstaðir in Seyðisfjördur, Gothenburg Archaeological Thesis, Series B.* Gothenburg: University of Gothenburg.

Kristjánsson, Jónas, Bjarni F. Einarsson, Kristján Jónasson, Þór Hjaltalín. 2012. Falling into Vínland: Newfoundland Hunting Pitfalls at the Edge of the Viking World. *Acta Archaeologica* 83:145–177.

Krogh, Knud J., and Bodil Leth-Larsen. 2007. *Hedensk og kristent: Fundene fra den kongelige gravhøj i Jelling. Vikingekongernes monumenter i Jelling 2.* Copenhagen: Carlsbergfondet and Nationalmuseet.

Krogh, Knud, and Olfert Voss. 1961. Fra hedenskab til kristendom i Hørning. *Nationalmuseets arbejdsmark* 1961:5–34.

Kruse, Arne. 2004. Norse Topographical Settlement Names on the Western Littoral of Scotland. In *Scandinavia and Europe 800–1350: Contact, Conflict, and Coexistence*, edited by Jonathan Adams and Katherine Holman, 97–107. Turnhout: Brepols.

Kuitems, Margot, Birgitta L. Wallace, Charles Lindsay, Andrea Scifo, Petra Doeve, Kevin Jenkins, Susanne Lindauer, Pınar Erdil, Paul M. Ledger, Véronique Forbes, Caroline Vermeeren, Ronny Friedrich, and Michael W. Dee. 2022. Evidence for European Presence in the Americas in AD 1021. *Nature* 601 (7893):388–391.

Kunin, Devra, and Carl Phelpstead. 2001. *A History of Norway and the Passion and Miracles of the Blessed Óláfr.* London: Viking Society for Northern Research.

Kunz, Keneva, trans. 2008. *Eirik the Red's Saga.* London: Penguin.

Kupiec, Patrycja, and Karen Milek. 2015. Roles and Perceptions of Shielings and the Mediation of Gender Identities in Viking and Medieval Iceland. In *Viking Worlds: Things, Spaces, and Movement*, edited by Marianne Hem Eriksen, Unn Pedersen, Bernt Rundberget, Irmelin Axelsen, and Heidi Lund Berg, 102–123. Oxford: Oxbow Books.

Kurze, Friedrich, ed. 1895. *Annales Regni Francorum.* Monumenta Germaniae historica, Scriptores rerum Germanicarum in usum scholarum 6. Hannover: Impensis Bibliopolii Hahniani.

Lamm, Jan Peder. 2007. Two Large Silver Hoards from Ocksarve on Gotland. Evidence for Viking Period Trade and Warfare in the Baltic Region. *Archaeologia Baltica* 8:328–333.

Larrington, Carolyne. 2004. "Undruðusk þá, sem fyrir var": wonder, Vínland and mediaeval travel narratives. *Mediaeval Scandinavia* 14:91–114.

Larrington, Carolyne. 2014. *The Poetic Edda.* Oxford: Oxford University Press.

Larsson, Mats G. 1992. The Vinland Sagas and Nova Scotia: A Reappraisal of an Old Theory. *Scandinavian Studies* 64 (3):305–335.

Lawson, Ian, Frederick Gathorne-Hardy, Mike Church, Anthony Newton, Kevin J. Edwards, Andrew Dugmore, and Árni Einarsson. 2007. Environmental Impacts of the Norse Settlement: Paleoenvironmental Data from Mývatnssveit, Northern Iceland. *Boreas* 36 (1):1–19.

Ledger, Paul M., Linus Girdland-Flink, and Véronique Forbes. 2019. New horizons at L'Anse aux Meadows. *Proceedings of the National Academy of Sciences* 116 (31):15341–15343.

Lee, Everett S. 1966. A Theory of Migration. *Demography* 3 (1):47–57.

Leifsson, Rúnar. 2012. Evolving Traditions: Horse Slaughter as Part of Viking Burial Customs in Iceland. In *The Ritual Killing and Burial of Animals: European Perspectives*, edited by Aleksander Pluskowski, 184–194. Oxford: Oxbow Books.

Lemus-Lauzon, Isabel, Najat Bhiry, and James Woollett. 2016. Assessing the Effects of Climate Change and Land Use on Northern Labrador Forest Stands Based on Paleoecological Data. *Quaternary Research* 86:260–270.

Leslie, Stephen, Bruce Winney, Garrett Hellenthal, Dan Davison, Abdelhamid Boumertit, Tammy Day, Katarzyna Hutnik, Ellen C. Royrvik, Barry Cunliffe, Wellcome Trust Case Control Consortium, International Multiple Sclerosis Genetics Consortium, Daniel J. Lawson, Daniel Falush, Colin Freeman, Matti Pirinen, Simon Myers, Mark Robinson, Peter Donnelly, and Walter Bodmer. 2015. The Fine-scale Genetic Structure of the British Population. *Nature* 519:309–314.

Leth, Peter Mygind, and Jesper Boldsen. 2009. Skeletterne i krypten. *Fynske årbøger* 2009:123–136.

Liebermann, Felix, ed. 1903. *Die Gesetze der Angelsachsen*, Vol. 1. Halle: Max Neimeyer.

Lincoln, Bruce. 2014. *Between History and Myth: Stories of Harald Fairhair and the Founding of the State.* Chicago: University of Chicago Press.

Linderholm, Anna, Charlotte Hedenstierna Jonson, Olle Svensk, and Kerstin Lidén. 2008. Diet and Status in Birka: Stable Isotopes and Grave Goods Compared. *Antiquity* 82:446–461.

Lindow, John. 2001. *Norse Mythology: A Guide to the Gods, Heroes, Rituals, and Beliefs.* Oxford: University of Oxford Press.

Lindow, John. 2021. *Old Norse Mythology.* New York: Oxford University Press.

Lindqvist, Sune. 1941. *Gotlands Bildsteine I.* Stockholm: Wahlström & Widstrand.

Lindqvist, Sune. 1942. *Gotlands Bildsteine II.* Stockholm: Wahlström & Widstrand.

Loe, Louise, Angela Boyle, Helen Webb, and David Score. 2014. *"Given to the Ground": A Viking Age Mass Grave on Ridgway Hill, Weymouth.* Oxford: Berforts Information Press.

Logan, F. Donald. 1983. *The Vikings in History.* London: Hutchinson & Co Ltd.

Lönnroth, Lars. 1971. Hjalmar's Death-Song and the Delivery of Eddic Poetry. *Speculum* 46 (1):1–20.

Lord, Albert B. 2000 (1960). *The Singer of Tales.* Edited by E. S. M. a. G. Nagy. 2nd ed. Cambridge, MA: Harvard University Press. Original edition, 1960.

Lowe, Chris. 2008. *Inchmarnock: An Early Historic Island and Its Archaeological Landscape.* Edinburgh: Society of Antiquaries of Scotland.

Lucas, Gavin. 2009. *Hofstaðir: Excavations of a Viking Age Feasting Hall in North-Eastern Iceland.* Reykjavík: Institute of Archaeology.

Lucas, Gavin, and Thomas McGovern. 2007. Bloody Slaughter: Ritual Decapitation and Display at the Viking Settlement of Hofstaðir, Iceland. *European Journal of Archaeology* 10 (1):7–30.

Lund, Julie. 2020. Rune Stones as Material Relations in Late Pagan and Early Christian South Scandinavia. *Danish Journal of Archaeology* 9:1–20.

Lunde, Paul, and Caroline Stone, trans. 2012. *Ibn Fadlan and the Land of Darkness: Arab Travellers in the Far North.* London: Penguin.

Luo, Shiyu, C. Alexander Valencia, Jinglan Zhang, Ni-Chung Lee, Jesse Slone, Baoheng Gui, Xinjian Wang, Zhuo Li, Sarah Dell, Jenice Brown, Stella Maris Chen, Yin-Hsiu Chien, Wuh-Liang Hwu, Pi-Chuan Fan, Lee-Jun Wong, Paldeep S. Atwal, and Taosheng Huang. 2018. Biparental Inheritance of Mitochondrial DNA in Humans. *Proceedings of the National Academy of Sciences* 115 (51):13039–13044.

MacLeod, Mindy, and Bernard Mees. 2006. *Runic Amulets and Magic Objects.* Woodbridge: Boydell & Brewer.

Magnusson, Magnus. 2000. *The Vikings.* Stroud: Tempus.

Magnusson, Magnus. 2003. Vínland: The Ultimate Outpost. In *Vinland Revisited: The Norse World at the Turn of the First Millenium*, edited by Shannon Lewis-Simpson, 83–96. St John's: Historic Sites Association of Newfoundland and Labrador.

Magnusson, Magnus, and Hermann Pálsson, eds. and trans. 1965. *The Vinland Sagas: The Norse Discovery of America.* London: Penguin.

Magnusson, Magnus, and Hermann Pálsson, eds. and trans. 1966. *King Harald's Saga.* London: Penguin.

Mainman, Ailsa, and Nicola Rogers. 2000. *Craft, Industry, and Everyday Life: Finds from Anglo-Scandinavian York.* York: Council for British Archaeology.

Mallery, Arlington H. 1951. *Lost America: The Story of Iron-Age Civilization Prior to Columbus.* Washington, DC: The Overlook Company.

Malmer, Brita. 2007. South Scandinavian Coinage in the Ninth Century. In *Silver Economy in the Viking Age*, edited by James Graham-Campbell and Gareth Williams, 13–28. London: Routledge.

Maltsberger, Anya. 2018. Currency and Kingship: An Examination of the Transformative Effect of Coins on the Viking Rulers of the Danelaw. MA Thesis: University of York.

Mann, Michael. 1986. *Sources of Social Power: A History of Power from the Beginning to A.D. 1760*: Cambridge University Press.

Mann, Michael E., Zhihua Zhang, Scott Rutherford, Raymond S. Bradley, Malcolm K. Hughes, Drew Shindell, Caspar Ammann, Greg Faluvegi, and Fenbiao Ni. 2009. Global Signatures and Dynamical Origins of the Little Ice Age and Medieval Climate Anomaly. *Science* 326:1256–1260.

Marchlewski, Ann-Kathrin. 2012. St Cnut of Denmark, King and Martyr: His Lives, Their Authors and the Politics of His Cult (c. 1086–1200). PhD dissertation, University of Leicester.

Mårtensson, Anders. 1976. *Uppgrävt förflutet för PKbanken i Lund: en investering i arkeologi,* *Archaeologica Lundensia* Lund: Kulturhistoriska museet.

Mauss, Marcel. 1990. *The Gift: The Form and Reason for Exchange in Archaic Societies.* Translated by W.D. Halls. New York: W.W. Norton [original French 1923–1924].

McAleese, Kevin. 2003. Skrælingar Abroad—Skrælingar at Home? In *Vínland Revisited: The* *Norse World at the Turn of the First Millenium,* edited by Shannon Lewis-Simpson, 353–264. St John's: Historic Sites Association of Newfoundland and Labrador.

McCormick, Finbar. 2009. Ritual Feasting in Iron Age Ireland. In *Relics of Old Decency: Archaeological* *Studies in Later Prehistory,* edited by G. Cooney, K. Becker, J. Coles, M. Ryan, and S. Sievers, 405–412. Bray: Wordwell.

McGovern, Thomas H. 1980. Cows, Harp Seals, and Churchbells: Adaptation and Extinction in Norse Greenland. *Human Ecology* 8 (3):245–275.

McGovern, Thomas H. 1990. The Archaeology of the Norse North Atlantic. *Annual Review of* *Anthropology* 19:331–351.

McGovern, Thomas. 2000. The Demise of Norse Greenland. In *Vikings: The North Atlantic Saga,* edited by William Fitzhugh and Elisabeth Ward, 327–339. Washington, DC: Smithsonian Institution Press.

McGovern, Thomas H. 2003. Herding Strategies at Sveigakot, N Iceland: An Interim Report. In *Archaeological Investigations at Sveigakot 2002,* edited by Orri Vésteinsson, 18–69. Reykjavík: Fornleifastofnun Íslands, FS206-00213.

McGovern, Thomas. 2005. The Midden. In *Hrísheimar 2004 Interim Report,* edited by Ragnar Edvardsson, 14–16. Reykjavík: Fornleifastofnun Íslands, FS278-03222.

McGovern, Thomas. 2009. The Archaeofauna. In *Hofstaðir: Excavations of a Viking Age Feasting Hall* *in North-Eastern Iceland,* edited by Gavin Lucas, 168–252. Reykjavík: Institute of Archaeology.

McGovern, Thomas, G.F. Bigelow, T. Amorosi, and D. Russell. 1988. Northern Islands, Human Errors, and Environmental Degradation: A View of Social and Ecological Change in the Medieval North Atlantic. *Human Ecology* 16:225–270.

McGovern, Thomas H., Sophia Perdikaris, Árni Einarsson, and Jane Sidell. 2006. Coastal Connections, Local Fishing, and Sustainable Egg Harvesting? patterns of Viking Age Inland Wild Resource Use in Mývatn District, Northern Iceland. *Environmental Archaeology* 11 (2):187–205.

McGovern, Thomas H., Orri Vésteinsson, Adolf Friðriksson, Mike J. Church, Ian Lawson, Ian Simpson, Arni Einarsson, Andrew Dugmore, Gordon Cook, Sophia Perdikaris, Kevin J. Edwards, Amanda M. Thomson, W. Paul Adderley, Anthony Newton, Gavin Lucas, Ragnar Edvardsson, Oscar Aldred, and Elaine Dunbar. 2007. Landscapes of Settlement in Northern Iceland: Historical Ecology of Human Impact and Climate Fluctuation on the Millennial Scale. *American* *Anthropologist* 109 (1):27–51.

Medelgaard, Jørgen. 1961. Fra Brattahlid til Vinland. *Naturens Verden* 45:353–384.

Merrill, William Stetson. 1935. The Vinland Problem through Four Centuries. *The Catholic Historical* *Review* 21 (1):21–48.

Metcalf, D. M. 1996. Viking-Age Numismatics 2. Coinage in the Northern Lands in Merovingian and Carolingian Times. *The Numismatic Chronicle* 156:399–428.

Metcalf, D. M. 1999. Viking-Age Numismatics 5. Denmark in the time of Cnut and Harthacnut. *The* *Numismatic Chronicle* 159:395–430.

Metcalf, Peter, and Richard Huntington. 1992. *Celebrations of Death: The Anthropology of Mortuary* *Ritual.* Cambridge: Cambridge University Press.

Mierow, Charles C., ed. and trans. 1908. *Jordanes: The Origin and Deeds of the Goths.* Princeton, NJ: Princeton University Press.

Migne, Jacques Paul, ed. 1853. *Magistri Adam Bremensis Gesta Hammaburgensis Ecclesiae* *Pontificum.* Patrologiae cursus completes 146. Paris: Tomus unicus.

Mikołajczyk, Łukasz, and Karen Milek. 2016. Geostatistical Approach to Spatial, Multi-elemental Dataset from an Archaeological Site in Vatnsfjörður, Iceland. *Journal of Archaeological* *Science: Reports* 9:577–585.

Milek, Karen. 2012. The Roles of Pit Houses and Gendered Spaces on Viking-Age Farmsteads in Iceland. *Medieval Archaeology* 56:85–130.

Milek, Karen, and Howell Roberts. 2013. Integrated Geoarchaeological Methods for the Determination of Site Activity Areas: A Study of a Viking Age House in Reykjavik, Iceland. *Journal of Archaeological Science* 40:1845–1865.

Milek, Karen, Davide Zori, Colin Connors, Waltraud Baier, Kate Baker, and Jesse Byock. 2014. The Organization and Use of Space in the House at Hrísbrú. In *Viking Age Archaeology in Iceland: Mosfell Archaeological Project*, edited by Davide Zori and Jesse Byock, 143–162. Turnhout: Brepols Publishers.

Miller, William Ian. 1990. *Bloodtaking and Peacemaking: Feud, Law, and Society in Saga Iceland*. Chicago: University of Chicago Press.

Miller, William Ian. 2014. *"Why Is Your Axe So Bloody": A Reading of Njáls Saga*. Oxford: Oxford University Press.

Moesgaard, Jens Christian, and Ole Kastholm. 2014. Making New Money: The Hedeby Coin. In *The World in the Viking Age*, edited by Søren M. Sindbæk and Athena Trakadas, 104–105. Roskilde: The Viking Ship Museum.

Møller, Stig Bergmann. 2008. Aalborgs ældste tid—perioden ca. 900–1200. In *De første 200 årene— nytt blikk på 27 skandinaviske middelalderbyer*, edited by Hans Andersson, Gitte Hansen, and Ingvild Øye, 195–214. Bergen: Universitetet i Bergen.

Moltke, Erik. 1976. *Runerne i Danmark og deres oprindelse*. Copenhagen: Forum.

Montgomery, James E. 2000. Ibn Fadlān and the Rūsiyyah. *Journal of Arabic and Islamic Studies* 3:1–25.

Mooney, Dawn Elise, and Lísabet Guðmundsdóttir. 2020. Barley Cultivation in Viking Age Iceland in Light of Evidence from Lækjargata 10–12, Reykjavík. In *Archaeobotanical Studies of Past Plant cultivation in Northern Europe*, edited by Santeri Vanhanen and Per Lagerås, in *Advances in Archaeobotany*, 5–20. Eelde: Barkhuis.

Munn, William. 1914. *The Wineland Voyages: The Location of Helluland, Markland, and Vinland from the Icelandic Sagas*. St. John's: Evening Telegram Limited.

Murray, Griffin. 2015. Insular crosiers from Viking-age Scandinavia. *Acta Archaeologica* 86 (2):95–12.

Müller-Wille, Michael. 1976. *Das Bootkammergrab von Haithabu*. Neumünster: Karl Wachholtz Verlag.

Myhre, Bjørn. 2000. The Early Viking Age in Norway. *Acta Archaeologica* 71:35–47.

Nansen, Fridtjof. 1911. *In Northern Mists: Arctic Exploration in Early Times*. Translated by Arthur Chater. New York: Frederick A. Stokes Company.

Näsman, Ulf. 2000. Raids, Migrations, and Kingdoms: The Danish Case. *Acta Archaeologica* 71:1–7.

Näsman, Ulf. 2006. Danerne og det danske kongeriges opkomst Om forskningsprogrammet "Fra Stamme til Stat i Danmark." *KUML: Årbog for Jysk Arkæologisk Selskab* 2006:205–241.

Naumann, Elise, Maja Krzewińska, Anders Götherström, and Gunilla Eriksson. 2014. Slaves as Burial Gifts in Viking Age Norway? Evidence from Stable Isotope and Ancient DNA Analyses. *Journal of Archaeological Science* 41:533–540.

Nelson, Janet L., ed. and trans. 1991. *The Annals of St-Bertin*. Manchester: Manchester University Press.

Ney, Agneta. 2012. The Welcoming Scene on Gotlandic Picture Stones, in Comparison with Viking Period and Medieval Literary Sources. In *Gotland's Picture Stones: Bearers of an Enigmatic Legacy*, edited by Maria Herlin Karnell, 73–82. Visby: Gotland Museum.

Nielsen, E. Levin. 1968. Pederstræde i Viborg: Købstadsarkæologiske undersøgelser. *KUML: Årbog for Jysk Arkæologisk Selskab* 1966/1967:23–81.

Nielsen, Gunhild Øeby. 2005. De danske runestens oprindelige plads. *KUML: Årbog for Jysk Arkæologisk Selskab* 2005:121–144.

Nielsen, Jens N. 2008. Sebbersund. In *The Viking World*, edited by Stefan Brink and Neil Price, 135–139. New York: Routledge.

Nielsen, Karl Martin. 1970. Om dateringen af de senurnordiske runeindskrifter, synkopen og 16 tegns futharken. *Aarbøger for Nordisk Oldkyndighed og Historie* 1969:5–51.

Nielsen, Leif-Christian. 1990. Trelleborg. *Årbog for Nordisk Olkyndighed og Historie* 1990:105–178.

Nordal, Sigurður. 1958. *Hrafnkels saga Freysgoða: A Study*. Translated by R. G. Thomas. Cardiff: University of Wales Press.

Nordeide, Sæbjørg Walaker, Niels Bonde, and Terje Thun. 2020. At the Threshold of the Viking Age: New Dendrochronological Dates for the Kvalsund Ship and Boat Bog Offerings (Norway). *Journal of Archaeological Science: Reports* 29:102192.

Nørlund, Poul. 1948. *Trelleborg*. Copenhagen: Det Kongelige Nordiske Oldskriftselskab.

Nydal, Reidar. 1985. Radiocarbon Dating of Material from L'Anse aux Meadows. In *The Norse Discovery of America*, Vol. 1, edited by Anne Stine Ingstad, 363–378. Oslo: Universitetsforlaget.

Oehrl, Sigmund. 2012. New Iconographic Interpretations of Gotlandic Picture Stones Based on Surface Re-Analysis. In *Gotland's Picture Stones: Bearers of an Enigmatic Legacy*, edited by Maria Herlin Karnell, 92–106. Visby: Gotland Museum.

Oehrl, Sigmund. 2019. Re-interpretations of Gotlandic Picture Stones Based on the Reflectance Transformation Imaging Method (RTI): Some Examples. In *Myth, Materiality, and Lived Religion in Merovingian and Viking Scandinavia*, edited by Klas Wikström af Edholm, Peter Jackson Rova, Andreas Nordberg, Olof Sundqvist, and Torun Zachrisson, 141–185. Stockholm: Stockholm University Press.

Okasha, Elisabeth. 1984. An Inscribed Anglo-Saxon lid from Lund. *Medieval Archaeology* 28:181–183.

Olesen, Martin Borring. 2000. Trelleborg eller ej? *KUML: Årbog for Jysk Arkæologisk Selskab* 2000:91–111.

Olsen, Magnus. 1951. *Norges Inskrifter med de Yngre Runer*, Vol. 2. Oslo: Norsk historisk kjeldeskrift-institutt.

Olsen, Magnus. 1971. *Hvad Våre Stedsnavn Lære Oss*. Oslo: Universitetsforlage.

Olsen, Olaf, and Holger Schmidt. 1977. *Fyrkat En Jysk Vikingeborg: I. Borgen og Bebyggelsen*. København: Det Kongelige Nordiske Oldskriftselskab.

Östergren, Majvor. 2011. The Spillings Hoard(s). In *Silver Economies, Monetisation and Society in Scandinavia, AD 800–1100*, edited by James Graham-Campbell, Søren M. Sindbæk, and Gareth Williams, 321–336. Aarhus: Aarhus University Press.

Owen, Olwyn, and Magnar Dalland. 2000. *Scar: A Viking Boat Burial on Sanday, Orkney* Edinburgh: Tuckwell Press.

Owen, Olwyn. 2015. Galloway's Viking Treasure: The Story of a Discovery. *British Archaeology* 140 (January–February):16–23.

Pálsdóttir, Albína Hulda, Marjorie Gorseline, and Thomas McGovern. 2008. The Archaeofauna from Vatnsfjörður. In *Vatnsfjörður 2007: Framvinduskýrslur/Interim Report*, edited by Karen Milek, 102–110. Reykjavík: Fornleifastofnun Íslands, FS383-03097.

Pálsdóttir, Lilja Björk, and Oddgeir Hansson. 2008. *Fornleifarannsóknir á Deiliskipulagssvæði í Leirvogstungu, Mosfellbæ: Framvinduskýrskla III*. Reykjavík: Fornleifastofnun Íslands, FS368-06353.

Pálsson, Hermann, and Paul Edwards, eds. and trans. 1972. *Landnámabók*. Winnipeg: University of Manitoba Press.

Pálsson, Hermann, and Paul Edwards, eds. and trans. 1976. *Egil's Saga*. New York: Penguin.

Pálsson, Hermann, and Paul Edwards, eds. and trans. 1986. *Knytlinga Saga*. Odense: Odense University Press.

Pálsson, Hermann, and Paul Edwards, eds. and trans. 1989. *Eyrbyggja Saga*. New York: Penguin.

Pálsson, Viðar. 2016. *Language of Power: Feasting and Gift-Giving in Medieval Iceland and Its Sagas*. Ithaca, NY, and London: Cornell University Press.

Papadopoulos, John. 1999. Archaeology, Myth-History and the Tyranny of the Text: Chalkidike, Torone and Thucydides. *Oxford Journal of Archaeology* 18 (4):377–394.

Parcak, Sarah. 2019. *Archaeology from Space: How the Future Shapes Our Past*. New York: Henry Holt and Company.

Park, Robert W. 2008. Contact between the Norse Vikings and the Dorset culture in Arctic Canada. *Antiquity* 82:189–198.

Pedersen, Anne. 1997. Similar Finds—Different Meanings? Some Preliminary Thoughts on the Viking-age Burials with Riding Equipment in Scandinavia. In *Burial and Society: The Chronological and Social Analysis of Archaeological Burial Data*, edited by Karen Høilund Nielsen and Claus Kjeld Jensen, 171–183. Aarhus: Aarhus University Press.

Pedersen, Anne. 2014a. *Dead Warriors in Living Memory: A Study of Weapon and Equestrian Burials in Viking Age Denmark, AD 800–1000. 1. Text*, Vol. 20:1.1: *Publications from the National Museum of Denmark. Studies in Archaeology and History*. Odense: University of Southern Denmark Press and the National Museum of Denmark.

Pedersen, Anne. 2014b. *Dead Warriors in Living Memory: A Study of Weapon and Equestrian Burials in Viking Age Denmark, AD 800–1000. 2 Catalogue*, Vol. 20:1.1: *Publications from the National Museum of Denmark. Studies in Archaeology and History*. Odense: University of Southern Denmark Press and the National Museum of Denmark.

Pedersen, Anne, and Else Roesdahl. 2014. Appendix 5. Botanical Finds from Aggersborg: ummary and Comments. In *Aggersborg: The Viking-Age settlement and fortress*, edited by Søren M. Sindbæk Else Roesdahl, Anne Pedersen, and David M. Wilson, 423–424. Moesgaard: Jutland Archaeological Society and The National Museum of Denmark.

Pierce, Elizabeth. 2009. Walrus Hunting and the Ivory Trade in early Iceland. *Archaeologia Islandica* 7:55–63.

Pluskowski, Aleks. 2010. The Zooarchaeology of Medieval "Christendom": Ideology, the Treatment of Animals and the Making of Medieval Europe. *World Archaeology* 42 (2):201–214.

Poole, Russell. 1987. Skaldic Verse and Anglo-Saxon History: Some Aspects of the Period 1009–1016. *Speculum* 62 (2):265–298.

Porsmose, Erland 1981. *Den regulerede landsby—studier over bebyggelsesudviklingen på Fyn i tiden fra ca. 1700 til ca. 1000 e.Kr. fødsel*. Odense: Odense Universitetsforlag.

Poulsen, Thomas Guntzelnick. 2019. Danish Coinage under the Reign of Cnut IV, 1080–1086. In *Life and cult of Cnut the Holy: The First Royal Saint of Denmark*, edited by Steffen Hope, Mikael Manøe Bjerregaard, Anne Hedeager Krag, and Mads Runge, 50–58. Odense: Odense Bys Museer and University Press of Southern Denmark.

Price, Neil. 1989. *The Vikings in Brittany*. London: Viking Society for Northern Research, University College London.

Price, Neil. 2002. *The Viking Way: Religion and War in Late Iron Age Scandinavia*. Uppsala: Uppsala Universitet.

Price, Neil. 2008. Dying and the Dead: Viking Age Mortuary Behaviour. In *The Viking World*, edited by Stefan Brink and Neil Price, 257–273. New York: Routledge.

Price, Neil. 2020. *Children of Ash and Elm: A History of the Vikings*. London: Allen Lane.

Price, T. Douglas, and Hildur Gestsdóttir. 2006. The First Settlers of Iceland: An Isotopic Approach to Colonization. *Antiquity* 80:130–144.

Price, T. Douglas, Karin Margarita Frei, Andres Siegfried Dobat, Niels Lynnerup, and Pia Bennike. 2011. Who Was in Harold Bluetooth's Army? Strontium Isotope Investigation of the Cemetery at the Viking Age Fortress at Trelleborg, Denmark. *Antiquity* 85:476–489.

Price, T. Douglas, Karin Margarita Frei, Vera Tiesler, and Hildur Gestsdóttir. 2012. Isotopes and Mobility: Case Studies with Large Samples. In *Population Dynamics in Prehistory and Early History: New Approaches by Using Stable Isotopes and Genetics*, edited by Elke Kaiser, Joachim Burger, and Wolfram Schier, 311–321. Berlin: De Gruyter.

Price, T. Douglas, Jüri Peets, Raili Allmäe, Liina Maldre, and Ester Oras. 2016. Isotopic Provenancing of the Salme Ship Burials in Pre-Viking Age Estonia. *Antiquity* 90 (352):1022–1037.

Quinn, Judy, trans. 1997. The Saga of the People of Eyri. In *The Complete Sagas of the Icelanders*, Vol. 5, edited by Viðar Hreinsson, 131–218. Reykjavík: Leifur Eiríksson.

Raffield, Ben. 2013. Antiquarians, Archaeologists, and Viking Fortifications. *Journal of the North Atlantic* 20:1–29.

Raffield, Ben. 2016. Bands of Brothers: A Re-appraisal of the Viking Great Army and Its Implications for the Scandinavian Colonization of England. *Early Medieval Europe* 24 (3):309–337.

Raffield, Ben. 2018. Raiding, Slaving, and the Economics of Unfreedom in the Viking Diaspora. *The SAA Archaeological Record* 18 (3):19–22.

Raffield, Ben, Claire Greenlow, Neil Price, and Mark Collard. 2016. Ingroup Identification, Identity Fusion and the Formation of Viking War Bands. *World Archaeology* 48 (1):35–50.

Raffield, Ben, Neil Price, and Mark Collard. 2017. Male-biased Operational Sex Ratios and the Viking Phenomenon: An Evolutionary Anthropological Perspective on Late Iron Age Scandinavian Raiding. *Evolution and Human Behavior* 38:315–324.

Rafnsson, Sveinbjörn. 1983. Fornleifaskýrsla Sera Markúsar Sigurðssonar á Mosfelli, Dag. 1. Ágúst 1817. In *Frásögur um Fornaldarleifar 1817–1823*, edited by Sveinbjörn Rafnsson, 258–259. Reykjavík: Rit Stofnun Árna Magnússonar.

Rafnsson, Sveinbjörn. 1999. The Atlantic Islands. In *The Oxford Illustrated History of the Vikings*, edited by Peter Sawyer, 110–133. Oxford University Press.

Ramskou, Thorkild. 1950. Viking Age Cremation Graves in Denmark. A Survey. *Acta Archaeologica* 21:137–182.

Ramskou, Thorkild. 1954. Lindholm: En gravplads fra yngre jernalder og en boplads fra tidlig middelalder. *Nationalmuseets arbejdsmark* 1954:37–48.

Ramskou, Thorkild. 1976. *Lindholm Høje Gravpladsen*. København: Det Kongelige Nordiske Oldskriftselskab.

Ramskou, Thorkild. 1981. *Vikingerne Som Ingeniører*. København: Rhodos.

Randsborg, Klavs. 1980. *The Viking Age in Denmark: The Formation of a State*. London: Gerald Duckworth.

Randsborg, Klavs. 2008. Kings' Jelling: Gorm and Thyra's Palace—Harald's Monument and Grave—Svend's Cathedral. *Acta Archaeologica* 79:1–23.

Rasmussen, Kaare Lund, Pia Bennike, Ulla Kjær, and Uffe Rahbek. 1997. Integrity and Characteristics of the Bones of the Danish King St. Knud (II) the Holy (+AD1086). *Journal of Danish Archaeology* 13:161–170.

Ravn, Mads, Christian Juel, Charlotta Lindblom, and Anne Pedersen. 2019. Erritsø: New Investigations of an Aristocratic, Early Viking Age Manor in Western Denmark c. 700–850 AD. In *Early Medieval Waterscapes Risks and Opportunities for (Im)material Cultural Exchange*, edited by Rica Annaert, 37–45. Wendeburg: Braunschweigischen Landesmuseum.

Resi, Heid Gjöstein. 1990. *Die Wetz- und Schleifsteine aus Haithabu, Berichte über die Ausgrabungen in Haithabu*. Neümunster: Bericht 28.

Reuter, Timothy, ed. and trans. 1992. *The Annals of Fulda*. Manchester: Manchester University Press.

Reuter, Timothy. 2002. Introduction to the 2002 Edition. In *History of the Archbishops of Hamburg-Bremen*, edited by Francis J. Tschan and Timothy Reuter, xi–xxi. New York: Columbia University Press.

Richards, Julian D. 2004. *Viking Age England*. Stroud: Tempus.

Richards, Julian D., Pauline Beswick, Julie Bond, Marcus Jecock, Jacqueline McKinley, Stephen Rowland, and Fay Worley. 2004. Excavations at the Viking Barrow Cemetery at Heath Wood, Ingleby, Derbyshire. *The Antiquaries Journal* 84:23–116.

Riddell, Scott, Egill Erlendsson, Guðrún Gísladóttir, Kevin J. Edwards, Jesse Byock, and Davide Zori. 2018. Cereal Cultivation as a Correlate of High Social Status in Medieval Iceland. *Vegetation History and Archaeobotany* 27:679–696.

Roach, Levi. 2011. Hosting the King: Hospitality and the Royal *iter* in Tenth-century England. *Journal of Medieval History* 37 (1):34–46.

Roberts, Howell M., and Elín Ósk Hreiðarsdóttir. 2013. The Litlu-Núpur Burials. *Archaeologia Islandica* 10:104–130.

Robinson, Charles H., ed. and trans. 1921. *Anskar, The Apostle of the North, 801–865: Translated from the Vita Anskarii by Bishop Rimbert His Fellow Missionary and Successor*. London: SPG.

Roesdahl, Else. 1977. *Fyrkat En Jysk Vikingeborg II: Oldsagerne og Gravpladsen*. København: Kongelige Nordiske Oldskriftselskab.

Roesdahl, Else. 1982. *Viking Age Denmark*. London: British Museum Publications Ltd.

Roesdahl, Else. 1998. *The Vikings*. 2nd ed. London: Penguin Books.

Roesdahl, Else. 2004a. En gravplads fra tidlig Kristen tid—Fyrkat. In *Kristendommen i Danmark før 1050*, edited by Niels Lund, 153–158. Roskilde: Roskilde Museums Forlag.

Roesdahl, Else. 2004b. Hvonår blev kirkerne bygget? In *Kristendommen i Danmark før 1050. Et symposium i Roskilde den 5–7 februar 2003*, edited by Niels Lund, 201–206. Roskilde: Roskilde Museums Forlag.

Roesdahl, Else. 2007. English Connections in the Time of Knut the Great: Material from Viborg. In *Cultural Interaction between East and West: Archaeology, Artefacts and Human Contacts in Northern Europe*, edited by Ulf Fransson, Marie Swedin, Sophie Bergerbrant, and Fedir Androshchuk, 276–278. Stockholm: Stockholm University.

Roesdahl, Else. 2018. *The Vikings*. 3rd ed. London: Penguin Books.

Roesdahl, Else, and Søren M. Sindbæk. 2014a. The Dating of Aggersborg. In *Aggersborg: The Viking-Age Settlement and Fortress*, edited by Else Roesdahl, Søren M. Sindbæk, Anne Pedersen, and David M. Wilson, 203–208. Moesgaard: Jutland Archaeological Society and The National Museum of Denmark.

Roesdahl, Else, and Søren M. Sindbæk. 2014b. The Purpose of the Fortress. In *Aggersborg: The Viking-Age Settlement and Fortress*, edited by Else Roesdahl, Søren M. Sindbæk, Anne Pedersen, and David M. Wilson, 383–414. Moesgaard: Jutland Archaeological Society and The National Museum of Denmark.

Roesdahl, Else, Søren M. Sindbæk, Anne Pedersen, and David M. Wilson, eds. 2014. *Aggersborg: The Viking-Age Settlement and Fortress*. Moesgaard: Jutland Archaeological Society and The National Museum of Denmark.

Rosenswig, Robert M. 2007. Beyond Identifying Elites: Feasting as a Means to Understand Early Middle Formative Society on the Pacific Coast of Mexico. *Journal of Anthropological Archaeology* 26:1–27.

Roussell, Aage. 1936. Sandnes and the Neighbouring Farms. *Meddelelser om Grønland* 88 (2):1–222.

Roy, Natasha, James Woollett, Najat Bhiry, Guillaume Haemmerli, Véronique Forbes, and Reinhard Pienitz. 2017. Perspective of Landscape Change Following Early Settlement (landnám) in Svalbarðstunga, Northeastern Iceland. *Boreas* 47(2):671–686.

Rubin, David. 1995. *Memory in Oral Traditions: The Cognitive Psychology of Epic, Ballads, and Counting-out Rhymes*. Oxford: Oxford University Press.

Rundkvist, Martin. 2011. *Mead-halls of the Eastern Geats: Elite Settlements and Political Geography AD 375–1000 in Östergötland, Sweden. Antikvariska serien* 49. Stockholm: Vitterhets Historie och Antikvitets Akademien (kvhaa), Handlingar.

Runge, Mads. 2018. New Archaeological Investigations at Nonnebakken, a Viking Age Fortress in Odense. In *The Fortified Viking Age: 36th Interdisciplinary Viking Symposium in Odense, May 17th, 2017*, edited by Jesper Hansen and Mette Bruus, 44–59. Odense: University Press of Southern Denmark.

Runge, Mads, and Mogens Bo Henriksen. 2018. The Origins of Odense: New Aspects of Early Urbanisation in Southern Scandinavia. *Danish Journal of Archaeology* 7 (1):2–68.

Sabo, Deborah, and George Sabo III. 1978. A Possible Thule Carving of a Viking from Baffin Island, N.W.T. *Canadian Journal of Archaeology* 2:33–42.

Sanmark, Alexandra. 2017. *Viking Law and Order: Places and Rituals of Assembly in the Medieval North*. Edinburgh: Edinburgh University Press.

Sawyer, Birgit. 1988. *Property and Inheritance in Viking Scandinavia: The Runic Evidence*. Alingsås: Viktoria Bokförlag.

Sawyer, Birgit. 2000. *The Viking-Age Rune Stones: Custom and Commemoration in Early Medieval Scandinavia*. Oxford: Oxford University Press.

Sawyer, Birgit. 2002. Runstenar och förmedeltida arvsförhållanden. In *Om runestenar i Jönköpings län*, edited by J. Agertz and L. Varenius, 55–78. Jönköping: Jönköpings läns museum.

Sawyer, Peter. 1962. *The Age of the Vikings*. London: Edward Arnold.

Sawyer, Peter. 1997. The Age of the Vikings and Before. In *The Oxford Illustrated History of the Vikings*, edited by Peter Sawyer, 1–18. Oxford: Oxford University Press.

Schledermann, Peter. 1980. Notes on Norse Finds from the East Coast of Ellesmere Island, N.W.T. *Arctic* 33 (3):454–463.

Schledermann, Peter, and K. M. McCullough. 2003. Inuit-Norse Contact in the Smith Sound Region. In *Contact, Continuity, and Collapse: The Norse Colonization of the North Atlantic*, edited by James H. Barrett, 183–205. Turnhout: Brepols.

Schmeidler, Bernhard, ed. 1917. *Magistri Adam Bremensis Gesta Hammaburgensis Ecclesiae Pontificum*. In *Hamburgische Kirchengeschichte*, 1–283. Hannover and Leipzig: Hansche Buchhandlung.

Schmid, Magdalena ME, Davide Zori, Egill Erlendsson, Cathy Batt, Brian N Damiata, and Jesse Byock. 2017. A Bayesian Approach to Linking Archaeological, Paleoenvironmental and Documentary Datasets Relating to the Settlement of Iceland (Landnám). *The Holocene* 28(1): 19–33.

Scholz, Bernhard Walter, ed. and trans. 1970. *Carolingian Chronicles: Royal Frankish Annals and Nithard's Histories*. Ann Arbor: University of Michigan Press.

Schwarcz, Henry P., and Margaret J. Schoeninger. 1991. Stable Isotope Analyses in Human Nutritional Ecology. *American Journal of Physical Anthropology* 34 (S13):283–321.

Scott, Forrest S., ed. 2003. *Eyrbyggja saga: The Vellum Tradition*, Vol. 18: *Editiones Arnamagnaeanae, Series A*. Copenhagen: C.A. Reitzel.

Seaver, Kirsten A. 2000. Unanswered Questions. In *Vikings: The North Atlantic Saga*, edited by William and Elisabeth Ward Fitzhugh, 270–279. Washington, DC: Smithsonian Institution Press.

Service, Elman. 1962. *Primitive Social Organization: An Evolutionary Perspective*. New York: Random House.

Shetelig, Haakon. 1912. *Vestlandske Graver fra Jernalderen*. Bergen Grieg.

Sigmundsson, Svavar. 1979. Íslensku staða-nöfnin. *Íslensk Mál og Almenn Málfræði* 1:238–248.

Sigurðsson, Gísli. 2000. The Quest for Vinland in Saga Scholarship. In *Vikings: The North Atlantic Saga*, edited by William W. Fitzhugh and Elisabeth I. Ward, 232–237. Washington, DC: Smithsonian Institution Press.

Sigurðsson, Gísli. 2004. *The Medieval Icelandic Saga and Oral Tradition: A Discourse on Method, The Milman Parry Collection of Oral Literature*. Cambridge, MA, and London: Harvard University Press.

Sigurðsson, Gísli. 2008. Introduction. In *The Vinland Sagas: The Icelandic Sagas about the First Documented Voyages across the North Atlantic*, edited by Gísli Sigurðsson, ix–xliii. London: Penguin.

Sigurðsson, Jón. 1857–76. *Diplomatarium Islandicum 834–1264*, Vol. 1. Copenhagen and Reykjavík: S.L. Möller.

Sigurðsson, Jón Viðar. 1999. *Chieftains and Power in the Icelandic Commonwealth*. Translated by J. Lundskær-Nielsen. Odense: Odense University Press.

Sigurðsson, Jón Viðar. 2011. Kings, Earls, and Chieftains. Rulers in Norway Orkney, and Iceland c. 900–1300. In *Ideology and Power in the Viking and Middle Ages: Scandinavia, Iceland, Ireland, Orkney and the Faroes*, edited by Gro Steinsland, Jón Viðar Sigurðsson, Jan Erik Rekdal, and Ian Beuermann, 69–108. Leiden: Brill.

Sigurðsson, Jón Viðar, Berit Gjerland, and Gaute Losnegård. 2005. *Ingólfr: Norsk-Islandsk Hopehav 870–1536*. Førde: Selja Forlag.

Sikora, Maeve. 2003. Diversity in Viking Age Horse Burial: A Comparative Study of Norway, Iceland, Scotland and Ireland. *The Journal of Irish Archaeology* 12/13:87–109.

Simpson, Ian, Orri Vésteinsson, W. Paul Adderley, and Thomas McGovern. 2003. Fuel Resource Utilisation in Landscapes of Settlement. *Journal of Archaeological Science* 30:1401–1420.

Sindbæk, Søren M. 2011a. Silver Economies and Social Ties: Long-Distance Interaction, Long-Term Investments—and Why the Viking Age Happened. In *Silver Economies, Monetisation and Society in Scandinavia AD 800–1100*, edited by Søren M. Sindbæk James Graham-Campbell, and Gareth Williams, 41–65. Aarhus: Aarhus University Press.

Sindbæk, Søren M. 2011b. Review of Gavin Lucas (ed.), 2009, *Hofstaðir: Excavations of a Viking Age Feasting Hall in North-eastern Iceland. Antiquity* 85 (329):1100–1101.

Sindbæk, Søren M. 2014. The Fortress. In *Aggersborg: The Viking-Age Settlement and Fortress*, edited by Else Roesdahl, Søren M. Sindbæk, Anne Pedersen, and David M. Wilson, 139–202. Moesgaard: Jutland Archaeological Society and The National Museum of Denmark.

Sindbæk, Søren M., ed. 2022a. *Northern Emporium*, Vol. 1: *The Making of Viking-age Ribe*. Moesgaard: Jutland Archaeological Society.

Sindbæk, Søren M. 2022b. The Making of a Northern Emporium. In *Northern Emporium*, Vol. 1: *The Making of Viking-age Ribe*, edited by Søren M. Sindbæk, 435–463. Moesgaard: Jutland Archaeological Society.

Sjøvold, Thorleif. 1974. *The Iron Age Settlement of Arctic Norway*, Vol. 2: *Late Iron Age*. Oslo: Norwegian Universities Press.

Skaaning, Poul. 1992. *Harald Blåtands Sidste Kamp: Trelleborgene og brydningerne i dansk vikingetid 979-983*. Lyngby: Dansk Historisk Håndbogsfolag.

Skov, Hans. 2005. Aros 700–1100. In *Vikingernes Aros*, edited by Hans Skov, 15–39. Højbjerg: Moesgård Museum.

Skov, Hans. 2008. Det ældste Århus—ca. 770–1200. In *De første 200 årene—nytt blikk på 27 skandinaviske middelalderbyer*, edited by Gitte Hansen, Ingvild Øye, and Hans Andersson, 215–226. Bergen: Universitetet i Bergen.

Skre, Dagfinn. 1996. Rural Settlements in Medieval Norway, AD 400–1400. *Ruralia* 1:53–71.

Skre, Dagfinn, ed. 2007. *Kaupang in Skiringssal, Kaupang Excavation Project Publication Series*, vol. 1: *Norske Oldfunn, vol. XXII*. Aarhus: Aarhus University Press.

Skre, Dagfinn, ed. 2008. *Means of Exchange: Dealing with Silver in the Viking Age, Kaupang Excavation Project Publication Series*, vol. 2: *Norske Oldfunn, vol. XXIII*. Aarhus: Aarhus University Press.

Smiarowski, Konrad, Ramona Harrison, Seth Brewington, Megan Hicks, Frank J. Feeley, Céline Dupont-Hébert, Brenda Prehal, George Hambrecht, James Woollett, and Thomas H. McGovern. 2017. Zooarchaeology of the Scandinavian Settlements in Iceland and Greenland: Diverging Pathways. In *The Oxford Handbook of Zooarchaeology*, edited by Umberto Albarella, Mauro Rizzetto, Hannah Russ, Kim Vickers, and Sarah Viner-Daniels, 1–23. Oxford: Oxford University Press.

Smith, Kevin P. 1995. Landnám: The Settlement of Iceland in Archaeological and Historical Perspective. *World Archaeology* 26 (3):319–346.

Smith, Kevin P. 2000. Jasper Cores from L'Anse aux Meadows. In *Vikings: The North Atlantic Saga*, edited by William W. Fitzhugh and Elisabeth I. Ward, 217. Washington, DC: Smithsonian Institution Press.

Snædal, Þórgunnur. 2002. Rúnaristur á Íslandi. *Árbók hins íslenzka fornleifafélags* 2000–2001:5–68.

Snædal, Thorgunn. 2016. Runes from Byzantium: Reconsidering the Piraeus Lion. In *Byzantium and the Viking World*, edited by Fedir Androshchuk, Jonathan Shepard, and Monica White, 187–214. Uppsala: Uppsala University Press.

Somerville, Angus A., and R. Andrew McDonald, eds. 2014. *The Viking Age: A Reader*. Toronto: University of Toronto Press.

Söderberg, Bengt. 2003. Integrating Power: Some Aspects of a Magnate's Farm and Presumed Central Place in Järrestad, South-east Scania. In *Centrality—Regionality: The Social Structure of Southern Sweden during the Iron Age*, edited by Lars Larsson and Birgitta Hårdh, 283–310. Lund: Acta archaeologica Lundensia 8/40.

Söderberg, Bengt. 2005. *Aristokratiskt rum och gränsöverskridande. Järrestad och sydöstra Skåne mellan region och rike 600–1100*. Stockholm: Riksantikvarieämbetet.

Sørensen, Anne C. 2001. *Ladby: A Danish Ship-Grave from the Viking Age*. Copenhagen: Viking Ship Museum/National Museum of Denmark.

Staecker, Jörn. 2005. The Concepts of imitatio and translatio: Perceptions of a Viking-Age Past. *Norwegian Archaeological Review* 38 (1):3–28.

Stefánsdóttir, Agnes, Rúna Tetzschner, Guðmundur Ólafsson, Ágúst Georgsson, Kristinn Magnússon, and Bjarni Einarsson. 2006. *Skráning Fornleifa í Mosfellsbæ*. Reykjavík: Þjóðminjasafn Íslands.

Steinberg, John, and Douglas Bolender. 2004. Rannsóknir á búsetuminjum í Skagafirði. *Árbók Hins Íslenzka fornleifafélags* 2002–2003:107–130.

Steinberg, John M., Douglas J. Bolender, and Brian N. Damiata. 2016. The Viking Age Settlement Pattern of Langholt, North Iceland: Results of the Skagafjörður Archaeological Settlement Survey. *Journal of Field Archaeology* 41 (4):389–412.

Steuer, Heiko. 1974. *Die Südsiedlung von Haithabu. Studien zur frümittelalterlichen Keramik im Nordseeküstenbereich und in Schleswig-Holstein.* Neumünster: Wachholtz.

Stolpe, Hjalmar. 1889. Ett och annat på Björkö. *Ny Illustrerad Tidning* 25:4–16.

Stylegar, Frans-Arne. 2007. The Kaupang Cemeteries Revisited. In *Kaupang in Skiringssal*, edited by Dagfinn Skre, 65–128. Aarhus: Aarhus University Press.

Sundt, Eilert. 1865. Lidt fra oldtiden. 1. Brygge-sten. *Folkevennen* 14:322–326.

Sutherland, Patricia D. 2000. The Norse and Native North Americans. In *Vikings: The North Atlantic Saga*, edited by William W. Fitzhugh and Elisabeth I. Ward, 238–247. Washington, DC: Smithsonian Institution Press.

Sutherland, Patricia. 2008. Norse and Natives in the Eastern Arctic. In *The Viking World*, edited by Stefan Brink and Neil Price, 613–617. New York: Routledge.

Sutherland, Patricia D. 2009. The Question of Contact between Dorset Paleo-Eskimos and Early Europeans in the Eastern Arctic. In *The Northern World, AD 900–1400*, edited by Herbert Maschner, Owen Mason, and Robert McGhee, 279–299. Salt Lake City: The University of Utah Press.

Svanberg, Fredrik. 2000. *Vikingatiden i Skåne.* Lund Historiska Media.

Sveinbjarnardóttir, Guðrún. 1992. *Farm Abandonment in Medieval and Post-medieval Iceland: An Interdisciplinary Study.* Oxford: Oxbow Books.

Sveinbjarnardóttir, Guðrún, Egill Erlendsson, Kim Vickers, Tom H. McGovern, Karen B. Milek, Kevin J. Edwards, Ian A. Simpson, and Gordon Cook. 2007. The Paleoecology of a High Status Icelandic Farm. *Environmental Archaeology* 12 (2):187–206.

Sveinbjarnardóttir, Guðrún, Ian A. Simpson, and Amanda M. Thomson. 2008. Land in Landscapes Circum *Landnám*: An Integrated Study of Settlements in Reykholtsdalur, Iceland. *Journal of the North Atlantic* 1:1–15.

Sveinsson, Einar Ól. 1953. *The Age of the Sturlungs: Icelandic Civilization in the Thirteenth Century*, Vol. 36: *Islandica.* Ithaca, NY: Cornell University Press.

Sveinsson, Einar Ólafur, and Matthías Þórðarson, eds. 1935. *Eyrbyggja saga, Brands þáttr örva, Eiríks saga rauða, Grœnlendinga saga, Grœnlendinga þáttr.* Reykjavík: Íslenzk Fornrit 4, Hið íslenzka fornritafélag.

Swanton, Michael, ed. and trans. 1998. *The Anglo-Saxon Chronicle.* New York: Routledge.

Taylor, Marvin, trans. 1997. The Tale of the Cairn-dweller. In *Complete Sagas of Icelanders*, Vol. 2, edited by Viðar Hreinsson, 443–444. Reykjavík: Leifur Eiríksson.

Taylor, P. B. 1976. The Hønen Runes: A Survey. *Neophilologus* 60 (1):1–7.

Thaastrup-Leth, Anne Katrine. 2004. Trækirker i det middelalderlige Danmark indtil ca. 1100. Hvornår blev de bygget? In *Kristendommen i Danmark før 1050. Et symposium i Roskilde den 5–7 februar 2003*, edited by Niels Lund, 207–214. Roskilde: Roskilde Museums Forlag.

Thalbitzer, William. 1951. Two Runic Stones, from Greenland and Minnesota. *Smithsonian Miscellaneous Collections* 116 (3):1–67.

Thomov, Thomas. 2014. Four Scandinavian Ship Grafitti from Hagia Sophia. *Byzantine and Modern Greek Studies* 38 (2):168–184.

Thorpe, Lewis, ed. and trans. 1969. *Einhard and Notker the Stammerer: Two Lives of Charlemagne.* New York: Penguin.

Þorláksson, Helgi. 1992. *Vaðmál og verðlag: Vaðmál í utanlandsviðskiptum og búskap Íslendinga á 13. og 14. öld.* Reykjavík: Sögufélag.

Þorláksson, Helgi. 2001. The Vínland Sagas in a Contemporary Light. In *Approaches to Vínland*, edited by Andrew Wawn and Þórunn Sigurðardóttir, 63–77. Reykjavík: Sigurður Nordal Institute.

Thórðarson, Björn Thráinn. 2014. Government's Partnership with the Mosfell Archaeological Project: Past, Present and Future. In *Viking Archaeology in Iceland: The Mosfell Archaeological Project*, edited by Davide Zori and Jesse Byock, 19–26. Turnhout: Brepols Publishers.

Þórarinsson, Sigurður. 1977. Gjóskulög og gamlar rústir: Brot úr íslenskri byggðasögu. *Árbók hins íslenzka fornleifafélags* 1976:5–38.

Thurston, Tina. 2001. *Landscapes of Power, Landscapes of Conflict: State Formation in the South Scandinavian Iron Age.* New York: Kluwer Academic/Plenum Publishers.

Tinsley, Clayton M., and Thomas H. McGovern. 2001. *Zooarchaeology of Aðalstræti 14–15, 2001: Report of the Viking Period Animal Bones.* NORSEC Laboratory Report 2. New York: NABO.

Tkocz, I., and K. R. Jensen. 1986. Antropologiske undersøgelser af skelettet i skrinet med de snoede søjler. In *Knuds-bogen 1986. Studier over Knud den Hellige*, edited by T. Nyberg, H. Bekker-Nielsen, and N. Oxenvad, 117–122. Odense: Fynske Studier XV.

Tonning, Christer, Petra Schneidhofer, Erich Nau, Terje Gansum, Vibeke Lia, Lars Gustavsen, Roland Filzwieser, Mario Wallner, Monica Kristiansen, Wolfgang Neubauer, Knut Paasche, and Immo Trinks. 2020. Halls at Borre: the discovery of three large buildings at a Late Iron and Viking Age royal burial site in Norway. *Antiquity* 94 (373):145–163.

Tomasson, Richard. 1980. *Iceland: The First New Society.* Minneapolis: University of Minnesota Press.

Tornbjerg, Svend Åge. 1998. Toftegård—en fundrig gård fra sen jernalder og vikingetid. In *Centrala Platser—Centrala Frågor*, edited by B. Stjernquist, 217–232. Lund: Acta Arch Lundensia 8° 28.

Townend, Matthew. 2002. *Language and History in Viking Age England: Linguistic Relations between Speakers of Old Norse and Old English.* Turnhout: Brepols.

Townend, Matthew. 2012. Óttarr svarti, Knútsdrápa. In *Poetry from the Kings' Sagas 1: From Mythical Times to c. 1035*, edited by Diana Whaley, 767. Turnhout: Brepols.

Townend, Matthew. 2014. *Viking Age Yorkshire.* Pickering: Blackthorn Press.

Trbojević, Nikola. 2016. The Impact of Settlement on Woodland Resources in Viking Age Iceland. PhD dissertation, University of Iceland.

Trigg, Heather B., Douglas J. Bolender, Katharine M. Johnson, Marisa D. Patalano, and John M. Steinberg. 2009. Note on Barley Found in Dung in the Lowest Levels of the Farm Mound Midden at Reynistaður, Skagafjörður Iceland. *Archaeologia Islandica* 7:64–72.

Trow, Meirion. 2005. *Cnut: Emperor of the North.* Stroud: Sutton.

Tschan, Francis J., and Timothy Reuter, eds. and trans. 2002. *Adam of Bremen: History of the Archbishops of Hamburg-Bremen.* New York: Columbia University Press.

Tulinius, Torfi. 2004. *Skáldið í Skriftinni: Snorri Sturluson og Egils saga.* Reykjavík: Hið Íslenska Bókmenntafélag.

Tummuscheit, Astrid, and Frauke Witte. 2018. The Danevirke in Light of Recent Excavations. In *The Fortified Viking Age*, edited by Jesper Hansen and Mette Bruus, 69–74. Odense: University of Southern Denmark.

Tummuscheit, Astrid, and Frauke Witte. 2019. The Danevirke: Preliminary Results of New Excavations (2010–2014) at the Defensive System in the German-Danish Borderland. *Offa's Dyke Journal* 1:114–136.

Turner, Victor. 1969. *The Ritual Process: Structure and Anti-structure.* Chicago: Aldine.

Ulriksen, Jens. 2008. Roskilde i 11. og 12. århundrede. In *De første 200 årene—nytt blikk på 27 skandinaviske middelalderbyer*, edited by Gitte Hansen and Ingvild Øye Hans Andersson, 165–180. Bergen: Universitetet i Bergen.

Ulriksen, Jens, Cille Krause, and Niels H. Jensen. 2014. Roskilde: En bygrundlæggelse i vanskeligt terræn. *KUML: Årbog for Jysk Arkæologisk Selskab* 2014:145–185.

Urbańczyk, Przemysław. 2002. Ethnic Aspects of the Settlement of Iceland. *Collegium Medieavale* 15:155–165.

Urbańczyk, Przemysław. 2012. An Archaeological Contribution to the Study of Icelandic Identity Formation. In *The Creation of Medieval Northern Europe: Christianisation, Social Transformations, and Historiography: Essays in Honor of Sverre Bagge*, edited by L. Melve and S. Sønnesyn, 176–219. Bergen: Dreyers forlag.

van Gennep, Arnold. 1960. *The Rites of Passage.* Chicago: University of Chicago Press.

Vansina, Jan. 1985. *Oral Tradition as History.* Madison: University of Wisconsin Press.

Vésteinsson, Orri. 1998. Patterns of Settlement in Iceland: A Study in Prehistory. *Saga-Book* 25:1–29.

Vésteinsson, Orri. 2000a. *The Christianization of Iceland: Priests, Power, and Social Change 1000–1300*. Oxford: Oxford University Press.

Vésteinsson, Orri. 2000b. The Archaeology of Landnám: Early Settlement in Iceland. In *Vikings: The North Atlantic Saga*, edited by William W. Fitzhugh and Elisabeth I. Ward, 164–174. Washington, DC: Smithsonian Institution Press.

Vésteinsson, Orri. 2004. Icelandic Farmhouse Excavations: Field Methods and Site Choices. *Archaeologia Islandica* 3:71–100.

Vésteinsson, Orri. 2006. The Building and Its Context. In *Reykjavík 871 ± 2: The Settlement Exhibition*, edited by Bryndís Sverrisdóttir, 116–121. Reykjavík: Reykjavík City Museum.

Vésteinsson, Orri. 2010. Ethnicity and Class in Settlement-period Iceland. Papers from the Proceedings of the Fifteenth Viking Congress, Cork 18–27 August 2005. In *The Viking Age: Ireland and the West*, edited by John Sheehan and Donnchadh Ó Corráin, 494–510. Dublin: Four Courts Press.

Vésteinsson, Orri, Thomas McGovern, and Christian Keller. 2002. Enduring Impacts: Social and Environmental Aspects of Viking Age Settlement in Iceland and Greenland. *Archaeologia Islandica* 2:98–136.

Vésteinsson, Orri, Mike Church, Andrew Dugmore, Thomas H. McGovern, and Anthony Newton. 2014. Expensive Errors or Rational Choices: The Pioneer Fringe in Late Viking Age Iceland. *European Journal of Post-Classical Archaeologies* 4:39–68.

Vilhjálmsson, Þorsteinn. 2001. Navigation and Vínland. In *Approaches to Vínland*, edited by Andrew Wawn and Þórunn Sigurðardóttir, 107–121. Reykjavík: Sigurður Nordal Institute.

von Heijne, Cecilia. 2011. Viking-age Coin Finds from South Scandinavia. In *Silver Economies, Monetisation and Society in Scandinavia, AD 800–1100*, edited by James Graham-Campbell, Søren M. Sindbæk and Gareth Williams, 185–202. Aarhus: Aarhus University Press.

Waggoner, Ben, ed. 2009. *The Sagas of Ragnar Lodbrok*. New Haven, CT: Troth Publications.

Wahlgren, Erik. 1958. *The Kensington Stone: A Mystery Solved*. Madison: University of Wisconsin Press.

Wahlgren, Erik. 1986. *The Vikings in America*. London: Thames & Hudson.

Waitz, G., ed. 1883. *Annales Bertiniani*. Monumenta Germaniae historica, Scriptores rerum Germanicarum in usum scholarum 5. Hannover: Impensis Bibliopolii Hahniani.

Waitz, G., ed. 1884. *Vita Anskarii auctore Rimberto, Monumenta Germaniae historica, Scriptores rerum Germanicarum in usum scholarum 55*. Hannover: Impensis Bibliopolii Hahniani.

Walker, Phillip, Jesse Byock, Jacqueline Eng, Jon Erlandson, Per Holck, Henry Schwarz, and Davide Zori. 2012. The Axed Man of Mosfell: Skeletal Evidence of a Viking Age Homicide and the Icelandic Sagas. In *The Bioarchaeology of Individuals*, edited by Ann Stodder and Ann Palkovich, 26–43. Gainesville: University of Florida Press.

Wallace, Birgitta Linderoth. 1991. L'Anse aux Meadows, Gateway to Vinland. *Acta Archaeologica* 61:166–198.

Wallace, Birgitta Linderoth. 2000. An Archaeologist's Interpretation of the *Vinland Sagas*. In *Vikings: The North Atlantic Saga*, edited by William W. Fitzhugh and Elisabeth I. Ward, 225–231. Washington, DC: Smithsonian Institution Press.

Wallace, Birgitta Linderoth. 2003. L'Anse aux Meadows and Vinland: An Abandoned Experiment. In *Contact, Continuity, and Collapse: The Norse Colonization of the North Atlantic*, edited by James H. Barrett, 207–238. Turnhout: Brepols.

Wallace, Birgitta Linderoth. 2006. *Westward Vikings: The Saga of L'Anse aux Meadows*. St. Johns: Historic Sites Association of Newfoundland and Labrador.

Wallace, Birgitta. 2009. L'Anse aux Meadows, Leif Eriksson's Home in Vinland. *Journal of the North Atlantic* Special Volume 2:114–125.

Wallace, Birgitta Linderoth, and William W. Fitzhugh. 2000. Stumbles and Pitfalls in the Search for Viking America. In *Vikings: The North Atlantic Saga*, edited by William W. Fitzhugh and Elisabeth I. Ward, 374–384. Washington, DC: Smithsonian Institution Press.

Walton, James. 1954. Hogback Tombstones and the Anglo-Danish House. *Antiquity* 28 (110):68–77.

Warner, David A., ed. and trans. 2001. *Ottonian Germany: The Chronicon of Thietmar of Merseberg.* Manchester: Manchester University Press.

Weber, Max. 1946. Politics as a Vocation. In *From Max Weber: Essays in Sociology,* edited by H. H. Gerth and C. Wright Mills, 77–128. Oxford: Oxford University Press.

Whaley, Diana. 1991. *Heimskringla: An Introduction.* London: Viking Society for Northern Research.

Wicker, Nancy L. 1998. Selective Female Infanticide as Partial Explanation for the Dearth of Women in Viking Age Scandinavia. In *Violence and Society in the Early Medieval West,* edited by Guy Halsall, 205–221. Woodbridge: Boydell.

Wiessner, Polly. 2001. Of Feasting and Value: Enga Feasts in Historical Perspective (Papua New Guinea). In *Feasts: Archaeological and Ethnographic Perspectives on Food, Politics, and Power,* edited by Michael Dietler and Brian Hayden, 115–143. Washington, DC: Smithsonian Institution Press.

Wigh, Bengt. 2001. *Animal Husbandry in the Viking Age Town of Birka and Its Hinterland: Excavations in the Black Earth 1990–95: Birka Studies.* Stockholm: Riksantikvarieämbetet.

Williams, Gareth. 2014. *The Viking Ship.* London: British Museum Press.

Williams, Gareth. 2015. Viking Camps and the Means of Exchange. In *The Vikings in Ireland and Beyond,* edited by Howard B. Clarke and Ruth Johnson, 93–116. Dublin: Four Courts Press.

Williams, Gareth, ed. 2020. *A Riverine Site near York: A Possible Viking Camp?* London: The British Museum.

Williams, Gareth, and Barry Ager. 2010. *The Vale of York Hoard.* London: The British Museum Press.

Williams, Gareth, and John Naylor. 2016. *King Alfred's Coins: The Watlington Viking Hoard.* Oxford: Ashmolean Museum.

Williams, Howard. 2016a. Citations in Stone: The Material World of Hogbacks. *European Journal of Archaeology* 19 (3):497–518.

Williams, Howard. 2016b. "Clumsy and Illogical"? Reconsidering the West Kirby Hogback. *The Antiquaries Journal* 96:69–100.

Williams, Thomas. 2017. *Viking Britain: An Exploration.* London: William Collins.

Wilson, David M. 2008. *The Vikings in the Isle of Man.* Aarhus: Aarhus University Press.

Wormald, Patrick. 1982. Viking Studies: Whence and Whither? In *The Vikings,* edited by Robert Farrell, 128–153. Chichester: Phillimore & Co.

Young, Bailey K. 1992. Text Aided or Text Misled? Reflections on the Uses of Archaeology in Medieval History. In *Text-Aided Archaeology,* edited by Barbara Little, 135–147. London: CRC Press.

Zachrisson, Torun. 1994. The Odal and Its Manifestation in the Landscape. *Current Swedish Archaeology* 2:219–238.

Zoëga, Guðný. 2014. Early Church Organization in Skagafjörður, North Iceland: The Results of the Skagafjörður Church Project. *Collegium Medievale* 27:23–62.

Zori, Davide. 2007. Nails, Rivets, and Clench Bolts: A Case for Typological Clarity. *Archaeologia Islandica* 6:32–47.

Zori, Davide. 2010. From Viking Chiefdoms to Medieval State in Iceland: The Evolution of Power Structures in the Mosfell Valley. PhD dissertation, University of California, Los Angeles.

Zori, Davide. 2014. Interdisciplinary Modelling of Viking Age and Medieval Settlement in the Mosfell Valley. In *Viking Archaeology in Iceland: Mosfell Archaeological Project,* edited by Davide Zori and Jesse Byock, 55–79. Turnhout: Brepols Publishers.

Zori, Davide, Jesse Byock, Egill Erlendsson, Steve Martin, Thomas Wake, and Kevin J. Edwards. 2013. Feasting in Viking Age Iceland: Sustaining a Chiefly Political Economy in a Marginal Environment. *Antiquity* 87 (335):150–165.

Zori, Davide, and Jesse Byock. 2014a. *Excavations at Skiphóll Mound in Leiruvogur and the Low-highland Site of Borg: Mosfell Archaeological Project 2014.* Reykjavík: Fornleifavernd Ríkisins.

Zori, Davide, Thomas Wake, Jon M. Erlandson, and Rúnar Leifsson. 2014. Viking Age Foodways at Hrísbrú. In *Viking Archaeology in Iceland: The Mosfell Archaeological Project,* edited by Davide Zori and Jesse Byock, 163–179. Turnhout: Brepols Publishers.

Index